*THE HISTORY AND FOLKLORE OF*

# NORTH AMERICAN WILDFLOWERS

# THE HISTORY AND FOLKLORE OF

# NORTH AMERICAN WILDFLOWERS

*Timothy Coffey*

Foreword by Stephen Foster

**Facts On File**

**The History and Folklore of North American Wildflowers**

Facts On File, Inc.
460 Park Avenue South
New York NY 10016
USA

**Library of Congress Cataloging-in-Publication Data**

Coffey, Timothy.
    The history and folklore of North American wildflowers / Timothy
Coffey.
        p.   cm.
    Includes bibliographical references (p.     ) and indexes.
    ISBN 0-8160-2624-6
    1. Wild flowers—North America.   2. Wild flowers—North America—
Utilization.   3. Wild flowers—North America—Folklore.
4. Medicinal plants—North America.   5. Plants, Useful—North
America.   6. Materia medica, Vegetable—North America.   I. Title.
QK110.C56   1993
582.13'097—dc20                                        92-18392

A British CIP catalogue record for this book is available from the British Library.

Facts On File books are available at special discounts when purchased in bulk quantities for businesses, associations, institutions or sales promotions. Please call our Special Sales Department in New York at 212/683-2244 (dial 800/322-8755 except in NY).

Text design by Donna Sinisgalli
Jacket design by Thomas Goddard
Composition by Vail Composition Services
Manufactured by R. R. Donnelley & Sons
Printed in the United States of America

10  9  8  7  6  5  4  3  2  1
This book is printed on acid-free paper.

# ACKNOWLEDGMENTS

The following publishers have generously given permission to use extended quotations from copyrighted works: From *The Collected Poems of A. E. Housman* by A. E. Housman. Copyright 1939, 1940, © 1965 by Holt, Rinehart and Winston. Copyright © 1967, 1968 by Robert E. Symons. Reprinted by permission of Henry Holt and Company, Inc. From *The Poetry of Robert Frost* edited by Edward Connery Lathem. Copyright 1936 by Robert Frost. Copyright © 1964 by Lesley Frost Ballantine.

Copyright © 1969 by Holt, Rinehart and Winston. Reprinted by permission of Henry Holt and Company, Inc. From Herbert Mitgang's obituary of E. B. White, *The New York Times,* October 2, 1985. Copyright © 1985 by The New York Times Company. Reprinted by permission. From "The Culinary Signs of Spring Across the Land," by Marian Burros, *The New York Times,* April 30, 1986. Copyright © 1986 by The New York Times Company. Reprinted by permission.

For my dear wife Aileen
and
Jennifer, Alexandra, Jacqueline
Siobhan, Paul and Francesca

# CONTENTS

# FOREWORD

## by Steven Foster

An interest in wildflowers usually begins in a similar sequence for most people. We may at first be struck by the beauty, color or curious form of a flower. We may want to know the plant's name and how to identify it. But more is here than meets the eye: Plants are an essential part of the human experience. Plants, in fact, allow us to exist. They transform carbon dioxide into oxygen, providing our very breath. Plants provide our food. Plants are essential for shelter and clothing. Throughout the world, from the beginnings of history to this day, plants have provided most of our medicine. The history of plants and people is an endless, intricate and fascinating tale of interdependence.

When early explorers and settlers arrived on the shores of the Americas, they were struck by the wealth of the new land—especially its plant wealth. The Plymouth colonies were partly financed by speculation on Sassafras, the aromatic bark of which was believed to be a 17th-century cure-all.

Five hundred years ago Columbus arrived on the shores of the Americas, not to find a new land, but to find an easier way to import herbs and spices to Europe from the Orient. Although he did not find the land he sought, the event opened the way for transoceanic migration of plants. Intentionally and vicariously, consciously and quietly, Columbus's arrival ushered in a new era of widespread and unabated worldwide distribution of plants through human intervention. The "herbs" of one culture became the herbs of another culture. While cayenne hails from the Americas, China is now the world's largest supplier of the plant.

Broadly defined, an herb is any plant used for its culinary, fragrant or medicinal qualities, meaning that many of our wildflowers are also herbs. About one-third of the more than quarter million known species of flowering plants have been used for medicinal purposes. Wildflowers, as medicinal plants, have always played an important role in human affairs. At least 80,000 plant species can be documented as folk medicines worldwide. In temperate regions, 20% of the plant species can be documented as being used for culinary or medicinal purposes. Hundreds of wildflowers, "herbs" if you will, serve as important source plants of medicine used in modern and traditional health care systems around the world.

Interest in medicinal plant use worldwide has continued to grow over the past two decades. The World Health Organization estimates that as many as 80% of the world's population relies on various forms of traditional medicine (rather than modern Western-style medicine). Herbal medicine is foremost among traditional medicine systems, the best-known example being the 5,000-year-old medical system of traditional Chinese medicine, which heavily relies on herbal treatments along with acupuncture. Over 500 different plants are "official drugs" of the 1985 *Pharmacopeia of the People's Republic of China*.

In North America, exclusive of Mexico, there are about 19,000 indigenous vascular plant species. Of these, something over 2,000 species can be documented as medicinal plants in the traditions of various native groups, as well as of the European populations that have settled the continent in the past 500 years. America, however, has no cohesive folk medicine, per se. Our written herbal tradition is only a few hundred years old, compared with the 5,000-year-old documented tradition of China.

Since the invention of the printing press, there have been thousands of books published on useful plants. To begin to explore the history and human utilization of our wildflowers, one must sift through endless dusty pages to find the facts. This is an enormous task, which, fortunately, Timothy Coffey has done for us. After searching more than 300 primary and rare references for information on the role of familiar wildflowers in human affairs, he has given us a veritable feast of information.

Why another book on wildflowers, their history, edibility and herbal uses? Undoubtedly there are at least as many wildflower and herb books in print today as there are publishers to offer them. As a reviewer of botanical and herb books for five periodicals, I have read or at least carefully perused nearly every new title in the field published in the last 10 years. I am also an avid book collector and have specialized in gathering titles on the uses of American wildflowers and woody plants. At one time or another, I have seen about every book published on wildflowers in America and their uses—or so I thought. Then I had the pleasure to read Timothy Coffey's book *The History and Folklore of North American Wildflowers*. He has dug deeper into the literature, beyond the titles a specialized bibliophile such as myself might know, and beyond the often-repeated quotes so typical of many plant books. Not only is this compilation unique, but it is also comprehensive, covering about 700 species of wildflowers. All interested in wildflowers, whether native or exotic, and their role in human affairs will enjoy these pages, then be pleased to give this book a place of honor on a book shelf—ready for the next stroll back into the history of human experience with plants.

# INTRODUCTION AND GUIDE TO THE USE OF THIS BOOK

A few generations ago most parents, cooks, gardeners, farmers, physicians and pharmacists would have recognized many of the plant names listed in this book, because plants were still an important ingredient of everyday life—of the medicines they gave their children and livestock, of the vegetable and flower garden and of the land on which they grazed their cattle and grew their food. Names like Colicroot, Garget-Plant, Mountain-Lettuce, Poverty-Weed, Devil's-Tether, Squawroot and Stagger-Grass had practical associations. But few North Americans now have the intimacy with the vegetable world that their ancestors had, and the names and even the plants are being lost and the roles that the plants had in American life are being forgotten. Most current guides to wildflowers provide only one or two names for each plant, a sad loss for us, since much of a plant's history can be learned from its names. It is that fast disappearing history and folklore of North American wildflowers that is the topic of this book.

The book contains entries for about 700 plants that have been described and illustrated in popular guides to North American wildflowers.[1] They have been included in this book because they have been used as a food, medicine, cosmetic, charm, poison or fiber by the Native Americans and the more recent colonists of this land.

The plants are arranged by family,[2] and the families are listed according to the classification system developed by Arthur Cronquist (1981, 1988). This is a so-called natural system that expresses the order of the plants' evo-

---

[1] These include the four Peterson Field Guides to wildflowers of Northeastern and North-Central North America (Peterson and McKenny), of the Rocky Mountains (Craighead, Craighead and Davis), of the Pacific states (Niehaus and Ripper) and of the Southwest and Texas (Niehaus, Ripper and Savage); the two *Audubon Society Field Guides to North American Wildflowers—Eastern Region* (Niering and Olmstead) and *Western Region* (Spellenberg); the *Golden Guide to Wildflowers of North America* (Venning and Saito); and Rickett's multivolume *Wildflowers of the United States*.

[2] Information in the brief descriptions of the families is taken from Heywood (1985) and Mabberly (1990).

lutionary development: Species of plants that are related by descent are placed in one genus, related genera are placed in a family, and the families are placed in a series that is supposed to represent their evolution from primitive to advanced. Thus the most primitive plants in this book are the two members of the Lizard's-Tail family (Saururaceae) and those that have evolved most recently are the Orchids. There appears to be less unanimity among botanists about the order of plants at the levels of genus and species, so in this book the genera within families and the species within genera are listed alphabetically.

## Common and botanical names of the plants

Each entry is headed by the plant's common (English) name or names; these are taken from popular field guides to wildflowers. The botanical name, in italics, appears just below the common name, with a translation, followed by the plant's vernacular names, if any. Most of these are in English, but some from Canada and a few from Louisiana and Missouri are in French,[3] and a few from the West are in Spanish. The sources of the vernacular names are described later in this introduction.

The botanical Latin names are from the checklist of John T. Kartesz.[4] The generic name starts with an initial capital, the species epithet with a lower-case letter.[5] The transla-

tion of the generic name starts with a capital; a semicolon follows; then a translation of the species epithet, which starts with a lower case letter, is given. Explanatory information is noted in parentheses. The meaning of many of the old botanic names is now obscure.[6] My guides to translation have been Coombes (1987), Gledhill (1985), Stearn (1983), Smith (1972), Fernald (1950) and Britton and Brown (1896), as well as Greek, Latin and English dictionaries.

The initial letters of the vernacular plant names in English have been capitalized, and, in most cases, the sensible rules for hyphens and spaces proposed by Rickett (1965)[7] have been followed:

1. Words that refer to plants in general (e.g., brier, plant, weed, wort) or to parts of plants (e.g., berry, leaf, root) are joined

name (e.g., *Acorus Calamus*), an aboriginal name (e.g., *Zephyranthes Atamasco*) or a personal genitive (e.g., *Lilium Michauxii*). A species epithet in the form of a person's Latinized name in the genitive was supposed to show that he or she had discovered or first described the plant. These distinctions are no longer kept.

[6]A frequent epithet for the plants that originated in Europe or are native also to Europe is *officinalis* or *officinale*. This is translated as "official," which means a pharmaceutical item that the pharmacist prepared or kept in stock, in contrast to a "magistral" preparation which was made up by a physician or prepared according to a physician's prescription.

[7]Kartesz and Thieret have recently (1991) published guidelines on the use and application of common names of plants, which, as regards hyphens and spaces, are not unlike those of Rickett; they are, however, much more precise and comprehensive. Kartesz has also prepared a book in which a common name for each North American plant (north of Mexico) is provided. Unfortunately, publication of this work was delayed, and it was not available at the time this book went to press.

---

[3]Most of the French Canadian names are taken from Frère Marie-Victorin's great work, *Flore Laurentienne* (1935).

[4]The second edition of the check list was still unpublished at the time this book went to press. But Professor Kartesz kindly allowed me access to a prepublication copy of his invaluable work.

[5]A convention followed in most botanical manuals until fairly recently was that the species epithet was given an initial capital if it was an old generic

to the preceding word without a hyphen, unless such a combined word would be awkward or difficult to grasp at first sight—thus, Beewort and Fireleaf but Memory-Root.

2. Words that are themselves names of a plant correctly applied are not joined or hyphenated to the preceding word. Thus, Canada Garlic, Freckled Lily, Moth Mullein, Water Cress.

3. Misapplied plant names are hyphenated to the preceding word. Thus, Water-Hyacinth, Bluebead-Lily, Rue-Anemone.

4. A hyphen is used when the second word is no part of a plant. Thus, Cuckoo-Pint, Bear-Tongue, Lady's-Slipper.

5. Names of over two words are hyphenated. Thus, Lords-and-Ladies, Star-of-Bethlehem. But if the first word is clearly an adjective (e.g., Yellow, False, Large, Lesser), then a hyphen is generally not used.

## Medicinal uses of the plants

The major sources of information on the medicinal uses of the plants[8] included in this book were the following:

"Dr. Bigelow" is Jacob Bigelow (p. xx), professor of medicine at Harvard College and author of *American Medical Botany,* Boston, 1817–1820. "Dr. Porcher" is Francis P. Porcher, surgeon in the Confederate Army and author of *Resources of Southern Fields and Forests,* Charleston, 1863. (The book was "prepared by direction of the Surgeon-General, for which

purpose the author was released temporarily from service in the field and hospital.") "Dr. Millspaugh" is Charles F. Millspaugh, a graduate of the New York Homeopathic College and Hospital, author of *American Medicinal Plants,* Philadelphia, 1887, and for many years curator of botany at the Field Museum of Natural History in Chicago.[9] "Rafinesque" is Constantine Samuel Rafinesque (page 272), botanical explorer and author of *Medical Flora of the United States,* Philadelphia, 1828–30. "The Lloyds" are the brothers John Uri and Curtis Gates Lloyd, authors of *Drugs and Medicines of North America,* Cincinnati, 1884–87, in which the histories, constituents, microscopic structures, physiologic effects and therapeutic uses of "every American medicinal plant of importance" were to be reviewed. Their ambitious project was never finished. Volume 1, 1884–85, published in two parts, contains accounts of 14 genera of the Buttercup family (Ranunculaceae), and Volume 2, 1886–87, adds another 15 plants from eight other families.[10]

"USD" cited without a date means the 25th edition of the *Dispensatory of the United States*

---

[8] That is, by North Americans of European ancestry. This book tends to exclude current uses of medicinal or edible plants and the results of modern pharmacologic research; its viewpoint is more historical. Information on medicinal and edible plants and their properties and current uses is available from many sources, including the Peterson Field Guides to medicinal plants (Foster and Duke) and to edible plants (L. A. Peterson).

[9] Unlike many 19th-century physicians who wrote on medicinal herbs, Bigelow, Porcher and Millspaugh critically evaluated contemporary medical beliefs and practices concerning medicinal plants and reported their own clinical and sometimes laboratory experiences with the plants and the plant products.

[10] The Lloyd Library in Cincinnati still has these two volumes for sale as well as other valuable historical American botanical works, published as part of the Reproduction Series of the *Bulletin of the Lloyd Library* (917 Plum Streeet, Cincinnati, Ohio 45202). In addition to being an innovative and successful manufacturing pharmacist and author of hundreds of scientific articles and monographs, J. U. Lloyd also wrote 60 short stories and eight novels.

(1955). This, like its predecessors, is a marvelous compendium of medicines, many of vegetable origin, prescribed by physicians and dispensed by pharmacists since the mid-19th century. By 1967 (the 26th edition), the USD had degenerated into a slim (1,277 pages versus 2,057 pages of the 1955 edition) and thoroughly boring manual of chemical preparations. Publication ceased thereafter.

"USP" is the *United States Pharmacopeia,* an official compendium of medicines prescribed by physicians, and "NF" is the *National Formulary,* a compendium of medicines and pharmaceutical preparations dispensed by pharmacists but not included in the USP.

Some of the medical concepts and terms appearing in the quotations may be unfamiliar. Conventional 19th-century medicine still emphasized the importance of releasing corrupting humors from the body, using clysters (enemas), phlebotomy (blood-letting), vomitives (emetics) and cathartics (laxatives). Medicinal herbs were classified according to their properties or virtues. Here is a list of properties and their definitions included in a Shaker catalog of herbs, roots and barks of 1864 (four terms that appear in this book but not in the Shaker list have been added with their definitions).[11]

| | |
|---|---|
| Acrid | Caustic, having a hot, biting taste |
| Alexiteric | Thwarting the action of venom |
| Alterative | Changing the morbid action of the secretions |

| | |
|---|---|
| Anodyne | Mitigating pain, quieting |
| Antibilious | Correcting the bilious secretions |
| Antilithic | Preventing the formation of calculus matter [kidney and bladder stones] |
| Antiscorbutic | Useful in scurvy |
| Antiseptic | Preventing mortification |
| Antispasmodic | Relaxing spasms, calming nervous irritation |
| Aperient | Gently purgative |
| Aromatic | Fragrant, spicy |
| Astringent | Producing contraction in the living tissue |
| Balsamic | Unctuous, mitigating, healing |
| Carminative | Causing the expulsion of wind |
| Cathartic | Cleansing the bowels, purgative |
| Cholalogue | Increasing the flow of bile into the intestine |
| Demulcent | Lubricating, softening, mollifying |
| Deobstruent | Having power to resolve viscidity |
| Depurative | Cleansing and purifying the system, particularly the blood |
| Diaphoretic | Increasing the cutaneous discharge [sweating] |
| Diuretic | Acting on the kidneys, increasing the urine |
| Discutient | Dissolving, discussing |
| Emetic | Producing vomiting |
| Emmenagogue | Promoting or increasing the menstrual flow |
| Emollient | Sheathing, softening, causing warmth and moisture |
| Expectorant | Augmenting and promoting the discharge from the lungs |
| Febrifuge | Expelling and allaying fever |
| Herpetic | Curing cutaneous diseases |

---

[11] Shaker herbs were greatly admired for their purity and their unusual method of preparation. Flowers and leaves were compressed into cakes and packed four to the pound, "neatly done up, and labelled for the especial accomodation of the retail trade" (United Society of New Gloucester).

| | |
|---|---|
| Narcotic | Relieving pain, stupefying, producing sleep |
| Nervine | Strengthening the nerves |
| Pectoral | Beneficial in diseases of the chest |
| Refrigerant | Diminishing animal temperature |
| Rubefacient | Producing inflammation and redness of the skin |
| Sialogogic | Promoting the flow of saliva |
| Stimulant | Increasing action |
| Stomachic | Strengthening the stomach |
| Styptic | Arresting bleeding |
| Sudorific | Producing sweat |
| Tonic | Permanently strengthening |
| Vermifuge | Expelling and destroying worms |
| Vulnerary | Promoting the healing of wounds |

These are essentially the same terms ("vertues") used in 16th-century English herbals.

The "eclectics," who are mentioned in several of the plant entries, were followers of the medical theory and practice of Wooster Beach, M.D., the "Eclectic," whose *American Practice of Medicine* was published in 1833, and of John King, M.D., co-author of *The Eclectic Dispensatory* (1852), the 18th edition of which (as *King's American Dispensatory*) was published in 1905. The medicines were based on the use of some 134 herbal preparations (Rothstein, 1972). At one stage the eclectic movement absorbed the Thomsonians (see p. 227).

**The Doctrine of Signatures.** It is an ancient idea that God or Nature or Providence has provided in the natural world all the cures for man's and woman's ills. And the cure, usually a plant but sometimes a mineral or animal, can be recognized by its "signature" of color, shape or smell. This is the doctrine of signatures, which is invoked, both directly and indirectly, by many of the writers who are quoted in this book. The same notions are evident in the medicine of the Native American. The doctrine was codified in Europe by Theophrastus Bombastus von Hohenheim (1493?-1541), who called himself Paracelsus, and by Giambattista Porta, the author of *Phytognomonica* (1588).

A prominent 17th-century English apostle of the doctrine of signatures was William Cole. An example from his *Adam in Eden* (1657) will be found in the entry for Jack-in-the-Pulpit (p. 288).

Astrological botanists believed in an association between certain plants and stars, planets and the moon. For example, 15th-century Albertus Magnus wrote of the Marigold that if it "be gathered, the Sunne beynge in the sygne Leo, in August, and be wrapped in the leafe of a Laurell or Baye tree, and a wolves toothe be added therto, no man shal be able to have a word to speake agaynst the bearer therof, but woordes of peace" (English translation of 1565, from Arber). Some botanists added a belief in astrology to the doctrine of signatures. A notorious English example was Nicholas Culpeper (1616–1654); the subtitle of his *The English Physician* of 1652 was *An Astrologo-physical Discourse of the Vulgar Herbs of this Nation*. A typical Astrologo-physical discourse can be found in the entry for Lesser Celandine (*Ranunculus ficaria,* p. 21).

### Indexes and illustrations

Two indexes follow the Bibliography: (1) An index of persons who are cited or quoted in the entries, (2) An index of families, genera and the common names.

Most of the plant drawings that appear in this book are taken from the first edition (1896) of Britton and Brown's *Illustrated Flora.* According to the Introduction to that work, the drawings were made by Mr. F. Emil, with the assistance of Miss Millie Timmerman ("now Mrs. Heinrich Ries"), Mr. Arthur Hollick, Mr. Joseph Bridgham, Mr. Theodor Holm, Miss Mary Wright and Mr. Rudolph Weber.

Several drawings of western plants have been taken from Margaret Armstrong's *Field Book of Western Wild Flowers.* Each of these is identified by the artist's initials, *MA.*

## Biographical notes

The quotations found throughout the book represent the classical world, the renewal of botanical knowledge in 16th- and 17th-century England and the shift of our interest to the New World in the 17th century.[12]

Following are biographical notes on some of the authors who are quoted:

**Pliny the Elder** (23–79), Caius Plinius Secundus, served in the Roman army in Germany and Africa and then as a senior colonial administrator in Spain. He was a man of prodigious industry, writing books on history, rhetoric, natural science and military tactics. Only one of his many works is extant, the 37 books of the *Natural History (Historia Naturalis).* This is an enthusiastic but uncritical encyclopedia of the natural sciences, compiled from the works, most of which are now lost, of 400 or 500 Greek and Latin writers. Sixteen of the books are concerned with the use of trees, vines, plants and flowers in farming, medicine and cooking. Pliny's nephew, Gaius Plinius Caecilius, or Pliny the Younger, was a historian and colonial governor. Pliny the Elder once admonished his nephew for wasting time by walking to the baths in the morning; he (the Elder) rode to the baths so that his reading and dictating to his ever-present scribes would not have to be interrupted. When Vesuvius erupted in A.D. 79, Pliny the Elder immediately went to investigate the volcano, was overcome by fumes and died.

**Dioscorides** (1st century A.D.), or Pedanius Dioscorides, was a Greek physician, born in Cilicia. He served in Nero's armies and then devoted himself to the study of physic (healing and medicine) and plants. His great work, *De Materia Medica,* a treatise on about 600 plant species, was probably written in about A.D. 70 or 80. He quotes many other, mostly Greek, writers and gives Latin, Dacian, Gallic and Egyptian names for some of the plants. *De Materia Medica* was the leading European work on pharmacology for the next 16 centuries, no drug being considered genuine that did not agree with his description. The book was translated into English by John Goodyer (see *Goodyera,* p. 327) in 1655. Pliny and Dioscorides were contemporaries but probably did not know of each other's work since neither quotes the other.

**William Turner** (1510–1568), who has been called the Father of English Botany, was a disputatious Protestant clergyman, constantly in trouble with his church and government, and twice exiled for his religious views to the Continent, where he studied botany and medicine. He is the author of a 20-page book of plant names, *Libellus de re Herbaria novus* (1538), a book on birds (1548), *The Names of Herbes in Greke, Latin, Englishe, Duche and Frenche* (1548) and a *Herball,* whose three parts were finally published in 1568 in Cologne. The chief aim of the herbal was to identify and describe the medicinal plants of Dioscorides.

**John Gerard** (1545–1612) was a member of the Barber-Surgeons Company in London

---

[12] The book's emphasis is on English-speaking North America, with some attention to French Canada. Most of the rich Native American botanical lore is excluded, except for that recorded by travelers, historians, ethnobotanists and anthropologists. Moreover, the experiences of the Spanish explorers and settlers and their botanical heritage are beyond the scope of this book.

and also a professional gardener. He supervised the gardens of several noblemen and had an elaborate garden of his own in Holborn. He is famous for his *Herbal or General Historie of Plants* (1597), an enormously successful and influential work in which Gerard expresses his great knowledge and love of plants in a strong and sometimes crude Elizabethan prose.[13] But much of his Herbal was plagiarized from an English translation by a Dr. Priest (then deceased) of the *Stirpium historiae pemptades* . . . of Rembert Dodoens (1583). Dodoens's book was itself based on the European herbals of the 15th and 16th centuries. Thus the many quotations from Gerard's Herbal in this book reflect Gerard's practical knowledge of plants and also the long tradition of the European herbalists. Gerard's Herbal was corrected, revised and amended by Thomas Johnson and republished in 1633; it is Johnson's edition of the Herbal that is quoted in this book.

**Thomas Harriot** (1560–1621), an eminent English scientist and mathematician, was hired by Sir Walter Raleigh to act as navigator, ethnologist and botanist on Sir Richard Grenville's fateful attempt to establish a colony on Roanoke Island in 1584. Harriot wrote an enthusiastic description of the New World, *A briefe and true report of the new found land of Virginia.* This was published in England in 1588 (by this time the Roanoke Colony had been abandoned) and then in 1590 in Theodore De Bry's folio edition, with illustrations by John White, who was the expedition's recording artist and later governor of the colony. Harriot's report, with White's drawings of Indian life, has been reprinted by Dover Publications (New York, 1972).

**John Parkinson** (1567–1650) was a London apothecary and gardener who in 1629 published a knowledgeable and charming book on ornamental plants, the vegetable garden and orchard called *Paradisi in Sole Paradisus Terrestris* (which is a pun on his name, Park-in-sun). He was appointed King's Botanist to Charles I and in 1640 published the *Theatrum Botanicum . . . a Herball of a Large Extent,* in which over 3,800 plants are grouped into 17 Tribes, including "Sweete smelling plants," "Venomous, sleepy, or hurtful plants," "Cooling or succory-like herbes" and "Hot and sharpe-biting plants."

**John Josselyn** (fl. 1630–1670) was born in the early 1600s and on two visits to the Colonies spent nine years in Massachusetts and Maine, where his brother, Henry, was a colonial administrator and large landowner. Based on his American experiences, Josselyn wrote two books, *New-England's Rarities Discovered in Birds, Beasts, Fishes, Serpents, and Plants of that Country* (London, 1672) and *An Account of Two Voyages to New-England, Made during the Years 1638, 1663* (London, 1674). The most valuable and original part of the two books is a chapter of the Rarities called "Fifthly, Of Plants," the first extended description of the plants of the region in English.

**John Bartram** (1699–1777) was a Quaker farmer in Pennsylvania who taught himself Latin and botany and became the first native-born American botanist. He made a series of botanical expeditions throughout the eastern states (colonies), collecting plants for botanists and gardeners in England, and established a botanic garden on the Schuylkill River (now in Philadelphia). In 1765 he was appointed "Botanist to the King" by George III at an annual salary of £50. Linnaeus called

---

[13] "Americans who have the proud distinction of being 'of Royal Indian descent' may be interested to know that a copy of Gerard's Herbal in Oxford has been identified as having belonged to Dorothy Rolfe, the mother-in-law of the Princess Pocahontas" (Rohde, 1922). The 1633 edition of Gerard's Herbal is still in print (New York: Dover, 1975).

him "the greatest living botanist in the world." But evidently he never gave up his simple ways or farmer's attire.

John Bartram's son William (1739–1823) accompanied his father on many collecting trips and was also a skilled natural-history artist. His *Travels* (Philadelphia, 1791), an account of his journeys through southeastern North America from 1773 to 1778, was greatly admired by, among others, Carlisle, Emerson, Coleridge (who used many of its gorgeous images in "Kubla Khan" and "The Ancient Mariner") and Wordsworth.

**Peter Kalm** (1715–1779) was professor of natural history and economy at Åbo when in 1748 he was sent to North America by the Swedish Academy of Sciences to obtain seed and plant material of useful herbs and trees that would be hardy enough to thrive in Sweden. He had been recommended for the job by his old teacher Linnaeus. He stayed four years in America, exploring Pennsylvania, New York, New Jersey (where he courted and married a Swedish clergyman's widow) and southern Canada. The account of his American experiences, *Travels into North America,* was first published in Stockholm, 1753–1761, followed by translations into German, English and French.

**Manasseh Cutler** (1742–1823) graduated from Yale College in 1765 and, after working as a schoolteacher, merchant and lawyer, was ordained pastor of the Congregational church in Ipswich (now Hamilton), Massachusetts, in 1771. He served as a chaplain in the American Revolution and was cited for heroism. He also studied medicine and, to help support his family, practiced medicine and ran a private school. In 1786 he helped organize the Ohio Company and negotiated with the Continental Congress for the purchase of a large tract of public land for the colonization of the Ohio Valley. Meanwhile he botanized, and

in 1785 published "An account of some of the vegetable productions naturally growing in this part of America." Cutler's was the first treatise on New England botany since John Josselyn's chapter on *New England's Varieties* 100 years previously.

**Jacob Bigelow** (1786–1879), son of a Congregational minister, was born in Sudbury, Massachusetts, and died in Boston. A Harvard graduate, he obtained his medical degree from the University of Pennsylvania in 1810. He subsequently became professor of materia medica and botany and Rumford Professor of Technology at Harvard. Among his publications were *Florula Bostoniensis,* 1814, and *American Medical Botany,* in three volumes, 1817 to 1820, which he also illustrated with meticulous paintings of each plant. He was an active and successful physician, teacher and botanist and a formidable medical and educational reformer and also found time to write poetry in English, Latin and Greek.

## Sources and origins of vernacular names

North America has nothing comparable to the *Dictionary of English Plant-Names* compiled by James Britten and Robert Holland for the English Dialect Society and published in 1886. But there were a few more modest attempts to collect names of American plants.

In the 1890s Fannie Bergen published eight lists of "popular American plant names" in the *Journal of American Folk-Lore.* She collected the names herself, and many were evidently sent to her by contributors from around the country; in her 1893 article she wrote that it would be impossible to thank every person who had contributed names, but she listed 28 people who had extended "substantial assistance." Some of her lists were reprinted in the *Botanical Gazette,* with an editorial note asking readers to send more names to her.

For the 1896 and 1913 editions of Britton and Brown's *Illustrated Flora,* "many thousand popular names" were compiled (and omitted in subsequent editions). Nathaniel Lord Britton (director of the New York Botanical Garden and professor of botany at Columbia University) and Addison Brown (jurist, botanist and president of the New York Botanical Garden) acknowledged "numerous general and special botanical works" and some individual contributors as their sources of names. The geographical origins of the names were not provided.

In 1909–1916 Gerth van Wijk, a Dutch schoolmaster, published his multilingual *Dictionary of Plant Names.* He acknowledged Bergen as his most frequent source of American plant names and also cited several 19th-century American botanical works, such as those by Pursh, Eaton and Wright and Asa Gray.

From 1913 to 1951 Waldo T. McAtee collected local plant names and published lists of them, mainly in the journal *Torreya.* McAtee collected the names himself on his extensive travels as an ornithologist; numerous correspondents appear to have sent him names, and he recorded names found in his wide reading in natural history.

In the 1920s and 1930s, Willard N. Clute made some collections of names, most of which had appeared in the former compilations, and published them in the *American Botanist* and in several editions of his book, *American Plant Names.* Clute acknowledged no sources for his names nor, unfortunately, did he note the geographical origins of the names.

Other sources of vernacular names include botanical lists, accounts of travel and exploration, books on drugs and pharmaceuticals and American herbals and manuals on medicinal plants.

Wherever possible, the names of the states or Canadian provinces where the plant names were recorded have been added. In some cases the notation is more general—for example, New England, "Canada," "South," "Plains Indian," "West"—or more specific—for example, Long Island, New York. Most of the information on geographical locations is from Bergen and McAtee.

The locations that Bergen provided are from several botanical works, from her own experiences in New England and from informants from around the country. Thus they are highly selective—it is evident from her lists that she had active correspondents in some parts of the country and none in others.

McAtee's locations came from his own research (he was a great traveler, particularly in watery and marshy country as befits an expert on water and shore birds), from contemporary informants and from extensive reading of books and periodicals on North American flora and fauna. Again, this is a highly biased method of collecting information.

Many of the plants that have been introduced or were adventive from Europe have vernacular names that are identified as local in the British Isles or included in the old English herbals.[14] The major American source for these names is Britton and Brown's *Illustrated Flora* of 1913 (most were also listed in the general index of the 1896 edition). Here is a paragraph about these names from Britton and Brown's introduction to their *Flora*

---

[14] Information on local or dialect plant names from the British Isles was obtained from Britten and Holland's *Dictionary of English Plant-Names,* the *English Dialect Dictionary* and Geoffrey Grigson's *The Englishman's Flora.*

(1913) that includes a relevant quotation from Britten and Holland's introduction to their *Dictionary of English Plant-Names* (1886):

> The popular names are full of interest, from their origin, history and significance. Hundreds of them, brought to this country by early English Colonists, are still in current use among us, though now obsolete in England. As observed in Britten & Holland's work cited below, "they are derived from a variety of languages, often carrying us back to the early days of our country's history, and to the various peoples who as conquerors or colonists have landed on our shores and left an impress on our language. Many of these old-world names are full of poetical associations, speaking to us of the thoughts and feelings of the people who invented them; others tell of the ancient mythology of our ancestors, of strange old medicinal usages, and of superstitions now almost forgotten."

## Abbreviations of states and Canadian provinces

| | |
|---|---|
| Ala. | Alabama |
| Ariz. | Arizona |
| Ark. | Arkansas |
| Calif. | California |
| Colo. | Colorado |
| Conn. | Connecticut |
| Del. | Delaware |
| Fla. | Florida |
| Ga. | Georgia |
| Ill. | Illinois |
| Ind. | Indiana |
| Kans. | Kansas |
| Ky. | Kentucky |
| La. | Louisiana |
| Md. | Maryland |
| Mass. | Massachusetts |
| Mich. | Michigan |
| Minn. | Minnesota |
| Mo. | Missouri |
| Mont. | Montana |
| Nebr. | Nebraska |
| Nev. | Nevada |
| N.H. | New Hampshire |
| N.J. | New Jersey |
| N.Mex. | New Mexico |
| N.Y. | New York |
| N.C. | North Carolina |
| N.Dak. | North Dakota |
| Okla. | Oklahoma |
| Oreg. | Oregon |
| Pa. | Pennsylvania |
| R.I. | Rhode Island |
| S.C. | South Carolina |
| S.Dak. | South Dakota |
| Tenn. | Tennessee |
| Vt. | Vermont |
| Wash. | Washington |
| W.Va. | West Virginia |
| Wis. | Wisconsin |
| Wyo. | Wyoming |
| | |
| Alta. | Alberta |
| B.C. | British Columbia |
| Man. | Manitoba |
| N.B. | New Brunswick |
| Nfd. | Newfoundland (includes Labrador, Lab.) |
| N.S. | Nova Scotia |
| Ont. | Ontario |
| P.E.I. | Prince Edward Island |
| P.Q. | Quebec |
| Sask. | Saskatchewan |

# PLANT FAMILIES
# INCLUDED IN THIS BOOK

*THE HISTORY AND FOLKLORE OF*

# NORTH AMERICAN WILDFLOWERS

# THE LIZARD'S-TAIL FAMILY

## *Saururaceae*

A family of five genera and only seven species; native to eastern Asia and western and eastern North America. One member of the family, *Houttuynia cordata,* is cultivated as a ground cover and ornamental. Greek *sauros* is a lizard, *oura* a tail.

## Yerba Mansa, Apache-Beads

*Anemopsis californica.* Like Anemone; of California.

Among the Costanoan Indians of California: "Root decoction used for menstrual cramps and for general pain remedy; tea used to wash sores; plant, dried and powdered, was sprinkled on wounds as a disenfectant" (Bocek, 1984). Charles Saunders wrote, "The Indian is also to be thanked for our knowledge of Yerba Mansa (or more correctly, Yerba del Manso, 'the herb of the tamed Indian'), common in wet, alkaline soil throughout much of the Southwest . . . The peppery, aromatic root is astringent, and is chewed raw, after drying, for affections of the mucous membrane, and also made into a tea for purifying the blood. It is one of the most popular of remedies among the Mexican population, who employ it also to relieve coughs and indigestion or pretty much anything." The rootstock was also dried and carved into "Apache beads," worn as a necklace.

## Lizard's-Tail, Water-Dragon

*Saururus cernuus.* Lizard tail; nodding. Breast-Weed, *Saurure penché* (P.Q.) Swamp-Dragon (S.C.), Swamp-Lily (Ark.).

John Bartram (1751) wrote, "It grows in wet places and produceth a long spike of white flowers; the root is spongy like a rush, and runs near the surface of the mud. It is of excellent virtue; being made into a poultice, and applied to sore and impostumated breasts, it ripens and heals them. The dried leaves made into a tea and drank, is commended for the pains of the breast and back." William Bartram (1776) called it Swamp-Lily, through whose "emollient and discutient" virtues "the lives of many thousands of the people of the southern states are preserved."

*Yerba Mansa*

# THE BIRTHWORT OR DUTCHMAN'S-PIPE FAMILY

## Aristolochiaceae

A family of seven genera and 410 species of woody vines and herbs; found in tropical and temperate regions. Its signature, the flower that was seen to resemble a swollen womb, suggested some of its ancient uses—to encourage conception, help delivery and purge the womb. Pliny wrote, "Among the most celebrated plants, aristolochia received its name, as is clear, from women, because they considered it to be *aristi lekhousais,* that is, excellent for women in childbed." Later generations decided that the flower was shaped like a Dutchman's curved pipe.

## Dutchman's-Pipe

*Aristolochia macrophylla.* Best birth; large-leaved.
*Aristoloche* (P.Q.), Big-Sarsparilla, Pipe-Vine, Wild-Ginger.

*Virginia Snakeroot*

## Virginia Snakeroot

*Aristolochia serpentaria.* Best birth; of serpents (the old generic name).
Birthwort, Black-Snakeroot, Pelican-Flower, Red-River Snakeroot, Sangree-Root, Sangrel, Sangrel-Snakeroot, Serpentary, Serpentary-Root, Snagrel, Snakeweed, Texas-Snakeroot, Thick-Birthwort, Virginia Serpentary

"The root of the Virginia *Pistolochia,* which is of a strong and aromatic scent, is a singular & much used antidote against the bite of the rattlesnake," according to Gerard's *Herbal* (1633), "and many also commend the use of this against the plague, small pox, measels, and such like maligne and contagious diseases." Mark Catesby reported that in the "1700s" "the usual price of this excellent root, both in Virginia and Carolina, is about six pence a pound when dried, which is money hardly earned. Yet the Negro slaves (who only dig it) employ much of the little time allowed them by their masters in search of it; which is the cause of there being seldom found any but very small plants."

In 1640 John Parkinson wrote, "Our people in Virginia do there call it the Snakeweed, or Snakeroote . . . But there is a cornuted Cornutus that among his American plants, calleth this (a horne plague on his head for his labour) *Snagroel* or *Snagrael nothae Angliae.*" The cornuted Cornutus was Jacob Cornut whose *Canadensium plantarium* was published in Paris in 1635. Somehow, Snakeroot of North America became *Snagrael nothae Angliae,* and then the American vernacular Snagrel and Sangrel. Virgil Vogel reports that "the Cherokees blew a decocotion of the root upon a patient for fever and feverish headaches and drank it for coughs. The root was chewed and spat upon snakebites, and the bruised root was placed in the hollow tooth for toothache. It was also held against the nose to relieve soreness by constant blowing in colds. The Louisiana Choctaws drank an extract of the root to relieve stomach pains. The Alabamas mashed the leaves for a snakebite poultice and drank a tea of the leaves to assist the cure. The Natchez boiled the whole plant for a warm infusion taken internally for fevers. The Penobscots steeped this plant 'for fits,' and the Mohegans applied a mash of the roots to snakebites."

The USD reports, "Serpentaria is to be classed among the aromatic bitters; in moderate doses it acts as a gastric stimulant and may therefore be of service in atonic types of dyspepsia." It has been included in the USP and NF and is still found in some European pharmacopeias. Red-River Snakeroot and Texas-Snakeroot are more properly names of *Aristolochia reticulata*.

## Wild-Ginger

*Asarum canadense*. (From the Greek name, *asaron*); of Canada.

Asarabacca, Asarabica, *Asaret* (P.Q.), Black-Snakeroot, Broad-Leaved Sarabacca, Canada-Snakeroot, Cat's-Foot, Colic-Root (W.Va.), Coltsfoot (N.Y.), Coltsfoot-Snakeroot (Mass.), False-Coltsfoot, False-Crowfoot, *Gingembre sauvage* (P.Q.), Hazelwort, Heart-Snakeroot (Mass.), Indian-Ginger, Southern-Snakeroot, Snakeroot (N.H.), Vermont-Snakeroot

John Pechey (1694) wrote of Asarabacca (*Asarum europaeum*) that it "purges violently upward and downward, flegm and choler. 'Tis diuretick also, and forces the courses; wherfore wenches use the decoction of it too frequently, when they think they are with child." In his *Flora Americana* of 1814, Frederick Pursh wrote of *Asarum canadense,* "The root is highly aromatic, and known by the

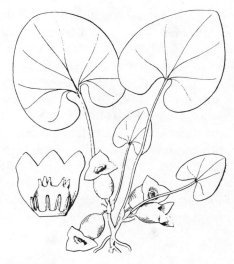

*Wild-Ginger*

inhabitants under the name of Wild Ginger. It is said to be made use of by the Indian females to prevent impregnation." The dried root is candied or ground and used as a kitchen spice and Eastern Canadian Indians drank an infusion to relieve heart pain and arrhythmias. Dr. Bigelow wrote that the "aromatic flavour of the root is more agreeable than that of the aristolochia serpentaria, which article it seems to resemble in its medicinal powers. Several country practitioners, who have employed it, have spoken to me favourably of its effect, as a warm stimulant and diaphoretic."

On the Yellowstone River, July 1806, George Gibson, one of the Lewis and Clark expedition hunters, severely injured his thigh. "The gentlest and strongest horse was therefore selected, and a sort of litter formed in such a manner as to enable the sick man to lie nearly at full length. They then proceeded gently, and at the distance of two miles passed a river entering from the southeast side, about 40 yards wide, called by the Indians Itchkeppearja, or Rose river; a name which it deserves, as well from its beauty as from the roses which we saw budding on its borders. Soon afterward they passed another Indian fort on an island; and after making nine miles halted to let the horses graze, and sent out a hunter to look for timber to make a canoe, and procure, if possible, some wild ginger to make a poultice for Gibson's thigh, which was now exceedingly painful, in consequence of his constrained position. He returned, however, without being able to find either; but brought back two bucks" (Lewis and Clark). Gibson recovered nevertheless. Lewis and Elvin-Lewis report that Wild Ginger root contains antibiotic substances A and B, effective against broad-spectrum bacteria and fungi.

## Western Wild-Ginger, Long-Tailed Wild-Ginger

*Asarum caudatum.* (From the Greek name, *asaron*); tailed (calyx lobes).

James Teit (1930) recorded that among the Thompson Indians "the whole plant, including the roots, but sometimes only the stems, are put in the bedding of infants when they are restless or ill, and this is said to make them quiet or well."

# THE LOTUS-LILY FAMILY

## *Nelumbonaceae*

A family of a single genus and two species; once included in the Nymphaeaceae family. The other species is *Nelumbo nucifera,* the Sacred Lotus of India, "introduced to Egypt about 500 BC where it was believed to contain the secrets of the gods and in particular was consecrated to the sun. The Pharaonic Egyptians both worshipped the Lotus and worshipped with it, offering the flowers upon their altars. It no longer grows beside the Nile but is venerated in all countries to the East for its association with creation, preservation, the afterlife, ultimate beauty, and holiness" (Whittle and Cook).

## American Lotus, Water-Chinquapin

*Nelumbo lutea.* (The Singhalese name); yellow.
Alligator-Buttons (S.C.), Alligator-Peas (S.C.), American Nelumbo, Big-Bonnet (Miss.), Bonnet (Tenn.), Can-Dock, Duck-Acorn, *Graine à voler* (La.), *Grand ovale* (La.), Great Yellow-Water-Lily (N.Y.), *Jac-quinot* (Mo.), Knock-Knocks (S.C.), Lily-Nut, Lotus (Wis.), Monaca-Nut (La.), Nelumbo, Pond-Nut, Rattle-Nut, Sacred-Bean, *Vole* (La.), Wampapin, Wankapin, Water-Bean, Water-Chinaquin, Water-

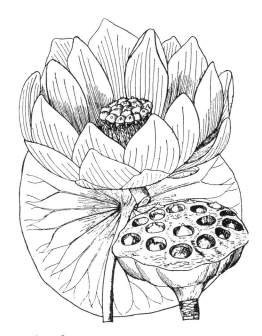

*American Lotus*

Chinkapin, Waterlily (Ill.), Water-Nut, Wonkapin (Ind.), Yankapin, Yawk-Nut (La.), Yellow-Lotus, Yellow Pond-Lily, Yonkapin (Ark.), Yonkapin-Bonnet (Tenn.)

Thomas Nuttall among the Quapaws in Arkansas (1821): "This morning I observed the wife of the chief, preparing for her family a breakfast from the nuts of the Cyamus (or Nelumbo). They are first steeped in water, and parched in sand, to extricate the kernels, which are afterwards mixed with fat, and made into a palatable soup. The tubers of the root, somewhat resembling patatas or sweet potatoes, when well-boiled, are but little inferior to a farinaceous potato." The young leaves and leaf stalks are cooked, the tubers baked, the young seeds eaten raw or cooked and the ripe seeds of winter are roasted, boiled or ground into meal. An edible oil is also extracted from the seeds.

According to Huron Smith (1933), "The Forest Potawatomi gather large quantities of the root of the yellow pond lily and give it the name of pine snake, because of the appearance of the roots when the water has dried away exposing them. The writer made a trip with Mrs. Spoon to obtain a supply of this root and gathered perhaps a two-bushel sack of it. The roots were cut in quarters to dry better. The root is pounded into a pulp, either fresh or dried, to use as a poulticing material for many inflammatory diseases." Chinquapin or chinkapin is the name of nut-bearing trees of the genera *Castanea* and *Castanopsis*. *Chechinkamin* is Algonquian for a chestnut.

# THE WATERLILY FAMILY

## *Nymphaeaceae*

A cosmopolitan family of six genera and 60 species of aquatic herbs. "According to tradition nymphaecea was born of a nymph who died of jealousy about Hercules," Pliny explained, "and therefore those who have taken it in drink for twelve days are incapable of intercourse and procreation." This idea is taken up by Rabelais in his botanical digression at the end of the Third Book of Pantagruel: Pantagruelion, which is hemp and from which ropes are made, "has proved more fearful and abhorrent to robbers than doddergrass and chokeweed are to flax . . . than nenuphar, lotus or water-lily to lascivious monks."

Manasseh Cutler listed two Nymphaeas: "Water Yellow Lily. Toad Lily. Blossoms yellow" and "Pond Lily. Water Lily. Blossoms white." He wrote of them that "the flowers open about seven in the morning, and close about four in the afternoon. A conserve is made of the leaves [petals] of the blossoms. The roots of both species are much used, in form of poultices, for producing suppuration in boils and painful tumors, and are very efficacious. The root of the water yellow lily is generally preferred. Dr. Withering says, the roots of the pond lily are used in Ireland, and in the island of Jura, to dye a dark brown."

## Yellow Pondlily, Spatterdock

*Nuphar luteum.* (From the Sanskrit *nilotpula,* the Blue Lotus of India); yellow. (Also found in Europe.)

Beaver-Lily (Maine), Beaver-Root, Bonnets (Fla.), Brandy-Bottle, Bullhead-Lily (Mass., N.H.), Can-Dock, Cow-Lily (Maine), Dog-Lily (New England), Ducks

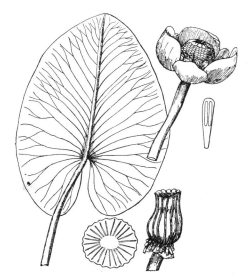

*Yellow Pondlily*

(Md.), Flatterdock, Frog-Lily, Globe-Lily, Gold-Watch (Pa.), Hog-Lily (Mass.), Holy-Trinity-Lily (Texas), Horse-Lily (Maine), Indian Pondlily, Kelp (Maine), Large Yellow-Pond-Lily, *Lis d'Eau* (P.Q.), Marsh-Collard, Mulefoot (Tenn.), Mulefoot-Bonnet (Tenn.), Mulefoot-Lily (Tenn.), Muleshoe (Tenn.), *Nénuphar jaune* (P.Q.), *Pied-de-cheval* (P.Q.), Splatterdock (Pa.), Three-Colored-Lily, Toad-Lily, Tuckahoe (Md.), Tuckey (Md.), Tucky-Lily (Md.), Water-Collard, Wokas, Yellow-Lanterns, Yellow Waterlily (Wis.)

The Klamath Indians "gather enormous quantities of it during the months of July and August, nearly all the old women of the tribe going to the marsh for the purpose," according to Coville (1897). "The large mucilaginous seed pods are gathered in boats, the seeds extracted after some process of drying the pods, and then stored for use during the year. The common method of preparing the seeds for use is to roast them either in an open basket with live coals, or more commonly in recent years in an iron frying pan over a fire. When treated thus the seeds swell and crack their coats much after the manner of parched corn. The roasted seeds are com-monly eaten dry without further preparation, tasting very much like popcorn, but sometimes they are ground into meal and made into a porridge or a bread." The large seeds, called Wokas, were an important farinaceous food of many western Indians.

In 1672 John Josselyn reported from New England that "the Indians eat the roots, which are long a boiling; they taste like the liver of a sheep. The moose deer feed much upon them, at which time the Indians kill them, when their heads are under water." Flatter-dock and Brandy-Bottles are local names in England—the flowers are said to smell of the stale dregs of brandy.

## Fragrant Waterlily

*Nymphaea odorata.* Of Nymphe (a water nymph); fragrant.

Alligator-Blankets (S.C.), Alligator-Bonnet (La.), Beaver-Root (Nfd.), Bonnets, Cow-Cabbage, Fairy-Boats (Texas), *Nénufar blanc* (P.Q.), *Pagayeur* (La., P.Q.), Pondlily, Sweet-Scented Pondlily, Sweet-Scented Waterlily, Toad-Lily, Water-Cabbage, Water-Nymph, Water-Queen (Texas), White Waterlily

On June 26, 1852, Thoreau wrote: "The *Nymphaea odorata,* water nymph, sweet water-lily, pond-lily, in bloom. A superb flower, our lotus queen of the waters. Now is the solstice in still waters. How sweet, innocent, whole-some its fragrance. How pure its white petals, though its root is in the mud! It must answer in my mind for what the Orientals say of the lotus flower. Probably the first a day or two since. To-morrow, then, will be the first Sab-bath when the young men, having bathed, will walk slowly and soberly to church in their best clothes, each with a lily in his hand or bosom, with as long a stem as he could get. At least I used to see them go by and come into church smelling a pond-lily, when I used to go myself. So that the flower is to some extent associated with bathing on Sab-bath mornings and going to church, its odor

*Fragrant Waterlily*

contrasting and atoning for that of the sermon."

Dr. Millspaugh reported that "the roots, in decoction, were much esteemed by Indian squaws as an internal remedy, and injection and wash for the worst forms of leukorrhoea, its properties in this direction being due to its astringency. The macerated root was also used as an application in the form of a poultice to suppurating glands; its styptic properties were also fully known and utilized." Most of the plant is edible—the leaves are eaten, raw or cooked, the flower buds are cooked or pickled, the rootstock boiled or roasted, and the ripe kernels cooked or dried and ground to meal.

# THE WATER-SHIELD FAMILY

## Cabombaceae

A family of two genera and eight species; found in tropical and warm temperate regions in both hemispheres.

### Water-Shield

*Brasenia schreberi.* (Origin obscure); of Schreber (Johann Christian Daniel Schreber, 1736–1810, a German botanist). (Also found in Europe, Asia, Africa and Australia.)
Deerfood, Egg-Bonnet (Tenn.), Frogleaf, Little Waterlily, Purple-Bonnet (Tenn.), Purple-Dock, Purple Wen-Dock, Small-Bonnet (Miss.), Water-Jelly, Water-Leaf, Water-Target

According to Rafinesque (1828), this plant was "unnoticed by all medical writers, but well known by the Indians." He reported, "The fresh leaves may be used like Lichen, in pulmonary complaints and dysentery: when dry the gelatinous matter almost disappears, yet they impart mucilage to the water. If no virose quality exists in this plant, as the taste of deer for it appears to indicate, it may become a useful substitute or auxiliary to Lichen in phthisis, inflammationa, debility,

*Water-Shield*

&c. boiled into decoction or jelly." The roots and leaves are eaten in many parts of the world, and the seeds are an important foodstuff for wildlife.

# THE BUTTERCUP OR CROWFOOT FAMILY

## *Ranunculaceae*

A large and diversified family of 58 genera and about 1,750 species of herbs, shrubs and woody vines; found in boreal and temperate regions of the New and Old World. Many species are cultivated as ornamentals, including Clematis, Columbine and Delphinium. *Ranunculus* is Latin for "a small frog" (*rana* means "frog"), presumably alluding to the watery habitat of many species.

## Aconites, Monkshoods, Wolfsbanes

*Aconitum.* (The Latin name from Greek *akoniton,* perhaps from *akonitos,* "dustless," i.e., an unconquerable poison).

"Fable has it that Aconite sprang out of the foam of the dog Cerberus when Hercules dragged him from the underworld" (Pliny). Al-Qazwini, a l3th-century physician, reported that "if the kings of India wished to betray enemy kings, they accustom a girl from her childhood to Aconite, by strewing it for a time under her cradle, then under her rug, then under her clothes, and continue gradually until the girl can consume Aconite without harm. In this way she develops a tolerance for it. The girl is then sent with presents to the king whom it is wished to betray, and if they copulate, he dies" (Copley and Boswell, 1944).

Garden Monkshood or Wolfsbane is *Aconitum napellus* ("little turnip," from the shape of the root). Gerard (1633) wrote that "Helmet-floure, or the great Monkes-hood, beareth very faire and goodly blew floures in shape like an helmet; which are so beautifull, that a man would thinke they were of some excellent vertue, but *non semper fides habenda fronte*"—appearances cannot always be trusted; the plant is exceedingly poisonous, and arrows were supposedly tipped with the juice to kill wolves. It contains at least three potent alkaloids, and on account of its local irritant effects and anesthetic action, affecting both the heart and central nervous system, it has had many medical uses (it was included in the USP), but because of "the closeness of the therapeutic and toxic doses it has lost the confidence of the profession" (USD).

## Monkshood

*Aconitum uncinatum.* (The Latin name); hooked (the tip of the "helmet"). Clambering Monkshood, Wild Monkshood, Wild Wolfsbane, Wolfbane

Dr. Porcher wrote that the tincture of Aconite is "useful as an external anaesthetic in frontal neuralgia, local pains, etc. No remedy, save chloroform, equals it when applied locally for relief of pain."

## White Baneberry

*Actaea pachypoda.* (From the Greek name of the Elder, transferred to this for the similarity of the leaves); with thick pedicels.

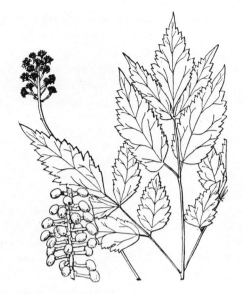

*White Baneberry*

American Herb-Christopher, Blue Cohosh (Maine), Button-Snakeroot, Chinaberry, Cohush, Doll's-Eyes, False-Aloe, Necklace-Weed, Pearl-Berry, Rattlesnake-Herb, Rattlesnake-Master, *Racine d'ours* (P.Q.), Richweed (Va.), Toadroot, White-Beads, White-Berry Snakeroot, White Cohosh (Maine)

"Cohush berries have just begun to be white, as if they contained a pearly venom,—wax white with a black spot (or very dark brown), imp-eyed," wrote Thoreau in 1852. Or like a doll's white china eyes. Dr. Millspaugh wrote that the root "will often be found useful in many forms of reflex uterine headache, some types of chronic fleeting rheumatism, congestion, in the female especially, and reflex uterine gastralgia." Among the Chippewa, the root was used to treat menorrhagia, while "the variety of this plant which had red berries . . . was used for diseases of men" (Densmore, 1928).

The Lloyds (1884–85) wrote that the two species of *Actaea,* "together with Cimicifuga racemosa, were used by the American Indians as emmenagogues and parturients, as well as in the cure of rheumatism. Thus they became

known to the whites, and by reason of their introduction were employed in domestic practice in the same manner. They accordingly were brought before the medical profession, and while the abundance of Cimicifuga racemosa enabled it to become a common remedy, the relative scarcity of the Actaeas kept them from being as well known."

## Red Baneberry

*Actaea rubra.* (From the Greek name for the Elder); red.

*Actée rouge* (P.Q.), Black Cohosh (Maine), Coral-Berry, Grapewort, Herb-Christopher, Necklace-Weed (Maine), *Pain de couleuvre* (P.Q.), Poison-Berry, *Poison de couleuvre* (P.Q.), Rattlesnake-Herb, Red-Berry, Red-Cohush, Snake-Berry (N.B.), Snakeroot, Toadroot

Manasseh Cutler called it Christopher and Baneberries and reported that "the berries are exceedingly poisonous. Dr. Withering says, the plant is powerfully repellant; and that the root is useful in some nervous cases, but it

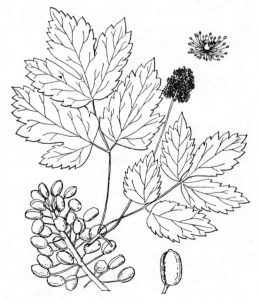

*Red Baneberry*

must be administered with caution. It is said, that toads, allured by the foetid smell of this plant, resort to it."

The Cheyenne cultural hero and prophet, Sweet Medicine or Sweet Root Standing, named this plant for himself, according to Jeffrey Hart (1980): "Sweet Medicine reputedly lived 445 years with the Cheyenne. Upon his death, he transformed his sacred powers into this plant. To this day, Cheyennes keep this root in the Sacred Arrow, Sacred Hat, and the Sun Dance bundles, thus benefiting from Sweet Medicine's sacred powers. It is the principal object in the chief's bundle, the one which Sweet Medicine gave to the Cheyenne after he returned from the Holy Mountain, Bear Butte. With the Sacred Arrows, he said to the Cheyennes: 'Don't forget me. This is my body I am giving you. Always think of me.' "

The Pillager Ojibwa make a tea from the root to be drunk by women after childbirth (Huron Smith, 1932), and the Thompson Indians of British Columbia drank a decoction as a remedy for syphilis and rheumatism (Teit, 1930). All parts of the plant are poisonous. Herb-Christopher is the British name for *Actaea spicata,* which Turner (1548) called Christophoriana or "Grapewurt, because it hath many blacke beries in the toppes lyke grapes."

## Anemones, Windflowers

*Anemone.* (From *Namaan,* a Semitic name for Adonis, from whose blood the flower supposedly sprang; or it grew from Aphrodite's tears as she wept for the slain Adonis.)
Lilies-of-the-Field

"Consider the lilies of the field, how they grow; they toil not, neither do they spin: And yet I say unto you, That even Solomon in all his glory was not arrayed like one of these" (Matthew 6:28–29). The "lilies of the field" are traditionally identified as Crown Anem-

one, *Anemone coronaria:* "In early spring thousands of crown anemones in scarlet (sometimes also in purple, pink, blue and white) dot every field, bush, wasteland and sandy hill in all the Mediterranean areas of the Land, and penetrate into the desert" (Zohary, 1982).

## Canada Anemone

*Anemone canadensis.* (From the Semitic name *Namaan*) of Canada.
Crowfoot (S.Dak), Little-Buffalo-Medicine, Round-Headed Anemone

"The root of this plant was one of the most highly esteemed medicines of the Omaha and Ponca," Gilmore (1914) reported. "The right to use this plant belonged to the medicine-men of the *Te-sinde* gens. To touch a buffalo was taboo to this gens; hence the name of the plant, little buffalo medicine."

## Long-Headed Thimbleweed

*Anemone cylindrica.* (From the Semitic name *Namaan*); cylindric.
Indian-Balm, Long-Fruited Anemone, Long-Headed Anemone, Nimbleweed, Thimbleweed

The fruiting head is shaped like a thimble. "Some Ponca used the woolly fruits of this plant as charms for good luck in playing cards, rubbing their hands in the smoke arising from burning some of the fruit" (Gilmore). Other Indian tribes made a poultice of the leaves to treat burns. Virginia Thimbleweed *(Anemone virginiana)* is called Nimbleweed, Tumbleweed, Wildflower and Windflower.

## Wood Anemone

*Anemone quinquefolia.* (From the Semitic name *Namaan*); five-leaved.
Bow-Bells, Drops-of-Snow, Granny's-Nightcap, Little-Buffalo-Medicine, Mayflower (Mass.), Nightcaps, Nimbleweed, Smell-Boxes, Snowboys, Snowdrops

(Mass.), Thimbleweed, Wild-Cucumber (N.H.), Wildflower, Windflower, Wood-Crowfoot, Wood-flower

According to Dr. Porcher, "It is said to be extremely acrid—even small doses producing a great disturbance of the stomach; employed as a rubefacient in fevers, gout, and rheumatism, and as a vesicatory in removing corns from the feet." Bow-Bells, Granny's-Nightcap and Smell-Foxes (Boxes in America) are local names in England for *Anemone nemerosa,* whose smell is said to be "foxy."

## Columbine, Wild Columbine
*Aquilegia canadensis.* (An obscure Medieval plant name); of Canada.
Akeley, *Ancolie* (P.Q.), Bells (Ohio), Cluckies (N.S.), Culverwort, *Gants de Notre-Dame* (P.Q.), Honey-Horns, Honeysuckle (Ill., Mass., N.H., Wis.), Jacket-and-Breeches, Jack-in-Trousers (Mass.), Lady's-Slipper (Mass.), Meetinghouses (New England), Red-Bells, Red Columbine, Rock-Bells, Rock-Lily (N.H.)

*Columba* is Latin for a dove. "The shape and proportion of the leaves [petals] do seem

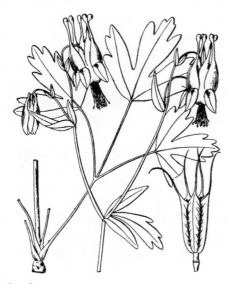

*Columbine*

to represent the figure of a dove or culver,—these floures produce hollows with a long crooked tayl like a Lark's-claw (and bending somewhat to the proportion of the neck of a Culver)" (Lyte, 1578). (A culver is a pigeon or dove.)

Among the Indians of the Missouri River Region, "The seeds are used by Omaha and Ponca, especially by bachelors, as a perfume. To obtain the odor the seeds must be crushed, a result which the Omaha commonly get by chewing to a paste. This paste is spread among the clothes, where its fragrant quality persists for a long time, being perceptible whenever dampened by dew or rain. Among the Pawnee the seeds are used for perfume and as a love charm" (Gilmore). "It has been used as a diuretic, diaphoretic, antiscorbutic, tonic, laxative, and emmenagogue. It is probably dangerous" (Jacobs and Burlage).

## Crimson Columbine, Red Columbine, Sitka Columbine
*Aquilegia formosa.* (An obscure Medieval plant name); beautiful.

Among the Thompson Indians, "Women use this plant as a charm to gain the affection of men and both sexes use it to retain wealth and possessions. It is also considered good luck in gambling" (James Teit, 1930).

## Western Marsh-Marigold, Elkslip
*Caltha leptosepala.* A Latin flower name (Greek *kalathos* means a cup); thin-sepaled.
Mountain Marsh-Marigold

Elk and moose feed on the leaves. Like the Cowslip (see below), this plant has been seen as a lip as well as a slip; to some observers, the leaf is the shape of an elk's lip.

## Marsh-Marigold, Cowslip
*Caltha palustris.* (A Latin flower name); of swamps. (Also found in Europe.)

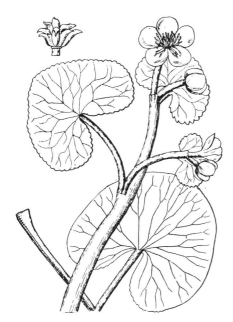

*Western Marsh-Marigold*

American-Cowslip, Boots, Bouts, Bullflower, Bull's-Eyes, Capers (Maine), Coltsfoot (Maine, N.H.), Coltsroot (Ohio), Cowlily (Mass.), Cowslops (Vt.), Crazy-Bets, Crowfoot (Maine), Drunkards, English-Marigold, Gollands, Gools, Great Bitter-Flower, Ground-Ivy, Horse-Blob, King-Cup, Mare-Blebs, Mare-Blobs, Mary-Buds, Mayblobs (Mass.), Meadow-Bouts, Meadow-Bright, Meadow-Buttercup (New England), Meadow-Gowan, Palsywort, *Populage* (P.Q.), Soldier's-Buttons, *Souci d'eau* (P.Q.), Spring-Cowslip, Water-Bowls, Water-Dragon, Water-Fennel, Water-Goggle, Water-Gowan, Water-Starwort

"Marsh Marigold hath great broad leaves, somewhat round, smooth, of a gallante green colour, slightly indented or purld about the edges, among which rise up thicke fat stalkes, likewise greene; whereupon doe grow goodly yellow flowers, glittering like gold" (Gerard, 1633). Marsh-Marigold may be derived from Anglo-Saxon *mersc,* a marsh, and *meargealla*—*mearh* meaning "horse" and *gealla* meaning "a gall or blister": "The Marsh Marigold was called *meargealla,* a Horse-Blob or

Mare-Blob, either because the tight round buds suggested a round swelling, or else because the flowers resemble large buttercups, and buttercup roots were used for raising blisters in counter-irritation" (Grigson). *Blob* is dialect for *bleb,* a blister.

"The flowers gathered, and preserved in salted vinegar, are a good substitute for capers," Manasseh Cutler wrote in 1785, and "it has been supposed, that the remarkable yellowness of butter in the spring, is caused by this plant: but Boerhaave says, if cows eat it, it will occasion such inflammation, that they generally die." Hermann Boerhaave (1668–1738) was professor of medicine and botany at the University of Leiden.

In Shakespeare's *Cymbeline,* (2.3.22),

> *And winking Mary-buds begin*
> *To ope their golden eyes;*
> *With everything that pretty is,*
> *My lady sweet arise!*

April 29, 1852: "But the season is most forward at the second Division Brook, where the cowslip is in blossom,—and nothing yet planted at home,—these bright-yellow *suns* of the meadow, in rich clusters, their flowers contrasting with the green leaves, from amidst the all-producing, dark-bottomed water. A flower-fire bursting up, as if through crevices in the meadow where they grow" (Thoreau). "And the wild marsh-marigold shines like fire in swamps and hollows gray" (Tennyson, *The May Queen*).

Cowslip in Britain is a Primrose, *Primula veris,* a common spring plant of fields and pastures with scented yellow flowers. Cowslip is conventionally derived from Old English *cuslyppe,* cow dung, presumably because they flourish in cow pastures. The *Oxford Dictionary of English Etymology* adds that *slyppe* also means "cow slobber." Ben Jonson in *Pan's Anniversary* wrote of "the prime-rose drop, the Spring's own spouse,/Bright day's eyes, and the lips of cows." Thoreau, writing of Marsh-Marigold in 1852, repeated the conceit: "Cowslips show at a distance in the meadows (Miles). The new butter is white still, but with these *cows' lips* in the grass it will soon be yellow, I trust. This yellowness in the spring, derived from the sun, affects even the cream in the cow's bag, and flowers in yellow butter at last. Who has not turned pale at the sight of hay butter? These are the cows's lips."

"In many parts of the country the Marsh Marigold is much used as a potherb, especially in the spring at or near the flowering season and before most garden greens are ready for use" (Medsger, 1939).

The names Gowan, Gowlan and Golland are English dialect names for many golden or yellow flowers; Gool is a Marigold. Drunkards comes "probably from the way they suck up water when placed in a vase" *(Oxford English Dictionary)*. English children also believed that staring at the flowers made one crazy (Crazy-Bets). Capers, Cowlily, Great Bitter-Flower, Palsywort and Water-Fennel appear to be American names.

## Black Cohosh, Bugbane

*Cimicifuga racemosa.* Bug repel (Latin, *cimex,* a bug, *fuga,* flight; the ground roots of European species have been used as an insect repellent); racemed.

Battle-Weed, Big-Snakeroot (Md.), Black-Snakeroot, Blueberry, Blue-Ginseng, Bugwort, Columbine-Leaved-Leontice, Cordate-Rattletop, Fairy-Candles, False-Cohosh, Heart-Leaved Rattletop, Meadow Rue-Leontice, Papoose-Root, Rattleroot, Rattle-Snakeroot, Rattletop, Rattleweed, Richweed, Squawroot, Squaw-Weed, Star-Lance, Tall-Snakeroot, Yellow-Ginseng

"Black snakeroot, remedying rheumatism, gout, and amenorrhea, found such wide usage

*Black Cohosh*

during the last half of the seventeenth century that its price per pound in Virginia on one occasion rose from ten shillings to three pounds sterling" (Hughes, 1957).

In their 48-page chapter on Black-Snakeroot, the Lloyds (1884–85) wrote that it has been used as a gargle in sore throats, as a drench for the murrain in cattle, for pulmonary affections (including tuberculosis), snakebite, rheumatic pains, hemorrhage, smallpox, dropsy, hysteria, chorea, nervous headaches, profound melancholy, aberration of mind, delirium tremens, and cerebrospinal diseases and "in abnormal conditions of the principal organs of reproduction." One researcher reported, "A lady patient of mine, who was taking five drops of the first dilution for rheumatism, was annoyed by an illusion of a mouse running from under her chair. This illusion disappeared upon suspending the medicine, and recurred when taking the same doses." Another wrote that "no drug in our materia medica uniformly causes such severe pain in the head both internal and external. Initially it causes passive congestion or anaemia, according to the constitution of the prover. Externally it causes pains in the muscles and the nerves supplying them."

"The aborigines of America already discovered medicinal virtues in this plant; finding it, as they did, growing in various parts of the country, they soon learned to use and value it highly for a variety of complaints, chief among which were rheumatism and amenorrhoea. In rheumatism they depended much more on a decoction of the roots externally than internally. A hole was made in the ground, into which they put a kettle containing a quantity of the hot decoction. The rheumatic limbs were placed over the kettle in such a manner as to receive the influence of the steam . . . In facilitating parturition and as an emmenagogue it was also highly esteemed by the Indian women, whence its name— squaw-root. It was also used by Indian doctors for ague and fevers, which it cured by profuse perspiration" (Sattler, in Lloyd & Lloyd, 1884–85).

The USD concluded that it has no therapeutic value but is "still used in the treatment of chorea, chronic rheumatism, and tinnitus aureum and as a tonic." It has been included in the USP and NF. "Although a plant of no Agricultural value—and probably over-rated as a medicine—the infusion of the bruised root is so generally regarded as a sort of *Panaceae* for stock (especially for sick cows) that every farmer ought to know it and be able with certainty to designate it " (Darlington, 1847).

## Vase-Flower, Sugarbowl, Leather-Flower

*Clematis hirsutissima*. (Greek name of a climbing plant); most hairy.
Hairy Leather-Flower, Headache-Weed, Lion's-Beard, Old-Man's-Whiskers, Vase-Vine

Geyer (1846) reported that "the Saptona Indians use the root of this plant as a stimu-

lant, when horses fall down during their innumerable races. They hold a scraped end of the root in the nostrils of the fallen horse. The effect of this is instantaneous: it produces trembling, the animal springs up, and is led to the water to refresh its limbs. I have been told that it never failed, nor produced bad consequences. The scraped root leaves a burning sensation for half a day, if touched with the tongue."

## Western Virgin's-Bower, Pipestems, Traveler's-Joy

*Clematis ligusticifolia*. (Greek name of a climbing plant); with leaves of *Ligusticum*.
Hill Clematis, Pepper-Vine, Western Clematis, Western Virgin's-Bower, Windflower (Calif.)

The peppery stems and leaves have been chewed as a remedy for colds and sore throats, but they may be poisonous. The Thompson Indians use the plant to make a head wash for scabs and eczema, and a mild decoction is drunk as a tonic (Teit, 1930).

## Purple Clematis

*Clematis occidentalis*. (Greek name of a climbing plant); of the west.
Blue Clematis, False Virgin's-Bower, Mountain Clematis, Purple Virgin's-Bower, Western Blue Traveler's-Joy, Whorl-Leaved Clematis

The Blackfoot name is "ghost's lariat," according to Alex Johnston, "because it crept over the ground and grew over nearby vegetation. As they walked along the trails, the Indians were sometimes tripped unexpectedly."

## Leather-Flower

*Clematis viorna*. (Greek name of a climbing plant); (a Latin name).
American Traveler's-Joy, Headache-Weed, Vase-Vine

Viorna is the old name for the European *Clematis vitalba* transferred to this plant. Gerard (1633) derived Viorna from "*vias ornans,* of decking and adorning waies and hedges, where people travel; and whereupon I have named it Travellers-Joy." This and the other Leather-Flowers have thick, leathery sepals.

## Virgin's-Bower

*Clematis virginiana.* (Greek name of a climbing plant); of Virginia.

Devil's-Darning-Needle (Vt.), Devil's-Hair (Va.), Devil's-Thread, Gander-Vine (South), *Herbe aux gueux* (P.Q.), Ladies'-Bower, Leather-Flower, Love-Vine, Old-Man's-Beard, Pipe-Stem, Traveler's-Ivy, Traveler's-Joy (N.H.), Wild-Hops (Maine, N.H.), Woodbine (Maine)

The Lloyds report (1884–85) that a tincture of the leaves and flowers has been found "particularly useful in the reflex neurosis of women, arising from irritation of the ovaries and urinary organs; also for the neurosis of men, when connected with painful affections of the testicles and bladder."

"It is Old Man's Beard (cf. German *Altermannsbart*) from the long feathery styles. But observe that the Old Man, as so frequently in English plant names, may also be the devil" (Grigson). In the French Canadian name above, *gueux* means "beggar or rascal."

## Common Larkspur

*Consolida ajacis.* Make firm (from its use in healing wounds); of Ajax. (From Europe.)

Annual Larkspur, Garden Larkspur, Knight's-Spur, Lark's-Claw, Lousewort, Rocket Larkspur

Gerard (1633) wrote that in English it was "Larks spur, Larks heele, Larks toes, and Larks claw: in High-Dutch Ridder spoozen, that is, Equitis calcar, Knights spur." Although it has had many medical uses, particularly as a parasiticide, "the only therapeutic purpose for which the use of delphiniums seems at all justifiable is for the destruction of lice in the hair. Even for this purpose their use is inadvisable because of their high toxiciy" (USD).

## Goldthread

*Coptis trifolia.* Cut (the divided leaves); three-leaved. (Also found in Asia.)

Canker-Root (Maine), Mouth-Root, *Sabouillane* (P.Q.), *Savoyane* (P.Q.), *Sibouillane* (P.Q.), *Tissavoyanne jaune* (P.Q.), Yellow-Root (Maine, N.H.)

Dr. Bigelow reported that "of this article larger quantities are sold in the druggists' shops in Boston than of almost any other indigenous production. The demand for it arises from its supposed efficacy in aphthous and other ulcerations of the mouth." By 1884, however, according to the Lloyds, "It is now so generally unimportant that, excepting an occasional call for domestic use, it is out of the market." The Lloyds quoted a letter written to them by a Mr. Chas. A. Peck of Albany, N.Y.: "I recall a fact that came under my observation several years ago. In a low piece of swampy woods abounding in sphagnum, situated in Rennselaer County in this state [New York], there was an abundance of Coptis. The Shakers were then paying 37½ cents a pound for the dried plants, roots and all. The women and children of several families

*Goldthread*

living in the vicinity of this piece of woods spent most of one summer in these woods (which were mostly of spruce and balsam trees), digging Goldthread to sell to the Shakers. They dug it out with their hands only, sitting down by a smudge built to keep off gnats and mosquitoes, while they pick out the 'roots' from among the sphagnum and other mosses among which they crept. They would take their lunch with them and spend the whole day in the swampy woods, and when they had accumulated a wagon-load of the dried material, one of the number would start with it for the Shaker settlement in Lebanon, forty miles away."

The yellow, thready roots contain berberine and "are astringent, and of a bitterish taste. Chewed in the mouth they cure aphthas and cankerous sores. It is frequently an ingredient in gargle for sore throats" (Cutler, 1785). It has been included in the USP and NF. In Maine "canker-root was used for children and adults with canker-sores or facial eruptions" (Perkins, 1929). Peter Kalm reported (1749), "This plant is called *Tissavoy-anne jaune* by the French in Canada. Its leaves and stalks are used by the Indians for giving a fine yellow color to several kinds of work which they make of prepared skins. The French who have learnt this from them, dye wool and other things yellow with this plant."

## Nuttall's Larkspur, Western Larkspur, Bilobed Delphinium

*Delphinium nuttallianum.* Like a dolphin; of Nuttall (Thomas Nuttall, 1786–1859).

The Indians extracted a blue dye from the flowers, and early western settlers made an ink from the dye.

Thomas Nuttall was born and died in England. At age 21, he arrived in Philadelphia as a printer, but he soon devoted himself to natural history. In 1809–1810, he made collecting trips to Delaware, Niagara Falls, Ontario and Detroit, and in 1811 he traveled 1,600 miles up the Missouri River. He made the dangerous ascent of the Arkansas River to the Great Salt River in 1819. He was curator of the Botanic Garden in Cambridge and professor of natural history at Harvard College from 1822 to 1832. During the 1830s, he crossed the Rocky Mountains, explored Oregon and Upper California and visited Hawaii. He returned to England in 1842, where he had inherited an estate from his uncle on the condition that he live there. His publications include *Genera of North American Plants,* 1818, volumes of journals of his travels, a geological survey of the Mississippi Valley and the *Manual of Ornithology,* 1832–1834. Asa Gray wrote in 1844 that "no botanist has visited so large a portion of the United States, or made such an amount of observations in the field and forest. Probably few naturalists have excelled him in aptitude for such observations, in quickness of eye, tact in discrimination and tenacity of memory."

## Liverwort

*Hepatica nobilis.* Of the liver; noble. (Two varieties are recognized: var. *acuta,* with sharp-lobed leaves, and var. *obtusa,* with round-lobed leaves.) (Also found in Eurasia.)
Blue-Anemone, Choisy, Common Liverleaf, Crystal-Wort, Edellebare, Golden-Trefoil, Heartleaf, Heartleaf-Liverwort, Heart-Liverleaf, Heart-Liverwort (N.Y.), Herb-Trinity, Ivy-Flower, Kidney-Liverleaf, Kidneywort, Livermoss, Mayflower (N.Y., P.Q.). Mouse-Ears (N.H.), Noble Liverwort (Maine, Ohio), Paas-Blumes (N.Y.), Pass-Blummies (N.Y.) , Red-Coonroot (southern Negro), Round-Leaved Hepatica, Round-Lobed Liverleaf, Sharp-Lobed Liverwort, Spring-Beauty (N.Y., Wis.), Squirrel-Cups (N.Y.,Vt.), Three-Leaf Liverwort, Trefoil, *Trinitaire* (P.Q.)

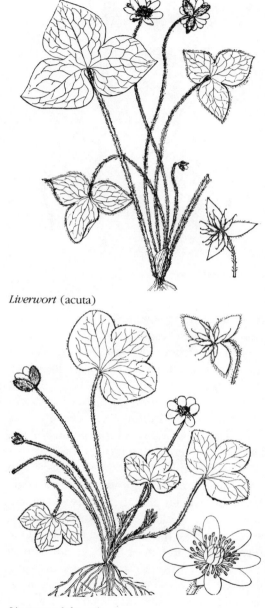

*Liverwort* (acuta)

*Liverwort* (obtusa)

"This herbe is called Lyverworte. His vertue is to destroy and clense the hardnes of the lyver" (Banckes, 1525). But 100 years later, Parkinson (1629) wrote, "These are thought to cool and strengthen the liver, the name

importing as much; but I never saw any great use of them by any of the physicians of our London College." Parkinson called the European Hepatica, "the great single blew Hepatica or noble Liverwort. In Latin *Hepatica nobilis, Hepatica trifolium, Trifolium nobile, Trifolium aureum, Trinitas, Herba Trinitatis.*" The leaves are shaped like a liver, heart or kidney.

The Lloyds report (1884–85) that there was little medical use of the plant in America until about 1880: "At this time a demand suddenly sprung up, and the country was afterwards scoured by the consumers or their agents. Circulars were scattered over the sections of our country where the plant was collected, urging gatherers of plants to give it special attention." Soon the supply from America became insufficient, and plants were imported from Germany. "From the importers of New York and the collectors of America," the Lloyds write, "we have statistics to show that in the aggregate 425,282 pounds of liver leaf were collected and imported to supply the demand during 1883. It is to be expected that some escape our notice; and we think it can be safely said that during the year 1883 an aggregate of 450,000 pounds were imported and gathered for our home market." The Lloyds conclude that "hepatica is as inefficient a plant as we can find," but "a demand was created for it by manufacturers of prominent proprietary medicines."

Pass-Blummies is a combination name for Liverwort. "Pass" or "Paas," from the Dutch *Paasch,* was a common name for Easter in New York State; Bartlett (1859) has explained the origin of "blummies." "A gentleman, ruralizing along the banks of the Hudson, stopped to pick some wildflowers near where sat an aged man, and said: 'These flowers are beautiful,—it is a treat for one from the city to gaze on them!' 'Flowers?' replied the old man, with an air of bewilderment. 'Flowers!

What be they?' 'Why these!' replied I, stooping and picking some. 'Oh, the *blummies!* Yes, the blummies be very thick hereabouts.'"

Susan Cooper (1850) wrote that "one often sees these flowers at the foot of trees, growing on their roots, as it were; and perhaps it is this position, which, added to their downy, furred leaves and stems, has given them the name of squirrel-cups—a prettier name certainly for a wood flower, than liverwort."

Among the Cherokees, "those who dream of snakes drink a decoction of this herb and the walking fern to produce vomiting, after which the dreams do not return. The traders buy large quantities of liverwort from the Cherokees, who may thus have learned to esteem it more highly than they otherwise would" (Mooney, 1891).

And in the Carolina mountains, "a girl can infallibly win the love of any sweetheart she may desire by secretly throwing over his clothing some of the powder made by rubbing together a few heart leaves which have been dried by the fire" (Mooney, 1889).

## Golden-Seal

*Hydrastis canadensis*. Water-acting (supposed medical properties); of Canada.

Curcuma, Eye-Balm, Eyeroot, Golden-Root, Ground-Raspberry, Indian-Dye, Indian-Iceroot, Indian-Plant, Indian-Turmeric, Jaundice-Root, Ohio-Curcuma, Orange-Root, Turmeric, Turmeric-Root, Wild-Curcuma, Yellow-Eye, Yellow-Eye-Wright, Yellow-Paintroot, Yellow-Puccoon, Yellow-Root, Yellow-Wort

In 1804 Dr. Barton reported, "The Hydrastis is a popular remedy in some parts of the United-States. A spirituous infusion of the root is employed as a tonic bitter, in the western parts of Pennsylvania, &c. and there can be little doubt that, both in this and in other shapes, our medicine may be used with much advantage. An infusion of the root, in cold

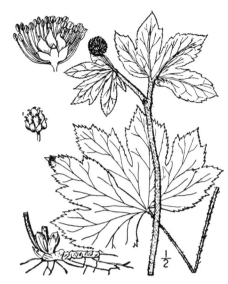

*Golden-Seal*

water, is also employed as a wash, in inflammations of the eyes." Barton also wrote, "The root of the Hydrastis supplies us with one of the most brilliant yellow colours with which we are acquainted."

In their *Drugs and Medicines of North America* (1884–85), the Lloyds devoted over 100 pages to Golden-Seal, recounting its botanical, commercial and medical history, analyzing its microscopical structure and constituents and describing its physiologic effects and many therapeutic uses—for example, in gastrointestinal disorders, cancer and diseases of the eyes, ears and skin. One researcher found it "efficacious in hemorrhages from myoma, from congestive dysmenorrhea, from subinvolution, also in those attending metritis and endometritis" and proposed that "the medicine acts upon the uterine mucous membrane, exciting vascular contractions, through which mechanisms it diminishes congestion of the genital organs." In 1950 the USD noted that "the effect of hydrastis in increasing the tonus and exciting rhythmic contractions of the uterus has been

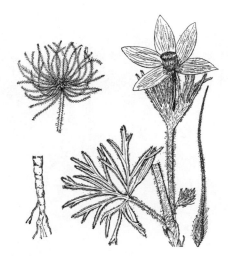

*Pasqueflower*

confirmed; its uterine hemostatic effect is thus attributable to compression of blood vessels." The root also contains an antibiotic that is effective against broad-spectrum bacteria and protozoa (Lewis and Elvin-Lewis). The 1918 USD estimated that between 200,000 and 300,000 pounds of the drug produced from the root were used annually. When the wild plant came close to extinction, much of this was supplied from cultivated plants. It was included in the USP and in the NF until 1955.

Puccoon is Algonquian for a number of plants that yield a red or yellow dye. The leaves and (inedible) fruit resemble those of raspberry. *Curcuma longa* of India yields the spice and yellow dye turmeric.

## Pasqueflower

*Pulsatilla patens.* Quiverer (they shake in the wind); spreading. (Also found in Eastern Europe and Siberia.)

American Pulsatilla, April-Fools (Ill.), Cat's-Eyes, Crocus (Iowa, Ill., Minn., Wyo.), Easter-Flower (Wis.), Gosling (Minn.), Hartshorn-Plant (Minn.), Headache-Plant (Minn.), Lion's-Beard, Mayflower, Meadow-Anemone, Old-Man (Alta.), Prairie-Anemone, Prairie-Crocus (Colo., Mont.,

N.Dak), Prairie-Hen-Flower, Prairie-Smoke (Minn.), Red-Calf-Flower (Prairie Indians), Rocklily (Wis.), Stone-Lily (Wis.), Wild-Crocus (Wis.), Wind Anemone (Wis.), Windflower (Wis.)

Pasqueflower in Britain is the similar *Pulsatilla vulgaris,* whose name was Passeflower (Lyte, 1578) until Gerard (1597) changed it: "They floure for the most part about Easter, which has mooved me to name it *Pasque Floure,* or Easter floure" (*pasque* is the Old French for Easter, from Greek *paskha;* related to Hebrew *pesakh,* Passover). He also noted that "when the whole floure is past there succedeth an head or knop, compact of many gray hairy lockes"—suggesting smoke or a badger, gosling or lion's mane. Among the Blackfoot Indians, "The grayish, silky seed heads of the species reminded the Indians of the gray heads of old men hence the name *[Napi].* The crushed leaves, which contain a vesicant, were rubbed on affected parts as a counter-irritant" (Johnston, 1970).

Gilmore wrote in 1914, "When an old Dakota first finds one of these flowers in the springtime it reminds him of his childhood, when he wandered over the prairie hills at play, as free from care and sorrow as the flowers and the birds. He sits down near the flower on the lap of Mother Earth, takes out his pipe and fills it with tobacco. Then he reverently holds the pipe toward the earth, then toward the sky, then toward the north, the east, the south, and the west. After this act of silent invocation he smokes."

Pasqueflowers have been called April-Fools, "perhaps because they blossom about April 1, and are afterwards sometimes snowed under" (Bergen, 1893). According to an eclectic physician cited by the Lloyds (1884–85), "The pulsatilla exerts a marked influence upon the reproductive organs of both male and female. I regard it as decidedly the best emmenagogue, when the suppression is not the result of, or attended by, irritation and determination of blood; where there is simple suppression from atony or nervous shock, it may be used with confidence. In male or female it lessens sexual excitement. It does not diminish sexual power, but rather strengthens it, by lessening morbid excitement."

## Buttercups, Crowfoots

*Ranunculus.* Small frog.

Gold-Cup, King's-Cup, Meadow-Bloom, *Renoncule* (P.Q.), Spearwort, Yellow-Weed

Cow pastures can be gold with Buttercups, which were believed to give butter its golden color in spring. Farmers have been known to rub the flowers on the cow's udder and hang them over the barn door to make the milk rich with golden cream. Actually, all grazing animals try to avoid these acrid plants, which can poison them and make cow's milk unpalatable.

## Kidneyleaf Buttercup, Small-Leaved Buttercup

*Ranunculus abortivus.* Small frog; abortive (reduced styles and petals).

Chicken-Pepper, Kidney-Leaved Crowfoot, Small-Flowered Crowfoot, Smooth-Leaved Crowfoot

According to John Bartram (1751), a decoction of this plant was drunk as a remedy for inveterate syphilis.

## Common Buttercup

*Ranunculus acris.* Small frog; acrid. (From Europe.)

Bachelor's-Buttons (Pa.), Biting Crowfoot, Blister-Plant, Blister-Wort, *Bouton d'or* (P.Q.), Burrwort, Butter-Cresses, Butter-Daisy, Butter-Flower, Butter-Rose, Gold-Balls, Gold-Knops, Goldweed, Horse-Gold, Kingcup (Maine), Meadow-Bloom, Meadow Buttercup, Queen's-Button (Ohio), Tall Crowfoot, Yellow-Daisy (Mass., N.H.), Yellow-Gowan, Yellow-Pilewort, Yellows

*Common Buttercup*

The Lloyds wrote (1884–85), "In the olden time the different acrid species of Ranunculus were used rather freely in medicine. As the practice of medicine inclined towards a humane system, physicians gradually substituted less virulent remedies; and in modern times we find that few who give large doses care to use such agents as the Ranunculus plants, even externally. They produce painful, sometimes deep ulcers, and blister some persons very quickly."

## Bulbous Buttercup

*Ranunculus bulbosus.* Small frog; bulbous (root). (From Europe.)

Biting Crowfoot, Blister-Flower, Bulbous Crowfoot, Buttercup, Butter-Cress, Butter-Daisy, Butter-Flower, Butter-Rose, Cuckoo-Buds, Frogwort, Giltcups, Gold-Balls, Goldcups, Golden-Knops, Gold-Knobs, Goldweed, Gowan, Horse-Gold, Kingcups, Meadow-Gold, Pilewort, Pissabed, St. Anthony's-Rape, St. Anthony's-Turnip, Turnip Buttercup, Yellow-Weed

"It is commonly called *Rapum D. Anthonij,* or Saint Anthonies Rape," according to Gerard (1633), the rape or turnip being the bulbous root, which, "being stamped with salt is good for those that have a plague sore, if it be presently in the beginning tied to the thigh, in the middle between the groin or flanke and the knee: by means whereof, the poyson and malignitie of the disease is drawn from the inward parts, by the emunctorie or clensing place of the flanke, into those outward parts of lesse account. For it exulcerateth and presently raiseth a blister to what part of the body soever it is applied." It had a reputation as a powerful diuretic (Pissabed) and was listed in the USP until 1870. Shakespeare wrote, "Cuckoo-buds of yellow hue do paint the meadows with delight" (*Love's Labour's Lost* 5.2.902).

## Lesser Celandine

*Ranunculus ficaria.* Small frog; like figs (the tubers; the old generic name). (From Europe.)

Burwort, Crain, *Ficaire* (P.Q.), Figwort Buttercup, Golden-Cup, Golden-Guineas, Pilewort

In 1652 Nicholas Culpeper wrote: "It is under the dominion of Mars, and behold here another verification of the learning of the Ancients, *viz.* that the virtue of an herb may be known by its Signature, as plainly appears in this: for if you dig up the roots of it, you shall perceive the perfect image of that disease which they commonly call the Piles. It is certain by good experience that the decoction of the leaves and roots doth wonderfully help Piles and Haemorrhoids, also kernels by the ear and throat, called the King's-Evil, or any other hard wens and tumours . . . With this I cured my own daughter of the King's Evil, broke the sore, drew out a quarter of a pint of corruption, cured without any scar at all in one week's time." The King's Evil, or

*Lesser Celandine*

scrofula, was marked by tuberculous swellings of the lymphatic glands of the neck, also known as scrofulous tumors or strumas. From the time of Philip I of France in the 11th century, the King's Evil was supposed to be cured by the king's or queen's touch. In 1712 Queen Anne touched 200 persons with the disease, including three-year-old Samuel Johnson. Crain is a local name in England. The other Figwort is *Scrophularia.* Celandine is *Chelidonium majus.*

## Small Yellow-Water-Buttercup

*Ranunculus gmelinii.* Small frog; of Gmelin (Johann Georg Gmelin, 1709–1755, its discoverer). (Also found in Asia.)

Pursh's Buttercup, Small Yellow-Water-Crowfoot, Yellow Water-Crowfoot

It has a "strong fresh-water marsh smell, rather agreeable sometimes as a bottle of salts, like the salt marsh and sea weeds, invigorating to my imagination" (Thoreau, 1853). A previous name was *Ranunculus purshii,* named afer Frederick Pursh. Gmelin, a member of a famous family of scientists, was born and died in Tübingen, Germany, where he was professor of botany and chemistry. He explored Siberia with Bering in the 1730s and 1740s.

## Macoun's Buttercup

*Ranunculus macounii.* Small frog; of Macoun (John Macoun, 1831–1920, its discoverer).

John Macoun was born in Ireland and died in British Columbia. He emigrated to Canada as a young man and farmed in Ontario for several years. In 1872 he served as botanist on an expedition across Canada to the Pacific, and in 1875, with one companion and mostly by canoe, he journeyed from the Canadian Rockies to Ontario, a journey of 8,000 miles. Subsequently he was professor of botany and natural sciences at Albert College, Belleville, Ontario, botanist to the Canadian government and naturalist to the Canadian Geological Survey.

## Cursed Buttercup

*Ranunculus sceleratus.* Small frog; cursed. (Also found in Eurasia.)

Biting Crowfoot, Blisterwort, Celery-Leaved Crowfoot, Cursed Crowfoot, Ditch Crowfoot, Marsh Crowfoot, Water-Celery

This flower is called "cursed" because of its blistering juice. "The bruised herb is said to raise a blister, which is not easily healed, and by which strolling beggars sometimes excite compassion" (Don, 1832). The plant has a high concentration of protoanemonin (the acrid component of all Buttercups) and is considered "especially dangerous" to livestock (Kingsbury, 1964).

## Meadow-Rues

*Thalictrum.* (A Greek name; *Thalia,* "the blooming one," is the muse of pastoral poetry and comedy.)

*Pigamon* (P.Q.)

The leaves resemble those of Rue *(Ruta).* Pliny wrote that Thalictrum "prevents hair falling out, or if it has already done so, restores it." But some Thalictrums contain thalictrine, a "very active cardiac poison" (USD).

## Early Meadow-Rue

*Thalictrum dioicum.* (A Greek plant name); dioecious.

Early Mountain-Rue, Feathered-Columbine, Poor-Man's-Rhubarb, Quicksilver-Weed (Maine), Shining-Grass (Vt.)

"The roots of the plant are purgative and diuretic; the plant has been used for sciatica, snake bite, and spruce beer" (Jacobs & Burlage). When placed in water, the leaves appear silvery.

## Tall Meadow-Rue

*Thalictrum pubescens.* (A Greek plant name); downy.

Celandine (Maine), Fall Meadow-Rue, Fall Mountain-Rue, Feather-Columbine, Fen-Rue (South), *Grand Pigamon* (P.Q.), Muskrat-Weed, Musquash-Weed (Maine, Mass.), Musket-Weed, King-of-the-Meadow (N.H.), Quicksilver-Weed, Rattlesnake-Bite (N.H.), Silver-Weed (Maine)

*Tall Meadow-Rue*

## Purple Meadow-Rue

*Thalictrum revolutum*. (A Greek plant name); with edge rolled back.

Maid-of-the-Mist, Skunk-Leaved Meadow-Rue, Wax-Leaved Meadow-Rue, Waxy Meadow-Rue

Among the Potawatomi, "the seed of the plant is used as a love medicine. When a man and his wife have been quarreling, the seeds are surreptitiously placed in their food to overcome the quarrelsome disposition. The Forest Potawatomi use the leaves and the seeds in combination with other materials to cure cramps" (Huron Smith, 1933). "The rue, just budded, smells remarkably like a skunk and also like a rank dog. Strange affinity" (Thoreau, 1854). It has waxlike glands on the undersurface of the leaves.

Gilmore (1914) wrote of the Midwestern Purple Meadow-Rue, *Thalictrum dasycarpum* ("hairy-fruited") that, among the Teton Dakota, "the fruits on approaching maturity in August are broken off and stored away for their pleasant odor; for this purpose they are rubbed and scattered over the clothing. The Indians say the effect is enhanced by dampness. This, like all other odors used by Indians, is of slight, evanescent fragrance. They use no heavy scents; all are delicate and give a suggestion of wholesomeness and of the freedom of the uncontaminated outdoors."

## Rue-Anemone

*Thalictrum thalictroides*. A Greek plant name; like *Thalictrum* (it was previously called *Anemonella thalictroides*).

Anemone (Ohio), Mayflower (Mass.), Starflower (Mass.), Wild-Potato (Pa.), Windflower (Ohio)

"I know of mountainous districts in Pennsylvania where these roots are collected and eaten under the name of 'wild potato'" (Medsger, 1939).

# THE BARBERRY FAMILY

## *Berberidaceae*

A family of 15 genera and 650 species of herbs, shrubs and small trees, found mainly in north temperate regions. The Old French *berberis,* Italian *berberi* and Spanish *berberis* are derived from the Arabic *barbaris.*

## Vanilla-Leaf, Deer-Foot

*Achlys triphylla*. Mist (Greek *akhlus*); three-leaved (one leaf cleft in three).

Mayleaf, Sweet-After-Death

Moldenke (1949) wrote of this "fragrant little plant" that "settlers on the Humboldt coast prize the plant's delicate fragrance and hang bunches of the leaves in their houses." In western Washington, "The Cowlitz use the leaves in an infusion drunk for tuberculosis.

*Blue Cohosh*

The Skagit also use it for tuberculosis, and they boil the leaves for a hair wash" (Gunther, 1945).

## Blue Cohosh

*Caulophyllum thalictroides.* Stem leaf; like Thalictrum.

Blueberry, Blueberry-Cohosh, Blueberry-Root, Blue-Ginseng, Columbine-Leaved Leontice, False Cohosh (Mass.), Green-Vivian, Lion's-Foot, Meadow-Rue Leontice, Papoose-Root, Poppoose-Root (Mass.), Squaw-Root, Yellow-Ginseng

Rafinesque reported that "the Indian women owe the facility of their parturition to a constant use of a tea of the root for two or three weeks before their time. As a powerful emmenagogue it promotes delivery, menstruation, and dropsical discharges." This notion was confirmed by Dr. John Gunn, author of the *New Domestic Physician* of 1857: "This is an Indian remedy, and considered by them as one of great value, principally used by the squaws as a parturient—that is to facilitate childbirth; hence the name Pappoose root . . . It has been abundantly proved as a valuable article in this respect by our white women." Huron Smith (1933) wrote, "This is known to the Forest Potawatomi as the Squaw Root and it seems to be of rather universal use amongst our Indian tribes to furnish a tea which suppresses profuse menstruation and aids in childbirth."

According to an eclectic physician cited by the Lloyds (1886–87), "its more prominent properties appear to be sedative, antispasmodic, and oxytocic; and, from its especial influences in these respects, upon certain maladies peculiar to the female generative organs, its use among Eclectic practitioners has become general in the treatment of several symptoms due to such maladies. Thus, it has been very efficacious in hysteria, not only having removed its attacks, but also any ovar-

ian or mammary pain or irritation that was present." The USD notes, however, that the plant "was also employed by the eclectics in hosts of other diseases such as chronic rheumatism, bronchitis, intestinal colic and hysteria. Its practical value is open to doubt." It has been included in the USP and NF.

Cohosh is an Indian name for species of Actaea and Cimicifuga. The name Lion's-Foot is a translation of Leontice, an old generic name.

## Twin-Leaf

*Jeffersonia diphylla.* Of Jefferson (Thomas Jefferson, 1743–1826); two-leaved.

Ground-Squirrel-Pea, Helmet-Pod, Rheumatism-Root, Yellow-Root

"The root is said to be emetic in large doses, and expectorant in smaller doses and not unlike senega, as a substitute for which it has sometimes been used" (USD) ("senega" is *Polygala senega*).

On May 18, 1792, at a meeting of the American Philosophical Society in Philadelphia, Benjamin Smith Barton announced that, since

*Twin-Leaf*

the plant had not been described "by any authors, except Linnaeus and Clayton, neither of whom had seen the flowers, and as it is, certainly, a new family, I take the liberty of making it known to the botanist by the name of JEFFERSONIA, in honour of Thomas Jefferson, Esq. Secretary of State to the United States. I beg leave to observe to you, in this place, that in imposing upon this genus the name of Mr. Jefferson, I have had no reference to his political character, or to his reputation for general science, and for literature. My business was with his knowledge of natural history. In the various departments of this science, but especially in botany and zoology, the information of this gentleman is equalled by that of few persons in the United States" (from Betts). Barton was a physician, naturalist, professor of natural history and botany at the University of Pennsylvania, author of *Collections for an Essay Towards a Materia Medica of the United States* (1798, 1801) and *Elements of Botany* (1803) and patron of Thomas Nuttall and Frederick Pursh.

## Creeping Oregon-Grape

*Mahonia repens.* Of Mahon (Bernard M'Mahon, 1755–1816); creeping.
Creeping-Barberry, Graproot, Holly-Leaf Barberry, Mountain-Holly, Oregon-Grape, Rocky-Mountain-Grape, Trailing Mahonia, Yerba de la Sangre (N.Mex.)

The ripe berries, the "grapes," are eaten raw and make a juice that tastes like grape juice. "California Indians used the berry decoction to stimulate the appetite. Said to be alterative, anaphrodisiac, antibilious, antiseptic, cholalogue, depurative, expectorant, febrifuge, laxative, purgative and tonic" (Duke, 1985). A yellow dye is also made from the bark and wood.

Bernard M'Mahon arrived in America from Ireland in 1796 and established a thriving plant nursery in Philadelphia. Thomas Jefferson regularly ordered plants from him for the gardens at Monticello. M'Mahon published a deservedy popular guide for gardeners in 1806, *The American Gardener's Calendar*; the 11th edition of this was published in 1857.

## Mayapple, Mandrake

*Podophyllum peltatum.* Foot leaf (a contraction of *Anapodophyllum,* duck foot leaf, the name given it by Catesby, and shortened to *Podophyllum* by Linnaeus); shield-shaped.
Behen, Citron (Mo.), *Citron sauvage* (P.Q.), Devil's-Apple, Duck's-Foot, Ground-Lemon, Hog-Apple (Iowa), Indian-Apple, Mandrake-Pear (N.J.), Maypop (Va.), Mug-Apple, Parasols (Ohio), *Pomme de mai* (P.Q.), Puck's-Foot, Raccoon-Berry, Umbrella-Plant, Umbrella-Root (Va.), Vegetable-Calomel, Vegetable-Mercury, Wild-Duckfoot, Wild-Jalap, Wild-Lemon, Wild-Mandrake, Yellow-Berry

In his *Rhymes of Childhood* (1890), the "Hoosier poet" James Whitcomb Riley wrote,

*And will any poet sing*
*Of a lusher, richer thing*

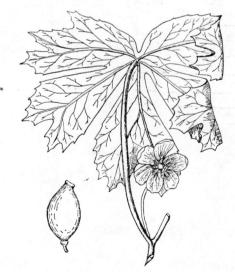

*Mayapple*

*Than a ripe May-apple, rolled*
*Like a pulpy lump of gold*
*Under thumb and finger tips,*
*And poured molten through the lips.*

Catherine Traill (1855) provided a recipe for May-Apple preserves: "Gather the fruit as soon as it begins to show any yellow tint on the green rind: lay them by in a sunny window for a day or two; cut them in quarters and throw them into a syrup of white sugar, in which ginger sliced and cloves have been boiled: boil the fruit till the outer rind is tender: take the fruit out, lay them in a basin, sift a handful of pounded sugar over them, and let them lie until cold. Next day boil your syrup a second time, pour it over the fruit, and when cold put it into jars or glasses, and tie down. It should not be used till a month or six weeks after making: if well spiced this preserve is more like some foreign fruit. It is very fine." Dr. Porcher recommends squeezing the pulp of the fruit into a wineglass, "and with the addition of a little old Madeira and sugar, it is said to be equal to the luscious golden granadilla of the tropics."

"Mayapple was used by the American Indians for a variety of ailments. Its strong physiological activity recommended itself to early settlers and preparations of the root, the most active part, soon entered the pharmacopeia and continued in use for many years. A crude resinous material having violent cathartic properties may be extracted from the root with alcohol and precipitated in water. This was given the name podophyllin" (Kingsbury, 1964). Podophyllin is now the drug of choice in the treatment of genital warts, and etoposide, prepared from the roots, is the first-choice treatment for small-cell carcinoma. Marie-Victorin reported that in Quebec *Pomme de mai* is used to treat "scrofulant, rheumatic, syphilitic disorders, and pulmonary or bronchial infections."

The famous and ancient herb Mandrake is the European *Mandragora officinarum,* whose root, supposedly shaped like the human body, was a powerful talisman and potent herb.

## Inside-Out Flower

*Vancouveria hexandra.* Of Vancouver (George Vancouver, 1757–1798); with six stamens.

Vancouver was a famous English navigator (the city in British Columbia is named after him) who entered the Royal Navy at age 13 and served on Captain James Cook's second and third voyages of discovery and then for several years in the West Indies. In 1791 he embarked on a four-and-a-half-year survey of Australia and New Zealand, Tahiti, the Hawaiian Islands, and the west coast of North America from southern California to British Columbia. Archibald Menzies (see pages 98) was the surgeon-naturalist on the voyage, which has been called the most arduous survey undertaken by any navigator.

# THE MOONSEED FAMILY

## *Menispermaceae*

A family of 78 genera and 520 species of lianas, shrubs and a few small trees and herbs, found mainly in tropical rain forests, but also in subtropical and warm temperate regions. One member of the Moonseed family is Pareira, *Chondodedron tomentosum,* which contains the alkaloid tubocurarine that is used as a neuromuscular blocking agent in surgery and to treat convulsions. Tubocurarine is also the chief ingredient of curare, the South American arrow poison.

## Canada Moonseed, Common Moonseed

*Menispermum canadense.* Moon seed (the seed is shaped like the crescent moon); of Canada.

American-Sarsparilla, Maple-Vine, Moon-Creeper, Moonseed-Sarsparilla, *Raisin de couleuvre* (P.Q.), Safarilla (Ky.), Sarsparilla (Ind., Ohio), Sasfriller (Ky.), Texas Moonseed, Texas-Sarsparilla, Vine-Maple, Yellow-Parilla, Yellow-Sarsparilla

"Our first knowledge of this plant as a remedy was undoubtedly handed down from the Aborigines, who are said by Rafinesque to have used the root in scrofulosis; the early settlers also found it useful as a diuretic in strangury in horses. Its employment generally by early practitioners has been very similar to that of Sarsparilla" (Millspaugh). "Menispermum has been used as a substitute for sarsparilla, but is probably inert" (USD). In Kentucky, to cleanse the blood, "one span of

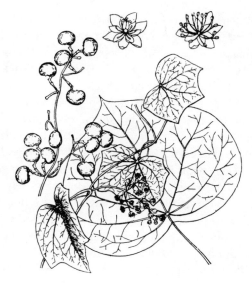

*Canada Moonseed*

sasfriller root is boiled in a quart of water until one-half pint of liquid remains. One-half pint of whiskey and a heaping tablespoon of sulfur are added to this. One spoonful is taken before each meal until it is all used" (Bolyard, 1981).

The grapelike fruit contain isoquinoline alkaloids and have been fatal to children eating them.

# THE POPPY FAMILY

## *Papaveraceae*

A family of 23 genera and 210 species of herbs and shrubs; found mainly in temperate and tropical regions of the Northern Hemisphere. Opium is extracted from *Papaver somniferum.* The name "Poppy" is derived from Middle English *popi,* Old English, *popig, popaeg,* ultimately from the Latin *papaver* and perhaps from the Sumerian *pa pa,* said to be the noise made when chewing poppy seeds.

## Prickly Poppy

*Argemone mexicana.* (A Latin plant name; *argemon* is a cataract which the plant was supposed to cure); of Mexico. (From tropical America.)

Bird-in-the-Bush (Mass.), Bull-Thistle (Kans.), Chicalote (Calif.), Devil's-Fig, Flowering-Thistle (Ohio), Jamaica-Thistle, Mexican-Poppy, Mexican Thorn-Poppy, Thistle Poppy (Calif.), Thornapple, Wild-Hollyhock (Texas), Yellow-Thistle

Prickly Poppy is "the golden Thistle of Peru, called in the West Indies, *Fique del Inferno*," whose fruit "doth much resemble a fig in shape and bignesse, but so full of sharpe and venomous prickles, that whosoever had one of them in his throat it would doubtless send him packing either to heaven or to hell" (Gerard, 1633). The whole plant, including the capsule (the Devil's-Fig), is prickly and "abounds in a milky acrid juice which turns yellow on exposure to the air and has been used locally as a domestic remedy for warts and various skin diseases" (USD). The seeds yield an oil that has been used in paints and to manufacture soap. In Texas "our prickle-guarded silken wild poppies, purest white, every shade of wine color, or clear deep yellow, are all known as wild hollyhocks" (Reid, 1951). White Prickly-Poppy is *Argemone albiflora*.

## Celandine

*Chelidonium majus.* Of swallows (the Latin name was *chelidonia* from the Greek *khelidonion*; the Greek *khelidōn* means "swallow"); larger. (From Europe.)

Cockfoot, Devil's-Milk, Elonwort, Felonwort, Grande Éclaire (P.Q.), Greater Celandine, *Herbe aux verrues* (P.Q.), Jacob's-Ladder, Kenningwort (Maine), Killwart, Killwort, Rock-Poppy, Sightwort, Swallowwort, Tetterwort, Wartflower, Wartwort, Wretweed

"It seems to be called Chelidonia because it springs out of the ground together with the swallows appearing, & doth wither with their departing. Some have related that if any of the swallows' young ones be blind, the dams bringing this herb, do heal the blindness"

*Celandine*

(Dioscorides). The herbalists took up this idea: "The juice is good to sharpen the sight, for it cleanseth and consumeth awaie slimie things that cleave about the ball of the eye" (Gerard, 1633). In Cotton Mather's *The Angel of Bethesda* (1724), he advises those with poor eyesight, "Ask now the fouls of the air and they shall tell thee. The swallows will carry thee to the Celandine. Feeble Eyes will not find a greater friend in the whole of the vegetable kingdom. Drop the juice of it in the eye. It may be diluted with fair-water." Manasseh Cutler (1785) reported that "diluted with milk, it is said to consume white opake spots upon the eye." Among the "Garden Herbs" grown in New England in the 17th century, Josselyn (1672) included "Celandine, by the West Country men called Kenning Wort, grows but slowly." Kenningwort is an old English name, a kenning being a cloudy spot on the eye.

The juice was also used to cure warts (tetters, or *verrues* in French), ringworm, eczema, corns and other skin diseases, including cancer (USD). Felonwort (a felon is a sore under or near a finger or toe nail), Jacob's-Ladder and Wartwort are local names in England. The plant contains sparteine, which "restores normal rhythm to feeble arrhythmic myocardia" (Lewis and Elvin-Lewis, 1977).

## California-Poppy, Gold-Poppy

*Eschscholtzia californica.* Of Eschscholtz (Johann Friedrich Gustav von Eschscholtz, 1793–1831, Russian botanist); of California. *Amapola del Campo, Amapola Dormidero, Copa del Oro,* Cups-of-Gold, Flame-Cups, Mexican Gold-Poppy, *Torosa*

This is the state flower of California. The early Spanish settlers called it *Copa del Ora* and told a legend that the orange petals, turning to gold, filled the soil with the precious metal. Among the Costanoan Indians of California, "flowers decocted, liquid rubbed in hair to kill lice; plant avoided by pregnant or lactating women, as smell believed to be poisonous; to put child to sleep, 1 or 2 flowers placed underneath bed" (Bocek). Among the Indians of Mendocino County, "the fresh root is placed in the cavity of a tooth to stop the toothache, and an extract from it as a wash or liniment for headache, suppurating sores, and to stop the excretion of milk in women; internally, to cause vomiting, cure stomach ache, and, to some extent, as a cure for consumption" (Chesnut, 1902). Mexican-Poppy is *Eschscholtzia californica,* subspecies *mexicana.*

## Corn Poppy

*Papaver rhoeas.* (The Latin name); (an old Greek name). (From Europe.)
African-Rose, Blind-Eye (South), Blue-Eyes, Canker-Root, Canker-Rose, Cheesebowl, Coquettes (Ohio), *Coquelicot* (P.Q.), Corn-Rose, Field Poppy, Flanders Poppy, Headache, Red Poppy, Red-Weed, Thunder-Flower

*Corn Poppy*

Long associated with cornfields (wheat, barley, oats, not maize), until the use of selective herbicides, Corn Poppy was the flower of Aphrodite and of Ceres, the Roman corn goddess. It was also the blood-red flower of the battlefield and has been the symbol of Memorial Day since John McCrae wrote his poem during the second battle of Ypres in 1915:

*In Flanders fields the poppies blow*
*Between the crosses, row on row,*
*That mark our place; and in the sky*
*The larks, still bravely singing, fly*
*Scarce heard amid the guns below.*
*We are the Dead. Short days ago*
*We lived, felt dawn, saw sunset glow,*
*Loved and were loved, and now we lie*
*In Flanders fields.*

*Take up our quarrel with the foe:*
*To you from failing hands we throw*
*The torch; be yours to hold it high.*
*If ye break faith with us who die*
*We shall not sleep, though poppies grow*
*In Flanders fields.*

Colonel McCrae, a medical officer in the Canadian Army, was himself killed two years later.

John Ruskin in the ruins of Rome (1879): "I have in my hand a small red poppy which I gathered on Whit Sunday in the palace of the Caesars. It is an intensely simple, intensely floral, flower. All silk and flame, a scarlet cup, perfect-edged all round, seen among the wild grass far away, like a burning coal fallen from Heaven's altars. You cannot have a more complete, a more stainless, type of flower absolute; inside and outside, all flower. No sparing of color anywhere—no outside coarseness—no interior secrecies; open as the sunshine that creates it; fine-finished on both sides, down to the extremest point of insertion on its narrow stalk; and robed in the purple of the Caesars." It was called Blind-Eye because of "a belief in Yorkshire that if placed too near the eye it will cause blindness" (Britten and Holland).

## Bloodroot

*Sanguinaria canadensis.* Bleeding; of Canada.

Boloroot, Coonroot (W.Va.), Cornroot, Large-Leaved Bloodwort, Large-Leaved-Sandwort, Panson, Pauson, Puccoon, Puccoon-Root (Ind.), Red-Indian-Paint, Red-Puccoon (Ohio), Redroot (Maine), *Sangdragon* (P.Q.), Snakebite (N.H.), Sweet-Slumber (Pa.), Tetterwort, White-Puccoon (N.Y.), Tumerick (Pa.), Turmeric

In 1728 William Byrd led an expedition to survey the border between Virginia and North Carolina, during which he and his men spent a night with the Notteway Indians: "We rested on our clean mats very comfortably, tho' alone, and the next morning went to the toilet of some of the Indian ladys, where, what with the charms of their persons and the smoak of their apartments, we were almost blinded. They offered to give us Silk-Grass baskets of their own making, which we modestly re-

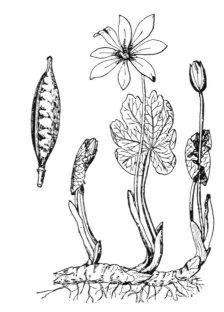

*Bloodroot*

fused, knowing that an Indian present, like that of a nun, is a liberality put out to interest, and a bribe plac'd to the greatest advantage. Our chaplain observ'd with concern, that the ruffles of some of our fellow travelers were a little discolor'd with pochoon, wherewith the good man had been told those ladies us'd to improve their invisible charms." Pochoon, or Puccoon, is Algonquian for the plant and its red juice. In Byrd's diary of the expedition (the "Secret History"), he had written, "I cou'd discern by some of our gentlemen's Linnen, discolour'd by the Soil of the Indian Ladys, that they had been convincing themselves in the point of their having no furr."

John Bartram (1751) called it "*Chelidonium,* or *Sanguinaria,* called by the country people, Red Root, or Turmerick . . . The root dried and powdered is commended by Dr. Colden, as a cure for the jaundice, the powder being given to the weight of a drachm in small beer; and by others, for the bite of rattle-snake." (Dr. Colden is Cadwallader Colden.) Manasseh Cutler reported that "when the fresh root is broken, a juice issues, in large drops, resembling blood. The Indians used it for painting themselves, and highly esteemed it for its medical virtues. It is emetic and cathartic, but must be given with caution. An infusion of the root in rum or brandy makes a good bitter. If it be planted in rich shady borders, it flourishes well in gardens; and the large leaves and blossoms make an agreeble appearance soon after the frost is out of the ground." Marie-Victorin writes that in Quebec "it is employed against hemopty-sis, no doubt an application of the ancient doctrine of signatures."

Bloodroot was given as a "Preventive of Bilious Fever" in 1854: "If you are bilious in the spring, it will be well to physic with a sirup made of four ounces of blood root, four ounces of mandrake root, ground or pounded fine, and stirred in half a pint of molasses, of which two tablespoons is a dose" (*The House-keeper's Guide*). It has been included in the USP and NF, "used chiefly as an expectorant, especially in the treatment of subacute and chronic bronchitis" (USD).

# THE FUMITORY FAMILY

## *Fumariaceae*

A family of 18 genera and 450 species of perennial herbs; found mainly in north temperate regions and in South Africa.

## Allegheny-Vine

*Adlumia fungosa.* Of Adlum (John Adlum, 1759–1836); spongy.
Alleghany-Fringe (Ohio), Canary-Vine (Wis.), Cliff-Harlequin, Climbing-Colicweed, Climbing-Fumitory, Cypress-Vine, Fairy-Creeper (N.B.), Mountain-Fringe (Maine, Mass., Vt.), Wood-Fringe (Maine)

John Adlum was born in York, Pennsylvania, and died in Georgetown. He enlisted in the Continental Army in July 1776, but by November 1777, as a corporal, he had been wounded, captured and sent home on parole. He saw active service in the War of 1812 and eventually became a Brigadier General in the Pennsylvania state militia. He worked as a surveyor, an associate judge, plantsman and agriculturist and in 1814 established a 200-acre experimental farm in Georgetown. In 1823 he published the first book on grape-growing based on American cultural practice and led a successful drive for the cultivation of native grapes. He introduced the Catawba grape into cultivation.

## Squirrel-Corn

*Dicentra canadensis.* Twice spurred; of Canada.
Colicweed, Ghost-Corn (N.Y.), Indian-Potatoes (Ohio), Ladies-and-Gentlemen (P.Q.), Lyre-Flower, Stagger-Weed (Va.), Turkey-Corn, Turkey-Pea, White-Hearts, Wild-Hyacinth (N.Y.)

The yellow corms of Squirrel-Corn resemble kernels of corn or peas. Among the Onondaga Indians, it was called " 'Ghost Corn,' that is, food for spirits" (Beaumont, 1891). "Turkey corn, corydalis, is a powerful and very valuable alterative and tonic. It is regarded by Eclectic physicians as very nearly specific in syphilis, and some other constitutional diseases" (Gunn, 1857). The medicine known as corydalis or corydalin was the dried tuber of this or *Dicentra cucullaria:* "Although there is no doubt that corydalis is physiologically active, the purposes for which it has been used in medicine have had no connection with the effect of its alkaloids" (USD).

## Dutchman's-Breeches

*Dicentra cucullaria.* Twice spurred; hood-like (an old generic name).

Bachelor's-Breeches, Boys-and-Girls (N.Y.), Breeches-Flower (N.Y.), Butterfly-Banners, Colicweed, *Dicentre à capuchon* (P.Q.), Eardrops (N.J.), Flyflower, Girls-and-Boys (Vt.), Indian Boys-and-Girls (Wis.), Kitten-Breeches (Ohio), Leather-Breeches (Ill.), Little-Blue-Stagger, Little-Boy's-Breeches (Iowa), Monkshood, Pearl-Harlequin, Soldier's-Cap, Stagger-Weed (Va.), Turkey, White-Eardrop, White-Hearts

"This is one of the most important love charms of the Menomini. The young swain tries to throw it at his intended and hit her with it. Another way is for him to chew the root, breathing out so that the scent will carry to her. He then circles around the girl, and when she catches the scent, she will follow him wherever he goes" (Huron Smith, 1923). Several species of Dicentra are toxic to grazing animals (Stagger-Weed).

The cultivated Bleeding-Heart is *Dicentra spectabilis* of Japan. Wild Bleeding-Heart is *Dicentra eximia* ("extraordinary"). Western Bleeding-Heart is *Dicentra formosa* ("beautiful").

## Earth-Smoke, Fumitory

*Fumaria officinalis.* Like smoke; officinal. (From Europe.)

Beggars, Common Fumaria, Earth-Smoke, *Fume-terre* (P.Q.), Hedge-Fumitory, Sax-Dolls, Wax-Dolls

Fumitory comes from the Latin words *fumus* (smoke) and *terrae* (of the earth). The smoke names have had many explanations.

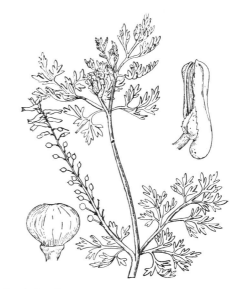

*Earth-Smoke*

Pliny called it *capnos* (Greek *kapnos* means "smoke") because "used as ointment for the eyes it improves the vision and, like smoke, produces tears, and to this fact it owes its name." In the Middle Ages, exorcists burned the leaves because the smoke was believed to have the power of expelling evil spirits. The *Grete Herball* of 1526 reported that Fumitory was "engendered of a coarse fumosity rising from the earth," and Cole in 1657 thought that it was of a "whitish blue colour as smoke is." Hill (1755) reported that "some smoke the dried leaves in the manner of tobacco for disorders of the head, with success," and Britten and Holland (1866) remarked that the root smells gaseous, "remarkably like the fumes of nitric acid." Frère Marie-Victorin wrote that the plant "seems to grow out of the ground like smoke." Peterson and McKenny (1968) add that the "gray-green plant has a smoky look in the distance, whence its name." Beggary and Wax-Dolls (from the waxy flowers) are local names in England.

# THE NETTLE FAMILY

## Urticaceae

A family of 52 genera and 1,050 species of herbs, shrubs, lianas and trees; found in tropical to temperate regions. One member of the family, *Boehmeria nivea,* China-Grass, is the source of ramie, a flaxlike fiber used in making fabrics and cordage. In Latin a Nettle is *urtica,* a word of obscure origin. Pliny wrote, "What can be more hateful than the nettle? Yet this plant, to say nothing of the oil which I have said is made from it in Egypt, simply abounds in remedies," and he lists over 50 disorders that had been treated with Nettles.

> *The Nettles stinke, yet they make recompense,*
> *If your belly by the Collicke pain endures,*
> *Against the Collicke Nettle-seed and honey*
> *Is Physick: better none is had for money.*
> *It breedeth sleepe, staies vomit, fleams doth soften,*
> *It helps him of the Gowte that eats it often.*
> Sir John Harington, 1607

## Wood Nettle

*Laportea canadensis.* Of Laporte (Frances de la Porte, Count of Castelnau, 1812–1880); of Canada.

Albany-Hemp, Canada Nettle

In Quebec in 1670, the Indians "also make thread of nettles, which they spin without a spindle, twisting it on their knees with the palm of the hand. With this they make their embroidery, ornamenting it with black and white porcupine quills, combined with others boiled in roots, which makes them as beautiful as cochineal makes scarlet in France"

*Wood Nettle*

(Marie de l'Incarnation). Ropes, canvas and fishing nets were also made with Albany-Hemp.

Castelnau was a French naturalist who traveled in Canada, the United States and Mexico (1837–1841) and then led a scientific expedition to South America. He died in Melbourne, Australia, where he was serving as the French consul.

## Pennsylvania Pellitory

*Parietaria pensylvanica.* Of the wall (from the Latin *paries,* "a wall," the habitat of *Parietaria diffusa*); of Pennsylvania.

Hammerwort, Helxine, Pellitory

"Helxine or Pardition is called in Englishe Parietorie or Pelletorie of the wall" (Turner, 1548). Pellitory is a corruption of *parietarius* (another plant name Pellitory is derived from Pyrethrum). Helxine is an old generic name of obscure origin. "To make a bath for Melancholy. Take Mallowes, Pellitory of the wall, of each three handfulls; Camomell flowers, Mellilot flowers, of each one handfull; Hollyhocks, two handfulls; Isop one great handfull; Senerick seeds one ounce, and boile them in nine gallons of water until they come to three, then put in a quart of new milke and go into it bloud warme or something warmer" (Lady Fairfax's still-room book, ca. 1632; from Rohde, 1922). Hammerwort is an old name (in Gerard, 1633) of *Parietaria officinalis.*

## Clearweed

*Pilea pumila.* A cap (from the Latin *pileus,* describing the larger sepal); dwarf.

Bastard-Nettle, Churle-Hemp (South), Coolweed, Coolwort, Dead-Nettle, False Nettle, *Petite ortie* (P.Q.), Richweed, Silverweed, Stingless Nettle, Waterweed (Ohio)

It has clear succulent stems which were used for healing. Churl Hemp is an old name (in Gerard, 1633) of the female plant of *Cannabis sativa.*

## Nettles

*Urtica.* (The Latin name.)

*Ortie* (P.Q.)

"Woodland is the natural home of the Nettle, but it travels round with man, grows out of his rubbish, gets a hold where he has disturbed the ground, clings to the site of his dwelling long after the dwellings themselves have disappeared. So not unnaturally in the Highlands and Islands [of Scotland] Nettles were believed to grow from the bodies of dead men" (Grigson).

In September 1859, Thoreau investigated the cellar of an old house that had been torn down that spring: "If, as here, an ancient cellar is uncovered, there springs up at once a crop of rank and noxious weeds, evidence of a certain unwholesome fertility,—by which perchance the earth relieves herself of the

poisonous qualities which have been imparted to her. As if what was foul, baleful, grovelling, or obscene in the inhabitants had sunk into the earth and infected it." In the cellar's ruins "there are mallows for food,— for cheeses at least; rich-weed for high living; the nettle for domestic felicity,—a happy disposition; black nightshade, tobacco, henbane, and Jamestown-weed as symbols of the moral atmosphere and influence of that house, the idiocy and insanity of it; dill and Jerusalem oak and catnep for senility grasping at a straw; and beggar ticks for poverty."

Nettles are used as a potherb, and the stem fibers were spun into cloths, table linens and sacking and into twine for fishing nets. Fresh and dried Nettles make an excellent fodder for animals. Grieve provided recipes for Nettle spring greens, Nettle Pudding and Nettle Beer and added that " 'urtication' or flogging with Nettles, was an old remedy for chronic rheumatism and loss of muscular power." The USD reports that Nettles were "once used medicinally as local irritants and to arrest uterine hemorrhages."

## Stinging Nettle

*Urtica dioica.* (The Latin name); dioecious.

Common Nettle, Great Nettle

Manasseh Cutler wrote that "the young shoots, early in spring, are a good pot-herb. A leaf put upon the tongue, and pressed against the roof of the mouth, is said to be efficacious in stopping a bleeding at the nose. The parts affected in paralytic cases have been recovered by stinging them with this plant. Dr. Withering says, the stings are very curious microscopic objects.—They consist of an exceeding fine pointed, tapering, hollow substance, with a perforation at the point, and a bag at the base. When the sting is pressed upon, it readily punctures the skin; and the

*Stinging Nettle*

same pressure forces up an acrimonious fluid from the bag, which instantly squirts into the wound, and produces an effect which almost everyone has experienced. The stalks are dressed like flax, for making cloth or paper.

The leaves cut fine, and mixed with dough, are very good for young turkeys."

Dr. Porcher reported that "flagellation with the branches, which, it is well known, contain stings which produce great irritation, followed by inflammation, has been recommended for bringing out cutaneous and febrile eruptions, as in scarlatina." In his 1672 list of "such plants as have sprung up since the English planted and kept cattle in New-England," Josselyn included "*Nettle stinging,* which was the first Plant taken notice of."

Among the Indians of the Missouri River Region, "the dried stalks were crumpled in the hands or gently pounded with a stone to free the fiber from the woody part. The first method was more common. The fiber of nettles was used by Nebraska tribes for spinning twine and cordage. Rope of this fiber was generally used to hobble horses. It was also used to weave into cloth. It is said that cloth of this fiber was used in the Sacred Bundle of the Tent of War" (Gilmore, 1914).

# THE POKEWEED FAMILY

## *Phytolaccaceae*

A family of 18 genera and 65 species of herbs, shrubs and trees; found mainly in tropical and warm regions of the New World. Greek *phuton* means "plant"; *lacca* means "crimson lake" (the dye obtained from the insect *Laccifer lacca*). One tropical member of the family, *Rivina humilis,* Blood-Berry or Rouge-Plant, is cultivated for its berries from which a dye is extracted.

An earlier name of the American Pokeweed appears to have been Pocan, shortened to Poke and corrupted to all the Cocum, Pokum, Skoke names listed below. Pocan is from the Algonquian *pakon,* meaning "bloody" and alluding to the plant's red juice. Puccoon has the same root.

## Pokeweed

*Phytolacca americana.* Crimson plant; of America.

American-Nightshade, American-Spinach, Bear's-Grape, Cancer-Jalap, Cancer-Root, *Chou gras* (La.), Coak (N.Y.), Coakum, Cocum, Cokan, Crowberry, Cunicum, Dyer's-Grape, Garget-Plant, Haystack-Weed (Conn.), Indian-Greens (Texas), Inkberry, Ink-Bush (Long Island), Jalap, Mockingbird-Berry (Texas), Pigeon-Berry, Pocan, Pocum, Poke, Poke-

*Pokeweed*

root, Red-Ink-Plant, Redweed, Scoke, Skoke, Virginia-Poke

The Widow Bedott, Ohio, 1850: "What seems to be the matter with you? Pain in yer chist! O! that's turrible! It always scares me to death to hear of any body's having a pain in ther chist . . . I dew beseech you, as a friend, to take skoke berries and rum afore it's too late. Temperance man, hey? So be I, tew; and you don't s'pose, dew you, Mr. Crane, that I'd advise you to take anything that would intosticate you? I'd die afore I'd dew it. I think tew much o' my repertation and yourn tew, to do such a thing. But it's the harmlessest stuff a body can take. You see the skoke berries counterects the alkyhall in the rum, and annyliates all the intosticatin' qualities" (Whitcher, 1856).

In 1847 Darlington wrote "The young shoots of this plant afford a good substitute for asparagus; the root is said to be actively emetic; and the tincture of the ripe berries is, or was,

a popular remedy for chronic rheumatism. The mature berries, moreover, have been used by the pastry cook in making pies of equivocal merit." Uncle Remus: "Yer I is, gwine on eighty year, en I aint tuck none er dat ar docter truck yit, ceppin' it's dish yer flas' er poke-root w'at ole Miss Favers fix up fer de stiffness in my j'ints" (Harris, 1911). In 1804 Dr. Barton had reported that "the ripe berries, infused in brandy or wine, especially the former, are a popular remedy for rheumatism in many parts of the United-States."

The root and mature leaves (and perhaps the berries) are poisonous. Jalap is the purgative root of *Exogonium jalapa,* a plant from Jalap, Mexico. It was a popular remedy and had many imitations. American farmers once applied a poultice of Pokeweed leaves to inflammatory diseases of the cow's udder, which were known as "garget." "Possibly Pokeweed is too commonly seen to be appreciated in its native North America. In Europe [where it was well established in cultivation by 1640] it is still grown for gourmets, boiled for a quarter of an hour in two lots of water, drained, and served on toasted whole grain bread, sauced with clarified butter" (Whittle and Cook, 1981). The 1853 USD classified the plant as "emetic, cathartic, alterative, antiherpetic, and somewhat narcotic." A variety is still included in the pharmacopeia of China.

Pokeweed is called Mocking-Bird Berry in Texas. "It is hard to get out of sight and hearing of a mocking bird in Texas, and where he is, there is almost certainly pokeweed, if it can possibly grow in the soil; the master singer scatters its seeds far and wide. Called also Indian greens, and still often used as 'greens' " (Reid, 1951).

# THE FOUR-O'CLOCK FAMILY

## *Nyctaginaceae*

A family of 34 genera and 350 species of herbs, shrubs and trees; found mainly in tropical and subtropical regions of the New and Old World. The genus name *Nyctago* means "of the night" (Greek *nuktos,* by night)—the flowers of many species, including the cultivated *Mirabilis jalapa,* open in late afternoon and stay open all night. Gerard (1633) wrote that this "admirable plant" was called "the marvell of Peru, or the marvell of the World."

*Desert Four-o'Clock*

*M. jalapa* is also cultivated for its tuberous roots, which are the source of a purgative drug. Another cultivated member of the family is *Bougainvillea,* many of whose species are grown as hedges and ornamental plants.

## Desert Four-o'Clock, Colorado Four-o'Clock, Maravilla

*Mirabilis multiflora.* Marvelous; many-flowered.

Zuñi Indian women "frequently slip a pinch of the powdered root into water to be drunk at meal time by the young men of the family, to prevent them overindulging their appetites. The powder is also put into *he'we* that is to be carried by men on long journeys, that they might not become too hungry to be satisfied with what they have" (Stevenson, 1915).

## Wild Four-o'Clock

*Mirabilis nyctaginea.* Marvelous; nightblooming.

Heart-Leaf Four-o'Clock, Snotweed, Umbrella-Wort

Gilmore wrote (1914) that among the Teton Dakota, "the root was boiled to make a decoction to drink in case of fever"; among the Ponka, "the root was used as a remedy for wounds, for this purpose being chewed and blown into them"; among the Pawnee, "the dried root, ground fine, was applied dry as a remedy for sore mouth in babies. A decoction of the root was drunk by women after childbirth to reduce abdominal swelling."

# THE CACTUS FAMILY

## *Cactaceae*

A family of 130 genera and 1,650 species; found in temperate and tropical regions of the New World.

## Prickly-Pear

*Opuntia humifusa.* (A Greek plant name); spreading.
Barberry, Devil's-Tongue (Ohio), Indian-Fig, Old-Man's-Hand (Kans.), *Pomme à raquet,* Prickly-Pear-Cactus

Gerard (1633) reported that "this plant groweth in all the tract of the East and West Indies, and also in the countrey Norembega, now called Virginia, from whence it hath beene brought into Italy, Spaine, England, and other countries; in Italy it sometimes beareth fruit, but more often in Spain, and never as yet in England, though I have be-stowed great pains and cost in keeping it from the injury of our cold clymat." Theophrastus had described a prickly plant (probably a Euphorbia) that grew near Opus, a city of Locris Opuntia, in central Greece. When the Prickly-Pear was introduced to Europe, herbalists decided that it was the same plant and called it Opuntium, the name given by Pliny to the plant described by Theophrastus.

Dr. Porcher wrote that "the decoction is mucilaginous, and I am informed that it is much used in Alabama as a demulcent drink in pneumonic and pleuritic inflammations." He also reported that hard tallow candles were made by boiling leaves of the Prickly-Pear in the tallow: "In this way we have made tallow candles nearly equal to the best adamantine and, at the same time, have the consolation of knowing that we are independent of the extortioners, who are next of kin to the villainous abolitionist makers of stearine candles in the North."

Among the Dakota and Pawnee, "The mucilaginous juice of the stem was utilized as sizing to fix the colors painted on hides or on receptacles made from hides. It was applied by rubbing the freshly peeled stem over the painted object" (Gilmore). After the bristles had been removed, the fruits were eaten fresh or dried for winter use.

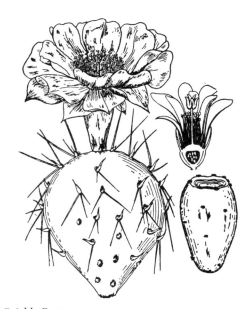

*Prickly-Pear*

## Plains Prickly-Pear

*Opuntia polyacantha.* (A Greek plant name); many-spined.
*Crapaud vert,* Hair-Spine Prickly-Pear, Many-Spined Opuntia, Plains Cactus

"For Southern Cheyenne women, especially, the gathering, drying and storing of this fruit was an important seasonal activity. They collected the fruits in parfleche sacks.

To remove the spines, they piled the fruits on the ground and stirred them with small sagebrush (*Artemesia* sp.) branches. They removed the remaining thorns from the fruits with their fingers which were protected with deerskin tips. The fruit was then split, the seeds were discarded, and the flesh was dried in the sun for use in stewing meat and game, thickening soup with its gelatinous content, etc." (Hart, 1980). *Crapaud vert* (green toad) was the name given by the Canadian voyageurs.

# THE GOOSEFOOT FAMILY

## Chenopodiaceae

A cosmopolitan family of 120 genera and 1,300 species of perennial herbs and a few shrubs and small trees or climbers. They are found mainly near the sea or in salt-rich steppes or alkaline prairies; they also grow as weeds in salt-rich soils around human habitations. Greek *khēn* means "goose," *pous* means "foot"—the leaves of many species are shaped like a goose's foot.

A cultivated member of the family is Quinoa, *Chenopoidum quinoa,* which is grown for its edible leaves and seeds that have long been a staple part of the diet of the Andean Indians. Several wild species are also used as potherbs and their seeds ground or parched into meal. Other members of the family include Beet *(Beta vulgaris)* and its many varieties that are used as a source of sugar and as animal fodder and Spinach *(Spinacia oleracea).*

## Orache

*Atriplex patula.* (The Latin name); spreading. (Also found in Eurasia.)

*Arroche* (P.Q.), Duck-Lettuce (Utah), Fat-Hen, Gooseweed, Lamb's-Quarters (Pa.), Orach, Spearscale

"Orach, Atriplex: is cooling, allays the Pituit Humor," wrote Evelyn (1699), "the tender leaves are mingl'd with other cold salleting; but 'tis better in pottage." In 1751 John Bartram noted that in Pennsylvania "the wild kind is called Lamb-Quarter." The dried seeds are ground and used for mush and bread. Orache is derived through the French from Latin *atriplex.*

## Goosefoots, Pigweeds

*Chenopodium.* Goosefoot.
*Ansérine* (P.Q.)

In Prison Lane, Boston, 1642, "Before this ugly edifice, and between it and the wheel-tracks of the street, was a grass-plot, much overgrown with burdock, pig-weed, apple-peru, and other unsightly vegetation, which evidently found something congenial in the soil that had so early borne the black flower of civilized society, a prison" (Nathaniel Hawthorne, *The Scarlet Letter*).

## Lamb's-Quarters, Pigweed

*Chenopodium album.* Goosefoot; white (the mealy undersurface of the leaves). (From Europe.)

Baconweed, Blackweed (Long Island), *Chou gras* (P.Q.), Dirty-Dick, Fat-Hen, Frost-Blite, Midden-Mylies, Muchweed, Muckweed, Mutton-Tops, *Poulette grasse* (P.Q.), Rag-Jag, White-Goosefoot, Wild-Spinach

Common on the dunghill (the midden), its seeds are full of fat and albumin and have been an important food from antiquity to modern times. The Indians of the Southwest eat the leaves and grind the seeds into meal or flour. "Part of August and September, 1934, I spent in New Mexico, where I studied the food habits of the Indians. The Lamb's-Quarter was growing about almost every pueblo visited, where it was apparently cultivated or at least protected. The natives call it 'Quelite' " (Medsger, 1939). The names Baconweed and Pigweed come from the plant's use as feed for hogs and Black-Weed "because it stains the fingers black" (Bergen, 1896). Fat-Hen is the British name for both this and Good-King-Henry (from the German *Fette Henne* and French *Poulette grasse*), having been used to fatten poultry. Dirty-Dick, Lamb's-Quarters, Rag-Jag, Muckweed and Mutton-Tops are local names in England and Midden-Mylies in Scotland.

## Mexican-Tea, Wormseed

*Chenopodium ambrosioides.* Goosefoot; like *Ambrosia.*

Ambrosia, American Wormseed, Epazote, Fishweed (Va.), Goosefoot, Herb Sancti Mariae, Jerusalem-Oak, Jerusalem-Tea, Jesuit-Tea, Spanish-Tea, Stinking-Weed, Wild Wormseed

Cotton Mather (1724) wrote that "this has been found a most surprising worm-killer. Tis incredible what cures have been wrought by it, on children troubled with worms. How many lives have been saved by this poor, mean, homely medicine! I am of the opinion that when raw fruits and cold things have brought the children into these maladies, this electuary may be then most proper for them. In many cases it may be too inflammatory. But then our countrey-people make almost a Panacæa of it. It strangely releeves pains in the stomach; and restores a ruined appetite." Here is his recipe: "Take half a pint of rhum; a quarter of an ounce of worm-seed; a penn'orth or two of aloes; lett these simmer together over a fire, till a quarter be con-

sumed; then add a convenient quantity of molasses, and boil the composition to little. So strain it and keep it for use. The dose is a spoonful or two for children; and thrice as much for a man." Until recently, a variety of this plant was being cultivated to make chenopodium oil for the treatment of intestinal parasites. It was included in the NF until 1955 and can still be found in some European pharmacopeias.

To the cook, this is *epazote,* "one of the pungent herbs used extensively in the cooking of central and southern Mexico," writes Diana Kennedy (1972). "A tea made of it is said to soothe the nerves and dispel intestinal parasites, while to cook a pot of black beans without it is unthinkable."

## Good-King-Henry

*Chenopodium bonus-henricus.* Goosefoot; good-Henry (the old generic name). (From Europe.)

All-Good, Blite, English-Mercury, Fat-Hen, Markery, Mercury-Goosefoot, Perennial Goosefoot, Roman-Plant, Shoemaker's-Heels, Smear-Dock, Smiddy-Leaves, Wild-Spinach

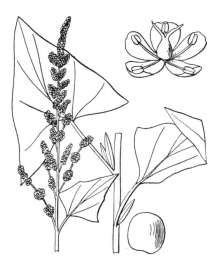

*Good-King-Henry*

The 16th-century name, Good-King-Henry, from the German *Guter Heinrich* (the English added "king"), distinguishes this plant from the poisonous Bad-Henry or Dog's-Mercury, *Mercurialis perennis* (of the Spurge family), whose leaves are similar. *Mercurialis annua* (Herb-Mercury) was known to the Romans as *mercurialis,* "the little herb of the god Mercury." In German folklore, Heinrich is a mischievous elf. John Evelyn (1699) wrote of "English Mercury, or (as our country housewives call it) Allgood, the gentle Turiones" that, "besides its humidity and detersive Nature, 'tis insipid enough." Pliny agreed: "Blite seems to be an inactive plant, without flavor or any sharp quality, for which reason in Menander husbands use the name as a term of abuse for their wives." "Nevertheless," Grieve wrote, "it is a very wholesome vegetable. If grown in rich soil, the young shoots, when as thick as a lead pencil, may be cut when 5 inches in height, peeled and boiled and eaten as Asparagus. They are gently laxative." *Bliton* was the Greek name. An ointment was made of the leaves to smear on chronic sores. Roman-Plant and Shoemaker's-Heels are local names in England, and Smeardock and Smiddy-Leaves are from Scotland (smiddy is the smithy, the blacksmith's shop).

## Jerusalem-Oak

*Chenopodium botrys.* Goosefoot; a bunch of grapes (the flower cluster; an old generic name). (From Eurasia.)

Ambrose, Ambrosia (Mass.), Feather-Geranium, *Herbe à printemps* (P.Q.), Hindheal, Hidin-Heal, Jewsly-Mose (N.C.), Turnpike-Geranium

Josselyn (1672) called this "Oak of Hierusalem" and reported that it "was excellent for stuffing of the lungs upon colds, shortness of wind, and the ptisick,—maladies that the natives are often troubled with. I helped several of the Indians with a drink made of two gallons of molosses wort (for in that part of

*Jerusalem-Oak*

the country where I abode, we made our beer of molosses, water, bran, chips of Sassafrass root, and a little Wormwood, well boiled,) into which I put of Oak of Hierusalem, Cat-mint, Sow-thistle, of each one handful, of *Enula campana* root, one ounce, Liquorice, scrap'd, brused and cut in pieces, one ounce, Sassafrass root, cut into thin chips, one ounce, Anny-seed and sweet Fennel-seed, of each one spoonful bruised. Boil these in a close pot, upon a soft fire to the consumption of one gallon, then take it off and strain it gently."

The leaves have oaklike lobes or, according to Dioscorides, are "like unto Cicorie, many, all of it is of a wonderful sweet scent, wherefore it is also laid amongst clothes." The Thompson Indians of British Columbia also enjoyed its scent: "This common plant is glandular-pubescent and viscid throughout, making it strongly scented, and is used in great quantities as scent. It is wound in necklaces and stuffed in pillows, bags, pouches, and baskets. The Indians often tie it on their clothes and in their hair, or wear it in little skin bags tied to parts of their clothing" (Teit, 1930).

The name Jewsly-Mose is a corruption of Jerusalem-Oak. Hind-Heal is an Anglo-Saxon name (and used by Gerard, 1633); presumably Hidin-Heal is an Americanization of the name from Gerard.

## Strawberry-Blite

*Chenopodium capitatum.* Goosefoot; in heads. (Also found in Europe.)

Garden-Strawberry (Maine), Indian-Paint (N.B.) Indian-Strawberry, Strawberry-Spinach

It is used as a potherb, and the strawberrylike, insipid but nutritious fruit are eaten.

## Fremont's Goosefoot

*Chenopodium fremontii.* Goosefoot; of Fremont (John Charles Frémont, 1813–1890).

Among the Klamath Indians, "the minute, black, lens-shaped, shining seeds are gathered at maturity, in late summer, and after the customary roasting and grinding are used for food. It is of interest to note that a species of the same genus, *Chenopodium Quinoa,* has for centuries constituted the chief farinaceous food of the inhabitants of the high plateau of Bolivia and Peru and has now become a cultivated plant" (Coville, 1897).

*Fremont's Goosefoot*

Frémont was an American explorer and army officer, born in Savannah, Georgia; his father was a French emigré. He led three expeditions into the Oregon Territory, 1842–1845, during which he mapped the Oregon Trail, penetrated northern Colorado and crossed the Rockies into California, and in 1848–49 and 1853–54, he led winter expeditions to locate passes for railroad lines. He was elected to the U.S. Senate from California and was nominated for president by the Republican Party in 1856 and 1864. He made and lost a fortune in California railroad ventures and accepted an appointment as governor of Arizona Territory in 1878. Some of his botanical observations are quoted in this book.

## Glassworts

*Salicornia.* Salt horn (salty plants with hornlike branches).

Baloney-Grass (Calif.), Barilla, Mutton-Sass (Conn.), Pickle-Grass (Va.), Saltgrass (Calif.), Saltwort, Samphire, Sausage-Grass (S.C.), Seacress (Va.), Seafennel, Seagrass (Calif.), Soapwort, Speargrass (Va.)

Many species of this genus and of *Salsola* and *Chenopodium* are rich in sodium salts and the ashes *(barilla)* of the burnt plants were used to make glass and soap. The salty stems are eaten raw or cooked and pickled and even the seeds are eaten. The name Mutton-Sass means "sheep forage."

## Slender Glasswort, Sea Saltwort

*Salicornia maritima.* Salt horn; of the seashore. (Also found in Eurasia and Africa.)

Chicken-Claws, Chicken's-Toes (Maine), *Corail* (P.Q.), Crabgrass, English-Seagrass, Frog-Grass, Jointed Glasswort, Marsh-Samphire, Pickle-Plant, Prickly-Grass, Pigeon-Foot, Seagrass, Saltweed (Utah), Saltwort, Samphire, Slender-Samphire

Manasseh Cutler wrote, "In Europe a fossil alkali is obtained from the ashes of this plant, which is in great request for making glass and soap. It is said to make a pickle little inferior to samphire." It is still eaten as a substitute for Samphire (a name derived from *herbe de St Pierre*) or *perce-pierre,* which is *Crithmum maritimum,* a tasty herb for sauces and pickles. In Shakespeare's *King Lear* (4.6.12) on the cliffs at Dover, Edgar sees that "half way down Hangs one that gathers samphire, dreadful trade."

### Woody Glasswort, Woody Saltwort

*Salicornia virginica.* Salt horn; of Virginia.
Cactus (La.), Leadgrass (Long Island), Leadweed (Long Island), Perennial-Saltwort

In New England, Glasswort, was "called berrelia. It grows abundantly in salt marshes" (Josselyn, 1672). The name Leadgrass came "from its weight in the salt-meadow hay" (Bergen, 1894).

### Saltwort, Russian Thistle

*Salsola australis.* Salty; of the south. (From Eurasia.)
Kelpwort, Prickly-Glasswort, Salt-Grape, Sea-Grape, Sea-Thrift, *Soude* (P.Q.), Tumbleweed

The plant is found on sea beaches in Asia, Europe and America and was accidentally introduced to South Dakota in the 1880s. It has now spread across the western United States and Canada. "On early spring ranges this species rates as fair forage for livestock. However, after the plant matures and the sharp spines form, it is worthless . . . After the first frost the exposed parts of Russian-thistle change from dark green to red. Later the plant breaks off and becomes a tumble-weed" (*Range Plant Handbook,* 1937). This is burned for the sodium ashes.

# THE AMARANTH FAMILY

## *Amaranthaceae*

A widespread family of 71 genera and 800 species of mostly herbs but also climbers, shrubs and small trees; found in tropical, subtropical and warm regions. Pliny reported that "the prize goes to the amaranth grown at Alexandria, which is gathered for keeping; in a wonderful way, after all the flowers are over, the amaranth, if moistened with water, revives and makes winter chaplets. Its special characteristic is implied in its name." Greek *amarantos* means "unfading."

In *Paradise Lost,* John Milton wrote of .

*Immortal Amaranth, a flower that once*
*In Paradise, fast by the Tree of Life*
*Began to bloom, but soon for man's*
 *offence*

*To heaven removed, where first it grew,*
 *there grows,*
*And flowers aloft shading the Font of Life.*

Inca's-Wheat is *Amaranthus caudatus,* whose seeds have been an important food-crop *(kiwicha)* in South America for centuries. The highly colored garden Amaranths are cultivars of *A. caudatus* and *Amaranthus tricolor.* Cockscomb, *Celosia cristata,* is another colorful family member.

## Tumbleweed

*Amaranthus blitoides.* Unfading; like Blitum (*Chenopodium*).
Matweed, Prostrate-Pigweed, Purslane (Kans.)

Among the Zuñi Indians, "the seeds of this plant are supposed to have been brought

*Tumbleweed*

from the underworld in the precious *el'leteliwe* of the rain priests and scattered by them over the earth. Originally seeds were eaten raw, but the Zuñi say that after they became possessed of corn, these seeds were ground with black corn meal, mixed with water, and the mixture was made into balls, or pats, and steamed, as are those eaten at the present time. A network of slender sticks or slats is fitted snugly inside the pot in the center, and the meal cakes or balls are placed thereon. The pot contains sufficient water to steam them" (Stevenson, 1915).

In winter the wind dislodges the shallow-rooted plants and tumbles them over the fields and plains.

## Smooth Pigweed, Spleen Amaranth

*Amaranthus hybridus.* Unfading; hybrid. (From Europe or tropical America.)

Balder-Herb, Careless, Cockscomb, Floramor, Flower-Gentle, Green Amaranth, Green-Opened Amaranth, Love-Lies-Bleeding, Pigweed, Pilewort, Prince's-Feather, Red Amaranth, Red-Coxcomb, Slender-Pigweed, Wild-Beet

Gerard (1633) reported that Amaranths were called in English "floure Gentle, purple Velvet floure, Floramor; and of some floure Velure . . . It is reported they stop all kinds of bleeding, which is not manifest by any apparent quality in them, except peradventure by the colour only that the red eares have: for some are of the opinion, that all red things stanch bleeding in any part of the body." Manasseh Cutler reported that "a decoction of this plant, drank freely, has been found efficacious in uterine haemorrhages, when other powerful styptics have failed." Baldare, after Balder the Scandinavian deity, is among the names of this plant listed by William Turner in 1548. Love-Lies-Bleeding is more commonly the name of a variety of *A. caudatus*. The tender leaves of this and the next plant are used as a potherb, and the tiny seeds are ground into flour.

## Green Amaranth, Pigweed

*Amaranthus retroflexus.* Unfading; bent-backward. (From Europe or tropical America.)

Abraham's-Cabbage (Mass.), Beetroot (Kans.), Borax (Maine), *Canne* (P.Q.), Careless-Weed (Kans., Mo.),

*Green Amaranth*

Curls (Ohio), Lighthouses (Long Island), Redroot (Kans., Ohio), Redroot-Pigweed, Rough-Pigweed, Wild-Beet (Maine)

In Maine this "was always 'Borax,' why I do not know" (Perkins, 1929). The leaves contain saponin and have been used to wash clothes.

Also, the leaves and seeds are eaten. It is called Lighthouses "from the speed with which they tower above crops in the field" (Bergen, 1897) and Careless-Weed because it is a careless farmer or gardener who will let them grow on his land.

# THE PURSLANE FAMILY

## Portulacaceae

A cosmopolitan family of 21 genera and 400 species of herbs and shrubs; best developed in western North America and the Andes. *Portula* is the diminutive of Latin *porta* (a gate), alluding to the gatelike covering of the capsule in Portulacas. Purslane, in its meaning of "herb of the womb," is derived from *porcella,* a sow, and a vulgar term for the pudendum. The word porcelain has the same root. Dioscorides wrote that Portulaca "doth assuage the stupidity of the teeth, and the burning of the stomach & entrails, and the flux, and doth help the eroded kidneys and the bladder, and doth dissolve the hot desire to conjunctions."

## Red-Maids, Rock-Purslane

*Calandrinia ciliata.* Of Calandrini (J. L. Calandrini, 18th-century Swiss botanist); fringed.
Mother's-Beauties (Calif.), Wild-Portulaca

The stems and leaves make a tasty salad or can be cooked as a potherb. Chesnut (1902) reported that in Mendocino County, California, "several pounds of the tiny jet-black seeds, which look like so many grains of gunpowder, were observed in the possession of a Numlaki squaw, who used them for pinole."

## Carolina Spring-Beauty

*Claytonia caroliniana.* Of Clayton (John Clayton, 1694–1773); of Carolina.
Rose-Elf, White-Leaved Spring-Beauty

John Clayton was born in Fulham, near London, England, and died in Gloucester County, Virginia. He came to Virginia in 1705 with his father, also John (and *his* father was Sir John), who was a lawyer and attorney general of the colony from 1714 until his death in 1737. Young John was appointed

*Carolina Spring-Beauty*

clerk of Gloucester County in 1722, a position he held for the remainder of his life, 51 years, and which provided him the means and leisure to travel and botanize throughout Virginia. He corresponded with many botanists and sent collections of plants to Johann Friedrich Gronovius, who systematized and listed them as *Flora Virginica,* published in two parts, 1739 and 1743 (both parts were published in an edition by L. T. Gronovius in 1762). "Clayton was esteemed in colonial Virginia not only for his scientific attainments, but also for his geniality, friendliness, and sterling integrity" (Swem, 1949).

## Miner's-Lettuce, Indian-Lettuce

*Claytonia perfoliata.* Of Clayton; perfoliate.
Petota (Calif.), Portuguese-Lettuce (Wash.), Spanish-Lettuce, Wild-Lettuce, Winter-Purslane

The succulent stems and leaves were a favorite food of the Indians and became a dietary staple for the miners of California's gold rush (the '49ers). "A Spanish Californian name for the plant is *petota.* A famous old time salad consists of a peeled *tuna* or prickly pear, nestling among *petota* leaves, served with a dressing of olive oil, salt, pepper and vinegar" (Saunders, 1934).

## Spring-Beauty

*Claytonia virginica* Of Clayton; of Virginia.
Fairy-Spuds, Good-Morning-Spring, Grass-Flower, Mayflower (P.Q.), Musquash, Wild-Potatoes (Pa.)

This is called Miskodeed in *The Song of Hiawatha.* In the following (from "XXI. The White Man's Foot") the youth Segwun is Spring:

> *And Segwun, the youthful stranger,*
> *More distinctly in the daylight*
> *Saw the icy face before him;*
> *It was Peboan, the Winter!*
> *From his eyes the tears were flowing,*

> *As from melting lakes the streamlets,*
> *And his body shrunk and dwindled*
> *As the shouting sun ascended,*
> *Till into the air it faded,*
> *Till into the ground it vanished,*
> *And the young man saw before him,*
> *On the hearth-stone of the wigwam,*
> *Where the fire had smoked and*
> *    smouldered,*
> *Saw the earliest flower of Spring-time,*
> *Saw the Beauty of the Spring-time,*
> *Saw the Miskodeed in blossom.*

"The roundish, irregular roots," wrote Fernald and Kinsey (1943), "when boiled in salted water, are palatable and nutritious, having the flavor of chestnuts."

## Bitterroot

*Lewisia rediviva.* Of Lewis (Meriwether Lewis, 1774–1809); revivable (apparently dead roots can be revived).
Konah, Mountain-Rose, *Racine amère,* Redhead-Louisa, Resurrection-Plant, Rock-Rose, Sand-Rose, Spatlum, Wild-Portulaca

Lewis and Clark found the root in a Shoshone Indian's bag in August 1805, and reported that "it had a bitter taste, which was nauseous to us, though the Indians seemed to relish it." Among the Indians of the Oregon Territory in 1844, the explorer Carl Geyer reported that "the root is dug during flower-time, when the cuticle is easily removed; by that it acquires a white colour, is brittle, and by transportation broken to small pieces. Before boiling, it is steeped in water, which makes it swell, and after boiling it becomes five to six times larger in size; resembling a jelly-like substance. As it is so small a root, it requires much labour to gather a sack, which commands generally the price of a good horse. Indians from the lower regions trade in this root by handfuls, paying a high price."

Brian Mathew writes that "there are several reported methods of preparing the roots for culinary purposes, including boiling and drying for later use, boiling with meat, frying with fish or making into flour for use in soups or bread: occasionally the roots were eaten raw. They were sometimes also eaten mixed with berries or meat and it is said that in modern times the Flathead Indians of Montana have been known to eat them with cream and sugar."

The first colored illustration of the plant was published in *Curtis's Botanical Magazine* (London) in 1863, accompanied by a report by W. J. Hooker, director of Kew Gardens. The specimen for the illustration had been collected in British Columbia in 1860. Since this was to be preserved for a herbarium, the plant, according to Hooker, "was immersed in boiling water on account of its well-known tenacity of life. More than a year and a half after, it notwithstanding showed symptoms of vitality, and produced its beautiful flowers in great profusion in May of the present year [1863], in the Royal Gardens of Kew" (Mathew, 1989). Spatlum is the Flathead name and Konah the Snake name. The plant is Montana's state flower. The Bitterroot River and the Bitterroot Mountains of western Montana are named after the plant.

Meriwether Lewis was born of a prominent family in Albemarle County, Virginia. He served in the army from 1795 until 1801 when his friend and neighbor, the newly elected president Thomas Jefferson, appointed him his private secretary. In 1803 Jefferson recommended to Congress that Lewis should lead an expedition to explore a land route to the Pacific. In his memoir of Meriwether Lewis (1813), Jefferson wrote, "Of courage undaunted; possessing a firmness and perserverance of purpose which nothing but impossibilities could divert from its direction; careful as a father of those committed to his charge, yet steady in the maintenance of order and discipline; intimate with the Indian character, customs, and principles; habituated to the hunting life; guarded, by exact observations of the vegetables and animals of his own country, against losing time in the description of objects already possessed; honest, disinterested, liberal, of sound understanding, and a fidelity to truth so scrupulous that whatever he should report would be as certain as if seen by ourselves—with all these qualifications, as if selected and implanted by nature in one body for this express purpose, I could have no hesitation in confiding the enterprise to him." Upon completion of the expedition, Lewis was appointed governor of the Louisiana Territory. According to the *Dictionary of American Biography,* "His services as governor were brief but useful. His evenhanded justice, his humanity and honesty gave the province the administration it needed." His death by shooting in central Tennessee has been attributed to homicide or suicide.

## Purslane

*Portulaca oleracea.* (The Latin name); of the vegetable garden. (Also found in Eurasia.)
Green Purslane, Kitchen-Garden Purslane, Little-Hogweed, *Pourpier gras* (P.Q.), Pressley, Purslance, Pursley (Ind., Ohio), Pusley (Ind., Minn.), Pussley

Manasseh Cutler reported, "It is eaten as a pot-herb, and esteemed by some as little inferior to asparagus." To John Evelyn (1699), it was "eminently moist and cooling, quickens appetite, asswages thirst, and is very profitable for hot and *Bilious* Tempers." It was probably introduced from Persia to Europe, where even its stems are pickled. In 1974, archaeologists reported finding Portulaca seeds at a site (Salts Cave) in Kentucky. Radiocarbon dating suggests that the seeds were gathered

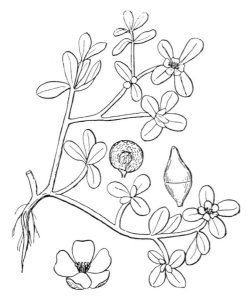

*Purslane*

there during the first millennium B.C. This evidence "establishes that *P. oleracea* was in the New World before historic times and indicates early prehistoric introduction or indigenous development. It may have been exploited by aboriginal Americans as 'greens' or valued for its medicinal properties" (Chapman, Stewart and Yarnell).

"I have made a satisfactory dinner, satisfactory on several accounts, simply off a dish of purslane *(Portulaca oleracea)* which I gathered in my cornfield. I give the Latin on account of the savoriness of the trivial name" (Thoreau, 1854). The seeds are used for mush or bread.

# THE PINK OR CARNATION FAMILY

## *Caryophyllaceae*

A widespread family of 89 genera and 2,070 species of herbs, shrubs and a few small trees; found in temperate and warm temperate regions. Latin *caryophylum* means "a clove," alluding to the clovelike scent of some Carnations.

## Corn-Cockle

*Agrostemma githago.* Field chaplet; the Latin name. (From Europe.)

Bastard-Nigelle, Cockle, Corn-Campion, Corn-Pink, Corn-Rose, Crown-of-the-Field, Licheta (Vt.), Mullein-Pink (N.S.), *Nielle des blés* (P.Q.), Old-Maid's-Pink (N.H.), Purple-Cockle, Rose-Campion, Rose-of-Heaven, Woolly-Pink

Dioscorides wrote that "the seed of it being drunk in the quantity of two dragms doth expell by the belly colerick matter & helpeth the scorpion-smitten. They say also that when this herb is laid by scorpions they become benumbed and not able to hurt." Before the development of selective herbicides, the plant was a pestilence in grain fields, the seeds being poisonous to man and beast. Gerard (1633) wrote of the "hurt it doth among corne, the spoyle unto bread, as well in colour, taste, and unwholsomnes." Cockle is the Old English name (Coccle in Turner, 1548), perhaps from Latin *coccus* (a seed or grain). Early herbalists called it Nigelle for its black seeds.

## Carnations, Pinks

*Dianthus.* God's flower (*dios,* "of Zeus"; *anthos,* "flower").

Josselyn (1674) wrote of New England that "Gilliflowers thrive exceedingly there and are very large, the collibuy or humming-Bird is much pleased with them. Our English dames make syrup of them without fire, they steep them in wine till it be of a deep colour, and then put to it syrup of vitriol." The 1683 inventory of Captain John Whipple's house in Ipswich (Mass.) included "Five bottles of syrup of clove gilly flowers" (Leighton, 1970). Carnation is derived either from the color carnation (flesh-colored) or from coronation—the flowers were used to make crowns and chaplets. "In English, garden Gillofers, Cloave gillofers, and the greatest and bravest sorte of them are called Coronations or Cornations" (Lyte, 1578). Pink is probably derived from obsolete Dutch *pinck oog* (small eye), from the shape of the flower (it is *oeillet*, "little eye," in French).

Spenser wrote in *The Shepheard's Calender*,

> *Bring hither the Pink and purple Columbine,*
> *With Gillyflowers:*
> *Bring Coronation, and Sops in wine,*
> *Worn of paramours.*

Gillyflower is from the Middle English *gilofre, gelofer*, Old French *girofre, girofle*, and Medieval Latin *caryophylum* (a clove, for the scent of some Carnations). Sops-in-Wine is because carnations were used to flavor wine.

In 1709 John Lawson wrote that "the flower-garden in Carolina is yet arriv'd but to a very poor and jejune perfection. We have only two sorts of Roses; the Clove-July-Flower, Violets, Princes Feather, and *Tres Colores*." The *American Herbal* of Samuel Stearns (1801) included "Clove July Flowers," whose "syrup is cordial, and proper to mix with juleps of that kind."

John Skelton wrote of that, "Mistress Jane Scrope" (ca. 1490):

> *She is the violet,*
> *The daisy delectable,*
> *The columbine commendable,*
> *The jelofer amiable;*
> *For this most goodly flower,*
> *This blossom of fresh colour,*
> *So Jupiter me succour,*
> *She flourisheth new and new*
> *In beauty and virtue.*

## Deptford Pink

*Dianthus armeria.* God's flower; (the Latin name of a Dianthus and a previous generic name). (From Europe.)
Grass Pink (Maine), Wild Pink

"There is a little wilde creeping Pinke, which groweth in our pastures neere about London, and in other places, but especially in the great field next to Deptford, by the path side as you go from Redriffe to Greenwich" (Gerard, 1633).

## Scarlet Lychnis, Maltese-Cross

*Lychnis chalcedonica.* (The Greek name of a scarlet flower); of Chalcedon (a city on the Bosphorus). (From Europe.)

*Scarlet Lychnis*

Cross-of-Jerusalem, Fire-Balls (Ohio), Knight's-Cross, London-Pride (Mass., N.H.), None-Such (Mass.), Scarlet-Lightning (P.Q.), Sweet-William (Ohio, Vt.)

In 1789 Erasmus Darwin (Charles's grandfather) published *The Loves of Flowers,* an explanation in rhymed couplets of the sexual classification of plants as established by Linnaeus. Here is his "Lychnis":

Five *sister-nymphs to join Diana's train*
*With thee, fair Lychnis! Vow,—but vow*
    *in vain;*
*Beneath one roof resides the virgin*
    *band,*
*Flies the fond swain, and scorns his*
    *offer'd hand;*
*But when soft hours on breezy pinions*
    *move,*
*And smiling May attunes her lute to*
    *love,*
*Each wanton beauty, trick'd in all her*
    *grace,*
*Shakes the bright dew-drops from her*
    *blushing face;*
*In gay undress displays her rival*
    *charms,*
*And calls her wandering lovers to her*
    *arms.*

This is explained in a footnote: "Ten males [stamens] and five females [styles]. The flowers which contain the five females, and those which contain the ten males, are found on different plants; and often at a great distance from each other. Five of the ten males arrive at their maturity some days before the other five, as may be seen by opening the corol before it naturally expands itself. When the females arrive at their maturity, they rise above the petals, as if looking abroad for their distant husbands; the scarlet ones contribute much to the beauties of our meadows in May and June."

The Maltese Cross, which the flower head

resembles, is the symbol of the Knights of Malta, the Hospitallers of St. John of Jerusalem, a military religious order founded in 1099 that still provides emergency medical services in some European countries. Sweet-William of the garden is *Dianthus barbatus.* London-Pride is a local name in England.

## Rose Campion, Mullein-Pink

*Lychnis coronaria.* (The Greek name of a scarlet flower); of crowns (the old generic name). (From Europe.)

Dusty-Miller, Gardener's-Delight, Gardener's-Eye, Mullein Lychnis

Campion is the 16th-century name for this "champion" of the garden, or the plant was used to make crowns for athletic champions. It is covered in white woolly down, like the Common Mullein, or is like a floury miller. Some of the other Campions have been placed in the *Silene* genus (below).

## Bouncing-Bet, Soapwort

*Saponaria officinalis.* Soapy; officinal. (From Europe.)

Boston-Pink (Maine, Mass.), Bouncing-Bess, Bruisewort, Chimney-Pink (N.H.), Crowsoap, Dog-Cloves, Flop-Top, Fuller's-Herb, Hedge-Pink, *Herbe à savon* (P.Q.), Lady-by-the-Gate (N.C.), Latherwort, London-Pride (Mass.), Mock-Gilliflower, Monthly-Pink (Mo.), My-Lady's-Washbowl (South), Old-Maid's-Pink (Mass.), Ragged-Sailor (Wis.), Scourweed, Sheepweed, Soaproot, Soapwort-Gentian, Sweet-Betty (Ind.), Wild-Sweet-William, Woods-Phlox (N.J.), World's-Wonder (Mass.)

"It is commonly called *Saponaria,* of the great scouring qualitie that the leaves have: for they yield out of themselves a certain juyce when they are bruised, which scoureth almost as well as sope" (Gerard, 1633). Dioscorides reported that the plant was used by fullers to full wool—that is to increase its weight by shrinking and beating. It was brought

*Bouncing-Bet*

to North America by settlers to use as a soap, balm and sheep dip and by fullers in cloth manufacturing. "In our Southern States a pretty local name that has come to my notice is 'My Lady's Wash-bowl.' It was in Saponaria, I believe, that the glucoside saponin—the detergent principle of soap plants—was first discovered and given its name" (Saunders, 1934).

Thomas Johnson (1633) reported that "it was one Zapata, a Spanish Empericke" who discovered "the singular effect of this herb against that filthy disease, the French Poxes"; but it has "somewhat an ungratefull taste, and therefore it must be reserved for the poorer sort." Culpeper claimed that it was "an absolute cure in the French Pox." Bouncing-Bett is a local west-country name in England, the common name in the British Isles being Soapwort.

## Sleepy Catchfly

*Silene antirrhina.* (A Greek plant name); like Antirrhinum (leaves).
Garter-Pink (South), Snapdragon Catchfly (Mass.)

"*Silene antirrhina,* sleepy catch-fly, or snapdragon catch-fly, the ordinarily curled-up petals scarcely noticeable at the end of the large oval calyx. Gray says opening only at night or cloudy weather. Bigelow says probably nocturnal for he never found it expanded by day" (Thoreau, 1852).

## Sweet-William-Catchfly

*Silene armeria.* (A Greek plant name); (the Latin name of a Dianthus). (From Europe.)
Bunch-Pink, Catchwort, Dwarf French-Pink (N.Y.), Garden Catchfly, Limewort, Lobel's Catchfly, Mice-Pink (Ill.), Mock-Sweet-William (Ind.), None-So-Pretty (Mass.), Old-Maid's-Pink (Mass., Canada), Pretty-Nancy (P.Q.), Sweet-Susan (Mass., N.H.), Waxplant (Ohio)

"The whole plant, as well leaves as stalks, as also the floures, are here and there covered over with the most thick and clammie matter like unto bird-lime, which if you take it into your hands, the sliminesse is such that your fingers will stick and cleave together . . . Whereupon I have called it Catchflie, or Lime woort" (Gerard). (Birdlime is a sticky substance smeared on twigs to catch small

*Sweet-William-Catchfly*

birds.) Pretty-Nancy is a local name in England for *Stellaria holostea*. Matthias de Lobel (1538–1616), honored in the name Lobel's catchfly, was a Flemish botanist.

## Red Campion, Bachelor's-Buttons

*Silene dioica*. (A Greek plant name); dioecious. (From Europe.)

Bull-Rattle, Cow-Rattle, Cuckoo-Flower, Evening-Lychnis, Poor-Robin, Red-Bird's-Eye, Red-Catchfly, Red-Robin, Red-Soapwort, Robins, Soldiers

Gerard wrote that "the similitude that these floures have to the jagged cloath buttons anciently worne in this kingdome gave occasion to our gentlewomen and other lovers of floures in those times to call them Bachelours Buttons." But the name evidently had another meaning: "I saw the Batchelers buttons, whose vertue is to make wanton maidens weepe when they have worne it fortye weekes under their Aprons for a favour" (Robert Greene, 1592). Grigson wrote that it is a "plant of snake (in Wales a local name is *blodau'r neidr,* 'snake's flower'), of devil, goblin (Robin Goodfellow and Jack a Lantern—see *Ge-*

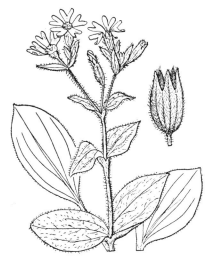

*Red Campion*

*ranium robertianum*), and of death, if it is picked." The name Silene is sometimes derived from Silenus, a satyr and foster father of Bacchus, who was described as covered with foam, like the Catchflies; or from Greek *sialon* (saliva), referring to the sticky secretions of the Catchflies.

## Starry Campion

*Silene stellata*. (A Greek plant name); starry.

King's-Cure-All, Thurman's-Snakeroot (N.C.), Widow's-Frill

Asa Gray at Jefferson, North Carolina, 1842: "We had frequently been told of an antidote to the bite of the Rattlesnake and Copperhead (not unfrequent through this region), which is thought to possess wonderful efficacy, called Thurman's Snake-root after an 'Indian Doctor,' who first employed it; the plant was brought to us by a man who was ready to attest its virtues from his personal knowledge, and proved to be the *Silene stellata!* Its use was suggested by the markings of the root beneath the bark, in which these people find a fancied resemblance to the skin of the Rattlesnake. Nearly all the reputed antidotes are equally inert; such herbs as the *Impatiens pallida,* etc., being sometimes employed; so that we are led to conclude that the bite of these reptiles is seldom fatal, or even very dangerous, in these cooler portions of the country."

## Bladder Campion

*Silene vulgaris*. (A Greek plant name); common. (From Europe.)

Behen, Bird's-Eggs, Bull-Rattle, Cowbell, Cow-Paps, Devil's-Rattle-Box (Mass.), Fairy-Potatoes (Mass.), Frothy-Poppy, Knap-Bottle, Maiden's-Tears (Maine), *Pétards* (P.Q.) *Péteux* (P.Q.), Rattle-Bags, Rattle-Box (Mass.), Sea-Pink, Snappers (Mass.), Snappery, Spattling-Poppy

*Bladder Campion*

Gerard invented the name Spattling-Poppy "in respect of that kinde of frothy spattle, or spume, which we call Cuckow spittle, that more aboundeth in the bosomes of the leaves of these plants than in any other." Cuckoo-spit (or snake's-spit) is the frothy secretion deposited on plants by nymphs of the spittle bugs. Behen is a corruption of the Arabic name of a root, applied by herbalists to Bladder Campion (White Behen or White Ben) and Sea-Lavender (Red Behen). In 1785 Manasseh Cutler called this plant Bladder Behen. "The leaves boiled have something of the flavour of pease, and proved of great use to the inhabitants of the island of Minorca in the year 1685, when a swarm of locusts had destroyed the vegetation. The Gothlanders apply the leaves to erysipelatous eruptions" (Withering, 1776).

## Corn Spurrey

*Spergula arvensis.* Scattered (Latin *spargere*); of fields. (From Europe.)

Cow-Quake, Devil's-Guts (Maine), *Grippe* (P.Q.), Pick-Purse, Pine-Cheat, Pine-Weed (Mass., N.H.), Piney, Poverty-Weed, Sandweed, *Spargoute des champs* (P.Q.), Spurrey, Wild-Flax (Wash.), Yarr

This was once a cultivated crop for livestock, and sometimes man—if he had nothing better. Yarr is the Scottish name, Cow-Quake a British name, and Pick-Purse and Poverty-Weed local names in England. Pine also means "hunger" or "starvation." Sand Spurrey is *Spergularia rubra* ("red"), which provided the medicine known as Tissa, "at one time employed in various diseases of the urinary bladder, including even calculi" (USD).

## Common Stitchwort, Lesser Stitchwort

*Stellaria graminea.* Starry; grasslike. (From Europe.)

"They are wont to drink it in wine with the powder of Acornes, against the paine in the side, stitches, and such like" (Gerard).

## Long-Leaved Stitchwort

*Stellaria longifolia.* Starry; long-leaved. (Also found in Eurasia.)

Eyebright, Stitchwort

Josselyn (1672) wrote that among the plants common to England and New England was the "Stitchwort, commonly taken here by ignorant people for Eyebright; it blows in June." Eyebright is the familiar name for Euphrasias and a local name in England for *Stellaria holostea.*

## Common Chickweed, Starwort

*Stellaria media.* Starry; intermediate. (From Europe.)

Adder's-Mouth, Chicken-Weed, Indian-Chickweed, *Mouron des oiseaux* (P.Q.), Satin-Flower, Tongue-Grass, White-Birdseye, Winterweed

*Common Chickweed*

Chickens and other birds love to pick at the leaves and seeds. "Little birds in cages (especially Linnets) are refreshed with the lesser Chickweed when they loath their meat" (Gerard). Withering (1776) reported that "the young shoots and leaves when boiled can hardly be distinguished from Spring Spinach, and are equally wholesome." He also noted that "this species is a notable instance of what is called the *Sleep of Plants*; for every night the leaves approach in pairs, so as to include within their upper surfaces, the tender rudiments of the new shoots; and the uppermost pair but at one end of the stalk, are furnished with longer leaf-stalks than the others, so that they can close upon the terminating pair and protect the end of the branch."

# THE SMARTWEED
# OR BUCKWHEAT FAMILY

## *Polygonaceae*

A family of 51 genera and 1,150 species of herbs, shrubs, lianas and trees; found chiefly in north temperate regions. *Polu* means "many," and *gonu* means "knee" (for the swollen stem joints of many species). Some members of the family are cultivated as ornamentals, including *Antigonon leptopus,* Coral-Vine or Rosa de montaña. Food plants include Buckwheat and Sorrel (see below) and Rhubarb, *Rheum rhaponticum.*

## Winged Eriogonum, Winged Wild Buckwheat

*Eriogonum alatum.* Woolly knee; winged.

Among the Zuñi Indians, "the root is ground by women on the grinding-slabs in the ceremonial chambers of all the fraternities and gathered into bowls by the officers of the fraternity. It is afterward distributed by the maker of medicine-water to each adult member of the fraternity. The powdered root is received in the palm of the hand and deposited in a piece of deerskin, which is tied securely. A pinch of the powder in a cup of warm water is taken morning, noon, and sunset to relieve 'general miserable feeling' or after a fall" (Stevenson, 1915).

## Desert-Trumpet, Bladder-Stem, Indian-Pipeweed

*Eriogonum inflatum.* Woolly knee; inflated (stems).

Bottle-Plant, Cigarette-Plant, Pickles

Charles Saunders (1934) wrote of "the so-called Desert Trumpet or Pickles, found

Many Erigerons are considered appropriate for the Navaho Life Medicine preparation: "Usually the roots only of the plant are used, being dried and ground by a virgin during a Life Way chant to the accompaniment of special songs. Life Medicine (and Life Way chants) is used to treat sprains, strains, fractures, swellings, bruises, wounds, burns, lameness, internal injuries, body pains, and any other results of accidents. Hence its reputation as a cure-all" (Wyman and Harris, 1941).

## Buckwheat

*Fagopyrum saggittatum.* Beech wheat; arrow-shaped. (From Asia.)

Beechwheat, *Blé noir* (P.Q.), Brank, Corn-Heath, Crap, Duck-Wheat, Goose Buckwheat, Indian-Wheat, Saracen's-Corn, Saracen's-Wheat, *Sarrasin* (P.Q.)

Buckwheat (from Middle Dutch *boecweite,* "beech-wheat," because the fruits resemble beechnuts) is supposed to have been brought to Europe by returning Crusaders, thus the Saracen names (it is also *grana Saraceno* in Italian). It was a good crop for the poor soils of New England and was once far more ex-

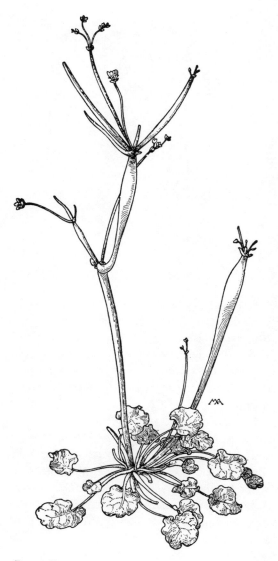

*Desert-Trumpet*

abundantly on the southwestern desert as far north as Utah and eastward to New Mexico. It is remarkable for its bluish-green, leafless stalks, hollow and puffed out like a trumpet, sometimes to the diameter of an inch or so, and rising out of a radical cluster of small heart-shaped leaves. The stems before flowering are tender and are eaten raw."

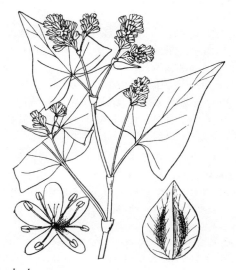

*Buckwheat*

tensively cultivated, for both human and live-stock consumption, than it is now; the groats make the cereal known as Kasha. In Pennsylvania in 1748, Kalm reported that "the buckwheat cakes are very good, and are common at Philadelphia and in other English colonies, especially in winter. In Philadelphia there were some people who baked them and in the morning carried them around while still warm, to be sold. Buckwheat is an excellent food for fowls: they eat it eagerly, and lay more eggs than they do from other food. Hogs are likewise fattened with it." Brank and Crap are obsolete dialect names in England.

## Knotweeds, Smartweeds

*Polygonum.* Many knees (the swollen stem joints of many species).

Bindweed, *Curage* (La.), Doorweed, Heart's-Ease (Pa.), Knotgrass, Pull-Down, *Renouée* (P.Q.)

The young shoots of many species are boiled and the leaves used as seasoning. The parched seeds are eaten as cereal or ground for flour, and the roots are eaten raw or cooked.

## Water Smartweed

*Polygonum amphibium.* Many knees; amphibious.

Devil's-Shoe-String (Kans.), Ground-Willow, Heart's-Ease (Nebr.), Red-Shanks, Water-Persicaria, Willowgrass, Willow-Weed

Manasseh Cutler listed this as "Bistort. Snakeweed. Blossoms red. In wet meadows." He reported that "the root is said to be one of the strongest vegetable astringents."

## Knotweed, Knotgrass

*Polygonum aviculare.* Many knees; of birds (which eat the leaves and seeds). (From Europe.)

Bindweed, Beggar-Weed, Birdgrass, Bird's-Knotgrass, Bird's-Tongue, Birdweed, Common Knotweed, Cowgrass, Crawl-Grass, Craw-Weed, Dog-

*Knotweed*

Tails (Mo.), Doorgrass (Ind.), Doorweed, Dooryard-Grass, Goosegrass, *Herbe à cochons* (P.Q.), Irongrass, Knotgrass, Ninety-Knot, Pigweed, Pinkweed, Prostrate Knotweed, Sparrow-Tongue, Stoneweed, Swinegrass, Tacker-Grass, *Traînasse* (P.Q.), Waygrass, Wiregrass (Ohio), Wireweed, Yard Knotweed

Many of the above are local names in England that describe the leaves or tough knotted stems. Tacker is a shoemaker's waxed thread. It had a reputation for stunting growth when eaten. In Shakespeare's *A Midsummer Night's Dream,* Lysander taunts Hermia about her height: "Get you gone; you dwarf; You minimus, of hindering knotgrass made" (3, 2, 338). And in Beaumont and Fletcher's *The Coxcomb* (ca. 1610), when someone small enough to creep into a house is needed, Dorothy tells the Tinker, "We want a boy extremely for this function, Kept under for a year with milk and knotgrass." Dioscorides reported that "it is commodious for the blood-spitters, & the fluxes by the belly, & for the sick of choler, & the strangury. It moves the urine manifestly."

Keats wrote of Knotgrass in *The Eve of St. Agnes:*

*A casement high and triple-arch'd there
was,
All garlanded with carven imag'ries
Of fruits, and flowers, and bunches of
knot-grass,
And diamonded with panes of quaint
device.*

## American Bistort, Western Bistort, Smokeweed

*Polygonum bistortoides.* Many knees; like bistort (*Polygonum bistorta*).

Bistort, Knotweed, Mountain-Meadow-Knotweed, Snakeweed

"When the Cheyennes ranged far and wide, in the former days, the roots were highly esteemed for food, especially in the stream bottoms of the Bighorn mountains. Women gathered, peeled and laid them in the sun to dry" (Hart, 1980). The starchy roots were roasted or added to stews by Cheyenne and Blackfoot Indians and by the Eskimo; the roots are also eaten by bears and rodents, and the foliage is grazed by deer and elk.

## Black-Bindweed

*Polygonum convolvulus.* Many knees; twining. (From Europe.)

Bearbind, Blackbird-Bindweed, Blindweed (Ohio), *Chevrier* (P.Q.), Climbing-Bindweed, Climbing-Buckwheat, Cornbind, Corn-Bindweed, Devil's-Tether, False Buckwheat, Ivy-Bindweed, Knot-Bindweed, Nimble-Will, Pull-Down (Ohio), *Renouée liseron* (P.Q.), Wild-Bean (Maine, Mass.)

William Turner (1548) wrote that "Elatine . . . hath seeds and floures lyk Buckwheat; it groweth among the corne & in hedges; it may be named in English Running Buckwheate or Bynde corn."

## Douglas's Knotweed

*Polygonum douglasii.* Many knees; of Douglas (David Douglas; 1798–1834).

Among the Klamath Indians, "at maturity the seeds are inclosed in the dry, papery calyx or 'hull,' and in this condition they are gathered. The hulls are rubbed off by hand, and the seeds parched and often ground. This meal is either eaten dry or mixed with water and boiled, a process which turns the material red" (Coville, 1897).

## Common Smartweed, Water-Pepper

*Polygonum hydropiper.* Many knees; water-pepper (the old generic name). (From Europe.)

Arsesmart, Arsmart, Bite-Tongue, Biting Knotweed, Biting-Know-Weed, Biting-Persicaria, *Curage* (P.Q.), Doorweed, Lakeweed, Pepper-Plant, Red-Knees, Red-Leaves, Red-Shanks, Red-Sharks, *Renouée poivre-d'eau* (P.Q.), Sickle-Weed, Smartweed (Mass.), Snakeweed, Wild-Buckwheat (Ore.)

Arsmart (or Arsesmart) appears to have been the common name for this plant in North America and the British Isles until the end of the 19th century, called thus "because if it touch the taile or other bare skinne, it maketh it smart, as often it doth, being laid

*Common Smartweed*

into the bed greene to kill fleas," according to John Minsheu's 1626 *Guide into Tongues*.

In his 1687 letter about the Indians of Virginia, the Reverend John Clayton wrote, "The great success they have in curing wounds and sores, I apprehend mostly to proceed from their manner of dressing them: For they first cleanse them by sucking, which though a very nasty, is no doubt the most effechual and best way imaginable; then they take the Biting Persicary, and chaw it in their mouths, and then squirt the juice thereof into the wound, which they will do as if out of a syringe. Then they apply their salve-herbs, either bruised or beaten into a salve with grease, binding it on with bark and silk grass."

Richmond, Virginia, 1797: "The *Arsmart* which grows plentifully in all the wet places, and on all the shores of the river and creeks, is a well-known poison to the fish. It is very common for the Negroes, when the tide retires, and in the low country leaves lakes or ponds of water full of fish, to throw in a basket full of the bruised Arsmart and stir it about. The fish soon come to the surface in a torpid state and are easily taken" (Latrobe).

Culpeper reported that "a good handful of the hot biting Arssmart put under a horse's saddle, will make him travel the better," a practice attributed to the Scythians, fierce horsemen of the seventh century B.C. According to the USD, the leaves have been used in "amenorrhea and other uterine disorders."

## Prince's-Feather

*Polygonum orientale.* Many knees; oriental. (From Europe.)
*Bâton de Saint-Jean* (P.Q.), Garden Persicary, Gentleman's-Cane (Ohio), Kiss-Me-over-the-Fence (Ohio), Kiss-Me-over-the-Garden-Gate, Loves-Lies-Bleeding, *Monte-au-ciel* (P.Q.), Princess-Feather, Ragged-Sailor (Maine)

More commonly, Kiss-Me-over-the-Garden-Gate is the name of the Pansy *(Viola tricolor),*

and Love-Lies-Bleeding is an *Adonis* (Pheasant's-Eye). The name Gentleman's-Cane was acquired because "the stems [were] cut by children into canes" (Bergen, 1894).

## Pennsylvania Smartweed, Pink Knotweed

*Polygonum pensylvanicum.* Many knees; of Pennsylvania.
Black-Heart (Kans.), Heart's-Ease (Maine, Ohio, Nebr., Vt.), Knee Knotweed, Pinkweed

"This is a bitter leaf which is dried by the Menomini for tea. When one has a hemorrhage of blood from the mouth, this is drunk to stop it. Mixed with other herbs, it is drunk by women after childbirth, and heals them internally" (Huron Smith, 1923).

## Lady's-Thumb, Redleg

*Polygonum persicaria.* Many knees; peach-like (the medieval name of a Knotweed). (From Europe.)
Adam's-Plaster (Nfd.), Black-Heart (Maine, Vt.), Common Persicary, Doorweed, Gandergrass (South), Heart's-Ease (Maine, Ohio, Nebr., Vt.), Heartspot Knotweed, Heartweed (Maine), Lover's-

*Lady's-Thumb*

Pride, Peachwort, Pinkweed, Red-Shanks, Red-weed, Spotted Arsesmart, Spotted Knotweed, Willow-Weed

The dark smudge on the leaf is heart-shaped or like a thumb print. In Britain it is also Pinchweed, Virgin Mary's Pinch and Useless: Our Lady pulled up a plant, leaving her thumb print on the leaf, tasted it and threw it away, saying "useless." In Gaelic it is *lus chrann ceusaidh* (the herb of the Crucifixion tree) because of the belief that it grew under the cross and was spotted with Christ's blood (Grigson). Heart's-Ease is usually a Pansy, or *Prunella vulgaris* (Self-Heal) in Ireland. In 1785 Manasseh Cutler called Lady's-Thumb "Heartsease" or "Spotted Arsmart" and noted that it "will dye woollen cloth yellow, after the cloth has been dipped in a solution of alum." From Maine in 1832, Williamson wrote that "Heart's-Ease resembles arsmart in appearance, except that it has a large reddish heart-formed spot on its leaf." Bergen (1894) reported that the name Heartsease was "used very generally by beekeepers" for several Polygonums. Marie-Victorin wrote that the English name Heart's-Ease "alludes to its use for relieving stomach pains (the people do not distinguish, in the expression, between the heart and the stomach)." Lover's-Pride is a local name in England. According to Pliny, if the seeds are taken in wine by the man and the woman before supper "for forty days before conception take place, the child will be of the male sex."

## Water Smartweed

*Polygonum punctatum.* Many knees; spotted. (Also found in Asia.)
Dotted Smartweed, Turkey-Troop (N.Y.), Water-Pepper

Marie-Victorin wrote that "the plant is found in both Americas; in South America it is one of the stupefying plants used by Indian fishermen to anesthetize and capture fishes."

## Alpine Smartweed

*Polygonum viviparum.* Many knees; viviparous (the young well-developed on the parent plant). (Also found in Asia.)
Alpine Bistort, Serpentgrass

The bistort or double-twisted rhizome suggests a coiled snake and thus it was given against snakebite. The rhizomes have been eaten by northern peoples in America and Asia. This plant was once called *Bistorta vivipara.*

## Docks, Sorrels

*Rumex.* (The Latin name).

Dock is from the Old English *docce,* perhaps meaning "a dark-colored plant." Sorrel is from the Old French *surele,* from *sur* (sour).

Chapter 49 of Cotton Mather's manual on medicine, *The Angel of Bethesda,* is on "*Scabiosus.* or, The ITCH . . . A Frequent, but a Grievous, Malady." He advised the patient to "Think: I am a Mangy Creature; And shall I not be an Humble One! The best friends I have shun me, are afraid of touching me. Did I know myself, I should even wish that I could gett away from myself. What an Abhorrence am I to the Holy Angels of God! I am advised unto Brimstone [sulfur] for my remedy; how much do I deserve to be thrown in the Lake that burns with Fire and Brimstone, for my Punishment!" However, those that have "an Horror of Brimstone think they have a Sufficient Remedy in Dock-root and Elecampane, sliced and mixed with hogs-fatt. Let the patient anoint himself a week, and then have the patience to forbear changing his cloaths for another week; and the business is done."

## Garden Sorrel

*Rumex acetosa.* (The Latin name); bitter (an old generic name). (From Europe.)
Cock Sorrel, English Sorrel, *Grande Oseille* (P.Q.), Green-Sauce, Green Sorrel, Meadow Sorrel, Red-

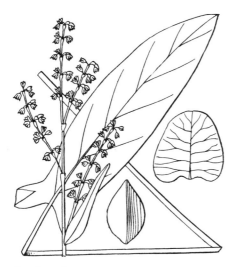

*Garden Sorrel*

Shanks, Sharp Dock, Sour Dock, Sourgrass, Sour-weed

"Sorrell is much used in sawces, both for the whole and the sicke, cooling the hot livers and stomackes of the sicke, and procuring unto them an appetite unto meate, when their spirits are almost spent with the violence of their furious or fierie fits; and is also of a pleasant relish for the whole, in quickning up a dull stomacke that is over-loaden with every daies plenty of dishes" (Parkinson, 1629). John Evelyn (1699) wrote that Sorrel was "never to be excluded" from his salads: "Abstersive, acid, sharpening appetite, asswages heat, cools the liver, strengthens the heart." This is the cultivated Sorrel. Cock Sorrel and Green-Sauce are local names in England.

## Sheep Sorrel, Common Sorrel

*Rumex acetosella.* (The Latin name); little Sorrel (an old generic name). (From Europe.)

Cow Sorrel (N.B.), Cuckoo-Bread, Field Sorrel, Flora-Carol-Sorrel, Gentleman's Sorrel (Mass.), Green-Sauce, Horse Sorrel (Md., Minn., Ohio),

Mountain Sorrel, *Oseille* (P.Q.), Ranty-Tanty, Red Sorrel (W. Va.), Red-Top Sorrel, Redweed (W. Va.), Sheep Sorrel (Iowa, Wis., Vt.), Sorrel Dock, Sour Dock, Sourgrass (Conn.), Sourleaf, Sour-Leek, *Surette* (P.Q.), Toad's Sorrel (N.H.), *Vignette* (P.Q.)

The young leaves are eaten as a salad or cooked as a potherb. Ranty-Tanty is a Scottish name for *Rumex obtusifolius,* and Cuckoo-Bread is a local name in England for this and *Rumex acetosa.*

## Curled Dock

*Rumex crispus.* (The Latin name); curled. (From Europe.)

Bitter Dock, Bloodwort (Ky.), *Cañaigre* (Texas), Coffee-Weed, Garden-Patience, Narrow Dock (Ohio), Out-Sting (Ky.), Sour Dock, Winter Dock (Texas), Yellow Dock

In New Jersey in 1749, Peter Kalm described this as "a kind of sorrel which grows at the edge of cultivated fields and elsewhere in rather low land. Farmers choose a variety which has green leaves instead of pale colored ones. All sorrel is not suitable for greens, for the leaves of some are very bitter. These green leaves are gathered at this time every-

*Curled Dock*

where and used by some people in the same way that Swedes prepare spinach. But they generally boil the leaves in the water in which they had cooked meat. Then they eat it alone or with the meat. It is served on a platter and eaten with a knife, which is different from the Swedish custom. Here also vinegar is placed in a special container on the table to be used on the kale. I must confess that this dish tastes very good."

In Maine "Rumex crispus was *Yaller dock,* and one of the constituents of a spring tonic" (Perkins, 1929). The USD reports that "dock root is mildly laxative and astringent and in the days of legendary therapeutics was employed in syphilis and chronic skin diseases." The powdered root was also used as a tooth powder. The seeds were roasted and used as a coffee substitute.

## Tanner's Dock, Desert-Rhubarb

*Rumex hymenosepalus.* (The Latin name); with membranous sepals.
*Cañaigre,* Sand Dock, Wild-Pie-Plant, Wild-Rhubarb

According to Charles Saunders, the plant, "common on the dry plains and deserts of the Southwest and becoming very showy when its ample panicles of dull crimson flowers and seed-vessels are set, is famous there as a satisfactory substitute for rhubarb, which, indeed, the plant somewhat resembles. The large leaves, nearly a foot long, are narrowed to a thick fleshy footstalk, which is crisp, juicy and tart. These stalks, stripped off before the toughness of age has come upon them, and cooked like rhubarb, are hardly distinguishable from it. Westerners know it as Wild Rhubarb, Wild Pie Plant, and Cañaigre. Under the last name it has some celebrity as tanning material, the tuberous roots being rich in tannin and having been long used by the Indians in treating skins."

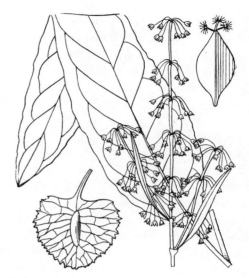

*Water Dock*

## Water Dock

*Rumex orbiculatus.* (The Latin name); disk-shaped (valves). (Also found in Europe.)
Horse Sorrel, Yellow-Rooted Water-Dock

In their *British Flora Medica* of 1877, Barton and Castle propose that this may be the "true Herba Britannica of the Ancients." According to Pliny, the Romans learned about the plant from the Frisians during the campaign of A.D. 11–16: "When Germanicus Caesar had moved forward his camp across the Rhine, in a maritime district of Germany there was only one source of fresh water. To drink it caused within two years the teeth to fall out and the use of the knee joints to fail. Physicians used to call these maladies stomacace [scurvy of the gums] and scelotyrbe [paralysis of the legs]. A remedy was found in the plant called britannica, which is good not only for the sinews and for diseases of the mouth, but also for the relief of quinsy and snake-bite." Manasseh Cutler reported that the "Indians used this root with great success in cleansing foul ulcers. It is said they endeavored to keep it a secret from the Europeans.

Dr. Withering says, he saw an ill-conditioned ulcer in the mouth, which had destroyed the palate, cured by washing the mouth with a decoction of this root, and drinking a small quantity of the same decoction daily."

## Patience Dock

*Rumex patientia*. (The Latin name); (the old colloquial name). (From Europe.)
Garden Dock, Garden Patience, Monk's-Rhubarb, Passions, Patience

"Monkes Rubarb or Patience is an excellent wholesome pot-herbe, for being put into the pottage in some reasonable quantitie, it doth loosen the belly, helps the jaunders, the timpany and such like diseases" (Gerard, 1633). The origin of the name Patience, which is recorded in the 15th century, is obscure.

## Winged Dock, Veined Dock

*Rumex venosus*. (The Latin name); veined (leaves).

Among the Northern Cheyenne of Montana, "this species was the source of a red, yellow and black dye. The roots were cut into small pieces and boiled. Feathers, quills, or hair were put into the solution to dye them yellow. For a darker yellow, the materials were left in a covered vessel overnight. For red, ashes were put into the yellow dye-bath overnight. For black, the bark of *Cornus stolonifera* shoots was scorched, pounded fine

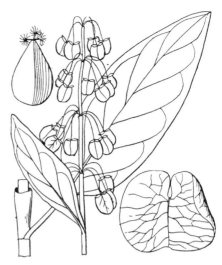

*Winged Dock*

and put into the red-yellow dye and boiled" (Hart, 1980).

According to Percy Train and his colleagues (1941), the Shoshones in Nevada call the plant "burn medicine." "Everywhere in the state, in fact, the root is the basis of a standard treatment for burns, wounds, sores, and sometimes swellings. Ordinarily the roots are dried, pulverized and applied as a powder, but occasionally the raw root is mashed and laid on as a wet dressing or poultice, and sometimes the solution from the boiled root can serve as an antiseptic wash. This treatment was mentioned as a means of drying up persistent sores, specifically those of syphilis."

# THE LEADWORT OR SEA-LAVENDER FAMILY

## *Plumbaginaceae*

A widely distributed family of 22 genera and 440 species of herbs, shrubs and lianas. *Plumbago* was the Latin name (derived from *plumbum*, "lead," and *ago*, "resemblance") of a European plant.

## Seathrift, Wild Thrift

*Armeria maritima*. (The Latin name of a Dianthus); of the seaside. (Also found in Eurasia.)

Cliff-Rose, Lady's-Cushion, Maiden-Pink, Marsh-Daisy, Redroot, Rockrose, Sea-Cushion, Sea-Gilliflower, Sea-Grass, Sea-Pink, Sea-Thrift, Statice

## Sea-Lavender, Statice, Marsh-Rosemary

*Limonium carolinianum*. Meadow plant (from Greek *leimon*, "a meadow"); of Carolina.

American-Thrift, Canker-Root, Ink-Root, *Lavande de mer* (P.Q.), Lavender-Thrift, Marshroot, Seaside-Lavender, Seaside-Thrift

Dr. Bigelow reported that "the Statice Caroliniana possesses much medicinal reputa-

*Sea-Lavender*

tion as an astringent, and large quantities are annually consumed in different parts of the United States. In Boston it is regularly kept by the druggists, and larger quantities are sold than of almost any other indigenous article." It has been included in the USP. Statice (from Greek *statikos*, "causing to stand") is a previous generic name. Manasseh Cutler called it Marsh Rosemary: "The roots are powerfully astringent. A decoction of them is given, and used as a gargle, with success, in cankers and ulcerated sore throats."

# THE PEONY FAMILY

## *Paeoniaceae*

A family of two genera and 34 species of herbs and soft shrubs. Peonies are named after Paeon, physician to the Greek gods. John

Parkinson (1629) wrote that the "Peony roote is farre above all the rest a most singular approved remedy for all Epilepticall diseases (in English, the Falling sicknesse) . . . if the disease be not too inveterate, to be boyled and drunke, as also to hang about the neckes of the younger sort that are troubled here-with."

## Western Peony, Wild Peony

*Paeonia brownii.* Of Paeon; of Brown (Robert Brown, 1773–1858).

Christmas-Rose (Calif.), Nigger-Heads (Calif.)

Among the Indians of Nevada, a decoction made from the boiled roots was used to treat tuberculosis, venereal diseases, coughs, nausea, diarrhea, and kidney troubles. "A Shoshone at Elko claimed that a three-year treatment by this method had been successful in curing her husband of kidney stones. It might be supposed that the informant was confused as to the exact nature of this disease, but in order to illustrate clearly the pain suffered by her husband she picked up a stone from the ground and placed it over her left kidney. She said that he had passed such a stone and that he had been very ill" (Train, Henrichs and Archer, 1941).

Robert Brown was a Scottish physican who served as surgeon and naturalist on the Flinders expedition to Australia (1801–1805) and collected many new species. He was curator of the botanical department at the British Museum and made several important discoveries, including gymnospermism and the Brownian movement. Asa Gray (1859) wrote of him that "no one since Linnaeus has brought such rare sagacity to bear upon the structure, and especially upon the ordinal characters and natural affinities of plants, as did Robert Brown . . . Perhaps no naturalist ever taught so much in writing so little, or made so few statements that had to be recalled, or even recast; and of no one can there be a stronger regret that he did not publish more."

# THE MANGOSTEEN
# OR ST. JOHNSWORT FAMILY

## *Clusiaceae or Guttiferae*

A family of 47 genera and 1,350 species of herbs, shrubs, lianas and trees; found chiefly in moist tropical regions. The North American genera belong to the subfamily Hypericoideae of the North Temperate Zone. Mangosteen is the fruit of the tropical *Garcinia mangostana.* Another family member is Mammy-Apple, *Mammea americana.* Members of the family also provide timber, drugs, dyes, gums, pigments, resins and oilseeds.

## St. Johnswort

*Hypericum.* Above a picture (the Greek name was *hupereikon*; plants were hung over religious images or pictures to ward off evil at the midsummer festival when St. Johnswort is in flower).

"Hypericon is called of barbarus writers Fuga demonum, in English saynt Iohans wurt or saynt Iohans grass, in Duch saynt Iohans kraut" (Turner, 1548). As Fuga demonum (demon chaser), St. John's Wort, one of the herbs of Saint John the Baptist, whom Christ called "a burning and shining light" (John 5:35), was collected and burnt on the day of Saint John, June 24, to protect the farm and its animals and men against goblins, devils and witches. "This is called saynt Johannes worte. The vertue of it is thus. If it be put in a mannes house, there shall come no wicked spyryte therein" (Banckes, 1525). Dr. Porcher (1863) wrote that *Hypericum perforatum* "was greatly in vogue at one time, and was thought to cure demoniacs."

## Pineweed

*Hypericum gentianoides.* Above a picture; like a Gentian.

Bastard-Gentian, False Johnswort, False St. Johnswort, Ground-Pine, Knitweed, Nits-and-Lice, Nitweed, Orange-Grass, Poverty-Grass, Sarothra

"It is reckoned a very good traumatic, and this quality Mr. Bartram himself experienced, for once being thrown and kicked by a vicious horse in such a manner as to have both his thighs greatly hurt, he boiled the Sarothra and applied it to his wounds. Thereupon it not only immediately appeased his pain, which before had been violent, but by its assistance he recovered in a short time" (Kalm, 1748). Indeed, John Bartram (1751), who called the plant *Centaurium Luteum,* reported that "it is of excellent virtue, being made into an ointment with Penny-royal, Hemlock and Henbane (or it may do alone made into an ointment) for bruises and strains, if it be green, for it loses much of its virtue when dry, it being of an active penetrating nature." Sarothra (from Greek *saron,* "broom") is a previous generic name. The minute, scalelike leaves resemble nits, the eggs of lice.

## St. Andrew's Cross

*Hypericum hypericoides.* Above a picture; like Hypericum (it was previously *Ascyrum hypericoides*).

Peterwort, St. Andrew's Wort, St. Peter's Wort

In 1728 in Virginia, William Byrd "observ'd abundance of St. Andrew's Cross in all the woods we passed thro', which is the common remedy used by the Indian traders to cure their horses when they are bitten by rattlesnakes . . . This antidote grows providentially all over the woods, and upon all sorts of soil, that it may be every where at hand in case a disaster should happen, and may be had all the hot months while the snakes are dangerous."

Dr. Clapp reported (1852) that "the infusion of the bruised root and branches of this plant was used by an Indian with success in the case of a female, under our observation, with an ulcerated breast, which had resisted all other attempts at relief. We have since seen it employed with entire satisfaction, on the person of an infant, having a painful enlargement of the submaxillary gland." The four petals form an oblique cross like that of Saint Andrew the Apostle, patron saint of Scotland, Russia and Greece, elder brother of Saint Peter and also a fisherman.

## Common St. Johnswort, Goatweed, Klamathweed

*Hypericum perforatum.* Above a picture; perforated (leaves). (From Europe.)

Amber, Balm-of-Warrior's-Wound, Cammock, *Chasse-diable* (P.Q.), Cola-Weed, Devil's-Sourage,

*Pineweed*

*Common St. Johnswort*

Eola-Weed, God's-Wonder-Plant, Herb-of-St.-John (Calif.), Herb-John, Johnswort, Klamathweed, *Millepertuis commun* (P.Q.), Penny-John, Penny-Join, Pertuisane (P.Q.), Rosin-Rose, St. John (W.Va.), St. John's-Bush, St John's-Wort, Speckled-John (Calif.), Tipton-Weed, Touch-and-Heal, *Toute-Saine,* Tutsan, Witch's-Herb

John Bartram wrote in 1758 that "the common English *Hypericum* is a very pernicious weed. It spreads over whole fields, and spoils their pasturage, not only by choking the grass, but infecting our horses and sheep with scabbed noses and feet, especially those that have white hair on their face and legs." The plant, which produces photosensitization in white or unpigmented animals that eat it, appeared in the Klamath River country in northern California about 1900 and soon spread throughout much of the drier ranges in the state; by 1951 Klamathweed had infested over 2 million acres and was judged the cause of the heaviest financial losses on pasture and range lands. All attempts at eradication failed until a large scale control project using a European beetle that eats the plant was initiated in 1951.

Amber (for its scent of ambergris), Balm-of-Warrior's-Wound, Cammock, Rosin-Rose (Dioscorides wrote that the seed "is like in smell to the rosin of the Pine") and Tipsen (changed to Tipton in America) are local names in England for this or *Hypericum androsaemum;* Touch-and-Heal is an Irish name. Tutsan (from the French name *toute-saine,* "all wholesome") is the British name for *H. androsaemum:* "The leaves laid upon broken shins and scabbed legs heal them, and many other hurts and griefes, whereof it took his name Tout-saine or Tutsane, of healing all things" (Gerard, 1633).

# THE MALLOW FAMILY

## *Malvaceae*

A cosmopolitan family of 116 genera and 1,550 species of herbs, shrubs and small trees. *Gossypium,* the source of cotton, is the most important economical member of the family. Okra is the young fruit of *Hibiscus esculentus.*

## Velvet-Leaf

*Abutilon theophrasti.* (From the Arabic name of the plant, given it by Avicenna, 11th-century physician); of Theophrastus. (From Asia.) American-Hemp, American-Jute (Kans., W.Va.), Buttercup (Kans.), Butter-Print (Ill., Iowa), Butter-weed (Ill.), Buttonweed (Ill., Md., Kans.), Cotton-

Weed, Indian-Hemp (Ohio), Indian-Mallow, Marsh-Mallow (Va.), Mormon-Weed (Ill.), Mountain-Lily (Maine), Old-Maid, Pie-Marker (Ohio), Pie-Print (Mo.), Sheepweed (Ill.), Stampweed (Ill.), Velvet-Weed (Ill.), Wild-Cotton (Va.), Wild-Okra (S.C.)

This was cultivated for the bast fiber called China jute. A native of China, it was introduced from England into the New World before 1750 as a potential fiber crop for use in bags, ropes and cordage. Philip Miller in 1741 wrote that "the common yellow mallow . . . is very common in Virginia and most of the other parts of America; where it is called by some of the inhabitants Marsh-Mallow." But it could not compete with hemp and has become a pestilential weed: "The current annual economic loss to velvetleaf in maize and soybeans is estimated to be approximately $343 million per year" (Spencer, 1984). It "is called 'butter print,' 'pie-print' and 'pie-marker,' because its pods are used to stamp butter or pie-crust" (Bergen, 1892).

## Marsh Mallow

*Althaea officinalis.* Healing (the Greek name, perhaps from *althaia,* "cure"); officinal. (From Europe.)

*Guimauve officinale* (P.Q.), Mortification-Root, Sweatweed, White Mallow, Wimot, Wymote

"Althea called also Hibiscus, and Euiscus, is named in Greek Althaia, in English Marish Mallow or Water Mallow" (Turner, 1548). Dioscorides listed dozens of complaints for which it was a remedy, as a salve ("mortification," as in one of the names above, is gangrene), pessary and cordial, and noted that the root "also doth thicken water being mixed when it is beaten small" and set in the open air. But marshmallows are now made with corn syrup and gelatin. Cotton Mather noted, "Tis no rare thing for people to be affected with gravel" (kidney stones). Here is one of his remedies: "Take an ounce of syrup of Marsh-Mallows; mix with two or three

*Marsh Mallow*

spoonfuls of white wine. Warm it on the fire; and add an ounce of oyl of Sweet Almonds; and slice into it a quarter of an ounce of Nutmeg. It has been a very successful remedy."

Manasseh Cutler wrote, "It is common in gardens, where it is cultivated for its medical virtues. The whole plant is mucilaginous, but the mucilage abounds most in the roots. It is much used in cataplasms and fomentations as an emollient." He noted that it grew wild in marshes on Martha's Vineyard. Wimote is a local name in England.

## Poppy-Mallow

*Callirhoë involucrata.* (In Greek mythology, the wife of Alcmaeon who died trying to obtain for her the fatal necklace of Harmonia); with an involucre.

On his expedition to Utah in 1849, Howard Stansbury found the plant growing in the Valley of the Little Blue, Kansas: "A splendid variety of the mallow, of a bright carmine colour, its trailing stems sending up flowers in little patches of a few yards square, pre-

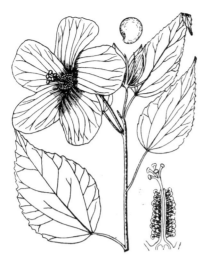

*Swamp Rose-Mallow*

sented a rich and beautiful appearance, enlivening the monotony of the prairie by its brilliant hues."

## Swamp Rose-Mallow, Crimson-Eyed Rose-Mallow

*Hibiscus moscheutos.* (The classical name); like the Musk Rose (scent).

Breast-Root (Va.), Mallow-Rose (N.Y.), Marsh Hibiscus, Marsh-Mallow, Musk (Ohio), Muskplant (Ohio), Rose-Mallow, Sea-Hollyhock, Swamp-Mallow, Swamp-Rose, Water-Mallow, Wild-Cotton

"In some parts of Virginia its root is used in the form of an emollient poultice in tumors of the breast, whence the name Breast-root" (Castiglioni, 1790).

## Flower-of-an-Hour

*Hibiscus trionum.* (The classical name); three-parted (the old generic name). (From Europe.)

Bladder-Ketmia, Black-Eyed-Susan (N.B., N.H.), Devils'-Head-in-a-Bush (N.H.), Modesty (Ohio), Shoofly (Iowa), Venice-Mallow

Gerard (1633) called it Venice Mallow and Goodnight at Noon because "it openeth it selfe about eight of the clocke, and shutteth up againe at noone, about twelve a clock when it hath receiveth the beams of the sun for two or three hours, whereon it should seeme to rejoice to look and for whose departure, being then upon the point of declension, it seemes to grieve, and so shuts up the floures that were open, and never opens them again; whereupon it might more properly be called *Malva horaria,* or the Mallow of an houre." Devil's-Head-in-a-Bush is a local name in England for *Nigella damascena* (Love-in-a-Mist).

## Low Mallow

*Malva pusilla.* (The Latin name; *malakhe* in Greek, both probably derived from a pre-Indo-European language); little. (From Europe.)

*Amours* (P.Q.), Blue Mallow, Buttonwood (Md.), Cheese-Flower, Cheeseplant, Cheeses (Maine), Cheesetts (Maine), Common Mallow, Country Mallow, Doll-Cheeses, Dutch-Cheese, Dwarf Mallow,

*Low Mallow*

Fairy-Cheeses, *Fromagère* (P.Q.), Malice (Vt.), Pancake-Plant, Pellas, Running Mallow

"Hippocrates employed it as we do, for gargles and collyriums, as an application to heated and inflamed parts, as a vehicle for pectoral and anodyne medicines" (Porcher). Dana (1900) wrote that the plant "overruns the country dooryards and village waysides" and "is used by country people for various medicinal purposes." The cheese names refer to the disk of nutlets, in shape like a round flat cheese but with a rather indistinguishable taste, not cheesy. Pancake-Plant is a local name in England, and in Cornwall the fruits are called Pellas. It has been included in the NF, used "as a household remedy in various 'catarrhal' conditions" (USD).

## High Mallow

*Malva sylvestris.* (The Latin name); of woods. (From Europe.)

Cheesecake, Cheese-Flower, Common Mallow, Country Mallow, Ground-Dock, Malice, Maul, Pancake-Plant (N.C.), Pick-Cheese, Pisk-Cheese, Round-Dock

Dioscorides wrote that Malva was "good for the belly, & especially the stalks which are profitable for the entrails and the bladder"; the seed, too, mixed with wine, "doth assuage the griefs about the bladder." Malice and Maul are local names in England.

## Narrow-Leaf Globemallow, Copper Globemallow

*Sphaeralcea angustifolia.* Globe mallow; narrow-leaved.

Nigger-Weed

According to Matilda Stevenson (1915), among the Zuñi, "The root, which is the only part of the plant used, is boiled and the tea drunk hot each evening during the ceremony of the Sword Swallowers fraternity. This root is also pulverized between stones, then taken into the mouth, ejected into the hands, and rubbed over the body, especially on the throat and chest, by the members of the fraternity of the Sword Swallowers and the order of the Sword Swallowers of the Great Fire fraternity, previous to swallowing the sword, to prevent injury from the weapon."

# THE PITCHER-PLANT FAMILY

## *Sarraceniaceae*

A family of three genera and 15 species of insectivorous herbs; found in marshy habitats of eastern and western North America and in the Guayana Highlands of northern South America. Michel Sarrasin de l'Etang (1659–1734) was a French physician and botanist who arrived in Canada (New France) in 1685, served as king's physician for the French colony and died in Quebec.

## Cobra-Plant, Cobra-Lily, California Pitcher-Plant

*Darlingtonia californica.* Of Darlington (William Darlington, 1782–1863); of California.

William Darlington was born in that hotbed of 19th-century American botany, Chester County, Pennsylvania, and received his medical degree from the University of Pennsylvania in 1804. After a voyage to India as ship's surgeon, he settled in Chester County, practiced medicine, busied himself in civic affairs, botanized and recorded the history of botany in the United States. He is the author of *The Memorials of John Bartram and Humphrey Marshall* (1849), a flora of Chester County and of *Agricultural Botany* (1847), quoted in this book.

## Trumpets, Yellow Pitcher-Plant

*Sarracenia flava.* Of Sarrasin; yellow.
Biscuits, Eve's-Cup, Flycatcher, Flytrap, Huntsman's-Horn, Sidesaddle-Flower, Southern-Trumpet, Trumpet-Leaf, Umbrella-Topped-Flycatcher, Watches, Water-Cup, Yellow-Trumpet, Yellow-Flowered Pitcher-Plant

## Pitcher-Plant, Northern Pitcher-Plant

*Sarracenia purpurea.* Of Sarrasin; purple.
Adam's-Cup (Mass.), Adam's-Pitcher, *Bleuets* (P.Q.), Bog-Bugle (South), *Cochons de pelé* (P.Q.), Devil's-Boot (south), Dumb, Dumb-Watches (N.J., Vt.),

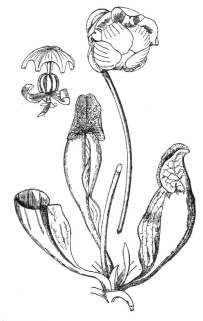

*Pitcher-Plant*

Eve's-Cup, Fever-Cup (N.B.), Flytrap (S.C.), Forefather's-Cup (New England), Forefather's-Pitcher (Maine, Mass.), Foxglove (Maine, N.H.), Frog-Bonnet (South), *Herbe crapaud* (P.Q.), Huntsman's-Cup (New England), Indian-Cup, Indian-Jug (Nfd.), Indian-Pipe (Nfd.), Indian-Pitcher (N.B.), Indian-Teakettle, Meadow-Cup (Maine, Mass.), *Petits cochons* (P.Q.), St. Jacob's- Dipper (Vt.), Sidesaddle-Flower (Va.), Skunk-Cabbage (Minn.), Smallpox-Plant, Watches (N.J.), Water-Cup, Whippoorwill's-Boots (Pa.), Whippoorwill's-Shoes (Maine)

John Josselyn (1672) called it Hollow Leaved Lavender, "with one straight stalk about the bigness of an Oat straw, better than a cubit high; upon the top standeth one fantastical flower, the leaves grow close from the root, in shape like a tankard, hollow, tough, and always full of water . . . I wonder where the knowledge of this plant has slept all this while, i.e., above forty years." He added, "It is excellent for all manner of fluxes." Dr. Millspaugh reports of an incident in Canada in 1861 "where an epidemic of small-pox having broken out among the Indians, the disease had proved virulent in the extreme among the unprotected, because unvaccinated, natives. However, the alarm had greatly diminished on an old squaw going amongst them, and treating the cases with an infusion. This treatment, it is said, was so successful as to cure every case." The "infusion" was subsequently shown to be of Sarracenia root.

Mark Catesby (1738) wrote that "the under part of the flower is somewhat the seat of a side-saddle, from which in Virginia it has received its name of side-saddle flower." In Vermont, "the more common name in this locality for the flowers is St. Jacob's-Dipper and Dumb-Watches, children playing with the hard shells of the stigmas after the purple petals have fallen, calling them watches. The convex surface of the stigma does indeed resemble the surface of a watch, although there are no hands to point the hour" (Niles,

1904). Crimson Pitcher-Plant or Fiddler's-Trumpet is *Sarracenia leucophylla* ("white-leaved"), and Hooded Pitcher-Plant (Flytrap in South Carolina) is *Sarracenia minor*.

# THE SUNDEW FAMILY

## *Droseraceae*

A widespread family of four genera and 85 species of carnivorous herbs and half shrubs. Greek *droseros* means "dewy." A viscid, dew-like fluid is exuded by the plant when the sun is at its height, and thus the Latin name of the plant, *ros solis* (*ros* means "dew").

## Sundews

*Drosera*. Dewy.

"The whole plant is sufficiently acrimonious to erode the skin. But Dr. Withering says, some ladies know how to mix the juice with milk, so as to make it an innocent and safe application to remove freckles and sunburn. The juice will destroy warts and corns. If the juice is put into a strainer, through which the warm milk from the cow is poured, and the milk set by for a day or two to become acescent [solid], it acquires a consistancy and tenacity—neither the whey nor the cream will separate. In this state it is used by the inhabitants in the north of Sweden, and called an extremely grateful food" (Cutler, 1785).

## Round-Leaved Sundew

*Drosera rotundifolia*. Dewy; round-leaved. (Also found in Eurasia.)
Bed-Rot, Dewgrass, Dewplant, Eyebright (N.H.), Lustwort, Moonwort, Moorgrass, Red-Rot, Rosa-Solis, *Rosée de soleil* (P.Q.), *Rossolis* (P.Q.), Sin-Dew, Youthroot, Youthwort

William Turner reported in 1568 that "our Englishmen nowadayes set very much by it,

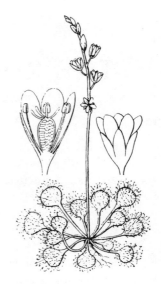

*Round-Leaved Sundew*

and holde that it is good for consumptions and swouning, and faintness of the harte." Gerard (1633) added that "the later physitions have thought this herbe to be a rare and singular remedie for all those that be in a consumption of the lungs, and especially the distilled water thereof: for as the herbe doth keep and hold fast the moisture and dew, and so fast that the extreme drying heate of the sun cannot consume and waste away the same; so likewise men thought that herewith the naturall and radical humidity in mens bodies is preserved and cherished." Dr. Millspaugh wrote in 1887 that many medical writers "recommend its use in 'different kinds' of coughs, arising from bronchial attacks, phthisis, and other diseases of the lungs."

Gerard (1633) also reported that the plant was called "in low Dutch, *Loopichecruit,* which in English signifieth Lustwoort, because sheepe and other catell, if they do but onely taste of it, are provoked to lust." The names Youthroot and Youthwort indicate that it is not only sheep and cattle that were provoked to lust by the plant. Grieve (1931) reported that "In America it has been advocated as a cure for old age." The plant is called Red-Rot because the leaves are reputed to give sheep the liver rot. Rosa-Solis was the name of the "distilled water" produced from the plant. Dewthread or Thread-Leaved Sundews is *Drosera filiformis* ("threadlike").

# THE ROCKROSE FAMILY

## *Cistaceae*

A family of seven genera and 175 species of herbs and shrubs; found in temperate and warm temperate regions, particularly in the Mediterranean region and the eastern United States. The name of the European genus *Cistus* is from the Greek name. *Cistus incanus* and other Cistus species of the Mediterranean are the source of labdanum, or ladanum, a fragrant resin now used in the scent industry and as incense. The resin on the leaves and branches is collected with rakelike instruments with leather thongs instead of teeth, which are drawn over the plant and to which the sticky juice adheres. "It can also be obtained by boiling the branches in water or, as on the island of Cyprus, by combing the beards of the goats which graze on the Cistus leaves" (Zohary, 1982). Dioscorides wrote that both the goats' beards and thighs were combed for the labdanum stuck to them.

## Frostweed

*Helianthemum canadense.* Sun flower (*helios,* "sun," *anthemon,* "flower"; the flowers only open in sunshine); of Canada.
Canadian Rockrose, Frostwort, Holly-Rose, Ice-plant, Long-Branched Frostweed, Male-Fluellin, Rockrose, Scrofula-Plant, Speedwell

The plant is called Frostweed because in late autumn crystals of ice sometimes extrude from cracks at the base of the stem. Dr. Millspaugh reported that "this plant has been long held as a remedy for scrofula and for many disorders arising in persons of strumous diatheses, especially, however, those diseases in such persons which have seemed to need an astringent, tonic, or alterative." It has been included in the USP and NF, "employed in diarrhea, syphilis, and, locally, in sore throat and skin diseases," according to the USD.

## False Heather, Hudsonia

*Hudsonia tomentosa.* Of Hudson (William Hudson, 1730–1793); densely woolly.
American-Heath, Beach-Heath, Beach-Heather, Bear's-Grass, Dog's-Dinner (Mass.), Ground-Cedar, Ground-Moss, Heath (Mass.), Lingwort, Poverty-Grass (Mass.), Poverty-Plant, Sand-Heather, Woolly Hudsonia

On Cape Cod, October 1849, Thoreau wrote, "The sand by the roadside was partially covered with bunches of a moss-like plant, *Hudsonia tomentosa,* which a woman in the stage told us was called 'poverty grass,' because it grew where nothing else would." William Hudson was a London apothecary, Praefectus of the Chelsea Physic Garden and author of *Flora Anglica* (1762). Ling is Heather.

# THE VIOLET FAMILY

## Violaceae

A cosmopolitan family of 23 genera and 830 species of herbs, shrubs and even lianas and small trees. Sweet Violets (*Viola odorata*) are cultivated, mainly in the south of France, for their essential oil, which is used in flavoring and to make scents: "100 kg of flowers giving 30 g of oil" (Mabberley). Gerard (1633) wrote that the Sweet Violets "have a great prerogative above others, not onely because the minde conceiveth a certaine pleasure and recreation by smelling and handling of those most odoriferous flours, but also for that very many by these Violets receive ornament and comely grace: for there bee made of them garlands for the head, nose-gaies, and poesies, which are delightfull to looke on, and pleasant to smell to, speaking nothing of their appropriate vertues; yea gardens themselves receive by these the greatest ornament of all, chiefest beauty and most gallant grace; and the recreation of the minde which is taken thereby, cannot be but very good and honest: for they admonish and stir up a man to that which is comely and honest; for floures through their beautie, variety of colour, and exquisite forme, do bring to a liberall and gentle manly minde, the remembrance of honestie, comelinesse, and all kindes of vertues."

The Violet is the state flower of Illinois, New Jersey, Rhode Island and Wisconsin.

## Marsh Blue Violet

*Viola cucullata*. (The Latin name); hooded. Blue Marsh Violet, Chicken-Fights (Md.), Common Blue Violet, Early Violet, Fighting-Cocks (N.B.), Hooded Blue Violet, Hoodleaf Violet (Mass.), Hookers, Johnny-Jump-Ups (N.C., Ohio), Long-Stemmed Purple Violet, Meadow Violet, Rooster-Hoods (N.C.), Roosters (N.Y.)

## Early Blue Violet, Wood Violet

*Viola palmata*. (The Latin name); palmate. Chicken-Fighters (N.C.), Hand-Leaf Violet, Hoodleaf Violet (Mass.), Johnny-Jump-Up, Roosters (Vt.), Wild-Okra

"The plant is very mucilaginous. It is employed by Negroes for making soup, and is commonly called wild okra. The bruised leaves are used as an emollient application" (Porcher).

## Birdfoot Violet

*Viola pedata*. (The Latin name); footlike (leaves). Crowfoot Violet (New England), Horseshoe Violet (Mass.), Horse Violet (New England), Johnny-Jump-Up (Ohio), Lavender Violet, Pansy (Ill.), Pansy Violet, Parsley Violet, Sand Violet (Conn.), Snake Violet (Mass.), Velvets (Ga.), Velvet Violet (Ga.), Wood Violet

Dr. Porcher reported that the roots "possess a nutritive and an emetic principle, called violine, allied to that of ipecacuanha, but more

*Birdfoot Violet*

*Common Blue Violet*

uncertain in its operation." It has been included in the USP, and the USD states the leaves "are mucilaginous and in sufficient dose slightly laxative."

## Round-Leaved Yellow Violet

*Viola rotundifolia.* (The Latin name); round-leaved.

Early Yellow Violet, Heal-All (Pa.), Stemless Yellow Violet

In Pennsylvania "the inhabitants know it by the name of Heal-all, being used by them in curing all sorts of wounds and sores" (Pursh, 1814). The following begins William Cullen Bryant's "The Yellow Violet":

*When beechen buds begin to swell,*
*And woods the blue-bird's warble*
*  know,*
*The yellow violet's modest bell*
*Peeps from the last year's leaves below.*

## Common Blue Violet

*Viola sororia.* The Latin name; sisterly (resembles other species).

Chicken-Fights (Md.), Confederate Violet, Fighting Cocks, Hooded Blue Violet, Johnny-Jump-Up, Johnny-Jump-Up-and-Kiss-Me, Long-Stemmed Purple Violet, Meadow Violet, Rooster-Hoods (N.C.), Roosters

"Fight rooster" or "chicken fight" is a boys' game in which the spur under the curved stem of a Violet is hooked with that of another's and pulled until the loser's Violet is decapitated. *Viola priceana* is the Confederate Violet, with pale gray-blue flowers and a violet eye.

## Pansy

*Viola tricolor.* (The Latin name); three-colored. (From Europe.)

Battlefield-Flower (Va.), Bird's-Eye, Cupid's-Delight (Mass.), Garden-Gate, Heartsease, Johnnies (Ohio), Johnny-Jump-Up (Ill., Mass., Ohio), Kit-

*Pansy*

ease, Paunsies, Love in idleness, Cull me to you, and Three faces in a hood." It was the juice of Love-in-Idleness (that is, love in vain) that Oberon squeezed on Titania's eyes in *Midsummer Night's Dream* (2.1.165–172) so that she would fall in love with the ass-headed Bottom:

Oberon. *Yet marked I where the bolt of*
   *Cupid fell.*
   *It fell upon a little western flower,*
*Before milk-white, now purple with*
   *love's wound,*
*And maidens call it love-in-idleness.*
*Fetch me that flower, the herb I showed*
   *thee once.*
*The juice of it on sleeping eyelids laid*
*Will make or man or woman madly*
   *dote*
   *Upon the next live creature that it*
   *sees.*

Run-About, Lady's-Delight (Mass.), None-So-Pretty (Mass.), *Pensée* (P.Q.)

Pansy is from the French name *pensée,* "thought." Gerard (1633) called it "Hearts-

Garden-Gate is presumably a contraction of the English name Kiss-Behind-the-Garden-Gate, and Johnny-Jump-Up is from Jump-Up-and-Kiss-Me, another name in England.

# THE PASSION-FLOWER FAMILY

## *Passifloraceae*

A family of 18 genera and 530 species of vines and a few shrubs and trees; best developed in tropical America and Africa. Many species of *Passiflora* in addition to *Passiflora edulis* bear edible fruit, including *Passiflora quadrangularis,* (Giant-Granadilla) and *Passiflora maliformis* (Sweet-Calabash).

## Passion-Flower, Maypops

*Passiflora incarnata.* Passion flower; flesh-colored.

Apricot (N.C.), Apricot-Vine, Granadilla, Holy-Trinity-Flower (Texas), Mayapple, Maypop, Molly-Pop (Ala., N.C.), Passion-Vine, Pop-Apple (N.C.)

In 1612 Captain Smith reported that in Virginia the Indians planted "Maracocks, a wild fruit like a lemmon, which also increase

*Passion-Flower*

in fruit: they begin to ripe in September and continue till the end of October." William Strachey described the maracock as "of the bigness of a green apple, and hath manie azurine or blew kernells, like as a pomegranate, a good sommer cooling fruit." The names of the fruit—Maracoc, Maracock and Maycock to early European settlers and Maypop, May-apple or Apricot more recently—are from the Powhatan *mahcawq*. Parkinson (1629) wrote that the plant "may be called in Latine, *Clematis Virginiana;* in English, The Virgin or Virginia Climer; of the Virginians, *Maracoc;* of the Spanish in the West Indies, *Granadillo,* because the fruit (as is before said) is in some fashion like a small Pomegranate on the out-

side, yet the seed within is flattish, round, and blackish. Some superstitious Jesuits would faine make men beleeve that in the flower of this plant are to be seene all the markes of our Saviours Passion; and therefore call it *Flos Passionis.*" According to *Brewer's Dictionary of Phrase and Fable,* "The *leaf* symbolizes the spear. The five *petals* and five *sepals,* the ten apostles (Peter who denied, and Judas who betrayed, being omitted). The five *anthers,* the five wounds. The *tendrils,* the scourges. The column of the *ovary,* the pillar of the cross. The *stamens,* the hammers. The three *stigmas,* the three nails. The *filaments* within the flower, the crown of thorns. The *calyx,* the glory or nimbus. The *white* tint, purity. The *blue* tint, HEAVEN."

Large quantities of the dried plant are exported to Europe where a tincture or fluid extract is used as an antispasmodic and sedative. "The drug contains alkaloids, glucosides, flavonids and bitter principles, and is used to combat insomnia and anxiety states, and as a hypotensive" (Bianchini and Corbetta). It is still included in the pharmacopeias of France, Spain and Italy. According to Tommie Bass of southern Appalachia, "It's the most wonderful sleep and pacifying plant, valuable for a nerve medicine. You can use it in many ways. They say it brings people together. After you have lived with someone for many years the little things they do start to bother you. So you take some passion-flower leaves and make you a tea. Pretty soon you start to relax and the little things don't bother you so much and you get along fine" (from Crellin and Philpott, 1990).

# THE GOURD FAMILY

## *Cucurbitaceae*

A family of 121 genera and 760 species of climbing or trailing plants found mainly in tropical and subtropical regions. Many members of the family are important sources of food, including species of *Cucurbita* (pumpkins, squashes, gourds), *Cucumis* (melons, cantaloupes, cucumbers) and *Citrullus* (watermelons). John Josselyn (1672) wrote of "Squashes, but truly *Squontersquashes,*" in 17th-century New England: "Some of these are green, some yellow, some longish like a gourd, others round like an apple, all of them pleasant food boyled and buttered, and season'd with spice. But the yellow Squash, called an apple Squash, because like an apple, and about the bigness of a Pomewater [a large apple], is the best kind. They are much eaten by the Indians and the English."

*Buffalo-Gourd*

## Buffalo-Gourd, Wild-Pumpkin, Stinking-Gourd

*Cucurbita foetidissima*. (The Latin name for a kind of gourd); most fetid.
Arizona-Gourd, Calabacilla Loca, Calabazilla, Calabrazilla, Chile-Coyote (Calif.), Desert-Gourd, Fetid-Gourd, Missouri-Gourd, Mock-Orange

Among the Indians of Nevada, "the large storage root of the plant is employed mainly as a cure for venereal diseases, apparently for both syphilis and gonorrhea," according to Percy Train and his colleagues; however, "many of the Indians warned of the poisonous nature of the plant and said that some deaths had occurred from overdoses of the medicine."

## Wild-Cucumber, Balsam-Apple

*Echinocystis lobata*. Hedgehog bladder; lobed.
*Concombre grimpant* (P.Q.), Creeper (Maine), Creeping-Jenny (Maine), Mock-Apple, Mock-Orange, Prickly Cucumber, Wild Balsam-Apple

The Menomini Indians brewed a bitter tea from the roots and used it as an analgesic and love potion (Huron Smith, 1923).

# THE LOASA FAMILY

## *Loasaceae*

A family of 15 genera and 260 species of herbs, shrubs and even small trees; found in temperate and tropical regions of North and South America.

## Whitestem Stickleaf

*Mentzelia albicaulis.* Of Mentzel (Christian Mentzel, 1622–1701, a German botanist); white-stemmed.

Among the Klamath Indians, "the minute, grayish seeds are much used for food" (Coville, 1897).

## Giant Blazing-Star

*Mentzelia laevicaulis.* Of Mentzel; smooth-stemmed.

Evening-Star, Sandlily, Stickleaf, White-Medicine (Mont.)

The Northern Cheyenne of Montana call the plant White-Medicine: "One of their old-est medicines, it was held in high esteem because of its powers. It was used only as an ingredient in medicinal preparations and never by itself. The root was dug before the plant had flowered, and was especially useful for fevers and complicated illnesses" (Hart, 1980).

## Stickleaf, Adonis Blazing-Star

*Mentzelia multiflora.* Of Mentzel; many-flowered.

"The plant is rough, covered with minute hairs, and clings to clothing tenaciously," according to Robbins and colleagues (1916). They reported that among the Tewa, "A young boy, before he is put on a horse for the first time, is stripped of his clothing and this rough plant rubbed briskly on the bare skin of his legs. His clothing is put on and he is placed on the back of the horse. The Tewa maintain that this treatment enables the boy to adhere to the horse."

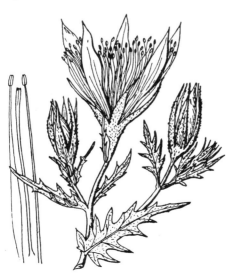

*Giant Blazing-Star*

*Stickleaf*

### Bullet Stickleaf, Golden Blazing-Star

*Mentzelia pumila.* Of Mentzel; dwarf.

The Navaho gathered the seeds by beating the seed capsules with a paddle over a basket; the seeds were then parched with hot coals in a basket and ground lightly with a special rock (Vestal, 1952).

# THE CAPER FAMILY

## *Capparaceae*

A widespread family of about 45 genera and 675 species of herbs, shrubs and a few trees; found chiefly in tropical and subtropical regions. Caper is a Mediterranean shrub, *Capparis spinosa,* whose flower buds are the pickled Capers. *Kapparis* was the Greek name.

### Rocky Mountain Beeplant, Pink Cleome, Spiderflower

*Cleome serrulata.* (An obscure name); finely saw-toothed.

Beeplant (Colo.), *Guaco* (N.Mex.), Pink Cleome, Skunkweed (Colo.), Stinking-Clover (Mont.), Stinkweed, Wild-Rocket (Kans.)

The flowers offer copious nectar for bees and are planted by apiarists. The plants smell of skunk, but the cooked leaves were an important potherb for Indians and settlers and even the seeds were ground to make flour.

"This is a very important plant with the Tewa, inasmuch as black paint for pottery decoration is made from it. Large quantities of young plants are collected, usually in July. The plants are boiled well in water; the woody parts are then removed and the decoction is again allowed to boil until it becomes thick and attains a black color. This thick fluid is

*Rocky Mountain Beeplant*

poured on a board to dry and soon becomes hardened. It may be kept in hard cakes for an indefinite period. When needed these are soaked in hot water until of the consistency needed for paint. Guaco is also used as a food. The hardened cakes are soaked in hot water, and then fried in grease" (Robbins, Harrington and Freire-Marreco, 1916). Yellow Beeplant or Yellow Spiderflower is *Cleome lutea.*

# THE MUSTARD
# OR CRUCIFER FAMILY

## *Brassicaceae or Cruciferae*

A widespread and well-traveled family of 390 genera and 3,000 species of herbs and shrubs; found in temperate and warm temperate regions. The flowers' four petals are in the shape of a cross (Latin *crucifer* means "cross-bearing"). The family includes many economically important plants, including the vegetables cabbage, kale, cauliflower, mustard greens, broccoli rabe, cress, turnip, radish, kohlrabi and rutabaga. The condiment mustard is the ground seed of *Brassica* or *Sinapis* species. The ancestral cabbage was cultivated about 8,000 years ago in coastal areas of nothern Europe. Cruciferous oil seeds, from species of *Brassica,* now rank fifth in economic importance after soybeans, cotton seed, ground nut and sunflower seed (Heywood). Some Mustard plants are called Rocket, which is derived from *eruca,* Latin for "cabbage."

## Garlic Mustard

*Alliaria petiolata.* Like Allium (Garlic; for its scent and taste); stalked (leaf). (From Europe.)
English-Treacle, Garlic-Root, Hedge-Garlic, Hedge-Mustard, Jack-by-the-Hedge, Jack-in-the-Bush, Leek-Cress, Penny-Hedge, Poor-Man's-Mustard, Sauce-Alone

"Alliaria is called in English Sauce alone or Jacke of the hedges" (Turner, 1548). In 1783 Bryant reported that "the poor people in the country eat the leaves of this plant with their bread, and on account of the relish they give, call them Sauce-alone. They also mix them with lettuce, use them as a stuffing herb to pork, and eat them with salt-fish." Sauce is English and Scottish dialect and colloquial for vegetables, especially green vegetables eaten with meat. In colonial Virginia, "Roots, herbs, vine, fruits, and salad-flowers—they dish up in various ways, and find them a very delicious sauce to their meat" (Beverley, 1705). The USD reports that the "herb and seeds have been used for reputed diuretic, diaphoretic, and expectorant effects, and were also used as an external stimulant and pustulant application." Jack-in-the-Bush, Jack-by-the-Hedge and Poor-Man's-Mustard are local names in England. Leek-Cress is the Anglo-Saxon name (Britten and Holland).

## Winter Cress

*Barbarea vulgaris.* Of St. Barbara; common. (From Europe.)
Bitter Cress, Creasy-Greens (N.C.), *Cresson d'hiver* (Quebec), *Cresson de terre* (P.Q.), Herb-Barbara, *Herbe de Sainte-Barbe* (P.Q.), Land Cress, Poor-Man's-Cabbage, Rocket, Rocket-Cress, Scurvygrass, Upland Cress, Water-Radish, Wound-Rocket, Yellow Cress, Yellow-Rocket

"Barbare herba groweth about brokes and water sydes. It hath leaves lyke Rocket, wherefore it may be called in English woundrocket, for it is good for wounds" (Turner, 1548). It grows in winter during warm periods, and the leaves may be picked to eat even on Saint Barbara's Day, December 4. "The plant is sometimes called Bitter Cress and is occasionally for sale in the markets under the name Upland Cress" (Medsger, 1939). Marie-Victorin writes that it "is considered a good antiscorbutic, and is applied as a resolvant on bruises." One of the most popular of the Catholic Church's saints, third-century Saint

*Winter Cress*

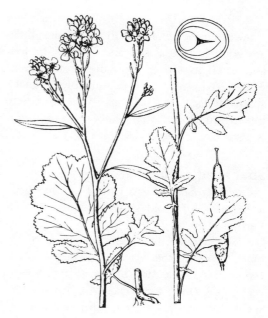

*Black Mustard*

Barbara was from Nicomedia, Asia Minor. She is the patron saint of firework makers, artillerymen, architects, founders, stonemasons and grave-diggers and a protectress against lightning, fire, sudden death and impenitence. She is usually represented holding a tower—her father locked her in a tower. When she was converted to Christianity, her father had her killed and was then struck dead by lightning. Cranach the Elder's painting of poor Barbara about to be beheaded by her father's henchmen is in New York's Metropolitan Museum.

## Cabbages

*Brassica.* Cabbage.

This remarkable genus gives us Savoy Cabbage, Red Cabbage, White Cabbage, Brussels-Sprouts, Broccoli and Cauliflower (all are *Brassica oleracea*), Turnips *(Brassica rapa)*, Rutabaga and Rapeseed and its oil *(Brassica napus)* and Mustard *(Brassica nigra* and *alba).*

## Black Mustard

*Brassica nigra.* Cabbage; black (seeds). (From Europe.)

Brown Mustard, Cadlock, Kerlock, *Moutarde Noire* (P.Q.), Red Mustard, Scurvie-Senvie, Warlock

This is the main source of the condiment mustard. Manasseh Cutler reported that "the seeds unbruised are frequently given in palsies and chronic rheumatisms, and are found beneficial. They may be taken in the quantity of a table-spoon full, or more, and will gently relax the bowels. Rheumatic pains in the stomach are often relieved by taking them in brandy. The powdered seeds, with crumbs of bread and vinegar, are made into cataplasms, and applied to the soles of the feet in fevers, when stimulants are necessary."

## Sea-Rocket

*Cakile edentula.* (An Arabic name); without teeth.

*Caquillier* (P.Q.), Sea-Kale (Va.), Wild Peppergrass (Maine)

In 1672 Josselyn reported, "Sea tears, they grow upon the sea banks in abundance, they are good for the scurvy and dropsie, boiled and eaten as sallade, and the broth drunk with it." The "tears" are presumably the tear-shaped pods. In Quebec, "its root is pounded, mixed with flour, and eaten here when there is a scarcity of bread" (Kalm, 1749).

## Shepherd's-Purse

*Capsella bursa-pastoris.* Little box; purse-of-a-shepherd (the old generic name). (From Europe.)

Blindweed, Caseweed, Cocowort, Hen-Pepper (Ind.), Lady's-Purse, Mother's-Heart, Pepper-and-Shot, Peppergrass (Iowa, Mass.), Pepperplant (Mass.), Pepperweed (Ind.), Pickpocket (Vt.), Pickpurse, St. James-Weed, Shepherd's-Bag, Shepherd's-Pouch, Shepherd's-Sprout (W.Va.), Shovelweed (Maine), *Tabouret* (P.Q.), Toothwort, Toywort, Windflower (Mass.), Witch's-Pouches

The seed pod is shaped like a purse. It is called a shepherd's purse in other languages also, because it is a thin purse on a poor plant and shepherds were poor men, as Grigson (1975) has noted. On the other hand, the Spanish botanist Correa de Serra in 1821 reported that this is "an esculent plant in Philadelphia, brought to market in large quantities in the early season. The taste, when boiled, approaches that of cabbage, but is softer and milder. The plant varies wonderfully in size and succulence of leaves, according to the nature and state of the soil where it grows. Those from the gardens and highly cultivated spots near Philadelphia come to a size and succulence of leaf scarcely to be believed without seeing them" (Fernald and Kinsey, 1943). Gerard (1633) wrote that it is called "Shepheards purse or scrip; of some Shepheards pouch, and poor mans Parmecitie: and in the North part of England, Toy-wort, Pick-purse, and Case-weed." Of the names Mother's-Heart and Pickpurse, Grigson writes of two children's games: In one, a child makes another pick one of the seed cases, and then when it breaks (as it always does), tells him that he has broken his mother's heart; in the other, when the seeds pour out, he chants "Pick pocket, penny nail,/ Put the rogue in jail."

The dried seeds are ground for flour. "Capsella at one time enjoyed considerable popularity as a uterine stimulant, especially in domestic practice. It had disappeared almost from medical notice but more recently has been attracting some attention in the treatment of uterine hemorrhages" (USD). Most of the vernacular names above are from the British Isles.

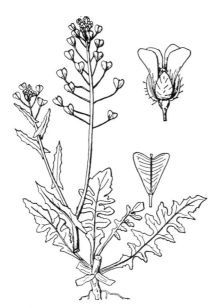

*Shepherd's-Purse*

## Toothwort, Pepperwort

*Cardamine diphylla.* (From the Greek name, *kardamon,* used by Dioscorides for some Cress); two-leaved.

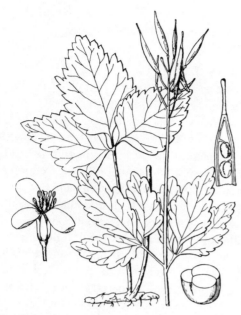

Toothwort

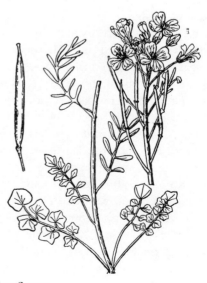

## Pennsylvania Bittercress

*Cardamine pensylvanica.* (A Greek plant name); of Pennsylvania.

Native Watercress

"The plant is an excellent substitute for the common Watercress. It is slightly bitter but not disagreeable. On hikes in the woods I have often gathered this cress to eat with my sandwiches and have found it a pleasing relish" (Medsger, 1939). The grated raw rootstocks of this and of Springcress *(Cardamine bulbosa)* are used as a condiment.

## Cuckooflower, Lady-Smocks

*Cardamine pratensis.* (A Greek plant name); of meadows. (Also found in Eurasia.)

Cuckoo-Spit, Mayflower, Meadow Bitter-Cress, Milkmaid, Smick-Smock, Spink

In *Love's Labour's Lost* (5.1.902) Shakespeare wrote

*When daisies pied and violets blue*
*And lady-smocks all silver white*
*And cuckoo-buds of yellow hue*
*Do paint the meadows with delight,*

Cuckooflower

Carcajou (P.Q.), Crinkleroot (N.Y., Pa.), Pepper-Root, *Snicroûte* (P.Q.), Toothache-Root, Toothroot, Trickle, Trinkle-Root, Two-Toothed Pepper-Root

"It is a 'potato' much relished by the Menomini, but has a pungent, acrid taste when it is freshly dug. The mass of cleaned roots is accordingly heaped on a blanket and covered to exclude the air. Then there is a natural process of fermentation for four or five days, following which the roots are found to be sweet. The Menomini cook it with corn, and say that, beside being good to eat, it is a good medicine for the stomach" (Huron Smith, 1923). Another Crinkleroot is Cut-Leaved Toothwort *(Cardamine laciniata),* whose segmented leaves give it the names of Crow's-Foot in Indiana and Crow-Toes in Ohio. Marie-Victorin writes that the French Canadian name Snicroûte is a corruption of Snakeroot. The previous generic name of the Toothworts was *Dentaria,* named for the toothlike swellings on the roots.

*The cuckoo then, on every tree,*
*Mocks married men; for this sings he,*
   *Cuckoo;*
*Cuckoo, cuckoo; O, word of fear,*
   *Unpleasing to a married ear!*

"These flower for the most part in Aprill and Maie, when the Cuckowe doth begin to sing her pleasant notes without stammering," according to Gerard (1597), who reported that they were called "Cuckowe flowers: in Northfolke Caunterburie bels: at the Namptwich in Cheshire where I had my beginning, Ladie smockes, which hath given me cause to christen it after my countrie fashion." Either Lady-Smocks was also the country name in Shakespeare's Warwickshire, or he was quoting Gerard's Herbal. They are evidently called Lady-Smocks because a thick patch in a field resembles linen put out to bleach in the sun. Milkmaids, Smick-Smock and Spink are local names in England.

## Desert-Candle, Squaw-Cabbage

*Caulanthus inflatus.* Stem flower; inflated (stem).
Wild-Cabbage (Calif.)

On the Death Valley expedition of 1891, Frederick Coville noted that "There grow in the desert several large crucifers, whose leaves and stems have about the taste of cabbage and are tender and probably easily digestible." The most abundant of these was this plant and *Stanleya pinnata* (p. 88) both of which were eaten by the Panamint Indians: "The leaves and young stems are gathered and thrown into boiling water for a few minutes, then taken out, washed in cold water, and squeezed. The operation of washing is repeated five or six times, and the leaves are finally dried, ready to be used as boiled cabbage. Washing removes the bitter taste and

certain substances that would be likely to produce nausea or diarrhoea."

## Scurvy-Weed

*Cochlearia officinalis.* Spoonlike (leaves); officinal. (Also found in Eurasia.)
Scrubby-Grass, Scurvy-Grass, Spoonwort

Manasseh Cutler reported that "it is acrimonious; and the acrimony is said to reside in a very subtile essential oil. It is frequently eaten by country people as a sallad. Writers on sea-voyages give high encomiums on the Scurvygrass for its antiscorbutic virtues. Dr. Withering says, it is a powerful remedy in the pituitous asthma, and in what Sydenham calls the scorbutic rheumatism. A distilled water and a conserve is prepared from the leaves. The juice is prescribed along with that of oranges, by the name of antiscorbutic juices." He also wrote that it was "frequently cultivated in gardens." The Sydenham cited by Withering is presumably Thomas Sydenham, the eminent 17th-century physician.

## Herb-Sophia, Flixweed

*Descurainia sophia.* Of Descourain (François Descourain, 1658–1740, French botanist and apothecary); (the old generic name). (From Europe.)
Fine-Leaved Hedge-Mustard, Flaxweed, Fluxweed, *Sagesse de chirurgiens* (P.Q.)

*Sophia* means "skill" or "wisdom" in Greek. Marie-Victorin wrote that it is called *Sagesse de chirurgiens* (wisdom of surgeons) because "it was once celebrated as an 'antiputrid,' vulnerary and vermifuge, and for the treatment of fractures." Withering (1776) reported that "the pods retain the seeds all winter, and small birds feed upon them—the force of a gun is said to be augmented if the gunpowder is mixed with a tenth part of these seeds—the plant is sometimes prescribed in

*Herb-Sophia*

Hysteric and Dysenteric cases; and the seeds are given to destroy worms." The USD reports that the plant has been used "externally in indolent ulcers and the seeds internally in worms, calculous complaints, etc."

## Whitlow-Grass

*Draba verna.* (The Greek name of a related plant); of spring. (From Europe.)
*Drave* (P.Q.), Nailwort, Shad-Blossom (Pa.), Shad-Flower (W.Va.), White-Blow

A whitlow is a sore under or around a finger or toe nail, for which this plant was a remedy. Aldo Leopold (1949) wrote, "Draba asks, and gets, but scant allowance of warmth and comfort; it subsists on the leavings of unwanted time and space. Botany books give it two or three lines, but never a plate or a portrait. Sand too poor and sun too weak for bigger, better blooms are good enough for Draba. After all it is no spring flower, but only a postscript to a hope . . . just a small

creature that does a small job quickly and well."

## Wormseed, Treacle Mustard

*Erysimum cheiranthoides.* (From the Greek name); like Cheiranthus (Wallflower). (From Europe.)
*Herbe au chantre* (P.Q.), Tarrify, *Vélar* (P.Q.), Wallflower

Pliny reported that it was "called by the Greeks erysimon" and when given with honey is "very good for coughs and for expectorations of pus." It was also a vermifuge—the seeds "stamped and given to children to drinke, killeth the wormes, and driveth them forth both by siege and vomit" (Gerard, 1633). Tarrify is a local name in England.

## Dame's-Rocket, Sweet-Rocket

*Hesperis matronalis.* Evening; matronly (from its name Mother-of-the-Evening). (From Europe.)
Damask-Rocket, Damask-Violet, Dame's-Violet (W.Va.), Damewort, Eveweed, Garden-Rocket, *Ju-*

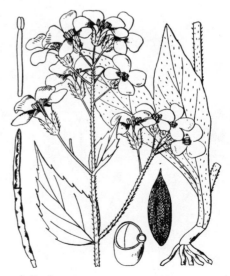

*Dame's-Rocket*

*lienne des dames* (P.Q.), Mother-of-the-Evening, Night-Rocket, Night-Scented-Gilliflower, Queen's-Gilliflower, Rocket, Rockset, Rogue's-Gilliflower, Summer-Lilac, Winter-Gilliflower

This is an old garden favorite whose scent is particularly strong in the evening. Many of the names listed above are from 16th- and 17th-century English herbals. Rocket is derived from the Old French *roquette,* Old Italian *ruchetta,* from the Latin *eruca,* "cabbage"; Gilliflower is a Carnation; Rogue is probably *rouge,* "red." Grieve wrote that "In the language of flowers, the Rocket has been taken to represent deceit, since it gives out a lovely perfume in the evening, but in the daytime has none. Hence its name of Hesperis, or Vesper-Flower, given it by the Ancients."

## Cowcress, Field Peppergrass

*Lepidium campestre.* Little scale (Greek *lepis,* "a scale"; for the shape of the pods); of fields. (From Europe.)

Bastard Cress, *Cresson de champs* (P.Q.), Crowd-Weed (W.Va.), English Peppergrass, False-Flax, Field Cress, Glenn-Pepper (W.Va.), Glenn-Weed (W.Va.),

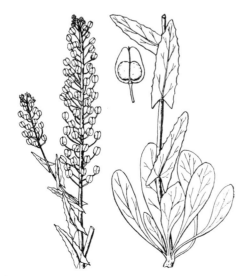

*Cowcress*

Hen-Pepper (Mo.), Mithridate Mustard, Poor-Man's-Pepper, Tonguegrass, Yellow-Seed

Dioscorides reported, "Lepidium, which some call Gingidum, is a little herb well known, preserved in brine with milk. The facultie of the leaves is sharp, exulcerating, wherefore it is a most singular plaster for the Sciatica, being beaten small with the root of Elycampane, & laid on for a quarter of an hour."

Gerard (1633) called the plant Mithridate Mustard, "whose seed is used in shops." Mithridate was a king of Pontus in the first century B.C. who made himself immune to poison by constantly taking antidotes.

A. E. Housman wrote of him in "A Shropshire Lad":

*And easy, smiling, seasoned sound,*
*Sate the king when healths went round.*
*They put arsenic in his meat*
*And stared aghast to watch him eat;*
*They poured strychnine in his cup*
*And shook to see him drink it up.*

Thus Mithridate came to mean a universal antidote against poison and infection.

The name Glenn-Weed came "from having been first noticed on a farm of a family named Glenn" (Bergen, 1893). Tonguegrass, for its hot flavor biting the tongue, is a local name in Ireland for *Lepidium sativum.* The young shoots and leaves and unripe seed pods are eaten.

## Peppergrass, Poor-Man's-Pepper

*Lepidium virginicum.* Little scale; of Virginia.

Bird's-Pepper (Neb.), *Cresson puant* (P.Q.), New England Mustard, Tonguegrass (Ind., Iowa), Wild-Cress, Wild Peppergrass

In 1672 Josselyn described this as "a plant like Knaves-Mustard, called New-England Mustard." Knave's Mustard ("for that it is too bad for honest men"—Gerard, 1633) is a Thlaspi. Lewis and Clark on the Missouri (June 5, 1804) encountered a "sand-bar extending several miles, which renders navigation difficult, and a small creek called Sand Creek on the south, where we stopped for dinner, and gathered wild cresses or tongue-grass."

## Honesty

*Lunaria annua.* Moonlike (the membranous pod partitions); annual. (From Europe.) Gold-and-Silver-Plant, Matrimony-Plant, Matrimony-Vine, Money-in-Both-Pockets, Money-Plant, Moonwort, Penny-Flower, Satin, Satin-Flower

"We call this herb in English Penny floure or Money floure, Silver plate, Pricke-song-woort; in Norfolke, Sattin and White Sattin, and among our women it is called Honestie" (Gerard, 1633).

## Watercress

*Rorippa nasturtium-aquaticum.* (From the Saxon name, *rorippen*); water-nasturtium (from Greek *mnastorgion,* "one that longs for wet soil"). (From Europe.) Brook-Lime, Brown Cress, Crashes, *Cresson* (P.Q.), Peppergrass, Sturshum (South), Water-Salad (Texas), Water-Sweet-Alice (Texas), Well Cress

"Water-Cresse being boyled in wine or milke and drunke for certaine dayes together, is very good against the scurvy or scorbute. Being chopped or boyled in the broth of flesh, and eaten for thirty dayes together at morning, noone, and night, it provoketh urine, wastes the stone, and driveth it forth. Taken in the same manner it doth cure yong maidens of the green sicknesse, bringeth down the termes, and sendeth into the face their accustomed lively colour lost by the stopping of their *Menstrua*" (Gerard, 1633). The green sickness, the mysterious illness that affected young women until the beginning of our century, also known as the Disease of Virgins, was chlorosis, a form of iron deficiency ane-

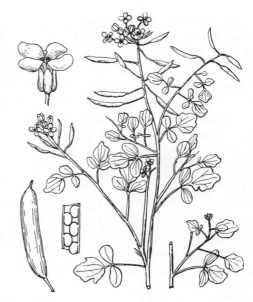

*Watercress*

mia. Viola in Shakespeare's *Twelfth Night* (2.4.111) told of the young woman who

. . . let concealment, like a worm i' the
    bud,
Feed on her damask cheek: she pin'd in
    thought;
And with a green and yellow melan-
    choly,
She sat like patience on a monument,
    Smiling at grief.

Gerard's treatment was most appropriate since Watercress is full of iron. Brooklime (a Veronica) and Crash are local names in England.

## Charlock

*Sinapis arvensis.* Mustard (the Greek name); cultivated. (From Europe.) Bastard-Rocket, California-Rape, Chadlock, Cornkale, Corn-Mustard, Crowd-Weed (W.Va.), Crunchweed, Curlock, Field-Kale, Herrick-Mustard, Kedlock, Kerlock, Kraut-Weed (W.Va.), *Moutarde d'été* (P.Q.), Runchweed, Water-Cress (W.Va.), Wild Mustard

"Kedlokes hath a leafe lyke rapes, and beareth a yelowe floure, and ys an yll weede, and groweth in al maner corn" (Fitzherbert, 1523). Cutler in 1785 told the same story in New England: "It is often very injurious to grain; and when it has once got into the ground it is extremely difficult to extirpate. The seeds will remain in the ground many years, in a vegetive state, after it is swarded over with grass, and will grow when the ground is again ploughed up." However, in 1727, Caleb Threlkeld reported that "it is called about the streets of Dublin, and used for a boiled sallet." Herrick is a corruption of Headridge, a local name in Wales. Chadlock is one of Gerard's names for the plant.

## Hedge Mustard

*Sisymbrium officinale.* (The Latinized Greek name of a Mustard); official. (From Europe.) Bank-Cress, California-Mustard (Maine), Hedge-Weed, *Herbe au chantre* (P.Q.), Scrabling-Rocket, Scrambling-Rocket, Wild Mustard (Maine)

"Taken with wine it is diuretic, the wild kind moreover even expels stone. Those who must remain awake are kept roused by an infusion in vinegar poured on the head" (Pliny). In 1776 Withering called this Hedge Mustard or Wormseed, Bank Cresses, Scrambling Rocket. The young leaves are cooked and eaten, and the seeds are ground for soups and stews. Dr. Porcher reported that "the seeds possess considerable pungency, and have been recommended in chronic cough, hoarseness, and ulceration of the mouth and fauces; the juice of the plant in honey or the seeds in substance may be used." The name in France and French Canada is *Herbe au chantre,* "herb of the singer."

## Prince's-Plume, Golden Prince's-Plume

*Stanleya pinnata.* Of Stanley (Lord Edward Stanley, 1775–1851, president of the Linnaean

and Zoological societies in London and patron of natural history); pinnate.

Desert-Plume, Paiute-Cabbage

The Paiute and Paramint Indians of California boiled and ate this as a cabbage (see *Caulanthus inflata,* above). Among the Indians of Nevada, "only the root is considered of value for the medicinal preparations, all but one of which were for external purposes, the exceptions being the use of a tonic tea to be given for general debility after an illness" (Train, Henrichs and Archer, 1941). To relieve toothache, the pulped root was placed on the gum or in the tooth cavity; it was also applied hot to stop an earache and to alleviate rheumatic pains.

## Field Pennycress

*Thlaspi arvense.* (The Greek name of a Cress); of fields. (From Europe.)

Bastard Cress, *Cents* (P.Q.), Dish-Mustard, False Cress, Fanweed (Mont.), Frenchweed, Jim Hill Weed, Mithridate Mustard, Pennycress, Stinkweed, Treacle Mustard, Treaclewort

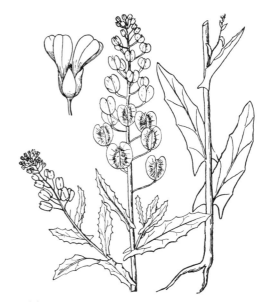

*Field Pennycress*

The round flat pods are the pennies, or *cents,* in Quebec. Gerard (1633) wrote that "the seed of Thlaspi or treacle Mustard eaten, purgeth choler both upward and downeward, provoketh flowers [menstruation], and breaketh inward aposthumes. The same used in clysters helpeth sciatica." Treacle is theriac or theriacle, the antidote against poison and the plague. The seed pods resemble fans, or according to Turner (1548), they are "lyke a disshe." The young leaves are eaten raw, and the seeds used as a condiment. Penny Cress is a local name in Scotland.

Jim Hill is James Jerome Hill (1838–1916), famous railroad builder and financier, also known as the "Empire Builder," along whose transcontinental railroads this and other plants spread westward; Jim Hill Mustard is *Erysimum inconspicuum* or *Sisymbrium altissimum.*

# THE CROWBERRY FAMILY

## *Empetraceae*

A family of three genera and only five species of evergreen shrubs; found mainly in the colder parts of the Northern Hemisphere and also in southern South America. Empetrum is derived from Greek *en,* "upon," and *petros,* "rock," alluding to the plants' habitat.

## Crowberry

*Empetrum nigrum.* On rocks; black (drupe). (Also found in Eurasia.)
Baby-Heathberry (Nfd.), Bearberry (Lab.), Black-Berried-Heath, Blackberry (Lab., Nfd.), Black Crowberry, *Camarine* (P.Q.), *Corbigeau* (P.Q.), Crakeberry, Crowpea, Curlew-Berry, Goules noires (P.Q.), *Graines à corbigeaux* (P.Q.), Heath, Heathberry (Nfd.), Hog-Cranberry (Maine), Monnocks, Monox, Monox-Heather, Pigeonberry, Redberry (Nfd.), Red-Heath (Nfd.), Rockberry (Nfd.), Squirt-Plum (Maine), Wineberry (Lab., N.S.), Wire-Ling

Among many northern peoples, the ripe berries are gathered from summer to early spring and eaten raw or cooked and dried for keeping or even fermented to make a mild alcoholic drink. Monnocks or Monox is from the Irish *moineog,* "bogberry" (*moin* means "bog" or "moor").

# THE HEATH FAMILY

## *Ericaceae*

A widespread family of 103 genera and 3,350 species of shrubs, lianas and small trees; found in temperate, cool and subtropical regions and in tropical mountains. Many members of the family are of great horticultural and gastronomic interest, including Rhododendrons, Azaleas, Heathers and Cranberries, Blueberries and Bilberries. "Heath" in Greek is *ereikē,* Latin *erica.*

## Bearberry

*Arctostaphylos uva-ursi.* Bear grape (from Greek *arktos,* "bear," *staphulē,* a bunch of

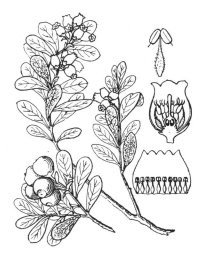

*Bearberry*

grapes—a translation of the popular name); bear-grape (Latin and previous generic name). (Also found in Eurasia.)

Barren-Bilberry, Barren-Myrtle, Bear's-Berry, Bear's-Grape-Bilberry, Bear's-Grapes (Mass.), Bear's-Weed, Bear's-Whortleberry, *Bousserole* (P.Q.), Box-Leaved Wintergreen, Bralins, Creashak, Crowberry (Mass.), Devil's-Tobacco (Canada), Foxberry, Foxplum, *Graine d'ours* (Canada), Ground-Holly, Hardberries (Lab., Nfd.), Hog-Cranberry (Mass.), Indian-Whort (Lab., Nfd.), Kinnikinnik, Manzanita, Mealberry, Mealyberry (Mass., N.J.), Mealplum, Mountain-Box, Mountain-Cranberry (Maine), *Raisin d'ours* (P.Q.), Rapper-Dandies, Red-Bearberry, Rockberry, *Sac à commis* (Canada), Sandberry (Ill.), Universe-Vine, Upland-Cranberry, Uversy, Wild-Cranberry

Prince Maximilian wrote from Fort McKenzie in 1833, "When the Blackfeet smoke, they put a piece of dried earth or a round mass made of the filaments and pods of certain water plants on the ground, to rest the pipe on. Their tobacco consists of the small, roundish, dried leaves of the sakakomi plant *[Arctostaphylos uva-ursi]*. When you visit an Indian in his tent, the pipe is immediately taken up and passes round in the company, each person handing it to his left-hand neighbour. The master of the tent often blows the smoke towards the sun and the earth; every one takes some puffs and hands it on." Erna Gunther reported that this was also the principal smoking mixture of the Northwest Indians: "The Chehalis say if one swallows the smoke of kinnikinnick, it produces a drunken feeling." In Quebec, 1749, the Bearberries "grow in great abundance. The Indians, French, English and Dutch, in those parts of North America which I have seen, call them Sagackhomi, and mix the leaves with tobacco for their use. Even the children use only the Indian name for these berries" (Kalm). Dr. Barton (1798) reported that the plant was "a most valuable medicine. It should be in the hands of every physician. I have used it with advantage in old gonorrhea. But its great virtue is that of a medicine in nephritis."

In the Fort Yukon Region of Alaska, the "Berries add a sweet flavor to fish (especially whitefish) intestines, liver, or eggs when cooked with plenty of grease. Formerly they were used to make Indian hash, a mixture of pounded dried meat, grease (fat from bear, caribou, or ducks, or vegetable shortening), and berries" (Holloway and Alexander, 1990). The berries are also made into jelly and cider. Rapper-Dandy is a local name in northern England and Scotland. Creashak (from the Gaelic *croiseagan*) and Brawlins (Americanized to Bralins) are local names in Scotland. Mealberry is from the Danish *meelboer* and Norwegian *miolboer*, "floury berry."

## Heather, Ling

*Calluna vulgaris.* Broom (from Greek *kallun;* brooms were made of the twigs); common. (From Europe.)

Grig, Moor-Besom, Scotch Heather

"In the upland zone of Great Britain heather has been a necessity of life time out of mind. It makes a springy bed, besoms for the home and the hearth, thatch for the roof, fuel, baskets, rope, an orange dye, and much else. It feeds the sheep and gives a dark honey to the bees. Highland settlers in North America took their heather beds with them, and so introduced heather to the New World" (Grigson). Grig is a local name in England.

## Trailing-Arbutus, Mayflower

*Epigaea repens.* Upon earth (Greek *epi,* "upon," *gaia,* "earth"); creeping.

Crocus, *Fleur de mai* (P.Q.), Gravel-Plant, Ground-Laurel, Ground-Sweet (Pa.), Mountain-Pink, Our-Beauties (N.Y.), Real-Mayflower (Maine), Rough-Leaf, Shadflower (New England, N.J.), Winter-Pink.

Legend has it that, on landing at Plymouth, Massachusetts, the Pilgrims saw this flower and named it after their ship:

> *Yet God be praised! the Pilgrim said,*
> *Who saw the blossoms peer*
> *Above the brown leaves, dry and dead,*
> *Behold our Mayflower here!*

> *God wills it, here our rest shall be,*
> *Our years of wandering o'er,*

*Trailing-Arbutus*

> *For us the Mayflower of the sea*
> *Shall spread her sails no more.*
> J. G. Whittier—

"This is the tribal flower of the Forest Potawatomi who consider that these flowers came direct from the hands of 'kitcimani-towwiwin,' their divinity" (Huron Smith, 1933). Arbutus is the name of an evergreen tree.

## Creeping Snowberry

*Gaultheria hispidula.* Of Gauthier (Jean-François Gauthier, 1708–1756, botanist and court physician at Quebec); fine-hairy.

Aromatic-Wintergreen, *Capillaire* (N.B., Nfd.), Ivory-Plums (Maine), Maidenhair (Nfd., N.B., P.E.I.), Maidenhair-Berry, Mountain-Partridgeberry, Moxa (Maine), Moxie (Maine), Moxie-Berry (Maine), Moxie-Vine (Maine), Moxie-Plum (Maine), *Oeufs de perdrix* (P.Q.), *Petit thé* (P.Q.), Running-Birch (Vt.), Running-Tea (Maine), Snakeberry (Maine), Snow-Plum (Maine), Spiceberry (N.B.), Sugarberry, Sugarplum (Maine), Teaberry (N.B.)

Thoreau's Indian guide in Maine told him that the leaves made the best tea of anything in the woods. Thoreau wrote, "He called it *cowosnebagosar,* which name implies that it grows where old prostrate trunks have collapsed and rotted. So we determined to have some tea made of this tonight. It had a slight checkerberry flavor, and we both agreed that it was really better than the black tea we had brought." The young leaves are also eaten raw.

"The berries, which are aromatic and pleasant, are employed to flavor spirituous liquors. An infusion of them in brandy is a convenient and useful substitute for the ordinary bitters" (Porcher).

## Wintergreen, Checkerberry, Teaberry

*Gaultheria procumbens.* Of Gauthier; procumbent.

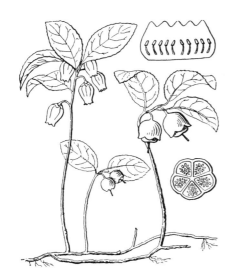

*Wintergreen*

Berried-Tea (N.C.), Boxberry (Mass.), Canada-Tea, Chickaberry (Conn.), Chickberry, Chickenberry (Pa.), Chidkerberry (N.C.), Chinks (Mass., N.H.), Clink (N.C.), Deerberry, Drunkards (Mass.), Eye-berry, Foxberry, Gingerberry, Gingerleaf (Mass.), Gingerplum (Mass.), Greenberry, Groundberry, Groundholly (Mass.), Grouseberry, Hillberry, Ivory (Maine), Ivory-Leaves (Maine, Mass.), Ivory-Plums (Maine, Mass., N.H.), Ivry-Leaves, Ivy (Maine), Ivy-Berry (N.B.), Jersey-Tea, Jinks (Mass., N.H.), Kinnikinnik, Little-Johnnies (Maine), Maidenhair (Nfd.), Mountain-Tea (Ky., Ohio, Pa.), Mountaineer-Tea (Nfd.), One-Berry, Partridge-Berry (N.H.), Partridge-Plant (N.Y.), Pine-Ivy, Pippins (Mass., N.H.), Pollom, Procalm, Redberry-Tea, Red-Pollom, Roxberry (N.C.), Spiceberry, Spicy Wintergreen, Spring Wintergreen, Teaberry, Tea-Leaves, *Thé des bois* (P.Q.), Winterberry (P.E.I.), Young-Chinks (N.H.), Young-Come-Ups (Vt.), Young-Ivories (N.H.), Young-Plantlets (Mass.), Youngsters (Maine, Mass.)

Jonathan Carver reported in the 1760s that "in winter it is full of red berries about the size of a sloe, which are smooth and round; these are preserved during the severe season by the snow, and are at that time in the highest perfection. The Indians eat these berries, esteeming them very balsamic, and invigorating to the stomach."

According to Rafinesque, it was "a popular remedy in many parts of the country. It is generally used as a tea, but the essence and oil possess eminently all the properties, and are kept in the shops. The tea is used as a palliative in asthma, to restore strength, promote menstruation, also in cases of debility, in the secondary stages of diarrhoea, and to promote the lacteal secretion of the breast, &c.: it is a very agreeable and refreshing beverage, much preferable to imported China Teas."

An oil, extracted from the leaves by distillation, became a prominent ingredient of many medicines. In the early 1800s, a French proprietary remedy called Rob de Laffecteur became fashionable among New York physicians. In 1811 Mr. Swaim, a bookbinder, procured the formula of the remedy from his physician, replaced some of its ingredients with oil of wintergreen and marketed it as Swaim's Panacea, which became celebrated. In 1831 the *American Journal of Pharmacy* reported that "the wonderful success of Swaim's Panacea has brought this oil into great vogue with all venders of Catholicons, Panaceas, and Syrups of Sarsparillas" (from Lloyd, 1929). Pollom is an Indian name for the plant. Kinnikinnik (or *killikinick*) is Algonquian for any smoking mixture.

## Salal

*Gaultheria shallon.* Of Gauthier; the Latinized Indian name.

Among the Clatsop Indians, December 1806: "Toward evening it began to rain and blow very violently from the southwest; Captain Clark therefore determined to remain during the night. When they thought his appetite had returned, an old woman presented him, in a bowl made of light-colored horn, a kind of syrup, pleasant to the taste, made from a

*Salal*

species of berry, common in this country, about the size of a cherry, called by the Indians shelwel; of these berries a bread is also prepared, which being boiled with roots, forms a soup, which was served in neat wooden trenchers; this, with some cockles, was his repast" (Lewis and Clark). The fruit (Salal or Shalal) was a valued food for many groups of Northwest Indians—large quantities were dried and pounded into slabs.

## Sheep-Laurel

*Kalmia angustifolia.* Of Kalm (Peter Kalm, 1716–1779); narrow-leaved.

Calf-Kill, Dwarf-Laurel, Goldwithy (Nfd.), Gold-worthy (Nfd.), Gouldwithy (Nfd.), Gouldworthy (Nfd.), Ivy (Va.), Kill-Kid, Lambkill, Mountain-Laurel (Maine), Pig-Laurel, Sheepkill, Sheep-Laurel, Sheep-Poison (New England), Spoonwood-Ivy (Conn.), Spurge-Laurel, Wicky

In 17th-century New England, "Spurge-Lawrel, called here Poyson berry, it kills the English cattle, if they chance to feed upon it, especially calves" (Josselyn, 1672). All the Kalmias and many Rhododendrons are poisonous to stock, which will generally avoid their tough leaves unless, in winter or early spring, there is nothing else green to eat. Goldwithy is a local name in England for Sweetgale *(Myrica gale).*

## Mountain-Laurel

*Kalmia latifolia.* Of Kalm; broad-leaved.
American-Laurel, Big-Leaved-Ivy, Broad-Leaved Kalmia, Calico-Bush (Mass.), Clamoun, Ivy (N.C., Tenn.), Ivybush, Little-Laurel (Md.), Poison-Laurel, Red-Stemmed-Ivy (Ky.), Sheepsbane (Long Island), Small-Laurel, Spoon-Hunt (N.H.), Spoonwood, Wocky, Wood-Laurel

In New Jersey, November 1748, Peter Kalm wrote that "the spoon tree, which never grows to a great height, was seen today in several places. The Swedes here have named it thus, because the Indians used to make their spoons and trowels of its wood." He reported that "Dr. Linné [Linnaeus], because of the peculiar friendship and kindness with which he has always honored me has been pleased to call this tree, *Kalmia foliis ovatis, corymbis terminalibus,* or *Kalmia latifolia.*"

Manasseh Cutler called it Great Laurel, Wintergreen, Spoon-haunch: "The Indians are said to have made small dishes, spoons, and other utensils, out of the roots. They are sometimes employed by people in the country for similar purposes. They are large, of a soft texture, and easily wrought when green; but when thoroughly dry, become very hard and smooth."

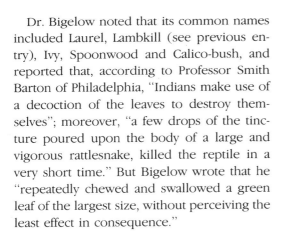

*Mountain-Laurel*

*Labrador-Tea*

Dr. Bigelow noted that its common names included Laurel, Lambkill (see previous entry), Ivy, Spoonwood and Calico-bush, and reported that, according to Professor Smith Barton of Philadelphia, "Indians make use of a decoction of the leaves to destroy themselves"; moreover, "a few drops of the tincture poured upon the body of a large and vigorous rattlesnake, killed the reptile in a very short time." But Bigelow wrote that he "repeatedly chewed and swallowed a green leaf of the largest size, without perceiving the least effect in consequence."

## Labrador-Tea

*Ledum groenlandicum.* (A Greek plant name); of Greenland.
*Bois de savane* (P.Q.), Country-Tea, Crystal-Tea (Lab.), Gowiddie (Nfd.), Hudson's-Bay-Tea, Indian-Tea (Nfd., Lab.), James-Tea, Labrador-Tea (Maine), St. James's-Tea, Swamp-Tea (Wash.), *Thé du Groënland* (P.Q.), Thé velouté (P.Q.)

Labrador Tea (or Country Tea or James Tea, named for James Bay) is brewed from the dried leaves of this or *Ledum palustre.* "It has a rather agreeable fragrance, between turpentine and strawberries. It is rather strong and penetrating, and sometimes reminds me of the peculiar scent of a bee. The young leaves, bruised and touched to the nose, even make it smart" (Thoreau, 1858).

In 1743 James Isham, the factor at Fort York on Hudson Bay for over 20 years, reported that the plant there was called Wishakapucka and that Wishakapucka-tea was of "a fine flavour and reckon'd very wholesome,—I was troubled very much my self with a nervous disorder, but by constant drinking 1 pint made strong for three months entirely cured me."

"It is apparently a mild narcotic; Indian women of certain tribes took some of it three times daily just before giving birth, and the powdered leaves are taken for a headache" (Marie-Victorin). Rafinesque reported that it was "useful in coughs, exanthema, itch, scabies, leprosy &c. In strong decoction kills lice and insects."

## Rhodora

*Rhododendron canadense.* Rose tree; of Canada.
Lambkill (N.B.), Laurel (Maine)

> *Rhodora! if the sages ask thee why*
> *This charm is wasted on the earth and*
> *    sky,*
> *Tell them, dear, that if eyes were made*
> *    for seeing,*
> *Then Beauty is its own excuse for*
> *    being.*
> > Emerson, from "The Rhodora"—

Rhodora, the previous generic name, is from the Latin variant of *rodarum,* Meadowsweet *(Spiraea),* from the Gaulish.

*Pink Azalea*

## Pink Azalea, Pinxter-Flower

*Rhododendron periclymenoides.* Rose tree; like Honeysuckle.
Early-Honeysuckle, Election-Pink (N.H.), Honeysuckle (Md.), Liberty-Bush, Mayapple, Mayflower (N.J.), Mountain-Pink (Vt.), Pinkster-Blummies (N.Y.), Pinxter-Blossoms (N.Y.), Pinxter-Blumachies (N.J., N.Y.), Purple Azalea, Purple-Honeysuckle, River-Pink (Vt.), Swamp-Apple (Mass.), Swamp-Honeysuckle, Swamp-Pink (New England), Wild-Honeysuckle (Ga., W.Va.)

In New Hampshire it was called "Election Pink, because in bloom at the old-time 'election,' when the governor took his seat in June" (Hayward, 1891).

Among the New York Dutch, Pinxter or Pinkster (from the Middle Dutch *pinxter* and the Greek *pentekoste*) is Whitsuntide, the feast of Pentecost, the seventh Sunday after Easter. It was an important holiday for the New York Dutch, especially in New York City and Al-bany. In the 18th century the holiday was taken over by the Negro slaves, who were given a three-day vacation, a tradition that lasted among their descendants at least until the late 1800s. James Fenimore Cooper, writing of 1757, called Pinkster "the great Saturnalia of the New York Blacks." In Albany the holiday procession was led by the "King of the Blacks" or "Charley of Pinkster Hill," according to an article in *Harper's Magazine* (1881), whose costume was that of a British brigadier-general, with scarlet broadcloth coat and a three-cornered cocked hat trimmed with lace. "Both he and his followers were covered with Pinkster blummies—the wild azalea."

Mayapple or Swamp-Apple is the edible gall of a fungus that grows on the shrub (also called Honeysuckle-Apple, Pinkster-Bloom-itje, Pinkster-Apple, Hog-Apple, Swamp-Cheese): "These May apples, as they are sometimes called, are excellent for pickling with spiced vinegar and have been used for that purpose since Pilgrim days" (Medsger, 1939). Azalea is New Latin for "dry plant" (Greek *azaleos* means "dry"), referring to some species that grew in dry soil, and the previous generic name for many plants now included among the Rhododendrons.

## Blueberries, Cranberries, Bilberries

*Vaccinium.* (A Latin plant name derived from a prehistoric Mediterranean language and transferred to these plants.)
*Airelles* (P.Q.), Bluets (N.B., Pa.), Ground-Hurts (Nfd.), Whortleberries (Nfd.)

In his *Key into the Language of America* (written at sea in 1643 on his way to England to secure a charter for his colony of Rhode Island), Roger Williams included "*Attitaash* (whortleberries), of which there are diverse sorts; sweet like currants; some opening, some of a binding nature. *Sautaash* are these currants dried by the natives, and so preserved all the year; which they beat to powder, and mingle it with their parched meal, and make a delicate dish which they call *sautauthig,* which is sweet to them as plum or spice cake to the English."

Josselyn (1672) called them "Cran Berry, or Bear Berry, because bears use much to feed upon them . . . The Indians and English use them much, boyling them with sugar for sauce to eat with their meat; and it is a delicate sauce, especially for roasted mutton: Some make tarts with them as with Goose Berries." Cranberry is from Low German *kraanbere,* "crane-berry," for the beaklike stamens. Bilberry is probably from Scandinavian *bolle,* "ball", *baer,* "berry." Whortleberry (*Vaccinium myrtillus* in Britain) is a variant of the dialect name Hurtleberry; *hurt* is of obscure origin.

## Large Cranberry

*Vaccinium macrocarpon.* (A Latin plant name); large-fruited.
American Cranberry, Bankberry (Nfd.), Bearberry (Nfd.), Bog Cranberry (Maine), *Gros atocas* (P.Q.), Marsh Cranberry (Maine, N.B.), Mossberry (N.C.), *Pommes de prée* (P.Q.), Swamp-Redberry

Josselyn (1672) wrote of "Bill Berries, two kinds, black and sky coloured, which is more frequent" and noted that "they are very good to allay the burning heat of feavers, and hot agues, either in syrup or conserve." He also described *A most excellent Summer Dish* of New England: "They usually eat of them put into a bason, with milk, and sweetened a little more with sugar and spice, or for cold stomachs, in sack. The Indians dry them in the sun, and sell them to the English by the bushell, who make use of them instead of currence, putting of them into puddens, both boyled and baked, and into water gruel." In 1722 Thomas More sent a package of plants and seeds from Boston to the English botanist Richard Sherard in London. The package included "Craneberry in a bottle, a drunken rogue that will neither grow or keep without swimming in water; he makes the best tarts in the world and therefore highly valued among gluttons and epicures for his fine taste."

## Small Cranberry

*Vaccinium oxycoccus.* (A Latin plant name); acid-berry (the old generic name). (Also found in Eurasia.)
*Atocas* (P.Q.), *Airelle des marais* (P.Q.), Bogberry, Bog Cranberry (Maine), Bogwort, *Canneberge* (P.Q.), Cramberry, Cranberry, Craneberry, Crawberry, Crowberry, Croneberry, European Cranberry, Fenberry, Hog Cranberry (Maine), Marshberry (Lab., Nfd.), Marsh Cranberry (N.B.), Marshwort, *Mocôques* (P.Q.), Moorberry, Mossberry, Moss-Mil-

*Small Cranberry*

lion, Sourberry, Sowberry, Swamp Cranberry, Swamp Redberry, Wren's-Egg Cranberry (Maine)

"Our employment generally is tinkering, mending the old worn-out teapot of society. Our stock in trade is solder. Better for me, says my genius, to go cranberrying this afternoon for the *Vaccinium Oxycoccus* in Gowing's Swamp, to get but a pocketful and learn its peculiar flavor, aye, and the flavor of Gowing's swamp and of *life* in New England, than to go consul to Liverpool and get I don't know how many thousand dollars for it, with no such flavor. Many of our days should be spent, not in vain expectations and lying on our oars, but in carrying out deliberately and faithfully the hundred little purposes which every man's genius must have suggested to him. Let not your life be wholly without an object, though it be only to ascertain the flavor of a cranberry, for it will not be only the quality of an insignificant berry that you will have tasted, but the flavor of your life to that extent, and it will be such a sauce as no wealth can buy" (Thoreau, 1856). (From 1853 to 1857, Nathaniel Hawthorne, once Thoreau's neighbor in Concord, was American consul in Liverpool.) Bogberry is an Irish name. Cramberry, Croneberry and Mossberry are local names in England. Moss-Million is a name in Ayrshire, "from the resemblance of the fruit to a pumpkin or melon in shape [*milion*], and the place of growth" (Britten and Holland). Another Scottish name is Moss-Mingin.

## Mountain Cranberry

*Vaccinium vitis-idaea.* (A Latin plant name); grape of Mount Ida (of Greek legend). (Also found in Eurasia.)

*Berris* (P.Q.), Cluster-Berries, Cowberry, Dry Cranberry, Flowering-Box, Foxberry (Lab., Nfd.), *Graines rouges* (P.Q.), Highland Cranberry (Maine), Lignonberry, Lingberry, Lingen, Lingonberry, Partridgeberry (Lab., Nfd.), *Pommes de terre* (P.Q.), Red Bilberry, Red Whortleberry, Rock Cranberry (N.B.), Teeter-Berry, Upland Cranberry (Mass.), Windberry, Wineberry, Woods Cranberry (Maine)

This is one of the staple foods of all northern peoples, particularly in Scandinavia; in 1846 in Maine the berries, "stewed and sweetened, were the common dessert" (Thoreau). Crowberry is the British name and Lingberry (Swedish *lingon*) a local name in England. Gerard (1633) wrote that the berries "are of an excellent red colour, and full of juyce; of so orient and beautifull a purple to limne [dye] withall . . . they make the fairest carnation colour in the world."

# THE SHINLEAF OR WINTERGREEN FAMILY

## *Pyrolaceae*

A family of four genera and 42 species of mycotrophic herbs and half-shrubs; chiefly found on acid soils in temperate and boreal regions of the Northern Hemisphere.

## Pipsissewas

*Chimaphila.* Winter love (Greek *kheima,* "winter," *phileo,* "to love"; referring to the evergreen leaves).
*Herbe à cles* (P.Q.), Sipsewa, Waxflower, Wintergreen

Pipsissewa is evidently from the Cree *pipisisikweu,* meaning "it breaks it into pieces," having been used to treat gallstones. The plants were also taken as a diuretic and tonic.

*Little Pipsissewa*

## Spotted Wintergreen, Striped Prince's-Pine

*Chimaphila maculata.* Winter love; spotted.
Dragon's-Tongue, Lion's-Tongue, Pepsissewa, Piperidge, Ratsbane (Va.), Rat's-Vein (Ky.), Rheumatism-Root, Spotted Pipsissewa, Striped Wintergreen, Waxflower (Long Island), Whiteleaf, Wild-Arsenic (Va.)

"The plant is in high esteem for its medicinal qualities among the natives; they call it *Sip-si-sewa.* I have myself been witness of a successful cure made by a decoction of this plant, in a very severe case of hysteria. It is a plant eminently deserving the attention of physicians" (Pursh, 1814). It has been included in the USP and is "said to be diuretic, sudorific, stimulant, and tonic" (Jacobs and Burlage).

## Little Pipsissewa, Little Prince's-Pine

*Chimaphila menziesii.* Winter love; of Menzies (Archibald Menzies, 1754–1842).

Archibald Menzies was born in Scotland and died in London. He was educated in Scotland and in 1782 became a Royal Navy surgeon. He botanized in the West Indies and on the east coast of North America and, in a voyage around the world, 1786–1789, in South America, the Pacific and South Africa. He was appointed surgeon and naturalist to Capt. Vancouver's (see *Vancouveria*) voyage of 1791–94 and collected plants in South Africa and the southern Pacific and particularly on the Northwest coast of North America; this four-and-half-year voyage was important for its zoological and botanical discoveries, and only one sailor died of disease.

## Pipsissewa

*Chimaphila umbellata.* Winter love; umbelled. (Also found in Europe.)

Bittersweet (N.H.), Bitter Wintergreen, Fragrant Wintergreen, Ground-Holly, *Herbe à peigne* (P.Q.), King's-Cure, Love-in-Winter (Maine), Noble-Pine (Maine, N.H.), Pine-Tulip, Prince's-Pine, Princess-Pine, Prince's-Pride, Pyrole, Rheumatism-Weed, Wintergreen (Maine)

Bigelow (1817) wrote that the plant, "though scarcely known as a medicine until within a few years past, has at the present day acquired a reputation of considerable extent in the treatment of various diseases. Its popular celebrity seems to have originated in its application to the treatment of fever and rheumatism." Marie-Victorin wrote, "In certain places they believe that to chew one leaf daily will prevent tuberculosis; the Indians used the plant against scrofula and rheumatism." It was included in the USP and NF.

## Pink Pyrola, Pink Wintergreen

*Pyrola asarifolia.* Little pear (*Pyrus* has similar leaves); with leaves of Asarum.

Liverleaf Wintergreen, Rheumatism-Weed

"It is said to have been considered by the Indians as an effective remedy in rheumatisms" (Cutler, 1785).

## Shinleaf

*Pyrola elliptica.* Little pear; elliptical (leaves). (Also found in Japan.)

Lesser Wintergreen, White Wintergreen, Wild-Lily-of-the-Valley (Mass., Maine), Wood-Lily

Pyrola leaves have an analgesic property and were a remedy for bruised shins and other sores and wounds.

## Round-Leaved Pyrola

*Pyrola americana.* Little pear; of America.

Canker-Lettuce, Coffee-Leaf, Consumption-Root, Consumption-Weed, Copalm, Copper-Leaf, Dollar-Leaf, False Wintergreen, Indian-Lettuce, Larger Wintergreen, Lettuce, Liverwort-Lettuce, Moose-mise (Vt.), *Muguet des bois* (P.Q.), Pear-Leaved Wintergreen, Round-Leaved American-Wintergreen, Shinleaf, Wild-Lettuce, Wild-Lily-of-the-Valley (Maine, Mass.)

Manasseh Cutler called it Consumption-Root in 1785. Moosemise is perhaps Algonquian for moose-shrub.

*Round-Leaved Pyrola*

# THE INDIAN-PIPE FAMILY

## *Monotropaceae*

A family of 10 genera and 15 species of mycotrophic herbs; found in temperate and cool
regions of the Northern Hemisphere and also
in Colombia and the Malay Peninsula.

## Pinesap

*Monotropa hypopytis.* One turn (to one side);
under pines. (Also found in Eurasia.)
False Beechdrop, Fir-Rape, Fire-Rope, Indian-Pipe,
Pinesap-Bird's-Nest, Yellow Pinesap, Yellow Bird's-
Nest

"Birds Nest hath many tangling roots plat-
ted or crossed one over another very intri-
cately, which resembleth a Crowes nest made
of sticks; from which riseth up a thicke soft
grosse stalk of a browne colour, set with short
leaves of the colour of a dry Oken leafe that
hath lien under the tree all the winter. On
the top of the stalke groweth a spikie eare or
tuft of floures"(Gerard, 1633). Gerard also
reported that "It is not used in Physicke that
I can finde in any authoritie either of the
antient or later writers, but is esteemed as a
degenerate kinde of Orchis, and therefore
not used."

## Indian-Pipe

*Monotropa uniflora.* One turn; one-flow-
ered. (Also found in Asia.)
American-Iceplant, Bird's-Nest, Broomrape, Con-
vulsion-Root (N.H.), Convulsion-Weed, Corpse-Plant,
Dutchman's-Pipe (N.J.), Eyebright, Fairy-Smoke
(Maine), Fitroot-Plant, Fitsroot, Ghost-Flower (Maine,
N.B.), Ghost-Plant (Lab., Nfd.), Iceplant, Nestplant,
Nestroot, One-Flowered-Waxplant, Ova-Ova, Pipe-
plant, Tobacco-Pipe, Waxplant

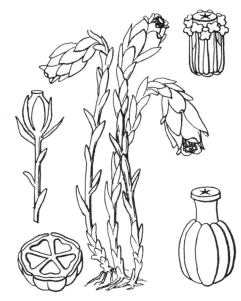

*Indian-Pipe*

Dr. Millspaugh reported that "the medical
history of the plant begins with its use by the
American Aborigines as an application in 'sore
eyes'; they valued a mixture of the juice with
water highly as a soothing and curative measure." He also noted that "this curious herb
well deserves its name of corpse plant, so
like is it to the general bluish waxy appearance of the dead; then, too, it is cool and
clammy to the touch, and rapidly decomposes
and turns black even when carefully handled."

"Indian pipe root makes a good remedy
for spasms, fainting spells, and various nervous conditions" (Lust, 1974) and thus earned
the names Convulsion-Root and Fitsroot.

## Giant Bird's-Nest, Pinedrops

*Pterospora andromedea.* Wing seed; like An-
dromeda (flowers).

Albany-Beechdrops, American-Dragonclaw, American-Dragonroot, False-Crawley, Fever-Root, Gall-of-the-Earth

This is called Nose-bleed Medicine by the Cheyenne Indians: "Used to prevent nose-bleeding and bleeding from the lungs. Grind the stem and berries together, make an infusion in boiling water, and let it cool. When cold, snuff some of the infusion up the nose and put some of it on the head for nose-bleed and drink it for bleeding at the lungs" (Grinnel, 1905).

# THE DIAPENSIA FAMILY

## *Diapensiaceae*

A circumpolar family of five genera and 13 species of herbs and dwarf shrubs found in Arctic and north temperate regions as far south as the Himalayas. Some members of the family are cultivated as ornamentals, including Galax and species of *Shortia*. Diapensia was the Greek name of a plant applied by Linnaeus to *Diapensia lapponica*.

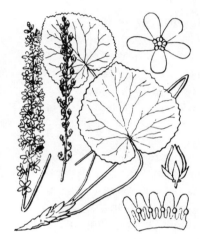

*Galax*

### Galax, Beetleweed

*Galax urceolata.* Milky (Greek *gala,* "milk"; perhaps color of the flower); urn-shaped
Carpenter's-Leaf (N.C.), Coltsfoot (N.C.), Galaxy, Heal-All, Wandflower

"In the Virginia mountains this plant is known by the name of Carpenter's-leaf, being used in healing of all kinds of wounds and cuts" (Pursh, 1814).

### Pyxie

*Pyxidanthera barbulata.* Small box anther (Greek *puxis* means "small box," for the structure of the anther); with a little beard.
Flowering-Moss, Pine-Barren-Beauty (N.J.), Pyxie-Moss (N.J.)

# THE PRIMROSE FAMILY

## *Primulaceae*

A family of 22 genera and 800 species of herbs and half-shrubs found chiefly in temperate and cold regions of the Northern Hemisphere and in tropical mountains. Some members of the family are cultivated as garden and house ornamentals, including species of *Primula* and *Cyclamen*; most Cyclamens grown in pots are cultivars of *Cyclamen persicum* ("of Persia").

The name Primrose is from the Middle English *primerose,* ultimately from the Medieval Latin *prima rosa* (first rose); the reason for so naming it is obscure. Primula is a diminutive of *primus* (first). The name *Primula veris* (little first one of spring) was applied both to the Cowslip and the Field Daisy *(Bellis perennis).*

## Scarlet Pimpernel

*Anagallis arvensis.* (The Greek name); of cultivated fields. (From Europe.)

Bird's-Eye, Bird's-Tongue, Eyebright, Poison-Chickweed (Calif.), Poor-Man's-Weatherglass, Red-Chickweed, Red Pimpernel, Shepherd's-Clock, Shepherd's-Delight, Shepherd's-Weatherglass, Sunflower, Wink-a-Peep

"They floure in Summer, and especially in the moneth of August, at what time the husbandmen having occasion to go unto their harvest work, will first behold the floures of Pimpernell, whereby they know the weather that shall follow the next day after: as for example, if the floures be shut close up, it betokeneth raine and foul weather; contrariwise, if they be spread abroad, faire weather" (Gerard, 1633). It is the shepherd's clock because the flowers are supposed to open promptly at 8 A.M. and shut at 3 P.M. or when it rains. The common red form is known as the male Pimpernel and the blue form the female. "Pliny and Dioscorides thought highly of Pimpernel in the removal of intestinal and hepatic obstructions; and it was, probably, from the happier condition of the mind following such action, that the latter called the plant *anagelao*" (Millspaugh). (*Anagelao* means "to laugh aloud.") The name Pimpernel was originally that of Burnet *(Sanguisorba officinalis).* Bird's-Eye, Eyebright, Poor-Man's-Weatherglass, Shepherd's-Clock, Shepherd's-Delight, Shepherd's-Weatherglass and Wink-a-Peep are local names in England.

## Shooting-Star

*Dodecatheon meadia.* Twelve gods (Pliny's name for the Primrose, which was under the care of 12 gods); of Mead (Richard Mead, 1673–1754).

American-Cowslip, Cyclamen (Ala.), Doty (Ohio), Gentlemen-and-Ladies, Indian-Chief (Ill.), Lamb's-Noses, Mosquito-Bells, Pinks, Poet's Shooting-Star, Prairie-Pointers (Ill.), Pride-of-Ohio, Rooster-Heads, Snake-Heads, Virginia-Cowslip

The flower with its swept-back petals is like the head of an Indian in a feathered headdress or a pointer or rooster's head. Richard Mead was an English physician, author of works on snakes, the influence of the sun and moon on human bodies and scabies. He was also a patron of Mark Catesby (page 305) who named this plant after him: "Linnaeus considered it a misplaced honor. Dr. Mead might be physician to the King of England, the Prime Minister, Sir Isaac Newton, and Alexander Pope, but botanically he was en-

*Scarlet Pimpernel*

*Shooting-Star*

tirely undistinguished. In an unusual burst of irritation the Great Systematist arbitrarily used Dr. Mead's name only for the species and the genus he renamed Dodecatheon" (Whittle and Cook, 1981).

## Western Shooting-Star, Few-Flowered Shooting-Star

*Dodecatheon pulchellum*. Twelve gods; beautiful.

American-Cowslip, Birdbills, Cyclamen (Calif.), Dark-Throat, Shooting-Star, Johnny-Jump (Calif.), Lady-Slipper (Wyo.), Mad-Violets (Calif.), Mosquito-Bills, Pinks, Pinky-Winky (Calif.), Rooster-Heads

"Shooting star has various fanciful names in Indian languages, such as rain's navel (Haida), curlew's bill (Okanagan), and beautiful maiden (Thompson)" (Ward-Harris). Noting that in California the plant is called Cyclamen and Mad-Violets, Bergen (1898) reported that "near Naples, Italy, the peasants call the true cyclamens mad violets."

## Rocky Mountain Dwarf-Primrose, Mountain Douglasia

*Douglasia montana*. Of Douglas (David Douglas, 1798–1834); of the mountains.

At age 11, David Douglas was apprenticed to the head gardener at Scone Palace in Perthshire, Scotland. He worked as a gardener for several years, during which he taught himself botany, and was then hired as an assistant by William Jackson Hooker, professor of botany at Glasgow University and later director at Kew Gardens. In 1823 Hooker recommended Douglas to the Horticultural Society of London as a plant collector, and in 1824 Douglas visited eastern North America and then sailed for the west coast. He explored British Columbia and Oregon for three years, making many important botanical discoveries.

He returned to North America in 1830, traveled in California, visited Hawaii and made further botanical trips in British Columbia, during which his canoe was wrecked on the Fraser River and he lost his journals and collections. He again visited Hawaii in 1834 and there accidentally fell into a pit trap and was gored to death by a wild bull. Asa Gray wrote in the *North American Review* (1844), "To give our readers some idea of the hardships which this indefatigable collector endured, and the risks at which our nurseries have been stocked with trees, and our gardens with the now familiar flowers of Oregon and California, we extract from the journal of Douglas a portion of the account of his visit to a group of these Lambert Pines [Sugar Pines, *Pinus lambertiana*]":

"Thursday, the 25th. Weather dull, cold, and cloudy . . . About an hour's walk from my camp I met an Indian, who, on perceiving me, instantly strung his bow, placed on his left arm a sleeve of raccoon skin, and stood on the defensive. Being quite satisfied that this conduct was prompted by fear, and not by hostile intentions, the poor fellow having probably never seen such a being as myself before, I laid my gun at my feet on the ground, and waved my hand for him to come to me, which he did, slowly and with great caution. I then made him place his bow and quiver of arrows beside my gun, and, striking a light, gave him a smoke out of my own pipe, and a present of a few beads. With my pencil I made a rough sketch of the cone and Pine-tree which I wanted to obtain, and drew his attention to it, when he instantly pointed with his hand to the hills fifteen or twenty miles distant towards the south; and when I expressed my intention of going hither, he cheerfully set about accompanying me. At mid-day I reached my long-wished-for Pines, and lost no time in examining them, and endeavoring to collect specimens and seeds."

## Loosestrifes

*Lysimachia.* (A classical plant name.)

"*Lysimachia,* as Dioscorides and Pliny write, took his name of a special vertue that it hath in appeasing the strife and unrulinesse which falleth out among oxen at the plough, if it be put about their yokes: but it rather retaineth and keepeth the name *Lysimachia,* of King Lysimachus the son of Agathocles, the first finder out of the nature and vertues of this herb" (Gerard, 1633). Thus the name Lysimachia is derived from either (or both) *lusimakhos,* "ending strife" (particularly between horses and oxen yoked together), or Lysimakhos, king of Thrace (or perhaps a Greek physician of the same name). Dioscorides described *lusimakhion* as having the "flower red, or of a golden color." Pliny wrote of *lysimachia* with purple flowers.

William Turner (1548) identified them as follows: "Lysimachia is of two sorts. The one is described of Dioscorides, and it hath a yealowe floure. Some cal it Lycimachiam luteam, it groweth by the Temes [Thames] syde beside Shene, it may be called in English yealow Lousstryfe or herbe Wylowe. The other kynde is described of Plinie, and it is called Lysimachia purpurea, it groweth by water sydes, also and may be called in English red Loos-

stryfe or purple Losestryfe." These became *Lysimachia vulgaris* and *Lythrum salicaria.* John Josselyn's "yellow Lysimachus of Virginia" (*Two Voyages,* p. 78) is an Evening Primrose, *Oenothera biennis.*

## Moneywort

*Lysimachia nummularia.* (A classical plant name); coin-like (old generic name, for the round leaves). (From Europe.)

Creeping-Charlie, Creeping-Jenny, Creeping Loose-strife, Creeping-Sally, Down-Hill-of-Life (N.C.), Herb-Two-Pence, Infant's-Breath (Maine), Meadow-Runagates, Moneybags (Mass.), Money-Myrtle, Money-Plant (Maine), *Monnayère* (P.Q.), Myrtle (Maine), String-of-Sovereigns, Two-Penny-Grass, Wandering-Jenny, Wandering-Sailor, Wandering-Sally, Yellow-Myrtle (Mass.)

"It may be called in English Herb II pence or Two penigrass because it hath two and two leaves standyng together of ech syde of the stalk lyke pence" (Turner, 1548). Grieve wrote that "the bruised fresh leaves were in popular use as an application to wounds, both fresh and old, a decoction of the fresh herb

*Moneywort*

being taken as a drink in wine or water, and also applied outwardly as a wash or cold compress." Manasseh Cutler called this Yellow Willowherb, Pimpernel, Loosestrife, Meadowsweet and Moneywort. Creeping-Jenny, Wandering-Jenny and Wandering-Sailor are local names in England.

## Whorled Loosestrife

*Lysimachia quadrifolia.* (A classical plant name); four-leaved.

Crosswort, Five-Sisters, Four-Leaved Loosestrife, Liberty-Tea (Maine, Mass.), Wild-Tea (Mass.), Yellow-Balm

"With the Revolution came the refusal to drink the tea of commerce, and our four-leaved loosestrife, being dried and steeped was used in its stead. This was known as 'Liberty-tea' " (*Essex Antiquarian,* 1898). Prairie Loosestrife or Prairie-Moneywort, *Lysimachia quadriflora* ("four-flowered"), was also called Liberty-Tea and Wild-Tea.

## Starflower

*Trientalis borealis.* One third of a foot (in height); of the north.

Chickweed-Wintergreen, Chick-Wintergreen (N.Y.), Indian-Potatoes (West), Maystar (N.Y.), Star-Anemone (Mass.), Star-Chickweed, Star-of-Bethlehem (Mass., N.H., Vt.)

In 1850 Susan Cooper wrote, "Some persons call this chick wintergreen, a name which

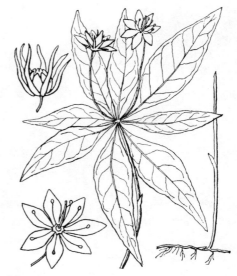

*Starflower*

is an insult to the plant, and to the common sense of the community. Why, it is one of the daintiest wood-flowers, with nothing in the world to do with chicks, or weeds, or winter. It is not the least of an evergreen, its leaves withering in autumn, as a matter of course, and there is not a chicken in the country that knows it by sight or taste. Discriminating people, when they first find its elegant silvery flower growing in the woods beside the violet, call it May-star."

The potatoes are the small swellings at the base of the stem, but apparently they are not edible.

# THE STONECROP FAMILY

## *Crassulaceae*

A cosmopolitan family of 35 genera and 1,500 species of succulent herbs and shrubs; found in arid, temperate or warm temperate regions, especially South Africa. Crassula is the diminutive of *crassus* (thick), for the thick leaves of some species. Many species are cultivated as ornamentals.

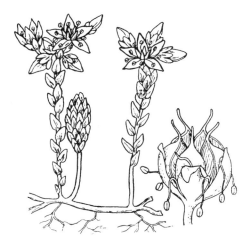

*Mossy Stonecrop*

## Mossy Stonecrop, Wallpepper

*Sedum acre.* Sitting (Latin *sedere*; many species affix themselves to rocks or walls); pungent. (From Europe.)

Bird's-Bread, Biting Stonecrop, Creeping-Charlie (N.Y.), Creeping-Jack, Creeping-Jennie, Ginger, Gold-Chain, Golden-Moss, Kit-of-the-Wall, Little-House-leek, Love-Entangled (Ohio), Mountain-Moss, Pepper-Crop, Poor-Man's-Pepper, Pricket, Prick-Madam, Rockplant, Tangle-Tail, Treasure-of-Love (Mass.), Wallmoss, Wallwort

*Trique-madame* was the French name, which became Prick-Madam in Gerard and other English herbals. A trique is a cudgel or stick, alluding to the upright flowering stems. "As *trique-madame,* the allied *Sedum album* was given in France for an aphrodisiac" (Grigson). John Evelyn (1699) called it Trick-Madame and Stone-Crop and wrote that it "is cooling and moist, grateful to the stomach. The cimata and tops, when young and tender, dress'd as Purselane, is a frequent ingredient in our cold sallet." The USD, however, reports that "it causes vomiting and purging; applied to the skin it produces inflammation and vesication. The fresh herb and the expressed juice have been used for reputed antiscorbutic, emetic, cathartic, and diuretic effects, and have been applied locally to old ulcers, warts, and other excrescences." Most of the names listed above are from Britain, but Treasure-of-Love appears to be American.

Rockmoss or Widow's-Cross is *Sedum pulchellum* (little beauty) and Wild Stonecrop or Shepherd's-Cress is *Sedum ternatum* (in threes).

## Pacific Sedum, Broad-Leaved Stonecrop

*Sedum spathulifolium.* Sitting; with spatulate leaves.

Among the Thompson Indians, "a heated decoction of the entire plant is used for washing babies, especially when they are cross, as it is said to have a soothing effect" (Teit, 1930).

## Live-Forever, Orpine

*Sedum telephium.* Sitting; (an old name of uncertain origin, perhaps named after Telephus, a king of Mysia). (From Europe.)

Aaron's-Rod (Maine, N.H.), Bagleaves, Bagplant (Maine, Mass.), Balloon-Purses, Blowleaf (N.H.), Bogleaves, Evergreen (Md.), Everlasting (P.Q.),

*Live-Forever*

Frog's-Bladder (N.Y.), Frog's-Mouth (N.Y.), Frog-plant (N.H.), Frog's-Throats (Mass.), Harping-Johnny, Heal-All, Houseleek (Mass.), Leeks (Vt.), Life-of-Man (Maine, Mass.), Live-Forever (Maine), Live-Long, Midsummer-Men, Pudding-Bag-Plant (Mass.), Toad-Bellies, *Vit-toujours* (P.Q.), Witch's-Money-Bags (Mass.)

It was called Live-Forever because a plant can be grown from a leaf fragment. In 1688 John Aubrey remembered that when he was a boy in Wiltshire, "the mayds (especially the cook mayds and dairymayds) would stick up in some chinks of the joists, etc., Midsommer-men, which are slips of Orpins. They placed them by pairs, sc: one for such a man, the other for such a mayd his sweetheart, and accordingly as the Orpin did incline to, or recline from, the other, that there would be love or aversion; if either did wither, death." J. G. Frazer reported in 1913 that "in Masuren, Westphalia, and Switzerland the method of forecasting the future by means of the orpine is exactly the same." Orpin is derived through the French *orpiment* from *auripigmentum* (pigment of gold), presumably applied to a yellow Sedum. "Live-forever or frog-plant is familiar to most children in regions where it occurs on account of the readily loosened epidermis of the leaf, loosened by holding the leaf between the tongue and the roof of the mouth; after which, by blowing into the opening, the loosened epidermis may be distended like a frog's throat" (Fernald and Kinsey, 1943)—or like a purse, money-bag or pudding-bag. The young leaves make a delicious salad, and the roots are pickled. Live-long and Midsummer-Men are British names; Heal-All is an Irish name; Aaron's-Rod and Harping-Johnny are local names in England.

## Houseleek

*Sempervivum tectorum.* Always alive; of roofs. (From Europe.)

Aye-Green, Bullock's-Eye, Bullock's-Plant, Healing-Blade, Hen-and-Chickens, Homewort, Jobarbe, Jupiter's-Beard, Leek (Mass.), Old-Man-and-Woman, Poor-Jan's-Leaf, Sengreen, Thunder-Plant

The Romans called it *Iovis caulis,* Jove's (Jupiter's) plant, since they believed it protected the house from lightning if planted on the roof. "Old wryters do call it Iovis Barba, Iupiter's Bearde, and hold an opinion supersticiously that in what house so ever it groweth, no Lyghtning or Tempest can take place to doe any harm there" (William Bullein, 1562). In Irish it is *luibh an toitean* (fire herb) and is still planted on roofs (Grigson). Most of the above are local names in England. Sengreen, from Old English *singrene,* and Aye-Green mean "evergreen." "The leek will apparently bloom very soon. I see the stigmas I think. What a surprising and stately plant! Its great flowerstem stands now a little aslant, some fifteen or eighteen inches high, regularly beset with its great thick leaves, gradually lessening upward to its great massy head. It has a peculiar columnar appearance, like the Leaning Tower of Pisa" (Thoreau, 1850).

# THE SAXIFRAGE FAMILY

## *Saxifragaceae*

A widespread family of 36 genera and 475 species of herbs and shrubs; best developed in temperate, cold and often mountainous parts of the Northern Hemisphere. The family provides us with edible berries (Currants and Gooseberries, both species of *Ribes*) and Hydrangeas and Saxifrages for the flower garden. The name Saxifrage is derived from *saxum* (a rock) and *frangere* (to break) since some species grow in rock crevices and were thus reputed to break rocks and, according to the doctrine of signatures, were a remedy for bladder and kidney stones.

## Alumroot

*Heuchera americana.* Of Heucher (Johann Heinrich Heucher, 1677–1747, professor of medicine at Wittenberg); of America.
American-Sanicle, Cliffweed, Crag-Jangle (South), Ground-Maple, Mapleleaf, Rock-Geranium, Split-Rock

In 1798 Dr. Barton reported, "This is sometimes called American Sanicle. It is more commonly called Alum-Root. The root is a very intense astringent. It is the basis of a powder which has lately acquired some reputation in the cure of cancer." According to Rafinesque (1828), "it was used by the Indians, and is still used in Kentucky and the Alleghany Mountains, in powder, as an external remedy in sores, wounds, ulcers, and even cancers."

## Miterwort, Bishop's-Cap

*Mitella diphylla.* Small cap (*mitra,* "a cap"; the form of the young pod); two-leaved.
American Bastard-Sanicle, Coolwort (Mass.), Crystal-Flower, Currant-Leaf, Fairy-Cup (N.Y.), False Sanicle (N.Y.), Fringe-Cup (N.Y.), Gem-Fruit, *Mitrelle* (P.Q.), Snowflake

The capsule resembles a miter, the tall pointed hat with two peaks worn by a bishop. The following is from the prelude to "Voices of the Night" by Longfellow:

> *Therefore at Pentecost, which brings*
> *The Spring, clothed like a bride,*
> *When nestling buds unfold their wings,*
> *And Bishop's Caps have golden rings,—*
> *Musing upon many things,*
> *I sought the woodlands wide.*

*Miterwort*

It was called Coolwort because a tea made of the leaves was used to treat a fever and Snowflake because of "the delicately fringed petals of the miterworts or bishopcaps *(Mitella),* resembling magnified snowflakes in their symmetrical and almost indescribable intricacy" (Moldenke, 1949). Marie-Victorin remarked that the flowers are "one of the marvels of our flora. The finely cut petals are extremely rare in the plant world, especially among the dicotyledons." Sanicle is a famous healing herb, for which this was evidently a substitute.

## Grass-Of-Parnassus

*Parnassia glauca.* Of Parnassus; blue-green.
Bog-Star, White-Buttercup, White-Liverwort
Dioscorides wrote of *Agrostis en parnasso* (the grass of Mount Parnassus) that it "bears leaves like Ivy, a white flower of a sweet scent, a small seed, not unuseful root, five or six, of a finger's thickness, white, soft, strong, of which the juice being sodden with wine, & as much honey, & an half part of myrrh & with pepper & a third part of Frankincense,

is an excellent medicine for eyes" *(Parnassia palustris)*.

## Ditch-Stonecrop

*Penthorum sedoides.* Five parts (Greek *pente,* "five," *horos,* "a boundary"; the plant's parts are in fives); like *Sedum.*

Grieve reported that "this plant has of late attracted much notice, especially in America, as a remedy for catarrh, catarrhal inflammation of the larynx, chronic bronchitis, with increased secretion of mucus and catarrhal affections of the stomach and bowels. It has also been employed with success in the treatment of diarrhoea, haemorrhoids and infantile cholera." This genus is often included among the Crassulaceae.

*Early Saxifrage*

## Lettuce Saxifrage

*Saxifraga micranthidifolia.* Stone break; with leaves of Micranthes (a previous genus name). Deer-Tongue, Lettuce (N.C.), Mountain-Lettuce

"In some of the mountain sections of Pennsylvania this plant is highly prized by the people. For salads it is probably used more than any other wild plant of the region" (Medsger, 1939). Swamp Saxifrage *(Saxifraga pensylvanica)* is called Swamp-Beet or Wild-Beet in Maine.

## Early Saxifrage

*Saxifraga virginiensis.* Stone break; of Virginia.
Bread-and-Butter (Conn.), Everlasting (Mass.), Lungwort (Maine), Mayflower (Mass.), Rockfoil, Rock Saxifrage, St. Peter's-Cabbage (South), Spring Saxifrage, Sweet Wilson (Mass.)

John Josselyn (1672) listed this twice in his *New-England's Rarities,* as "Jagged Rose-penny-wort" and "New-England Daysie, or Primrose . . . the second kind of Navel Wort in Johnson upon Gerard" (i.e., in Thomas Johnson's 1633 edition of Gerard's Herbal). It must have

reminded the settlers of the Wall Pennywort, *Umbilicus rupestris,* the little English Daisy, *Bellis perennis,* or the Primrose, *Primula vulgaris.* In *Two Voyages,* Josselyn wrote of the "New England daisie, it is good for hot humours, erisipelas, St. Anthonie's fire, all inflammations," echoing (with one mispelling) the virtues that Gerard (1633) attributed to Wall Pennywort: "a singular remedy against all inflammations and hot tumours, as erysipelas, Saint Anthonies fire, and such like." A name recorded in the American South for Early Saxifrage is St. Peter's-Cabbage; in the *Grete Herball* of 1526, the Primrose is called St. Peter's Wort. It was named Sweet-Wilson "by Mrs. Ward fifty years ago, to please Wilson Ward, who complained there was a sweet William but no sweet Wilson" (Bergen, 1896).

## Foamflower, False Miterwort

*Tiarella cordifolia.* Small crown (the form of the fruit); heart-leaved.
Coalwort, Colwort, Coolwort, False Bitterwort, Gem-Fruit, Nancy-over-the-Ground (Mass.), White Coolwort (N.Y.)

In 1850 Susan Cooper wrote from Cooperstown, New York, that "the cool-wort grows in patches upon many banks within the woods, or near them. It is a very pretty flower from its light, airy character, and the country people employ its broad, violet-shaped leaves for healing purposes. They lay them, freshly gathered, on scalds and burns, and, like all domestic receipts of the sort, they never fail, of course, but 'work like a charm.' " Bartlett (1859) wrote that Coolwort, "the properties of which are diuretic and tonic," was "prepared for sale by Shakers."

# THE ROSE FAMILY

## *Rosaceae*

A nearly cosmopolitan family of 107 genera and 3,100 species of herbs, shrubs and trees; most common in temperate and subtropical regions of the Northern Hemisphere. The family is of great economic importance, providing us with fruits (such as apples, cherries, plums, peaches, raspberries and strawberries) and ornamentals (Roses, *Spiraea, Filipendula, Cotoneaster,* for example).

## Tall Hairy Agrimony

*Agrimonia gryposepala.* (The Latin name, from Greek *argemone,* "poppy," perhaps from *argemon,* "white spot on the eye," which the plant was supposed to cure, or from Hebrew *'argaman,* red-purple); having hooked sepals.

Beggar-Lice, Beggar's-Ticks, Cocklebur, Feverfew, Harvest-Lice, Rough Agrimony, Stickleworth, Stickseed, Sweethearts

Dr. Porcher reported that "Colonel Seaborn, of Pendleton District, S.C., writes me word that he has known the plant, boiled in milk, given successfully in snake bites, and injuries arising from the stings of spiders." The hooked seed receptacles stick to clothing like ticks or lice.

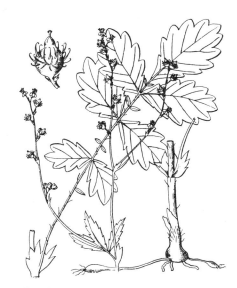

*Woodland Agrimony*

## Woodland Agrimony

*Agrimonia striata.* (The Latin name); scalloped (leaves).

Aaron's-Rod, Beggar-Ticks (W.Va.), Cocklebur, Harvest-Lice, Snakeweed (Mass.), Sweethearts, Stickseed

"The roots and the whole plant boiled in milk are used by herbalists for diabetes and incontinence of urine. One of their remedies for the tape-worm is Agrimony tea, with alum and honey. The roots are said to be more astringent than the leaves, the Indians use them in fever, and some empirics for jaundice with honey. It is said to be diuretic and vulnerary" (Rafinesque, 1828). Aaron's-Rod, Cocklebur, Harvest-Lice and Sweethearts are local names in England for *Agrimonia eupatoria,* which Grieve reported, "was one of the most famous vulnerary herbs. The Anglo-Saxons, who called it Garclive, taught that it would heal wounds, snake bites, warts, etc. In the time of Chaucer, where we find its name appearing in the form of Egrimoyne, it was used with Mugwort and vinegar for a 'bad back' and 'alle woundes'; and one of these old writers recommends it to be taken with a mixture of pounded frogs and human blood, as a remedy for all internal hemorrhages."

## Silverweed

*Argentina anserina.* Silver; of geese. (Also found in Eurasia.)

*Argentine* (P.Q.), Crampweed, Dog's-Tansy, Goosegrass, Goose-Tansy, Marsh-Tansy, *Richette* (P.Q.), Silver-Feather, Wild-Tansy

Gerard (1633) called it Silverweed, Wild-Tansy and Argentina and listed its many virtues, "especially against the stone, inward wounds, and wounds of the privie or secret parts, and closeth up all greene and fresh wounds. The distilled water taketh away freckles, spots, pimples in the face and sunburning." The thickened root fibers have been an important foodstuff for many northern peoples. Grigson reported that, before the introduction of the potato, the plant was cultivated for its roots in Ireland and the Highlands and Islands of Scotland. "American Indians are very fond of them, raw or cooked. They are said to taste in the early spring like sweet potatoes or parsnips. The northwestern Indians make regular pilgrimages to gather the Potentilla roots" (Fernald and Kinsey, 1943).

*Silverweed*

Marie-Victorin wrote that "the popular French name 'Richette' is charming; the plant is rich: from its flowers it has gold, from the leaves' undersurface it has gold." It was also called Crampweed because the Shakers made a tea of the leaves as a remedy in diarrhea. "It is named in English wylde Tansey" (Turner, 1548). The leaves are like those of Tansy, *Tanacetium vulgare.* Goose-Tansy and Goosegrass are local names in England and Dog-Tansy is a Scottish name.

## Purple Marshlocks, Marsh-Cinquefoil

*Comarum palustris.* Strawberry (Greek *Komaros*); of marshes. (Also found in Eurasia.)

*Argentine rouge* (P.Q.), Bog-Strawberry, *Comaret* (P.Q.), Marsh Five-Finger, Meadow-Nuts, Purple Cinquefoil, Purplewort

## Dryad, White Mountain-Avens

*Dryas octopetala.* Of the Dryads (wood nymphs); eight-petaled. (Also found in Eurasia.)

Alpine-Avens, Alpine-Rose, White Dryas, Wild-Betony

"No plant so much needs an apt English name. In Co. Clare [Ireland] they have called it Wild Betony from the close resemblance of Betony leaves to Dryas leaves . . . A leaf of Dryas also resembles an oak leaf, so it was named after the dryad, the wood-nymph of the oaks. Really it requires a name suggestive of gold, whiteness, and open sunlight" (Grigson).

## Queen-of-the-Meadow, Meadowsweet

*Filipendula ulmaria.* Hanging thread (roots of *Filipendula hexa-petala*); elmlike (leaflets; the old generic name). (From Europe.)

Bittersweet, Bridewort, Dropwort (Pa.), Herb-Christopher, Honey-Sweet, Meadow-Queen, Meadow-Wort, My-Lady's-Belt, Sweet-Bay, Sweet-Hay, Tea-Bush (Pa.)

This was originally Meadsweet or Meadwort, perhaps referring to mead (honey wine),

which it was used to flavor. John Parkinson (1640) wrote that "because both flowers and herbes are of so pleasing a sweet scent, many do much delight therein, to have layd it in their chambers, parlars &c. and Queen Elizabeth, of famous memory, did more desire it than any sweet herb to strew her chambers withall." According to Culpeper, "it is called Dropwort, because it helps such as piss by drops." It was previously called *Spiraea ulmaria* and contains salicylic acid, which combined with acetic acid becomes acetylsalicylic acid or aspirin (a[cetyl] + spir[aea] + in). Meadow-Queen and Sweet-Hay are local names in England. Manasseh Cutler called it Queen of the Meadow. Queen-of-the-Prairie is *Filipendula rubra* ("red"), called Sweet-William in New York.

## Wood Strawberry

*Fragaria vesca.* (From the Latin name *fraga*); weak. (Also found in Europe.)

Common Strawberry, *Fraisier des champs* (P.Q.), *Fraisier sauvage* (P.Q.), *Fraisier à vaches* (P.Q.), Hedge Strawberry, Sheep-Nose (Vt.), Sowberry (Maine), Sow-Teat Strawberry, Sow-Tit (Vt.), Woodland Strawberry

This appears to be indigenous in Newfoundland and Eastern Quebec. A more slender variety, var. *americana,* is indigenous from Nova Scotia and inland south to New Mexico.

In 1643 Roger Williams wrote of New England that "this berry is the wonder of all the fruits growing naturaly in those parts: It is of it self excellent: so that one of the chiefest doctors of England was wont to say, that God could have made, but God never did make, a better berry. In some parts where the natives have planted, I have many times seen as many as would fill a good ship within a few miles compass: the Indians bruise them in a mortar, and mix them with meal and make Strawberry bread." The "chiefest doctor" is

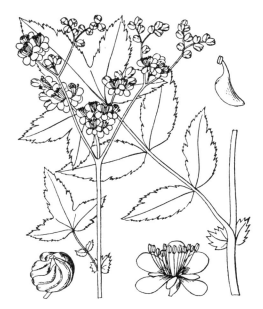

*Queen-of-the-Meadow*

*Wild Strawberry*

William Butler (1535–1618), an eminent but eccentric London physician, inventor of the medical drink called Dr. Butler's Ale. Izaac Walton (1653) quotes him thus: "Doubtless God could have made a better berry, but doubtless God never did."

## Wild Strawberry, Common Strawberry

*Fragaria virginiana.* (From the Latin name); of Virginia.
*Fraisier des champs* (P.Q.), *Fraisier sauvage* (P.Q.), Strawberry, Virginia Strawberry

The cultivated strawberry, *Fragaria ananassa,* is the offspring of this and Beach Strawberry *(Fragaria chiloensis),* an accidental hybridization that occurred in Holland in the l750s.

## Yellow Avens

*Geum aleppicum.* (The Latin name); of Aleppo. (Also found in Eurasia.)
*Benoîte* (P.Q.), Herb Bennet

In his *Account of Two Voyages to New-England* (1674), John Josselyn called it "Avens or herb-bennet" and wrote that "a neighbour of mine in hay-time, having overheat himself, and melted his grease, with striving to outmowe another man, fell dangerously sick, not being able to turn himself in his bed, his stomach gon, and his heart fainting ever and anon; to whom I administered the decoction of *Avens*-roots and leaves in water and wine, sweetning it with syrup of Clove-Gilliflowers; in one weeks time it recovered him, so that he was able to perform his daily work, being a poor planter or husbandman as we call them."

In Europe Herb Bennet is *Geum urbanum,* "called in English Avennes, in dutch Benedicten kraut" (Turner, 1548), from the Medieval Latin *herba benedicta,* the blessed herb whose spicy root protected the house from the Devil. Avens is from the Medieval Latin *avencia.*

## White Avens

*Geum canadense.* (The Latin name); of Canada.

American White Avens, Bennet, Black-Bur, Camproot, Cramproot, Chocolate-Root, Herb-Bennet, Redroot, Throatroot

Manasseh Cutler reported that, according to Dr. Withering, "the roots gathered in spring, before the stem grows up, and put into ale, give it a pleasant flavour, and prevent its going sour. Infused in wine it is a good stomachic. When it grows in warm dry situations, its taste is mildly austere and aromatic."

## Purple Avens, Water Avens

*Geum rivale.* (The Latin name); of river banks. (Also found in Eurasia.)
Bennet, Chocolate (Maine, N.H.), Chocolate-Plant (Maine), Chocolate-Root, Cureall, Drooping Avens, Evan's-Root, Indian-Chocolate, Maiden-Hair (Wis.), River Avens, Throatroot, Throatwort

*Purple Avens*

"Some use in the Spring time to put the root to steep for a time in wine, which giveth unto it a delicate favour and taste, which they drink fasting every morning, to comfort the heart, and to preserve it from noysome and infectious vapours of the plague" (Parkinson, 1640).

According to Dr. Millspaugh, "Geum at one time gained great renown as 'Indian Chocolate,'" given in decoction for most ailments of the digestive tract. Kalm (1749) reported that on the Mohawk River in New York both Indians and settlers used the powdered root, mixed with water or brandy, to treat malaria: "I was assured that this was one of the surest remedies, and more certain than Jesuit's bark." The roots also had a reputation as a cure for sore throats. "Any value they may possess can be attributed to the tannin which is present in large enough proportion to be perceptibly astringent" (USD).

## Long-Plumed Purple Avens, Prairie-Smoke

*Geum triflorum.* (The Latin name); three-flowered.

Apache-Plume, Johnny-Smokers (Ill.), Long-Plumed Avens, Old-Man's-Whiskers, Purple Avens, Three-Flowered-Avens, Torch-Flower

The long feathery hairs on the fruiting head suggest smoke, whiskers or feathers. "The large, bright pink rhizomes were used by the Thompson Indians both as a tea and, in stronger doses, as a tonic. A brew was made for use in the sweat-house as a body wash for aches and pains. Ripe seeds were crushed and used as perfume" (Ward-Harris).

## Golden-Hardhack, Shrubby Cinquefoil

*Pentaphylloides floribunda.* Little Pentaphyllon *(Potentilla);* freely blooming. (Also found in Eurasia.)

Hardhack (Mass.), Prairie-Weed, Widdy (Nfd.)

The leaves are brewed to make a tea. The Northern Cheyenne considered it a deadly arrow poison: "Leaves were made into a concoction, and the arrow tips were dipped into it; the poison was thought to go straight to the heart. The poison was also put into porcupine quills and was shot into the mouth. Only holy people could use it. At the time of Custer's battle with the Cheyenne and Sioux, a holy person, who was also the Keeper of the Sacred Hat, wished to use it against Custer, but the plant could not be found" (Hart, 1980).

## American Ipecac

*Porteranthus stipulatus.* Porter flower (Thomas Conrad Porter, 1822–1901, Pennsylvania botanist); stipuled.

Beaumont-Root, Bowman's-Root, Indian-Hippo, Indian-Physic, Injin-Physic (N.C.), Meadow-Sweet, Tulip-Tree, Western-Dropwort

Dr. Porcher reported that "it is emetic, and probably tonic, and is possessed of properties similar to those of [*P. trifoliatus*], though it is said to be more certain in its effects, and not to have been deteriorated by cultivation." It has been included in the USP.

## Bowman's-Root, Indian-Physic

*Porteranthus trifoliatus.* Porter flower; three-leaved.

American-Ipecac, Beaumont-Root, Dropwort, False Ipecac, Indian-Hippo, Ipecacuanha (Va.), Meadow-Sweet, Three-Leaved-Spiroea, Western-Dropwort

Eighteenth-century William Byrd of Westover called the plant Indian-Physic. In Virginia, 1732, he reported, "I found every body well at the Falls, blessed be God, tho' the bloody flux raged pretty much in the neighbourhood. Mr. Booker had receiv'd a letter from Mrs. Byrd, giving an account of great desolation made in our neighbourhood, by the death of Mr. Lightfoot, Mrs. Soan, Capt. Gerald and Colo. Henry Harrison. Finding the flux had been so fatal, I desired Mr. Booker to make use of the following remedy, in case it shou'd come amongst my people.

*Bowman's-Root*

To let them blood immediately about 8 ounces; the next day to give them a dose of Indian Physic, and to repeat the vomit again the day following, unless the symptoms abated. In the mean time, they shou'd eat nothing but chicken broth, and poacht eggs, and drink nothing but a quarter of a pint of milk boil'd with a quart of water, and medicated with a little Mullein root, or that of a Prickly Pear, to restore the mucus of the bowels, and heal the excoriation."

Dr. Barton (1798) concluded that "the active power of the root seems to reside exclusively in the bark. It is a safe and efficacious emetic, in doses of about thirty grains. Along with its emetic, it seems to possess a tonic power. It has accordingly been thought peculiarly beneficial in the intermittent fever, and it is often given to horses to mend their appetite. This plant has a number of different names, such as Ipecacuanha, Indian-Physic, Bowman's Root, &c." The origin of Bowman's- or Beaumont-Root is obscure. No pre-Revolutionary Dr. Beaumont appears to be involved, as some writers claim. Beaumont is perhaps derived from Bowman, which may be the man at the bow of a boat, or an Indian, the man with a bow, or bowman as a variant of batman, a military servant. Hippo is short for hippocras, a cordial originally made of wine and spices (Middle English *ypocras,* from the Latin *vinum Hippocrastum,* "wine of Hippocrates").

## Cinquefoils

*Potentilla.* Little powerful one (diminutive of *potens,* "powerful," originally applied to *Potentilla anserina*).

Five-Fingers, Starflower (Mass.)

"Quinquefolium is called in Greke Pentaphyllon, in English Cynkfoly, or Fyve Fyngered Grasse" (Turner, 1548).

## Rough-Fruited Cinquefoil

*Potentilla recta.* Little powerful one; upright. (From Europe.)

Septfoil, Sulphur Cinquefoil, Tormentil

"The ripest and largest dark-purple berries are just half an inch in diameter. You are surprised and delighted to see this handsome profusion in hollows so dry and usually so barren and bushes commonly so fruitless. The berries are peculiar in that the red are nearly as pleasant-tasted as the more fully ripe dark-purple ones" (Thoreau, 1860). Tormentil is the European *Potentilla erecta,* whose roots were given for colic (*tormina* in Latin); the plant known as American-Tormentil is Wild Geranium.

## Creeping Cinquefoil

*Potentilla reptans.* Little powerful one; creeping. (From Europe.)

Creeping-Jenny, Five-Fingers, Trailing-Tormentil, Wood Cinquefoil

Dioscorides called it *pentaphullon* (five fingers) and reported that "the decoction of the root being brought down to the third by

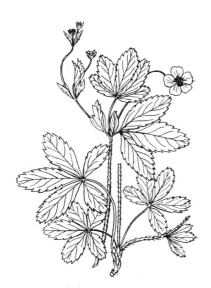

*Creeping Cinquefoil*

seething is of force being held in the mouth to assuage toothache, & it stays the rotten ulcers that are in the mouth." According to Culpeper, "this in an herb of Jupiter, and therefore strengthens the parts of the body it rules; let Jupiter be angular and strong when it is gather'd; and if you give but a scruple (which is but twenty grains) of it at a time, either in white-wine or whitewine vinegar, you shall very seldom miss the cure of an ague, be it what ague soever, in 3 fits, as I have ofen proved to the admiration both of my self and others; let no man despise it because it is plain and easy, the ways of God are all such."

## Common Cinquefoil

*Potentilla simplex.* Little powerful one; unbranched.

Decumbent Five-Finger, Old-Field-Cinquefoil

"It is mildly astringent and antiseptic. A decoction of it is used as a gargle for loose teeth and spungy gums" (Cutler, 1785).

## Roses

*Rosa.* (The Latin name).

On her visit to America in 1830, Frances Trollope wrote that the summer in Maryland was "delightful. The thermometer stood at 94, but the heat was by no means so oppressive as what we had felt in the West. In no part of North America are the natural productions of the soil more various, or more beautiful. Strawberries of the richest flavour sprung beneath our feet; and when these past away, every grove, every lane, every field looked like a cherry orchard, offering an inexhaustible profusion of fruit to all who would take the trouble to gather it. Then followed the peaches; every hedge-row was planted with them, and though the fruit did not equal in size or flavour those ripened on our garden walls, we found them good enough to afford a delicious refreshment on our long rambles. But it was the flowers, and the flowering shrubs that, beyond all else, rendered this region the most beautiful I had ever seen (the Alleghany always excepted). No description can give an idea of the variety, the profusion, the luxuriance of them. If I talk of wild roses, the English reader will fancy I mean the pale ephemeral blossoms of our bramble hedges; but the wild roses of Maryland and Virginia might be the choicest favourites of the flower-garden. They are rarely very double, but the brilliant eye atones for this. They are of all shades, from the deepest crimson to the tenderest pink. The scent is rich and delicate; in size they exceed any single roses I ever saw, often measuring above four inches in diameter. The leaf greatly resembles that of the china rose; it is large, dark, firm, and brilliant."

The Roses admired by Mrs. Trollope included the Smooth Rose, *Rosa blanda* ("mild" or thornless); Prairie Rose (Rose Blush in Missouri), *Rosa setigera* ("bristly"); Northeastern Rose, *Rosa nitida* ("shining"); Swamp Rose, *Rosa palustris* ("of swamps"); and the Pasture or Carolina Rose, *Rosa carolina*.

## Dog Rose

*Rosa canina*. (The Latin name); of dogs. (From Europe.)

Bedeguar, Bird-Brier, Bramble-Brier, Brere-Rose, Canker-Blooms, Cag-Whin, Dog-Thorn, Hedge-Peak, Horse-Bramble, Lawyers, Soldiers

Pliny the Elder wrote, "Down to recent years there has been no cure for the bite of a mad dog, a symptom of which is dread of water and aversion to drink of any kind. Recently the mother of a man serving in the praetorian guard saw in a dream how she was to send to her son, to be taken in drink, the root of the wild rose, called cynorrhodon, which had attracted her attention the day

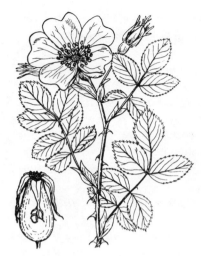

Dog Rose

before in the shrubbery. Operations were going on in Lacetania, the part of Spain nearest Italy, and by chance it happened that the soldier, after being bitten by a dog, was beginning to show a horror of water, when a letter arrived from his mother, begging him to obey the heavenly warning. So his life was unexpectedly saved, as was that of all who afterwards tried a similar remedy." So the Dog Rose (*kunorrhodon* in Greek) became the remedy for hydrophobia.

According to Manasseh Cutler, "the blossoms gathered before they expand, and dried, are astringent; but when full blown, are purgative. This species is generally preferred for conserves. A perfumed water may be distilled from the blossoms. The pulp of the berries, beat up with sugar, makes the conserve of hepps of the London dispensatory. The dried leaves of every species of rose have been recommended as a substitute for India tea, giving out a fine colour, a sub-astringent taste, and a grateful smell." The hips ("hepps") are full of vitamin C and a nutritious syrup is still made from them. The Dog Rose is also called Lawyers, "i.e., an old thorny stem" (Britton and Brown, 1913). Shakespeare called the flowers canker-blooms (Sonnet 65):

*O, how much more doth beauty beauteous seem*
*By that sweet ornament which truth doth give!*
*The Rose looks fair, but fairer we it deem*
*For that sweet odour which doth in it live.*
*The Canker-blooms have full as deep a dye*
*As the perfumed tincture of the Roses,*
*Hang on such thorns, and play as wantonly,*
*When summer's breath their masked buds discloses:*
*But—for their virtue only is their show—*
*They live unwoo'd, and unrespected fade;*
*Die to themselves. Sweet Roses do not so;*
*Of their sweet deaths are sweetest odours made:*
*And so of you, beauteous and lovely youth,*
*When that shall vade, my verse distills your truth.*

## Sweetbrier

*Rosa eglanteria.* (The Latin name); prickly (the old English name Eglantine is from the Old French *aiglantine,* from the Vulgar Latin *aguilentum,* "prickly"). (From Europe.)
Bedeguar, *Cébreur* (P.Q.), *Églantier* (P.Q.), Eglantine, Hip Brier, Hip Rose, Kitchen Rose, Primrose

"I think the blossom of the sweet-brier, now in prime,—eglantine,—is more delicate and interesting than that of the common roses, though smaller and paler and without their spicy fragrance; but its fragrance is in its leaves all summer, and the form of the bush is handsome, curving over from a considerable height in wreaths sprinkled with numerous flowers" (Thoreau, 1853). Bedeguar is the gall on roses made by the gall wasp; it has had many medicinal uses.

## Cloudberry, Bakeapple

*Rubus chamaemorus.* The Latin name, (from *ruber,* "red"); ground-mulberry (the old generic name). (Also found in Eurasia.)
Bake-Apple-Berry (N.B.), Baked-Apple, Baked-Apple-Berry, Baked-Apples (N.B.), *Blackbières* (P.Q.), *Chicoutés* (P.Q.), Dewater-Berry, Knotberry, Knoutberry, Molka, Mountain-Bramble, Mountain-Raspberry, Mulberry (N.H.), *Mûres blanches* (P.Q.), Outberry, *Plaquebières* (P.Q.), Salmon-Berry (Alaska), Yellowberry

The sweet yellow fruits taste of baked apples. "This species furnishes winter food to the western Eskimos, who collect the berries in autumn and preserve them by freezing. The fruit is also preserved by the Indians of Alaska. The Swedes and Norwegians preserve great quantities of the fruit in autumn to make tarts and other confections, and in Sweden,

*Cloudberry*

vinegar is made by fermenting the berries" (Sturtevant, 1919). Marie-Victorin wrote that the names Blackbières and Plaquebières are corruptions of *plat-de-bièvre,* "food for beavers."

## Northern Dewberry

*Rubus flagellaris.* (The Latin name); like a whip.

Bumblekites, Cloudberry-Root, Finger-Berry (N.Y.), *Ronce à flagelles* (P.Q.), Running Blackberry, Sow-teat Blackberry, Sow-Tit (Conn., N.H.), Thimble-berry (Mich., N.Y.)

Manasseh Cutler called it Sowteat and Bumblekites: "The fruit is pleasant to eat, and communicates a fine flavour to red wine. It is frequently infused in brandy and rum. The green twigs are said to be of great use in dying woollen, silk and mohair black." "Brambles are called Brumliekites in Cumberland," according to Canon Young (1945), "because children eat so many that their kites or bellies rumble." In *Song of Myself,* Walt Whitman wrote:

*I believe a leaf of grass is no less than
    the journeywork of the stars,
And the pismire is equally perfect, and
    a grain of sand, and the egg of the
    wren,
And the tree toad is a chef-d'oeuvre for
    the highest,
And the running blackberry would
    adorn the parlors of heaven*

## Purple-Flowering Raspberry

*Rubus odoratus.* (The Latin name); fragrant.
*Calottes* (P.Q.), *Chapeaux rouges* (P.Q.), Mulberry (Maine), Thimbleberry (N.Y., Vt., W.Va.), Virginia Raspberry

It was a valuable plant for the Cherokee Indians: "Chew root for cough; leaves highly astringent; decoction for bowel complaints;

*Purple-Flowering Raspberry*

wash for old and foul sores or ulcers; strong tea of red raspberry leaves for pains at childbirth; scratch rheumatism with thorny branch; ingredient in decoction for menstrual period; acts as emetic and purgative; tea drunk as tonic for boils; roots for toothache; fruit for food" (Hamel and Chiltoskey, 1975).

## Canadian Burnet

*Sanguisorba canadensis.* Blood absorber (supposed medicinal value of the official Burnet); of Canada.
American Burnet, *Herbe à pisser* (P.Q.), *Pimprenelle du canada* (P.Q.), Snakeweed

Burnet is from the Old French *burnette, brunette* (dark brown). It had a reputation as a diuretic.

## European Great Burnet

*Sanguisorba officinalis.* Blood absorber; officinal. (From Europe.)
Burnet-Bloodwort, Pimpernel

"The greatest use that Burnet is commonly put unto, is to put a few leaves into a cup with Claret wine, which is presently to be drunke, and giveth a pleasant quick taste thereunto, very delightful to the palate, and is accounted a help to make the heart merrie" (Parkinson, 1629). The leaves taste of cucumber, and the plant is still cultivated for salads. Pimpernel, from Old French *pimpernelle,* Latin *piperinus* (pepperlike), alluding to Burnet's fruit, was the old English name of Burnet (*pimpinella* in Italian, *pimpinela* in Spanish). Unaccountably, in English the name was transferred to *Anagallis arvensis* (Scarlet Pimpernel). John Evelyn (1699) wrote that "Pimpernel, *Pimpinella*; eaten by the French and Italians, is our common Burnet; of so chearing and exhilarating a quality, and so generally commended, as (giving it admittance into all sallets) 'tis passed into a proverb:

*L'Insalata non e buon, ne bella
Dove non e la Pimpinella.
[Salad is neither good nor beautiful
Where there is no pimpernella.]*

But a fresh sprig in Wine, recommends it to us as its most genuine element."

## Meadowsweet, Quaker-Lady

*Spiraea alba.* (From the Greek *speiraira,* a plant used for garlands); white.

*Bois d'inde* (P.Q.), Bridal-Wreath, Bridewort, Dead-Man's-Flower (Nfd.), Meadwort, Queen-of-the-Meadow (N.Y.), Spice-Hardhack (N.B.), Teaweed (Vt.), *Thé du Canada* (P.Q.)

July 16: "The meadow-sweet is now in bloom, and the yarrow prevails by all roadsides. I see the hardhack too, homely but dear plant, just opening its red clustered flowers" (Thoreau, 1851). An infusion of Meadowsweet leaves tastes like China tea and was esteemed as a restorative tonic. It has been called Dead-Man's-Flower because Newfoundland children believe that if you pick the flower, your father will die.

## Hardhack, Steeplebush

*Spiraea tomentosa.* (From the Greek *Speiraira*); downy.

Horseweed, Iron-Bush (Maine), Meadowsweet, Poor-Man's-Soap, Purple Hardhack, *Reine des prés* (P.Q.), Rosy-Bush, Silverleaf, Silverweed, Spice-Hardhack, Teaweed (Vt.), *Thé du Canada* (P.Q.), Wire-Bush (Maine)

Rafinesque reported that "the whole plant is inodorous, but the taste is pleasantly bitter and powerfully astringent. It contains tannin, gallic acid, bitter extractive &c. all soluble in water. Formerly used by the Mohegan tribe of Indians and the herbalists . . . The Honskokaogacha of the Osage Indians is probably this shrub; they use the dry root and stem as a powerful styptic and astringent, to stop bleeding and hemoptysis." In Maine, "Spiraea tomentosa, used as a country remedy for dysentry, had no name but 'Wire-bush' " (Perkins, 1929). It has been included in the USD: "The decoction of the flowers was at one time used as a diuretic in domestic practice. The roots are astringent, and have been used in the treatment of diarrhea." Hardhack means "hard to cut."

*Hardhack*

# THE PEA OR BEAN FAMILY

## *Fabaceae or Papilionaceae*

A widespread family of 495 genera and 14,400 species of herbs, shrubs, vines and trees; found in temperate, cold and tropical regions. The family is of major economic importance, providing numerous edible beans and peas, forage for grazing animals (Clover, Lucerne), ornamentals (Broom, Wisteria, Lupin, Sweet Pea) and dyes (indigo, for example).

## Leadplant, False Indigo

*Amorpha canescens.* Deformed (Greek *amorphos*; for the absence of four of the petals); grayish-pubescent.
False Indigo, Leadwort, Prairie-Shoestring, Shoestrings (Ill., Minn., S.Dak.), Wild-Tea

The Omaha-Ponca name of the plant was "buffalo bellow plant," according to Gilmore (1914). "The name is derived from the fact that its time of blooming is synchronous with the rutting season of the buffalo, being at that season the dominant blooming plant on the prairie of the loess plain. The stems were used by the Omaha for a moxa in cases of neuralgia and rheumatism. The small stems, broken in short pieces, were attached to the skin by moistening one end with the tongue. Then they were fired and allowed to burn down to the skin. An Oglala said the leaves were sometimes used to make a hot drink like tea, and sometimes for smoking material." It was once thought that the plant indicated the presence of lead. Shoestrings describes the long tough roots.

## Hog-Peanut

*Amphicarpea bracteata.* Both kinds of fruit (i.e., pods from the clusters of flowers in the leaf axils and often underground pods from the petalless flowers at the base); bracted.
American-Licorice, Hog-Pea (N.C.), Goober (South), Peavine, Wild Bean-Vine, Wild-Peanut

"The Hog Peanut was a very important food plant among the American Indians, especially those of the Missouri valley. The women in autumn and early winter robbed the nests of white-footed mice and other rodents, securing 'big piles of them.' The Dakota Nations when taking seeds from the nests of animals left corn or other food in exchange" (Medsger, 1939). Fernald and Kinsey reported that, "when boiled and properly seasoned with salt and pepper and dressed with butter or cream, they are not unlike the shelled beans from the garden." Goober, from the Angolese *nguba*, is a Peanut *(Arachis hypogaea).*

## Groundnut

*Apios americana.* Pear (Greek, for the shape of the tuberous enlargements, the nuts, on the rootstock); of America.

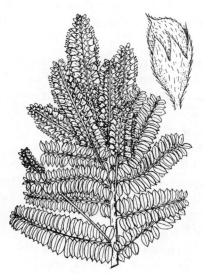

*Leadplant*

Chocolate (Maine), Cinnamon-Vine, Dacotah-Potato, Dakota-Potato (Minn.), Glycine, Ground-Pea, Hopnis (N.J.), Indian-Bean (N.J.), Indian-Potato, Micmac-Potato, *Patates en chapelet* (P.Q.), *Pénacs* (P.Q.), Pig Potato, Potato-Bean, Potato-Pea, Rabbit-Vine (S.C.), Trailing-Pea, Traveler's-Delight (Miss.), Tuberous-Wisteria, White-Apples, Wild-Bean (N.B.), Wild-Wisteria

In his *A briefe and true report of the new found land of Virginia* (1590), Thomas Harriot included *Openauk,* "a kind of roots of round forme, some of the bignes of walnuts, some far greater, which are found in moist & marish grounds growing many together one by another in ropes, or as thogh they were fastened with a string. Being boiled or sodden they are very good meate." In New Jersey, 1749, "Hopnis or Hapnis was the Indian name of a wild plant," according to Kalm, whose "roots resemble potatoes, and are boiled by the Indians, who eat them instead of bread."

"*Apios tuberosa* on the banks of streams and in alluvial bottoms is the true *pomme de terre* of the French and the modo or wild potato of the Sioux Indians, and is extensively used as an article of diet," according to the 1870 annual report of the U.S. Commissioner of Agriculture (Gilmore, 1914). During the Pilgrims' first hard winter in Massachusetts, they were sustained by eating the nutritious groundnuts. Attempts have been made both here and in Europe to cultivate the plant as a food crop but without much success. The "peas" in the pods are also edible. The plant is called Chocolate for the color of the flower, a brownish purple or cinnamon. *Glycine tuberosa* was a former name. *Glycine max* is the Soybean. Mic-mac is an Indian name.

## Milk-Vetch

*Astragalus canadensis.* (The Greek name of a legume); of Canada.

"When ripe, the stalks with their persistent pods were used by small boys as rattles in the games in which they imitated the tribal dances, hence the Omaha-Ponca name signifing 'rattle'. . . A decoction of the root was used among the Teton Dakota as a febrifuge for children" (Gilmore, 1914). Milk-Vetches had a reputation for increasing a cow's or goat's milk yield.

## Ground-Plum, Buffalo-Bean, Indian-Pea

*Astragalus crassicarpus.* (The Greek name of a legume); thick-fruited.
Buffalo-Apple, Buffalo-Pea

"The unripe seed pods, which resemble green plums, are used for food raw or cooked. When cooked, they are usually prepared and served in the same manner as the garden sugar pea where the entire pod is eaten," Oliver Medsger wrote. "In Lewis and Clark's westward journey in 1804, when in the region of South Dakota, they exchanged presents with the Indians. They record among the

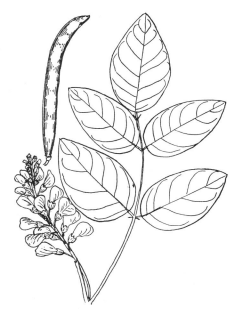

*Groundnut*

things received a quantity of a large, rich bean which grew wild and was collected by mice. The Indians hunted for these deposits, collected the beans, and cooked and ate them. The mice referred to were without doubt prairie dogs, then practically unknown, and the bean is Buffalo Pea."

## Woolly Locoweed, Crazyweed, Poison-Vetch

*Astragalus mollissimus.* (The Greek name of a legume); most soft (the dense hairy covering).

Garbanzilla, Texas Locoweed

Of the hundreds of species of *Astragalus* and *Oxytropis* (see below) in North America, several are poisonous to grazing livestock and are known as Poison-Vetches, Locoweeds or Crazyweeds. Kingsbury (1964) reports that a disease of stock called loco had been recognized long before it first received formal

attention by the U.S. Commissioner of Agriculture in 1873: "It is now known to occur in the Rocky Mountain states westward, south into Texas and Mexico, and north into British Columbia. The name derives from the Spanish word for crazy and is applied because of the characteristic symptoms. Plants causing loco in horses, cattle, sheep and goats on range constitute one of the most serious sources of domestic livestock loss." Some grazing animals develop a craving for locoweeds (they are known as "locoed") and have to be moved to ranges where Locoweeds are absent.

## Pursh's Sheeppod

*Astragalus purshii.* (The Greek name of a legume); of Pursh (Frederick Pursh, 1774–1820).

Locoweed, Milkvetch

James Teit (1930) reported that among the Thompson Indians "the flowers and leaves on the stems are tied in a bunch and used for bringing back the luck of fishing nets, traps, snares, guns, or any other such devices which have been contaminated by a widower touching or using them."

Friedrich Traugott Pursch, who changed his name to Frederick Pursh, was born in Saxony and died in Montreal. He worked at the Royal Botanical Garden in Dresden and then came to America in 1799 to manage a garden near Baltimore. Under the patronage of Benjamin Smith Barton, he made botanical excursions to Maryland, Virginia, the Carolinas, Pennsylvania and New York. He was chosen to classify the plants collected on the Lewis and Clark expedition, for which he went to London and published there the two volumes of *Flora Americae Septentrionalis.* He then traveled to Canada and worked for 12 years preparing a flora of Canada, but all his work was destroyed in a fire and he died virtually destitute.

*Woolly Locoweed*

*Wild-Indigo*

## Wild-Indigo

*Baptisia tinctoria.* Dye plant (from the Greek *baptistis,* "dyer"); used for dyeing.

Clover-Broom, Dyer's-Baptisia (N.C.), False Indigo, Horse-Fleaweed, Horsefly-Weed, Indigo-Broom, Indigo-Weed (Mass.), Shoofly (W.Va.), Rattlebush, Rattleweed, Yellow-Broom, Yellow-Indigo

"The Creek Indians boiled *Baptisia* roots in water and administered the decocotion externally and internally to children who seemed drowsy and lifeless and on the point of becoming sick. The Mohegans steeped the root and used it to bathe cuts and wounds" (Vogel, 1970). Dr. Millspaugh reported that "the young shoots of this plant resemble in form and general appearance those of asparagus and are used, especially in New England, in lieu of that herb for a pottage. As a dye, it is no longer used, being far inferior to Indigofera and its employment unnecessary. The most important previous use of the plant as a drug was as an 'antiseptic' dressing for gangrerous wounds, especially in such cases as were accompanied by a low form of fever; and in decoction in putrid fevers generally."

Thoreau wrote (1850), "I do not know whether the practice of putting indigo-weed

about horse's tackling to keep off flies is well founded, but I hope it is, for I have been pleased to notice that wherever I have occasion to tie a horse I am sure to find indigo-weed not far off, and therefore this, which is so universally dispersed, would be the fittest weed for this purpose." The seeds in the dry pod rattle—"a distinct rattling din,—like a small Indian's calabash," according to Thoreau (1860). The plant has been included in the USP and NF.

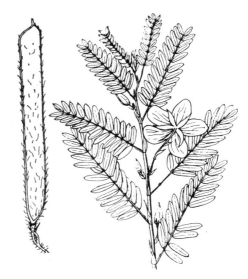

*Partridge-Pea*

## Partridge-Pea

*Chamaecrista fasciculata.* Low crest; in bunches.

Dwarf Cassia, Golden Cassia, Large-Flowered Sensitive-Pea, Maggoty-Boy-Bean (N.Y.), Locust-Weed, Prairie-Senna, Sleeping-Plant

It is called "Magothy-bay bean" in Darlington's *Agricultural Botany* of 1847, perhaps referring to the Magothy River in Maryland.

## Butterfly-Pea

*Clitoria mariana.* Clitoris (the shape of the flower); of Maryland.

Clabber-Spoon, Partridge-Pea (N.C.), Pigeon-Wings

*Butterfly-Pea*

Paul Fantz reports (1991) that "peoples in widely dispersed geographical areas reportedly use different species of *Clitoria* medicinally as a treatment to enhance fertility, to control menstrual discharge, to treat gonorrhea, and as a sexual stimulant. These peoples may follow an ancient principle called the Doctrine of Signatures, a belief that plant structures that resemble portions of the human body have been so structured by a creator as to indicate their ability to provide remedies or ailments for those body portions."

## Crown-Vetch

*Coronilla varia.* Small crown (the inflorescence); variable. (From Europe.)
Axseed, Axwort, Hive-Vine

"The seed of Axwoort openeth the stoppings of the liver, the obstruction of the spleen, and of all the inward parts" (Gerard, 1633); he also called it Axseed—the pods are shaped like an axehead.

## Rattlebox

*Crotalaria sagittalis.* Like a rattle; arrowlike (stipules).

Coffee-Peas, Crazy-Weed, Locoweed (Nebr.), Rattlebox (Iowa), Rattleweed, Rattlesnake-Weed (Ohio), Socoweed, Wild-Pea (Iowa)

The poisonous seeds, if boiled or roasted long enough, make a tasty substitute for coffee. "I detect the crotalaria behind the Wyman site, by hearing the now rattling seeds in its pods as I go through the grass, like trinkets about an Indian's leggings, or a rattlesnake" (Thoreau, 1856).

## Broom

*Cytisus scoparius.* (The Greek name of a legume); broomlike (Latin *scopa*, "broom"). (From Europe.)
Bannal, Besom, Broomflowers, Broomtops (N.C.), Ginster, Green Broom, Hagweed, Hayweed, Indian-Sage (Va.), Irish Broom, Scotch-Bloom (Wash.), Scotch Broom

The plant was famous for its magical and amorous virtues; as medicine—"That worthy Prince of famous memorie Henrie 8, King of England, was woont to drinke the distilled water of Broome floures against surfets and diseases thereof arising"; and as food—"the young buds of the floures are to be gathered and laid in pickle or salt, which afterwards being washed or boyled are used for sallads,

*Broom*

as capers be, and be eaten with no lesse delight" (Gerard, l633). The Old English name of the plant was *brom,* whence broom—a brush or besom made of this plant or Genista. Its name was once Planta Genista, the badge of the Angevin kings of England, who became known as the Plantagenets. Bannal is presumably an Americanization of the Cornish and Welsh name Bannadle, and Scotch-Bloom is a "very common error" in Washington State (McAtee, 1942). It has been included in the USP and NF, and the USD notes, "Scoparius is diuretic and cathartic, and in large doses emetic, and has been employed in dropsy."

## Tick-Trefoil

*Desmodium canadense.* Chain (Greek *desmos,* for the jointed stamens or pods); of Canada.

Beggar's-Lice (Mass.), Beggar-Ticks, Devil's-Thistle (Maine), Sainfoin, Showy Tick-Trefoil, Tick-Clover

"There is something witch-like about them; though so rare and remote, yet evidently, from those bur-like pods, expecting to come in contact with some travelling man or beast without their knowledge, to be transported to new hillsides; lying in wait, as it were, to catch by the hem of the berry-picker's garments and so get a lift to new quarters" (Thoreau, 1856).

## Dyer's-Greenweed

*Genista tinctoria.* (The Latin name, perhaps from Celtic *gen,* a bush used for dyeing); of dyers. (From Europe.)

Alleluia, Base-Broom, Dyer's-Broom, Dyer's-Weed, Dyer's-Whin, Dyeweed, Greenweed, Greenwood, Whin, Woad-Wax, Wood-Wash, Woodwax (Mass.), Woodwaxen

It is called Greenweed because the yellow dye this plant produces was mixed with the blue of Woad *(Isatis tinctoria)* to make a green dye. It was introduced to Massachusetts in the l630s: "The little yellow broom, *Genista tinctoria,* which no good farmer loves today,

*Dyer's-Greenweed*

was called 'witches blood' in Salem because it bloomed on Gallows Hill; but it was brought originally as a dye plant for 'sad' or sober colors" (Leighton, 1970). Josselyn (1672) wrote of Wood-wax "wherewith they dye many pretty Colours." Manasseh Cutler called it Greenwood, Dyer's Weed and Wood Waxen. Wood-wax or Woodwaxen is derived from the Old English *wuduweaxe* (*wudu,* "wood," *weaxe,* "to grow"); its association with Woad explains the common spelling of Woadwax both here and in the British Isles. Alleluia (see *Oxalis montana*) is a local name in England. Whin is Gorse *(Ulex).*

## Wild Licorice

*Glycyrrhiza lepidota.* Sweet root; scaly.

American Licorice, Licorice-Root (Calif.), Sweetroot, Sweetwood

In the Pacific Northwest, 1806: "The liquorice of this country does not differ from that common to the United States. It here delights in deep, loose, sandy soil, and grows very large and abundantly. It is prepared by roasting in the embers, and pounding it slightly with a small stick in order to separate the

*Wild Licorice*

strong ligament in the center of the root, which is then thrown away and the rest chewed and swallowed. In this way it has an agreeable flavour, not unlike that of the sweet potato" (Lewis & Clark). The Teton Dakota made a poultice for a horse's sore back by chewing the leaves, and "for toothache the sufferer chews the root and holds it in the mouth" (Gilmore, 1914).

Commercial licorice is made from the root of the European *Glycyrrhiza glabra.*

## Wild-Peas

*Lathyrus.* From the Greek name of a pea, *lathyros.*

Everlasting-Pea, *Gesse* (P.Q.), Vetchling

Many species are cultivated for fodder. *Lathyrus odoratus* is the Sweet-Pea of the garden.

## Beach-Pea

*Lathyrus japonicus.* (From the Greek name of a pea); of Japan. (Also found in Japan and Chile.)

*Pois de mer* (P.Q.), Sea-Pea, Seaside Everlasting-Pea, Seaside-Pea

Captain Thomas James, after whom James Bay is named, wrote of the spring of 1632 there: "Here I am to remember God's goodness towards us in sending those aforementioned green vetches. For now our feeble sick men that could not for their lives stir these two or three months [they had scurvy], can endure the air and walk about the house; our other sick men gathered strength also, and it is wonderful to see how soon they were recovered. We used them in this manner: Twice a day we went to gather the herb or leaf of these vetches as they first appeared out of the ground; then did we wash and boil them, and so with oil and vinegar that had been frozen, we did eat them. It was an excellent sustenance and refreshing; the most part of us ate nothing else."

The Cape Cod oysterman "liked the beach-pea . . . cooked green, as well as the cultivated. He had seen it growing abundantly in Newfoundland, where also the inhabitants ate them" (Thoreau, 1864).

## Birdfoot Trefoil

*Lotus corniculatus.* (From the Greek name, *lotos,* of several legumes); horned. (From Europe.)

Bastard-Indigo, Bird's-Eye, Bloom-Fell, Cat's-Clover, Claver, Cross-Toes, Crowtoes, Devil's-Fingers, Ground-Honeysuckle, Ladies'-Fingers, Lady's-Fingers-and-Thumbs, Lady's-Slipper, Sheepfoot, Shoes-and-Stockings

"Coronopus is a little herb, somewhat long, spreading upon the ground, having leaves indented; & this is also eaten as a pot herb, being sod; having a thinne roote, binding, which being eaten is good for the coeliaci" (Dioscorides). Most of the above are local names from England and Ireland, and Bloom-Fell is from Scotland. This plant has over 70 names in the British Isles, many referring to the bunch of hooked pods, seen as a Bird's-Claw or the Devil's-Fingers or a Witch's-Toe-nails, or, in contrast, God-Almighty's-Flower and Our-Lady's-Fingers.

## Wild Lupine, Sundial Lupin

*Lupinus perennis.* Wolfish (it was believed to destroy the soil); perennial.

Monkey-Faces (Ohio), Old-Maid's-Bonnets (Long Island, Mass.), Quaker-Bonnets, Sandflat-Sweet-Pea (Texas), Wild-Pea (Mass., Vt.)

"It paints a whole hillside with its blue, making such a field (if not a meadow), as Proserpine might have wandered in. Its leaf was made to be covered with dewdrops. I am quite excited by this prospect of blue flowers in clumps with narrow intervals. Such a profusion of the heavenly, the elysian color, as if these were the Elysian Fields. They say the seeds look like babies' faces, and hence the flower is so named" (Thoreau, 1852). Proserpine, gathering flowers in the Vale of Enna, was carried off by Pluto and made queen of the lower world. The baby-face name appears to be lost; it is seen as a monkey face in Ohio.

"Americans know the Lupines as popular garden subjects or (especially in the West) as among the most attractive of wild flowers. In the old world, they were cultivated by the ancient Egyptians as food, and in the Mediterranean region have continued to serve as such to the present day. The beans tend to be bitter but they are very nourishing and extremely rich in protein. Pliny says that no food is more wholesome or easier to digest; also that they produce a cheerful countenance and a fresh complexion" (Krutch, 1976).

## Alfalfa, Lucerne, Medick

*Medicago sativa.* Alfalfa (from Greek *medike,* perhaps because it came from Media [Persia]); sown. (From Asia.)

Brazilian-Clover, Burgundy-Clover, Burgundy-Trefoil, Chilean-Clover, Great-Trefoil, Holy-Hay, *Lentine* (P.Q.), *Luzerne* (P.Q.), Mail-Clover, Purple Medick, Sainfoin, Snail-Clover, Snail-Flower, Spanish Medick, Spanish-Trefoil

This is an important fodder crop. Alfalfa comes from the Arabic name, via the Spanish. Lucerne is ultimately derived from the Provençal *luzerno* (glowworm) for the shiny seeds. Dioscorides described the seed of Medice as "of the bigness of a lentil wreathed about as a little horn; which being dried, is mixed for its sweet savour's sake to salt sauces. Being laid on whilst it is green, it is good for whatsoever hath need of cooling, but they which breed beasts use the whole herb instead of grass."

## Melilot, White Sweet-Clover

*Melilotus alba.* Honey plant; white. (From Europe.)

Bokhara-Clover, Cabul-Clover, Honey, Honey-Clover (Mo.), Honey-Lotus, Sweet-Lucerne, Sweet Melilot, Trebol (Texas), Tree-Clover, White Melilot, White-Millet, *Vieux garçons* (P.Q.)

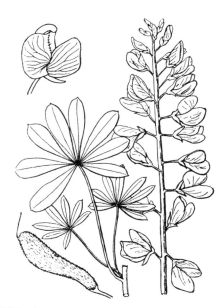

*Wild Lupine*

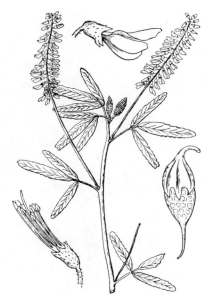

*Melilot*

The sweet scent of dried Sweet-Clover is that of coumarin, a fragrant organic compound also present in Bedstraws *(Galium)* and Sweet Woodruff. Research on a severe hemorrhagic disease of cattle, called sweet-clover poisoning, the result of eating moldy Sweet-Clover hay or silage, led to the development of the important anticlotting agent dicoumarin (which is the Guianan name of the Tonka Bean) and the rodenticide warfarin.

## Yellow Sweet-Clover

*Melilotus officinalis.* Honey plant; officinal. (From Europe.)

Balsam-Flowers, Hart's-Clover, Heartwort, King's-Clover, King's-Crown, Moonseed, Plaster-Clover, Sweet-Lucerne, *Trefle d'odeur* (P.Q.), Yellow Melilot, Yellow-Millet

King's-Clover or *Corona Regis,* King's-Crown, was the name given it by the herbalists and apothecaries who used it to make the popular Melilot Plaster. Gerard (1633) called it Melilot, Harts-Claver and Plaister Claver, for

"with the juice hereof, oile, wax, rosen and turpentine, is made a most soveraigne healing and drawing emplaster, called Melilote plaister," which "doth asswage and soften all manner of swellings, especially about the matrix, fundament and genitories, being applied unto those places hot." Dr. Millspaugh reported that "the flowers of the Melilots have been extensively used by the laity, boiled with lard, as a salve for ulcers, open indolent sores and broken breasts with much success."

## Stemless Loco, Purple Loco, Crazyweed

*Oxytropis lambertii.* Sharp keel (the beak at the tip of the two lowest petals); of Lambert (Aylmer Bourke Lambert, 1761–1842, English botanist).

Colorado Loco-Vetch, Rattleweed

"Normally, Crazyweed is unpalatable to livestock; cattle, horses, and sheep, however, eat it freely when palatable forage is scarce or absent," according to the *Range Plant Handbook.* "Among domesticated animals

*Stemless Loco*

probably horses are most seriously affected. In the early stages of loco poisoning, identification of a locoed horse is difficult, as the animal may appear normal except for occasional crazy spells. Locoed horses are usually hard to handle; they cannot be led or backed and can be stopped or turned only with difficulty; occasionally they leap over small pebbles in the road or try to step over a sizable stream."

## Silver Scurfpea

*Pediomelum argophylla.* Plains apple; silver-leaved.

Devil's-Turnip (Mont.), False-Turnip, Silver-Leaf Psoralea

According to Jeffrey Hart (1980), the following story explains why the Northern Cheyenne call the plant Devil's-Turnip: "A long time ago, some maidens went looking for wild turnips *(Psoralea esculenta)*. Whenever they thought they had found one, it turned out to be a false one. Finally, when they were far from camp, a medicine man from the village, realizing that the girls were being led away by the devil in the form of this plant, warned some of the people who then went to rescue the girls." *Psoralea* was the previous generic name of this and the next plant.

## Breadroot

*Pediomelum esculentum.* Plains apple; edible.

Cree-Potato, Cree-Turnip, Dakota-Tipsinna (S.Dak.), Dakota-Turnip (Minn.), Indian-Breadroot, Indian-Turnip, Missouri-Breadroot, *Navet de prairie* (Minn.), *Pomme blanche, Pomme de prairie,* Prairie-Apple, Prairie-Potato, Prairie-Turnip, Scurf-Pea, Tipsin (S.Dak.), Tipsinna (S.Dak)

The plant "has so important a place in the economy of the Plains tribes and has had for so long a time that it enters into their mythology, folklore, stories and sleight-of-hand

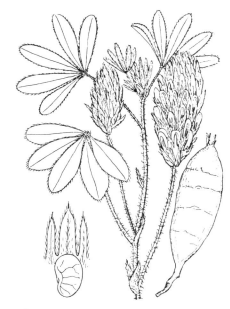

*Breadroot*

tricks" (Gilmore, 1914). The starchy root-tuber is tasty and nutritious and was eaten raw or boiled or roasted over an open fire or in the coals; for winter use it was sliced, dried and then ground into a meal. Father de Smet in South Dakota, 1868: "The plains are covered with a short but very nutritious grass called buffalo grass, which will some day serve to support and fatten numberless domestic herds. Everywhere the *pomme blanche* is found in abundance—a kind of wild potato, which Providence has sown here in profusion for the maintenance of its poor children of the desert. When an Indian is pressed by hunger, he has only to dismount from his horse, and armed with a little pointed stick of hard wood, which he always carries when traveling, he will pull out roots enough in ten minutes to satisfy him for the moment." The Dakota name is *tipsin* or *tipsinna.* This is the *Pomme blanche* or *Pomme de prairie* of the Canadian voyageurs across the prairies.

## Wild Senna

*Senna marilandica*. (The Latin name, from Arabic *sanā'* ); of Maryland.

American Senna, Locust-Plant, Teaweed, Wild-Indigo (Kans.), Wild Sensitive-Plant

Dr. Porcher reported that, as a cathartic, it was "as safe and as certain in its operation as the imported senna, but more apt to gripe; this may be corrected by infusing fennel seed or some other aromatic with leaves. It is prepared in large quantities by the Shakers." Dr. Bigelow concluded that it was milder than the "true Alexandrian Senna, which will prevent it from superseding the Senna of the shops, although the facility which it may be raised in any part of the United States, will render it a convenient medicine where cheapness is an object." It has been included in the USP. The dried leaves of *Cassia acutifolia* or *Cassia angustifolia* of the Middle East are the source of the commercial laxative.

## Coffee Senna

*Senna occidentalis*. (The Latin name); of the west. (From the tropics.)

Coffee-Weed (La.), Florida-Coffee (N.C.), Magdad-Coffee, Negro-Weed, Nigger-Coffee (South), Stinking-Weed, Styptic-Weed

"Once thought to be very valuable as a substitute for coffee," Dr. Porcher wrote, and the "Negroes apply the leaves, smeared with grease, as a dressing for sores." The plant is toxic to grazing animals.

## Goat's-Rue

*Tephrosia virginiana*. Ash color; of Virginia.

Catgut, Devil's-Shoestrings, Hoary-Pea, Rabbit-Pea, Turkey-Pea, Wild-Pea (Mo.), Wild-Sweet-Pea

The plant smells of goat. Toxic to grazing animals, the seeds are eaten by birds and esteemed by turkeys. The tough rootstock (like catgut or shoestrings) is a source of the insecticide rotenone and was used by Indians to poison and catch fish, and "employed in popular practice as a vermifuge" (Porcher).

## Clover

*Trifolium*. Three leaves (the Latin name).

"Many kinds of clover grow in great profusion in the limy soils of the West, and as a class they are considered excellent forage for all kinds of animals. In other parts of the world some of them have been occasionally eaten for food by man. In Ireland, for example, the dried flowers and seed heads of the common white or Dutch clover have in times of famine been ground into flour and converted into bread, and in the Eastern and Southern States the poorer Negro families occasionally eat one or two species with vinegar as a salad. With the Indians of Mendocino County [California], and especially of Round Valley, however, clover enters into their diet as an essential element even at the present time. The fresh green foliage taken before flowering is the part most generally eaten, but the flowers of three or four species and the seeds of one or two are also used. After flowering the leaves are apt to be tough and bitter. From the beginning of April along into July it is no uncommon sight to see small groups of Indians wallowing in the clover and eating it by handfuls, or to see an Indian squaw emerging from a patch of clover and carrying a red bandana handkerchief full of the crisp stems" (Chesnut, 1902).

## Rabbit-Foot Clover

*Trifolium arvense*. Three leaves; of cultivated fields. (From Europe.)

Bottlegrass (Mass.), Calf-Clover (Long Island), Dogs-and-Cats, Hare's-Foot-Clover, Old-Field-Clover, Poverty-Grass, Puss Clover (Mass.), Pussies (Long Island, Mass.), Pussy (Mass.), Pussy-Cats (Long Is-

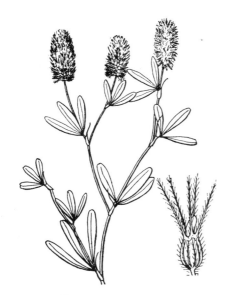

*Rabbit-Foot Clover*

land, Mass.), Pussy Clover, Pussy-Foot Clover (Maine), Stone Clover

It "groweth much among the corne, it hath a rough toppe lyke Doune, and leaves like Claver, wherefore it maye be named in Englishe rough Trifoly or Harefoote; the Duch men call it, Katzenklee" (Turner, 1548). Dogs-and-Cats is a local name in Scotland. Unlike most Clovers, this one is worthless as fodder, a Poverty-Grass.

## Least Hop-Clover, Shamrock

*Trifolium dubium.* Three leaves; doubtful. (From Europe.)

Least Hop-Trefoil, Yellow-Suckling, Yellow Trefoil, Wild Trefoil

Shamrock is from the Irish *seamrog,* a diminutive of *seamar,* "clover." In Ireland and Scotland, the plant was a potent charm against witches and fairies long before it was christianized as Saint Patrick's symbol of the Trinity. Other plants that have been called shamrock and sold as such include Wood Sorrel *(Oxalis acetosella),* Black Medick *(Med-*

*icago lupulina)* and even Red and White Clover (*T. pratense* and *T. repens*).

## Crimson Clover

*Trifolium incarnatum.* Three leaves; blood-red. (From Europe.)

Carnation Clover, French Clover, Italian Clover, Napoleons

Napoleon here is supposed to be a corruption of Trifolium, "but it looks like a deliberate 'corruption,' the bloody Frenchman of battles" (Grigson). Another name in England is Bloody-Triumph.

## Red Clover

*Trifolium pratense.* Three leaves; of meadows. (From Europe.)

Broad-Leaved Clover, Cowgrass, Cleaver-Grass, Honeysuckle Clover, Knap, Marlgrass, Meadow Clover, Purple Clover, Purplewort, Real Sweet Clover (Maine, Mass.), Suckles, Sugar-Plums

"The medow Trefoile (especially that with the blacke half moon upon the leafe) stamped with a little honie, takes away the pin and web in the eies, ceasing the pain and inflammation thereof, if it be strained and dropped therein" (Gerard, 1633). Most of the above are local names in England and Scotland. The plant is called Honeysuckle and Suckles because honey can be sucked from the flowers. It has been included in the NF, and the USD states "the eclectics attributed to clover antispasmodic and expectorant properties and employed it in the treatment of whooping cough and bronchitis." This is the state flower of Vermont.

## White Clover

*Trifolium repens.* Three leaves; creeping. (From Europe.)

Dutch Clover, Honeystalks, Honeysuckle (Maine), Honeysuckle Clover (Maine), Lamb-Sucklings, Purplegrass, Purplewort, Shamrock, Sheep's-Gowan, White Trefoil

This is the common clover of lawns and rich pastures and a sweet forage for sheep and cattle. It appears in Shakespeare's *Titus Andronicus* (4.4.89–91):

*I will enchant the old Andronicus*
*With words more sweet, and yet more*
*    dangerous,*
*Than baits to fish, or honeystalks to*
*    sheep.*

# THE LOOSESTRIFE FAMILY

## Lythraceae

A widespread family of 26 genera and 580 species of herbs and a few shrubs and trees; found mainly in tropical regions. Some members of the family are the source of certain dyes, including henna from *Lawsonia inermis* (the Mignonette Tree), a red dye from *Woodfordia fruticosa* and a yellow dye from *Lafoensia pacari*. One ornamental family member is Crepe Myrtle, *Lagerstroemia indica*.

## Swamp Loosestrife

*Decodon verticillatus*. Ten teeth (the calyx); whorled.

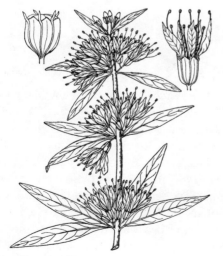

*Swamp Loosestrife*

Grass-Poly, Milk-Willow-Herb, Peatweed, Redroot (Mich.), Slinkweed, Swamp Willow-Herb, Water-Oleander, Water-Willow, Wild-Oleander, Willow-Herb

"The Lythrum verticillatum, or swamp loosestrife, or grass poly, but I think better named swamp-willow-herb" (Thoreau, 1851). The name Slinkweed refers to the belief that it causes cows to "slink" or abort.

## Hyssop-Leaved Loosestrife

*Lythrum hyssopifolia*. Blood (from Greek *luthron,* "gore"); hyssop-leaved (the old generic name). (Also found in South America and Europe.)

Grass-Poly, Hyssop-Loosestrife, Wild-Hyssop

It was Grasse Poly in Gerard's Herbal, and in America it was called Grasspoly (and Wild Hyssop) by Cutler (1785) and Grass poly by Bigelow (1814). Poly, Polly or Poley is an old English name for a Germander, *Teucrium polium* (from Greek *polios,* "hoary").

## Purple Loosestrife, Spiked Loosestrife

*Lythrum salicaria*. Blood; willowlike (the old generic name). (From Europe.)

*Bouquet violet* (P.Q.), Grass-Polly, Kill-Weed, Long-Purples, Milk-Willow-Herb, Purplegrass, Purple Willow-Herb, Rainbow-Weed, Red-Sally, Rosy-Strife, Sage-Willow, *Salicaire* (P.Q.), Soldiers, *Souillé de sang* (P.Q.), Spiked Willow-Herb, Willow-Weed

This is the *lysimachia* of Pliny, which Turner (1548) named "red loosestrife or purple loosestrife." The names are discussed under the Lysimachias. Long-Purples, Red-Sally and Soldiers are local names in England. Lythrum has become a pestilential weed in marshy areas, crowding out many valuable native species.

# THE EVENING-PRIMROSE FAMILY

## *Onagraceae*

A cosmopolitan family of 24 genera and 650 species of herbs, shrubs and a few trees; found mainly in temperate and subtropical regions, particularly in the New World. Many family members are cultivated as ornamentals, including Evening Primroses and Fuchsias.

## Enchanter's-Nightshade

*Circaea lutetiana.* Of Circe (the beautiful enchantress who turned all Ulysses' men into swine); of Paris. (Also found in Eurasia.)
Bindweed-Nightshade, Mandrake

Dioscorides and Pliny described a magical herb *kirkaia* or *circaea,* which in the 16th century was identified as *Circaea lutetiana.* Gerard (1633) reported that it was called Circaea's or the Enchanter's Nightshade since "doubtless it hath the vertue of Garden Nightshade, and may serve in its stead," but he noted, "There is no use of this herb either in physick or surgerie that I can read of." Dana (1900) wrote that "*C. alpina* is a smaller, less common species, which is found along the mountains and in deep woods. Both species are burdened with the singularly inappropriate name of enchanter's nightshade. There is nothing in their appearance to suggest an enchanter or any of the nightshades."

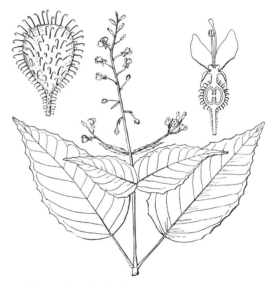

*Enchanter's-Nightshade*

## Deerhorn Clarkia

*Clarkia pulchella.* Of Clark (William Clark, 1770–1838); pretty.
Pink-Fairies, Ragged-Robin

William Clark was born in Caroline County, Virginia, served in the army on the frontier from 1789 to 1796 and then managed his family estate in Kentucky and traveled widely until in 1803 he was invited to share with Meriwether Lewis the leadership of the Lewis and Clark expedition. According to the *Dic-*

*tionary of American Biography,* "The success of the expedition, although Lewis was in ultimate command, was really due to the combined qualities of the two leaders, who worked in complete harmony and supplemented each other at every point. Clark had more enterprise, daring and resource than Lewis, since he had more frontier experience. By his quick thought and action he more than once saved the expedition from disaster. He was the mapmaker, and also the artist, drawing birds, fish and animals with meticulous care." Upon completion of the expedition, Clark was appointed superintendent of Indian affairs at St. Louis and then as governor of the Missouri Territory in 1813.

*Fireweed*

## Willow Herbs

*Epilobium.* On a capsule (*epi,* "on," *lobon,* "capsule"; the corolla surmounts the ovary).

The young shoots are cooked, and the "gelatinous interior of stalks cooked or used dried for making ale; leaves used to adulterate tea" (Morton, 1963).

## Fireweed

*Epilobium angustifolium.* On a capsule; narrow-leaved. (Also found in Eurasia.)

*Asperge* (P.Q.), Bay-Willow, Bay-Willow-Herb, Blooming-Sally, Blooming-Willow, *Bouquets rouges* (P.Q.), Burnt-Weed (Maine), Firetop (Maine), Flowering-Willow, French-Willow, French Willow-Herb, Great Willow-Herb, Herb-Wickopy, Indian-Wickup, Moose-Tongue (Maine), Persian-Willow, Pigweed (Canada), Purple-Racket (N.C.), Purple-Rocket (N.B.), Rosebay, Rose-Elder, Sally-Bloom (N.B.), Siberian-Flax (N.B.), Slinkweed, Spiked Willow-Herb, Wickapee, Wickop, Wickup (Maine, N.H.), Wild-Phlox (Mass.), Willow-Herb

Indians of the Northwest used the tough stem fibers to make twine and fishnets and still eat the young leaves and shoots and the sweet gelatinous pith. "The Flambeau Ojibwe say that the outer rind of this root lathers in water and they pound it to make a poultice. This is used to draw out inflammation from a boil or carbuncle" (Huron Smith, 1932). "Fireweed is well known as a nectar-producer, and bees and other insects are attracted by its flowers. In the coastal regions of Oregon and Washington apiarists follow logging operations, moving every 5 to 7 years to newer cut-over areas where fireweed is most abundant" *(Range Plant Handbook).* In New Hampshire, "Epilobium angustifolium we only knew by the name our grandmother taught us, Wickup" (Hayward, 1891). Blooming-Sally is an Irish name, and French-Willow a local name in England.

July 1944: "London, paradoxically, is the gayest where she has been the most blitzed. The wounds made this summer by flying bombs are, of course, still raw and bare, but cellars and courts shattered into rubble by the German raids of 1940–'41 have been taken over by an army of weeds which have turned them into wild gardens, sometimes as gay as any tilled by human hands. There is the brilliant rose-purple plant that Londoners call rose-bay willow herb. Americans call it fireweed because it blazes wherever a forest fire has raged. It will not grow in shade, but there is little shade as yet in the London ruins. It likes potash, and the ruins are full of wood ash. It sweeps across this pockmarked city and turns what might have been scars into flaming beauty. You see it everywhere—great meadows of it in Lambeth, where solid tracts were blitzed; waves of it about St. Paul's. Behind Westminster Abbey bits of it are high up where second-story fireplaces still cling to the hanging walls. The fireweed plant gives the characteristic rose-purple and green color tone to what look like vacant lots all over London—the blitz sites" (Lewis Gannett, *New York Herald Tribune*, 1944; from Krutch, 1959).

## Hairy Willow Herb

*Epilobium hirsutum*. On a capsule; hairy. (From Europe.)

Apple-Pie, Cherry-Pie, Codlins-and-Cream, Fiddle-Grass, Gooseberry-Pie, Great Hairy-Willow-Herb

The plant's many fruit and pie names (a codlin is a cooking apple) are supposed to allude to its smell, but since the plant and its flower are almost scentless, Grigson proposes that the names refer to the flowers' colors ("rosy petals, creamy white stigma," like an apple, cherry or gooseberry pie lapped with thick cream), "codlin" being an alteration of Gerard's name, Codded Willow Herb.

## Water-Purslane

*Ludwigia palustris*. Of Ludwig (Christian Gottlieb Ludwig, 1709–1773, professor of botany at Leipzig); of marshes. (Also found in Europe.)

Bastard-Loosestrife, False-Loosestrife, Isnardia, Marsh-Purslane, Phthisic-Weed, Waterweed

Phthisis is pulmonary tuberculosis: "It has been used in the treatment of asthma, chronic coughs, and tuberculosis" (Jacobs and Burlage). Isnardia is a previous generic name.

## Evening-Primroses

*Oenothera*. (From the Greek name, *oinotheras*, of a related plant).

Farewell-to-Spring (Calif.), Tree-Primrose

Oenothera (and its alternative spelling Onagra) either means "wine-scenting," since its roots were used for that purpose (Britton and Brown, 1913) or, inexplicably, "donkey-chase" (from *onos*, "donkey," *thera*, "chase, hunting"; Smith, 1972), "ass-catcher" (Gledhill, 1958) or "wine-imbibing" (from *oinos*, "wine," *thera*, "imbibing"; Plowden, 1970).

## Common Evening-Primrose

*Oenothera biennis*. (A Greek plant name); biennial.

Coffee-Plant, Cureall (N.C.), Fever-Plant, Four-O'Clock, German-Rampion, Golden-Candlestick (Kans.), King's-Cure-All (South), Large-Rampion, Night-Primrose, Night Willow-Herb, Scabious (Maine), Scabish (Maine), Scavey (Ont.), Scurvish (N.H.), Speckled-John (Kans.), Tree-Primrose

"*Lysimachus* or Loose-strife; there are several kinds, but the most noted is the yellow Lysimachus of Virginia," wrote Josselyn (1674); "the Flower yellow and like Primroses, and therefore called Tree-primrose" and also "taken by the English for Scabious." By the English, Josselyn meant the English settlers in New England. In 1814 Bigelow called it Tree Primrose and noted that "in the country it is vulgarly known by the name of Scabish, a corruption probably of Scabious, from which however it is a very different plant." Perhaps they had the same medicinal uses; Scabious (see *Knautia*) was a remedy for venereal disease and scaly eruptions.

The plant was once cultivated (as German Rampion) for its roots which, when boiled, are wholesome and nutritious and taste like those of Rampion (*Campanula rapuncu-*

*Common Evening-Primrose*

*loides).* The young shoots, fruit and seeds are also eaten, and the seed oil is being used experimentally to treat many conditions, including eczema, asthma, migraines, inflammations, the premenstrual syndrome, breast problems, metabolic disorders, arthritis and alcoholism; "extracts from this plant can alleviate imbalances and abnormalities of essential fatty acids in prostaglandin production" (Foster and Duke). Fever-Plant—"used as a diaphoretic in fevers"; Coffee-Plant—"infusion used as a drink in the harvest field"; King's Cure-All—"used in domestic medicine" (Bergen, 1893). Another common species, Sundrops *(Oenothera fruticosa),* is called

Wild-Beet in West Virginia and has been used as a potherb.

## Western Evening-Primrose, Hooker's Evening-Primrose

*Oenothera elata.* (A Greek plant name); exalted.

Frederick V. Coville (1897) wrote, "The Klamath name of the plant, derived from wäs, coyote, äm, plant, and chón·wäs, vomit, is associated with the following story, in which I have retained as nearly as possible the sentiment and sequence of the Indian narrator. A long time ago, when the animals lived and talked like men, the coyote, or prairie wolf, who was very keen and smart, but a good deal of the sneak, just as he is today, met one day the Indian Christ, Isis, who could do anything he wanted to—could make flowers, 'grub' (i.e., food), anything. The coyote said, in a bragging way, that he, too, could do these things just as well as Isis, and Isis said: 'Very well, go ahead and make a flower.' Then the coyote, who knew that he really couldn't make much of anything, was greatly ashamed, but he went off in the grass a little way and vomited, and on that spot pretty soon this great, rank, yellow-flowered weed came up. And that was the best the smart coyote could do."

The plant was previously called *Oenothera hookeri,* named for Sir Joseph Dalton Hooker (1817–1911), eminent English botanist, son of Sir William Jackson Hooker, whom he succeeded as director of the Royal Botanic Garden at Kew in 1865.

# THE MELASTOME OR MEADOW-BEAUTY FAMILY

## *Melastomataceae*

A widespread family of 215 genera and 4,750 species of herbs, shrubs and trees or lianas; found mainly in tropical and subtropical regions, particularly in South America. Greek *melas* means "black," *stoma* means "mouth"—the berries of the tropical shrub Melastoma stain the mouth black.

### Virginia Meadow-Beauty, Meadow-Pitchers

*Rhexia virginica*. (A name used by Pliny for an unknown plant); of Virginia.

Deergrass, Handsome-Harry, Robinhood, Virginia-Soapwort

September 1: "I am struck again by the richness of the meadow-beauty, though it will last some time, in little dense purple patches by the sides of the meadows. It is so low it escapes the scythe. It is not so much distinct flowers (it is so low and dense), but a colored patch on the meadow. Yet how few observe it! How, in one sense, is it wasted! How little thought the mower or cranberry-raker bestows on it! How few girls and boys come to see it!" September 14: "The chalices of *Rhexia*

*Virginia Meadow-Beauty*

*Virginica,* deer-grass or meadow-beauty, are literally little reddish chalices now, though many still have petals,—little cream pitchers" (Thoreau, 1853, 1851).

Manasseh Cutler called it Robinhood in 1785. Maryland Meadow-Beauty, *Rhexia mariana,* has pale pink flowers.

# THE DOGWOOD FAMILY

## *Cornaceae*

A widespread family of 12 genera and 90 species of trees, shrubs and a few herbs; found mainly in north temperate regions. Latin *cornus* means "horn," alluding to the hardness of the wood of the Dogwood trees. In Virgil's *Aeneid* (book 5),

*Now the boys ride in, before the eyes of*
*their fathers,*
*In perfect dressing, a brilliant sight on*
*their bridled horses—*
*Sicilians and Trojans greet them with*
*murmurs of admiration.*
*They wear on their hair ceremonial*
*garlands, well trimmed,*
*And each of them carries a couple of*
*steel-tipped cornel-wood lances.*

### Bunchberry, Dwarf Cornel

*Cornus canadensis.* Horn; of Canada. (Also found in Asia.)

Bearberry, Bunchplum (Maine, N.H.), *Cornouiller* (P.Q.), Crackerberry (Nfd.), Cuckoo-Plum (Maine), Dogberry, Frothberry (Nfd.), Low Cornel, Pigeon-berry (N.B.), Pudding-Berry (N.H.), *Quatre temps* (P.Q.), *Rougets* (P.Q.), Trailing Dogwood

Among the Hurons in 1624, Père Sagard wrote of "several other kinds of small fruits and berries unknown here of which we ate delicious dishes when we could find them. There are some red ones which appear almost like coral, that grow almost on the ground in little bunches with two or three leaves, resembling laurel, which give them charm; they seem like very fine bouquets and would serve as such."

John Josselyn (1672) wrote, "This plant I take for a variegated Herb Paris, True Love or One Berry, or rather One Flower, which

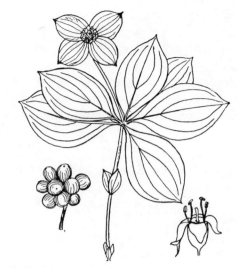

*Bunchberry*

is milk white, and made up with four leaves [petals], with many black threads in the middle, upon every thread grows a berry (when the leaves of the flower have fallen) as big as white pease, of a light red colour when they are ripe, and clustering together in a round form as big as a pullets egg, which at a distance shews but as one berry, very pleasant in taste, and not unwholesome." Herb Paris or True-Love is the European *Paris quadrifolia* (Liliaceae), for which an American Trillium has been mistaken. The ripe berries are eaten raw or cooked. Cracker is a crake or crow.

# THE SPURGE FAMILY

## *Euphorbiaceae*

A cosmopolitan family of 321 genera and 7,950 species of shrubs, lianas, trees and a few herbs; found particularly in tropical and subtropical regions. Family members provide rubber (from *Hevea brasiliensis,* the source of most of the world's rubber), castor oil (from *Ricinus communis*), tung oil (from *Vernicia* species), candlenut oil (from *Aleurites moluccana*), purgatives (from *Jatropha curcas* and *Croton tiglium*) and food (from *Manihot esculenta,* the manioc, cassava or tapioca plant).

Euphorbus was the Greek physician of King Juba of Numidia, a Roman province in North Africa. Spurge is derived from Old French *espurgier* (to purge).

## Ridge-Seeded Spurge, Rib-Seed Sandmat

*Chamaesyce glyptosperma.* Ground fig; carved-seed.

Thompson Indians rub the fresh plant on all snake bites, especially rattlesnake bites. "The plant is said to grow only in those parts of the country where rattlesnakes are found" (Teit, 1930).

## Milk-Purslane

*Chamaesyce maculata.* Ground fig; spotted (leaves).

Black-Pusley, Black Spurge, Blotched Spurge, Bowman's-Root, Corn-Pusley (Long Island), Emetic-Weed (N.C.), Eyebane, Eyebright, French-Pursley (Ohio), Milkweed, Rupterwort, Spotted-Eyebright, Spotted-Pusley, Spotted Sandmat, Spotted Spurge, Wart-weed, West-Indian-Eyebright

Josselyn (1672) called it "Spurge Time, it grows upon dry sandy sea banks, and is very like to Rupter-wort, it is full of milk." Gerard's Rupture Wort ("being drunk it is singularly good for ruptures") is *Herniaria glabra.*

## Spurge-Nettle

*Cnidoscolus stimulosus.* Nettle sting; stinging.

Bull-Nettle, Nettle (Ga.), Sand-Nettle, Stinging-Bush, Stinging-Nettle, Tread-Softly

"The present plant is a very injurious weed in some parts of Carolina, as it ruins the Negroes' feet when they tread upon it; from which it is known by the name of tread-softly" (Pursh, 1814).

## Turkey-Mullein

*Eremocarpus setigerus.* Solitary fruit; bristly. Yerba del Pescado

"The shining bean-like seeds, only a sixth of an inch long, are borne in great abundance, and in summer and autumn constitute one of the favorite foods of the wild mourning dove, which flocks to localities where the plant is particularly abundant, a circumstance which the Indians take advantage of in order to kill them in large numbers for food. Turkeys feed on the seed also, and on this account, and on account of the wooly, mullein-like appearance of the leaf, the plant has been called turkey mullein" (Chesnut, 1902). California Indians also used the plant to stupefy fish *(Yerba del Pescado),* as described in the entry for *Chlorogalum pomeridianum.*

## Flowering Spurge

*Euphorbia corollata.* Of Euphorbus; with corolla.

Apple-Root, Blooming Spurge, Boiling Spurge, Bowman's-Root, Emetic-Root, Go-Quick (Mich.), Hippo, Indian-Physic, Ipecacuanha, Milk-Ipecac,

*Flowering Spurge*

Milk-Purslane, Milk-Pusley, Milkweed, Peheca, Persley, Picac, Purging-Root, Smoke's-Milk, Snake-Milk, Tramp's-Purge, White-Purslane, White-Pursley, Wild-Hippo

In 1730 John Clayton reported that the Indians used "the roots of Tithymal, of which there are two sorts, the one *flore minimo herbaceo,* the other *flore albo.*" The former is presumably *Euphorbia ipecacuanhae* and the latter *E. corollata,* which, Clayton wrote, "is a most excellent purge, though it sometimes vomits. It is quick but moderate in its effect, and has this peculiarity, that it opens the body, when other more violent purgatives will not move it." *Tithymalus* (meaning "milky juice") is an old generic name of the Spurges.

Dr. Bigelow (1817) reported that "the *Euphorbia corollata* must undoubtedly be ranked among the most efficient medicines of the evacuating class." Hippo is short for hippocras, a cordial of wine and spices. It is called "Flowering" for the five round white petal-like bracts, and the name Go-Quick is "said to be the Indian name" (Bergen, 1898).

## Cypress Spurge

*Euphorbia cyparissias.* Of Euphorbus; like Cypress (the Latin name of a Spurge, from Greek *kuparissos,* "cypress," for the leaves). (From Europe.)

Balsam (N.Y.), Bonaparte's-Crown, Butternut (Maine), Cypress (Maine, N.H.), Garden-Spurge, Graveyard-Moss (Ind.), Graveyard-Weed (W.Va.), Irish-Moss (N.B.), Kiss-Me-Dick, Kiss-Me-Quick, Love-in-a-Huddle (Conn.), Milkweed (Vt., Wis.), Napoleon (Mass.), Quack-Salver's Spurge, *Rhubarbe des pauvres* (P.Q.), Squib-Knocket (Mass.), Tree-Moss (Ohio), Welcome-to-Our-Home

Kiss-Me-Dick and Welcome-Home-Husband are local names in England. Gerard (1633) wrote that it was called "among women, Welcome to our house." Quack-Salver's Spurge is an old English name; a quack-salver, from the Dutch, is a charlatan. The whorl of leaves at the base of the umbel perhaps resembles

*Wild Poinsettia*

the crown of laurel leaves worn by Napoleon in David's famous portrait.

## Wild Poinsettia, Mexican-fireplant

*Euphorbia heterophylla.* Of Euphorbus; various-leaved.

Fire-on-the-Mountain, Hypocrite-Plant, Mexican-Fireplant, Various-Leaved Spurge

This was previously *Poinsettia heterophylla,* named for Joel Roberts Poinsett (1779–1851), who was born and died in South Carolina. He served in the state legislature and in the U.S. House of Representatives and in 1822 and 1823 was sent on a special government mission to Mexico, from where he returned with the flower that was later named for him. He was a man of many accomplishments and interests, including the fine arts, agriculture and botany. The Christmas Poinsettia is *Euphorbia pulcherrima,* previously *Poinsettia pulcherrimo.*

## Wild-Ipecac

*Euphorbia ipecacuanhae.* Of Euphorbus; like Ipecacuanha (the early Virginian name, from its use as an emetic).

American White-Ipecac, Black Spurge, Carolina-Hippo, Carolina-Ipecac, Ipecac Spurge, Spurge-Ipecac

Dr. Millspaugh reported that "the emetic property of this root was well known to the Aborigines . . . Dr. Bigelow observes from his own experiments and those of Dr. McKeen at his instigation, that the species is an active emetic, safe when prudently administered, but injurious to the nervous system, and wanting in the mildness that characterizes officinal Ipecacuanha." It has been included in the USP. The emetic drug Ipecac is prepared from the roots of the South American shrub *Cephaelis ipecacuanha.*

## Caper Spurge

*Euphorbia lathyris.* Of Euphorbus; (a Latin name of a Spurge). (From Europe.)
Anti-Gopher-Plant, Caper-Bush, Cape-Spurge, Catepuce, Coper-Spurge (N.C.), Gopher-Plant, Moleplant, Moletree (Ohio), Moleweed (W.Va.), Myrtle-Spurge, Sassy-Jack (Va.), Springwort, Wild-Caper, Wolf's-Milk

Caper Spurge was supposed to keep moles and gophers out of the garden. The buds

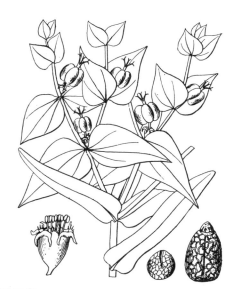

*Caper Spurge*

look like capers and have been mistaken for them—with drastic results, for they are dangerously poisonous, though evidently not lethal (Kingsbury, 1964). "The Caper Spurge is the *Cataputia minor* of old pharmacopoeias, and is one of the plants that Charlemagne ordered grown in every garden in France. The laity in England are said to use one capsule to cause catharsis, and the women, several to produce abortion" (Millspaugh).

In Chaucer's *The Nun's Priest's Tale,* the hen Pertelote tells her husband Chanticleer that his bad dreams are the result of "the superfluity and force of the red choler in your blood," and in the morning "on flying from these beams, for love of God do take some laxative":

> *Worms for a day or two I'll have to give*
> *As a digestive, then your laxative.*
> *Centaury, fumitory, caper-spurge*
> *And hellebore will make a splendid purge;*
> *And then there's laurel or the black-thorn berry,*
> *Ground-ivy too that makes our yard so merry;*
> *Peck them right up, my dear, and swallow whole.*
> *Be happy, husband, by your father's soul!*

## Snow-on-the-Mountain

*Euphorbia marginata.* Of Euphorbus; margined (with white).
Ghost-Weed (Texas), Milkweed (Texas), Mountain-Snow, Rattlesnake-Weed (Calif.), Variegated Spurge, White-Margined Spurge

## Queen's-Delight

*Stillingia sylvatica.* Of Stillingfleet (Benjamin Stillingfleet, 1702–1771, English naturalist); of woods.

*Queen's-Delight*

Cock-up-Hat (N.C.), Cocyshat, Marcony, Nettle-Potato, Queen-of-the-Lights (Ga.), Queen's-Root, Silver-Leaf, Yaw-Weed (Pa.), Yaw-Root

"A curious plant called in North Carolina Cockup Hat common all ye way" (John Bartram, 1765). In Stephen Vincent Benet's *John Brown's Body,* Sally Dupré, watching over her dyeing pots ("red is pokeberry juice . . . deep black is queen's delight"), thinks of Clay Wingate who is away at war:

> *I will dye my heart*
> *In a pot of queen's delight, in the poke-*
> *    berry sap,*
> *I will dye it red and black in the fool's*
> *    old colors*
> *And send it to him, wrapped in a cal-*
> *    ico rag,*
> *To keep him warm through the rain.*

"We are informed by a physician residing in South Carolina, that he has treated syphilis successfully with it. It is believed to be possessed of valuable properties" (Porcher). It has been included in the USP and the NF: small quantities were "supposed to exercise an 'alterative' effect upon the system" (USD). "The Creek Indians mashed *Stillingia* roots and boiled them, and a woman who had just borne a child drank the liquid and was bathed in it. A women suffering from irregular periods bathed in this liquid with devil's shoestring [*Tephrosia virginiana*] added" (Vogel, 1970).

# THE FLAX FAMILY

## Linaceae

A cosmopolitan family of 15 genera and 300 species of herbs and shrubs, most common in temperate and subtropical regions. Greek *linon* means "flax." Flax fibers from *Linum usitatissimum* have been woven into linen since at least 3000 B.C. in Babylon and Egypt. Its oil is linseed oil, and the residual oilcake is a valuable food for cattle.

## Prairie Flax, Blue-Flax

*Linum lewisii.* Flax (Latin); of Lewis (Meriwether Lewis, 1774–1809).

Lewis Flax, Lewis's Wild-Flax, Rocky Mountain Flax

Among the Klamath Indians in 1897, "the stems produce a remarkably strong fiber which is made into strings and cords. These are employed in certain parts of baskets and mats, in the meshes of snowshoes, and in the weaving of fish nets" (Coville). A young girl of the

Thompson Indians "would frequently wash her face and head with a decoction of the stems and flowers of the wild flax. She believed that this would give her a wealth of hair and a beautiful, fair face" (Teit, 1930).

## Flax

*Linum usitatissimum.* Flax; most useful. (From Europe.)

Common Flax, Flix, Lin, Linn, Linseed, Lint, Lintbells, *Lin utile* (P.Q.)

In 1847 Darlington wrote that "this valuable plant—once considered so indispensable among the crops of our farmers—is now but little cultivated. I have not seen a flax-patch for a number of years: whereas in the 'good old times'—before Spinning-Wheels were superseded by Pianos—every rural family cultivated and manufactured as much flax as was required for domestic purposes."

Flax also has its medicinal virtues: "Mollifying all inflammation inwardly & outwardly, being sod with honey. And being raw it takes away sun-burnings and the Vari, being applied as a cataplasm with nitre and figs," according to Dioscorides. It was called "Flax, lyne or lynte" by Turner (1548). Flix is a local name in England; Lintbells is from Scotland. It was included as a poultice and laxative in the USP and NF.

In "The Wreck of the Hesperus" by Longfellow:

Flax

> It was the schooner Hesperus,
> That sailed the wintry sea;
> And the skipper had taken his little
> daughter,
> To bear him company.

> Blue were her eyes as the fairy-flax
> Her cheeks like the dawn of day,
> And her bosom white as the hawthorn
> buds,
> That ope in the month of May.

Actually, Fairy Flax *(Linum catharticum)* has a white flower.

# THE MILKWORT FAMILY

## *Polygalaceae*

A nearly cosmopolitan family of 18 genera and 950 species of herbs, shrubs, lianas and trees. The Greek name *polugalon* (from *polus,* "much," and *gala,* "milk") was applied by Dioscorides to a plant, "harsh to the taste, and this also being drunk is thought to cause more milk." This was later identified as a Polygala, of which Dodoens wrote that it "engendreth plentie of milk; therefore it is good to be used of nurses that lack milk."

## Cross-Leaved Milkwort, Drumheads

*Polygala cruciata*. Much milk; cross-shaped (the four leaves).

"Polygala cruciata, cross-leaved polygala, in the meadow behind Trillium Woods and the railroad. This is rare and new to me. It has a very sweet, but as it were intermittent, fragrance, as of a checkerberry and mayflower combined" (Thoreau, 1851).

## Pink Milkwort

*Polygala incarnata*. Much milk; flesh-colored.

Procession-Flower, Rogation-Flower, Ink-Milkwort (N.C.)

Rogation Sunday, the fifth Sunday after Easter, is followed by Rogation Week during which church processions (or "gangs"), led by a Cross, bless the crops. Gerard (1633) wrote of *Polygala vulgaris*, also a pink Milkwort, that they "especially flourish in the Crosse or Gang weeke, or Rogation weeke; of which floures the maidens which use in the countries to walk the Procession doe make themselves garlands and nosegaies: in English we may call it Crosse-floure, Procession-floure, Gang floure, Rogation floure, and Milkewort, of their vertues in procuring milke in the breasts of nurses." Ink Milkwort is presumably from *incarnata*.

## Fringed Polygala

*Polygala paucifolia*. Much milk; few-leaved. Babies'-Feet (N.H.), Baby's-Slippers (Mass.), Baby's-Toes (Mass.), Bird-on-the-Wing (Maine), Dwarf-Milkwort, Evergreen-Snakeroot, Flavoring-Wintergreen (N.C.), Flowering-Wintergreen, Fringed Milkwort, Gaywings (N.Y., Vt.), Indian-Pink (Mass.), Lady's-Slipper (Maine), Little-Pollom, Maywings (Conn., N.Y.), Purple-Maywing (Maine), Satin-Flower

Susan Cooper (1850) in New York wrote of "May-wings, or 'gay-wings,' they are in truth one of the gayest little blossoms we have; growing low as they do and many of their winged flowers together, you might fancy them so many warm lilac, or deep rose-colored butterflies resting on the moss."

## Seneca-Snakeroot

*Polygala senega*. Much milk; of the Senecas (the old generic name).

Mountain-Flax, Rattlesnake-Snakeroot, Senega-Root, Seneca-Root, Senega-Snakeroot, Tennent's-Root, Virginian Milkwort

John Tennent was a controversial Virginia doctor whose wonderful discovery was that Seneca-Snakeroot, in addition to curing the bite of a rattlesnake (according to the Seneca Indians), was a specific treatment for pleurisy (the most prevalent disease in colonial Vir-

*Pink Milkwort*

*Seneca-Snakeroot*

was charged with bigamy, divorced and died in 1748. Meanwhile, Seneca-Snakeroot had become an accepted remedy for many diseases, particularly of the lungs. In 1770 Tennent's son petitioned the House of Burgesses for a reward since his father's discovery "hath become universal and by great experience found very serviceable to all." But the petition was rejected. The 1887 USD reported that collectors had exterminated the plant in the East but that supplies of the root were still available from the Northwest.

According to William Byrd of Virginia (1728), the most effective medicines for gout were those that "clear a passage through the narrow vessels, that are the seat of this cruel disease. Nothing will do this more suddenly than rattle-snake's oil, which will even penetrate the pores of glass when warm'd in the sun." Unfortunately, no rattlesnake oil was available to relieve the painful gout of one of the members of Byrd's 1728 boundary expedition, "but," Byrd wrote, "lately the Seneca Rattle-Snake-Root has been discover'd in this country, which being infus'd in wine, and drank morning and evening, has in several instances had a very happy effect upon the gout, and enabled cripples to throw away their crutches and walk several miles." The plant has been included in the USP and NF, used "as an expectorant in various forms of bronchitis and in asthma" (USD).

ginia) and pneumonia. He first published his findings in 1736 and in numerous subsequent publications fiercely defended his treatment against the attacks of other Virginia doctors. In 1738 he successfully petitioned the House of Burgesses to reward him for a discovery that was so beneficial to "this Country in Particular and Mankind in General." The hundred pounds granted him was immediately seized by his many creditors. He was equally unsuccessful in London, where he had gone, with a supply of Seneca-Snakeroots, to restore his reputation and fortune. There he was imprisoned for debt, married a rich widow,

# THE WOOD-SORREL FAMILY

## *Oxalidaceae*

A widespread family of eight genera and 575 species of herbs, shrubs and a few trees; found mainly in tropical and subtropical regions. These are the Wood-Sorrels to distinguish them from the field and meadow Sorrels (Rumex). One Mexican species, *Oxalis deppei,* is cultivated for its edible tubers.

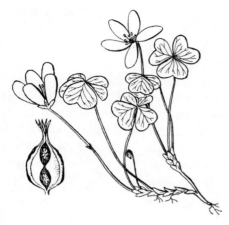

*Common Wood-Sorrel*

## Common Wood-Sorrel, Wood-Shamrock

*Oxalis montana.* Sour (from Greek *oxus*); of mountains. (Also found in Eurasia.)
Alleluia, Cuckoo-Bread, Cuckoo-Flower, Cuckoo's-Meat, Hearts, Lady's-Clover, *Pain de lièvre* (P.Q.), *Pain d'oiseau* (P.Q.), Shamrock, Sheep-Sorrel (Iowa), Sleeping-Beauty, Sleeping-Clover, Sleeping-Molly, Sour-Clover (N.C.), Sour-Trefoil, Sour-Trifoly, Stubwort, *Surette* (P.Q.), True Wood-Sorrel, White Wood-Sorrel, Wood-Sour, Wood-Sower

"This herbe Alleluya men call it Wood sowre or Stubworte" (Banckes, 1525). Turner (1548) wrote, "Oxys is called in English Alleluya, Cockowes meate, and Wood Sorel"—Alleluia "because it appeareth about Easter when Alleluya is sung again," after the mournful hymns of Lent. Or, as Canon Young (1945) suggests, "the plant may have been so named because its threefold leaf was thought to illustrate the Holy Trinity. Blooming about St. Patrick's Day, it has often been identified with the plant the saint is said to have used for that purpose, now commonly called Shamrock." It is also Alleluia in French, German and Dutch.

Dr. Porcher reported that "the herb is powerfuly and most agreeably acid, making a refreshing and wholesome conserve with fine sugar; its flavor resembles green tea." Sleeping Beauty (the leaves fold up at night), Woodsour, Stubwort (Stopwourt in the 14th century) and the Cuckoo names are local in the British Isles. Sleeping-Molly appears to be an American name.

## Yellow Wood-Sorrel

*Oxalis stricta.* Sour; erect.
Indian-Sorrel, Lady's-Sorrel (Mass., N.H.), Lady's-Sourgrass (N.J.), Poison-Sheep-Sorrel (Mo.), Rabbit-Clover (Ohio), Sheep-Sorrel (Ill., Ind., Mo., Ohio, Vt.), Sheep's-Clover (Mass.), Sourgrass (Ind.), Toad-Sorrel (Maine)

# THE GERANIUM FAMILY

## *Geraniaceae*

A widespread family of 14 genera and 730 species of herbs and shrubs; found chiefly in temperate and subtropical regions. Most of the garden and houseplants cultivated as Geraniums in fact belong to the South African genus *Pelargonium.* Some *Pelargonium* species are also cultivated for geranium oil, which is used in the scent and oil industries. Geranium is from the Greek name *geranion,* from *geranos* (crane), alluding to the long beak of the fruit.

## Storksbill, Alfilaria

*Erodium cicutarium.* Heron (from Greek *erodios*); like Cicuta (Water-Hemlock; the foliage). (From Europe.)

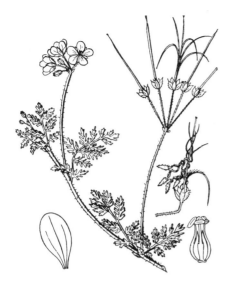

*Storksbill*

Alfileria, Alfilerilla, Alfiliria, Alfillarilla (Calif.), Clocks (West), Filagree, Filaree (Calif.), Hemlock Geranium, Hemlock-Stork's-Bill, Heron's-Bill, Nenn's-Bill (N.C.), Pinclover (Calif.), Pingrass (Calif.), Pink-Needle, Pinweed, Redstem-Filace, Red-stemmed-Filarel (Calif.), Redstem-Storksbill, Wild-Musk

March 1844, Oregon: "Continuing the next day down the river, we discovered three squaws in a little bottom, and surrounded them before they could make their escape. They had large conical baskets, which they were engaged in filling with a small leafy plant *[Erodium cicutarium]* just now beginning to bloom, and covering the ground like a sward of grass. These did not make any lamentations, but appeared very much impressed with our appearance, speaking to us only in a whisper, and offering us smaller baskets of the plant, which they signified to us was good to eat, making signs also that it was to be cooked by the fire" (Frémont).

The plant is a tasty and nutritious potherb, and the *Range Plant Handbook* reported that "Alfileria furnishes choice spring forage for all classes of livestock and is also relished by deer." In the Northeast, "the Storksbill is an occasional weed around towns and especially in the neighborhood of woolen mills, whence its seeds have been brought from the South-west entangled in wool" (Fernald and Kinsey, 1943). American Spanish *alfilerillo* is from the diminutive of *alfiler* (pin) alluding to the long pointed beak of the fruit. The plant was probably introduced into the Southwest by Spanish missionaries in the 18th century.

## Wild Geranium

*Geranium maculatum*. Crane flower; spotted.

Alum-Bloom, Alum-Root (Ky.), American Kino-Root, American-Tormentil, Astringent-Root, Chocolate-Flower (N.H.), Crowfoot, Crowfoot Geranium, Dove's-Foot, Fluxweed, Hemlock, Old-Maid's-Nightcap (Wis.), *Racine à becquet* (La., P.Q.), Rockweed, Sailor's-Knot, Shameface, Spotted Crane's-Bill, Spotted Geranium (Vt.), Wild Crane's-Bill

*Wild Geranium*

In his *New England's Rarities* of 1672, Jos-selyn called this "Raven's-Claw, which flowers in May, and is admirable for Agues." Accord-ing to Barton (1798), "the western Indian say it is the most effectual of all their remedies for the cure of the venereal disease . . . An aqueous infusion of the root forms an excel-lent injection in gonorrhoea. In old gonor-rhoeia, and in gleets, a more saturated infusion may be employed." In 1814 Pursh wrote, "This species is known in some parts of the Mountains by the name Alum-root, on ac-count of the astringent taste of its roots, which are very successfully employed in curing the flux among the the children, which is a dis-ease very prevalent in those countries" (the "Mountains" being the Appalachians). Wild Geranium has been included in the USP and NF, "used in diarrhea, also as a local astrin-gent in indolent ulcers, sore throat, etc. It was a popular domestic remedy in various parts of the United States, and is said to have been employed by the Indians" (USD). Raf-inesque reported that the plant was called *Racine à becquet* ("beaked") in Canada and Louisiana. Kino is a reddish resin obtained from some tropical trees. Tormentil, a Poten-tilla, is also a remedy for colic.

## Dove's-Foot Cranesbill

*Geranium molle*. Crane flower; soft. (From Europe.)

Pigeon-Foot, Culverfoot, Starlights

Gerard (1633) wrote that it was called *Pes Columbinus* in Latin, *Pied de Pigeon* in French and thus Dove's-Foot or Pigeon's-Foot in En-glish: "The herbe and roots dried, beaten into most fine pouder, and given halfe a spoonfull fasting, and the like quantitie to bedwards in red wine or old claret, for the space of one and twentie daies together, cureth miracu-lously ruptures or burstings." Culverfoot is a local name in England, a culver being a dove.

*Dove's-Foot Cranesbill*

## Richardson's Geranium

*Geranium richardsonii*. Crane flower; of Richardson (Sir John Richardson, 1787–1865, Scottish naturalist, physician and Arctic ex-plorer).

Crane's-Bill

This was called "nosebleed plant" by the Northern Cheyenne: "To stop nosebleed, the pulverized leaf was rubbed on the nose and the powder was snuffed into the nostrils" (Hart, 1980).

## Herb-Robert

*Geranium robertianum*. Crane flower; of Robert. (Also found in Eurasia and North Africa.)

Death-Come-Quickly, Dragon's-Blood, Fox Gera-nium, *Herbe à l'esquinancie* (P.Q.), Jenny-Wren, Mountain Geranium (N.H.), Red Bird's-Eye, Red-Robin, Red-Shanks, Robert, St. Robert, Wild Gera-nium (N.Y.), Wren's-Flower

In Medieval Latin it was *Herba Roberti*, named in honor of Robert, Duke of Nor-mandy (1054–1135), Saint Robert of Chaise-Dieu (died 1067) or Saint Rupert (died ca. 717), first archbishop of Salzburg. The plant

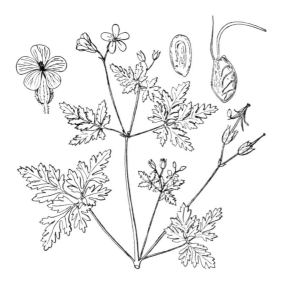

*Herb-Robert*

is associated with the little "house-haunting" Robin Redbreast, which in northern Europe was supposed to bring illness, death or misfortune when he flies indoors, and also of Jenny Wren, who was thought of as the Robin's wife, another bird of ill-omen (Grigson). Manasseh Cutler called the plant Mountain Cranesbill, Herb Robert and Stockbill and wrote that "it is considerably astringent, and smells somewhat like musk. A decoction of the plant has been known to give relief in calculous cases. It is given to cattle when they make bloody water." Most of the names listed above are from the British Isles, where the plant has over 100 more. Fox Geranium alludes to the scent of the leaves. Esquinancie is quinsy.

# THE TOUCH-ME-NOT FAMILY

## *Balsaminaceae*

A family of only two genera, *Impatiens,* which has about 850 species, native mainly to tropical Asia and Africa, and *Hydrocera,* which has a single species native to tropical Asia.

Touch-Me-Not Balsam is the British name for the European *Impatiens noli-tangere; "Noli me tangere"* ("Touch me not") were the words spoken by Christ to Mary Magdalene after the Resurrection (in the Vulgate, *John* 20:17). When ripe, the tight seed pods burst when touched, scattering the seeds. Or according to Erasmus Darwin *(see Lychnis chalcedonica),*

> With fierce distracted eye Impatiens
> stands
> Swells her pale cheeks and brandishes
> her hands,
> With rage and hate the astonished
> groves alarms

> And hurls her infants from her frantic
> arms.

## Spotted Touch-Me-Not, Jewelweed

*Impatiens capensis.* Impatience; of the Cape (of Good Hope, a mistake).

Balsam, Balsam-Weed (Ohio), Brook-Celandine, Celandine (Maine, Vt.), *Chou sauvage* (P.Q.), Cowslip (Ohio), Eardrop, Ear-Jewel (Vt.), Fireplant (Nfd.), Foxglove (Maine), Horns-of-Plenty (Mass.), Jack-Jump-Up-and-Kiss-Me (Nfd.), Kicking-Colt (Mass.), Kicking-Horse (Maine), Lady's-Eardrop (Ohio), Lady's-Earring, Lady's-Pocket (Ohio), Lady's-Slipper (N.Y., Ohio), Pocket-Drop, Shining-Grass (Vt.), Silverleaf, Silverweed (N.Y.), Slipperweed (Ohio), Snapdragon (Maine, N.H.), Snapweed (Maine, N.B.), Solentine (Maine), Speckled-Jewels, Sullendine (N.H.), Weathercock, Wild-Balsam (Mass.), Wild-Celandine (N.H.)

Josselyn called it the Humming-Bird Tree and wrote, "The Indians make use of it for

*Spotted Touch-Me-Not*

aches, being bruised between two stones, and laid to cold. But made (after the English manner) into an unguent with hog's grease, there is not a more sovereign remedy for bruises of what kind soever; and for aches upon stroaks." Manasseh Cutler called it Weathercock, Balsamine, Touch-Me-Not and Quick-in-the-Hand and reported that "it is generally known here by the name of Celan-

dine, and is much celebrated by the common people for curing their jaundice." It was called Celandine (or Solentine, Sullendine) because it is also a wart-wort—the juice removes warts. "Impatiens, noli-me-tangere, or touch-me-not, with its dangling yellow pitchers or horns of plenty which I have seen for a month by damp causeway thickets, but the whole plant was so tender and drooped so soon I could not get it home" (Thoreau, 1851). The young stems, raw or cooked, are eaten.

## Pale Touch-Me-Not, Jewelweed

*Impatiens pallida.* Impatience; pale.
Balsam, Lady's-Slipper (Ohio), Quick-in-the-Hand, Silverweed (N.Y.), Slippers, Slipperweed, Snapweed, Weathercock, Wild-Balsam, Wild-Celandine, Yellow Jewelweed

The soothing and medicinal juices of this and Spotted Touch-Me-Not are a remedy for Nettle stings and Poison-Ivy and other skin rashes. These are called Silverweeds because of the appearance of the leaves when put in water.

# THE GINSENG FAMILY

## *Araliaceae*

A widespread family of 57 genera and 800 species of shrubs, lianas, trees and a few herbs; found chiefly in tropical and subtropical regions. In addition to the notable plants discussed in the entries below, family members include Ivy (species of *Hedera*) and *Tetrapanax papyrifera,* from whose pith "rice paper" is obtained.

The name Ginseng is derived from the Chinese *jen-shen* (manlike), referring to the

branching root. Aralia is derived from the Indian name.

## Wild-Sarsparilla

*Aralia nudicaulis.* (The Indian name); naked-stemmed.
American-Sarsparilla, False Sarsparilla, Rabbit's-Foot, *Salsepareille* (P.Q.), Sasafafarilla (Maine), Sasafril (Maine), Sasapril (Maine), Sassafariller (N.C.), Sassafrilla (Maine), Saxapril (Maine), Shot-Bush, Small-Spikenard, Small-Spikeweed (N.C.), Sweetroot, Virginia-Sarsparilla, Wild-Licorice

*Wild-Sarsparilla*

"The roots are aromatic and nutritious. They have been found beneficial in debilitated habits. It is said the Indians would subsist upon them, for a long time, in their war and hunting excursions. They make an ingredient in diet drinks" (Cutler, 1785). The roots were used as a substitute for the official Sarsparilla. Marie-Victorin wrote that "under the name of Salsepareille, the root of this plant is one of the most important ingredients of the folk medicine of Canada. One knows that the true Sasparillas are not species of the genus *Aralia,* but of *Smilax* (Liliaceae)." It has been included in the USP. The young shoots of this and *A. racemosa* are cooked as a potherb, the roots are used for root beer, and the berries make jelly.

## Spikenard

*Aralia racemosa.* (The Indian name); racemose.
American-Spikenard, *Anis sauvage* (P.Q.), False-Sarsparilla (Wis.), Goutroot, Goutwort, *Grand Salsepareille* (P.Q.), Hungry-Root, Indian-Root (N.H.), King-of-the-Woods (southern Negro), Life-of-Man

(Maine, N.H.), Old-Maid's-Root, Old-Man's-Root (Maine), Petty-Morell, Pettymorell (Mass., N.H.), Pigeonweed, Spiceberry, Spicebush (Conn.), Spignet (Ky.), Spignut (Vt.), Whiteroot, Wild-Elder (Wis.)

John Bartram (1751) wrote of "*Aralia,* called by some Spikenard, by others Wild Licorice; this bears large clusters of berries, ripe in September, which are pleasant and wholesome to eat: The roots are of balsamick nature; the back inhabitants use them to cure fresh wounds." Manasseh Cutler called it Pettymorell and Life of Man and wrote, "It is aromatic. The berries give spirits an agreeable flavour. The bark of the root and berries are a good stomachic." Marie-Victorin reported that "the mature root is used to flavor beer." It was called Petty Morell and Spikenard by Bigelow (1814)—and "in high estimation with people in the country." Petty Morell was originally a name of the Common Nightshade.

In *The Canadian Settler's Guide* of 1855, Traill wrote of "Dysentry in Children. I lost two infants who were under the care of the most careful medical men; but saved another

*Spikenard*

by the use of a wild herb, that was given me by a Yankee settler's wife. A plant called spikenard (or spignet, as she called it) that grows in the forest with a long spindle root, scraped, and a small quantity boiled in milk, thickens it, as if flour had been put in it. It has a sweet astringent taste, slightly bitter. A teaspoon, thrice given in one day, cured the child, who was wasting fast under the disease."

Spikenard was included in the NF as a household remedy in rheumatic, syphilitic and cutaneous affections, and in medical practice "occasionally employed in pectoral complaints but now is practically never prescribed. Its therapeutic value is extremely questionable" (USD). Properly, Spikenard is the aromatic plant *Nardostachys jatamansi* of India from which the costly ointment of antiquity, nard, was made. Spike of Nard is a translation of the Greek name *nardostakhus.* "Micmac Indians made a salve of spikenard for use on cuts and wounds. The Ojibwe used the roots with wild ginger for a poultice on fractures. The Menominees used the root in blood poisoning, as a poultice on sores, and for a tea given in stomach ache. Potawatomis pounded the root to a pulp for a hot poultice in inflammations. Meskwaki mothers had a spikenard medicine sprayed on their heads in childbirth" (Vogel, 1970).

In his 1877 autobiography, Dr. James Still, the famous Black Doctor of the New Jersey Pine Barrens, included his recipe for a cough balsam, which "far excels anything that I have ever known used for pulmonary affections and coughs of long standing": eight ounces each of Spikenard root, Comfrey root, Horehound tops, Elecampane root, Bloodroot, Skunk-Cabbage root and Pleurisy-Root, all boiled in soft water, to which is added sugar, oil of anise, alcohol and tincture of Lobelia. The dose was one teaspoonful three to five times daily.

*Ginseng*

## Ginseng

*Panax quinquefolius.* Cure-all (Greek *panakeia,* "panacea"); five-leaved.

Chang, Cheng, Dwarf-Groundroot, Five-Fingers, Garantogen, Garantoqueen, Garentoquere, Gensang, Ginshang (Vt.), Grantogen, Jinshard (N.C.), Man's-Health, Ninsin, Redberry, Sang (Ky., W.Va.), Seng (Ky.), Shang, Tartar-Root

In 1714 a Jesuit priest in China published a report on Ginseng in a London periodical, a copy of which eventually reached a fellow Jesuit, Joseph François Lafitau, in Quebec. With the help of Indians, Lafitau collected native American Ginseng plants and sent them to China. The plants were sufficiently like the Asian species *(Panax ginseng)* to satisfy the Chinese, and the Ginseng trade had started. "This discovery produced in that epoch as much passion and greed as, much later, did the announcement of the gold mines of California" (Marie-Victorin). The Ginseng trade employed thousands of cheng, chang, sang or shang hunters, who were mainly Indians at first and then European settlers, from the Maritime Provinces to Minnesota and south into the Appalachians and the mountains of the southern states. In the Blue Ridge, 1842,

Asa Gray found "Ginseng, here called 'sang' (the roots of which are largely collected, and sold to the country merchants when fresh for about twelve cents per pound, or when dry for triple that price)." Successful cultivation of Ginseng was begun in the 1880s and is now dominated by growers in Wisconsin; 90% of the harvest is exported, mainly to Hong Kong.

Meanwhile, in Virginia William Byrd (1728) wrote of Ginseng, "Its vertues are, that it gives uncommon warmth and vigour to the blood, and frisks the spirits beyond any other cordial. It cheers the heart even of a man that has a bad wife, and makes him look down with great composure on the crosses of the world. It promotes insensible perspiration, dissolves all phlegmatick and viscous humours that are apt to obstruct the narrow channels of the nerves. It helps the memory, and would quicken even Helvetian dullness. 'Tis friendly to the lungs, much more than scolding itself. It comforts the stomach, and strengthens the bowels, preventing all colicks and fluxes. In one word, it will make a man live a great while, and very well while he does live. And what is more, it will even make

old age amiable, by rendering it lively, cheerful, and good-humour'd." At age 67 (in 1741), William Byrd wrote to his old London friend Sir Hans Sloane, "I take it a little unkindly, Sir, that my name is left out of the yearly list of the Royal Society, of which I have the honour to be one of its ancientest members. I suppose my long absence has made your secretarys rank me in the number of the dead, but pray let them know I am alive, and by the help of Ginseng hope to survive some years longer."

"According to conventional Chinese belief, ginseng is the crystallization of the essence of the earth in the form of man. It represents the vital spirit of the earth that dwells in a root. It is the manifestation of the spiritual phase of nature in material form. It is further believed that a small portion of ginseng can cure the sick, strengthen the weak, rejuvenate the aged, and revitalize the dying" (Shin Ying Hu, 1976). The USD concluded that "the extraordinary medicinal virtues formerly attributed to ginseng had no other existence than in the imagination of the Chinese. It is little more than a demulcent." Garantogen is an Indian name.

# THE CARROT OR PARSLEY FAMILY

## *Apiaceae or Umbelliferae*

A cosmopolitan family of 418 genera and 3,100 herbs and a few shrubs and trees, best developed in north temperate regions. Members of the family provide us with carrots *(Daucus carota)*, parsnips *(Pastinaca sativa)* and celery *(Apium graveolans)* for sustenance and, for flavor, chervil *(Anthriscus cerefolium)*, fennel *(Foeniculum vulgare)*, parsley *(Petroselinum crispum)*, dill *(Anethum graveolans)*, coriander *(Coriandrum sativum)*, cumin *(Cuminum cyminum)*, caraway *(Carum carvi)* and anise *(Pimpinella anisum)*.

Many species have umbrella-shaped flower clusters (New Latin *umbella,* "umbrella," from Latin *umbra,* "shadow").

## Angelica

*Angelica atropurpurea.* Angelic (medicinal properties); dark-purple.

Alexanders, American-Masterwort, Archangel, Aunt-Jerichos (New England), Belly-Ache-Root, Dead-Nettle, Great High-Angelica, Hunting-Root (Va.), Masterwort, Purple-Stemmed Angelica

Angelica is so named because people believed it could arrest the Plague or perhaps because it flowers on the feast of Saint Michael the Archangel. In his 1687 letter about the Virginia Indians, the Reverend John Clayton wrote that "it is mostly called by those who know it in Virginia by the name of Angelica. But showing a piece of the root to a great Woodsman to see whether he knew it and could tell me where it grew, he seemed surprized to see me have thereof, and told me that he kept an Indian once for several weeks with him, because he was an excellent Woodsman. And going a hunting . . . they came where some of this root grew. The Indian rejoycing gathered some of it, but was very carefull to cut off the top of the root and replant it. He then asked him why he was so careful, whereunto the Indian replyed, It was a very choice plant and very scarce for they sometimes travelled 100 or 200 miles without finding any of it. He then asked him what use it was of, to which the Indian answered you shall see by and by. After some time they spyed 4 deer at a distance; then the Indian, contrary to his usual custom, went to windward of them, and sitting down upon the trunk of an old tree, began to rub the root betwixt his hands, at which the deer toss up their heads and snuffing their noses, they fed towards the place where the Indian satt, till they came within easy shot of him, whereupon he fired at them, and killed a large buck . . . I have since learned from others that the Indians call it the Hunting Root."

William Byrd (1728) reported that the "root of this plant being very warm and aromatick, is coveted by woodsmen extremely as a dry dram, that is, when rum, that cordial for all distresses, is wanting." The leafstalks are boiled in sugar and eaten as candy or put in cakes. Writing of the very similar European *Angelica sylvestris,* Parkinson (1629) advised taking the "distilled water of Angelica" for "swounings, when the spirits are overcome and faint, or tremblings and passions of the heart" and the candied stem and roots "to comfort and warme a colde and weake stomach"; the powdered root "will abate the rage of lust in young persons," and a syrup made of Angelica is "very profitable to expectorate flegme out of the chest and lunges, and to procure a sweet breath." Here is Parkinson's recipe: "Into the green stalke of Angelica as it standeth growing, make a great gashe or incision, wherein put a quantitie of fine white sugar, letting it there abide for three days, and after take it forth by cutting a hole at the next joint under

*Angelica*

the cut, where the syrupe resteth, or cut off the stalke, and turne it downe, that the syrupe may drayne forth; which keepe for a most delicate medicine."

## Angelica-Root, Filmy Angelica

*Angelica fomentosa.* Angelic; densely pubescent.

In Mendocino County, California, "Angelica root, as it is most commonly called both by Indians and whites, is a most valued remedy and talisman. It is found in nearly every household and is frequently carried about the person for good luck in gambling or hunting . . . The root, after thorough mastication, is sometimes rubbed on the legs to prevent rattlesnake bites, and it is also tied around the head and ears in bad cases of headache and nightmare" (Chesnut, 1902).

## Caraway

*Carum carvi.* (From the Greek name, *karon*); (an old herbalists' name, also spelled *Carui;* the plant was widely grown in Caria, a district in Asia Minor). (From Europe.)
*Anis* (P.Q.), Carvies

In one of his chapters on "The Kitchen Garden," John Parkinson (1629) wrote, "The roots of Caraway being boyled may be eaten as carrots, and by reason of the spicie taste doth warm and comfort a cold weak stomacke, helping to dissolve wind (whereas carrots engender it) and to provoke urine, and is a very welcome and delightfull dish to a great many, yet they are somewhat stronger in taste than parsnips. The seed is much used to be put among baked fruit, or into bread, cakes, &c. to give them a rellish, and to help digest wind in them are subject thereunto." Caraway is cultivated for its aromatic seeds, and the young leaves are also eaten. Carvies is a local name in Scotland. It has been included in the USP and NF; "the seeds are a

*Caraway*

pleasant stomachic and carminative and have been used in flatulent colic" (Jacobs and Burlage).

## Water-Hemlock, Spotted Cowbane

*Cicuta maculata.* (The Latin name of Poison-Hemlock); spotted.
Beaver-Poison, *Carotte à Moreau* (P.Q.), Children's-Bane, Cowbane, Death-of-Man, False-Parsley, Fever-Root, Mock-Eelroot, Muskrat-Weed, Musquash-Poison, Musquash-Root, Poison-Hemlock, Poison-Parsnip, Snakeroot, Snakeweed, Scoots, Spotted-Hemlock, Spotted-Parsley, Wild-Carrot, Wild-Parsnip

"The most violently poisonous plant of the North Temperate Zone" (Kingsbury); the symptoms of Cicuta poisoning were "described several centuries ago, and are generally well known. They are specific and distinctive. Cicutoxin, acting directly on the central nervous system, is a violent convulsive." The symptoms appear 15 to 20 minutes after ingestion, usually of the root that was mistaken for a Wild Parsnip *(Pastinaca sativa)* or Wild Artichoke *(Helianthus annuus).* "Excessive salivation is first noted. This is quickly followed by tremors and then by spasmodic convulsions interspersed intermittently with periods of relaxation. The convulsions are extremely violent; head and neck are thrown rigidly back, legs may flex as though running, and clamping or chewing motions of the jaw and grinding of teeth may occur"—then pain, nausea, delirium, death. "Scores of cases of the loss of human life to this plant are on record in the United States."

John Richardson (1823) in Arctic Canada wrote of the Cicutas that "the poisonous kinds are called *manitoskatash,* and by the voyageurs *carotte de Moreau,* after a man who died from eating them."

## Poison Hemlock

*Conium maculatum.* (The Greek name); spotted. (From Europe.)

Bunk, California-Fern, Cashes, *Ciguë* (P.Q.), Herb-Bonnet, Kill-Cow, Nebraska-Fern, Poison-Parsley, Poisonroot, Poison-Snakeweed, St. Bennet's-Herb, Snakeweed, Spotted-Cowbane, Spotted-Parsley, Stinkweed, Wode-Whistle

"This herb is called humlock or herb Benet. The vertue of this herb is thus. The joyce of this herb kepeth maidens teets small"

*Poison Hemlock*

(Banckes, 1525). But Gerard (1633) wrote that it is "a very rash part to lay the leaves of Hemlocke to the stones of yong boyes, or virgins brests, by that means to keep those parts from growing great; for it doth not only easily cause those members to pine away, but also hurteth the heart and liver, being outwardly applied." It has been included in the USP and NF, "used in spasmodic disorders, such as tetanus and acute mania, and by some with asserted good results" (USD). Dr. Bigelow reported, "The Hemlock has been for many years a subject of attention with physicians, and has been found a remedy in many diseases," and he descibed its use in jaundice, "tic doloureux," "schirrus and cancer," and "old syphilitic affections." Bunk and Stinkweed are local names in England. Wode-Whistle is an old English name.

A plant called Conium (Greek *koneion*) was the source of a famous poison in antiquity and a favorite of suicides; old men in Athens, when they had become useless to the state and tired of their infirmities, would prepare a banquet and, after feasting, they would crown themselves, drink Conium and die. Plato has left us a detailed account of the death of Socrates: He had offended the state and was sentenced to death by poisoning. He calmly took the draught of Conium prepared by the executioner, drank it and serenely died among his friends. From Dioscorides's description of Conium, it is clearly an umbellate plant, and Linnaeus decided that it was this plant. But death from Hemlock poisoning (if one can get enough of it, for it is lethal only in large doses) is nasty and violent. Perhaps the Athenian executioners and suicides mixed Hemlock with other poisons or sedatives.

## Honewort, Wild-Chervil

*Cryptotaenia canadensis.* Hidden band (the oil tubes under the carpel ribs); of Canada.

In 1632 Thomas Johnson found Mistress Ursula Leigh gathering the English species of the plant in wheat fields near Mapledurham in Hampshire. She told him it was called Honewort and was used to cure swellings in the cheek, which her mother, Mistress Charitie Leigh, called Hones: "Take one handfull of the greene leaves of this Honewort, and stampe them, put to it about halfe a pint or more of beere, straine it and drinke it, and doe continue to drinke the like quantity every morning fasting till the swelling doth abate."

In Quebec "the French call it *cerfeuil sauvage,* and make use of it in spring, in green soups, like chervil. It is universally praised here as a wholesome, antiscorbutic plant, and as one of the best which can be had here in spring" (Kalm, 1749). The young leaves, the stems and the roots are eaten.

## Queen-Anne's-Lace, Wild Carrot

*Daucus carota.* (The Latin name); carrot (the old generic name). (From Europe.)
Bee's-Nest-Plant, Bird's-Nest (Maine, N.J., Texas), *Carotte sauvage* (P.Q.), Devil's-Plague (W.Va.), Fool's-Parsley (Maine), *Herbe à dinde* (Mo.), Lace-flower (Pa.), Parsnip (Maine), Rantipole

*Queen-Anne's-Lace*

Wild Carrot was William Turner's name (1548) and is still the British name for the plant. Queen-Anne's-Lace is an American name for this plant and a local name in England for Cow-Parsley *(Anthriscus sylvestris),* derived, Grigson suggests, not from a queen of England but from Saint Anne, the Virgin's mother. Saint Anne is the patron saint of lacemakers. The cultivated carrot is a descendant of this plant, whose first-year root is edible. Bee's-Nest-Plant and Crow's-Nest (the shape of the ripe seedhead) and Rantipole are local names in England. It is called *Herbe à Dinde* "because fed to young turkeys" (McAtee, 1937).

Dr. Porcher reported that "the root is edible, and possesses more aroma than any of our indigenous plants. It is used in spasmodic vomiting, flatulent colics, and nervous headaches; some say it is powerfully emmenagogue."

## Harbinger-of-Spring

*Erigenia bulbosa.* Born in the spring (Erigineia is another name for Aurora); bulbous.
Ground-Nut, Pepper-and-Salt (Ind.), Turkey-Pea (Ind., Ohio), Turkey-Foot

The white petals and dark stamens suggested salt and pepper. The tuber (Ground-Nut or Turkey-Pea) is eaten raw or cooked.

## Button-Snakeroot

*Eryngium aquaticum.* (From the Greek name); aquatic.
Contrayerva (N.C., S.C.), Corn Snakeroot, Eryngo, Feverweed, Rattlesnake-Flag, Rattlesnake-Weed, Water Eryngo

In Arkansas, February 1819, "the prairie, in consequence of the late rains, appeared almost one continued sheet of water. I observed springing up, the *Eryngium aquaticum,* occasionally employed as a medicine by the inhabitants, acting as a diuretic and in large doses proving almost emetic" (Nuttall, 1821).

The "button" is the round head of florets. The USD reported, "It is said to be diaphoretic, expectorant, in large doses emetic, and the plant has been used as a substitute for senega." Senega is Seneca-Snakeroot. Contrayerva is "counter-herb," an antidote, and usually refers to *Dorstenia contrayerva* (Moraceae) of tropical America.

## Rattlesnake Master

*Eryngium yuccifolium.* (From the Greek name); yucca-leaved.

Button-Snakeroot, Merrye-Curvye (La.)

Dr. Millspaugh reported that "this species was valued highly by the Aborigines as an alexiteric, and, combined with Iris versicolor, as a febrifuge and diuretic; since their time it has come into use by first the laity, then the physician, as a stimulant, diaphoretic, sialogogue, expectorant, diuretic, and alterative." He listed many conditions for which "a decoction of the root has been found useful," including "exhaustion from sexual depletion with loss of erectile power, seminal emis-

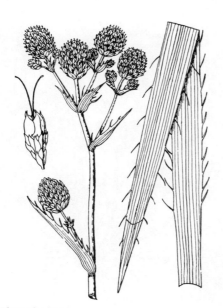

*Rattlesnake Master*

sions, and orchitis." The candied roots of the European *Eryngium maritimum,* called Eringos or Kissing Comfits, have also been esteemed for their aphrodisiac virtues. In the following (from Shakespeare's *The Merry Wives of Windsor,* 5.5) the aging Falstaff has a midnight assignation in the park:

> *Falstaff:* Who comes here? my doe?

> *Mrs. Ford:* Sir John? Art thou there, my deer?, my male deer?

> *Falstaff:* My doe with the black scut? Let the sky rain potatoes; let it thunder to the tune of Greensleeves; hail kissing-comfits and snow eringoes; let there come a tempest of provocation.

Luigi Castiglioni (1790) reported that "this plant was pointed out to me by Dr. Greenway, a Virginia physician . . . as an excellent remedy for rattlesnake bite; and Mr. Clayton, in his *Flora virginica,* after having alluded to the aforementioned quality, adds that in the treatment of fevers it is on a par with *Contrayerva.*" Of the name Merrye-Curvye in Louisiana, Touchstone (1983) wrote, "The only information I found on the name of the plant was that a 'Granny woman' with the name of Mary Curby brought the plant to the attention of local herbal users. Not knowing any other name, the people called it the merrye curvye plant. Everyone having knowledge of this herb made a tea from the root. They used the tea to treat hives, whooping cough, measles and other throat complaints." The Indians also used the plant to treat snakebite.

## Fennel

*Foeniculum vulgare.* (The Latin name); common. (From Europe.)

Dill, Finkel, Meeting-Seed, Spignel, Spingel

In his *Agricultural Botany* of 1847, Darlington wrote, "The whole plant is aromatic.

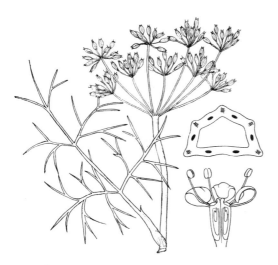

*Fennel*

Those who keep bees, in former years, were much in the practice, when those insects swarmed, of rubbing the inside of the beehive with this fragrant herb,—under the impression that the odor would attach them to their new domicile. It is chiefly cultivated for its aromatic fruit,—which is occasionally used in domestic economy; and is sometimes smoked like tobacco, as a popular remedy in cholic." "Some people call it 'caraway' and 'anise seed,' but we call it 'meetin seed,' cause we cal'late it keeps us awake in meetin'" (*Knickerbocker* 38:372, 1851).

John Evelyn wrote that it is "Aromatick, hot, and dry; expels wind, sharpens the sight, and recreates the brain; especially the tender umbella and seed-pods. The stalks are to be peel'd when young, and then dress'd like sellery. The tender tufts and leaves emerging, being minc'd, are eaten alone with vinegar, or oyl, and pepper." He added that "the Italians eat the blanch'd stalk (which they call *Cartucci*) all Winter long." Fennel seeds are used to flavor many foods. Spignel and Spingel are local names in England and Finkel in England and Scotland. It has been included in the USP and NF: "It is one of our most

grateful aromatics, and is employed as a carminative, and as a corrigent of other less pleasant medicine" (USD).

## Cow-Parsnip

*Heracleum lanatum.* Of Hercules *(Herakles);* woolly.

Beaver-Root (Neb.), *Berce laineuse* (P.Q.), Cow-Cabbage, Eltrot, Health-Root (Nfd.), Hell-Root (Nfd.), Heltrot, Hogweed, Madnep, Masterwort, Mouthwort

Among the Menomini, "on a deer hunt, as soon as the camp is established and the fire built, some of this cow parsnip is thrown on the fire, and the odor and smoke permeate the air for great distances, making it impossible for the sokenau [evil spirit] to approach too closely under ordinary circumstances. But if the sokenau is desperate and determined to steal one's hunting luck, he may come right into camp, but the smoke of pikiwunus (cow parsnip) will cause him to go blind" (Huron Smith, 1923). The Blackfoot Indians eat the spring stalks after roasting them on hot coals: "They were of two kinds, *napim,*

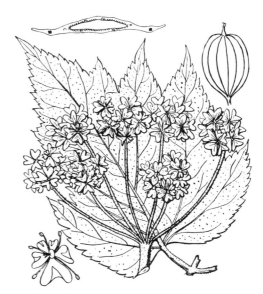

*Cow-Parsnip*

'he' or 'male beast,' which were immature flower stalks and had to be peeled before roasting, and *skim,* 'she' or 'female beast,' which were leaf stalks and had to be peeled and split before roasting. A stalk of cow parsnip was used in the Sun Dance ceremony. A strong decoction of the roots was used by several tribes in the treament of rheumatism and arthritis" (Alex Johnston).

The roots are cooked or dried and used as a salt substitute. Eltrot, altered to Heltrot in the United States and Health-Root or Hell-Root in Newfoundland, is dialect English for the hollow stems of many plants. Hogweed is a local name in England for *Heracleum sphondylium,* which Gerard (1633) called Cow Parsnep or Madnep: "If a phrenticke or melancholicke mans head bee annointed with oile wherein the leaves and roots have been sodden, it helpeth him very much, and such as be troubled with the head-ache and the lethargie, or sicknesse called the forgetfull evil."

## Canadian Lovage

*Ligusticum canadense.* Of Liguria (in Italy, where the medicinal Lovage came from); of Canada.

Angelica, Angelico, American-Savage, Bellyache-Root (Va.), *Livêche* (P.Q.), Nondo, Whiteroot

In the *Flora Virginica* of 1762, John Clayton called this "Angelica lucida canadensis fortesse, vulgo Belly-ach-root." In 1776 in South Carolina William Bartram wrote, "The Angelica Lucido or Nondo grows here in abundance; its aromatic carminative root is in taste much like that of the Ginseng (Panax) though more of the taste and scent of anise seed; it is in high estimation with the Indians as well as white inhabitants, and sells at a great price to the Southern Indians of Florida, who dwell near the sea coast where this never grows spontaneously." The young shoots and stems are cooked, and the roots are eaten raw or

*Canadian Lovage*

cooked. The cultivated Lovage is *Levisticum officinale.*

## Loveroot

*Ligusticum filicinum.* Of Liguria; fernlike (leaves).

Chuchupate, Colorado-Coughroot, Fernleaf Lovage, Fernleaf Loveroot, Icecream-Plant, Osha, Rocky-Mountain-Coughroot, Wild-Celery, Wild-Parsnip

The aromatic roots of this plant and of Porter Loveroot (*Ligusticum porterii*) "have a pleasant warm taste and are used in the treatment of coughs, colds, stomach disorders, and other ailments. In the drug trade they are sold under the names of Colorado or Rocky Mountain coughroot and osha" (*Range Plant Handbook,* 1937). Fernleaf Loveroot is highly prized as a forage plant because of its high palatability, but since it is also relatively scarce, it "is often referred to as an ice cream plant."

## Carrotleaf, Desert-Parsley, Fern-Leaved Lomatium

*Lomatium dissectum.* Fringed (the winged fruit); dissected (leaves).

Biscuitroot, Chocolate-Tips, Cough-Root, Indian-Balsam, Wild-Carrot, Wild-Celery, Wild-Parlsey

"For the preparation of medicinal remedies this plant is by far the best known in the State of Nevada, being used both by the Indians and by the whites. All Indian communities endeavor to maintain a stock to last through the winter months, for which purpose the root is peeled, sliced and laid away to dry. A number of years ago it was possible to purchase in local drugstores a commercial preparation of the plant under the name of Balsamea. Of all the ailments to which the Indian is heir, probably there is none which has not been treated in one way or another by remedies prepared from the root of this plant. Although considered universally as a panacea, the medicines most commonly used are for coughs and colds, and disorders such as hayfever, bronchitis, influenza, pneumonia and tuberculosis" (Train, Henrichs and Archer, 1941). The resinous balsamic roots were also roasted and eaten by the Indians.

## Biscuitroot, Indian-Biscuit

*Lomatium geyeri*. Fringed; of Geyer (Carl Andreas Geyer, 1809–1853).

Large quantities of Lomatium roots, called Cous, Cows, Cowas or Cowish, were gathered by Indians of the Rocky Mountain region. "The tubers may be consumed raw and in that state have a celery flavor. The most usual method of use among the Indians, however, was to remove the rind, dry the inside portion, and pulverise it. The flour would then be mixed with water, flattened into cakes and dried in the sun or baked. These cakes, according to Edward Palmer (1870), were customarily about half an inch thick but a yard long by a foot wide, with a hole in the middle, by which they could be tied to the saddle of the traveler. The taste of such cakes is rather like stale biscuits" (Saunders, 1934). Lomatium plants are closely related to the culti-

vated Parsnip. The roots are also prized by rodents and bears.

Lewis and Clark among the Chopunnish Indians, May 1806: "The hunters who have as yet come in brought nothing except a few pheasants, so that we still place our chief reliance on the mush made of roots, among which cows and quamash are the principal ones; with these we use a small onion, which grows in great abundance, and which corrects any bad effects they may have on the stomach. The cows and quamash incline to produce flatulency; to obviate which we employ a kind of fennel, called by the Shoshonees yearah, resembling anniseed in flavor and a very agreeable food." Quamash is Camas, Yearah is Yampa.

Geyer was a German botanist who collected plants in the American Northwest in 1844 and published an account of the Missouri and Oregon Territories in 1846.

## Pestle Lomatium

*Lomatium nudicaule*. Fringed; naked-stemmed.
Cous, Indian-Celery (B.C.), Indian Consumption-Plant, Licorice (B.C.), Pestle-Parsnip

In British Columbia, "we remember a school journey in which Indian children from Lytton were bused to Botannie Lake. As they jumped down from the bus, all the children at once pulled plants and roots of this species from the roadside, explaining that it was 'Licorice, ver' good!' The bus-driver's name for it was 'Indian Celery.' We thought the taste was rather like a hot, spicy parsnip" (Clark, 1976). The pestle is the enlarged stem just below the umbels. The name Indian Consumption-Plant suggests that the plant was a native remedy for the white man's tuberculosis.

## Sweet Cicely

*Osmorhiza claytonii*. Scented root; of Clayton (John Clayton, 1694–1773).

*Sweet Cicely*

Hairy Sweet-Cicely, Sweet-Jarvil (Maine), Sweet-Javril, Woolly Sweet-Cicely

The names Jarvil and Javril of this plant and the Chevril and Jowil of the next suggest that both plants were substitutes for the related Chervil *(Anthriscus cerefolium)* of the herb garden. Sweet Cicely is also the related *Myrrhis odorata* of Europe. Cicely is from the Latin and Greek name *seselis* of several related plants. The root of this and the next plant smell and taste of anise "and is often chewed by boys" according to Medsger (1939); the spicy green fruit is also a pleasant chew.

## Anise-Root

*Osmorhiza longistylis.* Scented root; long-styled.

Cicely-Root, Paregoric-Root, Sicily-Root, Smooth Sweet-Cicely, Sweet-Anise (Ohio), Sweet-Chevril, Sweet-Jarvil (Maine), Sweet-Javril, Sweet-Jowil (N.C.)

"The Omaha and Ponca say that horses were so fond of the roots . . . that if one whistled to them, while holding out the bag of roots, the horses came trotting up to get a taste, and so could easily be caught. An Omaha said the the roots were pounded up to make poultices to apply to boils. A Winnebago medicine-man reported the same treatment for wounds. A Pawnee said that a decoction of

the roots was taken for weakness and general debility" (Gilmore). The name Paregoric-Root suggests one of the medicinal uses of the sweet root; paregoric is an opium-containing remedy for diarrhea.

## Sweet-Anise

*Osmorhiza occidentalis.* Scented root; of the west.

Western Sweet-Cicely, Western Anise-Root

In Nevada, "as a source for remedies, this plant holds favor among all the Indians," Percy Train and his colleagues (1941) reported; "in most communities, the Shoshones and Paiutes look upon the root decoction as an important treatment for venereal disease, although many of the informants indicated that a long period of time was needed for the purpose." It was also used as a cure for colds, pneumonia, infuenza, fever, diarrhea, indigestion "and in one community to regulate menstrual disorders." According to the *Range Plant Handbook,* "sweet-anise is one of the choice range weeds. Its palatability is usually high for all classes of livestock."

*Sweet-Anise*

## Yampa

*Perideridia gairdneri.* With a leather coat (Greek *peri,* "around," *deris,* "leather coat," the dark skin of the tubers); of Gairdner (Meredith Gairdner, 1809–1837).

Breadroot, False-Caraway, Gairdner's Yampah, Indian-Potato, Ipo, Queen-Anne's-Lace, Squawroot, Wild-Caraway

In northern Colorado, 1843, Lieutenant Frémont reported, "At this place I became first acquainted with the *yampah,* which I found our Snake women engaged in digging in the low timbered bottom of the creek. Among the Indians along the Rocky mountains, and more particularly among the Shoshonee or Snake Indians, in whose territory it is very abundant, this is considered the best among the roots used for food . . . It grows more abundantly, and in greater luxuriance, on one of the neighboring tributaries of the Colorado than in any other part of this region; and on that stream, to which the Snakes are accustomed to resort every year to procure a supply of their favorite plant, they have bestowed the name Yampah river."

The *Range Plant Handbook* reported that the tubers "have a sweet, nutty, creamlike flavor" and suggested that the name Ipo is a corruption of the Spanish-Californian *apio,* meaning "celery": "Sacajawea, the famous Indian woman guide, counselor and interpreter for Lewis and Clark, appears to have been the first person to introduce this plant to the whites under that name . . . The roots were cleaned by placing them in baskets in running water where squaws trod them with bare feet to remove the dark outer skin and make them smooth and clean. They were then boiled or prepared as the Indians prepare other vegetables. The roots were also eaten raw, ground into flour and made into bread, or used with other roots and seeds to make a meal or gruel. The seeds have an aromatic caraway flavor and were used to season other foods."

Meredith Gairdner was born in London and died in Hawaii. He was surgeon to the Hudson Bay Company and collected plants in the American Northwest.

## Black Snakeroot, Maryland Sanicle

*Sanicula marilandica.* Healer (the Medieval Latin name; *sanus* means "healthy"); of Maryland.

Black Sanicle, Poolroot, Sanicle, Self-Heal

"The Flambeau Ojibwe use the root pounded as a poultice to cure rattlesnake bite or any snake bite. Bearskin, chief Flambeau medicine man, said that if this root be chewed it would cause eruptions on the epithelial lining of the mouth. They consider it a very potent remedy" (Huron Smith, 1932). Grieve reported that the root "contains resin and volatile oil, and it has been used with alleged success in intermittent fever and in chorea." Dr. Porcher reported that "the Indians used it as we do sarsparilla in syphilis, and also in diseases of the lungs."

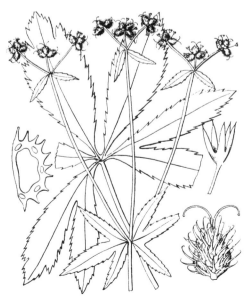

*Black Snakeroot*

Sanicle, *Sanicula europaea,* was famous for healing wounds in man and beast: "This is one of Venus's herbs to cure the wounds or mischiefs Mars inflicteth upon the body of man" (Culpeper). Poolroot and Self-Heal are names of the European species.

## Water-Parsnip

*Sium suave.* (From the Greek name of a marshy plant); fragrant. (Also found in Asia.) *Berle douce* (P.Q.), Hemlock-Water-Parsnip, *Queue de rat* (P.Q.), Skirret

"The seed of this is smoked over a fire by the Flambeau Ojibwe to drive away and blind Sokenau, the evil spirit that steals away one's hunting luck" (Huron Smith, 1932).

Skirret is the edible root, particularly of the European *Sium sisarum:* "hot and moist, corroborating, and good for the stomach, exceedingly nourishing, wholesome and deli-

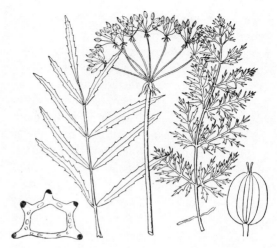

*Water-Parsnip*

cate; of all the root-kind, not subject to be windy, and so valued by the Emperor *Tiberius* that he accepted them for tribute" (Evelyn, 1699).

# THE LOGANIA FAMILY

## *Loganiaceae*

A widespread family of 29 genera and 600 species of herbs, shrubs, climbers and trees; found chiefly in tropical and subtropical regions. Many members of the family are extremely poisonous, including *Strychnos nux-vomita,* from whose seeds strychnine is obtained. One outstanding ornamental member of the family is *Buddleia.*

## Yellow Jessamine, Carolina-Jasmine

*Gelsemium sempervirens.* Jasmine (from the Italian name *Gelsemino*); ever-living. Carolina Jessamine, Cow-Itch, Evening Trumpet-Flower, Jasmine, Wild-Woodbine, Yellow-Jasmine

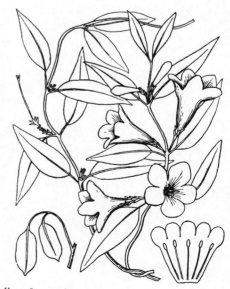

*Yellow Jessamine*

Lloyd (1911) reported that the drug, gelsemium, extracted from the roots of Yellow Jessamine, was discovered in the early 1800s "through the mistake of a servant of a Southern planter who was afflicted with fever. This servant, by error, gave his master a decoction of gelsemium root instead of the garden plant intended. Immediate loss of muscular power and great depression followed, all control of limbs was lost, the eyelids drooped and could not be voluntarily opened. Death seemed imminent. But the effects finally wore away and the man recovered, free from fever, which did not recur. An observer physician took this experience as a text, and prepared from gelsemium a remedy which he called the 'Electrical febrifuge,' which attained some popularity." It has been included in the USP and USD: "It is a primary stimulant to the motor centers of the cord, secondarily depressant, and in toxic doses produces almost complete paralysis" (USD). All parts of the plant are extremely poisonous, and eating just one flower has reportedly been fatal to children. The foliage can also cause contact dermatitis (Cow-Itch).

Jessamine is a variant of Jasmin (ultimately from the the Persian *Yasmin, Yasman*), plants of the genus *Jasminum* (Oleaceae); *Jasminum officinale* is the fragrant White Jasmin or Poet's Jessamine.

## Indian-Pink

*Spigelia marilandica.* Of Spieghel (Adriaan van den Spieghel, 1578–1625); of Maryland. American Wormroot, Carolina-Pink, Maryland Pinkroot, Pinkroot, Snakeroot, Starbloom, Unstilla, Wormgrass

Dr. Bigelow called it Carolina Pink Root and noted that its reputation as a vermifuge

*Indian-Pink*

"is now so generally established that the plant has become a considerable article of commerce to various parts of the world, from our southern states." It has been included in the USP. Dr. Millspaugh reported that "the colonists of the South received their information concerning its [anthelmintic] properties from the Cherokees, who called it *unsteetla,* and from the Osages, who used it also as a sudorific and sedative, under the name *mikaa.*"

In 1911 John Uri Lloyd wrote that "as a domestic remedy it was customary half a century ago, to use a mixture of pink root and senna, to which were added a few pieces of manna, a home decocotion being given to children and others afflicted with worms . . . In the days of this writer's experience as a prescription clerk in Cincinnati (1865–80) the mixture was in continual domestic demand as 'pink and senna.' " Spieghel, who Latinized his name to Spigelius, was a Flemish botanist and anatomist.

# THE GENTIAN FAMILY

## *Gentianaceae*

A cosmopolitan family of 74 genera and 1,200 species of herbs and a few shrubs and small trees; found chiefly in temperate and subtropical regions. Gentius, King of Illyria in the second century B.C., supposedly discovered the medicinal properties of Yellow Gentian *(Gentiana lutea)*. In 1983 E. B. White (aged 84) wrote from the Great Pond, Maine, "I sat out a New England boiled dinner this noon by anticipating it with martinis and cheese-and-crackers before walking up to the farmhouse, and after dinner (or lack of same) went fishing for bass in my canoe. There is a certain serenity here that heals my spirit, and I can still buy Moxie in a tiny supermarket six miles away. Moxie contains gentian root, which is the path to the good life. This was known in the second century before Christ, and it is a boon to me today" (Mitgang, 1985).

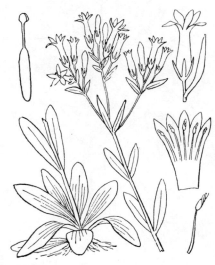

*Centaury*

## Centaury

*Centaurium erythraea.* Of the Centaur (Chiron the Centaur, who was famous for his knowledge of healing plants and used Centaury to cure an arrow wound in his foot); a previous generic name. (From Europe.)
Bitter-Herb, Bloodwort, Branching-Centaury, Christ's-Ladder, Earth-Gall, European Centaury, Fever-Few, Lesser Centaury, Mountain-Flax, Sanctuary

This is an ancient tonic and healing herb. Culpeper wrote that "the herb is so safe that you cannot fail in the using of it, only give it inwardly for inward diseases, use it outwardly for outward diseases. 'Tis very wholesome, but not very toothsome." The old herbalists recognized two plants named after Chiron the Centaur: this one, which Gerard called Small Centorie, and Great Centorie, a species of *Centaurea.* Small Centorie "cleanseth, scoureth, and maketh thinne humors that are thicke, and doth effectually performe whatsoever bitter things can" (Gerard, 1633). Bitter-Herb, Bloodwort, Earth-Gall and Sanctuary are local names in England.

## Charming Centaury

*Centaurium venustum.* Of the Centaur; graceful.
Canchalagua, Chill-and-Fever-Plant (Calif.), Wild-Quinine

In California this was a popular remedy for fevers and malaria.

## American Columbo

*Frasera caroliniensis.* Of Fraser (John Fraser, 1750–1811); of Carolina.
American Frasera, Colombo, Colombo-Root, Columbia, Columbo, Deer's-Ears, Felwort, Ground-Centaury, Indian-Lettuce, Meadow-Pride, Marsh-

*American Columbo*

Felwort, Monument-Plant, Pyramid-Flower, Pyramid-Plant, Quinine-Flower, Yellow-Gentian

Dr. Porcher reported that "This plant holds a deservedly high rank among our native tonics, and I would recommend its employment to those residing in localities where it may be found. The tincture is given as a tonic, and the powdered plant applied externally to ulcers in the form of a poultice." Columba or Columbo is the dried root of the African *Jateorhiza palmata* (*Kalumb* is the African name), once used "in functional atonic conditions of the digestive organ," according to the USD. American Columbo or Frasera is "a feeble, simple bitter" (USD).

John Fraser was born in Scotland and died in London. He was a hosier who established a nursery in London and collected plants in North America for the Czar of Russia, among others.

## Monument-Plant, Green-Gentian

*Frasera speciosa.* Of Fraser; showy.
Deer's-Ears, Deertongue, Elkweed, Giant Frasera, Green-Gentian

The Navaho rubbed a cold infusion of the leaves on the bodies of hunters and their horses "to strengthen them for a long expedition; dried leaves mixed with mountain tobacco, smoked in a corn husk cigarette or a hunting pipe, to give strength and to clear the mind if lost while hunting or if confused after returning from a hunt, enables clear thinking so the way to camp may be found" (Vestal, 1952).

## Closed Gentian

*Gentiana andrewsii.* Of Gentius; of Andrews (Henry C. Andrews, fl. 1794–1830, English botanical artist and engraver).
Bacral Gentian, Barrel Gentian (Mass.), Belmony (N.H.), Blind Gentian (Mass.), Bottle Gentian (Mass.), Cloistered-Heart, Dumb-Foxglove, Sampson's-Snakeroot

September 28: "The gentian (Andrewsii), now generally in prime, loves moist shady banks, and its transcendent blue shows best in the shade and suggests coolness; contrasts there with the fresh green; a splendid blue, light in the shade, turning to purple with age.

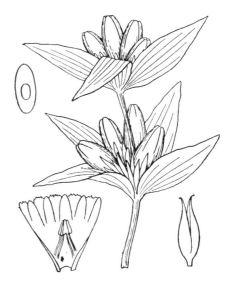

*Closed Gentian*

They are particularly abundant under the northside of the willow-row in Merrick's pasture. I counted fifteen in a single cluster there, and afterward twenty at Gentian Lane near Flint's Bridge, and there were other clusters below. Bluer than the bluest sky, they lurk in the moist and shady recesses of the banks."

## Catesby's Gentian

*Gentiana catesbaei.* Of Gentius; of Catesby (Mark Catesby, 1683–1749).

Bitter-Root, Bluebells, Blue Gentian, Sampson's-Snakeroot, Southern Gentian

It has been included in the USP and has been "reputed to be but little inferior to the official species [*G. lutea*], the most popular of all bitters in the treatment of atonic dyspepsia, anorexia, and similar complaints" (USD).

## Soapwort Gentian

*Gentiana saponaria.* Of Gentius; like Saponaria (Soapwort foliage).

*Soapwort Gentian*

Bluebells, Blue Gentian, Calathian-Violet, Harvest-Bells, Marsh Gentian, Rough Gentian, Sampson's-Snakeroot

Calathian Violet, Autumn Bel-floure and Harvest-bels were names used by Gerard (1633) for a similar Gentian. A calathus (from Greek *kalathos*) is a vase-shaped basket. September 2: "The soapwort gentian out abundantly in Flint's Bridge Lane, apparently for a week; a surprisingly deep, *faintly* purplish blue. Crowded bunches of ten or a dozen sessile and closed narrow or oblong diamond or sharp dome shape flowers. The whole bunch like many sharp domes of an Oriental city crowded together" (Thoreau, 1853).

## Fringed Gentian

*Gentianopsis crinita.* Like Gentian; with long hairs.

In "To the Fringed Gentian" (1832), William Cullen Bryant wrote,

> *Thou waitest late and com'st alone,*
> *When woods are bare and birds are*
> *flown,*
> *And frosts and shortening days portend*
> *The aged year is near his end.*

> *Then doth thy sweet and quiet eye*
> *Look through its fringes to the sky,*
> *Blue—blue—as if that sky let fall*
> *A flower from its cerulean wall.*

## Rose-Pink

*Sabatia angularis.* Of Sabbati (Liberato Sabbati, 18th-century curator of the Rome botanic garden); with angles (stem).

American-Centaury, Angular-Centaury, Bitter-Bloom, Bitter-Clover, Centory, Eyebright (N.C.), Pink-Bloom (W.Va.), Red-Centaury, Square-Stemmed Sabatia, Wild-Succory

According to Dr. Barton, this is the plant "which is called Centory or Centry in Philadelphia, &c., where it is so commonly employed both by physicians and as a domestic remedy in almost every family . . . I believe that no bitter has been more generally prescribed in the United-States, in febrile and other affections, than this common American plant, especially since the memorable year 1793, when it was much employed in certain stages of yellow-fever; and in which I believe it was very often used with much benefit." (There was a severe outbreak of yellow fever in Philadelphia in 1793.) It has been included in the USP and, according to the USD, "used as a bitter stomachic, similar in its action to the other gentians."

### Sea-Pink, Marsh-Pink

*Sabatia stellaris.* Of Sabbati; starry.
Rose-of-Plymouth (Mass.)

Dana (1900) wrote that "the advancing year has few fairer sights to show us than a salt meadow flushed with these radiant blossoms. They are so abundant, so deep-hued, so delicate!" She also reported that the inhabitants of Plymouth, Massachusetts, were convinced

*Sea-Pink*

that the Pilgrims of 1620 named the plant Sabatia after the Sabbath, the holy day on which they first saw the flower, and that "strong objections are made if any other flowers are irreverently mingled with it in church decorations."

# THE DOGBANE FAMILY

## *Apocynaceae*

A widespread family of 215 genera and 2,100 species of herbs, shrubs, lianas and trees; found chiefly in tropical and subtropical regions.

Members of the family provide medically important cardiac glycosides (ouabain, for example, from *Acokanthera* and *Strophanus* species) and alkaloids (reserpine is from *Rauvolfia serpentina*), and several are impor-

tant sources of latex. *Apocynum* means "Away, dog!" from the Greek *apo,* "away," and *kuon,* "dog." The plants were supposed to be poisonous to dogs, but apparently (Kingsbury, 1964) they are not as poisonous as the Latin name suggests. One member of the family, Oleander *(Nerium oleander),* however, is so poisonous that a single leaf is considered potentially lethal to a human being and "loss of human life, sometimes involving large numbers of persons during military exercises, has repeatedly occurred when meat was roasted while skewered on oleander branches" (Kingsbury).

## Blue Dogbane, Willow Amsonia, Bluestar

*Amsonia tabernaemontana.* Of Amson (Charles Amson, 18th century); of Tabernae-montanus (Jacobus Theodorus Tabernae-montanus, died 1590).

Charles Amson was a physician of Glouces-ter County, Virginia and a friend of John Clayton (1694–1773). Jacob Theodore Berg-zabern, who Latinized his name to Tabernae-montanus, was physician to the Count of the Palatine at Heidelberg and author of the cel-ebrated *Neuw Kreuterbuch (New Herb-book)* of 1588–1591. This was illustrated with wood-cuts, mostly copied from other herbals, which were then used to illustrate John Gerard's *Herbal* of 1597.

## Spreading Dogbane

*Apocynum androsaemifolium.* Away, dog!; with leaves of *Androsaemum.*

American-Ipecac, Angel's-Turnip (southern Ne-gro), Bitter-Root, Bitter Dogbane, Black Indian-Hemp, Buckbrush, Catchfly, Chickasaw (Maine), Colicroot (N.C.), Flytrap, *Herbe à la puce* (P.Q.), Honey-Bloom, Indian-Hemp, Milk-Ipecac, Milkweed (Maine), Rheumatism-Weed (W.Va.), Tutsan-Leaved Dogbane, Wandering-Milkweed, Western-Wallflower, Wild-Ipecac, Wildweed (Maine)

Rafinesque reported, "The Chickasaw and Choctaw Nations employ it in syphilis, and consider it a specific; they use the fresh root chewed, swallowing only the juice. This latter use has been introduced into Tennessee and Kentucky as a great secret. It must act as a tonic in all these cases, tonics being often emetic and antivenereal."

*Spreading Dogbane*

"The outer bark or rind of this herb fur-nished the finest Menomini thread material. The smallest divisions of this bast fiber are finer than our finest cotton thread and stronger. Just before the fruit has ripened the outer bark is peeled. By using three strands it is plaited so that a very strong cord is obtained. In the old days this was the way the Menomini made their bow strings" (Huron Smith, 1923). Dr. Millspaugh noted, "The flowers have the property of catching flies," thus the plant's names Catchfly and Flytrap. Dr. Millspaugh explained it as follows: "In consequence of the convergence of the anthers and their adherence to the zone of the stigma, a narrow fissure is formed, very contracted at the apex; the insect in search of honey from the nec-taries at the base of the corolla, inserts its proboscis between the short filaments of the stamens; thus when about to leave its feast, the proboscis is sometimes caught in this fissure; once fast, the greater the insect strug-gles the more firmly is it wedged." He added, "The only previous use of this herb is said to be that of the Indians who employed it in syphilis." It has been listed in the USP (see next entry) and NF.

## Indian-Hemp

*Apocynum cannabinum*. Away, dog!; hemp-like.

Amy-Root, Bitter-Root, Black Indian-Hemp, Bowman's-Root, Canadian-Hemp, *Chanvre du Canada* (P.Q.), Choctaw-Root, Coctaw-Root, Dog's-Bane, General-Marion's-Weed, Glabrous-Hemp, Indian-Physic, Milkweed (Maine), North-and-South-Root (Ky.), Old-Amy-Root, Rheumatism-Root, Rheumatism-Weed, St. John's-Dogbane, Silkweed, Snake's-Milk, Wandering-Milkweed, Wild-Cotton

In 1701 Charles Wolley in New York reported that the Indians make a "sort of brownish thread of a small weed almost like a willow, which grows in the Wood about three foot high, which is called Indian Hemp; of which they likewise make ropes and bring them to sell, which wears as strong as our hemp, only it wont endure wet so well; of this they make baggs, purses or sacks, which they call *Notas*, which word signifies a belly,

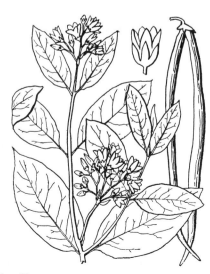

*Indian-Hemp*

and so they call any thing that's hollow to carry any thing." Kalm (1749) wrote that ropes made by Indians of Indian-Hemp "were stronger and kept longer in water than such as made of common hemp. The Swedes usually got thirty feet of these ropes for one piece of bread."

"This is a very active plant, highly valued by the Southern Indians. It is tonic, emetic, alterative and antisyphilitic. The root is the most powerful part: but it must be fresh, since time diminishes or destroys its power. At the dose of thirty grains of the fresh powdered root, it acts as an emetic, equal to ipecacuana; in smaller doses, it is a tonic, useful in dyspepsias. The Chickasaw and Choctaw Nations employ it in syphilis and consider it a specific" (Rafinesque). In the 18th century, the dried rhizome and roots of this and *A. androsaemifolium* were sent to Europe as a remedy for heart disease, and the constituent, the glycoside cymarin, was subsequently shown to have digitalis-like activity. It was listed in the USP as a cardiac medicine until 1952.

The name General-Marion's-Weed honors General Francis Marion, the American Revolutionary commander of troops in South Carolina who was known as the "Swamp Fox" for his tactics of harassing British troops and then disappearing into the swamps and forests. Choctaw-Root and Coctaw-Root refer to the Choctaws who occupied parts of Alabama and Mississippi. The plant is known as North-and-South-Root in southern Kentucky, and "For sunpain (a migraine headache, according to an anonymous local physician), a span of the root is infused in a half pint of whiskey. Take a spoonful before each meal" (Bolyard, 1981).

## Periwinkle, Myrtle

*Vinca minor*. (From the Latin name); lesser. (From Europe.)

*Periwinkle*

Blue-Myrtle, Hundred-Eyes, Joy-of-the-Ground, *Pervenche* (P.Q.), Running-Myrtle, Small Periwinkle, Wintergreen (Ohio)

The name used by Pliny was Vincapervinca, perhaps from *vincio,* "to bind," the long shoots having been used to bind wreaths. The name became Italian *pervinca,* French *pervenche* and English Periwinkle (the edible snail periwinkle is unrelated). Periwinkle has had a long reputation as a vulnerary herb, "used in fluxes of the belly, for dysentries, the piles, bleeding at nose, and for wounds with fluxion" (Pechey, 1694) and as an aphrodisiac: "Venus owns this herb, and saith, that the leaves eaten by man and his wife together, cause love between them" (Culpeper).

# THE MILKWEED FAMILY

## *Asclepiadaceae*

A family of 347 genera and 2,850 species of herbs, climbers and a few shrubs and trees; widespread in tropical and subtropical regions and with a few genera in temperate regions. The plants are named in honor of Asklepios, the Greek god of medicine (Aesculapius in Latin).

"During World War II a call went out from the government for milkweed pods. Boy and girl scouts, civic groups, farmers and collectors all over North America scoured the countryside for milkweeds, collected and dried the pods, and shipped them to central collecting stations. In Michigan and elsewhere milkweed farms were established where these suddenly valuable plants were grown in large fields, and the harvesting of the pods became a large-scale operation. Milkweed floss is 5 or 6 times as buoyant as cork, and it was soon discovered that a life jacket containing a few pounds of this floss could hold up a 150-pound man in the sea. It is warmer than wool and 6 times lighter. Flying suits lined with milkweed floss are warm and light-weight, and, if an aviator falls into the ocean, the suit will act as a life preserver" (Moldenke, 1949).

### Milkweeds, Swallowworts

*Asclepias.* Of Asklepios.

The buds, young shoots and flowers are cooked as potherbs and put into soup. The dewy flowers on summer mornings exude a sweet sugar, and the young pods of some species are blanched and then fried. Children collect the dried sap and chew it as chewing gum, but it is possibly toxic.

### Swamp Milkweed

*Asclepias incarnata.* Of Asklepios; flesh-colored (flesh of pink northern Europeans).

*Swamp Milkweed*

Flesh-Colored-Silkweed, Rabbit-Milk (N.C.) Rose-Milkweed, Rose-Silkweed, Silkplant, Swamp-Silkweed, Water-Nerve-Root, White Indian-Hemp

On his expedition to Utah in 1850, Howard Stansbury found the plant growing around springs near the Great Salt Lake: "The bark is tough, strong, and very much like that of flax. The root and the plant, when broken, exudes a milky viscous substance—that from the root intensely bitter. The Ottoes and Omahas make lariats of the bark, which are said to be stronger and better than those made of hide. It is said to grow abundantly near Council Bluffs, in Missouri. My Frenchman called it *vache à lait*. The Mexican Negro cook calls it *capote des acarte*. He says that the Pueblo Indians call it *noche*. They cut it down when ripe, rub it so as to separate the fibres, and make of it beautiful and very strong fishing-lines and fine sewing-thread. They also use a decoction of the root for medicinal purposes—the root itself is put into liquor to make bitters."

It has been listed in the USP, and, according to Jacobs and Burlage, has been used for dropsy, asthma and dysentry.

## Red Milkweed

*Asclepias rubra.* Of Asklepios; red.

An "Indian Swallow-wort" was included in Gerard's *Herbal* (1597), which from the illustration appears to be this plant: "There groweth in that part of Virginia, or Noremberga, where our English men dwelled (intending there to erect a certain colonie) a kind of Asclepias, or Swallow-woort, which the savages call Wisanck." Gerard wrote that the two "cods" (seed pods) were "stuffed full of most pure silke of a shining white colour . . . used of the people of Pomeioc and other of the provinces adjoining, being parts of Virginia, to cover the secret parts of maidens that never tasted man; as in other places they use a white kinde of mosse Wisanck. We have thought *Asclepias Virginiana,* or *Vincetoxicum Indianum* fit and proper names for it: in English, Virginia Swallow-wort, or the Silke-wort of Norembega." White Milkweed is *Asclepias variegata.*

## Common Milkweed, Silkweed

*Asclepias syriaca.* Of Asklepios; of Syria (it was early introduced to southern Europe and mistakenly supposed by Linnaeus to come from the Orient).

*Cochons de lait* (P.Q.), *Cotonnier* (P.Q.), *Herbe à coton* (P.Q.), Milkplant, *Petits cochons* (P.Q.), Silkgrass, Silky-Swallowwort, Virginia-Silk, Virginia Swallowwort, Wild-Cotton (W.Va.)

"And because it should not want an English name answerable to some peculiar property thereof, I have from the silken doune called it Virginia Silke" (Parkinson, 1629).

Manasseh Cutler wrote, "The seeds are contained in large pods, and are crowned with white down, extremely fine and soft, resembling silk, which has occasioned the name Silkweed. It may be carded and spun into an even thread, which makes excellent

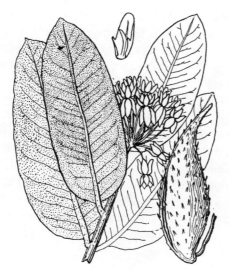

*Common Milkweed*

wickyarn. The candles will burn equally free, and afford a clearer light than those made with cotton wicks. They will not require so frequent snuffing and the smoke of the snuff is less offensive." Castiglioni reported in 1790 that "the mountaineers of Virginia made cloth from the outer covering of the stalks of this plant." In the 1860s, a number of articles were being manufactured from the fibers in Salem, Massachusetts, including "thread, netting, bags and purses, tapes, socks, knotting for fringes, etc. The silk from the pods forms an excellent article for stuffing cushions, pillows, mattresses" (Porcher).

Dr. Millspaugh wrote that "the young sprouts, just as they appear above the ground in the spring, are highly esteemed among housewives as a pot-herb, being cooked similarly to asparagus, for which they are an excellent substitute. The juice when applied to the skin forms a tough, adhesive pellicle; this has led to its use by the laity as a covering for ulcers and recent wounds to promote cicatrization." It has been included in the USP

and has been used "in amenorrhea, dropsy, retention of urine, dyspepsia, asthma and scrofulous diseases" (Jacobs and Burlage). Virginia-Silk is also *Yucca filamentosa*.

## Butterfly-Weed, Pleurisy-Root

*Asclepias tuberosa.* Of Asklepios; tuberous. Archangel (R.I.), Butterfly-Flower, Chigger-Flower (Mo.), Canada-Root, Colicroot, Fluxroot, Fly-Catcher, Indian-Bokay (Tex.), Indian-Nosy, Indian-Paint (Mich.), Indian-Plume (Mich.), Indian-Posy, Orange Swallowwort, Orangeroot, Rubber-Root, Silkgrass, Silkweed, Tuber-Root, Swallowwort, Whiteroot (Mass.), Windroot, Windweed, Yellow Milkweed (Mass.)

John Bartram (1751) wrote that for pleurisy "the root must be powdered and given in a spoonful of rum, or rather as the Indians give it, bruise the root and boil it in water and drink the decoction: Peter Kalm saith it is excellent for the hysteric passion." Jane Colden (ca. 1750) wrote that Silkgrass root was "an excellent cure for the colick, about half

*Butterfly-Weed*

a spoonfull at a time. This cure was learn'd from a Canada Indian, & is called in New England Canada Root." This was an important medicinal root for many Indian tribes, used both internally and as a poultice and powder for wounds and sores. The young shoots are a potherb. It has been listed in the USP and NF, "used not only in bronchitis and other pectoral complaints, but also in rheumatism and to promote the eruption in exanthematous fevers" (USD).

Like the Apocynums, the flowers of Asclepias also trap insects. Dr. Millspaugh wrote that, while he was drawing the plant, "a large blue-bottle alighted upon the crown; as he did so one of his legs slipped down between two hoods,—which neatly curve to such a shape that the foot of an insect is guided directly into the crevice between two adjacent anther cells—and upon attempting to withdraw it he was unable to do so. Noting this, I teased him into many strong tugs and pulls, but the more he struggled the tighter his foot became wedged, until finally after about ten minutes' hard work he flew off with a little yellow spot [the pollen mass] attached to the extremity . . . thus executing without design the will of Nature."

# THE NIGHTSHADE FAMILY

## Solanaceae

A nearly cosmopolitan family of 90 genera and 2,600 species of herbs, shrubs, lianas and small trees; best developed in South America. The family is of great economic importance, providing food (including peppers from *Capsicum,* tomatoes from *Lycopersicon* and potatoes and eggplants from *Solanum*), medically useful alkaloids and poisons—and tobacco:

"Tobacco, divine, rare, superexcellent tobacco, which goes far beyond all the panaceas, potable gold, and philosopher's stones, a sovereign remedy in all diseases. A good vomit, I confess, a vertuous herb, if it be well qualified, opportunely taken, and medicinally used; but as it is commonly abused by most men, which take it as tinkers do ale, 'tis a plague, a mischief, a violent purger of goods, lands, health, hellish, devilish and damned tobacco, the ruine and overthrow of the body and soul" (Robert Burton in *The Anatomy of Melancholy,* 1621).

## Western Jimsonweed

*Datura inoxia.* (The Latin name, from Hindi *dhatura,* Sanskrit *dhattura*); not spiny.
Jameston-Weed, Selguacha (Calif.), Southwestern Thornapple

The powdered root was used as a narcotic by American Indians. Stevenson wrote in 1915 that she once "observed the late Nai'uchi, the most renowned medicine-man of his time among the Zuñi, give this medicine before operating on a woman's breast. As soon as the patient became unconscious he cut deep into the breast with an agate lance, and, inserting his finger, removed all the pus; an antiseptic was then sprinkled over the wound, which was bandaged with a soiled cloth. (The writer obtained samples of the antiseptic, but each time the quantity proved too small for chemical analysis.) When the woman regained consciousness she declared that she had had a peaceful sleep and beautiful dreams. There was no evidence of any ill effect from the use of the drug." Among the Navaho, the

*Western Jimsonweed*

they could see and hear. In time, the Divine Ones (twin sons of the Sun Father) feared that the two children were learning too much and decided to banish them from this world for all time. "Flowers sprang up at the spot where the two descended—flowers exactly like those which they wore on each side of their heads when visiting the earth. The Divine Ones called the plant *a'neglakya,* after the boy's name. The original plant has many children scattered over the earth."

## Jimsonweed

*Datura stramonium.* (The Latin name); (the old generic name, (perhaps from *struma,* "swelling"). (From the Tropics.)

Apple-of-Peru, Devil's-Apple (Mass.), Devil's-Trumpet, Dewtry, Fireweed, *Herbe aux sorciers* (P.Q.), Jamestown-Lily (N.C.), Jamestown-Weed, Jimpson-Weed, Mad-Apple, Peru-Apple, *Pomme épineuse* (P.Q.), Purple Thorn-Apple (var. *Tatula*), Stink-Apple, Stinkweed (W.Va.), Stramonium, Thorn-Apple

patient is "restored to normal as follows: singer chews a bit of the leaf, makes a hole in another leaf, and passes the chewed portion through the hole into the patient's mouth who chews it a short time and then swallows it; dried tips of leaves and flowers are then smoked, so the plant will know the patient and not make him sick; treatment accompanied by songs and prayers" (Vestal, 1952). Beware! This and the next plant are violently toxic.

Stevenson also recounted a Zuñi legend about the plant: In the olden time, a brother and sister lived in the interior of the earth, but they often visited the outer world and walked about, closely observing everything

*Jimsonweed*

"The root being drunk with wine in the quantity of a dram, hath the power to effect not unpleasant phantasies. But two drams being drunk, make him beside himself for three days, and four being drunk kill him" (Dioscorides). In 1694 John Pechey reported that "wenches give half a dram of it to their lovers, in beer or wine. Some are so skill'd in dosing of it, that they can make a man mad for as many hours as they please."

On Cape Cod Thoreau (1864) wrote, "The *Datura stramonium*, or thorn apple, was in full bloom along the beach; and at sight of this cosmopolite,—this Captain Cook among plants,—carried in ballast all over the world, I felt as if I were on the highway of nations. Say, rather, this Viking, king of the Bays, for it is not an innocent plant; it suggests not merely commerce, but its attendant vices, as if its fibres were the stuff of which pirates spin their yarns." The plant contains extremely valuable alkaloids, hyoscyamine, atropine and scopolamine, used in the treatment of many diseases. Apple-of-Peru is the cultivated *Nicandra physalodes* of tropical America. In his discussion of the etymology of Datura, Heiser (1969) writes that *"Dhat* is the name of the poison derived from the plant, and the *Dhatureas* were a gang of thugs who used the plant to stupefy or poison their intended victims. Linnaeus, who adopted the name *Datura,* felt he should not use a barbaric name unless he could find a Latin root for the word and so he came up with *dare,* to give, because *Datura* is given to those whose sexual powers are weakened."

In Virginia, 1676, "This being an early plant, was gather'd very young for a boil'd salad, by some soldiers sent thither, to pacifie the troubles of Bacon; and some of them eat plentifully of it, the effect of which was a very pleasant comedy; for they turn'd natural fools upon it for several days; One would blow up a feather in the air; another wou'd dart straws at it with much fury; and another stark naked was sitting up in a corner, like a monkey, grinning and making mows at them; a fourth would fondly kiss, and paw his companions, and snear in their faces, with a countenance more antick, than any in a Dutch droll. In this frantick condition they were confined, lest they should in their folly destroy themselves; though it was observed, that all their actions were full of innocence and good nature. Indeed, they were not very cleanly; for they would have wallow'd in their own excrements, if they had not been prevented. A thousand such simple tricks they play'd, and after eleven days, return'd to themselves again, not remembring any thing that had pass'd" (Beverley, 1705). (The "troubles of Bacon" is now known as Bacon's Rebellion of 1676, a revolt in the Virginia colony led by Nathaniel Bacon, a planter, to protest the failure of the governor to provide adequate protection against the Indians.)

## Black Henbane

*Hyoscyamus niger.* Hog bean (a derogatory name given it by Dioscorides); black. (From Europe.)

Belene, Chenile, Devil's-Cabbage (Md.), Fetid-Nightshade, Henbeem (Md.), Henbean (Md.), Hog's-Bean, Insane-Root, *Jusquiame noire* (P.Q.), Poison-Tobacco, Stinking-Nightshade, Stinking-Roger

Henbane, both as a drink and more frequently as smoke, is used in many of the stories of *The Thousand and One Nights* to put people to sleep. In the story "The History of Gherib," when Selim wanted to rescue his captured brother Gherib, he "filled a cresset with firewood, on which he strewed powdered Henbane, and lighting it, went round about the tent with it till the smoke entered the nostrils of the guards, and they all fell asleep, drowned by the drug." Dr. Bigelow wrote that "the principal use which is made of hyoscyamous in medicine, is as a substitute for opium in cases where that article disagrees with the patient, or is contraindicated."

In a Babylonian clay tablet dated about 2250 B.C., the seeds are recommended for toothache, and William Cole (1657) wrote that "the husk, wherein the seed of Henbane is contained, is in figure like to a jaw tooth; and therefore the oyl of it, or the juyce by itself, or a decoction of the root with Arsmart in vinegar, being gargled warm in the mouth, is very effectual in easing the pains of the teeth." In 19th-century America, "the laity have often used the smoke of the smouldering leaves in odontalgia [toothache], by directing it into the caries by means of a paper funnel; but as convulsions, delirium, and other frightening symptoms have followed in some cases, this practice is now seldom resorted to" (Millspaugh).

Manasseh Cutler wrote that, "madness, convulsions, and death, are the general consequence" of eating any part of the plant; however, "the leaves scattered about a house will drive away mice." The plant is violently toxic and is a source of the medically active alkaloids hyoscyamine and scopolamine.

## Wild Tobacco

*Nicotinia rustica.* Of Nicot (Jean Nicot, 1530–1600); of the country.

Aztec Tobacco, Coyote Tobacco, Indian Tobacco (N.Y.), Real Tobacco (N.Y.), Syrian Tobacco

Jacques Cartier among the Iroquois, 1535–36: "They have also a herb, of which they harvest a lot during the summer for winter use, which they greatly esteem, and it is used only by the men in the following fashion. They dry it in the sun, and carry it in a little animal skin hung at their neck, with a pipe of stone, or of wood. Then at all hours, they powder the said herb, and putting it in one end of the pipe; they then put a hot coal on

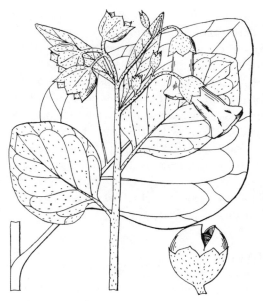

*Wild Tobacco*

top of it and suck from the other end of the pipe, so they fill their body with smoke, so much that it comes out of the mouth and the nostrils, like smoke from a chimney pot. They say this keeps them healthy and warm; and you never see them without these things" (from Biggar, 1924).

Roger Williams (1643) wrote that the New England Indians "generally all take tobacco; and it is commonly the only plant which men labor in; the women manage all the rest: they say they take tobacco for two causes; first, against the rheume, which causeth the toothake, which they are impatient of: secondly, to revive and refresh them, they drinking nothing but water." He also reported, "They take their *Wuttammauog* (that is, a weak Tobacco) which the men plant themselves very frequently; yet I never see any take so excessively, as I have seen men in Europe; and yet excess were more tolerable in them, because they want the refreshing of beer and wine, which God hath vouchsafed Europe."

Most of the tobacco of commerce is produced from *Nicotinia tabacum,* but *N. rustica* is still cultivated in some parts of the world for smoking tobacco. Josselyn (1672) wrote of *N. tabacum* that "there is not much of it planted in New England"; instead, "the Indians make use of a small kind with short round leaves called *Pooke*" (this must be *N. rustica*).

Jean Nicot was the French ambassador to Portugal who sent seeds of Tobacco to Catherine de Médicis, queen of France. The garden flower is *Nicotinia alata* or *Nicotinia sylvestris* from South America.

## Ground-Cherries

*Physalis.* Bladder (the inflated calyx).
Cape-Gooseberry, Cherry-Tomato (Long Island), *Coqueret* (P.Q.), Husk-Tomato, Wild-Cherry (N.J.)

Cape-Gooseberry is the yellow edible berry of the *Physalis peruviana.*

## Strawberry-Tomato

*Physalis pubescens.* Bladder; pubescent. (Also found in the Tropics.)
Alkekengi, Barbadoes-Gooseberry, Ground-Cherry, Husk-Tomato, Hairy-Ground-Cherry, Winter-Cherry

"The berries drop to the ground before they are ready to eat; but in a week or two the husk dries and the fruit within them turns a golden yellow. It is then very sweet and pleasant, but not sticky or glutinous. The plants are prolific and the berries will keep for weeks in the husk. They are excellent for preserves and sauce, and I have eaten wonderful pies made from them. Sometimes the berries are found for sale in the city markets" (Medsger, 1939).

Dr. Sturtevant reported in 1885 that "the alkekengi, or more usually called the strawberry tomato in our seed catalogues, is *Physalis pubescens* L., an American plant which furnishes one of our minor vegetable products"; the fruit "is much esteemed by some

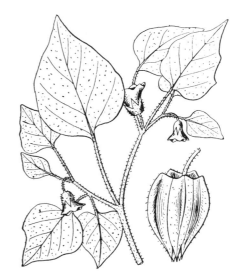

*Strawberry-Tomato*

people in a raw state or in preserves, and is disliked by others. It has a sweet acidulous taste with a pronounced flavor." Alkekengi (Alkakengie in Gerard, 1633) is from the Arabic and Persian. *Physalis alkekengi,* Chinese Lantern, is grown for its red fruiting calyx and was once cultivated for its edible Winter-Cherries.

## Virginia Ground-Cherry

*Physalis virginiana.* Bladder; of Virginia.
*Bonnets de grandmaman* (La.), Hog-Plum (N.Y.), Husk-Tomato, Wild-Cherry (Minn.), Wild-Pompion (N.Y.)

## Horse-Nettle

*Solanum carolinense.* Quietening (from Latin *solamen,* alluding to the sedative properties of some species); of Carolina.
Apple-of-Sodom, Bull-Nettle (Ind., Mo.), Irish-Plum, Poisonous-Potato, Radical (W.Va.), Radical-Weed, Sand-Brier (Kans., W.Va.), Thistle (Iowa), Thorn-Apple, Tread-Saft (southern Negro), Tread-Softly

Horse-Nettle is called Tread-Saft because of the prickly stems. Apple-of-Sodom is usually the Egg-Plant, *Solanum melongena*. The Irish-Plum (also spelled Irish-Plumb) is the orange-yellow fruit. It has been included in the NF, "used especially in the southern United States in the treatment of epilepsy" (USD) and "recommended as a remedy for asthma, bronchitis, and other convulsive disorders" (Jacobs and Burlage).

## Nightshade, Bittersweet

*Solanum dulcamara*. Quietening; bittersweet (the Latin name). (From Europe.)

Bitter Nightshade, Blue-Bindweed, Climbing-Nightshade, Dogwood, Fellen, Fellenwort, Felonwort, Fevertwig, *Herbe à la fièvre* (P.Q.), *Morelle douce-amère* (P.Q.), Myrtle-Vine (Ohio), Poison-Berry, Poison-Bittersweet, Poison-Flower, Scarlet-Berry, Snakeberry, *Vigne de Judée* (P.Q.), Violet-Bloom, Wolf-Grape, Wood-Nightshade

Manasseh Cutler (1785) called it Tivertwig or American Mezerion and reported that "farmers apply it to swellings in cows bags. Physicians of distinguished characters say, that the roots answer as valuable a purpose, in venereal cases, as the mezereon." (Once an

important medicine, Mezereon was prepared from the shrub *Daphne mezereum*.) Dr. Bigelow wrote that "the Bittersweet, both in substance and in a decoction appears to be a valuable auxiliary to mercury in the treatment of syphilitic eruptions." It has been included in the USP and NF, "used in the treatment of chronic rheumatism, bronchitis and various skin diseases but has, properly, been almost completely discarded" (USD).

## Common Nightshade, Black Nightshade

*Solanum nigrum*. Quietening; black. (From Europe.)

Blueberry (Ill.), Bonewort (West), Deadly Nightshade, Duscle, Garden-Huckleberry, Garden Nightshade, Hound's-Berry, Morel, Morelle, Petty-Morell, Prairie-Huckleberry (Ill.), Stubbleberry (N.Dak., S.Dak.), Stubby-Berry (N.C.), Sunberry, *Tue chien* (P.Q.), Wonderberry

The Common Nightshade was once locally cultivated for its berries, the "Garden Huckleberries," and the plants were marketed as "Wonderberries," even though the berries had a reputation among many as being poi-

*Nightshade*

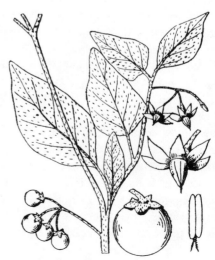

*Common Nightshade*

sonous—the unripe, green berry contains a poisonous alkaloid (Heiser, 1969). Dr. Millspaugh wrote, "This species has been in general practice, especially as a resolvant, from A.D. 54 (Dioscorides) to within a few years. The principal use of the plant has been in dropsy; gastritis; glandular enlargement; nervous affections; general inflammations of mucous membranes; herpetic, scorbutic, and syphilitic eruptions; and as a narcotic." Duscle is an old English name. Gerard (1633) called it "garden Nightshade, Morel, and petty Morel." Deadly Nightshade is *Atropa belladonna.*

# THE MORNING-GLORY FAMILY

## *Convolvulaceae*

A cosmopolitan family of 57 genera and 1,500 species of mostly twining and climbing vines, a few shrubs and one tall tree; found chiefly in tropical and subtropical regions. Latin *convolvere* means "to twine around."

## Hedge Bindweed

*Calystegia sepium.* Calyx sheath; of hedges. (Also found in Eurasia and New Zealand.) Bearbine, Bellbine, Bracted Bindweed, Creepers (Ohio), Devil's-Vine, German Scammony, Great Bindweed, *Gloire de matin* (P.Q.), Harvest-Lily, Hedge-Lily, Hellweed, Kentucky-Hunter (Maine, Ohio), Lady's-Nightcap, Lily-Bind, Lily-Vine, *Liserons des haies* (P.Q.), Morning-Glory, Peavine (Ohio), Pearvine, Rutland-Beauty (N.H., Ohio), Wild-Ivy (Nfd.), Wild Morning-Glory, Wild-Potato (Mo.), Woodbind, Woodbine (N.Y.)

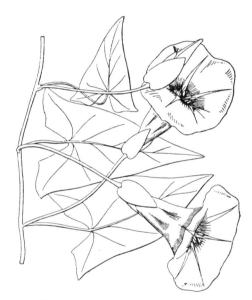

*Hedge Bindweed*

This is the original Morning-Glory, which is a local name for this plant in the West of England. Josselyn (1672) wrote, "Briony of Peru, we call it though it is grown here, or rather Scammony . . . The green juice is absolutely poison; yet the root when dry may safely be given to strong bodies." Scammony was a cathartic made from the roots of the Mediterranean *Convolvulus scammonia.*

Mannasseh Cutler suggested that, "as the imported Scammony is often very impure, and as there is so much difference in the purgative virtues of some masses of it, and that of others, that it is seldom to be depended upon alone in extemporaneous practice, might it not be prepared here much purer, and be more uniform in its virtue? Notwithstanding the roots of the Convolvulus is a very acrid purgative to the human race, hogs will eat it in large quantities without any ill effects."

"Well named morning glory. Its broad, bell- and trumpet-shaped flowers, faintly tinged with red, are like the dawn itself" (Thoreau, 1854). Bearbind (Old English *bere* means "barley"), Bellbind, Hellweed, Lady's Night-cap, Morning-Glory and Woodbind are local names in England.

## Field Bindweed

*Convolvulus arvensis.* Twining; of cultivated fields. (From Eurasia.)

Bearbine, Bellbind, Bellbine, Bellvine, Corn-Lily, Cornbind, Hedge-Bells, Lap-Love, *Liseron des champs* (P.Q.), Possession-Vine (Texas), Sheepbind, Sheepbine, Sheep-Blue, Small Bindweed, Tie-Vine (Miss.), Wild-Potato, Withwind

## Wild Potato-Vine

*Ipomoea pandurata.* Wormlike; fiddle-shaped.

Man-of-the-Earth, Man-Root, Mecha-meck, Mechoa-can, Mechoacanna (N.Y.), Morning-Glory, Peavine (Ohio), Scammonroot, Scammony, Wild-Jalap, Wild-Moonflower (N.Y.), Wild-Potato (Ala., Mo.), Wild Sweet-Potato (Ohio, W.Va.), Wild-Rhubarb

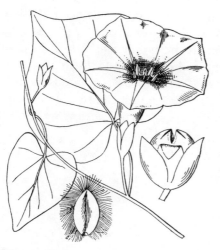

*Wild Potato-Vine*

Man-of-the-Earth and Man-Root allude to the size of the root: "I once dug up a root of the Wild Potato. It extended nearly vertically to a depth of three feet or more. The great fleshy root, resembling a large sweet potato, was two and a half feet long and weighed fifteen pounds," wrote Oliver Medsger (1939); "the Indians named this plant the Mecha-meck, and without doubt it was a favorite food among them." The roasted root evidently tastes of Sweet-Potato *(Ipomoea bata-tas)* but more bitter. The raw root is a drastic purge: "Taken in the place of Jalap, it has the same effect" (Pursh, 1814). Dr. Barton (1798) wrote that "its name Wild-Rhubarb implies that it is a purgative." Jalap is the cathartic from *Ipomoea purga,* which grew near Jalapa, Mexico.

## Cypress-Vine

*Ipomoea Quamoclit.* Wormlike; (a Mexican name). (From tropical America.)

American Red-Bellflower, China-Creeper, Cupid's-Flower, Indian-Pink, Jasmine-Bindweed, Red-Jasmine, Starglories, Sweet-William-of-the-Barbadoes, Wing-Leaved Ipomoea

## Glades Morning-Glory

*Ipomoea sagittata.* Wormlike; arrow-shaped (leaves).

Mark Catesby wrote that "Col. Moore, a gentleman of good reputation in Carolina, told me that he has seen an Indian daub himself with the juice of this plant; immediately after which, he handled a rattlesnake with his naked hands without receiving any harm from it." The Houma Indians of Louisiana called the plant *l'herbe à Congo* and used it to cure snake bites: "Let the patient chew the leaves and swallow the juice, then pack a poultice of the chewed leaves upon the place bitten" (Speck, 1941). *Congo* is Louisiana-French for the water moccasin.

# THE DODDER FAMILY

## *Cuscutaceae*

A family of a single genus and 150 species of parasitic twining herbs; nearly cosmopolitan, but best developed in the warmer regions of the New World.

## Dodder

*Cuscuta gronovii.* (The Medieval Latin name); of Gronovius (Jan Fredrik Gronov, 1690–1762).

Angel's-Hair (La.), Beggarweed, Cornsilk (Long Island), Devil's-Guts, Devil-Vine (Texas), Flaxvine, Goldthread (Va.), Gronovius's Dodder, Hellbind, Lover's-Knot (N.Y.), Lover's-Vine, Lovevine (Mo., Neb., N.C., Tex.), Robber-Vine (Texas), Scaldweed, Strangletare, Strangleweed

"The dodder vine was used by Pawnee maidens to divine whether their suitors were sincere. A girl having plucked a vine, with the thought of the young man in mind tossed the vine over her shoulder, into the weeds of host species of this dodder. Then, turning round, she marked the plant on which the vine fell. The second day after she would return to see whether the dodder had attached itself and was growing on the host. If so, she went away content with full assurance of her lover's sincerity and faithfulness. If the dodder had not twined and attached itself, she took it as a warning not to trust him" (Gilmore, 1914). This is a custom among

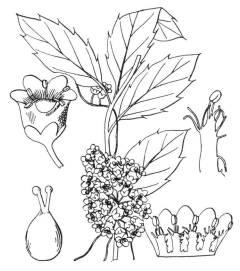

*Dodder*

many other young people, as the names Lover's-Knot and Lovevine indicate.

Devil's-Gut, Maiden's-Hair (becoming Angel's-Hair in Louisiana) and Scald are local names in England for the Lesser Dodder, *Cuscuta epithymum:* "This fawning parasite, and ungrateful guest, hugs the herb it hangs upon, with its long threads, and reddish twigs; and so closely embraces it, that at length it defrauds the hospitable herb of its nourishment, and destroys it by its treacherous embraces" (Pechey, 1694). Gronovius was a Dutch botanist who published lists of John Clayton's American plants in the *Flora Virginica* (1762).

# THE BUCKBEAN FAMILY

## *Menyanthaceae*

A cosmopolitan family of five genera and 40 species of aquatic or semiaquatic herbs.

## Buckbean

*Menyanthes trifoliata*. Moonflower; three-leaved. (Also found in Eurasia.)
Bean-Trefoil, Beckbean, Bitter-Trefoil, Bitter-Wort, Bogbean (Lab., Nfd.), Bog-Hop, Bog-Myrtle, Bognut, Brookbean, *Herbe à canards* (P.Q.), Marsh-Clover, Marsh-Trefoil, Marsh-Trifoil (Mass.), Moon-flower, *Trèfle d'eau* (P.Q.), Water-Shamrock, Water-Trefoil

"Of Water Trefoile, or Bucks Beanes. The great Marsh Trefoile hath thicke fat stalkes, weake and tender, full of a spungious pith, very smooth, and of a cubit long, whereon do grow leaves like to those of the garden Beane, set upon the stalks, three joined together like the other Trefoiles, smooth, shining, and of a deep greene colour: among which toward the top of the stalkes standeth a bush of feather-like floures of a white colour, dasht over slightly with a wash of light carnation" (Gerard, 1633).

Dr. Bigelow wrote that "the root of this vegetable is undoubtedly entitled to a high place in the list of tonics. In Europe it has long been entitled to a place in the Materia Medica, and has received the commendations of various physicians. When given in small doses, about ten grains, it imparts vigour to the stomach and strengthens digestion." The ground roots have also been used by Laplanders and Finns to make *missen* (famine) bread. Buckbean is a translation of the Dutch *boksboon*. Bogbean is a local name in England and Ireland.

# THE PHLOX FAMILY

## *Polemoniaceae*

A widespread family of 20 genera and 275 species of herbs and a few shrubs, lianas and small trees; found chiefly in temperate North America. *Polemonion* was the Greek name of a medicinal plant associated with Polemon, the philosopher of Cappadocia; or the plant is named after King Polemon of Pontus; or, according to Rabelais, "mighty and enduring wars were waged among certain kings in and about Cappadocia. What was the cause of the conflict? merely the naming of a plant. Because this was so eagerly disputed, the plant came down to us as polemonia, the warlike" (Greek *polemos* means "war").

## Skyrocket, Scarlet-Gilia, Desert-Trumpet

*Ipomopsis aggregata*. Wormlike; clustered.
Foxfire, Polecat-Plant, Skunk-Flower

In Nevada, "by far the principal employment of the plant, in the Shoshone communities at least, is for the treatment of venereal diseases, both gonorrhea and syphilis being mentioned in this connection. The whole plant is boiled for the purpose and a solution can

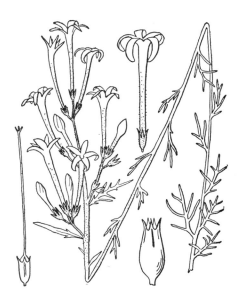

*Skyrocket*

be taken as a tea or used as a wash" (Train, Henrichs and Archer).

Coville (1897) reported that the Klamath Indian name of the plant, derived from *ōbls,* "dove," *am,* "plant," and *bōn-wäs,* "drink," "commemorates the legend, current among the Indian children, who pluck the flowers and suck the nectar, that in the old days when the beasts and birds lived together and understood each other's language the wild dove's drink was the nectar of this flower and nothing else." "Okanagan Indians prize the leaves for their tonic properties. Steeped until hot water turns bright green, the leaves are removed and the medicine taken in small doses" (Ward-Harris).

This and other *Ipomopsis* species were previously placed in the genus *Gilia,* named for Filippo Luigi Gilii (1756–1821), a scientist and astronomer at Rome who also wrote on botany.

## Annual Phlox, Drummond Phlox

*Phlox drummondii.* Flame (the Greek name of a plant with flame-colored petals); of

Drummond (Thomas Drummond, 1780–1835). Prairie Wild-Phlox (Texas), Pride-of-Texas (Texas)

Drummond was born in Scotland and died in Cuba. He was an indefatigable collector of plants in the Arctic (as botanist on Franklin's second expedition), Canada and the United States, particularly in Louisiana and Texas, from where he was reputed to have sent back 700 new plants to London. He applied for a tract of land in Texas and planned to bring his family over from Scotland and settle there, but he died soon after while botanizing in Cuba.

## Greek-Valerian

*Polemonium reptans.* (A Greek plant name); creeping (a misnomer).

Abscess-Root, American Great-Valerian, American Greek-Valerian, Bluebells (Ohio, Wis.), Blue-Valerian (Ind.), Creeping Great-Valerian, Jacob's-Ladder, Snakeroot, (Ind.), Sweatroot, Sweetroot

The Jacob's-Ladder or Greek-Valerian of the garden is *Polemonium caeruleum,* which Turner (1548) called "Valeriana greca, and

*Greek Valerian*

this is oure commune Valerian that we use agaynste cuttes wyth a blew floure"; Valerian is a famous healing herb. Grieve noted that Abscess-Root "is reported to have cured consumption; an infusion of the root in wine-glassful doses is useful in coughs, colds and all lung complaints, producing copious perspiration."

# THE WATERLEAF FAMILY

## Hydrophyllaceae

A widespread family of 22 genera and 275 species of herbs and shrubs, most common in the western United States. Greek *hudor* means "water," *phullon* means "leaf"; it is named after the watery or juicy leaves of the original species.

## Yerba Santa

*Eriodictyon californicum.* Wool net (leaf undersurface); of California.

Bear's-Weed, Consumptive's-Weed, Gumbush, Gumleaves, Holy-Herb, Mountain-Balm (Calif.), Palo Santo (Calif.), Sacred-Herb, Wild-Peach, Yerba Bueno (Calif.)

Among the Costanoan Indians of California: "Leaves woven into skirts and aprons; leaves heated and stuck to forehead for headache, also chewed or smoked to relieve asthma; decoction used for asthma, and for rheumatism, tuberculosis and to purify the blood" (Bocek). Grieve wrote that it was "Much used in California as a bitter tonic and a stimulating balsamic expectorant and is a most useful vehicle to disguise the unpleasant taste of quinine, Male Fern and Hydrastis. In asthma, the leaves are often smoked." According to Charles Saunders (1934), "it is abundant on dry hillsides and among the chaparral throughout much of California. A bitter tea is made of the dried leaves and taken freely; or

*Yerba Santa*

it may be prepared by boiling with sugar, if it is desired to disguise the bitterness."

## Dwarf Waterleaf, Ballhead Waterleaf

*Hydrophyllum capitatum.* Water leaf; in heads.
Bear-Cabbage, Cat's-Breeches, Pussyfoot, Ragged-Breeches, Woollen-Breeches

The young tender shoots and roots of this and of other Waterleaf species were used as potherbs by the Indians and settlers.

## Virginia Waterleaf

*Hydrophyllum virginianum.* Water leaf; of Virginia.
Brook-Flower, Burr-Flower, Indian-Salad, John's-Cabbage, Shawanese-Lettuce, Shawnee-Salad

"The young leaves serve in some localities as a salad, called Shawanese lettuce, and are eaten as a potage in other places, under the name of John's Cabbage" (Millspaugh).

# THE LENNOA FAMILY

## Lennoaceae

A family of three genera and six species of fleshy root-parasitic herbs found in the south-western states and south to Colombia and Venezuela.

## Sandroot, Sandfood, Sand-Sponge

*Pholisma sonorae.* (An obscure name); of Sonora (Mexico).

In 1889 Edward Palmer collected large quantities of the plant at Lerdo, Mexico, and reported that it "grows in deep sand, the deeper the sand the larger and juicier the plants. The Cocopa Indians gather them for food, which they relish under all circumstances. They eat it raw, boiled, or roasted. The plant is full of moisture, and whites and Indians alike resort to it in traveling, as a valuable substitute for water. It has a pleasant taste, much resembling the sweet potato. The stems are 2½ feet long and 1 to 4 inches in diameter, but almost buried, only the peculiar white tops appearing above the sand" (Vasey and Rose, 1890). Charles Saunders called it a "subterranean parasite, though not a fungus, that is of genuine worth as an edible."

# THE BORAGE OR FORGET-ME-NOT FAMILY

## Boraginaceae

A cosmopolitan family of 154 genera and 2,500 species of herbs and a few shrubs and trees; found in temperate and tropical regions, particularly the Mediterranean. The Latin name *borrago* is ultimately from the Arabic *abu'arag* (father of sweat), alluding to the medicinal use of Borage as a sudorific.

John Evelyn (1699) wrote that Borage (*Borago officinalis),* "hot and kindly moist, purifying the blood, is an exhilarating cordial, of a pleasant flavour: The tender leaves, and flowers especially, may be eaten in composition; but above all, the sprigs in wine, like those of baum, are of known vertue to revive the hypochondriac, and chear the hard student." Borage is cultivated as a salad and potherb; its leaves taste of cucumber and are used to flavor drinks. "Pliny calleth it *Euphrosinum,* because it makes a man merry and joyfull: which thing also the old verse concerning Borage doth testify: *Ego Borago gaudia semper ago.* I Borage bring always courage" (Gerard, 1633).

## Corn-Gromwell

*Buglossoides arvense.* Like Bugloss; of planted fields. (From Europe.)

Bastard-Alkanet, Batschia, False-Alkanet, Painting-Plant, Pearl-Plant, Pigeonweed, Redroot, Salfern, Stoneseed, Stoneweed, Wheat-Thief

"The girls in the North of Europe paint their faces with the juice of the root upon days of festivity. The bark of the root tinges wax and oil of a beautiful red, similar to that which is obtained from the root of the foreign

*Hound's-Tongue*

Alkanet that is kept in the shops" (Withering, 1776). Gerard (1633) called it Wild Bugloss or Alkanet and reported, "The roots of these are used to color sirrups, gellies, & such like confections . . . John of Arden hath set down a composition called *Sanguis Veneris,* which is most singular in deep punctures or wounds made with thrusts, as follows: take of oile olive a pint, the root of Alkanet two ounces, earth worms purged, in number twenty, boile them together & keep it to the use aforesaid." Salfern is an old English name for the plant, and Batschia is a previous generic name. The cultivated Alkanet, whose roots provide a red dye, is *Alkanna tinctoria.* American-Alkanet is Hoary Puccoon, *Lithospermum canescens.*

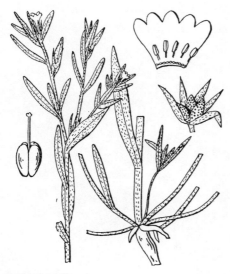

*Corn-Gromwell*

## Hound's-Tongue, Burgundy Hound's-Tongue

*Cynoglossum officinale.* Dog tongue (the shape and texture of the leaves); officinal. (From Europe.)

Beggar-Lice (Ohio), Beggar-Ticks, Canadian-Bur, Dog-Bur (Kans., W.Va.), Dog-Tongue, Gipsy-Flower, *Langue de chien* (P.Q.), Mouseleaf, Rose-Noble, Sheep-Lice (Ohio), Stickseed (W.Va.), Sticktights (Ind.), Tory-Bur (Kans., N.Y.), Tory-Weed, Wood-Mat, Wool-Mat (Kans., W.Va.)

Not only do the leaves look and feel like a dog's tongue, but according to Dioscorides, "the leaves beaten small with old swine grease hath the power to heal things bitten of dogs." Moreover, according to Culpeper, "the leaves laid under the feet, will keep dogs from barking at you; Hound's-tongue, because it ties the tongues of dogs." The fruits are covered with hooked spurs and stick to clothing and dogs' coats, thus the bur, tick and lice names.

The name Tory-Weed was used in 18th-century Vermont. In Montpelier, about 1800, while Dr. Timothy Todd was dressing a severe wound in his leg received in a carriage accident, an Indian chief visited him. " 'Ah!' exclaimed the old Indian, 'him velly bad! Indian do him good.' He went away immediately, and after a time returned with some leaves of a plant called 'tory weed,' and told the doctor to apply them to the wound, using fresh ones every day, and, when the leaves were gone, to make a decoction of the root. The learned physician followed the prescription of his savage professional brother, and the inflammation then first began to abate" (Todd, 1876).

Rose-Noble, a local name in Ireland for this plant, was the golden coin, stamped with a rose, introduced by Edward IV (15th century) which was a remedy for piles or the tubercular glands of the King's Evil, in lieu of the king's own touch, a supposed virtue shared by several plants of this family.

## Wild-Comfrey

*Cynoglossum virginianum*. Dog tongue; of Virginia.

Beggar's-Lice, Beggar's-Ticks (Mo.), Dog-Bur, Dysentry-Root, Dysentry-Weed, Sheep-Burr (Kans.), Soldiers (Mass.), Sticktight (Ind., Minn.), Virginia-Mouse-Ear, Virginia Stickseed

## Viper's Bugloss

*Echium vulgare*. (From the Greek name *ekhion*; *ekhis* is a viper); common. (From Europe.)

Adder's-Wort, Blue-Devil (Iowa), Blue-Dusil (N.C.), Bluestem (W.Va.), Blue-Thistle (N.Y., Va.), Blueweed (Iowa, W.Va.), Bluewort, Cat's-Tails, Snakeflower, *Vipérine* (P.Q.), Viper's-Grass, Viper's-Herb

Lyte (1578) wrote that the snake names were given the plant "because it is very good against the bitings of serpents and adders, and because also his seed is like the head of an adder or viper." Marie-Victorin noted that "the French name [*Vipérine*] is a reminder that in the old days the plant had a reputation of being able to neutralize viper venom. The seeds, it was claimed, resemble a viper's head, and the spots on the stem those on its skin; the doctrine of signatures evidently."

Bugloss is derived, via Middle English, Old French and Latin, from the Greek *bouglossus,*

*Viper's Bugloss*

ox-tongued, for the broad rough leaves. Blue-Devil, Blue-Thistle, Blueweed, Snake's-Flower and Viper's-Grass are local names in England.

This is a hateful invasive weed (a Blue-Devil) to the farmer, and the bristly hairs on leaves and stem can produce a severe dermatitis. Asa Gray in North Carolina, 1842, wrote, "This 'vile foreign weed,' as Dr. Darlington, agriculturally speaking, terms this showy plant, is occasionally seen along the roadside in the northern States; but here, for the distance of more than a hundred miles, it has taken complete possession even of many cultivated fields, especially where the limestone approaches the surface, presenting a broad expanse of brilliant blue." John Evelyn, however, found the flowers "greatly restorative, being conserv'd." And Nicholas Culpeper reported, "There is a syrup made hereof very effectual for comforting the heart, and expelling sadness and melancholy."

## Gromwells

*Lithospermum.* Stone seed (from Greek *lithos,* "stone," *sperma,* "seed;" i.e., the hard nutlets).

*Graines de lutin* (P.Q.), *Grémil* (P.Q.), *Herbes aux perles* (P.Q.), Puccoon

Gromwell is derived perhaps from the Vulgar Latin *gruinum milium* (crane's millet). Turner (1548) derived it from gray millet, "of the blewish gray colour" of *Lithospermum officinale.* Puccoon, from the Algonquian *pocoon,* is the name of many plants that yield a red or yellow dye.

## Hoary Puccoon

*Lithospermum canescens.* Stone seed; hoary.

American-Alkanet, Hoary-Poccoon, Indian-Paint (Minn., Mo.), Orange Puccoon, Perecron, Puccoon

"Pocones is a small roote," Captain Smith reported in 1612, "which being dried and beat in powder turneth red; and this they [the

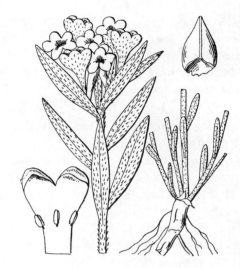

*Hoary Puccoon*

Indians] use for swellings, aches, annointing their joints, painting their heads and garments. They account it very pretious and of much worth." In his history of Virginia of 1705, Robert Beverley wrote that "the Indians also pulverize the roots of a kind of Anchuse or yellow Alkanet, which they call *Puccoon,* and of a sort of wild Angelica, and mixing them together with bears oyl, make a yellow ointment, with which, after they have bath'd, they anoint themselves capapee; this supples the skin, renders them nimble and active, and withal so closes up the pores, that they lose but few spirits by perspiration."

## Fringed Gromwell, Narrowleaf Gromwell, Stoneseed

*Lithospermum incisum.* Stone seed; cut (petals).

Indian-Paint, Puccoon

Jeffrey Hart reports that among the Northern Cheyenne, "for those suffering from the illness characterized by 'irrationless,' the tea made from the stems, leaves, and roots was rubbed on the face and head. To keep a very sleepy person awake, the plant was finally chewed and blown into the patient's face, and some of it was rubbed over the chest." The edible roots were gathered and cooked by many western Indians.

## Wayside Gromwell, Western Puccoon, Lemonweed

*Lithospermum ruderale.* Stone seed; rough.

Among the Thompson Indians, the plant is used "for inflicting sickness or bad luck on persons. The root is prayed over and some of the plant or any part of it is put on the person, or in his clothes, or in his bed" (Teit). The Shoshones of Nevada believe that the plant has contraceptive properties—"It is said that the cold water infusion from the roots, taken daily as a drink for a period of six months, will ensure sterility thereafter" (Train, Henrichs and Archer).

## Sea Mertensia, Oysterleaf

*Mertensia maritima.* Of Mertens (Franz Carl Mertens, 1764–1831, professor at Bremen); of sea shores. (Also found in Eurasia.)

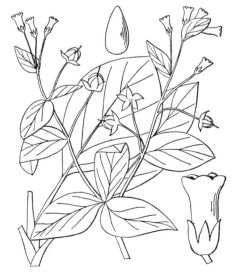

*Sea Mertensia*

Bluebells, Blue-Iris (Maine), Iceplant (Lab.), Oyster-Plant, Sea-Bugloss, Sea-Lungwort

The leaves taste of oysters. Mertensias were once classified as species of *Pulmonaria,* Lungworts, which have white spotted leaves and were thus a treatment for diseased lungs.

## Virginia Bluebells, Virginia-Cowslip

*Mertensia virginica.* Of Mertens; of Virginia. Bluebells, Blue-Iris, Bunchflower, Gentleman's-Breeches (Ohio), Old-Ladies'-Bonnets, Puccoon, Roanoke-Bells, Smooth-Lungwort, Tree-Lungwort, Virginia-Lungwort

## Forget-Me-Nots

*Myosotis.* Mouse ear (the name used by Dioscorides, for the short soft leaf of some species).

Scorpion-Weed

Forget-Me-Not is a translation of the Old French *ne m'oubliez mie.* Whoever wore the flower was not forgotten by his or her lover. In the German tale, a knight picked Forget-Me-Nots for his lady as they walked by the river; he tripped and fell in, but before he was drowned, he threw her the flowers, crying *"vergiss mein nicht,"* which is the German name of the flower. Gerard (1633) called them Scorpion-Grass because the flowers grow "upon one side of the stalke, . . . turning themselves back again like the taile of a scorpion." They were thus a remedy for the sting of a scorpion.

## Smaller Forget-Me-Not, Bay Forget-Me-Not

*Myosotis laxa.* Mouse ear; loose. (Also found in Eurasia and Chile.)

Mouse-Ear Forget-Me-Not

"The mouse-ear forget-me-not *(Myosotis laxa)* has now extended its racemes very much, and hangs over the edge of the brook.

*True Forget-Me-Not*

at the base of the young leaves is used by women and children to stain the cheeks crimson. The crisp, tender shoots and the flowers furnish a rather pleasant, sweet, and aromatic food, and the seeds are gathered in large quantities for pinole. After careful winnowing, the seeds are parched either in an ordinary frying pan or according to the old custom, which consists in tossing them about with hot oak-bark coals. When parched, the taste is much like that of popcorn" (Chesnut, 1902).

It is one of the most interesting minute flowers. It is the more beautiful for being small and unpretending, for even flowers should be modest" (Thoreau, 1852).

## True Forget-Me-Not

*Myosotis scorpioides.* Mouse ear; like a scorpion (the coiled raceme). (From Europe.)
Love-Me, Marsh Scorpion-Grass, Mouse-Ear Scorpion-Grass, Snake-Grass

In his *Boston Flora* of 1814, Jacob Bigelow called it "Mouse ear Scorpion grass," the name used by Gerard in 1597. Love-Me and Snake-Grass are local names in England. It is also *aimez-moi* in France.

## Popcorn-Flower

*Plagiobothrys fulvus.* Side-pit; yellow.
Snowdrop, White Forget-Me-Not

In Mendocino County, California, the plant "grows so profusely in Round Valley that whole acres of ground are made white with its delicately scented forget-me-not-like flowers. On account of its abundance and the similarity in the appearance of large masses to a light fall of snow, the Indian children call the plant snowdrops. The coloring matter

## Comfrey

*Symphytum officinale.* (From the Greek name; *sumphuo* means "to grow together"—the plant was used to heal wounds); officinal. (From Europe.)

Ass-Ear, Backwort, Blackwort, Boneset, Bruisewort, Bruisewort-Gumplant, Bugloss (Maine), Common-Conifrey (N.C.), Confrey (N.C.), Consound, *Consoude officinale* (P.Q.), Gumplant, Healing-Herb, Knitback, Slippery-Root

This was supposedly the *sumphuton* of Dioscorides, whose roots "beaten small and drunk, are good for the blood-spitters and

*Comfrey*

ruptures, and being applied they close up new wounds. And being sodden with them they join pieces of flesh together." John Pechey (1694) added that the flowers boiled in red wine "unite broken bones; wherefore 'tis called Bone-set." Gerard (1633) reported that in English it was called "Comfrey, Comfrey Consound; of some Knit backe and Blackewoorte," and that the "slimy substance of the root made into a posset of ale, and given to drink against the pain in the back gotten by any violent motion, as wrestling, or overmuch

use of women, doth in four or five days presently cure the same although the involuntarie flowing of the seed in man be gotten thereby." Manasseh Cutler remarked that "the roots are much used by the common people for sprains. They are glutinous and mucilaginous. The leaves give a grateful flavour to cakes and panadoes." (A panada or panado is a dish of bread cooked with sugar and fruit.) Comfrey is derived, through the French and Medieval Latin, from the Latin name *conferva,* which is from *confervere,* "to grow together."

# THE VERVAIN FAMILY

## *Verbenaceae*

A family of 91 genera and 1,900 species of herbs, shrubs, lianas and trees; mainly tropical, with a few species in temperate regions. Some members of the family are important sources of timber, particularly *Tectona grandis* (Teak), and others are cultivated as ornamentals, including species of *Lippia, Lantana* and *Verbena.* In Latin, *verbenae* were the sacred boughs of laurel, olive or myrtle used in religious ceremonies. Marie-Victorin suggested that "the generic name means the vein of Venus, alluding to the supposed aphrodisiac properties."

Vervain was one of the remedies for consumption included in Cotton Mather's *The Angel of Bethesda* (1724): "Take Vervain, a convenient quantity. Make a strong decoction. Then add unto the decoction an æqual quantity of honey; and boil them together into the consistency of a syrup. Of this, take now and then a spoonful. Tis a very remarkable, and often experimented, cure for the consumptions." Manasseh Cutler wrote that there were two or three varieties of Vervain and called

them Simpler's Joy (see European Vervain below); he noted that during the American Revolution "the Surgeons of the American army, at a certain period when a supply of medicine could not be obtained, substituted a species of Verbena for an emetic and expectorant, and found its operation kind and beneficial." In Texas, Vervains are called Bit-

*Blue Vervain*

terweed, Indian-Quinine and Indian-Tea (Reid, 1951).

## Blue Vervain

*Verbena hastata.* (From the Latin); halberd-shaped.

American Vervain, Common Vervain, False Vervain, Ironweed (Iowa), Purvain, Purvane, Simpler's-Joy, Wild-Hyssop

John Josselyn (1674) wrote that "it will heal a green wound in 24 hours, if a wise man have the ordering of it." In 1858 Thoreau wrote, "Mrs. Monroe says that her mother respected my grandfather very much, because he was a religious man. She remembers his calling one day and inquiring where blue vervain grew, which he wanted, to make a syrup for his cough, and she, a girl, happening to know, ran and gathered some." Thoreau also noted (1852) that Vervain has an "interesting progressive history in its rising ring of blossoms. It has a story."

## European Vervain

*Verbena officinalis.* (From the Latin); officinal. (From Europe.)

Berbine, Enchanter's-Plant, Herb-Grace, Herb-of-the-Cross, Holy-Herb, Holy-Plant, Juno's-Tears, Pigeon's-Grass, Simpler's-Joy, Turkey-Grass (La.)

Dioscorides called it *Peristereōn* (dove-cote) because "doves do gladly stay about it." He listed numerous medical uses and wrote "now they call it sacra herba, because it is of fit use in the expiations to serve for amulets." As a holy herb it was used throughout Europe as an amulet, charm or garland against witches, demons and the devil. "Many odde old wives fables are written of Vervaine, tending to witchcraft and sorcerie, which you may read elsewhere for I am not willing to trouble your eares with reporting such trifles, as honest ears abhorre to hear" (Gerard, 1633). He noted it was called in English "Junos tears,

*European Vervain*

Mercuries moist bloud, Holie herbe, and of some Pigeons grasse, or Columbine, because Pigeons are delighted to be amongst it." A simpler was one who collected simples (medicinal plants), a herbalist.

The calyx is covered with viscid hairs and adheres to cloth and long-haired animals and is thus dispersed. Henry Ridley (1930) reported that this Vervain "is found all over Europe (except the north), Morocco, Canaries and Azores, Asia Minor, through Palestine to India, Siam, China and Japan, Philippines (rare), Australia (in 1904), Rapa Island, in Polynesia, Cape Verde Islands and Africa, chiefly in mountain districts to the Cape. In North America, Bermudas, and West Indies, and the Pampas and Chile it is probably introduced. Its original home appears to be Northern India, whence it has radiated as far as climate would allow it."

## Hoary Vervain

*Verbena stricta.* (From the Latin); upright.
Burvine (Mo.), Fever-Weed (Ill.), Mullein-Leaved Vervain, Thimble-Weed (Mo.)

It was called Fever-Weed because it was "thought to be specific for fever and ague" (Bergen, 1892).

## White Vervain

*Verbena urticifolia.* (From the Latin); nettle-leaved.

Burbine (Ky.), Burvine (Ky., Mo.), Feverweed (Ky.), Nettle-Leaved Vervain

In Kentucky, "the root is boiled and a small amount of the decoction is given to babies to break out the hives. The sweetened root decoction is drunk as an aid for flu" (Bolyard, 1981).

# THE MINT FAMILY

## *Lamiaceae*

A cosmopolitan family of 221 genera and 5,600 species of herbs, shrubs and a few trees; particularly abundant in the Mediterranean region and eastward into Central Asia. This is the preeminent family of culinary and medicinal herbs—of Lavender, Rosemary, Sage, Thyme, Mint, Balm, Marjoram, Savory and Basil.

## Blue Giant-Hyssop, Anise-Hyssop

*Agastache foeniculum.* Many spikes (of flowers); like Fennel (scent).

Among the Cheyenne, this was called Elk-Mint and was "used as tea by boiling the leaves and forming a pleasant drink. An infusion of the leaves when allowed to get cold is good for pain in the chest (as when the lungs are sore from much coughing), or from a weak heart" (Grinnel, 1905).

## Bugle

*Ajuga reptans.* (An obscure name); creeping. (From Europe.)

Brown Bugle, Carpenter's-Herb, Carpet-Bugle-weed, Middle-Comfrey, Middle-Consound, Sickle-wort

William Turner (1548) called it Bugle, from the Latin name *bugillo,* which is from the Gaulish. Nicholas Culpeper claimed that "it

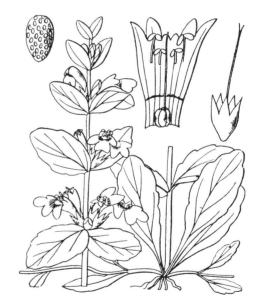

*Bugle*

is so efficacious for all sorts of hurts in the body, that none should be without it." He also used it to treat alcoholic hallucinations: "Drunkard are troubled with strange fancies, strange sights in the night time, and some with voices, as also with the nightmare. I take the reason for this to be . . . a melancholy vapour made thin by excessive drinking strong liquor, and so flies up and disturbs the brain, and breeds imaginations, fearful and troublesome; these I have known cured by taking only two spoonfuls of the syrup of this herb after supper."

Carpenter's-Herb is a local name in England; it resembles the more esteemed Carpenter's-Herb or Sicklewort, *Prunella vulgaris.*

## Wild-Basil, Horse-Thyme

*Clinopodium vulgaris.* Bed-foot (the Greek name); common. (Also found in Europe.)
Basil-Weed, Bed's-Foot, Dogmint, Field-Basil, Field-Thyme, Stone-Basil

"It may be called in English Horse Tyme, because it is like great Tyme" (Turner, 1548). The cultivated Basil, to eat with slices of fresh mozarella cheese and ripe New Jersey tomatoes, is *Ocimum basilicum* or *Ocimum minimum.* Basil is from the Greek *basilikos* (royal), "because the smell thereof being so excellent, is fit for a king's house" (Parkinson, 1640).

The plant was called Bed's-Foot, according to Liddell and Scott's *Greek Lexicon,* because the leaves "are like the feet of a bed"; or, according to Britten and Holland's *Dictionary of English Plant Names,* because the flowers were "likened to a bed-castor." Both explanations seem unlikely. In John Donne's "A

*Horse-Balm*

Nocturnal upon S. Lucy's Day, being the shortest day,"

> *The world's whole sap is sunk:*
> *The general balm th' hydroptic earth*
> *hath drunk,*
> *Whither, as to the bed's-feet, life is*
> *shrunk,*
> *Dead and interr'd.*

"Life *in extremis* shrinks down into the earth, as a dying man huddles at the foot of the bed. One of Hippocrates' signs of imminent death is when the sick man 'makes the beds feet where the head should be'" (Gardner, 1972).

## Horse-Balm, Richweed

*Collinsonia canadensis.* Of Collinson (Peter Collinson, 1694–1768); of Canada.
Archangel, Citronella, Collinson's-Flower, Gravelroot, Hardhack, Heal-All, Horseweed, Knobgrass, Knobroot, Knobweed, Mountain-Balm (Va.), Oxbalm, Rattlesnake-Root (W.Va.), Richleaf, Stoneroot

"I had discovered this singular flower there new to me, and, having a botany by me,

*Wild Basil*

looked it out. What a surprise and a disappointment, what an insult and impertinence to my curiosity and expectation, to have given me the name 'horseweed'!" (Thoreau, 1851). John Bartram (1751) wrote that it was called Horseweed, "not only because horses are very greedy of it, but it also is good for sore gall'd backs. The root is hard and knobby, and is much commended for womens afterpains, being pounded, boiled and the decoction drank." Rafinesque reported that "it is one of the plants called Heal-all in the United States because they cure sores and wounds: the Indians employ this plant for that purpose. In the mountains and hills of Virginia, Kentucky, Tennessee and Carolina, this genus is considered a panacea, and used outwardly and inwardly in many disorders." It was called Gravelroot and Stoneroot because it was used to treat the "gravel" or the "stone" (bladder or kidney stones).

In 1749 Peter Kalm wrote, "The Collinsonia has a peculiar scent, which is agreeable, but very strong. It always gave me a pretty violent headache whenever I passed a place where it stood in plenty, and especially when it was in flower. Mr. Bartram was acquainted with a better characteristic of this plant, namely that of being an excellent remedy against all sorts of pain in the limbs, and for a cold, when the parts affected were rubbed with it. And Mr. Conrad Weiser, interpreter of the language of the Indians in Pennsylvania, had told him of a more wonderful cure with this plant. He had once been among a company of Indians, one of whom had been stung by a rattlesnake. The savages gave him up, but Mr. Weiser boiled the Collinsonia and made the poor wretch drink the water, from which he happily recovered."

Peter Collinson was a London cloth merchant and naturalist who used his overseas agents to collect plants for his and his friends' gardens in England. His chief plant collector in North America was John Bartram.

*American Dittany*

## American Dittany, Stonemint

*Cunila mariana.* (The Latin name of a mint); of Maryland.

Dittany, Frostweed, High-Pennyroyal, Maryland Cunila, Mountain Dittany, Pennyroyal, Sweet Horsemint, Thyme, Wild-Basil

In 1728 William Byrd wrote that horseflies "are a great nuisance to travellers; insomuch that it is no wonder they were formerly employed for one of the Plagues of Egypt. But Dittany, which is to be had in the woods all the while those insects remain in vigour, is a sure defense against them. For this purpose, if you stick a bunch of it in the head-stall of your bridle, they will be sure to keep a respectful distance. Thus, in what part of the woods soever any thing mischievous or troublesome is found, kind providence is sure to provide a remedy. And 'tis probably one great reason why God was pleas'd to create these, and many other vexatious animals, that men sho'd exercise their wits and industry, to guard themselves against them."

Dr. Porcher reported, "A gentleman in Spartanburg district, S.C., tells me that in his day 'everybody cured everything with dittany.' Doubtless they took less mercury and drastic purgatives in consequence." American Indians made a tea of the leaves to treat colds and fevers. The plant is called Frostweed because of the "frost flowers" that sometimes form on the stem in late autumn. Moldenke (1949) wrote of the frost flowers on Dittany that "the outer edges are often beautifully wavy, fluted, or crisped. Sometimes two or three of these vertical plates of ice are grown together around the stem, giving the appearance of a snow-white clam or mussel shell. Thoreau described such 'frost bodkins' as these from the dead stems on timothy grass at Concord in 1859."

Dittany (from Middle English *ditane* and ultimately from Greek *diktamon,* which is perhaps from Dikte, a mountain in Crete) is more properly the name of *Origanum dictamnus* of Greece and Crete or of *Dictamnus albus,* of Eurasia.

## Gill-Over-the-Ground, Ground-Ivy

*Glechoma hederacea.* Mint (Greek *glekhon*); ivylike (*Hedera*). (From Europe.)

Ale-Gill, Alehoof, Bluebells (Mass.), Catnip (Iowa), Cat's-Foot, Cat's-Paw, Creeping-Charlie (Mass., Wis.), Creeping-Jenny, Crow-Victuals (Md.), Field-Balm, Furn-Hoof, Gill, Gill-Ale, Gill-Go-Over-the-Ground (Maine), Gill-Over-the-Ground (Mass.), Gill-Run, Gill-Run-Over-Grass (Mass.), Gill-Run-Over-the-Ground (Conn.), Hayhofe, Hathove, Haymaids, Hedgemaids, Hove, Jack-Over-the-Ground (Mass.), *Lierre terrestre* (P.Q.), Robin-Runaway (Maine, N.H.), Robin-Run-in-the-Hedge, Roving-Charlie, Run-Away-Jack (Mass.), Run-Away-Nell (Mass.), Run-Away-Robin, Scarlet-Runner (Nfd.), Tunhoof, Wild-Snakeroot (Mass.)

Gill-Over-the-Ground is the American version of several such Gill names in the British Isles. Gill or Jill is short for Gillian. Gerard (1633) called it "Ground-Ivy, Ale-hoofe, Gill go by ground, Tune-hoofe and Cats-foot." He wrote, "The women of our Northerne parts, especially about Wales and Cheshire, do tunne the herb Ale-hoof into their ale." Cotton Mather included Alehoof in his medical manual, *The Angel of Bethesda* (1724): "This is the plant with which our ancestors made their common drink, when the inhabitants of England were esteemed the longest livers in the world. In Old English, the name signifies, What was necessary to the making of ale. Tis a mighty cleanser. Hear what Sir Kenelm Digby sais: 'A good handful of leaves of Ground-Ivy, boil'd in a draught of ale, drunk morning and evening; it is admirable to cure all head-aches, pains, inflammations, defluxions in the eyes; jaundices; coughs, consumptions, spleen, stone, and gravel, and all obstructions. The herb stamped and applied like a plaister to a felon, cures it marvellously and speedily. It is admirable for old sores.' " (Sir Kenelm Digby, scientist, naval commander and diplomat, was also author of *Choice and Experimental Receipts in Physick and Chirurgery* [1668].) Manasseh Cutler (1785) reported, "A decoction of the leaves is esteemed by the common people a remedy for the jaundice. Dr. Withering says, the leaves are thrown into the vat with ale, to clarify it, and give it a flavour: and that ale thus prepared is often drank as an antiscorbutic."

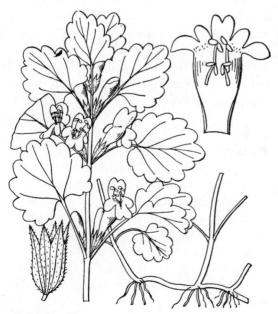

*Gill-Over-the-Ground*

In Chaucer's *The Nun's Priest's Tale,* "Ground-ivy that makes our yard so merry" is one of the herbs that Pertelote gives Chanticleer to "purge you well beneath and well above." American names include Creeping- and Roving-Charlie, Crow-Victuals (by blacks in Maryland according to Bergen, 1892), Field-Balm, Furn-Hoof, Run-Away-Nell and Wild-Snakeroot. Hofe is Old English for the plant. Marie-Victorin noted, "Constantly visited by bees, this is an interesting plant for the bee-keeper because it can be grown around a hive without harming other plants."

## American Pennyroyal

*Hedeoma pulegioides.* Sweet scent (from *hedus,* "sweet," *osme,* "scent"); like Pulegium (the old name of *Mentha pulegium*).

Mock Pennyroyal, Pennyr'yal (Maine), Pennyrile (Ky.), Pudding-Grass (West), Squaw-Mint, Squaw-Weed, Stinking-Balm, Thickweed, Tickseed, Tick-weed

"It was used by the Indians in the form of decoctions and infusions, and was introduced by them to the settlers, coming thence to the attention of the medical profession" (Lloyd, 1911). Peter Kalm (1748) reported that "an extract from it is reckoned very wholesome to drink as a tea when a person has a cold,

as it promotes perspiration. I was likewise told that on feeling a pain in any limb, this plant, if applied to it, would give immediate relief." In Virginia ticks are "apt to be troublesome during the warm season, but have such an aversion to Penny Royal, that they will attack no part that is rubb'd with the juice of that fragrant vegetable" (Byrd, 1728). It was called Squaw-Mint because "formerly thought to have emmenagogue powers and was much used as a hot tea for suppression of menses" (USD).

Pennyroyal *(Mentha pulegium)* is an ancient medicinal herb that was also used to flavor meat puddings: "It is yet to this day, as it hath beene in former times, used to bee put into puddings, and such like meates of all sorts, and therefore in divers places they know it by no other name than Pudding-grasse. The former age of our great grandfathers had all these hot herbes in much and familiar use, both for their meates and medicines, and therewith preserved themselves in long life and much health: but this delicate age of ours, which is not pleased with anything almost, be it meat or medicine, that is not pleasant to the palate, doth wholly refuse these almost, and therefore cannot be partaker of the benefit of them" (Parkinson, 1629). Pennyroyal is derived from Anglo-Norman *puliol real,* which is Royal Pulegium, *pulegium* being the Latin name for Fleabane.

## Hyssop

*Hyssopus officinalis.* (An ancient name of another plant); official. (From Europe.)

"Hyssope is much used in ptisans and other drinkes to help to expectorate flegme. It is many countrey peoples medicine for a cut or greene wound, being bruised with sugar and applyed," Parkinson reported (1629); moreover, he wrote, "an oyle made of the herbe and flowers, being anointed, doth comfort benummed sinews and joynts." The USD re-

*American Pennyroyal*

*Hyssop*

ports that "hyssop is a warm, gently stimulant aromatic."

This was once thought to be the Hyssop of the Bible, but Zohary (1982) writes that the Biblical Hyssop (*ezov* in Hebrew, from which Hyssop is derived), used for sprinkling in purefactory rites (for example in Exodus 12:21–22)), was not this plant, which does not grow in Israel, but Syrian Hyssop, *Origanum syriacum*.

## White Dead-Nettle, Snowflake

*Lamium album*. (The Latin name); white. (From Europe.)
Bee-Nettle, Blind-Nettle, Day-Nettle, Deaf-Nettle, Dog-Nettle, Dumb-Nettle, Snakeflower, Suck-Bottle, White-Archangel

These are Dead, Blind, Deaf (Day is an Americanization of *dea,* "deaf") and Dumb Nettles because they do not have the stinging hairs of the real Nettles (Urtica). "A tincture of the leaves and flowers has been used upon mucous membranes in general and upon the female generative organs in particular, to cause a kind of inflammatory excitement" (USD).

Turner in 1548 called this "dead nettle or white nettle." Bee-Nettle, Dea-Nettle, Snake's-Flower and Suck-Bottle are local names in England.

## Motherwort

*Leonurus cardiaca*. Lion tail; of the heart (previous generic name). (From Europe.)
*Agripaume cardiaque* (P.Q.), Cowthwort, Lion's-Ear, Lion's-Tail, Throw-Wort

"We do call it Motherwort in English, as truly from the effects to help the Mother, as they call it *Cardiaca* from the effects to help the heart" (Parkinson, 1640). Mother here refers to the womb. In 1814 Bigelow wrote that it was "a popular remedy in considerable request," and the USD reports that "an infusion or decoction has been used in amenorrhea."

*Motherwort*

## Gypsywort, Cut-Leaved Water-Horehound

*Lycopus americanus*. Wolf foot (from *lukos,* "wolf," *pous,* "foot"); of America.
Bitter-Bugle, Paul's-Betony, Rattlesnake-Weed

Manasseh Cutler called it Water Hore-hound and Gipsie: "This plant has been mistaken for a species of the Veronica, and is generally known by the name *Paul's Betony.* It is said the juice will give a permanent colour to linen, wool and silk, that will not wash out." Gypsywort is the British name for the genus and of *Lycopus europaeus* in particular: "Some also thinke good to call it *Herba Aegyptia,* because they that feine themselves Egyptians (such as many times wander like vagabonds from citie to citie in Germanie and other places) do use with this herb to give themselves a swart colour, such as the Egyptians and the people of Africke are of" (Gerard, 1633).

Dr. Porcher reported that "it appears to act like *digitalis* in abating the frequency of the pulse; its use, however, not being attended with the disagreeable symptoms sometimes accompanying the employment of the latter." The roots are eaten raw, boiled, pickled or dried. "Herb said to be an antidote for the bite of rattlesnakes" (Bergen, 1897).

## Bugleweed

*Lycopus virginicus.* Wolf foot; of Virginia. Archangel (Maine), Betony, Buglewort, Carpenter's-Herb, Gipsy-Weed, Sprig-of-Jerusalem (Maine), Sweet Bugleweed, Water-Bugle, Water Horehound, Wolf-Foot, Virginia-Horehound, Wood-Betony

Dr. Millspaugh wrote, "Most writers accept the idea that the plant is narcotic; we, however, infer, both from our own experience and that of others, that it is only sedative in that it removes, by checking hemorrhage, that nervous excitability and mental fear always accompanying such conditions."

## Horehound

*Marrubium vulgare.* (The classical name, perhaps related to Hebrew *marrob,* "bitter"); common. (From Europe.)

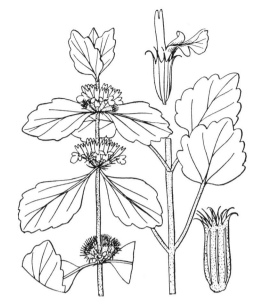

*Horehound*

Common Horehound, Hoarhound, Houndbene, Hound's-Bane, Marrhue, Marrube, Marvel, White Horehound

Dr. Sturtevant (1888) wrote, "This plant affords a popular domestic remedy, and seems in this country to be an inmate of the medicinal herb garden only. In Europe the leaves are sometimes employed as a condiment." This is the horehound of cough remedies. Dioscorides wrote that it was good for the "phthisical and asthmatical and to such as cough, and for the venomous-beast-bitten." In Texas this is "Marrubio; candy, cough, or croup, weed. Still made into candy or syrups, with sorghum or sugar, for dosing youngsters with throat ailments" (Reid, 1951). "There is a syrup made of Hore-hound to be had at the Apothecaries, very good for old coughs, to rid the tough phlegm; as also to avoid cold rheums from the lungs of old folks" (Culpeper). The Old English name was *hune,* which has nothing to do with hounds (hore is hoary, the white pubescence on the leaves). Marvel is a local name in England.

Dr. Schöpf (1783–84) reported that this was an ingredient of a "tried remedy" for the bite of a rattlesnake, "made known not many years ago by Caesar, a Carolina Negro, who was rewarded by the state of North Carolina with his freedom and a considerable sum of money. Having been many times tried, the especial efficacy of this remedy seemed to be admitted. It consists of the roots of the Hoarhound [*Marrubium vulgare*] and Plantain [*Plantago major* or *lanceolata*]. These roots are mixed in equal parts, and three ounces of the mixture boiled in two quarts of water until reduced by half; the patient takes a third of this decoction three mornings together on an empty stomach."

## Wild Mint

*Mentha arvensis.* Mint (the Latin name; in Greek legend the plant is named after the nymph Menthe who was changed into the plant by the jealous Proserpine, queen of the lower world); of cultivated ground. (Circumboreal.)

American Mint, Brook Mint (Maine), Cornmint, Fieldmint, Lamb's-Tongue, Wild-Bergamont (Maine),

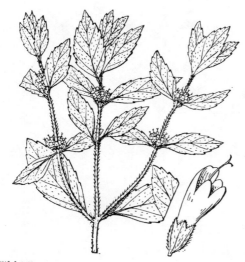

*Wild Mint*

Wild-Bergamot (Maine), Water-Calamint, Wild-Pennyroyal, Wild-Peppermint (Iowa, Wis.)

David Douglas on his walk to the headwaters of the Willamette River, Oregon, to find the Sugar Pine, September 13, 1826: "After resting a short time, Mackay made us some fine steaks, and roasted a shoulder of the doe for breakfast, with an infusion of [*Mentha arvensis*], sweetened with a small portion of sugar. The meal laid on the clean mossy foliage of *Gaultheria shallon* in lieu of a plate and our tea in a large wooden dish hewn out of the solid, and supping it with spoons made from the horns of the mountain sheep or Mouton Gris of the voyageurs. A stranger can hardly imagine the hospitality and kindness shown among these people." (Jean Baptist Mackay was a local hunter.)

## Peppermint

*Mentha piperita.* Mint; peppery. (From Europe.)

American Mint, Brandy-Mint, Lambmint, Lammint (N.C.)

This is a hybrid between Spearmint and Watermint, not discovered in England until the late 17th century. In 1696 the English botanist John Ray wrote that to his taste it was peppery; the pepper name persisted. Lambmint and Lammint are local names in England for this and *Mentha spicata.* According to Gerard (1633), "the smell of mint, saith Pliny, doth stir up the minde and the taste to a greedy desire to meate." It has been included in the USP and, according to the USD, was "formerly much used to allay nausea, relieve spasmodic pains of the stomach and bowels, expel flatus."

## Spearmint

*Mentha spicata.* Mint; spiked. (From Europe.)

*Spearmint*

*Baume* (P.Q.), Brownmint, Common Mint, Creek-mint (Ky.), Garden Mint, Greenmint, Lambmint, Mackerel Mint, *Menthe verte* (P.Q.), Our Lady's Mint, Sage-of-Bethlehem

Manasseh Cutler concluded that "it has a more agreeable flavour than the Horse Mint, and is preferred for culinary and medical purposes. The juice of the leaves, boiled up with sugar, is formed into tablets. The leaves make an agreeable conserve. The distilled waters, both simple and spiritous, are generally esteemed pleasant. The essential oil and distilled waters are considered as carminative. They are given with success for removing sickness at the stomach." Marie-Victorin wrote, "Spearmint is an important ingredient in the popular medicine of Quebec, where it is found along ditches. It is usually used as an infusion. In the old days, in summer every family in the country would lay in a store of 'baume.'" Mackerel Mint, Our Lady's Mint and Sage-of-Bethlehem are local names in England. It was included in both the USP and NF. John Evelyn wrote that Spearmint, "dry and warm, very fragrant, a little press'd, is friendly to the weak stomach, and powerful against all nervous crudities."

## Horsemints

*Monarda.* Of Monardes (Nicolas Monardes, 1493–1588).

Bee-Balm, Sweet-Mary (N.H.), Wild-Bergamot

Nicolas Monardes, physician and botanist of Seville, was author of the first European book on American medicinal plants, *Historia medicinal de las cosas quese traen de nuestras Indias occidentales* (1569). This was translated into English in 1577 as *Joyfull Newes out of the newe founde Worlde.*

## Bee-Balm, Oswego-Tea

*Monarda didyma.* Of Monardes; twin (paired stamens).

American Bee-Balm, Fragrant-Balm, Horsemint, Indian-Plume, Low-Balm, Mountain-Balm (N.C.), Mountain-Mint, Oswego, Red-Balm, Red Bergamot, Rose-Balm, Scarlet-Balm, Square-Stem, Sweet-Mary

Oswego Tea was a popular healthful concoction "used in flatulence, nausea, vomiting, and in suppression of urine and menstruation" (Jacobs and Burlage).

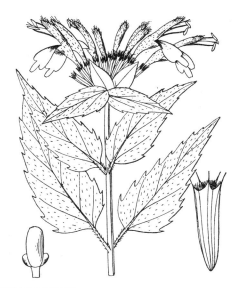

*Wild-Bergamot*

## Wild-Bergamot

*Monarda fistulosa.* Of Monardes; tubular.

Beebalm, Horsemint, Lemon-Mint, Oswego-Tea, Purple-Bergamot

Among the Ojibwa Indians, "the root is used by making a decoction and drinking several swallows, at intervals, for pain in the stomach and intestines" (Hoffman, 1891). The scent is like that of oil of bergamot (used in scent making and to flavor foods—Earl Gray Tea, for example), which is extracted from the Bergamot, *Citrus aurantium bergamia,* a small Mediterranean tree. The leaves and blossoms are brewed for a medicinal tea and cooked as a potherb. "At roadside opposite Leighton's, just this side his barn, *Monarda fistulosa,* wild bergamot, nearly done, with terminal whorls and fragrance mixed of balm and summer savory" (Thoreau, 1856).

## Horsemint

*Monarda punctata.* Of Monardes; dotted.

American-Origanum, Dotted Horsemint, Dotted Monarda, Gravel-Wort, Origanum, Rignum, Spotted Bee-Balm, Spotted Horsemint

Dr. Porcher reported that "this is another of our very aromatic indigenous plants, possessing stimulant and carminative powers and regarded as a very popular emmenagogue among those residing in this country. The French authorities speak favorably of it; an aromatic oil is obtained from this; and the infusion of the leaves, recent or dried, is very efficient in allaying nausea and vomiting in bilious fevers." It has been included in the USP, "employed as a domestic remedy for flatulent colic and sick stomach" (USD). The plant was once cultivated as a source of thymol, which is now produced synthetically.

## Catnip

*Nepeta cataria.* (The Latin name, from Nepi in Italy); of cats (the old generic name; Late Latin *cattus* means "cat"). (From Europe.)

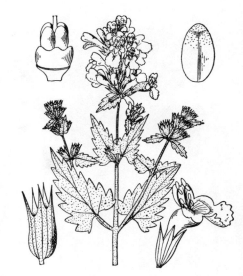

*Catnip*

*Cataire* (P.Q.), Catmint, Catnep, Catrup, Cat's-Heal-All, Cat's-Wort, *Chataire* (P.Q.), Field-Balm, *Herbe à chats* (P.Q.)

Turner (1548) reported that it was called "in Latin Nepeta, in English Nepe, in Dutch Katzenkraut oder Katzenmuntz, in French Herbe au Chat." In 19th-century Pennsylvania, "the dried herb, in infusion, is a highly popular medicine among the good ladies who deal in simples,—and is probably often useful" (Darlington, 1847). Included in the USP and NF, "Catnep has no therapeutic virtues other than that of a mild aromatic" (USD).

## Wild-Marjoram, Oregano

*Origanum vulgare.* (From the Greek name of an aromatic herb); common. (From Europe.)

Organs, Organy, Origanum, Pot-Marjoram, Sweet-Marjoram, Winter-Marjoram, Winter-Sweet

Gerard (1633) called it Goat's Marjerome or Organy and reported that it "is very good against the wamblings of the stomache." Manasseh Cutler wrote, "It is warm and aromatic. Dr. Withering says, the essential oil is

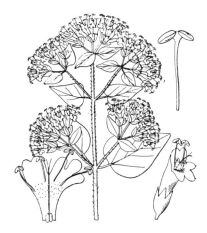

*Wild-Marjoram*

so acrid that it may be considered as a caustic, and is much used with that intention by far-riers. A little cotton wool moistened with it, and put into the hollow of an aching tooth, frequently relieves the pain. The dried leaves make an exceedingly grateful tea." This is one of the sources of the kitchen herb ore-gano. Sweet Marjoram usually means *Origanum majorana;* the Medieval Latin name *majorana* is of obscure origin. Wild Mar-joram has been listed in the USP.

> *Venus showered a dew of peaceful*
> *sleep on the limbs of*
> *Ascanius, snuggled him in her breast,*
> *and divinely bore him*
> *Up to Idalian groves, where the tender*
> *Marjoram puts him*
> *To bed in a cradle of flowers and*
> *shade and entrancing fragrance.*
> *The Aeneid, 691–695*

Ascanius was Aeneas's son.

## Douglas's Pogogyne, Mesa-Mint

*Pogogyne douglasii.* Bearded female (the hairy style); of Douglas (David Douglas, 1798–1834).

In Mendocino County, California, "the seed is gathered in surprisingly large quantities and is highly valued by the Yukis and Num-lakis as a sweet aromatic ingredient of wheat and barley pinole. The taste of the leaf when taken before the flowers appear is much like that of some of the finer species of mint" (Chesnut, 1902).

## Heal-All, Self-Heal

*Prunella vulgaris.* (An old name; herbalists in the 15th and 16th centuries used both Prunella and Brunella, perhaps derived from German *braun,* "purple," from Latin *prunum,* or *Braune,* "quinsy," which was supposedly cured by this herb); common. (From Europe.)
All-Heal, Blue-Curls, Blue-Lucy (Maine), *Brunelle* (P.Q.), Brown-Wort, Carpenter's-Herb, Carpenter's-Square, Carpenter's-Weed (N.H.), Cure-All (West), Dragonhead (Mont.), Heart-of-the-Earth, Heart's-Ease (Mass.), *Herbe au charpentier* (P.Q.),

*Heal-All*

Hook-Heal, Hookweed, Sicklewort, Slough-Heal, Thimble-Flower, Wild-Sage

Gerard (1633) wrote that it was called "Carpenters herbe, Selfe-heale, and Hook-heale, & Sicklewoort" because "the decoction of Prunell made with wine or water doth joine together and make whole and sound all wounds, both inward and outward." The corolla is shaped like a billhook, which would suggest its medicinal virtues, according to the doctrine of signatures. Heart's-Ease and Heart-of-the-Earth are local names in England. This is Robert Frost's "Design":

> I found a dimpled spider, fat and
>   white,
> On a white heal-all, holding up a moth
> Like a white piece of rigid satin cloth—
> Assorted characters of death and blight
> Mixed ready to begin the morning
>   right,
> Like the ingredients of a witch's broth—
> A snow-drop spider, a flower like froth,
> And dead wings carried like a paper
>   kite.
>
> What had that flower to do with being
>   white,
> The wayside blue and innocent heal-
>   all?
> What brought the kindred spider to that
>   height,
> Then steered the white moth thither in
>   the night?
> What but design of darkness to ap-
>   pall?—
> If design govern in a thing so small.

## Appalachian Mountain-Mint

*Pycnanthemum flexuosum.* Dense flower (*puknos,* "dense," *anthemon,* "flower"); flexuous.

Basil, Dysentery-Weed, Flax-Leaved Basil, Wild-Marjoram

"This American mint was popularly used in bowel complaints; its hot infusion is diaphoretic" (USD).

## Virginia Mountain-Mint

*Pycnanthemum virginianum.* Dense flower; of Virginia.

Calamint, Common Mountain-Mint, Horsemint, Wild-Basil (Mass.)

The Chippewa Indians made a decoction of the leaves for the treatment of fevers: "If a person feels chilly he should take 1 cup of this medicine as hot as possible, repeating the dose after a short time. He should also wrap up and go to bed; when the fever comes on he should take the same decoction, but cold and whenever desired" (Densmore, 1928).

## Sage

*Salvia.* Healing plant (the Latin name for Sage, from *salvus,* "healthy, safe").

"Sage is much used of many in the month of May fasting, with butter and Parsley, and is held of most much to conduce to the health of mans body. It is also much used among other good herbes to be tunn'd up with ale, which thereupon is term'd Sage Ale, whereof many barrels full are made, and drunke in the said month chiefly for the purpose afore recited: and also for teeming women, to help them the better forward in their childbearing" (Parkinson, 1629). John Evelyn (1699) wrote that "'tis a plant endu'd with so many and wonderful properties, as that the assiduous use of it is said to render men Immortal." Both were writing of *Salvia officinalis,* the kitchen and garden herb. The popular garden flower is *Salvia splendens* from Brazil.

## Chia, California Sage

*Salvia columbariae.* Healing plant; of the dove-cote.

Wild-Sage, Winter-Oat (Calif.)

*Chia*

"The small, blue flowers, crowded in dense, prickly, globular heads, interrupted on the stalk (which passes through the midst like a skewer), appear from March to June, and the seeds are ripe a month or so later. They are easily gathered by bending the stalks over a bowl or finely woven basket, and beating the heads with a paddle or fan, which shatters out the seeds. That is the Indian method; but when the plants grow plentifully, as they sometimes do as thick as grass in a field, or

as they may be made to do so by sowing the seed in cultivated ground, they can be cut, threshed and winnowed like flax or wheat" (Saunders, 1934).

Saunders also reported, "At the present day, Chia is better known as a drink than a food. A teaspoonful of the seeds steeped in a tumbler of cold water for a few minutes communicates a mucilaginous quality to the liquid. This may be drunk plain, but among the Mexicans, who are very fond of it as a refreshment, the customary mode of serving it is with the addition of a little sugar and a dash of lemon juice." The seeds are also parched and ground to make pinole, and the leaves are used as a poultice.

## Lyre-Leaved Sage

*Salvia lyrata.* Healing plant; lyre-shaped. Cancer-Weed, Meadow-Sage, Wild Sage

The fresh leaves were applied to remove warts, and the leaves and seeds were made into an ointment to cure wounds and sores.

## Yerba Buena, Tea-Vine, Oregon-Tea

*Satureja douglasii.* Savory (the Latin name); of Douglas (David Douglas, 1798–1834).

"Its dried leaves steeped for a few minutes in hot water make a palatable beverage mildly stimulating to the digestion, and, like real tea, even provocative of gossip; for it is an historic little plant, this Yerba Buena, which gave name to the Mexican village out of which the city of San Francisco afterwards arose. The two words, which mean literally 'good herb,' are merely the Spanish for our term 'garden mint,' of whose qualities the wild plant somewhat partakes" (Saunders, 1934).

## Mad-Dog Skullcap

*Scutellaria laterifolia.* Little dish (Latin *scutella* means "dish," alluding to the pouch on the fruiting calyx); lateral-flowered.

Mad-Dog Skullcap

any peculiar taste or smell, the possession of medical virtues. It is even destitute of the aromatic properties which are found in many of the labiate plants. When taken internally it produces no very obvious effects, and probably is of no remedial value, although at one time it was esteemed as a remedy in hydrophobia. It is also used by some practitioners as a nervine in neuralgic and convulsive affections, chorea, delirium tremens, and nervous exhaustion." It has been included in the USP and NF.

## California Hedge-Nettle

*Stachys bullata.* Spike (the Greek name of a mint); knobbed.

Grandmother, Purissima

"An infusion of stem and leaves is made by soaking them for a few minutes in boiling water. This is applied as a wash to wounds and sores. The soaked leaves may also be bound upon the parts as a poultice" (Saunders, 1934). It was called Grandmother because "the flower looks like an old dame with a high cap" (Bergen, 1897).

## Woundwort

*Stachys palustris.* Spike; of marshes. (From Europe.)

All-Heal, Betony, Clownheal, Clown's-Woundwort, Cockhead, Dead-Nettle, *Épiaire des marais* (P.Q.), Hedge-Nettle, Marsh-Woundwort, Roughweed

Clownheal and Clown's-Woundwort are names from Gerard's *Herbal:* "A very poor man in mowing of Peason did cut his leg with the sithe, wherein he made a wound to the bones, & withall very large and wide, and also with great effusion of bloud. The poore man crept unto this herbe which he bruised in his hands, and tied a great quantity of it unto the wound with a piece of his shirt." Gerard offered to treat the wound, but the man refused, "Saying that I could not heale it so well as himselfe; a clownish answer I

American Skullcap, Blue-Pimpernel, Blue Skullcap, Helmet-Flower, Hooded-Willowherb, Hoodwort, Mad-Dog, Mad-Dog-Herb, Madweed, Side-Flowered Skullcap, Skullcap

In the 1770s Dr. Lawrence Vander Veer of Roycefield (now Hillsborough), New Jersey, started to treat persons and animals bitten by mad dogs with this plant, with remarkable success. Over a 40-year period "he treated as many as four hundred persons (an average of ten a year), with but one death." For example: "A man, two hogs, and two cattle, were bitten by a mad dog. Scutellaria was given the man and one hog. Both recovered. The other animals died of hydrophobia." In 1783 Mr. Daniel Lewis of North Castle, New York, was bitten by a mad dog and was sent to Dr. Vander Veer for treatment. Lewis was shown the plant and instructed how to use it. He then went home and advertized himself as the "Mad Dog Doctor" with the "Lewis Secret Cure" for hydrophobia. This became celebrated and was later shown to be powdered Scutellaria leaves (Lloyd, 1929).

The cure enjoyed a reputation for some years, but by 1887 the USD concluded that "to the senses skullcap does not indicate, by

*Woundwort*

confesse, without any thankes for my good will, whereupon I have named it Clownes Wound-wort." Manasseh Cutler called it Clownheal and Hedge Nettle and noted that "it has a foetid smell, and toads are thought to be fond of living under its shade. It will dye yellow." Betony is *Stachys officinalis,* an ancient healing herb, from Latin *betonica,* after the Vettones, an Iberian tribe. Cockhead is a local name in Scotland.

## Germander, Wood-Sage

*Teucrium canadense.* Of Teucer (the first king of Troy); of Canada.

American Germander, Betony, *Germandrée du Canada* (P.Q.), Groundpine, Head-Betony, Wood-Betony

Germander *(Teucrium chamaedrys)* is an ancient vulnerary or healing herb "and is still prescribed today for healing sores and ulcers" (Bianchini and Corbetta, 1975). In his list of New England plants "common with us in England," Josselyn called this "Pellamount or Mountain time," which are names for Teucrium species in Gerard's *Herbal.* Pellamount is a corruption of *Polium montanum, polium* being the Latin name of a Germander.

## Blue-Curls

*Trichostema dichotomum.* Hairy stamen (from Greek *thrix,* "hair," *stemon,* "stamen"); forked in pairs.

Bastard-Pennyroyal, Blue-Gentian, Fluxweed (Ind.), Heart's-Angel (Maine), Pennyroyal (Md.)

## Vinegar-Weed, Western Blue-Curls

*Trichostema lanceolatum.* Hairy stamen; lanceolate (leaves).

Camphor-Weed (Calif.), Tarweed

"The very peculiar little blue-flowered annual, which covers dry grassy hillsides with its ashy-gray verdure throughout the summer months, exhales a strong pungent odor, somewhat like that of a mixture of vinegar and turpentine," according to Chesnut (1902); "the plant is best known as a fish poison, its use for this purpose being especially well known to the Concow and Numlaki Indians who formerly inhabited the Sacramento Valley. These tribes mash up the fresh plants with rocks and throw this product, without any additional ingredient, into pools or sluggish streams. The fish are quickly intoxicated and float to the surface, when they are easily caught by hand or scooped out of the water with shallow sieve baskets made of small wands of willow."

# THE PLANTAIN FAMILY

## Plantaginaceae

A cosmopolitan family of three genera and 255 species (of which *Plantago* has 250) of herbs and a few shrubs. Plantain is derived from the Latin *planta* (the sole of the foot), from the shape of the broad leaves of many species. Two Eurasian species are of medical importance, *Plantago afra,* which provides the laxative psyllium (Metamucil is one brand), and *Plantago ovata,* which is used in the treatment of dysentery.

## English Plantain

*Plantago lanceolata.* Footlike; lance-shaped. (From Europe.)

Black-Jacks, Buckhorn, Buckhorn Plantain (W.Va.), Buck Plantain (W.Va.), Cat's-Cradles, Chimney-Sweeps, Clock, Cocks, Dog's-Ribs, Headsman, Hen-Plant, He-Plantain (Ky.), Hock-Cockle (Long Island), Jackstraws, Kemps, Kempseed, Klops, Knock-Heads, Lance-Leaved Plantain, Leechwort, Long Plantain, Nigger-Heads (Long Island), Pig-Grass (N.C.), *Queue de rat* (P.Q.), Ram's-Tongue, Rattail, Ribgrass, Ribwort (W.Va.), Ripple (W.Va.), Ripple-grass, Ripple Plantain, Snake Plantain, Soldiers (Mass.), Windles

Kemp is a name from northern England: "The origin of this name is to be found in the Danish *koempe,* a warrior, and the reason for its being so called is to be found in the game which children in most parts of the kingdom play with the flower-stalks of the plantain, by endeavoring to knock off the heads of each other's mimic weapons" (Thiselton-Dyer). Black-Jacks, Cock-Grass, Chimney-Sweeper, Clock, Jackstraw, Nigger-Heads and Soldiers are other local names in England.

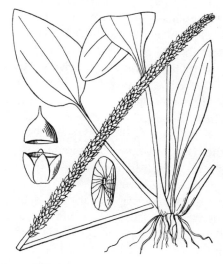

*Common Plantain*

## Common Plantain

*Plantago major.* Footlike; larger. (From Europe.)

Birdseed, Broadleaf Plantain, Cart-Track-Plant, Cocks, Devil's-Shoestring, Dooryard Plantain, Englishman's-Foot, Englishman's-Weed, Greater Plantain, Healing-Blade, Hen-Plant, Lamb's-Foot, Psyllium, Rat-Tail (Nfd.), Round-Leaved Plantain, Silkplant, Waybread, Wayside Plantain, Whiteman's-Foot

"Heres a noble Hæmoptoic Draught. Take Plantain-water, four ounces; wine vinegar, and syrup of Comfrey, each half an ounce; the white of an egg beat up. Mix. It mightily quiets and thickens the blood; and constringes and consolidates the apertures of the vessels. This is for all bleeding" (Cotton Mather, 1724). In the Highlands of Scotland "it is still called *Slan-lus,* or plant of healing, from a firm belief in its healing virtues. Pliny goes so far as to state, 'on high authority,' that if 'it be put into a pot where many pieces of flesh are boiling, it will sodden them together' " (Grieve, 1931).

In his list "Of such Plants as have sprung up since the English Planted and kept Cattle in New-England," Josselyn (1672) included "Plantain, which the Indians call English-Mans Foot, as though produced by their treading." In his 1865 edition of Josselyn's *New-England's Rarities,* Edward Tuckerman wrote that "the old vulgar names of the plant in Northern languages—as *Wegerich* and *Wegetritt* of the German, *Weegblad* and *Weegbree* of the Dutch, *Veibred* of the Danish, and *Weybred* of the old English, all pointing to the plantain's growing on ways trodden by man—suggest, perhaps, a far older supposed relation between this plant and the human foot than that mentioned above." Birdseed, Lamb's-Foot and Waybread (Old English *wegbroede,* way-breadth) are local names in England and Healing-Blade in Scotland. Psyllium is the old generic name and the name of a medicine produced from an African species.

*Sea Plantain*

## Sea Plantain

*Plantago maritima.* Footlike; of the seacoast. Buck's-Horn, Gibbals, Goosetongue, Sea-Kemps, Seaside Plantain

"Seaside Plantain is not very generally known as one of the available summer vegetables, but on the New England coast, especially by the fishermen of eastern Maine and in Nova Scotia, where the plant is regularly gathered under the name Goosetongue, it is exten-sively used" (Fernald and Kinsey, 1943). And in 1749 Peter Kalm wrote that in Canada "the French boil its leaves in a broth on their sea voyages or eat them as a salad. It may likewise be pickled like samphire."

## Indian-Wheat, Woolly Plantin

*Plantago patagonica.* Footlike; of Patagonia.

"On some ranges it is considered fairly good or even good spring forage for sheep and cattle, and is one of the most valuable winter annual weeds," according to the *Range Plant Handbook;* "the dense and relatively large seed heads are the most palatable part of the plant, and are reputedly nutritious and fattening. Elsewhere than in the Southwest, woolly Indian-wheat ranks as poor forage."

# THE FIGWORT OR SNAPDRAGON FAMILY

## *Scrophulariaceae*

A cosmopolitan family of 224 genera and 4,450 species of herbs and a few shrubs and trees; most abundant in temperate regions and in tropical mountains. Many members of the family are cultivated as ornamentals, including *Antirrhinum* (Snapdragons), *Veronica* and *Calceolaria* (Slipper-Flowers) and *Paulownia tomentosa,* the Empress-Tree.

John Parkinson (1640) wrote that the tubercled roots of the Knotted Figwort (*Scrophularia nodosa*) were "effectual for the Kings Evil, or any other knots, kernels, bunches or wennes growing in the flesh wheresoever: it is of singular good use to be applyed for the hemorrhoids or piles, when they grow painefull and fall down, and for other such knobbes or kernells as sometimes grow in and about the Fundament." The King's Evil is scrofula, which is marked by scrofulous tumors or strumas, swellings of the lymphatic glands of the neck. Hemorrhoids were called figs.

## Foothills Kittentails, White River Coraldrops

*Besseya plantaginea.* Of Bessey (Charles E. Bessey, 1845–1915, American botanist and teacher); like Plantago (leaves).

Among the Navaho, "if a hunter cuts the bladder in butchering a deer, he chews the leaves of this plant and blows them over the cut 'so the deer will not feel badly about it'; otherwise the mistake causes anuria in the hunter, which may be cured by drinking quantities of a cold infusion of the plant (diuretic); to prevent this the hunter chews the dried root while hunting and adds the leaves to his smoking materials" (Vestal, 1952).

## Paintbrushes, Painted-Cups

*Castilleja.* Of Castillejo (Domingo Castillejo, an 18th-century Spanish botanist).
Bloody-Noses (Colo.), Mexican-Blanket (Texas)

## Painted-Cup

*Castilleja coccinea.* Of Castillejo; scarlet.
Bloody-Noses, Bloody-Warrior (Minn.), Election-Posies (Mass.), Fire-Pink (Wis.), Honeysuckle (S.Dak.), Indian-Blanket, Indian-Paintbrush, Indian-Pink (Ill.), Nosebleed (Conn.), Paintbrush (Ill, N.H., P.Q.), Prairie-Fire (Wis.), Red-Indians (Mass.), Scarlet Painted-Cup, Wickackee (Mass.), Wickawee

On May 8, 1853, Thoreau wrote, "At the foot of Annursnack, rising from the Jesse Hos-

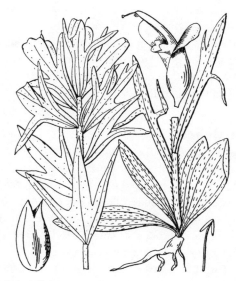

*Painted-Cup*

mer meadow, was surprised by the brilliant scarlet flowers of the painted-cup *(Castilleia coccinea)* just coming into bloom. Some may have been out a day or two. Methinks this is the most high-colored and brilliant flower yet, not excepting the columbine. In color it matches Sophia's cactus blossoms exactly. It is all the more interesting for being a painted leaf and not a petal, and its spidery leaves, pinnatifid with linear divisions, increases its strangeness." (Sophia was Thoreau's sister.) Wickackee and Wickawee are said to be from the Indian.

## Indian-Paintbrush, Wyoming-Paintbrush

*Castilleja linariifolia.* Of Castillejo; with leaves of Linaria.

Among the Tewa Indians, "the red flower is prominent in decorative art at Hano; it is painted on pottery, painted and carved in wood, and imitated in colored yarn on a wooden framework" (Robbins, Harrington and Freire-Marreco). According to Percy Train and his colleagues, "prized particularly as a remedy for venereal diseases, the Beatty Indians travel long distances to secure the plant. A solution of boiled roots, taken in small amounts as a drink, is said to cure venereal disease, if the treatment is continued for a long time." This is the state flower of Wyoming.

## Turtlehead

*Chelone glabra.* Tortoise (the flower is shaped like the head of a tortoise or turtle); white.
Balmony, Bammany (N.B.), Bitter-Herb, Bitterweed, Codhead, Fishhead, Fishmouth, *Galane glabre* (P.Q.), Rheumatism-Root, Salt-Rheumweed, Shell-Flower, Snakehead, Snakemouth (N.C.), *Tête de tortue* (P.Q.), Turtlebloom

"The Indians use a strong decoction of the whole plant in eruptive diseases, biles, hemorrhoids, sores, &c. Few plants promise to

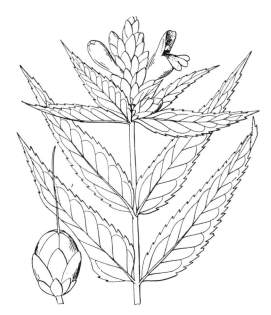

*Turtlehead*

become more useful in skillful hands: it ought to be tried in yellow fever and bilious fever, the tropical liver complaint" (Rafinesque). Dr. Porcher reported, "It is administered by the vegetable practitioners as an anthelmintic; also in jaundice, in hepatic disorders generally, and in constipation." Balmony and Bammany are presumably variants of Baldmoney, an early name for some Gentians, which are also Bitterworts.

## Blue-Eyed-Mary

*Collinsia verna.* Of Collins (Zaccheus Collins, 1764–1831, naturalist of Philadelphia); of spring.
Blue-Bonnet-White-Apron, Blue-Eye, Innocence, Lady-by-the-Lake, Prairie-Innocence, Tall-Pink

Maiden Blue-Eyed-Mary of the West (also called Blue-Lips) is *Collinsia parviflora.*

## Kenilworth-Ivy

*Cymbalaria muralis.* Like a cymbal (the leaves); of walls. (From Europe.)

Aaron's-Beard, Climbing-Sailor, Coliseum-Ivy, Ivy-Leaved-Toadflax, Ivy-Weed, Mother-of-Thousands, Oxford-Weed, Pennywort, Roving-Sailor, Wandering-Jew

Kenilworth may be derived from Kernelwort, a name for species of *Scrophularia* that were used to treat the kernels or tubercular glands of scrofula. In Britain the common name of the plant is Ivy-Leaved-Toadflax, which was introduced as a garden plant to England in the 17th century, and soon spread wild, earning all the other names above and many more in England and Scotland.

Foxglove

Kenilworth-Ivy

## Foxglove

*Digitalis purpurea.* Thimble; purple. (From Europe.)

Cottager's, Dog's-Finger, Fairy-Bells, Fairy-Cap, Fairy-Glove, Fairy-Thimbles, Finger-Flower, Flapdock, Folk's-Glove, Ladies'-Thimbles, Lady's-Fingers, Lady's-Glove, Lion's-Mouth, Popdock, Rabbit-Flower, Scotch-Mercury, Thimbles, Throatwort, Witch's-Thimbles

William Withering (1741–1799) was an English physician and botanist, author of a British flora (1776) frequently cited by Manasseh Cutler in his account of American plants (he is the "Dr. Withering" who appears in Cutler quotations in this book). Withering is also the author of *An Account of the Foxglove* (1785), in which he presented 10 years of clinical data on the patients he had treated with Foxglove: "In the year 1775, my opinion was asked concerning a family receipt for the cure of dropsy. I was told that it had long been kept secret by an old woman in Shropshire, who had sometimes made cures after the more regular practitioners had failed. I was informed also, that the effects produced were violent vomiting and purging; for the diuretic effects seem to have been overlooked. This medicine was composed of twenty or more different herbs; but it was not very difficult for one conversant in these subjects, to perceive, that the active herb could be no other than the foxglove." Withering concluded that Foxglove was a diuretic, stimulating urination and thus draining the body of the excess fluid. His treatment of this type of dropsy with Foxglove was remarkably effective, but not because it is a diuretic. One of the major causes of dropsy (fluid accumulation in body tissue or cavity) is congestive heart failure. A damaged heart pumps blood at low pressure, allowing fluid to leak out of the capillaries into tissues, which then swell into dropsy. Digitalis, the active constituent of Foxglove, strengthens cardiac contraction and enables the heart to deliver blood to the rest of the body at higher pressure, thus keeping fluid from leaking out of the capillaries. Digitalis preparations are used to treat almost every type of heart disease.

Evidently Foxglove does mean "the glove of a fox," despite all attempts to make it "the glove of the folk" (fairies, goblins). The other names listed above are among the 90 local names in the British Isles.

## Eyebright

*Euphrasia nemorosa.* Mirth; of woods. (Also found in Eurasia.)

Hairy Eyebright, Mouthwort

"Have you never seen a very common plant call'd Eye-bright? It forever sais to the eye that looks upon it; Make use of me, and I will do thee good and not hurt, all the days of thy life. A plain Eye-bright water constantly or frequently used will continue to the eye-sight a brightness to be wondered at" (Cotton Mather, 1724).

*Euphrasia officinalis* was called "Eye bryghte" by William Turner in 1548. John Pechey (1694) reported that "the oculists in England and Beyond-Sea, use the herb in sallets, in broths, in bread, and in table-beer; and apply it outwardly in fomentations, and other external medicines for the eyes."

John Milton suggested in *Paradise Lost* that it was man's first medicine:

*Michael from Adam's eyes the film re-*
*moved,*
*Which the false fruit, that promised*
*clearer sight,*
*Had bred; then purged with euphrasy*
*and rue*
*The visual nerve, for he had much to*
*see.*

Euphrosyne was one of the three Graces, daughters of Zeus, distinguished for her joy and mirth, feelings evidently shared by persons whose eyesight has been restored by applying Eyebright. The black pupil-like spot in the corolla perhaps indicated its medicinal virtues, according to the doctrine of signatures.

## Golden Hedge-Hyssop, Golden Pert

*Gratiola aurea.* Little favor (for its medicinal properties); golden.

"What a miserable name has the *Gratiola aurea,* hedge hyssop! Whose hedge does it grow by, pray, in this part of the world" (Thoreau, 1851). The European Hedge-Hyssop, *Gratiola officinalis,* was an important medicinal herb ("a drastic cathartic and emetic," according to Grieve) and was named *Gratia Dei* by the herbalists and placed among the Hyssops *(Hyssopus).*

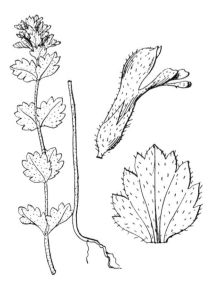

*Eyebright*

*Butter-and-Eggs*

## Butter-and-Eggs, Toadflax

*Linaria vulgaris*. Like Linum (Flax); common. (From Europe.)

Bread-and-Butter (Mass.), Brideweed, Bridewort, Continental-Weed, Dead-Men's-Bones (N.Y.), Devil's-Flax (W.Va.), Devil's-Flower, Eggs-and-Bacon, Flaxweed, Fluellin, Gallweed, Gallwort, *Gueule de lion* (P.Q.), Hogmouth (N.Y.), Impudent-Lawyer (W.Va.), Indian-Hemp (W.Va.), Jacob's-Ladder (New England, Long Island), Ladies'-Slippers (Mass.), Mother-of-Millions, Rabbit-Ears, Rabbit-Flower, Rancid, Ranstead (Pa.), Snapdragon (Mass., Pa.), Snapdragon-Ramsted, Wax-Candles (Ky.), Wild-Flax (W.Va.), Wild-Snapdragon (Ky.), Wild-Tobacco (W.Va.), Yellow Toadflax

"If it have no name it may be called in English Lynary or Todes flax, for the Poticaries cal it Linarium, and the Duch cal it Krotenflaks" (Turner, 1548). In his "brief account of those plants that are most troublesome in our pastures and fields in Pennsylvania," John Bartram (1758) wrote that "the most mischievous of these is, first, the stinking yellow *Linaria*. It is the most hurtful plant to our pastures that can grow in our northern climate. Neither the spade, plough, nor hoe can eradicate it when it is spread in pasture. Every little fibre that is left will soon increase prodigiously; nay, some people have rolled great heaps of logs upon it, and burnt them to ashes, whereby the earth was burnt half a foot deep, yet it put up again, as fresh as ever, covering the ground so close as not to let any grass grow amongst it; and the cattle can't abide it." Thoreau wrote in 1852 of "butter-and-eggs, toad-flax, on Fair Haven . . . It is rather rich-colored, with a not disagreeable scent. It is called a troublesome weed. Flowers must not be too profuse nor obtrusive; else they acquire the reputation of weeds." Manasseh Cutler called it Snapdragon and Fluellin. Darlington (1847) noted that in Philadelphia it was called Ranstead-Weed because it was introduced from Wales, as a garden flower, by a Mr. Ranstead, a Welsh resident of Philadelphia. According to Marie-Victorin, "an unguent of Linaria was previously celebrated as a remedy for hemorrhoids." According to Dr. Clapp (1852), it was "reputed to be cathartic, diuretic and somewhat anodyne."

Devil's-Flax, Devil's-Flower and Impudent-Lawyer are American farmers' names, and the "bride" in Bridewort and Brideweed is a disease of pigs that was treated with this plant. Dead-Man's-Bones is a local name in Scotland for Chickweed.

## Seepspring Monkeyflower, Yellow Monkeyflower

*Mimulus guttatus*. Little mimic (Latin *mimus*, "a mimic," for it looks like a monkey's face); spotted (petals).

Wild-Lettuce

This was a salad plant for the Indians and early settlers of the Rocky Mountains.

## Wood-Betony, Lousewort

*Pedicularis canadensis*. Of lice (it was believed that cattle grazing on or among the

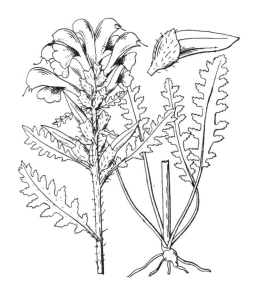

*Wood-Betony*

European Lousewort become covered with lice); of Canada.

Betong, Beton Lousewort, Betony (N.Y.), Beefsteak-Plant, Chicken's-Heads (Long Island), Common Lousewort, Head-Betony, High-Head-All, Louse-wort-Foxglove, Snaffles

Jane Colden (ca. 1750) wrote, "This pedicularis is call'd by the country people Betony. They make Thee [tea] of the leaves, et use it for the fever & ague et for sikness of the stomack." (Betony is *Stachys officinalis*.) Among the Potawatomi, "the use of the root is rather different in the two tribes. The Forest Potawatomi use it as a physic, whereas the Prairie Potawatomi use it for reducing both internal and external swellings" (Huron Smith, 1933). Snaffles is a local name in England for a Rhinanthus.

## Hot-Rock Beardtongue, White Penstemon

*Penstemon deustus.* Five stamens; burnt.

In Nevada "often the plant is known to the Shoshones under the name 'timbah-hay nut-zoo,' meaning 'bad disease medicine.' Appar-ently it is one of the more important remedies for venereal diseases. Medicine men collect the plant, grind it to a fine powder and sell it to other Indians in small quantities for as much as five dollars" (Train, Henrichs and Archer).

## Foxglove Beardtongue

*Penstemon digitalis.* Five stamens; like Digitalis.

Dead-Men's-Bells (West)

Bergen (1897) wrote that it is called Dead-Men's-Bells in the West "from growing on graves." This is also a local name in Scotland for Foxglove (Digitalis).

## Rydberg's Penstemon, Meadow Beardtongue

*Penstemon rydbergii.* Five stamens; of Rydberg (Per Axel Rydberg, 1860–1931).

Rydberg was born in Sweden and came to the United States in 1882. He was on the staff of the New York Botanical Garden for over 30 years and botanized across the American West. His publications include *Flora of the Sand Hills of Nebraska* (1895), *Flora of Colorado* (1906) and *Flora of the Prairies and Plains* (1932).

## Yellow-Rattle

*Rhinanthus minor.* Nose flower (originally the name of another plant); lesser. (Also found in Eurasia.)

*Claquette* (P.Q.), *Cocrête* (P.Q.), Cow-Wheat, *Graines de Boston* (P.Q.), Money-Grass, Penny-Grass, Penny-Rattle, Rattlebag, Rattlebox, Shepherd's-Coffin (Lab., Nfd.), *Sonette* (P.Q.), *Tartarie* (P.Q.), Yellow-Cockscomb

The early round calyx is flat as a penny, and the ripe seeds rattle in the pod. Penny-Grass is a name from Gerard (1633). Penny-Rattle is a local name in England.

*Moth Mullein*

## Moth Mullein

*Verbascum blattaria.* (The Latin name, perhaps related to *barbascum,* "bearded"); of cockroaches. (From Europe.)

Slippery Mullein (Long Island)

"Said to repel the cockroach (Blatta), whence the name *Blattaria;* frequented by moths hence moth-mullein" (Britton and Brown, 1913). However, "although Plinie saith that moths do most frequently haunt where Blattaria either groweth, or is laid, yet it is not observed sufficiently in our country so to do, notwithstanding the name of Moth Mullein is generally given them" (Parkinson, 1629). The curved furry stamens are astonishingly like a moth's antennae.

## Common Mullein

*Verbascum thapsus.* (The Latin name); from Thapsus (an ancient town in North Africa; the old generic name). (From Europe.)

Aaron's-Rod, Adam's-Flannel, Blanket-Leaf, *Bonhomme* (P.Q.), *Bouillon blanc* (La., Mo., P.Q.), Bullock's-Lungwort, Candlewick, Candlewick Mullein, Cow's-Lungwort, Feltwort, Flannel-Leaf, Flannel-Plant, Flannel-Weed (Texas), Fuzzy Mullein (Long Island), Goosegrass, Hag-Taper, Hare's-Beard, Hedge-Tapers, Iceleaf, Indian-Tobacco, Jacob's-Staff, Jupiter's-Staff, Lady's-Foxglove, Lamb's-Tongue (Maine), Lucernaria, Miner's-Candle (West), *Molène vulgaire* (P.Q.), Mullein-Dock, Old-Man's-Flannel, Peter's-Staff, Poultice-Weed (Tex.), Shepherd's-Club, *Tabac du diable* (P.Q.), Torches, Torchwort, Velvet-Dock

Such names as Candlewick, Lucernaria, Miner's-Candle and Torchwort allude to the use of the leaves as lamp wicks and of the stalk as a torch: "The elder age used the stalks dipped in suet to burn, whether at funerals or for private use" (Cole, 1657), and evidently miners in the American West did the same. It is also a Hag (*haga* is Anglo-Saxon for "hedge") Taper: "The whole toppe, with his pleasant yellow floures, showeth like to a Waxecandle, a taper, cunningly wrought" (Dodoens). Gerard (1633) wrote that the husbandmen of Kent "do give their cattel the leaves to drink against the cough of the lungs, being an excellent approved medicine for the same, whereupon they call it Bullocks Lungwoort." Most of the above are names from the old herbals or are local names in England and Scotland. Poultice-Weed and Indian-Tobacco are American; in Pennsylvania, "the Swedes here call it wild tobacco, but confessed that they did not know whether or not the Indians really used this plant instead of tobacco. The Swedes tie the leaves round their feet and arms when they have the ague. Some of them prepare a tea from the leaves for dysentery" (Kalm, 1748).

In his medical manual, *The Angel of Bethesda* (1724), Cotton Mather included a chapter on The Gout: "O Thou Sword Causing Terrour in the Land of the Living; How do the Sons of the Mighty tremble before thee! Even, the Swift-footed Achilles cannot escape thee! Yea, All the People, all the Inhabitants of the World, Both Low and High, Rich and Poor together, feel the Strokes of this Terrible One. Tis, *Dominus Morborum;* But Especially, *Morbus Dominorum."* He reported that "a gentleman in Germany re-leeved his gout in this manner. He gathered Mullein, when it was in flowre, and cutt off a good quantitie of it small, stalk, flowre, leaf, and all; and boiled it in a pail-full of forge-water taken from a smith's trough; and then putt into it a large piece of chalk in powder. In this water he bathed his feet, legs, and knees, as hott as he could endure it in a tub till the water grew cold; he then buried this water, with the ingredients, in his garden."

According to Dr. Porcher, "a large quantity of the flowers will even induce sleep, so active is the narcotic principle it contains." Mullein, via Middle English *moleyne* and Old French *moleine,* is derived from Latin *mollis* (soft), alluding to the woolly leaves. The name *Bouillon blanc* refers to "a decoction used to reduce swellings" (McAtee).

## Speedwells, Paul's-Betony

*Veronica.* True image.

Gerard (1633) wrote that Veronicas were called in English "Pauls Betonye, or Speed-well; in Welch it is called Fluellen, and the Welch people do attribute great vertues to the same." Saint Veronica was the woman who wiped Jesus's face when he fell while carrying the cross on the road to Calvary, and her towel preserved the true image *(Veron Ikon)* of His face. Paul is the great Byzantine physician Paul of Aegina (late 7th century). Betony is a *Stachys.* Speedwells because they grow by waysides to greet the traveler.

## American Brooklime

*Veronica americana.* True image; of America. (Also found in Asia.)
Bluebells (Maine), Wallink (W.Va.), Wild Forget-Me-Not (Wash.)

Brooklime (from Middle English *brok,* "brook," and *lemok,* the name of the plant)

in Britain is *Veronica beccabunga.* Wellink, changed to Wallink in West Virginia, is a Scottish and Irish name for *V. beccabunga.* The leaves are eaten raw or cooked.

## Water Speedwell

*Veronica anagallis-aquatica.* True image; aquatic-Anagallis (Pimpernel). (Also found in Eurasia.)
Brook-Pimpernel, Faverell, Great Water-Speedwell, Long-Leaved Brooklime, Neckweed (N.J.), Water-Pimpernel, Water-Purslane

Rafinesque reported that the plants "are chiefly used with us as weak stimulants, discutient, antiscrofulous, hepatic, antiscorbutic, and diuretic; while the *V. officinalis,* which is highly valued in Europe, and the base of the Faltrank or Swiss herb tea, is deemed tonic, vulnerary, astringent, aperient, pectoral, diuretic, &c." He added that "in New Jersey they are called Neckweed, because usefully applied to the scrofulous tumors of the neck."

Faverell as a name for this plant is listed in the supplement of names "gathered out of antient written and printed copies, and from the mouthes of plaine and simple country people" in Gerard's *Herbal* (1597).

*Water Speedwell*

## Common Speedwell

*Veronica officinalis.* True image; officinal. (Also found in Europe.)

Fluellin, Ground-Hale, Gypsy-Weed (W.Va.), Male-Fluellin, Paul's-Betony, *Thé d'Europe* (P.Q.), Upland Speedwell, *Véronique mâle* (P.Q.)

According to Gerard (1633), its virtues were that it "sodereth and healeth all fresh and old wounds, clenseth the bloud from all corruption, and is good to be drunk for the kidneys, and against scurvinesse and foul spreading tetters, and consuming and fretting sores, the small pox and measels." In New England, Josselyn (1672) called this "Male fluellin or Speed-well." The name Ground-Hale is presumably Growndheill, the "high Dutch" name in Gerard's *Herbal*.

## Thyme-Leaved Speedwell

*Veronica serpyllifolia.* True image; thyme-leaved. (From Europe.)

Paul's-Betony, Smooth Speedwell, Spiked Speedwell

May 24: "The smooth speedwell is in its prime now, whitening the sides of the backroad, above the Swamp Bridge and front of Hubbard's. Its sweet pansy-like face looks up on all sides. This and the *Myosotis laxa* are the two most beautiful *little* flowers yet" (Thoreau, 1853).

## Culver's-Root

*Veronicastrum virginicum.* False Veronica; of Virginia.

Beaumont's-Root, Blackroot (Mo.), Bowman's-Root, Brinton's-Root, Cubeno-Root, Cubeun's-Root, Cubuno-Physic, Culver's-Physic, Hini, Leptandra, Leptandra-Wurzel, Oxadaddy, Purple-Leptandra (the purple variety), Quitch, Quitel, Tall-Speedwell, Virginia-Hini, Whorlywort

"The various species are known under many local names, such as black root, Culver's root,

*Culver's-Root*

Brinton root, Bowman root, physic root, etc., as used by the settlers. They derived their knowledge of the drug from the American Indians, and designated the plant from its characteristics, or from the name of the man who used it in his practice. The Delaware Indians called the plant *quitel,* and the Missouri and Osage tribes knew it as *hini.* Leptandra was employed in decoction by settlers and savages alike, as a violent purgative, and in the practice of early physicians of the United States it was used for bilious fevers" (Lloyd, 1911). The name "Culver's root" is recorded in Massachusetts in 1716. Two of the common names listed by Rafinesque in 1826 were Brinton Root and Culvert Root, named "for men who used it in practice." But no pre-1716 Dr. Culver/Culvert or Brinton can be found.

John Bartram wrote that "one handful of the roots of this plant, boiled in a pint of milk, and drank, is used by the back inhabitants for a powerful vomit." Leptandra, a previous generic name, is the medicine made from the roots. Quitch is a grass, but "in Co. Donegal, every weed is so called" (Britten and Holland).

# THE BROOMRAPE FAMILY

## *Orobanchaceae*

A family of 17 genera and 230 species of herbaceous root-parasites, widely distributed in the Northern Hemisphere. Broomrape is a translation of the Medieval Latin *Rapum genistae,* meaning "a knob or tuber of Genista," referring to the parasitic growths of Orobanche on the roots of Broom (Genista) and other plants. William Turner (1548) wrote that "Orobanche . . . may of his properties be called Chokeweed, because it destroyeth and choketh the herbes that it tyeth and claspeth with his roote."

## Beechdrops

*Epifagus virginiana.* Upon Beech; of Virginia.

Broomrape, Cancer-Drops, Cancer-Root, Clapwort (N.C.), Virginia Brown-Rape

Dr. Barton (1804) called it the Virginian Broom-rape and Beach-drops because "it is generally, if not always, found under the shade of the American Beach-tree . . . But it is much more generally known by the name of Cancer-root." He reported that "some of the medical powers of this plant have long been known to the people of the United-States. It has been celebrated as a remedy in dysentery. There are, I think, cases of dysentery in which much advantage might be expected from the exhibition of a medicine possessed of the powers of Cancer-root. But this vegetable has acquired its principal reputation as a remedy in cancerous affections." "There is a folk-legend that it is useful as a local application to cancerous ulcers, hence its popular name" (USD). In the names above, "Clap" is gonorrhea.

## Lesser Broomrape

*Orobanche minor.* Vetch strangle (from Greek *orobos,* "Vetch," *ankheim,* "strangle"); lesser. (From Europe.)

Clover Broomrape, Devil's-Root, Hell-Root, Herb-Bane, Strangle-Tare

"Orobanch or Broom rape sliced and put into oyle of Olive to infuse or macerate in the same, as ye do Roses for oil of Roses, scoureth and putteth away all spots, lentils, freckles, pimples, wheals and pushes from the face . . . Dioscorides writeth that Orobanch may be eaten raw or boiled, in manner as we use to eat the sprigs or young shoots of Asparagus" (Gerard, 1633).

## One-Flowered Cancer-Root

*Orobanche uniflora.* Vetch strangler; one-flowered.

Cancer-Root, Naked Broomrape, One-Flowered Broomrape, Pale Broomrape, Pipes (Maine),

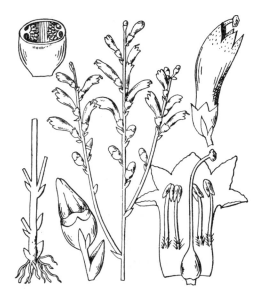

*Beechdrops*

Squawdrops, Squawroot (N.C.), Squirrel's-Grandfather (Calif.)

Medsger (1939), writing of the Western Broomrape, *Orobanche ludoviciana,* noted that "all the plant except the fruiting part grows underground; therefore the thick stems are white and tender. They are much consumed by the Pah Ute Indians."

# THE SESAME FAMILY

## *Pedaliaceae*

A family of 18 genera and 95 species of herbs and a few shrubs; found chiefly in tropical regions. Sesame is *Sesamum indicum* of tropical Asia, which is cultivated for its seeds. The subfamily Martynioideae was previously considered a separate family, the Martyniaceae, named after John Martyn (1699–1768), a London physician and professor of botany at Cambridge University, author of *Historia Plantarium rariorum* (1728–1737) and translator of Virgil's *Georgics* and *Bucolics.*

## Unicorn-Plant, Devil's-Claw

*Proboscidea louisiana.* Like an elephant's trunk; of Louisiana.

Cockle-Horn (Va.), Cuckold's-Horn (Texas, Va.), Devil's-Darning-Needle (Mo.), Devil's-Horn (Texas), Double-Claw, Elephant's-Trunk (Texas), Goat's-Horn, Martinoe, Martynia, Mouse-Bur, Pickled-Rats (N.Y.), Proboscis-Flower, Ram's-Horns, Toenails

In 1847 Darlington wrote, "This plant—a native of the valley of the Mississippi, and the plains of Mexico—is much cultivated of late, for its singular fruit,—which, in its young state—before it becomes hard and woody—

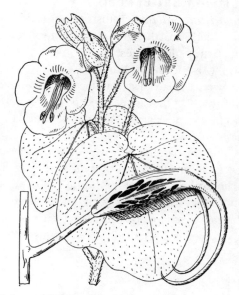

*Unicorn-Plant*

is used for making that kind of condiment called *Pickles.*" The immature fruit has a straight spine like a unicorn's horn, which then becomes curved like a proboscis. The seeds, rich in oil and protein, are eaten in Mexico. In the early 1900s, the plant was grown as a field crop in Massachusetts and Michigan, and the fruit was canned commercially.

# THE BLADDERWORT FAMILY

## *Lentibulariaceae*

A cosmopolitan family of four genera and 245 species of insectivorous aquatic or semi-aquatic herbs.

## Common Butterwort

*Pinguicula vulgaris.* Fattish (from Latin *pinguis,* "fat," for the greasy or buttery leaves which trap and digest small insects); common. (Also found in Eurasia.)

Beanweed, Bog-Violet, Earning-Grass, *Grassette vulgaire* (P.Q.), Rotgrass, Sheeproot, Sheeprot, Sheepweed, Steepgrass, Valentine's-Flower (Fla.), Yorkshire-Sanicle

"The husbandmens wives of Yorkshire do use to anoint the dugs of their kine with the fat and oilous juice of the herbe Butterwoort, when they are bitten with any venomous worme, or chapped, rifted, and hurt by any other means" (Gerard, 1633)—thus, York-shire-Sanicle. Marie-Victorin wrote that farmers in the Alps did the same. Earning-Grass, a name from the north of England, and Steep-Grass, from Ireland, mean "curdling-grass"—the leaves were steeped in milk to curdle it. It was reputed to give sheep the rot. Torrey (1894) explained the name Valentine's-Flower: "If you put one under your pillow and think of some one you would like to see, you will be pretty likely to dream of him." Beanweed and Bog-Violet are local names in England.

"When we see a midge being slowly digested on the pale sticky leaf-rosette of Butterwort, our sympathy is with the midge, a creature we usually do not care for; yet all we are seeing is how our own stomach works. The plant is not ashamed of eating any more than we are. It holds up its beautiful blue flower, described with admirable inaccuracy as 'a violet springing from a starfish'; perhaps it is amused at its botanical name, Pinguicula, Little Fat One. But the offense in our eyes is that such plants invade our animal kingdom" (Young, 1945).

## Common Bladderwort

*Utricularia macrorhiza.* Little bladder (the floating bladders on the branches or leaves); large-rooted.

Bladder-Snout, Greater Bladderwort, Hooded Water-Milfoil, *Lentille des prés* (P.Q.), Popweed

Thoreau (1852) called it "a dirty-conditioned flower, like a sluttish woman with a gaudy yellow bonnet."

Hylander (1939) has described how "each of the pale green bladders of the Bladderwort is flattened on the bottom, where there is a small opening surrounded by a mass of stiff bristles. Closing the opening from the inside is a delicate trapdoor, a flap of tissue hinged

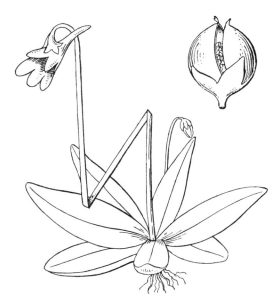

*Common Butterwort*

on the inside and closing against the doorway. A small larva, pursued by a minnow, frantically rushing for a place of safety, can swim freely through the bristles around the opening into the bladder, while the same bristles repel the larger animal. Pushing against the trapdoor, perhaps by chance, the larva gets inside of the bladder; once there he finds himself in a death chamber already containing other small animals similarly trapped. When they push against the door from the inside, it cannot open. Eventually the larva and its neighbors die and their bodies decompose to form a nitrogenous food for the plant . . . That such a perfect mechanical trap should be developed from ordinary foliage parts of the plant is one of the marvels of plant evolution."

# THE BELLFLOWER FAMILY

## Campanulaceae

A cosmopolitan family of 87 genera and 1,950 species of herbs, shrubs and a few small trees.

### Clustered Bellflower

*Campanula glomerata.* Small bell (diminutive of Latin *campana*); clustered. (From Europe.)

*Clustered Bellflower*

Canterbury-Bells, Dane's-Blood

The Canterbury-Bells of the garden is *Campanula media,* whose flowers resemble the bells on the horses of pilgrims to the shrine of Thomas à Becket at Canterbury in Kent, England, who was murdered in 1170 and canonized in 1172: "Some other pilgrims will have with them bagpipes; so that in everie towne they come through, what with the noise of their piping, and with the sound of their singing and the jangling of their Canterburie bells" (from Britten and Holland). Dane's-Blood is a local name in England—they were supposed to have sprung up from the blood of Danes killed in battle.

### Harebell

*Campanula rotundifolia.* Small bell; round-leaved. (Also found in Eurasia.)
Bluebells, Bluebells of Scotland, *Clochettes bleues* (P.Q.), Heathbells, Heatherbells (Mich.), Lady's-Thimble, Round-Leaved Bellflower, Thimbles, Wild-Thimbles (Nfd.), Witch's-Bells

"I lingered round [the graves], under that benign sky: watched the moths fluttering among the heath and hare-bells; listened to the soft wind breathing through the grass; and wondered how any one could ever imag-

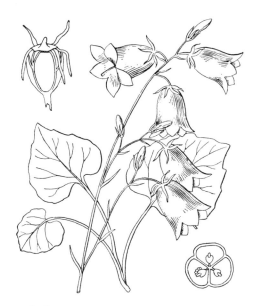

*Harebell*

ine unquiet slumbers for the sleepers in that quiet earth" (Emily Brontë; this is the final scene in *Wuthering Heights*). In Shakespeare's Cymbeline (4.2.220), Imogen is assured that she would not lack "the flower that's like thy face, pale primrose, nor/ The azur'd harebell, like thy veins." But evidently Shakespeare's Hare-Bell was a Hyacinth (Liliaceae). It is not clear whether it is hair bell, for the hairlike stems, hare bell, for hares romp in it, Hea'erbell, a contraction of Heather-Bell, or Ayr-bell, a corruption of the Welsh *awyr-pel,* a "balloon."

## Cardinal Flower

*Lobelia cardinalis.* Of Lobel (Matthias de Lobel, 1538–1616); of cardinals (it is as red as a cardinal's robe; the old generic name).
Cardinal Lobelia, Highbelia, Hog-Physic (Mass.), Queen-of-the-Meadow (Long Island), Red-Bay, Redbelia, Red-Betty (Vt.), Red-Cardinal, Red Lobelia, Slinkweed (Mass.)

Rafinesque reported, "The root has been chiefly employed in decoction by the Cherokee Indians in syphilis and against worms.

It is said to be equivalent to *Spigelia* or Pink-root." A slinkweed is supposed to "slink" or abort cows.

Lobel, who called himself Lobelius, was a Flemish botanist who died in London where he had served as physician to James I.

## Indian-Tobacco

*Lobelia inflata.* Of Lobel; inflated (capsule). Asthma-Weed (Maine), Bladder-Pod Lobelia, Colicweed, Emetic-Herb, Emeticweed, Eyebright, Gagroot, *Herbe à l'asthme* (P.Q.), Kinnikinnick, Lowbelia, Obelia (N.C.), Pukeweeed (Maine), Thomson's-Herb, Vomitroot, Vomitwort, Wild-Tobacco

Manasseh Cutler called it Emeticweed and reported that "the leaves chewed in the mouth are, at first, insipid, but soon become pungent, occasioning a copious discharge of saliva. If they are held in the mouth for some time, they produce giddiness and pain in the head, with a trembling agitation of the whole body: at length they bring an extreme nausea and vomiting. The taste resembles that of tartar emetic. A plant possessed of such active

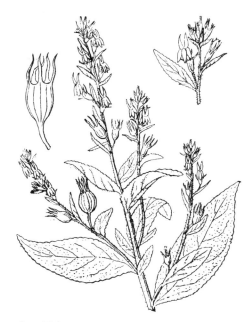

*Indian-Tobacco*

properties, notwithstanding the violent effects from chewing the leaves, may possibly become a valuable medicine."

Samuel Thomson (1769–1843) was born to poor parents in New Hampshire. From childhood he was curious about herbs and when his mother sickened of the "galloping consumption" and "the doctors gave her over . . . for they are the riders, and their whip is mercury, opium and vitriol, and they galloped her out of the world in about nine weeks"— and his wife after childbirth nearly succumbed to the conventional, and expensive, heroic treatment of purging and bleeding— he gave up his poor farm to become an itinerant herb doctor (Thomson, 1822). He developed a course of medicines that cleaned out the system with emetics and restored it with tonics. The *Number 1* of the course was this Lobelia, "to cleanse the Stomach, overpower the Cold, and promote a free perspiration." This was followed by steam baths, cayenne pepper and herbal teas and tonics. He not only treated his patients but taught them his method and enrolled them in his lay medical society for their mutual care and treatment. In 1809 Thomson was arrested for the wilful murder of one of his patients, a young man named Lovel. His accuser, a "regular" doctor, charged that he "did kill and murder the same Lovel with lobelia, a deadly poison." At his trial, the prosecution tried to show that the powder given to Lovel was Lobelia, while Thomson claimed that it was Marsh-Rosemary (*Limonium carolinianum*). The defense was able to show that the prosecution expert witness, a Dr. Howe, could not even identify Lobelia, and the court eventually acquitted Thomson. The Lloyds (1886–87) have reviewed the evidence and conclude that both Lobelia and Marsh-Rosemary were administered. They wrote, "This was the memorable 'Trial of Thomson,' but it did not end the assault of his adversaries . . . In 1811 a doctor in Eastport, Me., while Thomson was

passing his office door, tried to kill him with a scythe." Nevertheless, within a few years there were thousands of Thomsonians (or "Thompsonians"), members of his Friendly Botanical Societies; in 1839 Thomson claimed three million adherents (Jordan, 1943). In 1836 Alva Curtis, one of Thomson's lieutenants, broke with the movement and formed his own Botanico-Medical School and Infirmary in Columbus, Ohio. "After 1838, there were no more national conventions of the Friendly Botanical Societies. Instead Thomson and Curtis organized separate societies, both using the word 'Thomsonian' in the title. The movement rapidly fragmented, and Thomson's branch soon disintegrated altogether" (Rothstein, 1972).

In 1852 Dr. Clapp wrote, "No medicine has been more used or more abused by empirics, especially the Thompsonians, than lobelia; yet it is a valuable article when judiciously employed. Although cases of its fatal effects, from the recklessness and ignorance of quacks, are not very unfrequent, it may admit of a doubt whether many active articles, as frequently and injudiciously employed, would be less dangerous."

The leaves taste of tobacco, and thus its name Wild-Tobacco. "From Wild Tobacco it is quite natural that it should acquire the name Indian tobacco, as it would be presumed a tobacco that was wild would be used by the Indians. As a matter of fact, however, we have no record that the Indians ever made use of the plant in the manner of a tobacco" (Lloyd and Lloyd, 1886–87). It has been included in the USP and NF.

## Great Lobelia

*Lobelia siphilitica*. Of Lobel; of syphilis.
Blue Cardinal-Flower, Blue Lobelia, Cardinal, Highbelia

Among the plants included in John Bartram's appendix to Benjamin Franklin's 1751

*Great Lobelia*

reprint of the *Medicina Britannica* was "the newly discovered Indian Cure for the Venereal Disease," the root of this Lobelia: "The learned Peter Kalm (who gained the knowledge of it from Colonel Johnson, who learned it of the Indians, who, after great rewards bestowed on several of them, revealed the secret to him) saith that the roots of the plant cureth the pox much more perfectly and easily than any mercurial preparations, and is generally used by the Canada Indians, for the cure of themselves, and the French that trade amongst them, tho' deeply infected with it." This cure for syphilis was popular for a while

here and in Europe, but studies eventually showed that it was valueless and it became obsolete.

William Johnson arrived in America from Ireland in 1738 and established an enormously successful trading business with the Indians on the Mohawk above Albany, New York. He was a trusted friend of the neighboring tribes of the Six Nations, a scholar of Indian languages and customs and held a royal commission as colonel of the Six Nations and superintendent of Indian affairs. He led the colonial forces and Indian allies against the French and Indians at the Battle of Lake George (1755) and was created a baronet for his victory and given a tract of 100,000 acres of land north of the Mohawk. He retired to live in baronial splendor on his estate, called Fort Johnson, with his favorite Indian maiden, Molly, and their eight children.

## Venus's-Looking-Glass

*Triodanis perfoliata.* Three teeth (seed); perfoliate.
Clasping Bellflower

This was previously *Specularia perfoliata.* Latin *specula* is a looking-glass. The European Venus'-Looking-Glass is *Legousia speculum-veneris:* "When the long capsule opens, the looking-glasses of the Virgin or Venus are revealed, the seeds of which are oval or elliptical, pale brown, exquisitely polished, and pellucid like a speculum" (Grigson).

# THE MADDER OR BEDSTRAW FAMILY

## *Rubiaceae*

A cosmopolitan family of 630 genera and 10,400 species of shrubs, lianas, trees and a few herbs. The family provides us with coffee *(Coffea)*, quinine *(Cinchona)*, ipecacuanha *(Cephaelis)*, yohimbine *(Pausinystalia)*, dyes, timber and ornamental shrubs *(Gardenia,* for example).

## Bedstraws

*Galium*. Milk (from Greek *gala;* the plants were used to curdle milk in cheese-making). Beggar-Lice (Mo.), Chicken-Weed (Md.), Cleavers (Ohio), Robin-Run-Ahead (Ohio)

It is called "Chicken-weed, because small chickens get caught in it" (McAtee, 1926). The dried plants are fragrant with coumarin and were used as bedstraw in pillows and mattresses.

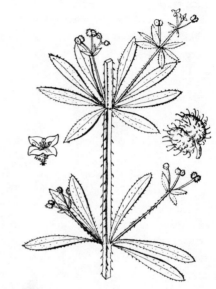

*Cleavers*

## Cleavers, Goosegrass, Clabber-Grass

*Galium aparine*. Milk; scratching (old generic name). (Also found in Eurasia.)

Airif, Beggar-Lice, Bird-Lime, Burhead, Catchweed, Chicus (N.C.), Cheese-Rennet-Herb, Claver-Grass, Cleaver-Wort, Cling-Rascal, Coachweed, Gosling-Grass, Gosling-Weed, *Gratte-cul* (P.Q.), Grip, Gripgrass, Hairif, Harvest-Lice, Loveman, Milksweet, Pigtail, Poor-Robin, Savoyan-Scratchgrass, Scratchweed, Spring-Cleavers, Stick-a-Back, Stickleback, Sticky-Willy, Sweethearts, Turkey-Grass, Wild-Hedge-Burs

Clabber is American for curdled milk, shortened from Anglo-Irish *bonny clabber* (Jonathan Swift wrote in 1730 that the Irish country people "live with comfort on potatoes and bonny clabber"), which is from Irish *bainne,* "milk," *claba,* "thick." Rennet is a curdler of milk used in cheese making.

The young spring shoots of Cleavers are cooked, the seeds are roasted as a coffee substitute, and the whole dried plant is steeped for tea. In Gerard's day, it was a diet food: "Women do usually make pottage of Clevers with a little mutton and Otemeal, to cause lankness, and keep them from fatnesse." John Evelyn (1699) wrote of "Clavers, *Aparine;* the tender Winders with young Nettle-Tops, are us'd in Lenten pottages." Evidently geese and turkeys also love this bristly plant. A Stickleback is a small freshwater fish with a spiny back. Savoyanne, of Savoyan-Scratchgrass, is French Canadian for *Coptis* (see *Galium tinctorium* below). Hayriff, a local name in parts of England, became Airif and Hairif in America. Most of the other names are from the old herbals or are local in England and Scotland.

## Rough Bedstraw

*Galium asprellum.* Milk; somewhat rough.
*Caille-lait des marais* (P.Q.), Clivers (Maine), Kidney-Vine (Maine), Pointed Cleavers

In Maine Kidney-Vine is "used in kidney troubles by the country people" (Perkins, 1929).

## Stiff Marsh-Bedstraw

*Galium tinctorium.* Milk; used for dyeing.
Wild Madder

In northern Saskatchewan, in 1820: "The Crees extract some beautiful colours from several of their native vegetables. They dye their porcupine quills a beautiful scarlet, with the roots of two species of bed-straw (galium tinctorium, and boreale), which they indiscriminately term *sawoyan*. The roots, after being carefully washed, are boiled gently in a clean copper kettle, and a quantity of the juice of the moose berry, strawberry, cranberry, or arctic raspberry, is added, together with a few red tufts of pistils of the larch. The porcupine quills are plunged into the liquor before it becomes quite cold, and are soon tinged of a beautiful scarlet" (Richardson).

## Fragrant Bedstraw

*Galium triflorum.* Milk; three-flowered. (Also found in Eurasia.)
Fragrant-Cleavers, Sweet-Scented Bedstraw, Three-Flowered Bed-straw, Wild-Woodruff

In western Washington State, "a Quileute woman will get some hairs of the man she wishes to attract and press them with some of her own, together with some bedstraw. Just as they stick together so will this desired man stick to her. The woman who told the informant this had had eight husbands and

as each died she did this and got another by the action" (Gunther, 1973). Woodruff is the European *Galium odorata,* a fragrant herb with whorled ruffs of shiny leaves, used to flavor May wine.

## Yellow Bedstraw, Lady's Bedstraw

*Galium verum.* Milk; true. (From Europe.)
Bedflower, *Caille-lait* (P.Q.), Cheese-Rennet, Curdwort, Fleawort, Goosegrass, Gravel-Grass, Maid's-Hair, Milksweet, Our-Lady's-Bedstraw, Poor-Robin, Savoyan-Clabbergrass, Yellow-Cleavers

This was believed to be the "true" Bedstraw of Mary (Our Lady) that filled the manger at Bethlehem. When dry, it has a delicious scent, like a maid's hair perhaps, and was placed in mattresses (evidently it also kept fleas away).

"The people in Cheshire, especially about Namptwich, where the best cheese is made, do use it in their Rennet, esteeming greatly of that Cheese above other made without it" (Gerard, 1633). *Caille-lait* is French for cheese-rennet. Marie-Victorin wrote that "the flowers were employed in ancient medicine as sudorific, diuretic, astringent and antispas-

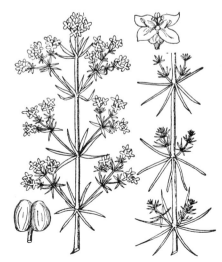

*Yellow Bedstraw*

modic. A yellow dye is obtained when the foliage is boiled with alum, and the root provides a red dye."

## Bluets, Quaker-Ladies, Innocence

*Houstonia caerulea.* Of Houston (William Houston, 1695–1733); blue (Latin *caeruleus*). Angel-Eyes, Blue-Eyed-Babies (Mass.), Blue-Eyed-Grass (Wis.), Bright-Eyes (Md., Mass.), Dwarf-Pink, Eyebright (Maine, Mass., N.H.), Forget-Me-Not (Ky., Maine), Little-Washerwoman (Pa.), Nuns, Quaker-Beauty, Quaker-Bonnets, Quaker-Girls (N.J.), Sky-Flower (Conn.), Starflower (Mass.), Starlights (Mass.), Star-of-Bethlehem (Miss.), Star-Violet, Venus's-Pride (Conn.), Wild-Forget-Me-Not

William Houston was a Scottish physician and botanist who, as a ship's surgeon, collected plants in Mexico and the West Indies.

## Partridge-Berry, Twin-Berry

*Mitchella repens.* Of Mitchell (John Mitchell, 1711–1768); creeping.
Boxberry (Mass.), Checkerberry, Chicken-Berry (West), Cowberry (N.Y.), Deer-Berry, Eyeberry, Foxberry (Mass.), Heath-Hen-Plum (Long Island), Hive-Vine, Jesuit-Berry, Mountain-Tea, One-Berry (N.Y.), *Pain de perdrix* (P.Q.), Partridge-Vine, Pheasant-Berry (Va.), Pigeon-Berry (Mass.), Pigeon-Plum (Maine), Pudding-Plum, Running-Box, Snake-berry (N.Y.), Snake-Plum (Maine), Squawberry (Mich.), Squaw-Plum, Squaw-Vine (New England), Teaberry, Turkey-Berry (Ala.), Twin-Berry, Two-Eye-Berry (Mass.), Two-Eyed-Plum (Maine), Winter-Clover

In 1723 Thomas More sent a package of plant specimens from Boston to the botanist William Sherard in London, including "a small red berry white in the middle, but, while not fully ripe, white and red prettily streaked like a Pomgranate," whose leaves make "the best tea in the world and is counted a great catholicon among us. Colonel Brown, a man of

*Partridge-Berry*

great figure here, told me his body was so big of a dropsie as a sack of malt, but by drinking this tea he soon recovered a very healthy state of body, which he has for some years enjoyed, and mynds to drink it to his dying day." More noted that the berries were the "beloved food" of partridges "and that I take to be the reason why we have the best Partridges in the world."

Manasseh Cutler called it Foxberry and Checkerberry and wrote, "The leaves are much celebrated by the common people as a diuretic and sweetner of the blood, but are of very little efficacy. It makes an ingredient in their diet drinks. The berries are rather of an agreeable taste, and are sometimes eaten by children in milk." American Indians used the plant as a parturient, pregnant women taking frequent doses during the few weeks before giving birth. The edible berries are found 10 months of the year.

John Mitchell was born in Lancaster County, Virginia, and died in England. He was educated at the University of Edinburgh and then returned to Virginia and established a medical practice in Urbanna, spending his leisure time studying the local flora and fauna. Ill health forced him to give up his practice in 1746, and he settled in London, where he became active in scientific, social and political circles. He was elected a Fellow of the Royal Society in 1748. In 1750 he was commissioned to prepare a map of the North American colonies. This *Map of the British and French Dominions in North America* was completed in 1755 and was used in many important boundary negotiations in later history.

# THE HONEYSUCKLE FAMILY

## *Caprifoliaceae*

A family of 16 genera and 365 species of shrubs, lianas, small trees and few herbs; found chiefly in north temperate and boreal regions and tropical mountains. Family members include the ornamental shrubs Snowberry *(Symphoricarpus)*, Elder *(Sambucus)* and species of *Viburnum, Abelia* and *Weigelia*.

## Bush-Honeysuckle

*Diervilla lonicera*. Of Dièreville; like Lonicera.

Gravel-Weed, *Herbe bleue* (P.Q.), Life-of-Man (N.B.), Northern Bush-Honeysuckle

Jacobs and Burlage (1958) report that "the leaves possess a narcotic principle inducing nausea; it is used as a gargle in catarrhal angina." Doctor Dièreville was a 17th-century traveler who carried the plant from Canada to France.

## Twinflower

*Linnaea borealis*. Of Linnaeus (Carolus Linnaeus, 1707–1778); northern. (Also found in Eurasia.)

Deer-Vine, Ground-Ivy (Lab., Nfd.), Ground-Vine, Trumpet-Flower (Lab., Nfd.), Twin-Sisters, Two-Eyed-Berries (N.B.)

Linnaeus, the father of modern systematic botany, was born in Råshult, southern Swe-

*Twinflower*

den, where his father was the Lutheran pastor. Members of the family took their names (Linné, Linnaeus, Lindelius, Tiliander) from a tall Linden tree growing at their farm. Linnaeus was educated at the universities of Lund and Uppsala, where he became assistant to the aged Dr. Olaf Celsius, who was preparing a treatise on plants of the Bible, and to Olaf Rudbeck, professor of botany (Linnaeus called our Black-Eyed Susans *Rudbeckia*). He made a botanical exploration of Lapland for the Swedish Academy of Sciences in 1732 and found growing "a little northern plant, long overlooked, depressed, abject, flowering early," which he chose to name after himself. Gronovius later described the plant as *Linnaea borealis.* He first published his sexual system of plant classification in *Systema Naturae* and *Genera Plantarum* in 1737 and *Classes Plantarum* in 1738. These were followed by other important publications, and then in 1753 he published his *Species Plantarum,* which is considered the foundation for botanical nomenclature and from which all the earliest plant names now in use are taken. Linnaeus was appointed professor of medicine in 1741 and succeeded Rudbeck as professor of botany at Uppsala in 1742. In 1761 he was granted a patent of nobility by Gustavus III of Sweden and henceforth called himself Carl von Linné.

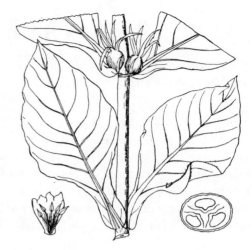

*Feverwort*

## Fly-Honeysuckle

*Lonicera canadensis.* Of Lonitzer (Adam Lonitzer, 1528–1586, a German herbalist); of Canada.

American Fly-Honeysuckle, *Chèvrefeuille du Canada* (P.Q.), Medaddy-Bush (Maine), Twin-Berry, Vernal Honeysuckle

Among the Montagnais Indians north of the St. Lawrence, the branches "are steeped for urinary trouble. As an example of efficiency, a boy at Tadousac whose abdomen was distended with retained water was relieved in twenty minutes after taking this medicine" (Speck, 1917).

## Trumpet Honeysuckle

*Lonicera sempervirens.* Of Lonitzer; evergreen.

Coral Honeysuckle, Scarlet Honeysuckle, Woodbine

"The fruit is emetic, cathartic, and the expressed juice of the plant is beneficial for the treatment of bee stings" (Jacobs and Burlage, 1958).

## Feverwort, Tinker's-Weed, Wild-Coffee

*Triosteum perfoliatum.* Three-bone (the nutlets; shortened from *triosteospermum*); perfoliate.

Bastard-Ipecacuanha (Pa.), Cinque (N.C.), Fever-Root, Feverwort, Genson (N.C.), Gentian (Pa., Va.), Horse-Gentian, Horse-Ginseng, Indian-Purge (Va.), Narrow Fever-Wort, Sweet-Bitter (N.C.), White-Gentian, White-Ginseng, Wild-Ipecac, Wood-Ipecac

John Bartram (1751) wrote of "*Triosteospermum,* called in our Northern Colonies Dr. Tinker's Weed; in Pennsylvania, Gentian; and to the Southward, Fever Root, where it is used for the fever and ague; With us it was used with good success for the pleurisy, and in New-England for a vomit. It is a powerful worker, a little churlish, yet may be a noble medicine in skilful hands."

Dr. Millspaugh reported that "the dried and toasted berries of this plant were considered by some of the Germans of Lancaster County, Pa., an excellent substitute for coffee . . . Having great respect for German taste I tried an infusion, but came to the conclusion that it was not the Lancaster County Germans' taste that I held in regard."

# THE VALERIAN FAMILY

## *Valerianaceae*

A cosmopolitan family of 17 genera and about 400 species of herbs and a few shrubs; found chiefly in north temperate regions and in the Andes. The red Valerian or Pretty-Betsy of the flower garden is *Centranthus ruber.* Another family member, *Nardostachys jatamansi,* is the source of nard or spikenard, the costly ointment of antiquity.

## Tobacco-Root

*Valeriana edulis.* Health (the medieval name; from Latin *valere,* "to be strong"); edible.

Edible Valerian, Kooyah, Oregon-Tobacco

Among the Shoshonee Indians in 1843, Lieutenant Frémont reported, "We obtained from them also a considerable quantity of berries of different kinds, among which service berries were the most abundant; and several kinds of roots and seeds, which we could eat with pleasure, as any kind of vegetable food was gratifying to us. I ate here, for the first time, the *kooyah,* or tobacco root [*Valeriana edulis*], the principal edible root among the Indians who inhabit the upper waters of the streams on the western side of the mountains. It has a very strong and remarkably peculiar taste and odor, which I can compare to no other vegetable that I am acquainted with, and which to some persons is extremely offensive . . . To others, however, the taste is rather an agreeable one, and I was afterwards always glad when it formed an addition to our scanty meals. It is full of nutriment; and in its unprepared state is said by the Indians to have very strong poisonous qualities, of which it is deprived by a peculiar process, being baked in the ground for about two days."

*Valerian*

## Valerian, All-Heal

*Valeriana officinalis.* Health; officinal. (From Europe.)

Cat's Valerian, Common Valerian, Cut-Heal, English Valerian, Fragrant Valerian, Garden Valerian, Garden-Heliotrope, German Valerian, Great Wild-Valerian, Hardy-Heliotrope, *Herbe de la femme meurtrie* (P.Q.), *Herbe de Saint-Sebastien* (P.Q.), St. George's-Herb, Setwell, Summer-Heliotrope, Vandal-Root, Wild Valerian

Gerard (1633) wrote that the dried root "is put into counterpoisons and medicines preservative against the pestilence, as are treacles, mithridates, and such like: whereupon it hath been held (and is to this day among the poore people of our Northern parts) in such veneration amongst them, that no broths, pottage, or physicall meats are worth anything if Setwall were not at an end." "Strangely enough also the odor of valerian, now considered exceedingly disagreeable, was in the

16th century accepted as a perfume, and as a perfume is still used in the Orient" (Lloyd, 1911). "Equally fond, too, are cats of valerian, being said to dig up the roots and gnaw them to pieces, an allusion to which occurs in Topsell's 'Four-footed Beasts' (1658–81):— 'The root of the herb valerian (commonly called Phu) is very like to the eye of a cat, and wheresoever it groweth, if cats come thereunto they instantly dig it up for the love thereof, as I myself have seen in my own garden, for it smelleth moreover like a cat' " (Thiselton-Dyer).

Since antiquity, the root has been esteemed as a sedative in nervous disorders. The USD reports that "there is considerable evidence that it has a depressant effect upon the central nervous system . . . It is still prescribed by many physicians as a remedy for hysteria, hypochondriasis, nervous unrest and similar emotional states." It has been included in the USP and NF. The herbalists' name Setwall (it grows on walls) became Setwell in America.

### Sitka Valerian

*Valeriana sitchensis.* Health; of Sitka.

James Teit (1930) recorded that the Thompson Indians pounded the roots into a pulp and applied it to cuts and wounds: "It is said by some of the older Indians that in the early days the warriors always had some of the roots in their medicine bags to be handy when needed"; hunters "wash their bodies with it, believing that after this treat-ment the deer will become tame and the hunter will be able to approach them easily."

### Corn-Salad, Lamb's-Lettuce

*Valerianella locusta.* Little Valerian; (a pre-vious generic name). (From Europe.)
*Doucette* (P.Q.), European Corn-Salad, Fetticus, Milkgrass, Pawnee-Lettuce, White-Potherb

John Evelyn (1699) reported that Corn-sallet was "loos'ning and refreshing: The tops and leaves are a sallet of themselves, season-able eaten with other salleting the whole Winter long, and early Spring: The French call them *Salad de Prêtre,* for their being generally eaten in Lent." It is still cultivated and marketed as Mâche.

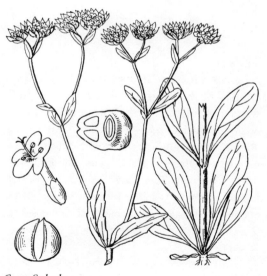

*Corn-Salad*

# THE TEASEL FAMILY

## *Dipsacaceae*

A family of eight genera and 250 species of herbs and a few shrubs; found in Eurasia and Africa, particularly in the Mediterranean re-gion. Some species of *Knautia* and *Scabiosa* are cultivated as ornamentals, and species of *Dipsacus* for their teasels.

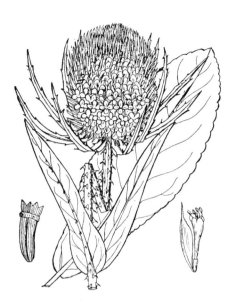

*Teasel*

## Teasel

*Dipsacus fullonum.* Thirsty (from Greek *dipsa,* "thirst"—the leaves of some species hold water); of fullers. (From Europe.)

Adam's-Flannel, *Cardère* (P.Q.), Card-Teasel, Card-Thistle, Church-Broom, Clothier's-Brush, Common-Teasel, Draper's Teasel, English-Thistle (W.Va.), Fuller's Teasel, Fuller's-Thistle, Gipsy-Combs, Hutton-Weed (W.Va.), Indian's-Thistle, Prickly-Back, Shepherd's-Thistle, Shepherd's-Staff, Venus's-Bath, Venus's-Cup, Water-Thistle (W.Va.), Wild-Teasel, Wood-Brooms

Gerard (1633) wrote that the Teasel "bringeth forth a stalke that is straight, very long, jointed, and ful of prickles: the leaves grow forth of the joints by couples, not onely opposite or set one right against another, but also compassing the stalke about, and fastened together; and so fastened that they hold dew and raine water in manner of a little bason . . . on the tops of the stalkes stand heads with sharpe prickles like those of the hedgehog, and crooking backward at the point like hookes."

One species, *Dipsacus sativus,* was cultivated for the heads which were used by fullers to dress or tease cloth to raise the nap. Apparently the design of the ubiquitous Velcro fastener was suggested by the hooked spines of the Teasel head. The plant was called Venus' Bath and Venus' Basin by Lyte and Gerard; in Latin it was *Labrum Veneris* (Venus's bath). A little pool of rainwater can often be found in the concavity of the leaves next the stem. A card is a wire-toothed brush used to tease cloth. Adam's-Flannel, Church-Broom, Gipsy's-Comb and Shepherd's-Staff are local names in England. Huttonweed: "Because found on the farm of a man named Hutton" (Bergen, 1894).

## Field-Scabious, Bluebuttons

*Knautia arvensis.* Of Knaut (Christian Knaut, 1654–1716, Saxon physician and botanist); of cultivated fields. (From Europe.)

"The decoction of the roots taken for forty daies together, or a dram of the powder of them taken at a time in whey, doth (as Mathiolus saith) wonderfully help those that are troubled with running or spreading scabs, tetters, ringworms, yea, though they proceed from the French Pox" (Culpeper). Dr. Withering wrote that "a strong decoction of it, used in continuance, is an empirical secret for gonorrhea." Devil's-Bit Scabious is *Succisa pratensis* of Europe.

# THE ASTER OR COMPOSITE FAMILY

## Asteraceae or Compositae

A cosmopolitan family of 1,314 genera and 21,000 species of herbs, shrubs, climbers and a few trees; found chiefly in temperate and subtropical regions that are not densely forested. "Compared with other large families," Mabberley writes, the Compositae "are of little value to man except as ornamentals, the edible ones having low levels of toxins or, as in lettuce, having had them selected out; some are insecticides and fish poisons, but many are noxious weeds . . . With increasing clearance of vegetation throughout the world, these aggressive toxic plants will inherit it."

*Yarrow*

## Yarrow, Milfoil

*Achillea millefolium.* Of Achilles (who cured the wounds of his Myrmidon warriors with it); thousand-leaved (the old generic name). (Also found in Eurasia.)

Achillée (P.Q.), Carpenter's-Grass, Bloodwort, Deadman's-Daisy (Nfd.), Dog-Daisy, Gordaldo, Gordoloba (Calif.), Green-Arrow, *Herbe à dinde* (P.Q.), *Herbe aux charpentiers,* Hundred-Leaf-Grass, Knight's-Milfoil, Ladies'-Mantle, *Mille feuille* (P.Q.), Noble Yarrow, Nosebleed, Nosebleed-Plant (Maine), Old-Man's-Pepper, Plumajillo (West), Sanguinary, Sneezefoil, Soldier's-Woundwort, Staunchweed, Thousand-Leaf, Thousand-Seal, *Yerba-de-San-Juan*

Dioscorides wrote that the leaf "beaten small is conglutinative of bloody wounds, and uninflaming, and a stayer of their bleeding." In the *Grete Herball* of 1526, it is called Bloudworte, Sanguinary and Carpenter-grasse, for "it is good to rejoine and soudre wounds." Soldier's-Woundwort is a name from the

American Civil War when the crushed plant was applied to battle wounds. American Indians used it to treat bruises, sprains and swollen tissues and to heal wounds and relieve rashes and itching. Stevenson (1915) reported that among the Zuñi Indians "such fraternity men as manipulate with fire chew the blossoms and root of this plant and rub the mixture on their limbs and chests previous to passing live coals over their bodies. The same mixture, in liquid form, is employed for bathing the bodies of those who dance in fire, and is placed in the mouth before placing live coals into it."

Britten and Holland write that the name Nosebleed is from an old English superstition that if a boy puts a leaf of Yarrow in the nose and turns it thrice round, if the nose bleeds, he is sure to get his sweetheart. In Suffolk a rhyme is recited:

> *Green 'arrow, Green 'arrow, you bears*
> *a white blow;*
> *If my love love me, my nose will bleed*
> *now;*
> *If my love don't love me, it 'ont bleed a*
> *drop;*
> *If my love do love me, 'twill bleed ivery*
> *drop.*

Green-Arrow became an American name for the plant. It has been included in the USP, "used chiefly as a folk-remedy in the form of a tea, as a sudorific and in amenorrhea" (USD). Hundred-Leaf-Grass, Nosebleed, Old-Man's-Pepper (it is supposed to have aphrodisiac virtues) and Thousand-Leaf are local names in England and Dog-Daisy in Ireland. *Gordolobo* is the Spanish name.

## Sneezeweed Yarrow

*Achillea ptarmica.* Of Achilles; sneezeweed (from Greek *ptairō,* "to sneeze"; the old generic name). (From Europe.)

Bastard-Pellitory, European-Pellitory, Fair-Maid-of-France, Goose-Tongue, *Herbe à éternuer* (P.Q.), Pearl Yarrow, Seven-Year's-Love, Sneezewort, Sneezewort-Tansy, White-Tansy, Wild-Pellitory

"Ptarmica is a little shrub, having small branches, many, round, like unto Sothernwood, about which are many leaves somewhat like to those of the Olive tree; on the top a little head, as of Anthemis, small, round, with a sharp smell, provoking of sneezing, from whence it is named" (Dioscorides). Sneezewort was dried, crumbled and used as snuff. It received the Pellitory names because it was chewed to relieve toothache, as was Pellitory *(Anacyclus pyrethrum)*. Pellitory is also the name of a Nettle.

*Smaller White-Snakeroot*

## Smaller White-Snakeroot

*Ageratina aromaticum.* Little *Ageratum;* aromatic.

Aromatic Eupatorium, Poolroot, Poolwort, Poor-Root, Upland Wild-Horehound, White-Sanicle (N.C.), Wild-Horehound

"The root is diaphoretic, antispasmodic, expectorant, aromatic, diuretic, and is used in ague, stomach complaints, nervous diseases, and pulmonary affections" (Jacobs and Burlage).

## White-Snakeroot

*Ageratina rugosum.* Little *Ageratum;* rough.

Deerwort-Boneset, Hemp-Agrimony, Indian-Sanicle, Milk-Sickness-Plant, Richweed, Squaw-Weed (N.C.), Stevia (Wis.), Thoroughwort, White-Sanicle, White-Top

Milk sickness or morbeo lacteo, the "trembles," was a mysterious and dreaded disease that attacked 19th-century farm families and their livestock in the South and Midwest, particularly in North Carolina, Ohio, Indiana

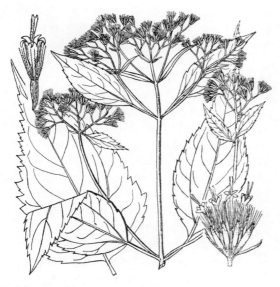

*White-Snakeroot*

and Illinois. The progressive symptoms of the disease include lassitude, nausea, vomiting, stomach pains, intense thirst, prostration, coma and death. In 1818, Nancy Hanks Lincoln, Abraham Lincoln's mother, died of milk sickness in Little Pigeon Creek, Indiana, and because of milk sickness Thomas Lincoln and his new wife, Sarah, moved to Illinois. In some areas the population was decimated by milk sickness (children were particularly vulnerable), and in 1852 county officials in Kentucky complained that the disease was so rife as to deter settlers. The cause of milk sickness was identified by an Illinois doctor, Anna Pierce, in the 1830s: "Pierce finally learned the identity of the poisonous plant when she befriended a Shawnee woman, identified only as Aunt Shawnee, who was a fugitive from the forced relocations of Native Americans. Aunt Shawnee took the doctor into the woods and showed her white snakeroot, saying that it caused both milk sickness and trembles and that it was used by the Shawnee for the treatment of snakebite. Other tribes are also known to have used snakeroot for diarrhea,

fever, and urinary infections" (Duffy, 1990). *A. rugosum* as the cause of milk sickness was not confirmed until 1917. The plant contains a toxic alcohol, tremetol, that causes ketosis and is transmitted through the milk of cows foraging on the plant.

## Common Ragweed

*Ambrosia artemisiifolia.* Immortal (the food of the gods that imparted immortality); with leaves of Artemisia.

Bastard-Wormwood, Bitterweed (Kans., Nebr., N.Y., Ohio, Pa.), Blackweed (Long Island), Carrot-Weed, Hayfever-Weed, Hayweed (Kans.), *Herbe à poux* (P.Q.), Hogweed, Oxtail (Kans.), *Petite herbe à poux* (P.Q.), Roman-Wormwood, *Sarriette* (P.Q.), Stammerwort, Stickweed, Tassel-Weed (Mass.), Wild-Tansy, Wild-Wormwood

Manasseh Cutler called it Conot-Weed. He wrote that it was mistaken for an Artemisia and "generally called Roman Wormwood . . . used in antisceptic fomentations. When it abounds amongst rye or barley, the seeds are thrashed out with the grain, and will give bread, made of it, a bitter and disagreeable taste"—and thus Bitterweed. John Josselyn (1672) called it Oak of Cappadocia (after Gerard) and reported that, like Oak of Hierusalem, it was "excellent for stuffing of the lungs upon colds."

Gerard (1633) wrote that the "fragrant smell" of *Ambrosia* "hath moved the poets to suppose that this herbe was meate and food for the gods." Fernald (1950), however, concludes that the name is "most inappropriate since the pollen of these and related bitter plants is the worst cause of hayfever."

## Great Ragweed

*Ambrosia trifida.* Immortal; three-cleft (leaves).

Bitterweed, Bloodweed (Miss., Texas), Buffalo-Weed, *Grande herbe à poux* (P.Q.), Hayfever-Weed, Horsecane, Horseweed (Kans., Ohio), King-Head, Richweed, Wild-Hemp (Kans.)

*Great Ragweed*

Marie-Victorin wrote that the plant "is cultivated by several Indian tribes as a food or medicinal plant. A red color is obtained from the crushed heads. The species was cultivated by the pre-Columbian Indians, and the seeds found in prehistoric sites are four or five times larger than those of the present wild plant, which seems to indicate culture by selection."

## Pearly Everlasting

*Anaphalis margaritacea.* (The Greek name); pearly (from Greek *margaritēs*, Latin *margarita*, "pearl"). (Also found in eastern Asia and early introduced to Europe from North America.)

Cottonweed, Cudweed, Everlasting-Cottonweed, Everwhite, *Immortelle blanche* (P.Q.), Indian-Posy, Indian-Tobacco (Mich.), Ladies'-Tobacco (N.H.), Lady-Never-Fade, Life-Everlasting, Life-of-Man (N.H.), Live-Long, Moonshine, None-So-Pretty, Pasture Everlasting (Maine), Poverty-Weed (Maine), Silver-Button, Silver-Leaf

In *Two Voyages to New-England* (1674), John Josselyn wrote, "Live forever, it is a kind of Cud-weed, flourisheth all summer long till cold weather comes in. It growes now plentifully in our English gardens; it is good for cough of the lungs, and to cleanse the breast taken as you do Tobacco; and for pain in the head the decoction; or the juice strained and drunk in beer, wine or Acqua vitae, killeth worms. The Fishermen when they want Tobacco take this herb being cut and dried." John Bartram (1751) wrote that "Cotton-weed, or Life-everlasting, is very good for baths or fomentations for cold tumors, bruises or strains." In Quebec "it is a popular remedy for burns" (Marie-Victorin).

Among the Northern Cheyenne of Montana, "Men often carried the dried and powdered flowers in their medicine bundles. Before going to battle, men protected themselves by chewing and rubbing it on arms, legs, and bodies to impart strength, energy, and dash"; and for horses, "some of it was put on the soles of each hoof and blown between the animal's ears to make it enduring and untiring" (Hart, 1980). Gerard (1633) wrote that the flower, if gathered young, could be kept for "the space of a whole year after in your chest or elsewhere; wherefore our

*Pearly Everlasting*

English women have called it Live Long, or Live for ever."

## Everlastings, Pussytoes

*Antennaria.* Like an insect's antennae (the sterile pappus).

*Immortelle* (P.Q.), Indian-Tobacco (Maine), Lady's-Tobacco

## Plantain-Leaved Pussytoes

*Antennaria plantaginifolia.* Like antennae; plantain-leaved.

Cudweed, Dog's-Foot (Mass.), Dog's-Toes (Mass., N.H.), Early Everlasting, Four-Toes (Mass.), Indian-Tobacco (Nebr., New England), Ladies'-Chewing-Tobacco, Ladies'-Tobacco, Love's-Test (Ind.), Mouse's-Ear (Maine, Mass.), Pearly Everlasting (Mass.), Pincushions (Mass.), Plantain-Leaf Everlasting, Poverty-Weed (Maine), Pussy's-Toes (Mass.), Splinterweed (Ill.), Spring Everlasting, White-Plantain, Woman's-Tobacco (Mass.)

Of the name Love's-Test, Bergen (1896) wrote, "The test is in this wise: A leaf is taken by the ends, a person of the opposite sex is

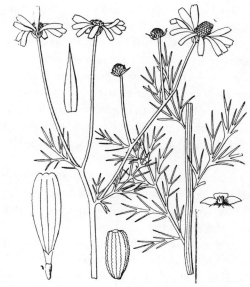

*Mayweed*

thought of, and the ends are pulled apart. If the tomentum beneath is drawn out long, the affection is supposed to be proportionate. Sometimes this is varied by naming both ends, when the relative length of the tomentum determines the stronger love." Rafinesque reported that "for a small fee, the Indians, who call this plant *sinjachu,* will allow themselves to be bitten by a rattlesnake, and immediately cure themselves with this herb." The dog's toes are the staminate flowers, and the pussy's toes the pistillate flowers.

## Mayweed

*Anthemis cotula.* (The Greek name); (the old generic name). (From Europe.)

Balders, Bald-Eye-Grow, *Camomille des chiens* (P.Q.), Chigger-Weed (Ind.), Dilweed, Dilly, Dog-Daisy, Dog-Fennel, Dog-Finkle, Dog's-Camomile, Fetid-Camomile, Fieldweed, Fieldwort, Hay-Fennel (N.C.), Hog's-Fennel, Horse-Daisy, Madder-Mayweed, Maidweed, Maise, *Maroute* (P.Q.), Mather, Morgan, Pathweed, Pigsty-Daisy (Maine, Mass.), Poison-Daisy, Stinking-Camomile (N.Y.), Stinking-

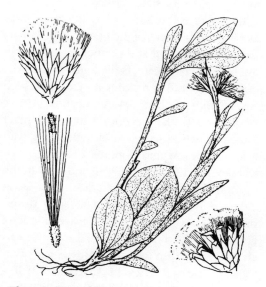

*Plantain-Leaved Pussytoes*

Mayweed (Maine), Stinkweed (Maine), Wild-Cam-
omile

"These Mayweeds have nothing to do with
the month of May," Canon Young writes, but
"they cure mays or young women." In his
*New-England's Rarities* (1672), John Josselyn
wrote of Mayweed that it was "excellent for
the Mother; some of our English Housewives
call it Iron Wort, and make a good unguent
for old Sores."

In the Prose Edda of Scandinavian mythology, the god Balder is described as, "So fair
and dazzling is he in form and features, that
rays of light seem to issue from him; and
thou mayst have some idea of his beauty
when I tell thee that the whitest of all plants
is called Baldur's Brow" (from Britten and
Holland). The white plant was Mayweed, which
became Balder's-Brae in the north of England
and then Balders and Bald-Eye-Grow in
America. Rafinesque reported that the plant
was "extensively used throughout the country
for rheumatism, hysterics, epilepsy, dropsy,
asthma, scrofula, &c., both internally and externally."

It was called Chigger-Weed because it was
"supposed to harbor the 'chigger,' a trouble-
some mite which burrows under the skin"
(Bergen, 1896). Dog-Fennel, Dog-Finkle (i.e.,
Fennel), Madders, Maise, Margon (Morgan in
America) and Mathers are local names in
England.

## Great Burdock

*Arctium lappa.* (From the Greek name, *ark-
tion,* from Greek *arktos,* "bear," for the rough
involucre); rough (the old generic name).
(From Europe.)

*Artichaut* (P.Q.), Badweed, Bardana, Bardane, Beggar's-Buttons, Buzzies (Long Island), Clotbur, Coc-
kle-Bur, Cockle-Button, Cuckle-Buttons (Maine),
Cuckold-Dock, Cuckoo-Button, *Grande Bardane*
(P.Q.), *Graquias* (P.Q.), Great-Bur, Hardane, Har-

*Great Burdock*

dock, Hare-Bur, Hare-Lock, Horse-Burr, Hurr-Burr,
*Rapace* (P.Q.), *Rhubarbe sauvage* (P.Q.), Stick-
Button, *Toques* (P.Q.), Turkey-Bur

Manasseh Cutler wrote, "The young stems
boiled, divested of the bark, are esteemed as
little inferior to asparagus. They are also eaten
raw with oil and vinegar. Dr. Withering says,
a decoction of the roots is esteemed, by some
very sensible physicians, as equal, if not superior, to that of sarsaparilla."

Gerard (1633) called it Clote Burre or Burre
Dock and reported that the peeled stalk, "being
eaten raw with salt and pepper, or boyled in
the broth of fat meate, is pleasant to be eaten;
being taken in that manner it increaseth seed
and stirreth up lust." More recently (1958),
Jacobs and Burlage reported that "the plant
causes increased secretion of milky urine with
frequent desire and copious discharges." It
has been included in the USP and NF. "In the
bygone days when the medical profession
believed in the 'alterative' effects of drugs,
burdock root was used in the treatment of
gouty and syphilitic disorders; also in various
chronic skin diseases" (USD). Beggar's-Buttons, Bazzies (Buzzies in America), Cockly-
Bur, Cuckold-Button (Cuckle-Button in Amer-

ica), Hurr-Burr and Stick-Button are local names in England.

## Common Burdock

*Arctium minus.* (From the Greek name); lesser. (From Europe.)

*Artichaut* (P.Q.), *Bardane* (P.Q.), *Cibourroche* (P.Q.), Cuckoo-Button, Lesser Burdock, *Tabac du diable* (P.Q.)

"A tea and syrup have been made from the berries or roots and have been used in coughs, asthma, diseases of the lungs, as a stimulant in menstrual obstruction, also used as a cold plasma in inveterate ulcers" (Jacobs and Burlage). Marie-Victorin wrote that "the decoction, used to treat chronic infections of the skin and scalp, has given it the name *Herbe aux teigneux* in France." (*Teigneux* is a dirty person or one with scurvy.)

## Heartleaf Arnica

*Arnica cordifolia.* (An obscure name); heartleaved.

Leopard's-Bane

"In countries where Arnica is indigenous, it has long been a popular remedy. In the North American colonies the flowers are used in preference to the rhizome. They have a discutient property. The tincture is used for external application to sprains, bruises, and wounds . . . A homoeopathic tincture, ×6, has been used successfully in the treatment of epilepsy; also for seasickness, 3× before sailing, and every hour on board till comfortable" (Grieve).

## Southernwood

*Artemisia abrotanum.* Of Artemis (virgin goddess of the hunt and the moon, the Roman Diana); a Greek plant name. (From Europe.)

Boy's-Love (New England), Kiss-Me-Quick-and-Go, Lad's-Love (New England), Old-Man (Ill., Maine,

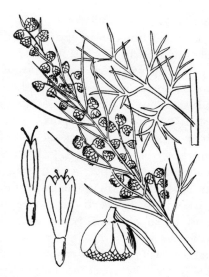

*Southernwood*

Mass., Ohio), Old-Woman (Maine, Ohio), Slovenwood, Smelling-Wood, Sothernwood, Sweet-Benjamin (Mass.)

In Massachusetts in the 1850s, "A favorite shrub in our garden, as in every country dooryard, was southernwood, or lad's love. A sprig of it was carried to Meeting each summer Sunday by many old ladies, and with its finely dissected, bluish-green foliage, and clean pungent scent, it was pleasant to see in the meeting house, and pleasant to sniff at" (Alice Morse Earle).

In *Some Bits of Plant Lore* (1892), Fanny Bergen wrote that "in many parts of England and also in Scotland the familiar southernwood, *Artemisia abrotanum,* according to Britten and Holland's 'Dictionary of English Plant-names,' is known as lad's love, lad-love-lass, or lad's-love-and-lasses'-delight. Another British name for the plant is old man's love, or simply old man, from its use as recommended by Pliny . . . and explained by Macer in the line,

*'Haec etiam venerum, pulvino subdita tantum, incitat.'*

"Now in Maine and in Woburn, Mass., this herb is called boy's love, and in the latter locality it is said that if a girl tucks a bit of it in her shoe she will marry the first boy whom she meets. In Salem a popular name for the plant is lad's love. In other parts of Massachusetts it is said that if a girl puts a piece of southernwood down her back she will marry the first boy whom she meets. In Boston, if a marriageable woman puts a bit of southernwood under the pillow on retiring, the first man whom she meets in the morning will (so says the superstition) be the one whom she is to marry.

"In these half-playful observances we have merely survivals of what three hundred years ago was a matter of serious belief. For William Turner in his fine old English 'Herball' writes in 1551, 'some hold that thys herbe [Sothernwode] layd but under a mannys bolster, provoketh men to the multyplyenge of their kynde, and that it is good agaynst chermynge and wychyng of men, which by chermynge are not able to exercise the worke of generacion.' " The line from Macer (a 15th-century herbalist) above can be translated as, "This even incites lust if merely put under the pillow."

## Absinthe Wormwood

*Artemisia absinthium.* Of Artemis; absinthe (the old generic name, from the Greek name *absinthion*). (From Europe.)

Absinth, *Armoise absinth* (P.Q.), Boy's-Love (Mass.), Green-Ginger (La.), Madderwort, Mingwort, Mugwort, Old-Woman, Warmot, Wormwood

Manasseh Cutler wrote, "The leaves and flowers are well known to be bitter, and to resist putrefaction. They are made a principle ingredient in antisceptic fomentations. The roots are warm and aromatic. The plant affords a considerable quantity of essential oil, by distillation, which is used both internally and externally to destroy worms."

*Absinthe Wormwood*

In Shakespeare's *Romeo and Juliet* (1.3.30–36) Juliet's nurse remembers the day Juliet was weaned:

> *For I had then laid wormwood to my*
> *    dug,*
> *Sitting in the sun under the dovehouse*
> *    wall,*

and

> *When it did taste the wormwood on the*
> *    nipple*
> *Of my dug and felt it bitter, pretty fool,*
> *To see it tetchy and fall out with the*
> *    dug.*

Soon after, the plant was carried to New England and put to the same use: "Some children are hardly weaned; although the teat be rubbed with wormwood or mustard, they will either wipe it off, or else suck down sweet and bitter together." (Ann Bradstreet, 1664).

In Louisiana "Wormwood (Absinthe/Green ginger) was better known by the rural backwoods folks who operated 'white lightning' stills many years back. They would take the best 'drippings' for their own use. An infusion of wormwood would be added to the remainder of a given batch. This would be sold to 'outsiders.' This would give the white lightning the kick of a mule" (Touchstone, 1983). The toxic and intoxicating properties of its volatile oil, thujone, have been known since ancient times; thujone was once an ingredient in the alcoholic beverage Absinthe. Madderwort is Mader (Mother) Wort, an old English name. Mingwort and Warmot are local names in England. It has been included in the USP and NF, "used as a stimulant, tonic, anthelmintic, narcotic, and in beverages and as a flavor" (Jacobs and Burlage).

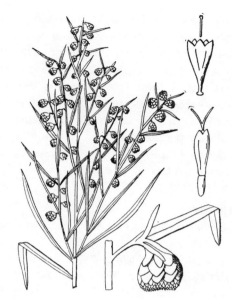

*Linear-Leaved Wormwood*

## Linear-Leaved Wormwood, Dragon Wormwood

*Artemisia dracunculus.* Of Artemis; little-dragon (former generic name).

James Teit (1930) recorded how the Thompson Indians use the plant to steam out rheumatism and aching bones, muscles and joints: "A considerable quantity of the entire plants or the fresh stems and leaves are gathered. A sufficient number of stones are collected and heated red-hot in a fire as for an ordinary sweat bath. Smooth waterworn stones are chosen. When they are hot they are arranged so as to make as smooth a surface as possible. Such a bed of stones is made the full length and breadth of the person to be treated. Fine dry sand is collected and spread over the stones until their surfaces are just covered. The fresh plants are spread evenly on the top of the hot stones and sand until they form a thick bed, generally about 6 inches in depth. The patients lies naked and full length on top of the plants and is covered with a blanket to keep in the heat and steam. He lies there for several hours, perspiring

freely, until the stones become cool." Teit added that "steaming is probably truly helpful, but directly after rising from this steam bed they usually dash into an ice-cold stream, which sometimes has a fatal result."

Among the Indians of the Missouri River region, "The immaterial essence or, to use the Dakota word, the *ton,* of Artemisia was believed to be effectual as a protection against maleficent powers; therefore it was always proper to begin any ceremonial by using Artemisia in order to drive away any evil influences" (Gilmore).

## Western Wormwood, White-Sage

*Artemisia ludoviciana.* Of Artemis; of St. Louis. Cudweed Mugwort, Dark-Leaved Mugwort, Man-Sage (Mont.), Prairie-Sage, Sage (Minn.), Western-Sage

" 'Man sage' was perhaps the most important ceremonial plant of the Cheyennes. It was spread along the borders in almost every ceremonial lodge, the tops of the stems pointing to the fire. The leaves were burned as incense which was believed to have the power to drive away bad spirits, evil influences, and ominous and persistent dreams of sick persons. A small pinch of *Actaea rubra* was often mixed with it for this purpose. Its use for purification was widespread: the leaves were burned as incense to purify implements, utensils, or people in various ceremonies; or in a bundle employed to wipe a person guilty of breaking a taboo" (Hart, 1980).

## Mugwort

*Artemisia vulgaris.* Of Artemis; common. (From Europe.)

Apple-Pie, *Armoise vulgaire* (P.Q.), Bulwand, Fellon-Herb, Green-Ginger, *Herbe Saint-Jean* (P.Q.), Motherwort (Maine), Sailor's-Tobacco, Smotherwood, Wormwood

"This herb is called Mugwort. The vertue of this herb is thus. If a man bear this herb about him he shall not be weary of travelynge in his way. Also if this herb be pounded with tallow, it healeth the soreness of mannes feet and akyng also. And if it be within a house, there shall no wicked spirit abyde" (Banckes, 1525). William Cole (1656) wrote that "if a

*Mugwort*

footman takes Mugwort and puts it in his shoes in the morning, he may go forty miles before noon and not be weary." Country people picked Mugwort and smoked it over bonfires on Midsummer Eve and hung it over doors to keep off evil spirits. Remains of smoked Mugwort wreaths have been found in Irish archaeological sites. Mugwort is the first of nine sacred herbs in the *Lacnunga,* written in the Wessex dialect in the 10th century but, according to Rohde, "in its origin a heathen lay of great antiquity preserved down to Christian times":

> *Have in mind, Mugwort, what you*
> *made known,*
> *What you laid down, at the great de-*
> *nouncing.*
> *Una your name is, oldest of herbs*
> *Of might against thirty, and against*
> *three,*
> *Of might against venom and the onfly-*
> *ing,*
> *Of might against the vile She who fares*
> *through the land.*

Mugwort is from Old English *mucgwyrt, mucg* meaning "midge"; it was used to repel flies and midges. Bulwand is a local name in Scotland, and Green-Ginger and Sailor's-Tobacco are local names in England. It was called Motherwort in 19th-century Maine and in the Banckes *Herbal* (1525): "This herb helpeth a woman to conceyve a chylde, and clenseth the mother, and maketh a woman to have her flowers."

## Asters, Michaelmas Daisies

*Aster.* Starry.

Daisy, Fall-Rose (Ohio), Frost-Flower (Maine, N.B., N.H.), Frostweed (Maine), Goodbye-Summer (N.C.), It-Brings-the-Fall (N.Y. Indian), (N.Y.), Sharewort, Starwort

Michaelmas is a church festival on September 29 celebrating the Archangel Michael;

cultivated Michaelmas Daisies are hybrid As-ters. Asters are also called Starwoorts and Sharewoorts in Gerard's *Herbal* (1633) and also *Inguinalis,* because "stamped, and ap-plied unto botches, imposthumes, and vener-eous bubones (which for the most part happen *in Inguine,* that is the flanke or share) doth mightily maturate and suppurate them."

## Heart-Leaved Aster

*Aster cordifolius.* Starry; heart-leaved.
Beeweed (W.Va.), Blue-Devil (W.Va.), Common Blue Wood-Aster, Fall Aster (W.Va.), Stickweed (W.Va.), Tongue (Maine)

In Maine this was known as Tongue and "used as greens" (Perkins, 1929). In North Carolina "it is used as an aromatic nervine in the form of a decoction and as an infusion for rheumatism and by old women, as *partus accelerandum*" (Jacobs and Burlage). Rafin-esque also reported that it was "an excellent aromatic nervine, in many cases preferable to Valerian." Among the Flambeau Ojibwa, "the root of this aster is but one of nineteen that can be used to make a smoke or incense

*Heart-Leaved Aster*

when smoked in a pipe, which attracts the deer near enough to shoot it with a bow and arrow. The deer carries its scent or spoor in between its toes . . . It is a peculiar scent and the Ojibwe tries successfully to counter-feit it with roots and herbs" (Huron Smith, 1932).

## Panicled Aster, Western Aster

*Aster lanceolatus.* Starry; lance-shaped.
Among the Zuñi, "The entire plant is ground between stones in the fraternity chamber of the Shu'maakwe, at noon during the elabo-rate ceremony of the preparation of the fraternity medicine in August, by the A'wantsi'ta ('great mother' of the fraternity), to the ac-companiment of the pottery drum, rattle, and song. This medicine is in the exclusive pos-session of the a'kwamosi (director of medi-cine), and is used only on the faces of the personators of the Shu'maikoli, patron god of this fraternity" (Stevenson, 1915). The plant was also used to treat arrow or bullet wounds, and for "bleeding at the nose the blossoms are crushed and sprinkled on live coals, and the smoke is inhaled. The remedy is said to be specific for this ailment. When used for this purpose it belongs to all the people."

## Calico Aster

*Aster lateriflorus.* Starry; one-side-flowering.
Devil-Weed (W.Va.), Farewell-Summer (W.Va.), Hairy-Stemmed Aster, Michaelmas Daisy, Nail-Rod, Old-Field-Sweet (W.Va.), Old-Virginia-Stickweed (W.Va.), Rosemary (Md.), Starved Aster, Trades-cant's Aster, White-Devil (W.Va.), Wireweed (W.Va.)

Among the Meskwaki, "the entire plant is used as a smoke or steam in the sweat bath. The blossoms only are smudged to cure a crazy person" (Huron Smith, 1928).

A previous name was *Aster tradescantii.* September 14, 1856: "Now for the *Aster Tra-descanti* along low roads, like the Turnpike,

*Calico Aster*

*Large-Leaved Aster*

swarming with butterflies and bees. Some of them are pink. How ever unexpected these later flowers! You thought that Nature had about wound up her affairs. You had seen what she could do this year, and had not noticed a few weeds by the roadside, or mistook them for the remains of summer flowers now hastening to their fall; you thought you knew every twig and leaf by the roadside, and nothing more was to be looked for there; and now to your surprise, the ditches are crowded with millions of little stars" (Thoreau).

## Large-Leaved Aster

*Aster macrophyllus.* Starry; large-leaved.
*Pétouane* (P.Q.), Rough-Tongues

August 26, 1856: "Sailed across to Bee Tree Hill. This hillside, laid bare two years ago and partly last winter, is almost covered with the *Aster macrophyllus,* now in its prime. It grows large and rank, two feet high. On one count seventeen central flowers withered, one hundred and thirty in bloom, and half as many buds. As I looked down from the hilltop over the sprout land, its rounded grayish tops

amid the bushes I mistook for gray, lichen-clad rocks, such was its profusion and harmony with the scenery, like hoary rocky hilltops amid bushes" (Thoreau).

"The Flambeau Ojibwe consider this a feeble remedy but also a good charm in hunting. Young roots were used to make a tea to bathe the head for headache" (Huron Smith, 1932). Marie-Victorin wrote, "It is reported that the Indians smoked the large basal leaf in lieu of tobacco."

## New England Aster

*Aster novae-angliae.* Starry; of New England.
Farewell-Summer, Hardy Aster (Ohio), Last-Rose-of-Summer, Michaelmas-Daisy (Ohio)

"The *Aster novae-angliae* is employed in decoction internally, with a strong decoction externally, in many eruptive diseases of the skin," according to Rafinesque, and Densmore (1928) reported that among the Chippewa the root was smoked in a pipe to attract game. Marie-Victorin wrote that when the flowering heads are rubbed between the fingers, "they emit an odor sui generis, recalling camphor and turpentine."

## Purple-Stemmed Aster

*Aster puniceus.* Starry; purple.

Cocash, Cold-Water-Root, Early Purple-Aster, Meadow-Scabish, Red-Stalk Aster, Squaw-Weed, Starflower, Swamp-Weed, Swan-Weed

This was one of the ingredients of the Thomsonian system of botanic medicine (see *Lobelia inflata*), used "to scour the stomach and bowels, and remove the canker."

## Groundsel-Tree

*Baccharis halimifolia.* Of Bacchus (the name of a shrub dedicated to Bacchus); with leaves of *Halimus.*

Consumption-Weed (N.C.), Cottonbush (Ga.), Cottonseed-Tree, Groundsel-Bush, Kink-Bush (Md., Va.), Lavender (S.C.), Mangle, *Manglier* (La.), Mangrove (La.), Marsh-Elder (Long Island), Marsh-Laurel (Texas), Mung (La.), Oil-Willow (Texas), Pencil-Tree, Plowman's-Spikenard (N.Y.), Saltwater-Bush (Va.), Sand-Myrtle (S.C.), Sea-Island-Myrtle (Ga., S.C.), Sea-Myrtle, Waterbush (Va.), Water-Gall (Va.), White-Mangle

"This plant is of undoubted value, and of very general use in popular practice in South Carolina, as a palliative and demulcent in consumption and cough" (Porcher). Gerard (1633) wrote of a Baccharis that, "The learned Herbarists of Montpellier have called this plant *Baccharis* . . . by reason of that sweet and aromaticall savour which his root containeth and yeeldeth: in English it may be called the Cinamon root, or Plowmans Spiknard." Spikenard is an Aralia.

It is called Oil-Willow because in Texas, "it so happens that oil has been found by drilling in many of the flats where these bushes are abundant; hence a legend has grown up to the effect that they indicate oil-sand areas" (Reid, 1951).

## Arrowleaf Balsamroot

*Balsamorhiza sagittata.* Balsam root; arrow-shaped.

Bigroot, Big-Sunflower, Spring-Sunflower

In Utah, "This brilliantly flowered plant, which is abundant over the hills and mountain-sides throughout the territory of the Gosiutes, was formerly of much economic importance to them. In the spring the large leaves and their petioles were boiled and eaten. Later when the seeds were ripe these were beaten out of the heads into baskets and used as food as in the case of those of Helianthus. The root was applied as a remedy upon fresh wounds, being chewed or pounded up and used as a paste or salve upon the affected part" (Chamberlin, 1911). Among the Northern Cheyenne, "A medicinal tea of the leaves, roots, and stems was drunk for pains in the stomach and for colds. For headache, the Cheyennes held their heads over the hot, steaming infusion. The root was given to facilitate childbirth" (Hart, 1980).

## European Daisy

*Bellis perennis.* Pretty one (the name in Pliny); perennial. (From Europe.)

Bairnwort, Banwort, Bennert, Boneflower, Bonewort, Bruisewort, Childing-Daisy, Common Daisy,

*Groundsel-Tree*

Ewe-Gowan, Garden Daisy, Hen-and-Chickens, Herb-Margaret, Lawn Daisy, March Daisy, Marguerite, May-Gowan

Robert Burns's poem "To a Mountain Daisy, on turning one down with the plough, in April, 1786" is about this plant:

> *Wee modest crimson-tippèd flow'r,*
> *Thou's met me in an evil hour;*
> *For I maun crush amang the stoure*
> > *Thy slender stem:*
> *To spare thee now is past my pow'r,*
> > *Thou bonnie gem.*

This is the "day's eye" (Old English *daeges-eage*) that shuts at night and opens in the morning. "The Northren men call this herbe a Banwort, because it helpeth bones to knyt agayne" (Turner, 1548). Bairnwort, Bone-flower, Ewe-Gowan and Mary-Gowlan (May-Gowan in America) are local names in England.

## Bur-Marigolds, Beggar-Ticks, Cuckolds

*Bidens.* Two teeth (awns).

Beggar's-Needles (N.J.), *Bident* (P.Q.), *Fourchettes* (P.Q.), Harvest-Lice, Spanish-Needles, Sticktights

Manasseh Cutler called them Harvest-Lice and Cuckolds. Most of the names refer to the barbed fruit, some of which have two curved awns like a cuckold's horns.

## Tickseed-Sunflower, Bearded Beggar-Ticks, Great Bidens

*Bidens aristosa.* Two teeth; bristly.

September 14, 1854: the Water-Marigold is "drowned or dried up, and has given place to the great bidens, *the* flower and ornament of the riversides at present, and now in its glory, especially at I. Rice's shore, where there are dense beds. It is a splendid yellow—

*Tickseed-Sunflower*

Channing says a lemon yellow—and looks larger than it is (two inches in diameter, more or less). Full of the sun. It needs a name" (Thoreau).

## Spanish-Needles

*Bidens bipinnata.* Two teeth; bipinnate (leaves).

Cuckolds, High-Brighties (southern Appalachia)

In 1748 in Pennsylvania, Peter Kalm wrote that it was called "Spanish needles" and complained that its black seeds stuck to his clothing. The young shoots and leaves are cooked, and the flowering tops make tea. The USD reports that "the root and seeds were popularly used as emmenagogues, and by the eclectics in laryngeal and bronchial diseases."

## Beggar-Ticks, Sticktight

*Bidens frondosa.* Two teeth; leafy.

Beggar's-Lice (Maine), Boot-Jacks (Conn., Pa.), Cockles, Common Bur-Marigold, Cuckles (Mass., N.Y.), Devil's-Pitchfork (Mass., Vt.), Old-Ladies'-Clothes-Pins (Mass.), Rayless-Marigold, Stickseed

*Bachelor's-Button*

## Bachelor's-Button, Cornflower

*Centaurea cyanus.* Of the Centaur (who was famed for his gift of healing; the other healing plant named for the Centaur is Centaury); dark-blue (the old generic name). (From Europe.)

Barbeau (La.), Blaver, *Bleuet* (P.Q.), Blue-Bonnets, Bluebottle, Blue-Caps, Blue-Poppy, *Bluet* (P.Q.), Brushes, Corn-Blinks, Corn-Bluebottle, Cornbottle, Corn-Centaury, Cornpink, Cyani, French-Pink (Ohio), Hurt-Sickle, Ragged-Ladies, Ragged-Robin (Md., Ohio), Ragged-Sailor, Witch's-Bells, Witch's-Thimbles

Parkinson (1629) wrote, "We doe call them in English, Blew Bottles, and in some places, Corne flowers," and reported that they were used "as a cooling cordiall, and commended by some to be a remedy, not onely against the plague and pestilentiall diseases, but against the poison of scorpions and spiders." Grieve wrote that, "the Cornflower, with its starlike blossoms of brilliant blue, is one of our most striking wild-flowers, though it is always looked on as an unwelcome weed by the farmer, for not only does it by its presence withdraw nourishment from the ground that is needed for the corn, but its tough stems in former days of hand-reaping were wont to blunt the reaper's sickle, earning it the name of Hurt-Sickle."

Barbeau was "a name common along the Mississippi a generation and more ago, from a M. Barbeau who brought it from France" (Bergen, 1896). Bachelor's-Buttons, Cornbottle, Corn-Blink and the Witch's names are local in England. Blaver and Brushes are from Scotland.

## Dusty-Maiden, Morning-Brides

*Chaenactis douglasii.* Gape ray (the marginal flower of some species); of Douglas (David Douglas, 1798–1834).

Bride's-Bouquet, False-Yarrow, Hoary Chaenactis

In Nevada "One of the Paiute names commonly applied to this plant is 'bawa na-tizua,'

*Dusty-Maiden*

meaning 'swelling medicine,' and it is utilized mostly in that capacity. The fresh plants, or sometimes only the leaves, are crushed and applied as a poultice" (Train, Henrichs and Archer, 1941).

## Wild Chamomile

*Chamomilla recutita.* Chamomile (from the Greek *khamaemēlon,* "earth apple"); circumcised (appearance of the flowering head with reflexed petals). (From Europe.)
Bachelor's-Buttons, German Chamomile, Horse-Gowan, Scented-Mayweed

Chamomile (or Camomile) tea is made from the leaves of this plant or of *Chamaemelum nobile* (Roman Chamomile). "Camomill is put to divers and sundry uses, both for pleasure and profit, both for inward and outward diseases, both for the sick and the sound, in bathings to comfort and strengthen the sound, and to ease pains in the diseased" (Parkinson, 1629). Cotton Mather (1724) recommended it as a remedy in dropsy: "Take little handfuls of Camomile-flowers. Boil them

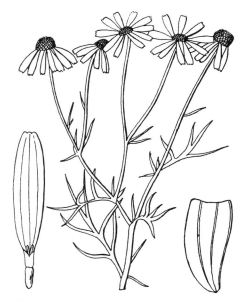

*Wild Chamomile*

a little in a mess of thin water-gruel; strain the gruel and sweeten it. It has been said, This never fails to procure sweat. It also provokes the urine; quenches the thirst; and abates the fever. Woodman sais, Tho' this look like a simple medicine, lett it be tried; and not be despised for the seeming meanness of it."

The previous generic name was *Matricaria,* called thus, according to Gerard (1633), because "it is a great remedie against the diseases of the matrix; it procureth womens sicknesse with speed; it bringeth forth the afterbirth and the dead child, whether it bee drunke in a decoction, or boiled in a bath and the woman sit over it; or the herbes sodden and applied to the privie part, in manner of a cataplasme or pultis."

In their enthnobotany of the Fort Yukon Region, Alaska, Holloway and Alexander (1990) report that the flowerheads are harvested to make a tea for the "relief of hangovers." It has been included in the USP: "Matricaria is a mild tonic, very similar to chamomile [*C. nobile*] in medicinal properties, and, like it, in very large doses an emetic" (USD). Horse-Gowan is a local name in Scotland.

## Chicory

*Cichorium intybus.* (From the Greek name, *kikhora*); (the old generic name, from the Egyptian *tybi,* January, the month in which the plant grows). (From Europe.)
Bachelor's-Buttons (Calif., Mass.), Blue-Daisies (Long Island), Blue-Dandelion (N.H.), Blue-Sailors, Bunk, Coffee-Weed, Horseweed (W.Va.), Ragged-Sailors (Long Island), Succory, Wild-Bachelor's-Buttons (Mass.), Wild-Endive, Wild Succory

The plant is cultivated for the roots which are roasted and ground as a coffee substitute or flavoring. The young leaves and roots are also boiled and eaten. Manasseh Cutler called it Blue Succory and noted that "it is said to be a good stomachic." The name Blue-Sailors refers to the legend about a beautiful girl who fell in love with a sailor. He left her for the sea, and she sat patiently by the roadside waiting for his return, until the gods took pity on her and turned her into a chicory plant, which still wears its sailor-blue blossoms and waits for his return. Dioscorides called the plant Seris, which "is of a twofold kind, for the one is more like lettuce, and broad-leaved, the other is narrow-leaved and bitter. But they are all of them binding, cooling, and good for the stomach." The broad-leaved plant is Endive, *Cichorium endiva.*

*Chicory*

## Canada Thistle

*Cirsium arvense.* (From the Greek name, *kirsion,* from *kirsos,* a swollen vein for which one species was a remedy); of cultivated fields. (From Europe.)

California Thistle, Corn Thistle, Creeping Thistle, Cursed Thistle, Hard Thistle, Prickly Thistle, Way Thistle

"The root is tonic, diuretic, astringent, antiphlogistic and hepatic; the leaves are antiphlogistic. It causes inflammation and has irritating properties" (Jacobs and Burlage).

*Canada Thistle*

## Elk Thistle

*Cirsium foliosum.* (From the Greek name); leafy.

Evert's Thistle

In September 1843, on their journey up the Bear River, Lieutenant Frémont and his companions "found on the way this morning a small encampment of two families of Snake Indians, from whom we purchased a small quantity of *kooyah.* They had piles of seeds, of three different kinds, spread out on pieces of buffalo robe; and the squaws had just gathered a bushel of the roots of a thistle *[Cirsium foliosum].* They were about the ordinary size of carrots, and, as I have previously mentioned, are sweet and well flavored, requiring only a long preparation. They had a band of twelve or fifteen horses, and appeared to be growing in the sunshine with about as little labor as the plants they were eating." (Kooyah is *Valeriana edulis.*)

On an expedition to explore Yellowstone National Park in 1870, Truman Everts became separated from his companions and was then thrown from his horse. Lost and without food, he subsisted for a month on the root of this

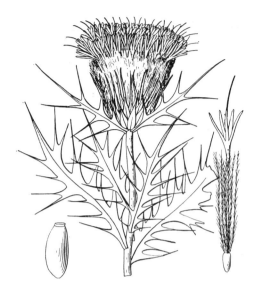

*Santa Fe Thistle*

Thistle until rescued; thus the name Evert's Thistle. The peeled stems are a sweet pot-herb. This is a favorite early summer food of elk and bears.

## Santa Fe Thistle, Yellow-Spine Thistle

*Cirsium ochrocentrum.* (From the Greek name); yellow-prickled.

Among the Zuñi Indians, "The entire plant is placed overnight in a vessel of cold water. The water is drunk morning, noon, and at sunset as a cure for syphilis *(su'towe).* Immediately after taking each dose the patient, if a man, runs rapidly to promote perspiration and to accelerate action of the kidneys. On returning to the house he is wrapped in blankets. If the patient is a woman she does not run, but sits bundled in heavy blankets. The medicine often induces vomiting" (Stevenson, 1915).

## Pasture Thistle

*Cirsium pumilum.* (From the Greek name); dwarf.

Bull Thistle (New England), Fragrant Thistle

"How many insects a single one attracts! While you sit by it, bee after bee will visit it, and busy himself probing for honey and loading himself with pollen, regardless of your overshadowing presence" (Thoreau, 1851).

## Blessed Thistle

*Cnicus benedictus.* (A Latin name); blessed (it was believed to provide protection against evil). (From Europe.)

Bitter Thistle, Holy Thistle, Our Lady's Thistle, St. Benedict's Thistle, Stickers (N.B.), Sweet-Sultan (Mass.)

It has been cultivated for centuries as a medicinal herb, considered effective even against the plague and thus blessed. Grieve (1931) wrote, "It is chiefly used now for nursing mothers, the warm infusion scarcely ever failing to procure a proper supply of milk." There is an herbal tea on the market, packaged in California, called Mother's Milk whose active ingredient is listed as "blessed thistle leaf."

Dr. Porcher reported, "The plant is emetic, tonic, and febrifugal; one drachm of the powder of the flowers in wine, with a decoction

*Blessed Thistle*

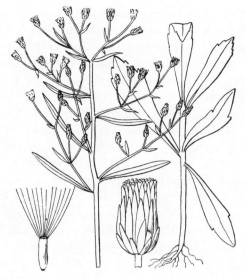

*Horseweed*

of the leaves, is said to be invaluable in anorexia, weak stomach, impaired by irregularities of diet, atony, jaundice and tertian fevers." In Shakespeare's *Much Ado About Nothing*, Beatrice complains, "by my troth I am sick," and she is told, "Get you some of this distill'd carduus benedictus and lay it to your heart. It is the only thing for a qualm."

## Horseweed

*Conyza canadensis*. (A Greek plant name); of Canada.

Bittersweet, Bitterweed, Blood-Staunch, Butterweed, Buttonweed, Canada Fleabane, Cocash (Canada), Colt's-Tail, Cow-Tail (Ill.), Fireweed, Hogweed, Horseweed, Mare's-Tail, Prideweed, Scabious (N.C.), Squaw-Weed (Canada)

Rafinesque wrote, "I highly recommend these plants to medical attention. They were known to the northern Indians by the name of Cocash or Squaw weed as emmenagogues and diuretics, and are often employed by herbalists. They may be collected for medical use at any time when in blossom."

This was previously *Erigeron canadensis,* introduced to Europe in the early 1600s and,

according to John Parkinson (1640), "bound to the forehead is a great help to cure one of the frensie." Oil of Canada Fleabane (once included in the USP) "has been used in diarrhea, dysentry, and internal hemorrhages" (USD).

## Coreopsis, Tickseed

*Coreopsis lanceolata*. Like a bedbug (the achene); lanceolate (leaves).

Dye-Flowers (N.C.), Lady's-Breast-Pin, Old-Maid's-Breast-Pin (Ohio)

## Garden Coreopsis, Garden Tickseed

*Coreopsis tinctoria*. Like a bedbug; used in dyeing.

Calliopsis, Golden Coreopsis, Nuttall's-Weed, Rocky-Mountain-Flower (Ohio), Wild-Flax (S.Dak.)

Calliopsis is New Latin for "having beautiful eyes," describing the flower's reddish central disk. A red dye was extracted from the petals.

## Coneflowers

*Echinacea*. Spiny (from Greek *ekhinos,* a hedgehog or sea urchin).

*Garden Coreopsis*

"As was the case with many other American medicinal plants, the early settlers learned the uses of Echinacea from the Indians. Echinacea species were popularly known as Indian Head, Scurvy Root, Black Sampson, Niggerhead, Comb Flower, Hedgehog, Red Sunflower, Purple Coneflower, Missouri Snakeroot, and in the Ozarks, Droops, referring to the reflexed ray flowers of *E. pallida* . . . Dr. J. S. Leachman of Sharon, Oklahoma, writing in the October 1914 edition of *The Gleaner* states, 'Old settlers all believe firmly in the virtues of Echinacea root, and use it as an aid in nearly every sickness. If a cow or horse does not eat well, the people administer Echinacea, cut up and put in feed. I have noticed that puny stock treated in this manner soon begin to thrive' " (Foster, 1991).

## Purple Coneflower

*Echinacea pallida.* Spiny; pale.
Black-Sampson, Comb (S.Dak.), Black-Susans, Comb-Flower, Droops (Ark., Mo.), Hedgehog Cone-

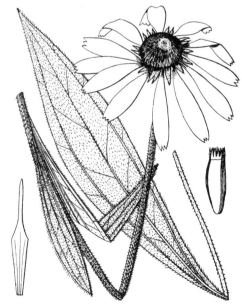

*Purple Coneflower*

flower, Indian-Head, Kansas Snakeroot, Nigger-head (Okla.), Purple-Daisy, Rattlesnake-Weed, Red-Sunflower, Scurvy-Root, Snakeroot (Kans.)

Among the Indians of the Northern Great Plains, "This plant was universally used as an antidote for snake bite and other venomous bites and stings and poisonous conditions. Echinacea seems to have been used as a remedy for more ailments than any other plant. It was employed in the smoke treatment for headache in persons and distemper in horses. It was used also as a remedy for toothache, a piece being kept on the painful tooth until there was relief, and for enlarged glands, as in the mumps. It was said that jugglers bathed their hands and arms in the juice of this plant so that they could take out a piece of meat from a boiling kettle with the bare hand without suffering pain, to the wonderment of onlookers" (Gilmore).

In 1871 Dr. H. C. F. Meyer, a patent medicine salesman of Pawnee City, Nebraska, who had heard about the use of the plant by the Indians, marketed a tincture of the root as Meyer's Blood Purifier: "This is a powerful drug as an Alterative and Antiseptic in all tumorous and Syphilitic indications: old chronic wounds, such as fever sores, old ulcers, Carbuncles, Piles, eczema, wet or dry, can be cured quick and active . . . It will not fail in gangrene . . . In fever it is a specific . . . It relieves pain, swelling and inflammation . . . It has not and will not fail to cure Diptheria quick. . . It has cured hydrophobia" (Foster, 1991). Echinacea was then discovered by the eclectic physicians, and despite denunciations by the American Medical Association, its use grew: "Case reports and verbal commendations of clinical success with the plant made it one of the most widely used American medicinal plants of the late nineteenth and early twentieth centuries. By 1921, Echinacea and its preparations became the most widely sold medicines from an American medicinal plant" (Foster, 1991). It was included in the NF from 1916 to 1950. Kindscher (1989) reports that recent research on *Echinacea* species demonstrates that they possess immunostimulatory activity and that "on a visit to the Rosebud Reservation in South Dakota during summer 1987, I learned that the purple coneflower is still widely harvested by the Lakota for a variety of medicinal uses."

The spiny bristles among the disk flowers are the "comb" in South Dakota (particularly in *Echinacea purpurea*), the "brush" being Long-Headed Coneflower *(Ratibida columniferis)*.

## Brittlebush, Incienso, Golden-Hills

*Encelia farinosa.* Of Encel (Christopher Encel, 16th-century botanist); floury.

A medicinal tea is brewed from the leaves and stems by Southwestern Indians, who also chew the scented gum exuded by the stems. "The gum is widely used in northern Mexico as a church incense or smelly-cigar incense, dropped on coals like Copal or frankincense. Delightfully elegant" (Moore, 1989).

## Pilewort, Fireweed

*Erechtites hieracifolia.* (A Greek plant name); with leaves of Hieracium.

Crenate-Milkweed (Canada), *Crève-z-yeux* (P.Q.)

Dr. Millspaugh reported that "the whole plant is succulent, bitter, and somewhat acrid, and has been used by the laity principally as an emetic, alterative, cathartic, acrid tonic, and astringent, in various forms of eczema, muco-sanguineous diarrhoea, and hemorrhages. The oil, as well as the herb itself, has been found highly seviceable in piles and dysentery." It was called fireweed because "it abounds in new plantations where the ground has been burnt over" (Cutler, 1785).

*Brittlebush*

## Fleabanes, Horseweeds

*Erigeron.* Early old man (from Greek *eri,* "early," *geron,* "old man," "because the flowers in spring turn gray like hair," according to Dioscorides).

Farewell-to-Summer (Lab., Nfd.), *Vergerette* (P.Q.)

"The herb burned where flies, gnats, fleas, or any venomous things are, doth drive them away" (Gerard, 1633).

## Daisy Fleabane

*Erigeron annuus.* Early old man; annual.

Lace-Buttons, Little-Daisies (Maine), Muletail-Weed (Okla.), Sweet-Scabious, Tall-Daisy, White-Top-Weed (Ohio)

John Bartram (1751) wrote of "*Erigeron,* used by some for the bite of a snake: it bears a white flower in the Spring, something like a large Daisy, about a foot high, the roots run under the surface of the ground in small fibres or threads, of a hot taste; the Indians pound this root, and apply it to cold tumours to dissolve them."

## Common Fleabane, Philadelphia Fleabane

*Erigeron philadelphicus.* Early old man; of Philadelphia.

Cocash, Daisy (N.Dak., Ohio), Daisy-Fleabane, Frostroot, Mourning-Bride (N.C.), Mourning-Widow (N.C.), Scabish, Skevish (Pa.), Squaw-Weed, Sweet-Scabious

According to Dr. Barton, "A decoction or infusion of the plant has been used in Philadelphia, by several persons, for gouty and gravelly complaints, and some of them have informed me, that they have been much benefited by the use of the plant. It operates powerfully as a diuretic and also as a sudorific. This Erigeron is known in Pennsylvania by the name of Skevish, which I suspect is a corruption of the word Scabious." Rafinesque

reported that "these weeds . . . act in a mode peculiar to themselves, by means of their acrid quality. Their oil is so powerful that two or three drops dissolved in alcohol have arrested suddenly uterine hemorrhages." Mournful Widow and Mourning Widow are local names in England for Sweet Scabious *(Scabiosa atropurpurea)* and Dusky Cranesbill *(Geranium phaeum).* "The name *widow* is applied to other plants with very dark or dingy flowers" (Britten and Holland).

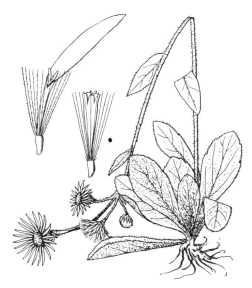

*Robin's-Plantain*

*Common Fleabane*

## Robin's-Plantain

*Erigeron pulchellus.* Early old man; little pretty.

Blue Spring-Daisy, Plantain-Fleabane, Poor-Robin's-Plantain, Rattlesnake-Plantain, Robert's-Plantain, Rose-Betty

During his travels in eastern North America in 1783 and 1784, Dr. Schöpf was shown 38 plants that were used to cure the bite of the rattlesnake. "Aristolochia Serpenteria and Polygala Senega have especially held the general esteem; and to these must be added the Robert's Plantain, which has been praised by several, particularly the worthy Dr. Otto at Bethlehem, from positive and often confirmed experience, having many times been of excellent use where signs of the poison taken up into the blood were already plainly manifest. This plant, little known as yet, grows well in hilly regions and is found in plenty about Bethlehem; it is raised there foresightedly in gardens, so as to be found in the night if occasion arises." The other Robin's-Plantain is a Hawkweed.

## Joe-Pye Weeds, Thoroughworts

*Eupatorium.* Of Eupator (Mithridates Eupator, king of Parthia, 120–63 B.C., and one of Rome's most formidable opponents, who was supposed to have discovered the medicinal virtues of the Eupatoriums).

In Amos Eaton's *Manual of Botany* of 1818, *Eupatorium verticillatum* (now *Eupatorium dubium*) was "joe-pye's weed" and *Eupatorium purpureum* was "joe-pye weed." By 1893 "Joe Pye" had become "the name of an Indian who cured typhus fever in New England by means of this plant" (Dana). But the existence of Joe Pye is in doubt. These are called Thoroughworts because the stem of the most renowned species, *Eupatorium perfoliatum,* appears to grow thorough (through) the leaves.

"This forenoon I was disagreeably surprised by a slight attack of the intermittent fever," or malaria, wrote Thomas Nuttall on his 1819 trip up the Arkansas River. "No medicines being at hand, as imprudently I had not calculated upon sickness, I took in the evening about a pint of a strong and very bitter concoction of the *Eupatorium* . . . This dose, though very nauseous, did not prove sufficient to operate as an emetic, but acted as a diaphoretic and gentle laxative, and prevented the proximate return of the disease."

## Hyssop-Leaved Thoroughwort, Justice-Weed

*Eupatorium hyssopifolium.* Of Eupator; hyssop-leaved.

"The entire plant is antivenomous and may be used as a remedy for bites of reptiles and insects by bruising and applying to the wound" (Jacobs and Burlage).

## Boneset

*Eupatorium perfoliatum.* Of Eupator; perfoliate.

Agueweed, Common Thoroughwort, Crosswort (Va.), Feverwort (N.C.), Indian-Sage, Joepye (N.C.), Sweating-Plant, Teasel, Thoroughgrow (Pa.), Thoroughstem, Thoroughwax, Thoroughwort, Vegetable-Antimony, Wild-Isaac (N.C.), Wild-Sage, Wood Boneset

"To one whose childhood was passed in the country some fifty years ago the name and sight of this plant is fraught with unpleasant memories. The attic or woodshed was hung with bunches of the dried herb, which served so many grewsome warnings against

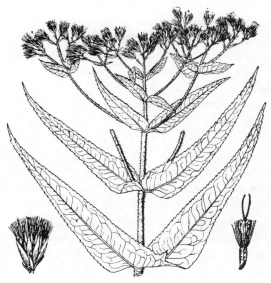

*Boneset*

wet feet, or any over-exposure which might result in cold or malaria. A certain Nemesis, in the shape of a nauseous draught which was poured down the throat under the name of 'boneset tea,' attended such a catastrophe. The Indians first discovered its virtues, and named the plant ague-weed. Possibly this is one of the few herbs whose efficacy has not been overrated. Dr. Millspaugh says: 'It is prominently adapted to cure a disease peculiar to the South, known as break-bone fever (Dengue), and it is without doubt from this property that the name boneset was derived' " (Dana, 1900). Dr. Millspaugh also noted that "there is probably no plant in American domestic practice that has more extensive or frequent use as this." It was included in both the USP and NF but probably "possesses no therapeutic virtues which are not explicable on the ground of its nauseating properties" (USD).

*Sweet Joe-Pye-Weed*

## Sweet Joe-Pye-Weed

*Eupatorium purpureum*. Of Eupator; purple.

Gravelroot, Gravelweed, Green-Stemmed Joe-Pye-Weed, Hemp-Agrimony, Indian Gravel-Root, Jopi-Root (N.C.), Jopi-Weed, Kidney-Root, Kidneywort, King-of-the-Meadow (N.H.), King-of-the-Prairie, Knotroot (D.C.), Marsh-Milkweed (Mass.), Motherwort (Mass.), Niggerweed (Ind.), Pride-of-the-Meadow, Purple Boneset, Purple Thoroughwort, Queen-of-the-Meadow (Ind., Maine, Mass.), Queen-of-the-Prairie, Quillwort (W.Va.), Skunkweed, Stinkweed, Tall Boneset, Trumpet-Weed, Turnip-weed

"Brought home a great *Eupatorium purpureum* from Miles's swamp," wrote Thoreau in August 1854. "It is ten and a half feet high and one inch in diameter; said to grow to twelve feet. The corymb, eighteen and a half inches wide by fifteen inches deep; the largest leaves, thirteen by three inches. The stem hollow throughout. This I found, to my sur-

prise, when I undertook to make a flute of it, trusting it was closed at the leaves; but there is no more pith there than elsewhere."

Manasseh Cutler called it Liver-Hemp, Honesty and Hemp-Agrimony and wrote, "Dr. Withering says, an infusion of an handful of it, vomits and purges smartly." In Britain *Eupatorium cannabinum* is Hemp-Agrimony, named for its resemblance to Hemp and its use in jaundice, for which Agrimony was a remedy. It was called Gravelroot and Gravelweed because it was "a remedy for calculi" (Bergen, 1894). "The roots and herb are diuretic, stimulant, tonic, and astringent and were used by the Indians" (Jacobs and Burlage).

## Sweet Everlasting, Catfoot, Cudweed

*Gnaphalium obtusifolium*. Woolly (Greek *gnaphallon,* a lock of wool); blunt-leaved (the lower ones).

Balsam (N.Y.), Balsam-Weed, Chafeweed, Feather-Weed (N.Y.), Field Balsam, Fragrant Life-Everlasting, Fuzzy-Guzzy (Ohio), Golden-Motherwort (N.C.),

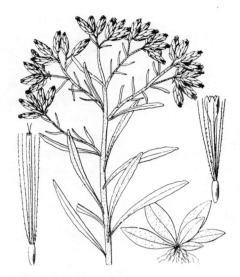

*Sweet Everlasting*

Indian-Posy (Long Island), Ladies'-Tobacco (Wis.), Life-Everlasting (New England, Ohio), Life-of-Man (N.H.), Moonshine (Vt.), None-So-Pretty, Old-Field-Balsam (New England), Owl's-Crown, Poverty-Weed (Maine), Rabbit-Tobacco (Ga., Ky.), Sweet-Balsam, Sweet Life-Everlasting, White-Balsam

August 21, 1852: "The leaves of the dogs-bane are turning yellow. There are as few or fewer birds heard than flowers seen. The red-eye still occasionally. Agrimony still. 'The dry, pearly, and almost incorruptible heads of the Life Everlasting.' Ah! this is a truly elysian flower now, beyond change and decay, not lusty but immortal,—pure ascetics, suggesting a widowed virginity" (Thoreau).

Among the Menomini, when a person has fainted, a smudge made from the leaves "is used to bring him back to consciousness again, the smoke being blown into his nostrils. Then again, when one in the family has died, his spirit or ghost is supposed to come back to trouble the living. Bad luck and nightmares will result to the family from the troublesome ghost. This smudge discourages and displeases the ghost which, after a fumigation

of the premises with this smudge, leaves and never returns" (Huron Smith, 1923).

In Georgia "a tea is made by boiling rabbit tobacco and pine twigs. Strain the tea and take a small amount every three hours, but no more than a juiceglassful in twelve hours. The plant is also smoked or used as snuff for asthma" (Bolyard, 1981). Feather-Weed was a "name given because the heads were used by poor people to fill beds, as a substitute for feathers" (Bergen, 1892).

Gerard (1633) wrote of a yellow-flowered Cudweed that it was called Golden Moth-wort because "branches and leaves laid amongst cloathes keepeth them from moths, where-upon it hath been called of some Moth-weed or Mothwort." This appears to have become Golden-Motherwort in America. "It may be called in Englishe Chafeweed; it is called in Yorkshyre Cudweede" (Turner, 1548). The soft leaves of a similar British species were used to prevent chafing and, mixed with fat, were given to cattle that had lost their cud.

## Gumweed, Tarweed, Sticky-Heads

*Grindelia squarrosa.* Of Grindel (David Hieronymus Grindel, 1776–1836, professor at Riga, Latvia); spreading (bracts).

August-Flower (Calif.), Broad-Leaved Gumplant, Curlycup Grindelia, Curlycup Gumweed, *Epinette des prairies,* Gumplant, Rosinweed (Calif., Wyo.), Scaly Grindelia, Subalpine Gumweed

"Curlycup gumweed has little forage value and is unpalatable to livestock, although sheep occasionally crop the flower heads on poor, overgrazed ranges. The leaves and flowering tops of this species and of the closely related shore gumweed *(G. robusta),* of California, are the official source of fluid extract of grindelia, a valuable spasmodic, also used because of its stimulating effect upon the mucous membrane in the treatment of chronic bronchitis and asthma. It is also used as a tonic"

*Gumweed*

(*Range Plant Handbook,* 1937). The Dakota and Ponca used it to treat colic and consumption, and the Pawnee boiled the tops and leaves to make a wash for saddle sores (Gilmore). *Epinette des prairies* was the name used by western explorer John C. Frémont, presumably the name given the plant by the Canadian voyageurs.

## Broom-Snakeweed, Turpentine-Weed

*Gutierrezia sarothrae.* Of Gutiérrez (Pedro Gutiérrez, 19th-century botanist of Madrid); like Sarothra (*Hypericum sarothra*; Greek *sarotron* means "broom").

Broomweed, Fireweed (Utah), Kindling-Weed, Lightning-Brush (Utah), Matchbrush, Matchbush (Calif.), Matchweed (Calif.), Rabbit-Brush, Snakeroot, Yellowtop

The Zuñi name for the plant means "waters gathered together," according to Matilda Stevenson (1915); "This plant is supposed to

have received its name from the Gods of War 'because they observed that it was very fond of drinking water, and drew about it waters from all directions just as the people of fraternities meet together under one roof.' A small quantity of the blossoms of this plant is steeped for a short time in boiling water and the tea given to relieve retention of urine." The plant also had a reputation as a remedy for snakebite, and the dried plants were used to make brooms. It is poisonous to livestock and now covers thousands of square miles of overgrazed range land.

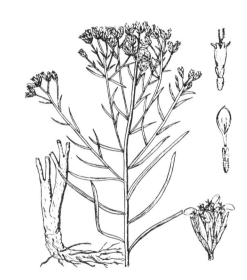

*Broom-Snakeweed*

## Sneezeweed

*Helenium autumnale.* Of Helen (the name of another plant dedicated to Helen of Troy); of autumn.

Autumn Sneezeweed, False Sunflower, Ox-Eye, Staggerwort, Swamp-Sunflower, Yellow-Star

"The American Indians used the dry, nearly mature flower heads in powdered form to sniff for colds and an infusion of the leaves as a laxative and alterative" (Jacobs and Burlage).

*Sneezeweed*

## Rosilla

*Helenium puberulum.* Of Helen; with tiny hairs.

In Mendocino County, California, "the flower heads are extremely acrid and bitter, the taste being compared by one Indian to that of 'Wizard Oil.' He remarked at the same time that they were as hot as red pepper, and stronger than whisky. As a medicine for a certain venereal complaint it is claimed to be almost specific" (Chesnut, 1902).

## Sunflowers

*Helianthus.* Sun flower.

In his *Two Voyages to New-England* (1674), John Josselyn wrote, "The plants in New-England for the variety, number, beauty, and vertues, may stand in competition with the plants of any country in Europe. Johnson hath added to Gerard's Herbal 300 and Parkinson mentioneth many more; had they been in New-England they might have found 1000 at least never heard of nor seen by any Englishman before: 'Tis true, the country hath

no Bonerets, or Tartarlambs, no glittering coloured Tuleps; but here you have the American Mary-Gold, the Earth-nut bearing a princely flower, the beautiful leaved Pirola, the honied Colibry, &c." His American Mary-Golds were the Sunflowers.

## Common Sunflower

*Helianthus annuus.* Sun flower; annual.
Comb-Flower, Gold, Golden, Larea-Bell, *Soleil* (P.Q.), *Tourne soleil* (P.Q.)

In western Montana, July 1805: "Along the bottoms, which have a covering of high grass, we observed the sunflower blooming in great abundance. The Indians of the Missouri, more especially those who do not cultivate maize, make great use of the seed of this plant for bread, or in thickening their soup. They first parch and then pound it between two stones, until it is reduced to a fine meal. Sometimes they add a portion of water, and drink it thus diluted; at other times they add a sufficient proportion of marrow grease to reduce it to the consistency of common dough, and eat it in that manner. This last composition we preferred to all the rest, and thought it at that time a very palatable dish" (Lewis & Clark).

*Common Sunflower*

Thomas Harriot (1590) wrote that in Virginia there is a "great hearbe in forme of a Marigolde, about six foote in height; the head with the floure is a spanne in breadth. Some take it to bee *Planta Solis*; of the seedes heereof they make both a kind of bread and broth." Gerard (1633) wrote that "some have called it *corona Solis,* and *Sol Indianus,* the Indian Sun-floure: others *Chrysanthemum Peruvianum,* or the Golden floure of Peru: in English, the floure of the Sun, or Sun-floure." He reported that "the buds before they be floured, boiled and eaten with butter, vineger, and pepper, after the manner of Artichokes, are exceeding pleasant meat, surpassing the Artichoke far in procuring bodily lust." The plant has been cultivated since pre-Columbian times for flour and oil from its nutritious seeds. Lareabell is an old English name.

## Maximilian's Sunflower

*Helianthus maximilianii.* Sun flower; of Maximilian (Prince Maximilian zu Wied, 1782–1867).

Prince Maximilian attained the rank of major-general in the Prussian army and then devoted himself to natural history, ethnology and exploration. He traveled in Brazil, 1815–1817, and in North America, 1832–1834, ascending the Missouri and spending the winter at Fort Clark (now Bismarck, North Dakota) with the Mandan and Minnetaree Indians. Some of his botanical observations are quoted in this book. The artist on his North American expedition was Karl Bodmer, who painted some fine landscapes and splendid portraits of Plains Indians.

## Jerusalem Artichoke

*Helianthus tuberosus.* Sun flower; tuberous. Canada-Potato, *Chiben* (P.Q.), *Chibequi* (P.Q.), Earth-Apple, *Girasole, Topinambour* (P.Q.)

*Jerusalem Artichoke*

April 9, 1805: "When we stopped for dinner the squaw went out, and after penetrating with a sharp stick the holes of the mice, near some driftwood, brought to us a quantity of wild artichokes, which the mice collect and hoard in large numbers. The root is white, of an ovate form, from one to three inches long, and generally of the size of a man's finger, and two, four, and sometimes six roots are attached to a single stalk. Its flavor as well as the stalk which issues from it resemble those of the Jerusalem artichoke, except that the latter is much bigger" (Lewis and Clark). This was the wild Jerusalem Artichoke. The "mice" were gophers or prairie dogs, both of which store the tubers. There is evidence that the Indians of the Northeast and the Mississippi Valley cultivated the plant.

In 1617 in England, John Goodyer was sent two small roots, "no bigger than hens eggs," one of which he planted and which "brought me a pecke of roots." He reported that "these rootes are dressed divers waies; some boile them in water, and after stew them with sacke and butter, adding a little ginger: others bake them in pies, putting marrow, dates, ginger, raisons of the sun, sacke, &c. Others some other way, as they are led by their skill in cookerie. But in my judgement, which way soever they be drest and eaten, they stirre and cause a filthie loathsome stinking winde within the bodie, thereby causing the belly to bee pained and tormented, and are a meat more fit for swine than men." John Parkinson (1629) disagreed: "Being put into water they are soon boiled tender, after which they be peeled, sliced and stewed with butter and a little wine, was a dish for a Queen, being as pleasant as the bottom of an Artichoke." Italian *girasole* means "sunflower" and is the source of the Jerusalem in the name. *Topinambour* is the French name (and *Topinambur* in German). The Globe Artichoke is a thistle, *Cynara scolymus*.

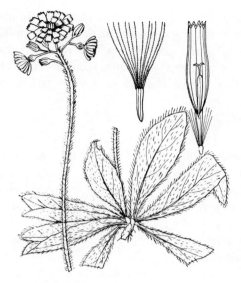

*Orange Hawkweed*

## Orange Hawkweed, Devil's-Paintbrush

*Hieracium aurantiacum*. Hawk plant (from Greek *hierax*, "hawk"; Pliny reported that hawks ate the plant to sharpen their eyesight); orange-colored. (From Europe.)

Arnica (N.Y.), Artist's-Brush (Maine), *Bouquets rouges* (P.Q.), Burmah-Weed (Maine), Devil's-Paintbrush, *Épervière* (P.Q.), Fairy's-Paintbrush, Fireweed (Maine), Flora's-Paintbrush (Maine), Golden Mouse-Ear Hawkweed, Grim-the-Collier, *Marguerite rouge* (P.Q.), Missionary-Weed (Maine), Red-Daisy, Redweed (Maine), Tawny Hawkweed, Venus's-Paintbrush (Maine)

Gerard (1633) reported that "The decoction or the distilled water of this herbe taken inwardly, or outwardly applied, conduce much to the mundifying and healing of greene wounds; for some boyle the herb in wine, and so give it to the wounded patient, and also apply it outwardly." He also noted that "the stalkes and cups of the floures are all set thicke with a blackish downe or hairinesse as

it were the dust of coles; whence the women, who keep it in gardens for noveltie sake, have named it Grim the Collier." Grim the Collier was the title of a popular comedy in 16th-century England: "The name of Grim the Collier, whereby it is called by many, is both idle and foolish" (Parkinson, 1629).

It was called Burmah-Weed in Maine "because its appearance in the region [Penobscot County] coincided with the return of a missionary" (Bergen, 1898); presumably Missionary-Weed has the same origin.

## Rattlesnake-Weed

*Hieracium venosum*. Hawk plant; veined (leaves).

Adder's-Tongue, Bloodwort, Early Hawkweed, Hawkbit, Poor-Robin's-Plantain, Robin's-Plantain, Rattlesnake-Plantain, Snake-Plantain, Striped-Bloodwort, Vein-Leaf Hawkweed

Manasseh Cutler called it Rattlesnake-Plantain and Poor-Robin's-Plantain: "It is said to have been considered by the Indians as an infallible cure for the bite of rattle-snakes.

They chewed the leaves in the mouth, and, after swallowing part of the juice, applied them to the wound." The patterned leaf must have suggested the plant's name and use. The other Robin's-Plantain is *Erigeron pulchellus*.

## Elecampane

*Inula helenium.* (The Latin name); (old generic name, for its resemblance to *Helenium*). (From Europe.)

Elfdock, Elfwort, Horse-Elder, Horseheal, Inul, Scabwort, Starwort, Velvet-Dock, Wild-Sunflower, Yellow-Starwort

Elecampane is from the Medieval Latin *enula campana*; *enula* is Pliny's *helenium* and the *helenion* of Dioscorides, a famous medicinal plant for man and his horse. The *Grete Herball* of 1526 called it Elf docke, Scabwoort and Horsehale, names that have survived in America. It was brought here by early colonists for the sake of the roots which have been included in the USP and NF, "employed by the ancients in amenorrhea and diseases of women, also in phthisis, in various bronchial catarrhs, and in skin infections, in all of

*Elecampane*

which diseases it was probably of no service" (USD).

## Lettuces

*Lactuca.* Milky (the Latin name, alluding to the juice).

*Laitue* (P.Q.), Milkweed (Maine, N.B.), Sowthistle (Wis.)

The cultivated Lettuce is *Lactuca sativa* and its many varieties. In 1699 John Evelyn wrote that Lettuce, "by reason of its *Soporiferous* quality, ever was, and still continues the principal foundation of the universal tribe of sallets." He reported that "it allays heat, bridles choler, extinguishes thirst, excites appetite, kindly nourishes, and above all represses vapours, conciliates sleep, mitigates pain; besides the effect it has upon the morals, temperance and chastity. Galen (whose beloved sallet it was) from its pinguid [fat], subdulcid [soft] and agreeable nature, says it breeds the most laudable blood. No marvel then that they were by the Ancients called *Sana,* by way of eminency, and so highly valu'd by the great *Augustus,* that attributing his recovery of a dangerous sickness to them, 'tis reported, he erected a statue, and built an altar to this noble plant." Evelyn described "a few in present use" in the London of his day; they totaled 19, "with divers more." In the 1885 report of the New York Agricultural Experiment Station, 87 varieties were described with 585 names of synonyms (Sturtevant). Culpeper reported that lettuce "abateth bodily lust, outwardly applied to the testicles with a little camphire."

Lettuce plants (including the two listed below) were sources of lactucarium, or Lettuce Opium, the dried milky sap that looks and smells like opium and was listed in the USP. "Once used to falsify opium, there is some evidence that the latex possesses some opiate qualities, at least as a sedative" (Duke, 1985).

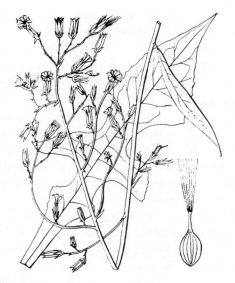

*Wild Lettuce*

## Wild Lettuce

*Lactuca canadensis.* Milky; of Canada.
Butterweed (Ohio), Devil's-Ironweed (Kans., W.Va.),
Devil's-Weed (W.Va.), Fall Lettuce, Fallweed, Fire-
weed, Florida Blue Lettuce, Horseweed (Kans.,
W.Va.), Milkweed (N.H.), Prickly Lettuce, Trumpet-
Milkweed, Trumpetweed, Trumpets, Tall Lettuce,
Wild-Opium

"The milky juice is said to possess the
properties of opium. It may be collected in
shells, dried by a gentle heat, and made into
pills" (Cutler).

## Prickly Lettuce

*Lactuca serriola.* Milky; (from the Arabic
name). (From Europe.)
Horse-Thistle, Milk-Thistle, Wild Lettuce, Wild-
Opium

"The young leaves are tender, and for that
reason it makes a very good salad plant. Some
prefer it cut in pieces with a little chopped
onion and served with French dressing. As a
potherb, it needs very litle cooking and is
excellent when served with a hot dressing of
melted butter and vinegar" (Medsger, 1939).

## Nipplewort

*Lapsana communis.* (From a Greek plant
name); common. (From Europe.)
Bolgan-Leaves, Ballogan, Dock-Cress, *Herbe aux
mamelles* (P.Q.), Succory

John Parkinson (1640) named it Nipplewort: "In Prussia they call it *Papillaris,* because it is good to heal the ulcers of the
nipples of womens breasts, and thereupon I
have intituled it Nipplewort in English." Bal-
lagan and Bolgan-Leaves are local names in
Scotland; a bolgan is a swelling.

*Nipplewort*

## Fall-Dandelion

*Leontodon autumnalis.* Lion tooth (leaves);
of autumn. (From Europe.)
Arnica (Maine, Mass.), Arnica-Bud (Mass.), August-
Flower (Nfd), Autumnal-Hawkbit, Dog-Dandelion
(Mass.), Horse-Dandelion (Nfd.), Lion's-Tooth, *Pis-
senlit* (P.Q.)

The names suggest that this was mistaken
for a species of *Arnica*; or perhaps it had the
same medicinal uses—a remedy for sprains
and bruises is made from the dried flower
heads of *Arnica montana.* The name Pissenlit
is from the Magdalen Islands, where, Marie-
Victorin wrote, "it is one of the commonest
plants, and in the nearly total absence of

*Taraxacum* [Dandelion], it has been given the name Pissenlit."

## Ox-Eye Daisy, Marguerite

*Leucanthemum vulgare.* White flower; (Common.) (From Europe.)

Bachelor's-Buttons (Lab., Nfd.), Big Daisy, Bull Daisy, Bull's-Eye (Maine, N.B., W.Va.), Bull's-Eye Daisy (N.B.), Butter Daisy, Daisy, Dog Daisy, Dog-Blow, Dutch-Curse, Dutch-Cuss (N.J.), Dutch-Morgan, Field Daisy, Goldens, Great White Ox-Eye, Herb-Margaret, Horse Daisy, Hungarian-Daisy, Kellup-Weed (Vt.), Maudlin Daisy, Maudlinwort, Midsummer Daisy, Moon Daisy, Moonflower, Moon-Penny, Pismire (Mass.), Poorland Daisy, Poverty-Weed, Rhode-Island-Clover (Vt.), Russian Daisy, Sheriff-Pink (W.Va.), White Daisy, White-Man's-Weed, White-weed

Gerard (1633) called it the "great Daisie, or Maudlin-wort. It groweth in medowes, and in the borders of fields almost everywhere." In November 1631, John Winthrop, Junior, son of the first governor of Massachusetts Bay Colony and later a colonial governor (of Con-

necticut) himself, landed in New England with seeds he had bought in London three months earlier. The bill of sale from the London merchant lists seeds for the herb and vegetable garden, including Alisander, Bassil, Burradge, Cabedg, Lettice, Radish, Rockett, and Spynadg, and some flowers, such as Cullumbine, Hollihocks, Marigold, and ½ oz. Maudlin seed for 2d (two pence) (Leighton, 1970). Maudlin is Mary Magdalen, one of the witnesses of the Resurrection, who is also identified as the harlot whom Jesus forgave (Luke 7:37). Grieve (1931) wrote that the ancients dedicated the plant "to Artemis, the goddess of women, considering it useful in women's complaints. In Christian days it was transferred to St. Mary Magdalen and called Maudelyn or Maudlin Daisy after her." She added that the plant is "Antispasmodic, diuretic, tonic. Oxe-Eye Daisy has been successfully employed in whooping cough, asthma and nervous excitability . . . In America, the root is also employed successfully for checking the night-sweats of pulmonary consumption." John Evelyn (1699) reported, "The young roots are frequently eaten by the Spaniards and Italians all the Spring till June."

Bull's-Eye, Butter Daisy, Dutch-Morgan, Moon Daisy, Moon-Penny, Poorland Daisy and Poverty-Weed are local names in England. *Herba Margarita* is *Bellis perennis.*

## Large Blazing-Star

*Liatris scariosa.* (An obscure name); scarious (thin and dry).

Blue Blazing-Star, Colicroot (Maine), Devil's-Bite (Mass.), Gay-Feather, Large Button-Snakeroot, Rattlesnake-Master

Among the Omaha, "the corm after being chewed was blown into the nostrils of horses to enable them to run well without getting out of breath. It was supposed to strengthen and help them. The flower heads mixed with

*Ox-Eye Daisy*

shelled corn were fed to horses to make them swift and put them in good condition" (Gilmore).

## Blazing-Star, Button-Snakeroot

*Liatris spicata*. (An obscure name); spiked.
Backache-Root, Button-Snakeroot, Colic-Root, Corn-Snakeroot, Dense Blazing-Star, Dense-Button-Snakeroot, Devil's-Bit, Devil's-Bite, Gay-Feather, Marsh Blazing-Star, Prairie-Pine, Rough-Root, Spiked Saw-Wort (Pa.), Throatwort

In his appendix to the *Medicina Brittanica* of 1751, John Bartram included "*Jacea,* called by some Throat-wort, because of its virtue for the cure of sore-throats." Barton (1798) wrote that "From their ignorance of botany, many persons in the western country have been using a plant which they call Lobelia [to treat gonorrhea]. I have received specimens of the plant under the name Lobelia. It proves to be the *[Liatris spicata],* or Spiked Sawwort. There is good reason to believe that it has been found useful, not only in venereal complaint, but also in cases of nephritis calculosa, or gravel. Thus ignorance sometimes leads to knowledge."

Grieve wrote that the plant is "useful for its diuretic properties and as a local application for sore throat and gonorrhea, for which it is exceedingly efficacious. Being an active diuretic it is valuable in the treatment of Bright's disease. Its agreeable odour is due to Coumarin, which may be detected on the surface of its spatulate leaves."

## Tahoka-Daisy, Tansy-Aster, Tansyleaf Spine-Aster

*Machaeranthera tanacetifolia*. Sickle anther; with leaves of Tansy.
Dagger-Flower

The Zuñi name for the plant means "flower woman," which is explained by the following legend: "Once when the Zuñi were on the warpath, several of their number, leaving the camp and cautiously approaching the Navaho, their hated enemy, found many of the warriors sleeping in a hogan. One of the Zuñi threw over the Navaho a quantity of the blossoms and delicate twigs of the plant, ground together, while others made a circle of the medicine around the hogan; then all hastened

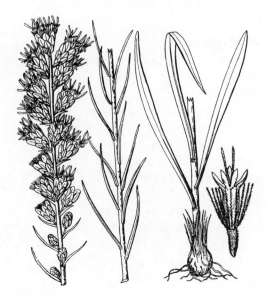

*Blazing-Star*

*Tahoka-Daisy*

back to their camp. They called their fellow warriors to arms and made an attack on the enemy. When the Zuñi gave the war-whoop on approaching the enemy's camp, the Navaho awoke and endeavored to use their arrows, but they were so weak from the effect of the medicine that they could not hold them firmly—'they were as weak and helpless as women'" (Stevenson, 1915).

## Tarweed, Mountain Tarplant

*Madia glomerata.* (From the Chilean name, *Madi*); clustered.

"This was a Cheyenne love medicine. Men often kept the dried plants; the mere aroma of it was enough to attract a woman. Men also vaporized the hot infusion and inhaled it underneath a blanket" (Hart, 1980). This is called a tarweed for its scent ("strongly and unpleasantly odorous," according to Munz and Keck).

## Scotch Thistle

*Onopordum acanthium.* Donkey flatulence (from *onos,* "donkey," *pordē,* "to break wind"; a windy plant according to Pliny); thistle (a previous generic name; Greek *akantha* is a thistle). (From Europe.)

Ass's-Oats, Cotton Thistle, Down Thistle, Musk Thistle, Oak Thistle, Queen Mary's Thistle, Scotch Thrissel, Silver Thistle.

In Scotland, during the reign of Malcolm I in the 10th century, the Norsemen, on one of their many forays of rape and pillage, made a midnight attack on Staines Castle. They stripped to swim across the moat and jumped in, but the moat was dry, filled instead with Thistles. The raiders' shrieks of pain roused the guard, and the raid was repulsed. Thus the Thistle became the national emblem of Scotland. John Bartram (1758) reported, "The Scotch Thistle is a very troublesome weed

*Scotch Thistle*

along our sea-coast. The people say, a Scotch minister brought with him a bed stuffed with thistledown, in which was contained some seed. The inhabitants, having plenty of feathers, soon turned out the down, and filled the bed with feathers. The seed coming up, filled that part of the country with Thistles."

## Wild-Quinine

*Parthenium integrifolium.* Virgin (from Greek *parthenos*; only the pistillate flowers are fertile); entire-leaved.

American Feverfew, Cutting-Almond, Nephritic-Plant (N.C.), Prairie-Dock

"It is used for inflammation of the urinary passages and kidneys, in amenorrhea, as a substitute for quinine, and as a lithontryptic [stone crusher]" (Jacobs and Burlage). Feverfew is *Tanacetum parthenium,* whose old name was *febrifuga,* "from whence I think our English names Featherfew or Feaverfew is derived, it being good to expell feavers or agues" (Parkinson, 1640).

*Western Coltsfoot*

## Western Coltsfoot, Sweet Coltsfoot

*Petasites frigidus.* Like a hat (from Greek *petasos*; the large leaves); of the cold (climate).

In Mendocino County, California, "so far as history is concerned, this plant might very appropriately be called the Yuki salt plant. Hedged in from the sea by enemies, this tribe, together with the Wailakis, formerly used the ashes of various plants, but more especially of this one, for the salt which they contain, and being essentially a herbivorous people, salt was as prime a necessity for them as it is for cows and other herbivorous animals. I was told that frequent battles were fought for the possession of a certain salt supply on Stony Creek in Colusa County. To obtain the ash the stem and leaves were first rolled up into balls while still green, and after being carefully dried they were placed on top of a very small fire on a rock and burned. It was a very acceptable ingredient for their pinole, but no kind of salt is or was ever used in their acorn bread or soup" (Chesnut, 1902). Chesnut also reported, "The young stems and leaves are used as food by the Concow . . . The root, which they call *pe'-we,* is valued medicinally in the first stages of consumption and for grippe; when dry, and coarsely grated like nutmeg, it is applied to boils and running sores to dry them up." Common Coltsfoot is *Tussilago farfara* (see page 281).

## Lion's-Foot, Gall-of-the-Earth

*Prenanthes serpentaria.* Drooping flower; of serpents (old name).

Cancerweed, Cankerweed, Earthgall, Ivyleaf, Joy-Leaf, Milkweed, Rattlesnake-Root, Snake-Gentian, Snakeweed, White Cankerweed, White Canker-Root, Wild-Lettuce

Dr. Millspaugh reported that, "as Gall-of-the-Earth, it has been known in domestic practice from an early date, and is said to be an excellent antidote to the bite of the rattlesnake and other poisonous serpents,—one who searches through the domestic literature of medicinal plants, wonders why the bite of snakes ever has a chance to prove fatal.—As an alexiteric, the milky juice of the plant is recommended to be taken internally, while

*Lion's Foot*

the leaves steeped in water, are to be frequently applied to the wound, or a decoction of the root taken."

William Byrd (1728) of Virginia wrote, "The rattle-snake has an utter antipathy to this plant, insomuch that if you smear your hands with the juice of it, you may handle the viper safely. Thus much can I say of my own experience, that once in July, when these snakes are in their greatest vigour, I besmear'd a dog's nose with the powder of this root, and made him trample on a large snake several times, which, however, was so far from biting him, that it perfectly sicken'd at the dog's approach, and turn'd its head away from him with the utmost aversion."

## Desert-Chicory, Plumeseed

*Rafinesquia neomexicana.* Of Rafinesque (Constantine Samuel Rafinesque, 1783–1840); of New Mexico.

Rafinesque was born in Constantinople of French parents and, according to his autobiography, started to collect plants at the age of 11. He arrived in Philadelphia in 1802, got a job as a merchant's clerk and in his spare time classified the bird collection of a local museum and botanized enthusiastically. He spent the period from 1805 to 1815 in Europe. Then, ambitious to write the first comprehensive flora of eastern North America, he sailed for America with books, manuscripts, drawings and plant collections but was wrecked off Block Island and lost it all. He then spent many years exploring the wilderness on foot, studying the flora and the languages and customs of the American Indians. He taught for a while at Transylvania University in Lexington, performing "with such enthusiasm and originality, using living botanical specimens to illustrate his lectures, that no one who had sat in any of his classes ever forgot him" (Leighton, 1987). He was ridiculed during his lifetime for his eccentric

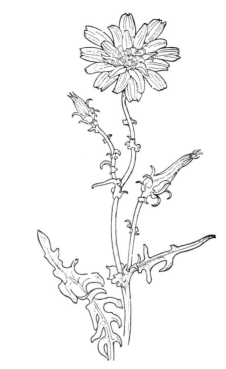

*Desert-Chicory*

manners and appearance ("I like the free range of woods and glades. I hate the sight of fences like an Indian") and what seemed to be exaggerated botanical and zoological claims; but for the past 50 years his reputation has grown, and many of his previously rejected discoveries in botany and zoology have finally been accepted. "He published a modest *Medical Flora* [quoted in this book], which must have seemed to bring him almost a full circle, and wrote an enormous poem on the whole world, which he did not sign as he intended to review it himself. Sadly he died a pauper in Philadelphia, where only the intervention of friends—come a little late— saved his body from being sold to medical students by his landlord" (Leighton). His publications also included *New Flora and Botany of North America* (four volumes, 1836–38), *Flora telluriana* (four volumes, 1837–38),

*American Manual of the Mulberry Trees* (1839) and *A Life of Travels and Researches* (1836).

## Black-Eyed-Susan

*Rudbeckia hirta.* Of Rudbeck (Professor Olaf Rudbeck, 1630–1702, and his son, Professor Olaf Rudbeck, 1660–1740, of Uppsala, Sweden); rough.

Black-Eyed-Daisy (Md.), Brown-Betty (N.J.), Brown-Daisy (Mass.), Brown-Eyed-Susan (Mass.), Bull's-Eyes (Maine), Darkey-Head, English-Bullseye (Maine), Golden-Jerusalem (N.H.), *Marguerite jaune* (P.Q.), Nigger-Daisy (Mass.), Niggerheads (Md., N.B.), Ox-Eye-Daisy (Maine, Mass.), Ox-Eye-Daisy (Maine), Poor-Land-Daisy, Poor-Man's-Daisy, Yellow-Daisy, Yellow Ox-Eye-Daisy

In 1720 John Gay wrote the ballad "Sweet William's Farewell to Black-ey'd Susan," which begins:

> *All in the Downs the fleet was moor'd,*
> *The streamers waving in the wind,*
> *When black-ey'd Susan came aboard.*
> *"Oh! where shall I my true love find!*
> *Tell me, ye jovial sailors, tell me true,*
> *If my sweet William sails among the*
> *crew."*

## Golden Ragwort

*Senecio aureus.* Old man (alluding to the hoariness of many species); golden.

Cocash-Weed, Cough-Weed, Ebbens-Root (N.Y.), False Valerian, Female-Regulator (N.C.), Fireweed, Golden-Rod, Golden Senecio, Groundsel (Lab., Nfd.), Grundy-Swallow, Life-Root, Piunkum, *Sénecon doré* (P.Q.), Snakeroot (Mass.), Squaw-Weed, Uncum (N.C.), Uncum-Piuncum, Wild-Valerian

Dr. Millspaugh reported that "Senecio has been found useful in Aboriginal medicine as an anti-hemorrhagic, abortivant and vulnerary. Later it has been recommended as a substitute for ergot, as an excellent drug to control pulmonary hemorrhage, generally as

*Golden Ragwort*

a diuretic, pectoral, diaphoretic, tonic, and a substance to be thought of in various forms of uterine trouble." "As suggested by the name 'squaw-weed,' this plant was used among the Indians as a female remedy. The Catawbas made a tea of all parts of the plant to check the pains of childbirth, to hasten the birth of the child, and for female troubles in general" (Vogel, 1970). It has been included in the NF. It was called Snakeroot "From the aromatic and bitterish flavor of the roots, like that of *Polygala Senega*" (Bergen, 1894).

## Tansy Ragwort, Horseweed

*Senecio jacobaea.* Old man; of St. James. (From Europe.)

Cankerweed, European-Ragwort, Fairies'-Horse, Felonweed, Kettle-Dock, Ragweed, St. James-Wort, Saracen's-Consound, Staggerwort, Starwort, Staverwort, Stinking-Alexanders, Stinking-Willie, Tansy

Gerard (1633) called it Saint James his Wort: "the country people do call it Staggerwort and Staver-wort, and also Rag-wort." Staggers or stavers is a cerebrospinal disease

*Tansy Ragwort*

of horses and other livestock. Parkinson (1640) wrote that "it is held to be a certain remedie to help the staggers in horses." Stinking-Willie is the Scottish name, given in memory of William, the Duke of Cumberland, "Butcher Cumberland," the English general who defeated the Scots at the battle of Culloden Moor in 1726 and then brutally suppressed Jacobitism. The weed is supposed to have entered Scotland with his army's forage. Fairies' Horse is an Irish name—Irish fairies and fairies of the Scottish Highlands and Islands rode Ragwort stalks. Keedle-Dock (Kettle-Dock in America) is from England. Saracen's-Consound is an old herbalists' name for Broad-Leaved Ragwort, *Senecio fluviatilis,* of Europe.

Saint James the Greater, one of the 12 Apostles (the other Apostle called James is known as Saint James the Less), is Santiago, whose shrine is at Compostela in Spain. He is reputed to have liberated Spain from the Moors and is thus often represented on horseback and has become the patron saint of Spain and of veterinary surgeons who used the plant as a remedy for sick or lame horses.

The plant is said to flower on his day, July 25.

## Arrowleaf Groundsel, Arrowleaf Butterweed, Arrowhead Butterweed

*Senecio triangularis.* Old man; triangular (leaves).

According to the *Range Plant Handbook,* the plant "is one of the most palatable of the species of groundsels in the western range States," and the name "Butterweed is appropriate because of the high palatability of the plant whose yellow flowers are the same color as butter."

## Groundsel, Ragwort

*Senecio vulgaris.* Old man; common. (From Europe.)

Birdseed, Chickenweed, Fleawort, Grinsel, Pigflower (Nfd.), *Séneçon* (P.Q.), *Séneçon vulgaire* (P.Q.), Squaw-Weed, Simson

Manasseh Cutler called it Stanchblood: "This plant has been found very efficacious in stop-

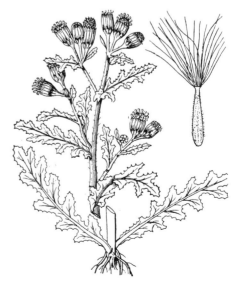

*Groundsel*

ping hemorrhages in certain persons, subject to a very singular kind of constitutional bleeding, when other means have failed. If the bleeding be occasioned by the rupture of internal blood-vessels, they drink a strong decoction of the plant: if it be external, they both drink the decoction, and apply to the wound the fresh leaves bruised, or the dried plant in form of a poultice." It has had many other medical uses in Europe.

Grieve wrote, "The name Groundsel is of old origin, being derived from the Anglo-Saxon *groundeswelge,* meaning literally, 'ground swallower,' referring to the rapid way the weed spreads. In Scotland and the north of England it is still in some localities called Grundy Swallow," a name in America applied to Golden Ragwort. It is called Birdseed because it is fed to caged birds. Chickenweed, Grinsel and Simson are local names in England.

## Compass-Plant

*Silphium laciniatum.* (The Greek name, *silphion,* of some resinous plant); slashed (leaves).

Cut-Leaf Silphium, Gumplant, Pilot-Weed, Polar-Plant, Rosinweed, Turpentine-Weed

"It is an ordinary graveyard, bordered by the usual spruces, and studded with the usual pink granite or white marble headstones, each with the usual Sunday bouquet of red or pink geraniums. It is extraordinary only in being triangular instead of square, and in harboring, within the sharp angle of its fence, a pin-point remnant of the native prairie on which the graveyard was established in the 1840s. Heretofore unreachable by scythe or mower, this yard-square relic of original Wisconsin gives birth, each July, to a man-high stalk of compass plant or cutleaf Silphium, spangled with saucer-sized yellow blooms resembling sunflowers. It is the sole remnant of this plant along this highway, and perhaps the sole

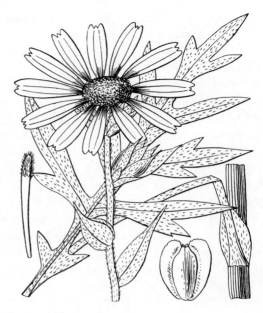

*Compass-Plant*

remnant in the western half of our county. What a thousand acres of Silphiums looked like when they tickled the bellies of buffaloes is a question never again to be answered, and perhaps not even asked" (Aldo Leopold, 1949). The basal leaves tend to point north and south, thus the name Compass-Plant.

## Cup-Plant

*Silphium perfoliatum.* (From a Greek plant name); perfoliate.

Compass-Plant, Indian-Cup, Indian-Gum, Pitcher-Plant (Kans.), Prairie-Dock, Ragged-Cup, Rosinweed

Among the Indians of the Missouri River region, "The root stock of this plant was very commonly used in the smoke treatment for cold in the head, neuralgia, and rheumatism. It was also used in the vapor bath. A Winnebago medicine-man said a decoction was made of the root stock which was used as an emetic in preparatory cleansing and lustration before going on the buffalo hunt or on any other important undertaking" (Gilmore). The two upper perfoliate leaves form a shallow cup.

## Prairie-Dock

*Silphium terebinthinaceum.* (From a Greek plant name); like turpentine.

Polar-Plant (Ind.), Prairie-Burdock, Rosin-Plant, Rosinweed

William Bartram in West Florida (1776) wrote that "the stem is usually seen bowing on one side or other, occasioned by the weight of the flowers, and many of them are broken, just under the panicle or spike, by their own weight, after storms and heavy rains, which often crack or split the stem, from whence exudes a gummy or resinous substance, which the sun and air harden into semi-pellucid drops or tears of a pale amber colour. This resin possesses a very agreeable fragrance and bitterish taste, somewhat like frankincense or turpentine; it is chewed by the Indians and traders, to cleanse their teeth and mouth."

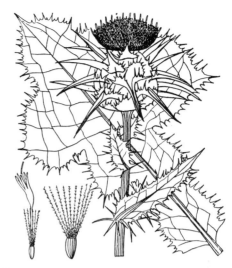

*Milk Thistle*

## Milk Thistle

*Silybum marianum.* (From Greek name, *silubon,* of some thistlelike plant); of Mary (whose milk is supposed to have fallen on the plant and veined the leaves). (From Europe.)

*Chardon-Marie* (P.Q.), Holy Thistle, Lady's-Milk, St. Mary's Thistle, Virgin-Mary's-Thistle

Evelyn (1699) called it "our Lady's milky or dappl'd Thistle" and reported that "disarm'd of its prickles, is worth esteem: The young stalk about May, being peel'd and soak'd in water, to extract the bitterness, boil'd or raw, is a very wholesome sallet, eaten with oyl, salt, and peper; some eat them sodden in proper broth, or bak'd in pies, like the Artichoak; but the tender stalk boil'd or fry'd, some prefer; both nourishing and restorative." Nursing mothers were encouraged to eat the plant. Gerard (1633) reported that the root "is the best remedy that grows against all melancholy diseases."

## Goldenrods

*Solidago.* Make whole.

Flowers-of-Gold, *Verges d'or* (P.Q.), Yellow-Tops (N.B., Pa.), Yellow-Weeds (Vt.)

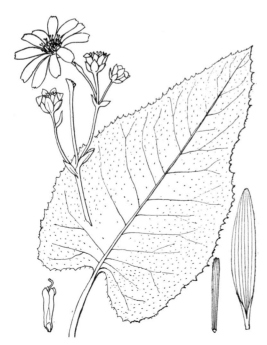

*Prairie-Dock*

"It is extolled above all other herbes for the stopping of bloud in sanguinolent ulcers and bleeding wounds; and hath in times past beene had in greater estimation and regard than in these dayes: for in my remembrance I have knowne the dry herbe which came from beyond the sea sold in Bucklers Bury in London for halfe a crowne an ounce. But since it was found in Hampstead wood, even as it were at our townes end, no man will give halfe a crowne for an hundred weight of it; which plainly setteth forth our inconstancie and sudden mutabilitie, esteeming no longer of any thing, how pretious soever it be, than while it is strange and rare. This verifieth our English proverbe, Far fetcht and deare bought is best for ladies" (Gerard, 1633).

## Silver-Rod

*Solidago bicolor.* Make whole; two-colored.
Belly-Ache-Weed (Maine), Pale Goldenrod, Silver-weed (N.Y.), Silvery-Rod, White Goldenrod (Maine)

In the Carolinas, 1705, "The Indians of these parts use sweating very much. If any pain seize their limbs, or body, immediately

*Silver-Rod*

they take reeds, or small wands, and bend them umbrella-fashion, covering them with skins and matchcoats: They have a large fire not far off, where they heat stones, or (where they are wanting) bark, putting it into this stove, which casts an extraordinary heat: There is a pot of water in the *Bagnio,* in which is put a bunch of an herb, bearing a silver tassle, not much unlike the *Aurea Virga.* With this vegetable they rub the head, temples, and other parts, which is reckon'd a preserver of sight and strengthener of the brain" (Lawson, 1709).

## Blue-Stemmed Goldenrod

*Solidago caesia.* Make whole; blue-gray.
Slender Goldenrod, Sylvan Goldenrod, Woodland Goldenrod, Wreath Goldenrod

John Bartram called it "*Virga-aurea,* or that species of Golden Rod, that is so famous for the bite of a Rattle-Snake." *Solidago virgaurea* is the common British Goldenrod (from Latin *vira,* "rod," *aurea,* "golden").

## California Goldenrod

*Solidago californica.* Make whole; of California.
*Oreja de liebre* (Calif.)

"Spanish Californians make a lotion of the boiled leaves and stems of *Solidago californica* for sores and cuts in man or beast, finishing off with a sprinkling of the powdered leaves. Their name for the species is *oreja de liebre,* jack-rabbit's ear, from a fancied resemblance in the leaf" (Saunders, 1934).

## Sweet Goldenrod

*Solidago odora.* Make whole; odorous.
Anise-Scented Goldenrod, Blue-Mountain Tea, Bohea-Tea, Fragrant Goldenrod, Sweet-Scented Goldenrod, True Goldenrod, Woundweed

"This easily known by its sweet scent near to aniseed. Essential oil of it has the same

*Sweet Goldenrod*

It is called the Hare's Thistle in the *Agnus Castus,* a 15th-century herbal: "The vertu of this herb is quanne [when] an hare is wood [mad] in somer he wele etyn of this herbe and thanne schal he ben hol." It is the Hare's Palace in the *Grete Herball* of 1526: "For yf the hare come under it, he is sure that no beast can touche him" (its Latin name was *palatium leporis*). The leaves are eaten as a salad and potherb and the root cooked. "Sow-thistle given in broth taketh away the gnaw-ings of the stomacke proceeding of an hot cause: and increaseth milk in the brests of nurses, causing the children whom they nurse to have a good colour" (Gerard, 1633). "It is reputed to contain a narcotic and has been used by the Chinese in California as an anti-opiate" (Jacobs and Burlage).

sweet scent, much used for head ache, in frictions. Whole plant aromatic, stimulant, dia-phoretic, carminative, useful in flatulence, nausea, spasms of the stomach; chiefly used as a grateful tea. Leaves prepared like tea have been sent to China, much used in some parts of our country, used in fevers by Cher-okees" (Rafinesque). Dr. Bigelow wrote, "The claims of the Solidago to stand as an article of the Materia Medica are of a humble, but not despicable kind. We import and consume many foreign drugs which possess no virtue beyond that of being aromatic, pleasant to the taste, gently stimulant, diaphoretic and carminative. All these properties the Golden Rod seems fully to possess."

## Common Sow-Thistle, Hare's-Thistle

*Sonchus oleraceus.* (From the Greek name); of the vegetable garden. (From Europe.)
Annual Sow-Thistle, Hare's-Colewort, Hare's-Let-tuce, *Laiteron potager* (P.Q.), Low-Thistle, Mary's-Seed, Milk-Thistle (Calif.), Milk-Weed, Milky-Tassel, Swinies

## Spiny Skeletonweed, Wreath-Plant

*Stephanomeria spinosa.* Crown divided (the petals); spiny.
Indian-Gumplant, Skeletonweed, Thorny Wire-Let-tuce

*Common Sow-Thistle*

This is called "big medicine" by the Northern Cheyenne Indians: "Stands-in-Timber [1967] stated that it was used in every medicine made, and that Indians could not make medicine without it. For colds, the root was pulverized and boiled; the patient enclosed himself in a blanket and trapped the vapor from the hot infusion, causing sweating; the brew was also drunk. The vapor from the boiled root was also taken as a remedy for mumps" (Hart, 1980). In Nevada "this plant is best known to the Indians for the rubber-like exudate which is collected from the stems and roots and used as chewing gum" (Train, Henrichs and Archer, 1941).

*Common Tansy*

## Common Tansy

*Tanacetum vulgare.* Immortality (from Old French *tanesie,* Medieval Latin *athanasia,* an elixir of life, Greek *athanatos,* "without death"); common. (From Europe.)

Bitter-Buttons, English-Cost, Ginger-Plant, Golden-Buttons, Hindheal, Parsley-Fern, *Tanaisie vulgaire* (P.Q.)

"The leaves are frequently used to give colour and flavour to pudding," Manasseh Cutler wrote in 1785, and "fresh meat may be preserved from the attacks of the flesh-fly, by rubbing it with this plant."

"It is connected with some interesting old customs observed at Easter time, when even archbishops and bishops played handball with men of their congregation, and a Tansy cake was the reward of the victors. These Tansy cakes were made from the young leaves of the plant, mixed with eggs, and were thought to purify the humours of the body after the limited fare of Lent. In time, this custom obtained a kind of symbolism, and Tansies, as these cakes were called, came to be eaten on Easter day as a remembrance of the bitter herbs eaten by the Jews at the Passover" (Grieve, 1931). John Evelyn found the leaves "hot and cleansing; but in regard of its domineering relish, sparingly mixt with our cold sallet." But Tansy is not for modern palates; according to the Park Seed catalog, the leaves are "used fresh as a dye, dried as an insect repellent." Bitter-Buttons, Ginger-Plant and Hindheal are local names in England. It has been included in the USP: "recommended in hysteria and amenorrhea, but is probably no longer used by physicians. The seeds are said to be effectual as a vermifuge" (USD). The USD also reports several cases of fatal poisoning from drinking Tansy tea, perhaps from its use as a supposed abortificant.

## Common Dandelion

*Taraxacum officinale.* (From the Arabic name); officinal. (From Europe.)

Blowball, Cankerwort, Dashaloga (R.I.), Doonhead Clock (N.C.), Dumbledore (Lab., Nfd.), Faceclock (Nfd.), Fortune-Teller, Horse-Gowan, Grunsel, Irish-Daisy, Lion's-Tooth, Milk-Gowan, Monk's-Head, One-O'Clock, Pee-da-Bed (New England), Pissabed (Nfd.),

*Common Dandelion*

*Pissenlit* (P.Q.), Priest's-Crown, Puffball, Swine-Snout, White-Endive, Wild-Endive, Witch-Gowan, Yellow-Gowan

John Evelyn called it Dandelion, *Dens Leonis, Condrilla:* "Macerated in several Waters, to extract the bitterness; tho' somewhat open-ing, is very wholesome, and little inferior to Succory, Endive, &c. The French country-peo-ple eat the roots; and 'twas with this homely sallet, the Good-Wife *Hecale* entertain'd *The-seus.*" (Hecale was the poor woman who gave Theseus a dish of Dandelions or Sow Thistles to eat just before he was to fight the Mara-thonian Bull.)

> Dandelion this,
> A college youth that flashes for a day
> All gold; anon he doffs his gaudy suit,
> Touch'd by the magic hand of some
>    grave Bishop,
> And all at once, by commutation
>    strange,
> Becomes a Reverend Divine.
>   From "The Village Curate" by James
> Hurdis, 1788

The plant is cultivated for the young leaves, and the roots in the fall are eaten raw or dried, roasted and ground as a coffee substi-tute. A wine is made from the flower heads. Pishamoolag is an Irish name; perhaps this became Dashaloga in Rhode Island. Irish-Daisy, Monk's-head, One-o'Clock, Priest's-Crown and Swine-Snout are local names in England and Doonhead-Clock, Horse-Gowan and Witch-Gowan in Scotland. It has been included in the USP and NF and was "sup-posed to possess cholagogic as well as di-uretic power" (USD)—thus the names Pissabed and *Pissenlit.*

## Oyster-Plant, Salsify

*Tragopogon porrifolius.* Goat beard (from Greek *tragos,* "goat," *pogon,* "beard"); with leaves of Leek *(Allium porrium).* (From Eu-rope.)

Jerusalem-Star, Nap-at-Noon (Ill.), Oyster-Root, Purple Goat's-Beard, Vegetable-Oyster

This is the cultivated Salsify whose root tastes of oysters. John Evelyn wrote that the

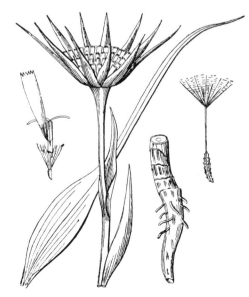

*Oyster-Plant*

roots, "tho' medicinal, and excellent against the palpitation of the heart, faintings, obstruction of the bowels, &c. are besides a very pleasant sallet; being laid to soak out the bitterness, then peel'd, may be eaten raw, or condited; but best of all stewed with marrow, spice, wine, &c. as Artichoak, Skirrets, &c. sliced or whole. They likewise may bake, fry, or boil them; a more excellent root there is hardly growing." (Skirret is a Water-Parsnip, *Sium Sisarum*.)

## Goat's-Beard, Meadow-Salsify

*Tragopogon pratensis.* Goat beard; of meadows. (From Europe.)

Buck's-Beard, Go-to-Bed-at-Noon, Joseph's-Flower, Noonflower, Noontide, Star-of-Jerusalem, Yellow Goat's-Beard

Turner (1548) called it Goat's Beard, and it was *tragopogon* to Theophrastus and Dioscorides, named for the long silky pappus. It is Joseph's Flower because Joseph, the Virgin Mary's husband, is always bearded in pictures of the Nativity (Britten and Holland). Jack-Go-to-Bed-at-Noon is the British name, because "it shutteth itself at twelve of the clock, and showeth not his face open untill the next dayes Sun doth make it flower anew. Whereupon it was called Go to bed at noone" (Gerard, 1633). "In some provinces in France, farmers determine when it is dinner hour from the closing of the Salsify involucre" (Marie-Victorin). Yellow-Goats-Beard is *Tragopogon dubius.*

## Coltsfoot

*Tussilago farfara.* For coughs (from Latin *tussis,* "cough"); the Latin name. (From Europe.)

Ass's-Foot, British-Tobacco, Bull's-Foot, Butterbur, Clayweed, Cleats, Coughwort, Dove-Dock, Colt-Herb, Dummy-Weed, Flower-Velure, Foal-Foot, Ginger, Ginger-Root (Minn.), Horse-Foot, Horse-Hoof, Hoofs, *Pas-d'âne* (P.Q.), Sow-Foot

*Coltsfoot*

"The smoke of this plant," wrote Pliny, "is said to cure, if inhaled deeply through a reed, an inveterate cough, but the patient must take a sip of raisin wine at each inhalation." Later physicians omitted the raisin wine: "Dr. Withering says, the leaves are the basis of the British herb tobacco.—They are somewhat austere, bitterish, and mucilaginous to the taste. They have been much used in coughs and consumptive complaints" (Cutler, 1785). William Wood in New England (1634) called this Pooke, perhaps in reference to its being smoked (see *Nicotinia rustica*).

William Byrd in southern Virginia, October 1728: "We observ'd abundance of Colt's foot and Maiden-hair in many places, and nowhere a larger quantity than here. They are both excellent pectoral plants, and seem to have greater vertues much in this part of the world than in more northern climates; and I believe it may pass for a rule in Botanicks, that where any vegetable is planted by the hand of nature, it has more vertue than in places whereto it is transplanted by the curiosity of man." Cleats ("beer made from the flowers is called cleats beer"—Britten and

Holland), Dummy-Weed, Hoofs and Horse-Hoof are local names in England; Dove-Dock is from Scotland. The dried leaf, called Far-fara, was included in the NF.

## Cowpen-Daisy, Añil Del Muerto

*Verbesina encelioides.* (Name was changed from Verbena); like Encelia.

Golden-Crownbeard, Goldweed, Skunk-Daisy

The plant, which smells of a cowpen, rotting meat *(añil del muerto)* or a skunk, was used by Indians to make a salve for skin ailments.

## New York Ironweed, Flat-Top

*Vernonia noveboracensis.* Of Vernon (William Vernon, fl.1680s-1710s); of New York.

Bluetop-Stickweed (Ky.), Devil's-Bit (W.Va.)

Dr. Porcher reported that "the root is used by the Negroes in South Carolina as a remedy for the bite of serpents. It is also considered by them to be aphrodisiac." In Kentucky, "to promote sweating in children, boil roots and drink the tea. For pneumonia, give a tea made with bluetop stickweed roots and black draught

tea" (Bolyard, 1981). Tall Ironweed is *Vernonia gigantea* ("gigantic"). William Vernon was an English botanist who collected plants in Maryland in 1698.

## Mule-Ears

*Wyethia amplexicaulis.* Of Wyeth (Nathaniel Wyeth, 1802–1856); stem-clasping.

Black-Sunflower, Green-Dock, Mountain Wyethia, Pik, Smooth Dwarf-Sunflower

The seeds were a source of food for the Gosiute Indians of Utah, and the "roots furnished a remedy applied externally upon bruised and swollen limbs" (Chamberlin, 1911). Pik or Pe-ik was the Indian name of the plant. Nathaniel Wyeth was born in Cambridge, Massachusetts, where his father was a member of a prominent colonial family. After graduation from Harvard College, Nathaniel became a successful ice merchant. In 1832 and 1834 he led two overland expeditions to Oregon, with the intention of establishing a commercial and agricultural colony there. The botanist Thomas Nuttall and the ornithologist John Kirk Townsend accompanied the second expedition. His western ventures were not a financial success, and Wyeth returned to his ice business.

## Clotbur, Cocklebur

*Xanthium strumarium.* (From the Greek name, *xanthion*); rough. (Also found in Europe.)

Beach-Clotbur, Butter-Bur, *Lampourde piquant* (P.Q.), Lesser-Burdock, Louse-Bur, Sea-Burdock, Sheep-Bur, Small-Burdock, Pigs (Calif.)

Gerard (1633) wrote that "it seemeth to be called Xanthium of the effect, for the Burre or fruite before it be fully withered, being stamped and put into an earthen vessel, and afterwards when need requireth, the weight of two ounces thereof and somewhat more, being steeped in warme water and rubbed

*New York Ironweed*

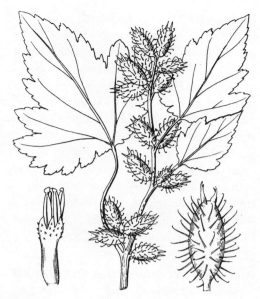

*Clotbur*

on, maketh the haires of the head red." Greek *xanthos* means yellow.

Among the Zuñi, "Seeds of the bur are ground with native squash seeds and with grains of corn that have been buried by crows and found by members of the Cactus fraternity. The grinding is done on stone slabs in the fraternity chamber. This mixture is applied externally to extract cactus needles or splinters, to heal wounds from nails, and for similar purposes. The theurgist expectorates on the wound, then on the medicine, which he applies to the wound, patting it until it adheres firmly to the flesh. He then binds on a cloth when this can be done; but in instances when the medicine is applied after a ceremony, in the performance of which the entire body has been exposed to the cactus, and no bandaging can be done, the medicine is used more freely. The officiating theurgist expectorates on the body wherever the pain indicates the presence of cactus needles, and applies the paste. The Zuñi claim that this medicine usually causes the spines or splinters to come to the surface in a day" (Stevenson, 1915).

### Little Golden Zinnia, Rocky Mountain Zinnia, Plains Zinnia

*Zinnia grandiflora.* Of Zinn (Johann Gottfried Zinn, 1727–1759); large-flowered.
Prairie Zinnia

Among the Zuñi Indians, "the entire plant is reduced to powder between stones; this is sprinkled over hot stones, beside which sits a fever patient, who inhales the fumes. This treatment is accompanied by a sweat bath, both the patient and the stones with the medicine being covered with a heavy blanket" (Stevenson, 1915). J. G. Zinn was a German botanist and physician who wrote the first book on the anatomy of the eye (1755).

# THE WATER-PLANTAIN OR ARROWHEAD FAMILY

### *Alismataceae*

A cosmopolitan family of 11 genera and 95 species of aquatic and marsh herbs; best developed in the Northern Hemisphere. *Alisma* was the Greek name. According to Dioscorides, the root of Alisma taken with wine "is good for such as have eaten a sea hare, & those who are bitten by a toad & such as have drunk opium."

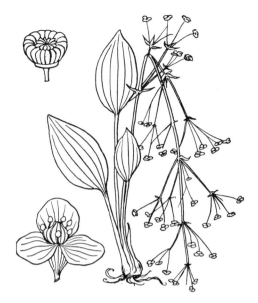

*Water-Plantain*

## Water-Plantain

*Alisma triviale.* (The Greek name); ordinary. (Also found in Eurasia.)

Deil's-Spoons, Great-Thrumwort, Mad-Dog-Weed, Scurvy-Leaves

According to John Josselyn, in New England "Water-plantane" was called "Water Suck-leaves, and Scurvie-leaves. You must lay them whole to the leggs to draw out water between the skin and the flesh." Thrumwort and Mad-Dog-Weed (the leaves were used to treat the bites of rabid dogs) are local names in England and Deil-Spoon (Deil is the Devil) in Scotland. The USD lists the plant as a "rubefacient" and the leaves were used to treat kidney and urinary tract infections. The American plants are var. *americanum.*

## Arrowheads, Swamp-Potatoes

*Sagittaria.* Arrowlike.

Adder's-Tongue, Arrowroot, Bull-Tongue (La.), Duck-Potato (Texas), *Flèche d'Eau* (P.Q.), Indian-Potato (Tex.), Wapato, White-Bull Tongue (La.)

## Engelmann's Arrowhead

*Sagittaria engelmanniana.* Arrowlike; of Engelmann (George Engelmann, 1809–1884).

George Engelmann was born in Frankfurt am Main and died in St. Louis, Missouri. He received his medical and scientific training in Germany and sailed for Philadelpia in 1832. He traveled in the South and Midwest and then settled in St. Louis, where he was a successful physician (gaining a national reputation as a gynecologist) and active botanist (in the Appalachians, the Rockies and the Pacific States). He published accounts of a variety of plants, particularly Cactaceae.

## Broad-Leaved Arrowhead, Wapato

*Sagittaria latifolia.* Arrowlike; broad-leaved.

Arrowleaf (N.Y.), Bull-Tongue (La.), Chinese-Onion (Wis.), Duck-Potato, Katniss (N.J., Pa.), *Langue de boeuf* (La.), Muskrat-Potato (Wis.), Swan-Potato, Swanroot (Calif.), Tule-Potato, Wappata, Water-Archer, Water-Lily (Mo.), Waxflower (Maine)

Lewis and Clark on Wappatoo Island (now Sauvie Island), on the lower Columbia River, 1806: "The chief wealth of this island consists of the numerous ponds in the interior abounding with the common arrowhead (sagittaria sagittifolia), to the root of which is

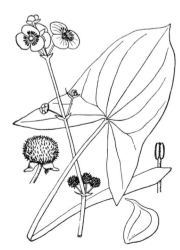

*Broad-leaved Arrowhead*

attached a bulb growing beneath it in the mud. This bulb, to which the Indians gave the name of wappatoo, is the great article of food, and almost the staple article of commerce, on the Columbia. It is never out of season, so that at all times of the year the valley is frequented by the neighbouring Indians who come to gather it. It is collected chiefly by the women, who employ for the purpose canoes from 10 to 14 feet in length, about 2 feet wide, and 9 inches deep, and tapering from the middle, where they are about 20 inches wide. They are sufficient to contain a single person and several bushels of roots, yet so very light that a woman can carry them with ease. She takes one of these canoes into a pond where the water is as high as the breast, and by means of her toes separates from the root this bulb, which on being freed from the mud rises immediately to the surface of the water, and is thrown into the canoe. In this manner these patient females remain in the water for several hours, even in the depth of winter."

Among the Blackfeet in 1845, Father De Smet wrote that the roots were "prized by the Indians, who call them Swan potatoes." Peter Kalm (1749) reported from New Jersey that "Katniss is another Indian name of a plant, the root of which they were also accustomed to eat" and that "some of the Swedes likewise ate them with much relish." The roots are also esteemed by ducks, swans and muskrats. "This is the famous wapato, wappatoo, or duck potato of the Northwestern states. It is known as Chinese onion and muskrat potato at Oshkosh, Wisconsin" (McAtee, 1913).

# THE TAPEGRASS OR FROG'S-BIT FAMILY

## *Hydrocharitaceae*

A cosmopolitan family of 16 genera and 90 species of aquatic herbs. *Hudor* is Greek for water; *kharis* is grace. "There floteth upon the upper parts of the water a small plant, which we usually call Frog-bit, having little round leaves, thick and full of juyce" (Gerard, 1633). The family is named after *Hydrocharis morsus-ranae* ("a morsel for frogs") of Eurasia.

## Eelgrass, Water-Celery

*Vallisneria americana*. Of Vallisneri (Antonio Vallisneri, 1661–1730); of America. Canvasback-Grass (Md.), *Celeri d'eau* (P.Q.), Celery-Grass (Va.), Channel-Weed, Duck-Celery (Texas), Duck-Grass, *Herbe aux anguilles* (P.Q.), *Herbe aux*

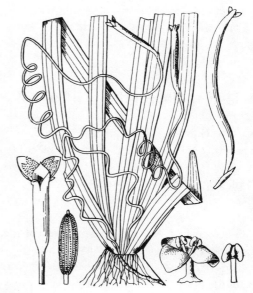

*Eelgrass*

*canards* (P.Q.), Ox-Tongue (La.), Poppy (N.Y.), Riverweed (Fla.), Sharpless, Tapegrass, Wild-Celery, Zhebes-Plantain (La.)

This is "the 'Wild or Water Celery' of Chesapeke Bay and a favorite food of the canvasback duck" (Britton and Brown, 1913). The female flowers rise on long, coiling, eel-like pedicels to the surface of the water, where they meet the tiny male plants that have just been propelled to the surface from the staminate spathes at the bottom of the pond. The male and female flowers open, pollination

occurs, and the fertilized female flowers contract their pedicels into tight spirals and sink to the bottom where the fruits ripen. Marie-Victorin wrote that "this astonishing ensemble of phenomena, one of the most beautiful poems in nature . . . has inspired the poets, among others Castel, the abbé Delille, Mistral in his immortal *Mirèio,* and Maeterlinck in *La mesure des heures.*" Zhebes is a corruption of *des herbes.* Antonio Vallisneri was professor of medicine at the University of Padua and a noted naturalist.

# THE SWEETFLAG FAMILY

## *Acoraceae*

A family of one genus and two species, the other being Asian. *Acorus calamus* is an ancient medicinal herb of Europe and Asia. The leaves were strewn on floors for their pleasant orangy scent when crushed underfoot, and "having a very grateful flavour are by some nice cooks put into sauce for fish" (Culpeper). Book Five of Walt Whitman's *Leaves of Grass* is titled "Calamus," whose parts evidently symbolize the love of male comrades.

## Calamus, Flagroot, Sweetflag

*Acorus calamus.* (The Latin name; *akoron* was the Greek name of an Iris); a reed.
Beewort, *Belle-Angélique* (Mo., P.Q.), Bitter-Pepper-Root, Calamus-Root, Calmus (N.J.), Kalamus, Myrtle-Flag, Myrtle-Grass, Myrtle-Rush, Myrtle-Sedge, Pineroot, *Redote* (P.Q.), Reed-Acorus, Sea-Sedge, Sedge-Cane, Sedge-Grass, Sedge-Rush, Swamproot (Mo.), Sweetcane, Sweet-Cinnamon, Sweet-Myrtle, Sweet-Segg, Wild-Flag (Mo.), Wild-Iris (Mo.)

The herbalist John Pechey (1694) wrote that "the root of it candied tastes very pleas-

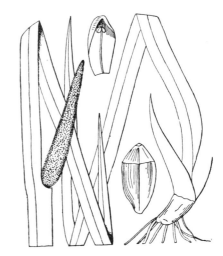

*Calamus*

antly," and in 1943 Fernald and Kinsey reported that "The making of candied flag-root was one of the few frivolities of our great-great-grandmothers. The candied roots have been much sold by Shakers and others in New England." In the 1880s Sturtevant noted that "These rhizomes are to be seen for sale on the street corners of Boston and are frequently chewed to sweeten the breath."

May 27, 1852: "The fruit of the sweet flag is now just fit to eat, and reminds me of childhood,—the critchicrotches. They would help sustain a famished traveller. The inmost tender leaf, also, near the base, is quite palatable, as children know. I love it as well as muskrats" (Thoreau). The plant is extensively cultivated for the "oil of calamus," which is extracted from the roots and used as a flavoring agent and in scents.

Among the Northern Cheyenne of Montana, "it was sometimes called 'ghost medicine,' as it had the power to ward off ghosts. A bit of the root tied to a child's necklet, dress or blanket was believed to keep night spirits away" (Hart, 1980).

In the mid-1830s in Connersville, Indiana, Thomas T. Chinn, "constable three weeks before, and barely able to write his name," became "Dr. Chinn, Root Doctor and No Calomel," as his sign proclaimed. Some months later he reported, "I lost nine fine patients last week, one of them an old lady that I wanted to cure very bad, but she died in spite of all I could do. I tried every root I could find but she still grew worse, and there being nobody here to detect my practice, like the other regular doctors I concluded to try calamus, and dug up a root about nine inches long and made a tea of it. She drank it with some difficulty, turned over in the bed and died. Still I don't think it was the calamus that killed her, as all the calamus doctors are giving it in heavier doses than I did" (from Pickard and Buley, 1946). Dr. Chinn had "No Calomel" on his sign: Calomel is mercurous chloride (or subchloride of mercury), a laxative with severe and sometimes permanent side effects that was generously prescribed by all physicians to their often reluctant patients. According to Zohary (1982), the "sweet calamus" or "sweetcane" of the Bible is Ginger-Grass, *Cymbopogon martinii*.

---

# THE ARUM OR CALLA FAMILY

## *Araceae*

A family of 105 genera and about 2,950 species of herbs, shrubs and climbers; found chiefly in tropical and subtropical regions. *Aron* was the Greek name. *Calla* is evidently derived from Greek *kallaia* (cock's wattles), which is perhaps related to *kalos* (beautiful). Pliny claimed that Aron "dissipates the effects of drunkenness. The fumes arising from it when it burns keeps away serpents, especially asps, or make them so tipsy they are found in a state of torpor." The "Calla Lily" of the florist is a species of *Zantedeschia* from South Africa.

## Dragonroot, Green-Dragon, Dragon-Arum

*Arisaema dracontium*. Arum blood (i.e., related to Arum or a blood-red Arum); (the Greek name of an Arum).

American Wake-Robin, Dragon-Tail, Edderwort, Jack-in-the-Pulpit

"The Menomini Indians called it 'owl's foot' and used it to treat female disorders. Among other Indians the root is often found in sacred bundles, where it is thought to give the owner the power of supernatural dreams" (Plowman, 1969). Edder is an adder.

*Jack-in-the-Pulpit*

## Jack-in-the-Pulpit, Indian-Turnip

*Arisaema triphyllum.* Arum blood; three-leaved.

Adam's-Apple, Bog-Onion (Maine, Mass.), Brown-Dragon, Cooter-Wampee, Cuckoo-Pint, Cuckoo-Plant, Devil's-Ear, Dragonroot (Mass.), Hopnis, Indian-Cherries (Texas), Indian-Cradle (N.Y.), Iroquois-Breadroot, Lady-in-a-Chaise (Mass.), Lords-and-Ladies, Marsh-Turnip, Memory-Root (Mass.), *Oignon sauvage* (P.Q.), Parson-in-the-Pulpit (South), *Petit prêcheur* (P.Q.), Pepper-Turnip, Plant-of-Peace (southern Negro), Preacher-in-the-Pulpit, Priest's-Pintle, Starchwort, Swamp-Cherries (Texas), Swamp-Turnip, Thrice-Leaved-Arum, Thrice-Leaved Indian-Turnip, Tuckahoe, Wake-Ribin, Wake-Robin, Wampee (S.C.), Wild-Pepper, Wild-Turnip (Vt.)

The cooked or dried fruit and peppery root were important foods for Indians and early settlers. The spathe curves over the erect spadix like a canopied pulpit. Jack-in-the-Pulpit, Lords-and-Ladies, Wake-Robin (the common name of a Trillium in America) and Cuckoo-Pint and Priest's-Pintle (pint, pintle = penis) are British names for the very similar *Arum maculatum* of Europe. William Cole, who was the English apostle of the doctrine of signatures, wrote in 1657 that, "It hath not only the signature [the erect spadix] which will sufficiently declare itself but the virtues also according to the signature, for they are notable for stirring up of the inclination to copulation."

Dr. Millspaugh reported that "The corms, when fresh, especially, and all parts of the plant, have a severely acrid juice, imparting an almost caustic sensation to the mucous membranes, and swelling of the parts when chewed. This action upon the mouths of school-boys, who often play the trick of inviting bites of the corm upon each other, gave rise to the common name, 'memory-root,' as they never forget its effects." Jonathan Carver (1768) called it Wake Robin and reported that the root, when dried, "loses its astringent quality and becomes beneficial to mankind, for if grated into cold water and taken internally, it is very good for all complaints of the bowels." According to Virgil Vogel (1970), Pawnee Indians dusted the powdered root on top of the head and on the temples as a cure for headache, and Ojibwa and Menomini Indians used the root for treating sore eyes. Hopnis is Seneca for the root of this and Groundnut (*Apios americana*). The USD lists it as a "stimulant to the secretions, especially in asthma, whooping cough, and rheumatism."

Starch was obtained from the roots of this and *A. maculatum,* "the most pure and white starch," according to Gerard (1633), "but most hurtful to the hands of the Laundresse that hath the handling of it"; and fashionable gentlemen complained of the neck rash produced by the starched ruffs.

## Water-Arum, Wild Calla

*Calla palustris.* (The Greek name); of marshes. (Also found in Eurasia.)

Female-Dragon, Female Water-Dragon, *Gouet des marais* (P.Q.), Swamp-Robin, Water-Dragon, Water-Lily

The acrid rootstock and seeds are dried or cooked and ground into flour. Female-Dragon is a name from the old herbals.

## Yellow Skunk-Cabbage

*Lysichiton americanum.* Unfasten frock (from Greek *lusi, khitōn;* the spathe is shed); of America.

Yellow-Arum

The Kathlamet Indians of Western Washington tell a story about the Yellow Skunk-Cabbage: "In the ancient days, they say, there were no salmon. The Indians had nothing to eat save roots and leaves. Principal among these was the skunk cabbage. Finally the spring salmon came for the first time. As they passed up the river a person stood upon the shore and shouted: 'Here come our relatives whose bodies are full of eggs. If it had not been for me all the people would have starved.' 'Who speaks to us?' asked the salmon. 'Your uncle, skunk cabbage,' was the reply. Then the salmon went ashore to see him, and as a reward for having fed the people, skunk cabbage was given an elk-skin blanket and a war club, and was set in the rich, soft soil near the river. There he stands to this day wrapped in his elk-skin blanket and holding aloft his war club" (Gunther, 1973). The Indians roasted or dried the root from which they prepared a flour and cooked the young leaves as a potherb. Bears eat the whole plant, including the roots.

## Golden-Club

*Orontium aquaticum.* Of the Orontes (a river in Syria that gave its name to a plant in classical Greece; "ardent" Orontes was one of Aeneas's companions in the *Aeneid*); aquatic.

Bog-Torch, Bull-Tongue (Ga.), Fireleaf, Floating-

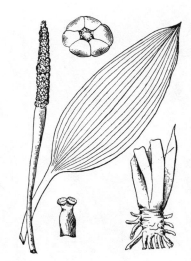

*Golden-Club*

Arum, Never-Wets, Tawkee (N.J., Pa.), Tawkin, Tuckahoe, Water-Dock

The waxy leaves shed water instantly and thus are never wet. The Indians boiled and ate the thick starchy roots or pounded them into flour and, according to Kalm (1749) in New Jersey, used the seeds "instead of bread; and they taste like peas. Some of the Swedes likewise ate them; and the old men among them told me, they liked this food better than any of the other plants which the Indians formerly made use of."

## Arrow-Arum, Green-Arrow, Tuckahoe

*Peltandra virginica.* Shield stamen (i.e., its shape); of Virginia.

Arrow-Weed (Mich.), Breadroot, Cruel-Man-of-the-Woods (southern Negro), Duck-Corn, Green-Arum, Hog-Wampee (S.C.), Poison-Arum, Taw-ho, Tawkee (N.J., Pa.), Tuckahoo (N.C.), Virginia Wake-Robin

Captain John Smith reported of the Indians in Virginia that "The chief root they have for food is called *Tockawhoughe.* It groweth like a flagge in low muddy freshes. In one day a

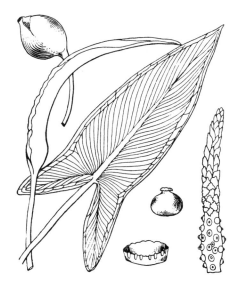

*Arrow-Arum*

Savage will gather sufficient for a week. These roots are much of a greatness and taste of Potatoes. They use to cover a great many of them with oke leaves and fern, and then cover all over with earth in the manner of a colepit; over it, on each side, they continue a great fire 24 hours before they dare eat it. Raw it is no better than poison, and being roasted, except it be tender and the heat abated, or sliced and dried in the sun, mixed with sorrell and meal or such like, it will prickle and torment the throat extreamely, and yet in sommer they use this ordinarily for bread." *Taccaho* is Algonquian for various edible roots.

The fruits of this and Jack-in-the-Pulpit were called Ocoughtanamins (Strachey, 1612), Cuttanimmons (Beverley, 1705) or "Sacquenummener, a kinde of berries almost like unto capers but somewhat greater which grow together in clusters upon a plant or herb that is found in shallow waters; being boiled eight or nine hours according to their kind are very good meat and holesome, otherwise if they be eaten they will make a man for the time frantick or extremely sick" (Harriot, 1590).

In 1748, according to John Bartram, "the savages boiled the spadex and the berries of this flower and devoured them as a great delicacy" (from Kalm).

## Water-Lettuce

*Pistia stratiotes.* Watery; solider (name used by Dioscorides for an Egyptian water plant). (Also found in Africa and Asia.)

Pondweed, Water-Bonnets (Fla.), Water-Houseleek

In 1774 William Bartram wrote that the vast floating islands of Water-Lettuce on the St. John's River in Florida "present a very entertaining prospect; for although we behold an assemblage of the primary productions of nature only, yet the imagination seems to remain in suspence and doubt; as in order to enliven the delusion and form a most picturesque appearance, we see not only flowering plants, clumps of shrubs, old weather-beaten trees, hoary and barbed, with the long moss waving from their snags, but we see them compleatly inhabited, and alive, with crocodiles, serpents, frogs, otters, crows, herons, curlews, jackdaws, &c. There seems, in short, nothing wanted but the appearance of a wigwam and a canoe to complete the scene." The former masses of Water-Lettuce seen by Bartram on the St. John's have been replaced by Water-Hyacinth, introduced from the tropics in 1884.

The whole plant and particularly the young leaves are eaten. The burnt plant is used as a substitute for salt.

## Skunk Cabbage

*Symplocarpus foetidus.* Fused fruit (the ovary); fetid. (Also found in East Asia.)

Bear's-Foot, Bear's-Leaf, Bear's-Root, Byron-Blad (N.J.), Byron-Ritter (N.J.), *Chou puant* (P.Q.), Clumpfoot-Cabbage, Collard, Cow-Collard, Dracontium, Fetid-Hellebore, Irish-Cabbage, Meadow-Cabbage, Midas-Ears, Parson-in-the-Pillory (South),

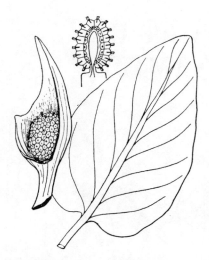

*Skunk Cabbage*

Poke, Pokeweed, Polecat-Weed, Polkweed (Mass.), Rockweed, Skunkweed, Stink-Cabbage, Swamp-Cabbage, *Tabac du diable* (P.Q.)

In 1723 Thomas More sent a package of botanical specimens from Boston to the botanist William Sherard in London. It included "a pod with a seed enclosed which the natives call Skunkroot because of his stinking smell; the Indians call him Poke or Smoak because they smoak it when they want tobacco, and ere the knowledge of Rum was brought among them by the Christians they used to make a fuddling drink of it at their gambols and merry making." He also reported that "I dryd & smoakt some on't but it stunk so wretchedly as to make me spew; but the Indians have a way of dressing it so as to make it less hideous."

The name Collard is colewort, a name for any plant of the cabbage kind. Midas, the fabled king of Phrygia whose touch turned all to gold, was given ass's ears by Apollo for being bored by his lyre-playing. Byron-Blad and Byron-Ritter are from Swedish names; in 1749 Kalm reported from Raccoon, now Swedesboro, New Jersey, that "the Swedes call it björnblad (bear's leaf) or björnrötter (bear's root) . . . from the fact that the bears, when they leave their winter quarters in spring, are fond of it."

Kalm also reported, "Dr. Colden told me that he had employed the root in all cases where the root of the arum is used, especially against the scurvy, etc." This is Cadwallader Colden (1688–1776), colonial administrator (lieutenant governor of New York, 1761–1766), historian (*The History of the Five Indian Nations,* 1727), physician (University of Edinburgh, 1705) and botanist who classified the plants around his New York estate for Linnaeus. The botanist Jane Colden (1724–1776) was his daughter. According to Manasseh Cutler (1785), "Scunk cabbage . . . is given in the fit, and repeated as the case may require. This knowledge is said to have been obtained from the Indians." Jonathan Carver reported (1768) that a lotion prepared from the root "is made use of by the people in the colonies for the cure of the itch." The leaves are a potherb, and the acrid starchy rhizome was a source of flour for the Indians and was once used as a "nerve sedative in whooping cough, hysteria, etc." (USD).

# THE SPIDERWORT OR DAYFLOWER FAMILY

## Commelinaceae

A widespread family of 42 genera and 620 species of herbs found chiefly in tropical and subtropical regions. The family was named after the Dutch botanists Johan (1629–1692) and his nephew Caspar (1667–1731) Commelijn, who are represented by the two large petals, and Caspar's son, represented by the small lower petal since he died young "before accomplishing anything in botany" (Linnaeus).

## Western Dayflower, Birdbill-Flower

*Commelina dianthifolia.* Of the Commelijns; with leaves of Dianthus.

The plant was considered an aphrodisiac by the Navaho Indians: "For aged men, women, or stud animals. Infusions are drunk" (Wyman and Harris). An infusion of the pulverized roots was given to rams in the breeding season to increase fertility and to ewes if twin lambs were desired (Vestal).

## Spiderworts

*Tradescantia.* Of Tradescant (John Tradescant, fl.1608–1637).
Indian-Paint (Wis.), Moses-in-the-Bulrushes (Fla.), Twelve-o'Clock (Ky.)

The plant is called Spiderwort either because the sap from the broken stem forms filaments like a spider's web or the angular leaf arrangement suggests a squatting spider. It was called Indian-Paint because "the juice is said to irritate the skin and make it red" (Bergen, 1896). John Tradescant visited Archangel in 1618 and sailed on Sir Robert Max-

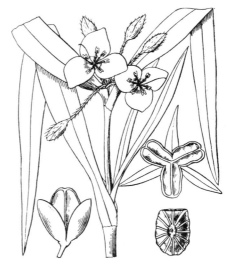

*Spiderwort*

well's 1620 expedition against the dreaded Barbary pirates. He then settled in Lambeth and established a celebrated garden and museum and became gardener to Charles I. His son John Tradescant the Younger (1608–1662) was collecting plants in North America in 1637 when his father died and he returned to succeed him as royal gardener.

## Spiderwort

*Tradescantia virginiana.* Of Tradescant; of Virginia.
Flower-of-a-Day, Job's-Tears, Snake-Grass, Spider-Lily (La., N.Y.), Trinity, Trinity-Lily, Virginia Spiderwort, Widow's-Tears

The three-petaled flower lasts only one day, like a widow's tears. John Parkinson (1629) called it "the soon fading Spider-wort of Virginia, or Tradescant his Spider-wort. This Spider-wort is of late knowledge, and for it the Christian world is indebted unto that painfull industrious teacher, and lover of all nature's varieties, John Tradescant."

# THE CATTAIL FAMILY

## *Typhaceae*

A cosmopolitan family of one genus and 10 to 12 species of aquatic and marsh herbs. *Tuphe* was the Greek name.

Julia Morton (1975) has reviewed the many human uses of Cattails: The stems and leaves are made into fans in Guatemala; burial shrouds and sandals in Peru; rafts on Lake Titicaca; chair seats in New York; dolls and toys for Chippewa children; thatch, screens and barrel caulking in Africa; spear handles in Queensland; rope in the Philippines; bedding in Bermuda; and mats, pads, baskets, slippers and socks in New Zealand. The woolly seed heads are used for quilts and diapers, torches, pillows, mattresses, upholstery and filling for baseballs and life-jackets. Much of the plant is eaten—the flower spikes, raw or boiled, in North America and Africa; the pollen and seeds in New Zealand, India, China, Iraq and North America; and the tender blanched heart, Cossack-Asparagus, by the Cossacks of the Don Valley. Also, in Russia, the root is "a common source of alcohol." Cattails are also an important source of food for wildlife.

## Common Cattail, Reedmace

*Typha latifolia.* (From the Greek name); broad-leaved. (Also found in Eurasia and North Africa.)

Blackamoor, Blackcap, Bubrush, Bulrush, Bull-Segg, Candlewick, Cat-o'Nine-Tails, Cattail-Flag, Cooper's-Reed, Cossack-Asparagus, Deer-Marsh-Grass

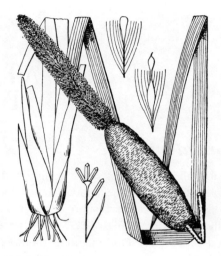

*Common Cattail*

(Texas), Flag-Grass (La.), Flag-Tule, Flatgrass (N.C.), Flat-Rush (La.), Flaxtail, Fox-Tail, Great Reedmace, Indian-Leek (Texas), Indian-Onion (Texas), *Jonc matelas* (La.), *Jonc plat* (La.), Marsh-Beetle, Marsh-Pestle, *Massette* (P.Q.), Nail-Rod, *Quenouille* (P.Q.), *Queue de chat* (La.), *Queue de rat* (La.), *Queue de renard* (P.Q.), Water-Torch

"Typha groweth in fennes & water sydes among the reedes; it hath a black thing almost at the head of the stalk lyke black velvet. It is called in English Cattes tayle or a Reedmace" (Turner, 1548). The flowering spike, shaped like a mace (the weapon) or a beetle (a type of pestle), blackens with age.

In 1749 in New Jersey, Peter Kalm reported, "Its leaves are here twisted together, and formed into great oblong rings, which are put upon the horse's neck, between the mane and the collar, in order to prevent the horse's neck from being hurt by the collar. Formerly the Swedes employed the down which surrounds its seeds and put it into their beds instead of feathers." On Cape Cod, "At the Pond Village we saw a pond three eighths of a mile long densely filled with cat-tail flags, seven feet high—enough for all the coopers in New England" (Thoreau, 1864). The leaves were twisted into bands to hold barrels together (Cooper's-Reed). Tule (pronounced too-ly) is a western Bulrush *(Scirpus)*. Blackamoor, Blackcap and Candlewick are local names in England and Bull-Segg in Scotland (segg is sedge).

# THE WATER-HYACINTH FAMILY

## *Pontederiaceae*

A widespread family of seven genera and 31 species of aquatic and semiaquatic herbs; found chiefly in tropical and subtropical regions. Giulio Pontedera (1688–1757) was a professor at Padua, Italy. One infamous member of the family, and a pestilential weed in many waterways, is Water-Hyacinth *(Eichornia crassipes)*.

## Pickerelweed

*Pontederia cordata*. Of Pontedera (Giulio Pontedera, 1688–1757); heart-shaped (leaves). Alligator-Wampee (S.C.), Black-Potato (La.), Blue-Bull-Tongue (La.), Cooter-Wampee (S.C.), Cow-Wampee (S.C.), Dog-Tongue, Dog-Tongue-Wampee (S.C.), *Glayeul bleu* (P.Q.), *Langue de boeuf* (La.), Moose-Ear (Maine, N.B.), Pickerel-Plant, Tuckahoe, Wake-Robin, Water-Hyacinth, Wild-Gentian (S.C.)

"These plants were called *Wampi* by the Indians and the seeds eaten by them. They are now called Pickerelweed in the Northern States" (Rafinesque). In Britain a pickerel is a young pike, whose "feeding is usually of fish or frogs and sometimes a weed of his own called Pickerel-weed" (Izaac Walton,

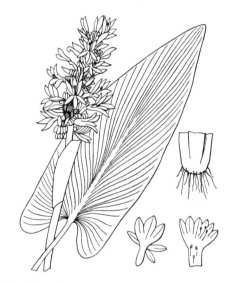

*Pickerelweed*

1676). Walton noted that some believed that some pickerel were bred from Pickerelweed, that it "both breeds and feeds them; but whether those Pikes so bred will ever breed by generation as the others do, I shall leave to the disquisitions of men of more curiosity and leisure than I profess myself to have." The ripe seeds are eaten or ground to make flour. A cooter is a fresh-water terrapin, which eats the leaves.

# THE LILY FAMILY

## Liliaceae

A widespread family of 294 genera and 4,500 species of herbs and a few shrubs; most abundant in temperate to tropical regions. Lily in Latin is *lilium*, in Greek *leirion*, in Persian *laleh*. Celtic *li* means "white."

## Stargrass, Colicroot

*Aletris farinosa*. The slave who ground the corn in Greek households; floury.

Ague-Grass, Ague-Horn, Ague-Root, Aloeroot, Backache-Root, Bettie-Grass, Bitter-Grass, Bitter-Plant, Blackroot, Blazing-Star, Crow-Corn, Devil's-Bit, False Unicorn-Root, Huskroot (Mass.), Husk-wood, Huskwort, Mealy-Starwort, Miller's-Maid, Rheumatism-Root, Star-Root, Starwort, True Unicorn-Root, Unicorn, Unicorn-Horn, Unicorn-Root, White-Tube-Stargrass

"Known by the name of Stargrass or Colic-root; the last name from its being considered an excellent remedy in this disease" (Pursh, 1814). Dr. Porcher reported that, "infused in vinegar, it is given in intermittent fever. The decoction of the root and leaves in liberal doses is much employed in popular practice in the lower portions of South Carolina." The tapering raceme of white flowers, which seem to be dipped in flour, resembles a unicorn's horn. In 1904 Henkel of the U.S. Department of Agriculture classified this as the "false" and *Chamaelirium luteum* as the "true" Unicorn-Root.

In 1856 Thoreau visited Martha Simons, the only pureblooded Indian left near New Bedford, Massachusetts: "The question she answered with the most interest was, 'What do you call that plant' and I reached her the aletris from my hat. She took it, looked at it a moment, and said, 'That's husk-root. It's good to be put into bitters for a weak stomach.' The last year's light-colored and withered leaves surround the present green stem like a husk. This must be the origin of the name. Its root is described as intensely bitter. I ought to have had my hat full of plants." Jacob Bigelow included it in his *American Medical Botany*. He wrote of its "genuine, intense, and permanent bitterness" and proposed that it "may hereafter become an article of more consequence in the Materia Medica." Subsequently, it was used for "expelling flatulence" and to treat "various uterine disorders" (USD).

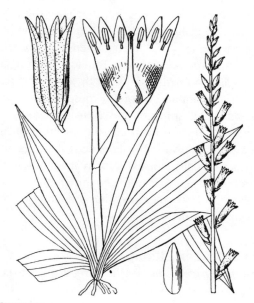

*Stargrass*

## Wild Garlic

*Allium canadense*. Garlic; of Canada.

Canada Garlic, Meadow Garlic, Meadow-Leek, Meadow-Shallot, Onion-Tree, Rose-Leek, Wild-Onion

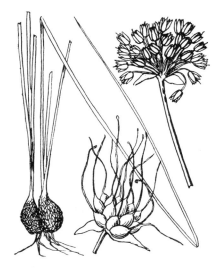

*Wild Garlic*

In *The American Gardener's Calendar* of 1830, Bernard M'Mahon wrote, "The *Allium canadense,* or tree onion, merits culture both as a curiosity in producing onions at the top of the stalk, as well as for their value in domestic use, particularly for pickling, in which they are excellent, and superior in flavor to the common kind; they may also be used for any other purposes that onions are."

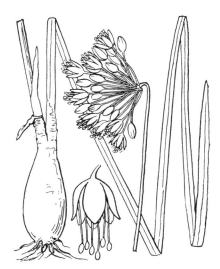

*Wild Onion*

## Wild Onion, Nodding Wild Onion

*Allium cernuum.* Garlic; nodding.
Chicago, Lady's-Leek

On an island on the upper Missouri: "Here we found great quantities of a small onion about the size of a musket-ball, though some were larger; it is white, crisp, and as well flavoured as any of our garden onions; the seed is just ripening, and as the plant bears a large quantity to the square foot, and stands the rigours of the climate, it will no doubt be an acquisition to settlers. From this production we called it Onion Island" (Lewis and Clark, 1805).

## Prairie Wild Onion

*Allium textile.* Garlic; woven (the fibrous outer coat of the bulb).

At Fort Clark (Fort Mandan, North Dakota), April 1834, Prince Maximilian wrote that he was "in a hopeless condition, and so very ill, that the people who visited me did not think that my life would be prolonged beyond three or, at the most, four days." The fort's cook, a Negro from St. Louis, diagnosed scurvy and recommended "the green herbs in the prairie, especially the small white flowering [*Allium textile*] . . . I was advised to make trial of this recipe, and the Indian children accordingly furnished me with an abundance of this plant and its bulbs: these were cut up small, like spinage, and I ate a quantity of them. On the fourth day the swelling of my leg had considerably subsided, and I gained strength daily. The evident prospect of speedy recovery quite reanimated me, and we carried on with pleasure the preparations for our departure."

## Wild-Leek, Ramp

*Allium tricoccum.* Garlic; three-lobed (fruit).
*Ail des bois* (P.Q.), *Ail sauvage* (P.Q.), Lance-Leaved Garlic, Ramp-Scallions (South), Three-Sided Leek

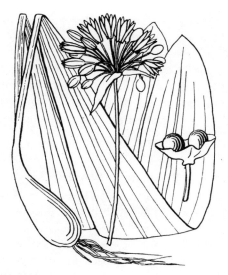

*Wild-Leek*

"April is ramp eating season in West Virginia, when the pungent smell of the wild leeks permeates every hill and hollow. 'They're synonymous with spring,' says Jim Comstock, editor of the West Virginia Hillbilly. 'Ramps go with changing the oil or your underwear'" (Burros, 1986). Ramps, from Old English *hramas* (garlic), is a local name in England, Scotland and Ireland for the similar *Allium ursinum,* Ramsons being the British name. Gerard (1633) wrote that the leaves of Ramsons "may very well be eaten in April and Maye with butter, of such as have a strong constitution, and labouring men."

## Field Garlic

*Allium vineale.* Garlic; of the vineyard. (From Europe.)

Crow Garlic, Jamestown-Grass, Rush-Leek, Scallion, Stag's Garlic, Wild Garlic

"Crow Garlick is greatly loved by the horses, cows, and sheep, and is very wholesome early pasture for them; yet our people generally hate it, because it makes the milk, butter, cheese, and indeed the flesh of those cattle that feed much upon it taste so strong that we can hardly eat of it; but for horses and young cattle, it doth very well" (John Bartram, 1758). Crow Garlic is the British name: "A leek fit for crows distinguishes the wild and useless and harmful leek from the 'spear leek' of the garden" (Grigson). Garlic is derived from Old English *gar,* "spear," plus leek; the cultivated Garlic, *Allium sativum,* has a long spathe pointed like a spear.

John Evelyn (1699) wrote of Garlic that "tho' both by Spaniards and Italians, and the more southern people, familiarly eaten, with almost everything, and esteem'd of such singular vertue to help concoction, and thought a charm against all infection and poyson (by which it has obtain'd the name of the Country-man's Theriacle) we yet think it more proper for our northern rustics, especially living in uliginous and moist places, or such as use the sea: Whilst we absolutely forbid it entrance into our salleting, by reason of its intolerable rankness, and which made it so detested of old; that the eating of it was (as we read) part of the punishment for such as had committed the horrid'st crimes. To be

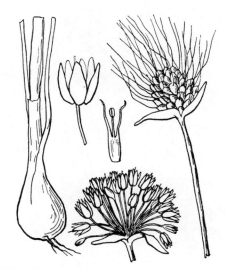

*Field Garlic*

sure, 'tis not for ladies palates, nor those who court them, farther than to permit a light touch on the dish, with a clove thereof."

## Fly-Poison

*Amianthium muscaetoxicum.* Unspotted flower; flies-poisonous.

Crow-Poison (N.C.), Fall-Poison (N.C.), Hellebore, Puppy-Tails, St. Elmo's-Feather (South), Stagger-Grass

In North Carolina, 1842, Asa Gray reported that the plant, "which is common in the low country of the southern States, we here found only in the rich open woods of the Bluff Mountain, and in similar places further south. The flowers are pure white or cream-color, in a dense and very showy raceme, at length turning to green. The cattle which roam in the woods for a great part of the year are sometimes poisoned by feeding, as is supposed, on the foliage of this plant during the autumn: hence its name of Fall-poison." The name Stagger-Grass indicates that livestock get the "staggers," a cerebrospinal disease,

from eating the plant. "The bulbs when mixed with honey or syrup make an excellent fly poison" (Jacobs and Burlage, 1958). Saint Elmo or Erasmus, martyred under Diocletian in 303, is the patron saint of sailors. St. Elmo's fire or light is the electrical discharge sometimes seen on mast tops or mountain peaks before or during a thunderstorm.

## Harvest Brodiaea, Cluster-Lily

*Brodiaea coronaria.* Of Brodie (James Brodie, 1744–1824, Scottish botanist); crowned.

Fool's-Onion, Large-Flowered Brodiaea

The round corms, raw or cooked, were a favorite food of the Indians and early settlers of the Pacific Northwest. Archibald Menzies, surgeon and botanist on the *Discoverer,* Captain Vancouver's ship, reported in May 1792 that on Restoration Point, Puget Sound, "a few families of Indians live in very mean huts or sheds formed of slender rafters & covered with mats. Several of the women were digging on the point, which excited my curiosity to know what they were digging for & found it to be a little bulbous root of a liliacious plant, which on searching about for the flower of it, I discovered to be a new genus of the Triandria monogina [i.e., *Brodiaea*]" (from Clark, 1976).

## Sego-Lily

*Calochortus nuttallii.* Beautiful grass (from Greek *kallos,* "beautiful," *chortos,* "grass"); of Nuttall (Thomas Nuttall, 1786–1859).

Butterfly-Tulip, Mariposa-Lily (Mont.), Nuttall's Calochortus, Nuttall's Mariposa-Lily, Prairie-Lily (Mont.), Star-Tulip

This is the state flower of Utah. The bulbous root is sweet and nutritious and can be eaten cooked or raw or ground into a meal, as the Indians did. Sego is Shoshone for any edible bulb. "It is reported that when the Mormon pioneers in Utah faced famine con-

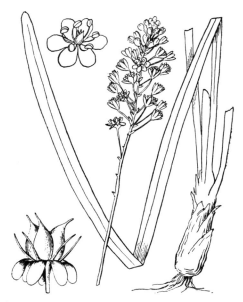

*Fly-Poison*

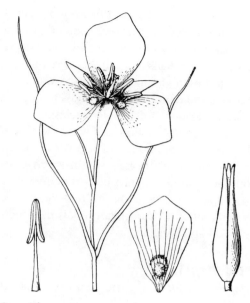

*Sego-Lily*

ditions in 1848–49 due to inroads of crickets, drought, and frost on their grain fields, the sego-lily was an outstanding means of tiding them over" *(Range Plant Handbook).*

## Globe-Tulip, Mount Diablo Mariposa-Lily

*Calochortus pulchellus.* Beautiful grass; little pretty.

Among the Indians of Mendocino County, California, "the corms are small, being only occasionally as large as one's thumb, but they are easily gathered in considerable quantity. They are eaten raw or are roasted in the ashes for about an hour" (Chesnut, 1902). The Yokia name means "deer potato" and the Pomo name "forest potato."

## Common Camas

*Camassia quamash.* (The Latinized American Indian name); (the Indian name).

Indian-Potatoes, Swamp-Sego

Lewis and Clark (1805) among the Nez Percés: "They now set before them a small

*Common Camas*

piece of buffalo-meat, some dried salmon, berries, and several kinds of roots. Among the last is one which is round, much like an onion in appearance, and sweet to the taste. It is called quamash, and is eaten either in its natural state, or boiled into a kind of soup, or made into a cake which is then called a pasheco. After the long abstinence this was a sumptuous treat. They returned the kindness of the people by a few small presents, and then went on." The root was an important part of the diet of the Northwest Indians and of the trappers and settlers. Charles F. Saunders wrote that "white settlers, in the days before their orchards and gardens were established, found in Camas a welcome addition to their meager and monotonous bill of fare, and Camas pie was a not uncommon dish in many an old time Oregon or California household."

In 1854 Father de Smet was among the Flatbow Indians of Montana. He wrote, "I cannot pass over in silence the Camas root, and the peculiar manner in which it is prepared. It is abundant, and, I may say, is the queen root of this clime. It is a small, white, vapid onion, when removed from the earth, but becomes black and sweet when prepared for food. The women arm themselves with long crooked sticks to go in search of the Camas. After having procured a certain quantity of these roots, by dint of long and painful labor, they make an excavation in the earth from twelve to fifteen inches deep, and of proportional diameter, to contain the roots. They cover the bottom with closely cemented pavement, which they make red hot by means of a fire. After having carefully withdrawn all the coals, they cover the stones with grass or wet hay; then place a layer of Camas, another of wet hay, a third of bark overlaid with mold, whereon is kept a glowing fire for fifty, sixty, and sometimes seventy hours. The Camas thus acquires a consistency equal to that of the jujube." Saunders described the product as "soft, dark brown in color, and sweet—almost chestnutty. The cooked mass, if pressed into cakes and then dried in the sun, may be preserved for future use."

Camas roots were the cause of the Bannock War of 1878. By treaty, the Bannock and Paiute Indians had retained the right to dig camas roots on the Camus Prairie, 100 miles south-

east of Fort Boise, Idaho. But white ranchers introduced hogs, which were soon despoiling this rich source of one of the Indians' staple foods. The Indians first threatened the settlers, and then violence erupted. A war party of about 200 Bannocks and Paiutes under the Bannock leader Buffalo Horn clashed with volunteers, and Buffalo Horn was killed. Regular troops mobilized out of Fort Boise chased the Indian force through southeastern Oregon and southern Idaho until they met in a major battle fought at Birch Creek on July 8. By September all the Indian rebels had been defeated and were in prison.

## Wild-Hyacinth

*Camassia scilloides.* (The Latinized Native American name); like *Scilla*.
Atlantic Camas, Eastern Camas, Indigo-Squill, Meadow-Hyacinth, Quamash

Hyacinth (usually meaning a *Hyacinthus* species) is apparently derived from a pre-Greek word having to do with the color of the sea. In mythology, Hyacinths sprang either

*Wild-Hyacinth*

from the blood of the beautiful youth Hyakin-thos when he was accidentally killed by his lover Apollo or from the blood of the brave Greek warrior Ajax; and thus the petals are supposed to be inscribed with the words *AI, AI* (Alas, alas.)

## Blazing-Star, Devil's-Bit, Fairy-Wand

*Chamaelirium luteum*. Dwarf lily; yellow (apparently describing the original shriveled specimen, for it is not dwarf and bears white flowers).

Angel's-Wand, Colicwort, Drooping-Starwort, False-Unicorn, Grubroot, Rattlesnake-Root, Squirrel-Tail, True Unicorn-Root

In John Bartram's appendix to the *Medicina Britannica,* printed by Benjamin Franklin in 1751, he wrote of "Blazing Star, as it is called by the back [country] inhabitants, by others, Devil's-bit, both fanciful names . . . This precious root is a great resister of fermenting poisons, and the previous pains of bowels, taken in powder, or the root bruised and steeped in rum."

*Blazing-Star*

The thick and abrupt tuberous rhizome of Chamaelirium is another Devil's Bit, originally a name for Scabious, *Succisa pratensis:* "It is commonly called *Morsus Diaboli,* or Divils bit, of the root (as it seemeth) that is bitten off. For the superstitious people hold opinion that the divell for envie that he beareth to mankinde bit it off, because it would be otherwise good for many uses" (Gerard, 1633). The dried rhizomes, called Helonias (the plant was formerly *Helonias scabiosa*), were supposed to have a "tonic action upon the uterus and used in amenorrhea, dysmenorrhea, and leukorrhea" (USD).

## Soap-Plant, Amole

*Chlorogalum pomeridianum.* Green milk (sap); of the morning.

California Soap-Plant, Soaproot, Wavy-Leaf Soap-Plant

Among the Pomo Indians of Mendocino County, California, "After the last June freshet, when the river was running very low, all of the inhabitants of a village or of several neighboring rancherias would assemble together at some convenient place on the river. The squaws were each provided with a quantity of the fleshy bulbs, which they deposited in a common heap and proceeded to mash up on the rocks. A weir 6 to 7 feet high had in the meantime been constructed by the men by driving willow sticks into the river bed and then lashing them together by means of redbud bark. Bushel after bushel of the crushed pulp was thrown into the water and thoroughly stirred in. Much of the finer material passed through the weir; the larger pieces were again taken out and again crushed and thrown into the water. The Indians, stationed all along the stream for 3 miles or so, added fresh bulbs here and there and kept the water in a state of thorough agitation. After a very short time all of the fish, and also

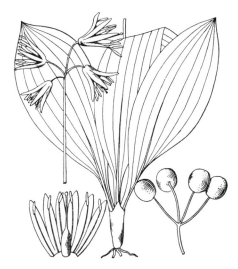

*Bluebead Lily*

*Soap-Plant*

the eels, but not the frogs, were so stupefied by the poison that they floated to the surface and were quickly captured, either by hand or by the use of a shallow, coarse-meshed basket" (Chesnut, 1902). The bulb was also crushed and used as a soap by many Indian tribes and by the early Spanish settlers (Spanish *amole,* from the Nahuatl *amol(li),* means "soap").

### Bluebead Lily, Clintonia, Cornlily

*Clintonia borealis.* Of Clinton (De Witt Clinton, 1769–1828); of the north.

Balsam-Bell (South), Bead-Lily, Bearberry (Maine), Bear-Plum (N.H.), Bear-Tongue, Bear's-Corn (Maine), Bluebead-Lily, Blueberry (Nfd.), Calf-Corn (Maine), Canada-Mayflower (N.H.), Clinton's-Lily, Cornflower (Maine), Cow-Tongue (Maine, N.B.), Dogberry (Maine), Dragoness-Plant, Heal-All (Mass., N.B.), Hound's-Tongue (Maine), Northern-Lily (Maine), Poison-Berries (Nfd.), Wild-Corn (Maine), Wild Lily-of-the-Valley (Maine, Mass.), Wood-Lily, Yellow Clintonia, Yellow Wood-Lily

It bears bright blue tasteless berries. "The very young leaves of this plant are extensively used as a potherb by country people in parts of Maine under the name Cow Tongue" (Fernald and Kinsey, 1943).

De Witt Clinton was born in Little Britain, New York, and died in Albany. He was educated at Columbia College and in 1795 became secretary to his uncle, George Clinton, governor of New York. He was elected to the state senate in 1798, became mayor of New York City in 1803 (for the first of three terms), served again as state senator from 1806 to

1811 and was lieutenant governor from 1811 to 1813. He was the presidential candidate for the Peace Party in 1812 but lost to James Madison. He was elected governor of New York for two terms (1817 to 1823) and then again in 1825 and served until his death. In addition to his interests in politics, public improvements (he was responsible for the construction of the Erie Canal), education, the conditions of the poor and the abolition of slavery, he also wrote books on natural history.

## Lily-of-the-Valley

*Convallaria majalis.* Of the valley; of May. (From Europe.)

Conval-Lily, Lady's-Tears, May-Blossoms, May-flower, May-Lily, *Muguet* (P.Q.,), Pack-Lily, Wood-Lily

In European folklore, these lilies sprang from Our Lady's tears as she wept at the foot of the Cross or from Mary Magdalene's tears when she found Christ's tomb empty. Gerard (1633) wrote that "it is called in English Lillie of the Valley, or the Conval Lillie, and May Lillies, and in some places Liriconfancie." The root, which "exerts an effect upon the heart very similar to digitalis" (USD), contains a cardiac glycoside called convallotoxin and is still included in some European pharmaco-peias. The flowers "have a delightful odor, resembling that of musk, and when dried and powdered are much employed as a sternu-tatory, acting sometimes quite violently" (Porcher).

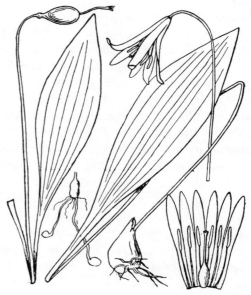

*Trout-Lily*

## Trout-Lily, Adder's-Tongue, Fawn-Lily, Dogtooth-Violet

*Erythronium americanum.* Red (from the Greek name of an Orchid); of America.

Adderleaf, *Ail doux* (P.Q.), Amberbell, Chamise-Lily, Common Fawn-Lily (Pa.), Cornflower (Maine), Deer's-Tongue (Ind.), Easter-Lily (Kans.), Fawn-Lily, Jonquil (Maine), Lamb's-Tongue (N.C.), Lillette, Rattlesnake-Violet, Scrofula-Root, Serpent's-Tongue, Snakeleaf, Snakeroot, Star-Strikers, Trout-Flower (N.Y.), Wild Yellow-Lily (Maine), Yellow

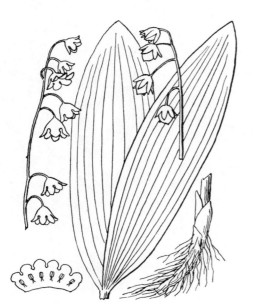

*Lily-of-the-Valley*

Adder's-Tongue, Yellow Bastard-Lily, Yellow-Bells (Mass., N.J.), Yellow-Hookers, Yellow-Lily (Vt.), Yellow-Snowdrop

"How it came to be called 'adder's tongue' I do not know; probably from the spotted character of the leaf, which might suggest a snake, though it in no wise resembles a snake's tongue. A fawn is spotted too, and 'fawn lily' would be better than adder's tongue. Still better is the name 'trout lily' which has been recently proposed. It blooms along the trout streams, and its leaf is as mottled as a trout's back" (John Burroughs, 1894). The adder's tongue is surely the protruding stamens.

Dodoens wrote that the names of the European species were "*Denticulus* and *Dens canis,* others call it *Satyrion Erythronium,* wherewithal notwithstanding it has no similitude." And wherewithal notwithstanding, Linnaeus called the genus *Erythronium.* The bulbs of the European *Erythronium denscaninus* are like a dog's teeth. The leaves and juice of Trout-Lily have had many medical uses (it was once included in the USP), and the young bulbs are eaten, raw or cooked. Chamise (from the Spanish *chamiso*) is more commonly the western *Lilium rubescens.* "We have had from Virginia a root sent unto us that we may well judge, by the form and colour thereof being dry, to be either the root of this, or of an orchis, which the naturall people hold not only to be singular to procure lust, but hold it a secret, loth to reveal it" (Parkinson, 1629). In 1672 Josselyn called it "Yellow-bastard daffodil."

## Yellow Trout-Lily, Yellow Fawn-Lily

*Erythronium grandiflorum.* Red; large-flowered.

Adam-and-Eve (Calif.), Adder's-Tongue, Chamise-Lily (Calif.), Dogtooth-Violet, Glacier-Lily, Snow-Lily, Yellow Avalanche-Lily

The bulbs were cooked by the Indians or dried for winter use and are prized by bears

and rodents. The green pods are grazed by elk, deer, sheep and Rocky Mountain goats.

## Glacier Trout-Lily, Glacier Fawn-Lily, Avalanche-Lily

*Erythronium montanum.* Red; of the mountains.

Adder's-Tongue, Alpine Fawn-Lily, Dogtooth-Violet, Fawn-Lily, Glacier-Lily, Snow-Lily, White Avalanche-Lily

The bulbs were an important food for Northwest Indians: "A Shuswap family might

*Glacier Trout-Lily*

harvest up to 200 lbs/90 kg a year, which they cooked and ate immediately or threaded and hung to dry for winter use" (Ward-Harris).

## Oregon Trout-Lily, Oregon Fawn-Lily, Easter-Lily

*Erythronium oregonum.* Red; of Oregon.

Dogtooth-Violet, White Fawn-Lily, White Trout-Lily

In California, "the Wailakis use the crushed corm as a poultice for boils and have a peculiar superstition that if they wash themselves with a decoction of it they can stop a rattlesnake from having dreams, which, they say, make them more irritable and dangerous" (Chesnut, 1902).

## Kamchatka Mission-Bells

*Fritillaria camschatcensis.* Like a dicebox (the checkered flowers); of Kamchatka (a peninsula on the Bering Sea).

Black-Lily, Eskimo-Potato, Indian-Rice, Northern Rice-Root, Sarana

"The bulbs, found an inch or two below the surface, resemble a cluster of cooked rice grains. They are, in fact, good sources of starches and sugars, and since prehistoric times have been dug in the fall, dried and powdered for winter use. David Nelson, botanist on the *Resolution,* visited 'Kamtschatka' in 1778 (shortly before Captain Cook's murder in 1779) and found the natives eating the bulbs of a plant with flowers of 'an exceeding dark red colour,' now thought to be the present species" (Clark, 1976). The bulbs ("rice-roots") of many Fritillaries were a valuable food source for Indians, Eskimos and early explorers and are eagerly sought by small mammals.

## Canada Lily, Meadow Lily, Wild Yellow Lily

*Lilium canadense.* Lily (the Latin name); of Canada.

Bitter-Root, Canadian Martagon, Field Lily (N.Y.), Mountain Lily, Nodding Lily (N.Y.), Yellow Bell-Lily

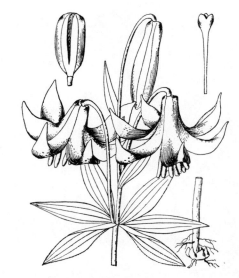

*Canada Lily, Meadow Lily*

On the Penobscot River in Maine, July 1857, Thoreau and his Indian guide "saw a splendid yellow lily *(Lilium canadense)* by the shore, which I plucked. It was six feet high, and had twelve flowers, in two whorls, forming a pyramid, such as I have seen in Concord. We afterward saw many more thus tall along this stream, and also still more on the East Branch, and, on the latter, one which I thought approached nearer to the *Lilium superbum.* The Indian asked what we called it and said that the 'loots' (roots) were good for soup, that is, to cook with meat, to thicken it, taking the place of flour. They get them in the fall. I dug some, and found a mass of bulbs pretty deep in the earth, two inches in diameter, looking and even tasting somewhat like raw green corn on the ear." John Parkinson (1629) called this "*Martagon Canadense maculatum.* The spotted Martagon of Canada."

## Leopard Lily, Pine Lily

*Lilium catesbaei.* Lily; of Catesby (Mark Catesby, 1683–1749).

Catesby's Lily, Showy Lily, Southern Red Lily

Mark Catesby was born in Essex, England and died in London. On two trips to America,

*Leopard Lily*

he collected flora and fauna in Virginia, 1712–1719, Jamaica, 1715, and in Carolina, Florida and the Bahamas, 1722–1726. He then returned to London and for the next 20 years wrote and illustrated his *Natural History of Carolina, Florida and the Bahama Islands,* published in two volumes from 1730 to 1747, "the most outstanding work on the natural history of the British possessions in North America published before the American revolution" (Frick and Stearns, 1961).

## Carolina Lily

*Lilium michauxii.* Lily; of Michaux (André Michaux, 1746–1802).

André Michaux was born in Versailles, France and died on a botanical expedition to Madagascar. Asa Gray wrote in 1844 that "the foundation of the North American Sylva was laid by the laborious researches of the elder Michaux; who, under the auspices of the French government, devoted ten years, from 1785 to 1796, to a thorough exploration of the country, from the sunny, sub-tropical groves of Florida to the cold and inhospitable shores of Hudson's Bay; repeatedly visiting nearly all the higher peaks and deepest recesses of the Alleghany Mountains, and extending his toilsome journeys westward to the prairies of Illinois and the banks of the Mississippi." His study of American oaks was published in 1801 and the *Flora Boreali-Americana* in 1803. His son François André Michaux (1770–1855) accompanied him on his North American travels and made further extensive explorations in 1801–1802 and 1807. "Having thus faithfully collected the requisite information, his great work upon our forest trees—the fruit of so much labor—was published at Paris in 1810–13." This was the *Histoire des Arbres Forestières de l'Amérique Septentrionale,* translated as *The North American Sylva.*

## Wood Lily, Rocky-Mountain Lily

*Lilium philadelphicum.* Lily; of Philadelphia. Fire-Lily, Flame Lily, Freckled Lily (Maine), Glade Lily (W.Va.), Huckleberry Lily, Mouse-Root, Orange-Cup Lily, Philadelphia-Martagon, Prairie Lily (Wis.), Red Lily, Rocky-Mountain Lily, Tiger Lily (N.J.), Wild Orange-Red Lily, Wild Tiger Lily

## Turk's-Cap Lily

*Lilium superbum.* Lily; superb. American Martagon, Jack-in-the-Pulpit (Pa.), Lily Royal, Nodding Lily (Mass.), Martagon, Supen's Lily, Swamp Lily, Turk's-Head (Mass.), Wild Nodding-Lily, Wild Tiger-Lily (Minn.)

In New England, Josselyn (1672) found "Mountain-Lillies, bearing many yellow flowers, turning up their leaves like the *Martagon,* or Turks Cap, spotted with small spots as deep as Safforn." The flower of the European *Lilium martagon* resembles a *martagan,* a special kind of turban worn by the Ottoman sultan of Turkey. Mark Catesby reported that "the Indians boiled these Martagon-Roots, and esteemed them dainties."

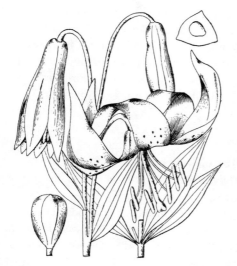

*Turk's-Cap Lily*

## Canada Mayflower, Wild Lily-of-the-Valley

*Maianthemum canadense.* May flower; of Canada.

Bead-Ruby (N.Y.), Cowslip (Maine), Dwarf Solomon's-Seal, Elf-Feather, False Lily-of-the-Valley, Heartleaf, Lily-of-the-Valley (N.H.), *Muguet* (P.Q.), One-Blade, One-Leaf, Ruby-Bead, Scurvy-Berries, Solomon's-Plume, Tobacco-Berries (Nfd.), Two-Leaved Solomon's-Seal (N.H.)

## False Solomon's-Seal, False Spikenard

*Maianthemum racemosa.* May flower; race-mose.

Clustered Solomon's-Seal, Feather Solomon's-Seal, Golden-Seal (N.C.), Jacob's-Ladder (Maine), Job's-Tears (N.Y.), Snake-Corn (Mass.), Solomon's-Feathers (South), Solomon-Plume, Solomon's-Zigzag, Spiked Solomon's-Seal, Tobacco-Berry (Nfd.), Treacle-Berry (Mass.), Wild-Spikenard, Wood-Lily (Mass.)

It is called "false" since it has none of the magical or medicinal properties of the "real" Solomon's-Seal or Spikenard. In 1672 John

Josselyn wrote of "*Treacle Berries,* having the perfect taste of treacle when they are ripe; and will keep good a long while; certainly a very wholsome berry, and medicinable." And William Wood in 1634 called the plant "trea-cle-beries." Since the use of "treacle" to mean molasses is not reported until 1694 (*Oxford English Dictionary*) and elsewhere Josselyn wrote of "molosses," he and Wood probably meant the earlier treacle (theriac, theriacle), a widely used antidote against poison and the plague; many of the concoctions of theriac contained herbs, honey and snake venom or flesh. The berries' taste is quite sweet but medicinal. June 18, 1857, Cape Cod: "Reached the Highland Light about 2 p.m. The Smila-cina is *just* out of bloom on the bank. They call it the 'wood lily' there. Uncle Sam called it 'snake corn,' and said it looked like corn when it first came up" (Thoreau). A previous name was *Smilacina racemosa.* The rootstock is soaked in lye and then cooked or pickled for a relish. Job's-Tears is a local name in England for Solomon's-Seal.

*False Solomon's-Seal*

Among the Ojibwa Indians: "1. Warm decoction of the leaves used by lying-in women. 2. The roots are placed upon a red-hot stone, the patient, with a blanket thrown over his head, inhaling the fumes to relieve headache. 3. Fresh leaves are crushed and applied to cuts to stop bleeding" (Hoffman, 1891).

## Indian Cucumber-Root

*Medeola virginiana.* Of Medea (the mythical sorceress); of Virginia.

Cushat-Lily (South), *Concombre sauvage* (P.Q.), *Jarnotte* (P.Q.)

"I seem to perceive a pleasant fugacious fragrance from the rather delicate but inconspicuous green flowers. Its whorl of leaves of two stages are the most remarkable. I do not perceive the smell of cucumber in its roots" (Thoreau, 1852). The white tuber, a food and medicine for the Indians, tastes of cucumber and was "at one time used as a diuretic in dropsies" (USD). "Several of our harmless wild flowers have been absurdly named out of the old mythologies," wrote John Bur-

roughs (1894); this "is named after the sorceress Medea and is called 'medeola,' because it was at one time thought to possess rare medicinal properties, and medicine and sorcery have always been more or less confounded in the opinion of mankind." A cushat is a pigeon.

## Bunchflower

*Melanthium virginicum.* Dark flower; of Virginia.

Blackflower, Quaffidilla, Quaffodil

Manasseh Cutler (1785) used the name Quaffidilla; this and Quaffodil appear to be American inventions. The roots and stems are poisonous to livestock, and the root has been used as a fly and crow poison and to kill intestinal parasites. The flower turns black with age.

## Bog-Asphodel

*Narthecium americanum.* Little rod (Greek *narthīs* was the tall plant with a pithy stem in which Prometheus carried the spark of fire from heaven to earth); of America.

Moor-Grass, New Jersey Bog-Asphodel, Rosa-Solis, Yellow-Asphodel, Yellow-Grass

Asphodel is a Lily of southern Europe *(Asphodeline* or *Asphodelus)* and the flower that grew in the Elysian Fields of Greek mythology.

## Star-of-Bethlehem

*Ornithogalum umbellatum.* Bird milk; umbelled. (From Europe.)

Bethlem-Star, Chinkerichee, Dove's-Dung, Eleven-O'Clock-Lady, Nap-at-Noon, Sleepy-Dick, Snowdrops (Ky.), Starflower, Summer-Snowflake, Ten-O'Clock-Lady

Dioscorides named it *ornithogalon (ornis,* "bird," *gala,* "milk") because the flowers

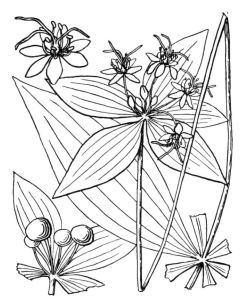

*Indian Cucumber-Root*

*Star-of-Bethlehem*

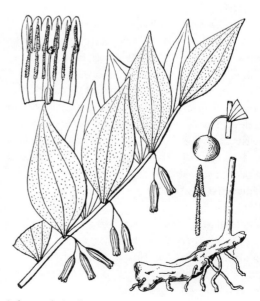

## Solomon's-Seal, Smooth Solomon's-Seal

*Polygonatum biflorum.* Many joints (the rhizome); two-flowered.

Conquer-John (Mo.), Drop-Berry, John-the-Conqueror-Root (Ala., La.), Lady's-Seal, Lily-of-the-Valley Vine (Texas), St. Mary's-Seal, *Sceau-de-Salomon* (P.Q.), Sealwort, Wild Lily-of-the-Valley (Maine)

"Dioscorides writeth that the roots are excellent good for to seale or close up greene wounds being stamped and laid thereon: whereupon it was called *Sigillum Salomonis,* of the singular vertue that it hath in sealing, or healing up wounds, broken bones, and such like. Some have thought it took the name *Sigillum,* of the marks upon the roots: but the first reason seemeth to me more probable." Gerard (1597) is here writing of the European *Polygonatum multiflorum.* He also wrote, "The root of Solomons Seale stamped while it is fresh and greene, and applied, taketh away in one night, or two at the most, any bruise, blacke or blew spots gotten by falls or womens wilfulnesse, in

"being opened they are like milk." It is "dove's dung" in Hebrew and Arabic—perhaps the blotchy appearance of a mass of the white flowers suggests bird droppings. "Dove's dung" was sold as a food for a large sum during the siege of Samaria (2 Kings 6:25), and "the plants are still familiar to Muslim pilgrims because a flour manufactured from the dried bulbs is part of their diet en route to Mecca" (Whittle and Cook, 1981). John Evelyn (1699) reported that "the Ornithogalons roasted as they do chestnuts, are eaten by the Italians, with oyl, vineger and pepper." The edible spring shoots of the European *Ornithogalum pyrenaicum* are known as Bath-Asparagus in Britain. Nevertheless, Kingsbury (1964) notes that sheep and cattle have been poisoned by the bulbs and children by the flowers and bulbs. Presumably drying or cooking makes them harmless. Chinkerichee, the name of a cultivated South African species, is of unknown origin. The flowers do not open until late morning and shut early, particularly on a cloudy day.

*Solomon's-Seal*

stumbling upon their hasty husbands fists, or such like." The root of *P. biflorum* is a powerful Voodoo "conjure" in Alabama (Carmer, 1934), and Louisiana (Hurston, 1935) and no doubt elsewhere. "Ah totes mah Big John de Conquerer wid me. And Ah sprinkles mustard seed round mah door every night before Ah goes tuh bed" (Hurston). The boiled young shoots are eaten and the dried rootstock ground for flour.

## Twisted-Stalk, White Mandarin

*Streptopus amplexifolius.* Twisted foot; stem-clasping-leaved.

Claspleaf Twisted-Stalk, Liverberry (Maine), Scootberry, Pagoda-Bells, Watermelon (Alaska)

The flower stalk twists under the leaf. The name Liverberry is "from the supposed medicinal value of the cathartic fruit, which is freely eaten by children wherever the Streptopus grows" (Bergen, 1894). The berries' taste is said to be like cucumber, despite the Alaskan name of Watermelon.

## Pink Mandarin, Rose Twisted-Stalk

*Streptopus roseus.* Twisted foot; rosy.

Jacob's-Ladder (Maine), Liverberry (Maine), *Rognons de coq* (P.Q.), Rose-Bellwort, Rose Mandarin, Scootberry (N.H.), Solomon's-Seal

"*Streptopus roseus* I learned to call Scootberry long before I understood why it was so called. The sweetish berries were quite eagerly eaten by boys, always acting as physic, and as the diarrhea was locally called 'the scoots,' the plant at once received the name" (Hayward, 1891).

## Trilliums, Wake-Robins

*Trillium.* Three whorl (leaves).

Benjamin (N.B.), Birthroot, Bethroot, Corn-Lily (Mich.), Mooseflower (N.Y.), Much-Hunger (Maine), Three-Flowered Nightshade, *Trille* (P.Q.), Wood-Lily

*Pink Mandarin*

In 1830 Constantine Rafinesque announced, "I have pleasure to introduce this fine genus into the Materia Medica. It has been neglected by all our writers, although well known to our herbalists." He reported that Trilliums were "a popular remedy in the Northern States, and used also by the Shakers. The roots are the officinal parts; almost all the species may be used indifferently, although the Indians have a notion that those with red blossoms (which they call male) are the best, and those with white blossoms (called female) are best for women's complaints."

Wake-Robin, a name applied to many spring flowers (in Britain particularly to an Arum), alludes perhaps to the danger of rousing the goblin Robin Goodfellow if the flower is picked or to the plant's reputation as an aphrodisiac ("a use of Robin as a pet name for the penis," Grigson): "They have eaten so much Wake Robin, that they cannot sleep for love" (John Lyly, 1602). Birthroot refers to the plant's use in childbirth: bath, beth, bett = birth. In

Cooperstown, New York, Susan Cooper (1850) wrote that "botanists call them all Trilliums, and a countrywoman told me, the other day, they were all 'moose flowers.'" Fernald and Kinsey (1943) reported that "the young, unfolding plants of Trilliums are eaten as greens by country people in Franklin County, Maine, under the name of 'Much hunger.'"

## Nodding Trillium

*Trillium cernuum.* Three whorl; nodding.
Benjamin, Coughroot, Drooping Trillium, Ground-Lily, Indian-Shamrock, Jewsharp-Plant, Rattlesnake-Root, Snakebite, Stinking-Willie, Wake-Robin, White-Benjamin (Maine)

Benjamin is a corruption of benjoin or benzoin, for the ill scent of the flowers.

## Purple Trillium, Red Trillium, Wake-Robin, Stinking-Benjamin

*Trillium erectum.* Three whorl; erect.
Bathflower, Bathroot (Mass.), Benjamin (Maine, Mass., N.B., N.H., Vt.), Bethroot, Birthroot (N.Y.), Bloody-Nose, Brown-Beth, Bumblebee-Root (New

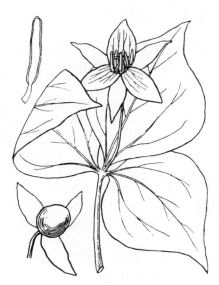

*Purple Trillium*

England), Daffy-Down-Lily (Vt.), Deathroot, Dish-cloth (P.Q.), Dogflower, Ground-Lily, Herb-Paris, Herb-True-Love (N.Y.), Ill-Scented Wake-Robin, Indian-Balm, Lamb's-Quarters, Mountain-Lettuce, Nosebleed (N.Y.), One-Berry, Orange-Blossom (Vt.), Paris (N.Y.), Rattlesnake-Root, Red-Benjamin (Maine), Red-Death (Canada), Rule-Of-Three (Vt.), Shamrock, Squawflower (Vt.), Squawroot (N.H.), Stinking-Dishcloth (P.Q.), Three-Leaved-Nightshade, *Trille* (P.Q.), True-Love, Wild-Peony (Maine), Wild-Piny (Maine), Wood-Lily

In New Hampshire "my father used to gather the early plants for greens, and called them *Benjamins*" (Hayward, 1891). And in Penobscot County, Maine, "*Trillium erectum* is here called Benjamin, and every spring the children go hunting Benjamins and Sarahs" (Bergen, 1894). It is another ill-scented Trillium. If placed in the nose, the petals were reputed to make it bleed, or "merely smelling the freshly exposed surface of red Beth roots will check bleeding from the nose" (Grieve, 1931).

Jane Colden (ca. 1750) called the plant "Paris. The three Leaved purple flower'd Herb Trulove." Paris is from *par* (equal), for the equal numbers of the plant's parts. Herb Paris is more commonly the *Paris quadrifolia* of Europe, "at the very top whereof come forth foure leaves directly set one against the other in manner of a Burgundian crosse or true love knot; for which cause among the Antients it hath been called Herbe True Love" (Gerard, 1633). The plant has been included in the NF.

## Large-Flowered Trillium, White Wake-Robin

*Trillium grandiflorum.* Three whorl; large-flowered.
Bathflower (P.Q.), Buttermilk-Lily, Easter-Flower, Ground-Lily, Large White Trillium, Mooseflower, Snow Trillium, Trinity-Lily (Wis.), White-Lily (Md., Ohio), Wood-Lily

Among the Menomini Indians, "this root was used to reduce the swelling of the eye. The raw root is grated and applied as a poultice to the eye. For cramps, it is grated, steeped and drunk as a tea. For irregularity of the menses, this root is grated and put into water to simmer, and then drunk" (Huron Smith, 1923).

## Western Wake-Robin, Western Trillium, Coast Trillium

*Trillium ovatum.* Three whorl; egg-shaped (leaves).

Birthroot, Large White-Trillium

In western Washington, "the Makah pound the bulb and rub it on the body as a love medicine. The Quinault also attribute this power to the plant, for a woman will cook the bulb and drop it in the food of a man she wants as a lover" (Gunther). James Teit recorded that among the Thompson Indians the root is dug up in the fall, cleaned, dried and powdered as a medicine for sore eyes.

## Prairie Trillium, Prairie Wake-Robin

*Trillium recurvatum.* Three whorl; recurved (the sepals bend down).

Beck (Wis.), Brown-Bess (Wis.), Brown-Beths (Wis.), Brown-Betts (Wis.), Bloody-Nose, Cowslip (Ind.), Jack-in-the-Pulpit (Ill.), Purple Wake-Robin, Whippoorwill-Flower (South)

## Sessile Trillium, Toadshade

*Trillium sessile.* Three whorl; stemless.

Beefsteak, Bettroot, Bloody-Butchers, Nigger-Heads (Ind.), Nosebleed, Three-Leaved Nightshade, Toad Trillium

The flower's scent is like that of raw beef or a butcher's shop. Bloody Butchers is a local name in England for an Orchid, *Orchis mascula.* Petiver (1715) called this "trefoil Herb Paris of Virginia."

## Painted Trillium

*Trillium undulatum.* Three whorl; wavy (petals).

Benjamin, Bettroot, Painted-Lady, Sarah (Maine), Smiling Wake-Robin, White-Benjamin (Maine), White-Death (Canada), Wild-Pepper

## Douglas's Triteleia, Wild-Hyacinth, Triplet-Lily

*Triteleia grandiflora.* Thrice perfect (from Greek *tri, teleos;* the flower parts); large-flowered.

Blue-Dicks, Cluster-Lily, Douglas's-Brodiaea

The corms were gathered in large quantities by the Indians and early settlers in the

*Western Wake-Robin*

West and eaten raw or cooked; they are also a favorite food of grizzly bears. The young seed pods are a potherb. The Thompson Indians "put the bulb, which they call the root, into the medicine bag, believing that it will make the medicine bag more potent" (Teit, 1930). "*Triteleia grandiflora* should be rigorously protected. Though for untold centuries it survived digging by Indian tribes (who were essentially conservationists) for food, the bulldozer and plough have almost completed its rout in the span of a generation. The corm is reported by many authorities to be perhaps the tastiest of our edible 'bulbs' " (Clark, 1976). This was previously called *Brodiaea douglasii*.

## Ithuriel's-Spear, Grassnut, Wally-Basket

*Triteleia laxa.* Thrice perfect; loose.

Blue-Milla (Calif.), Grass-Lily (Calif.), Triplet-Lily

In John Milton's *Paradise Lost,* Ithuriel was one of the cherubim sent by Gabriel to search for Satan, who had disguised himself and was hiding in Paradise. Touched by Ithuriel's spear, which "no falsehood can endure," Satan was revealed.

In Mendocino County, California, this is the "most abundant and widespread of all the Indian potatoes," according to Chesnut (1902); "it grows in fields, especially on the hills, and is known as 'highland potato.' In one clump observed by the writer it was estimated that there were over 200 plants in 1 square foot of ground . . . The sweet bulbs are especially esteemed for food by the Yakis."

## Perfoliate Bellwort, Merry-Bells

*Uvularia perfoliata.* Like the uvula; perfoliate.

Cow-Bells, Fragrant Bellwort, Haybells, Mealy Bellwort, Mohawk-Weed, Strawbell, Strawflower

The flower is shaped like the uvula, and thus the European species was called "Throote

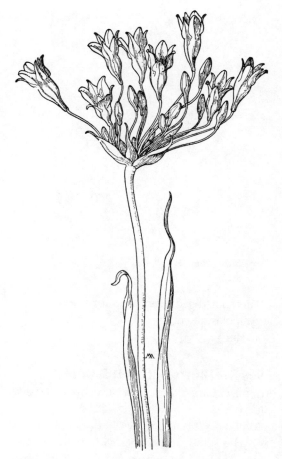

*Ithuriel's-Spear*

wort or Uvula woort, of the vertue it hath against the pain and swelling thereof" (Gerard, 1633). John Bartram (1751) called it "*Uvulary.* It was formerly taken for a species of Solomon's Seal, having smooth leaves like it; but the stalk grows through the leaf and the little yellowish flowers something resemble a Lilly; it grows about a foot high, the root is white, and spreads like a Crow's Foot; some people call it by that name for that reason. It is a good root for gathering and breaking a boil, and makes a fine salve for healing wounds and ulcers; it makes a fine maturating poultice." The insides of the flowers are mealy or rough with orange grains.

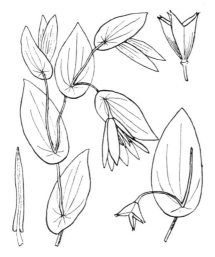

*Perfoliate Bellwort*

"The roots have been used for the nerves, in erysipelas, wounds and sores" (Jacobs and Burlage).

## Sessile Bellwort, Wild-Oats

*Uvularia sessilifolia*. Like the uvula; sessile-leaved.

Cornflower (Maine), Straw-Lilies (Conn.)

"The sessile-leaved bellwort, with three or four delicate pale-green leaves with reflexed

*Sessile Bellwort*

edges, on a tender-looking stalk. The single modest-colored flower gracefully drooping, neat, with a fugacious, richly spiced fragrance, facing the ground, the dry leaves, as if unworthy to face the heavens" (Thoreau, 1852). Cutler (1785) reported that "the young shoots may be eaten as asparagus. The roots are nutritious, and are used in diet-drinks."

## California False Hellebore, California Corn-Lily

*Veratrum californicum*. Truly black (roots of *Veratrum album*); of California.

False Hellebore, Skunk-Cabbage

In Nevada "this plant is of interest chiefly because the Indians employ it as a contraceptive measure," according to Percy Train and his colleagues; "the liquid is made by boiling the root of the plant. A dosage of one teaspoonful three times a day for three weeks was said to ensure permanent sterility." Among the Thompson Indians, "a small quantity of the roots are dried, then burned, and the ashes are boiled for a long time. This decoction is taken in small doses for blood disorders, and particularly for syphilis" (Teit, 1930). The plant is toxic to grazing animals, and an insecticide was once made from the powdered roots.

## False Hellebore, Indian-Poke, White-Hellebore

*Veratrum viride*. Truly black; green.

American White-Hellebore, American Veratrum, Bear-Corn, Bigbane, Big Hellebore, Branch-Eliber (N.C.), Bugbane, Bugwort, Cornlily, Crow-Poison, Devil's-Bite, Duck-Retter (N.J.), Earth-Gall, Elever (Conn.), Green Hellebore, Green Veratrum, *Hellébore* (P.Q.), Itchweed, Pepper-Root, Pokeroot (N.H.), Poor-Annie, Rattlesnake-Root, Rattlesnake-Weed, Skunk-Cabbage, Swamp-Hellebore, *Tabac du diable* (P.Q.), Tickleweed, True Veratrum, *Varaire* (P.Q.), Vernal-Varebell (South), *Veratre* (P.Q.)

In New England, Josselyn (1672) wrote of "White Hellibore . . . the Indians cure their

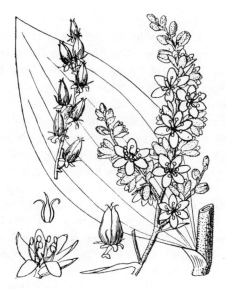

*False Hellebore*

*rötter* (doll-root) "because the children make dolls of its stalks and leaves." "Cherokees used a plant decoction to relieve body pains. It is now known to contain ester alkaloids that are potent hypotensive agents" (Lewis and Elvin-Lewis, 1977). It has been included in the USP and NF and is still included in some European pharmacopeias as a hypotensive agent.

## Bear-Grass, Indian Basket-Grass, Elk-Grass

*Xerophyllum tenax.* Dry leaf; tenacious.
Basket-Grass (B.C., Wash.), Bear-Lily, Deer-Grass (Calif.), Elk-Grass, Sour-Grass (Calif.), Squawgrass (B.C.), Turkey-Beard, Turk's-Beard (Wash.)

Northwest Indians dried and bleached great quantities of the leaves to weave into hats, capes and baskets. The flowers, stalks and seed pods are avidly eaten by rodents, deer and elk, and the tough leaves are eaten by Rocky Mountain goats.

## Atamasco-Lily, Zephyr-Lily, Easter-Lily

*Zephyranthes atamasca.* West-wind flower; (from the Indian name).
Amaryllis (South), Easter-Lily (Ga.), Fairy-Lily, Rain-Lily, Stagger-Grass, Swamp-Lily

"The Indians in Virginia do call it *Atamusco,* some among us do call it *Lilionarcissus Virginianus,* of the likeness of the flower to a Lilly, and the leaves and root to a Daffodill. We for brevity do call it Narcissus Virgineus, that is, the Daffodill of Virginia" (Parkinson, 1629). Mark Catesby wrote that "the flower just before opening is stained with a rose colour, which, as the flower declines, grows fainter. It is a native of Virginia and Carolina, where in particular places the pastures are as thick sprinkled with them and martagons, as cowslips and orchis's are with us in England." Horses get the "staggers," a

wounds with it, annointing the wound first with raccoons greese, or wild-cats greese, and strewing upon it the powder of the roots; and for aches they scarifie the grieved part, and annoint it with one of the foresaid oyls, then strew upon it the powder. The powder of the root put into a hollow tooth, is good for the tooth-ache. The root sliced thin and boyled in vineager, is very good against *Herpes Milliaris.*" The White Hellebore of Europe, a famous and ancient poison and potent herb, is *Veratrum album.* Hellebore is from a Greek name now applied to a genus of the Buttercup family; *Helleborus niger* is Black Hellebore, another ancient poison.

The early leaves are like those of Poke but are poisonous and can irritate the skin. "The root is a most drastic cathartic and sternunatory. The fresh roots, beaten up with hog's lard, cures the itch," Manasseh Cutler reported, and "crows may be destroyed by boiling Indian corn in a strong concoction of the fresh roots, and strewing it on the ground where they resort."

Of the name Duck-Retter, Kalm (1749) wrote that the Swedes in New Jersey called it *dock-*

*Atamasco-Lily*

cerebrospinal disease, from eating the leaves or bulbs.

## Black-Snakeroot, Crow-Poison

*Zigadenus densus.* Paired glands; dense.
Osceola's-Plume, St. Agnes-Feather

Osceola was the American Indian who led the Seminoles in the Second Seminole War (1835–1837); he was captured and died in imprisonment. Saint Agnes, martyred under Diocletian in 304, is a patroness of chastity.

## Elegant-Camas, Mountain Death-Camas

*Zigadenus elegans.* Paired glands; elegant.
Alakali-Grass, Glaucous Anticlea, Poison-Camas, Poison-Sego, Wandlily, White-Camas

"Since these bulbs are difficult to distinguish from those of the edible Camas, especially *Camassia Quamash,* many fatalities have occurred from this confusion, particularly since native peoples commonly dug the bulbs in the hunger-time of early spring, before the appearance of the distinctive flowers. Some species of Poison Camas grow in the same

prized meadows as *C. Quamash,* but the Nez Percé were careful to dig out and destroy Zigadenus bulbs while the blooming plants were easily told apart" (Clark, 1976). The *Range Plant Handbook* reported that "all North American species [of Zigadenus] are poisonous, to a greater or lesser degree, to both animals and man. Grassy Deathcamas *(Z. gramineus),* Meadow Deathcamas *(Z. venenosus),* Foothill Deathcamas *(Z. paniculatus),* and Mountain Deathcamus *(Z. elegans)* are the most common and important species in the West. However, Grassy and Meadow Deathcamases are the most dangerous. *Z. elegans* is only slightly poisonous and probably is never injurious to livestock."

Among the Thompson Indians, "Hunting or trapping for about a month cannot be done successfully by a man who has a daughter reaching puberty. He has to snare a grouse, cut off its head, remove its eyes, and in their place put two small roots of this plant and another in its mouth. If this were not done he would not be able to snare any more grouse" (Teit, 1930). Anticlea, who was the mother of Ulysses, was a previous name of the genus.

*Elegant-Camas*

# THE AGAVE FAMILY

## Agavaceae

A family of 18 genera and 410 species of shrubs and trees; found chiefly in arid regions. Several members of the family, including species of *Agave, Sansevieria* and *Phormium,* are the source of strong fibers used in cordage, matting and fishing nets. The fermented sap of *Agave americana* is the source of pulque.

### Blue Yucca, Banana Yucca, Datil

*Yucca baccata.* (From the Spanish *yuca* which is from Carib); fruited.

Amole, Hosh-Kawn, Spanish-Bayonet, Spanish-Dagger, Wild-Date

"The fruit of this plant is regarded by the Zuñi as a great luxury. Before they obtained wagons it was gathered and carried in blankets on their backs, and later on the backs of burros. The fruit, which is called *tsu'piyaně* (pl. *tsu'piyawě,* 'long oval'), after being pared is eaten raw, and is also boiled. When the boiled fruit becomes cold, the skin is loosened with a knife and pulled off. The fruit is greatly relished when prepared this way, but is still more highly esteemed as a conserve" (Stevenson, 1915). Other Indian tribes baked the sweet fruit and gathered and ate the flowers. Hoskawn is the Navaho name.

Amole is the vegetable soap prepared from several Yuccas, particularly *Y. baccata* and *Yucca glauca* (Soapweed). "The Tewa of Hano, like the Hopi, accompany all ceremonies of adoption and name-giving by washing with yucca suds. Thus, when an infant is named before sunrise on the twentieth day after birth, its head is washed by the paternal grandmother, and each member of the father's clan who gives an additional name smears the child's head with suds. The bride is bathed by the bridegroom's mother at the beginning of her bridal visit to the bridegroom's house, and at the end of the visit, when she is about to return to her own clan-house, women of the bridegroom's clan wash her hair before sunrise and give her a new name" (Robbins, Harrington and Freire-Marreco, 1916). Southwestern Indians also twisted Yucca fibers to make bowstrings, fishing nets and fabric (sometimes combined with cotton or animal fur); paintbrushes were made of Yucca needles; and strips of Yucca were plaited into sandals and baskets.

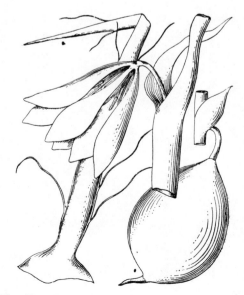

*Blue Yucca*

### Adam's-Needle, Spanish-Bayonet, Bear-Grass

*Yucca filamentosa.* (From the Spanish *Yucca*); filamentous.

Beargrass, Bear's-Thread, Christmas-Bells, Confederate-Flax, Curly-Hair (South), Eve's-Darning-Needle (Texas), Eve's-Thread, Grass-Cactus, Needle-Palm,

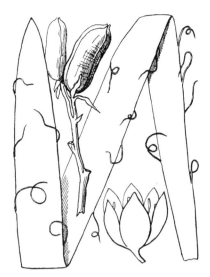

*Adam's-Needle*

Our-Lord's-Candles, Silkgrass, Soaproot, Soapweed (Iowa), Spanish-Dagger, Spoonleaf Yucca, Thread-and-Needle (Mass., N.Y.)

In Virginia Thomas Harriot (1590) reported, "Here is a kind of grasse in the countrey uppon the blades whereof there groweth very good silke in forme of a thin glittering skin to bee stript off." In 1610, Sir Thomas Gates, governor of Virginia, described some Indian "womens girdles of silke of the Grassesilke, not without art, and much neatnesse finely wrought" (Purchas, 1625). In his history of Virginia of 1705, Robert Beverley reported, "In the First Discovery of this part of the World, they presented *Q. Elizabeth* with a piece of grogram that had been made of this plant. And yet to this day they make no manner of use of this plant, no, not so much as the Indians did, before the English came among them, who then made their baskets, fishing nets, and lines of it." William Byrd of Virginia (1728) reported that "the Indians use it in all their manufactures, twisting a thread of it that is prodigiously strong. Of this they make their baskets and the aprons which their women wear about their middles, for decency's sake. These are long enough to wrap quite round them and reach down to their knees, with a fringe on the under part by way of ornament."

According to Dr. Porcher, in July 1862 there was "an article in the Charlestone Courier, entitled 'Confederate Flax,' in which it is stated that Mr. D. Ewart, of Florida, had presented for exhibition 'specimens of scutched fibre, and of cordage and twine of different sizes, made from the very common plant familiarly known as bear-grass, or Adam's needles.'" The flowers are eaten raw or cooked. The roots contain saponin and were used to make a soapy lather and to treat rheumatism and gonorrhea.

# THE CATBRIER FAMILY

## Smilacaceae

A family of 10 genera and 225 species of lianas or climbers and a few herbs and shrubs; widespread in tropical and subtropical regions and in the North Temperate Zone.

## Catbriers, Greenbriers

*Smilax*. (The Greek name of the Bindweed). Bullgrip (S.C.), Devil's-Clothesline (Md.), Hell-Ropes (Ark.), Horsebrier

Many species form impenetrable green-stemmed vines that bear thorns like a cat's claws. The young shoots and roots and the fruit are eaten, and the mature roots are boiled for tea or pulverized to make a flour.

## Carrion-Flower

*Smilax herbacea*. (A Greek plant name); herbaceous.

Bohea-Tea (Pa.), Field-Yam-Root (Wis.), Jacob's-Ladder, *Raisin de couleuvre* (P.Q.)

"It smells exactly like a dead rat in the wall, and apparently attracts flies like carrion" (Thoreau, 1854). Bohea is a black Chinese tea. *Couleuvre* is French for an adder. "The fruits were eaten at times by the Omaha for their pleasant taste. They were said to be effectual in relieving hoarseness" (Gilmore).

## American Chinaroot

*Smilax pseudochina*. (A Greek plant name); false-China (i.e., *Smilax china*, a medicinal herb from Asia).

Bamboo-Brier, Bastard-China, Bristly Greenbrier, Bryony-Leaved Jacob's-Ladder, Bullbrier, Carrion-Flower, Chinabrier, Dead-Man's-Bryony (South), False Chinaroot, False Sarsparilla, Helfetter, Long-Stalked Greenbrier, Sarsparilla, Virginia-Sarsparilla

*American Chinaroot*

In 1774 William Bartram was given a "noble entertainment and repast" by the Seminoles, "consisting of bears ribs, venison, varieties of fish, roasted turkeys (which they call the white man's dish), hot corn cakes, and a very agreeable, cooling sort of jelly, which they call conte; this is prepared from the root of the China brier." The Indians ground the root, mixed it with water and then dried the reddish flour: "A small quantity of this, mixed with warm water and sweetened with honey, when cooled, becomes a beautiful delicious jelly, very nourishing and wholesome. They also mix it with fine corn flour, which being fried in fresh bear's oil makes very good hot cakes or fritters" (Bartram).

Among the Houma Indians of Louisiana, "the large tuberous roots are grated with a knife or spoon to clean them of the outside coating, then cut into pieces and boiled to make a tea which is taken internally to cure kidney trouble symptomized by urinary disturbance" (Speck, 1941). The Houma also ground the root into a flour, as did the Seminoles. The medicinal and flavoring sarsparilla (from Spanish *zarzparilla*) comes from tropical species. It is also the name of an Aralia.

## Catbrier, Greenbrier

*Smilax rotundifolia.* (A Greek plant name); round-leaved.

Bamboo-Brier, Biscuit-Leaves (Mass.), Biscuit-Plant (Mass.), Blaspheme-Vine, Bread-and-Butter (Mass.), Bullbrier, Bullgrip, Devil's-Hop-Vine, Devil's-Wrapping-Yarn (Mass.), Dogbrier (Mass.), Horsebrier (Mass.), Hunger-Root, Hungry-Vine, Indian-Brier, Nigger-Head (N.B.), Rough-Bindweed, Sawbrier, Wait-a-Bit (Mass.)

Thomas Harriot (1590) called it Tsinaw and reported, "From these roots while they be new or fresh beeing chopt into small pieces and stampt is strained with water a juice that makes bread, and also being boiled a very

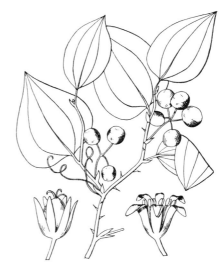

*Catbrier*

good spoonemeat in maner of a gelly, and is much better in taste if it bee tempered with oyle." In New Bedford, "Catbrier (Smilax) they call here 'the devil's wrapping yarn'" (Thoreau, 1857).

# THE IRIS FAMILY

## *Iridaceae*

A cosmopolitan family of 92 genera and 1,800 species of herbs and a few half-shrubs; most abundant in Africa. Iris was the rainbow goddess, the messenger of the gods, the rainbow being her bridge from heaven to earth. The flower is said to be named after her for its rainbow of colors. The Iris was the origin of the scepter, the symbol of power and majesty. The Egyptians placed the Iris on the brow of the Sphinx, the three "falls" (the drooping petals) representing faith, wisdom and valor.

The names Fleur-de-Lis, Fleur-de-Lys and Flower-de-Luce are from the Old French *flor de lis,* which means "flower of lily." A more colorful, but evidently wrong, origin is *fleur de Louis,* the flower of King Louis of France, who in the 12th century adopted it as the armorial emblem of the kings of France. Marie-Victorin has suggested that *fleur-de-lis* is an abbreviation of *fleur de la Lys,* a river in Flanders where the plant grows abundantly. The "Flag" in some names is from Middle English *flagge,* a rush. Josselyn (1672) called a blue Iris of New England "Blew Flower-de-luce; the roots are not knobby, but long and streight, and very white, with a multitude of strings." He reported that "it is excellent for to promote vomiting, and for bruises on the feet or face."

## Crested Dwarf Iris

*Iris cristata.* Iris; crested.

"The roots of this species when chewed are very remarkable; they at first occasion a pleasant sweet taste, which in a few minutes turns to a burning sensation, by far more pungent than capsicum. The hunters of Virginia, notwithstanding these properties, use it very frequently to alleviate thirst" (Pursh, 1814). Dwarf or Vernal Iris is *Iris verna* ("of spring"), also called Violet or Violet Iris in South Carolina.

## Mountain Iris, Douglas's Iris

*Iris douglasiana.* Iris; of Douglas (David Douglas, 1798–1834).

Among the Indians of Mendocino County, California: "The edges of the leaves are as fine and strong as silk and used to be gathered for the purpose of making the strongest kinds of nets and ropes. As the margin of the leaf is alone used, the work of making anything of it was exceedingly laborious. The

*Mountain Iris*

silky strands were separated from the leaf and thoroughly cleaned from other tissues by means of a sharp-edged oblong piece of abalone shell, which was fastened to the thumb and used to scrape the fiber. Frank Youree informed me that it took nearly six weeks to make a rope twelve feet long. The rope, which was exceedingly strong and very pliable, was especially valuable in making snares to catch deer, and on this account it was known as 'deer rope'" (Chesnut, 1902).

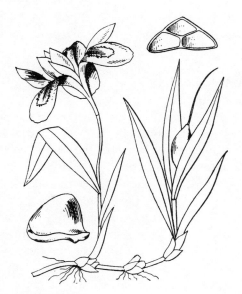

*Crested Dwarf Iris*

*Rocky Mountain Iris*

## Rocky Mountain Iris, Western Blue-Flag

*Iris missouriensis.* Iris; of Missouri.

Flag, Fleur-de-Lis, Snakelily, Water-Flag

In Nevada "the most extensive use for this plant is as a toothache remedy, being so reported from most of the Paiute and Shoshone communities. The usual procedure was merely to insert entire pieces, or a portion of the pulped, raw root, directly into the tooth cavity, but some of the people said that the pulped root would serve just as well if placed against the gum" (Train, Henrichs and Archer, 1941). Western Indians also made an arrow poison from the ground roots soaked in animal bile.

## Yellow Iris

*Iris pseudacorus.* Iris; false Acorus (the old generic name). (From Europe.)

Corn Flag, Daggers, False Sweet-Flag, Flagons, Jacob's-Sword, Sword Flag, Water Flag, Water-Skegs, Yellow Flag

"The root of the common Floure-de-luce cleane washed, and stamped with a few drops of Rose-water, and laid plaisterwise upon the face of a man or woman, doth in two dayes at the most take away the blacknesse or blewnesse of any stroke or bruse" (Gerard, 1633). Moreover, Manasseh Cutler reported, "the fresh roots of the yellow water flag have been mixed with food of swine bitten by a mad dog, and they escaped the disease, when others, bitten by the same dog, died raving mad." Water-Skegg is a local name in Scotland and Flaggon in Ireland.

## Tough-Leaf Iris

*Iris tenax.* Iris; tenacious.

This Iris was discovered by David Douglas who, according to Mathew (1991), "suggested the name *tenax* because 'the native tribes about the Anguilac River, in California, make a fine cord from the fibres of the leaves, of which they weave their fishing nets, a purpose to which it is admirably suited on account of its buoyancy, strength and durability. Snares are made of it for deer and bears, of such strength, that one not thicker than a sixteen-thread line is sufficient to strangle the great stag of California, *Cervus alces.*' "

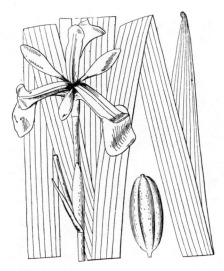

*Larger Blue-Flag*

## Larger Blue-Flag

*Iris versicolor.* Iris; variously colored.
Blue Flag, Blue-Lily (Wis.), *Clajeux* (P.Q.), Dagger-Flower Flag-Lily, Dragon-Flower, Fleur-de-Lis, Flower-de-Luce, Flowering Flag, *Glaieul des marais* (P.Q.), Harlequin Blue-Flag, Liver-Lily, Marsh Iris, Poison Flag, Poison Flagroot (Mass.), Snake-Lily, Water Flag, Wild Iris

Among the Atasi Indians of Alabama in 1775, William Bartram reported, "At this time the town was fasting, taking medicine, and I think I may say praying, to avert a grevious calamity of sickness, which had lately affected them, and laid in the grave abundance of their citizens; they fast seven or eight days, during which time they eat or drink nothing but a meagre gruel, made of a little corn-flour and water; taking at the same time by way of medicine or physic, a strong decoction of the roots of Iris versicolor, which is a powerful cathartic; they hold this root in high estimation: every town cultivates a little plantation of it, having a large artificial pond, just without the town, planted and almost over-grown with it." It has been included in the USP and NF, and eclectic physicians attributed "alterative powers" to it and used it for various skin diseases and chronic rheumatism (USD). Longfellow wrote a poem called "Flower-de-Luce"; here is the final stanza:

> *Thou art the muse, who far from*
> *crowded cities*
> *Hauntest the sylvan streams,*
> *Playing on pipes of reed the artless dit-*
> *ties*
> *That come to us as dreams.*
> *O flower-de-luce, bloom on, and let the*
> *river*
> *Linger to kiss thy feet!*
> *O flower of song, bloom on, and make*
> *forever*
> *The world more fair and sweet.*

## Blue-Eyed-Grass

*Sisyrinchium angustifolium.* Swine snout (the Greek name of a plant whose roots were much sought after by swine); narrow-leaved.
Bachelor's-Button (Mass.), Bermuda-Flag, *Bermudienne* (P.Q.), Blue-Eyed-Lily, Blue-Eyed-Mary, Bluegrass (Mass.), Forget-Me-Not (Maine), Grass-flower (Mass.), Pigroot, Pointed Blue-Eyed-Grass, Rush-Lily, Satin-Flower, Satin-Lily, Spanish-Nut, Star-Eyed-Grass (Mass.), Stargrass (Mass.)

The Bermuda names allude to *Sisyrinchium bermudiana,* a native Irish species now extensively naturalized elsewhere in Europe (*bermudiana,* "of Bermuda," is erroneous). Spanish-Nut in Gerard's *Herbal* (1633) was *Sisynrichium majus,* whose sweet edible corms were evidently aphrodisiac: "The Spanish nut is eaten at the tables of rich and delicious, nay vicious persons, in sallads or otherwise, to procure lust and lecherie."

# THE ORCHID FAMILY

## *Orchidaceae*

A cosmopolitan family of 769 genera and 17,500 species of terrestrial and even subterranean herbs. *Orchis* in Greek means "testicle" and is the name given by Theophrastus to *Orchis morio* for the shape of its pair of rounded tubers. Thus Orchids were widely esteemed as aphrodisiacs: "In the mornynge and at nyght dronke of the same water at eche tyme an ounce and a half causeth great hete, therefore it giveth lust unto the works of generacyon and multiplicacyon of sperm" (Braunschweig, 1500; 1527 translation). And in Puritan New England, "I once took notice of a wanton womans compounding of the solid roots of this plant with wine, for an amorous cup; which wrought the desired effect" (Josselyn, 1672).

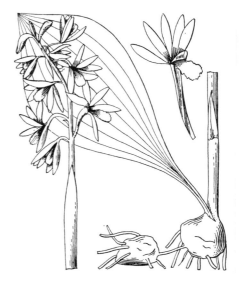

*Putty-Root*

## Putty-Root, Adam-and-Eve

*Aplectrum hyemale*. Without spur; of winter (the evergreen leaf).

The two joined corms, lying side by side, yield a glutinous putty. "The roots bruised, with a small addition of water, give a strong cement, which when applied to broken china and glass is exceedingly durable" (Pursh, 1814). "The two joined bulbs are called 'Adam-and-Eve' by the Negroes and poor whites in Georgia and the Southern States, where the orchid grows freely. They wear them as amulets, and tell each other's fortunes by placing the separated bulbs in water, and according as Adam or Eve pops up calculate the chances of retaining a friend's affection, getting work, or living in peace with neighbors" (Gibson, 1905). Indians of the southeast beat and macerate

the roots and corms to a paste and apply it to boils.

## Dragon's-Mouth, Arethusa

*Arethusa bulbosa*. Of Arethusa (a nymph of Greek legend); bulbous.

Adam-and-Eve (Nfd.), *Arethuse* (P.Q.), Bog-Rose, Indian-Pink (Mass.), Laughing-Jackass, Meadow-Pink (Mass.), Swamp-Pink (Mass.), Wild-Pink (N.J.),

"In Plymouth County, Massachusetts, where the arethusa seems common, I have heard it called Indian pink" (Burroughs, 1894). The flower is held quite erect and the two swollen upper petals and the pendulous lower lip look not unlike a braying ass. The only other species of Arethusa is found in Japan. The nymph Arethusa, while bathing in the river, was seen by the river god and pursued. To save her, Artemis changed her into an underground stream, and she became the nymph of fountains.

## Grass-Pink

*Calopogon tuberosus.* Beautiful beard (the fringed lip); tuberous.

Bearded-Pink, Meadow-Gift, Pretty Calopogon, Swamp-Pink (Mass.), Tuberous-Rooted Calopogon

"The very handsome 'pink purple' flowers of the *Calopogon* (!) *pulchellus* enrich the grass all around the edge of Hubbard's blueberry swamp, and are now in their prime. The *Arethusa bulbosa,* 'crystalline purple'; *Pogonia ophioglossoides,* snake-mouthed arethusa, 'pale purple'; and the *Calopogon pulchellus,* grass pink, 'pink purple,' make one family in my mind,—next to the purple orchid, or with it,—being flowers par excellence, all flower, all color, with inconspicuous leaves, naked flowers, and difficult—at least the calopogon—to preserve. But they are flowers, excepting the first, at least, without a name. Pogonia! Calopogon!! They would blush still deeper if they knew what names man had given them" (Thoreau, 1852). *C. tuberosus* was previously *C. pulchellus.*

## Spotted Coralroot, Summer Coralroot

*Corallorhiza maculata.* Coral root, spotted.

Crawley (N.C.), Crawley-Root, Dragon's-Claws (N.Y.), Large Coralroot, Scahose-Herb

"The rhizome of this orchid has been used as a diaphoretic, febrifuge and sedative, and the dried stems are said to be used by the Paiute and Shoshone Indians of Nevada to make a tea so as to build up blood in pneumonia patients. Doubtless the latter fancied attribute rests on the existence of a reddish tone and coloration in some of the plants" (Correll, 1950).

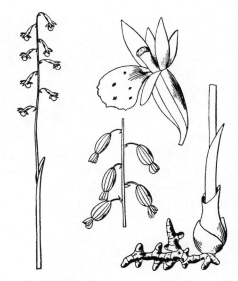

*Autumn Coralroot*

## Autumn Coralroot

*Corallorhiza odontorhiza.* Coral root; toothrooted (i.e., their shape).

Chicken-Toes, Crawley-Root, Dragon's-Claw, Deverroot, Fever-Root, Late Coralroot, Turkey-Claw

"This parasitic plant has been used by herbalists for centuries," according to Grieve, "but its scarcity and high price prevent its being more generally used. It provokes perspiration without producing any excitement in the system, so is of value in pleurisy, typhus fever and other inflammatory diseases. In addition to being a powerful diaphoretic, its action has a sedative effect."

## Lady's-Slippers, Moccasin-Flowers

*Cypripedium.* Venus slipper (Venus was born in the foam off the shores of Cyprus and was commonly given that island's name).

Ducks (Pa.), Nervine (Wis.), Pitcher-Plant (Mich.), Whippoorwill-Shoe (N.Y.)

Yellow Lady's-Slipper was called *Calceolus Marianus,* St. Mary's Shoe, by Dodoens in 1554, a Latinization of the vernacular name;

Gerard called it Our Lady's Shoe or Slipper, and it is Sabot de la Vierge in French. But Linnaeus, that good Lutheran, changed it to Venus's shoe (Greek *pedilon* means "sandal" or "slipper," and the plant name should be *Cypripedilum*). In Virginia in 1669 John Banister wrote of "three kinds of Lady-Slipper, we call them, Mockason flowers; the Indians call their shoes so, which they much resemble." "When the flower is partly filled with sand and set afloat, it looks like a duck" (Bergen, 1894), hence the name Ducks.

## Moccasin-Flower, Pink Lady's-Slipper

*Cypripedium acaule*. Venus slipper; stemless.

Brown Lady's-Slipper, Camel's-Foot, Common Lady's-Slipper, Dwarf-Umbil, Hare's-Lip, Heal-All (N.H.), Indian-Moccasin, Indian-Slipper (Maine), Male-Nervine, Nerve-Root (Maine, N.B.), Noah's-Ark, Old-Goose, Pink Moccasin-Flower, Purple-Slipper, Rose-Vein-Moccasin, *Sabot de la Vierge* (P.Q.), Squirrel's-Shoes (Conn.), Two-Leaved Lady's-Slipper, Two-Lips, Valerian (Maine, N.H.), Ve-

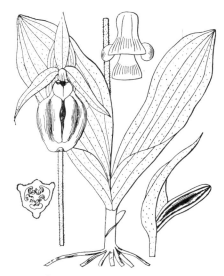

*Moccasin-Flower*

nus'-Slipper (South), Whippoorwill (Mass.), Whippoorwill's-Shoes (Conn.), Wild Calceolaria (Lab., Nfd.)

Mark Catesby wrote that "this plant produces the most elegant flower of all the Helleborine tribe, and is in great esteem with the North American Indians for decking their hair, etc. They call it the moccasin flower, which also signifies in their language, a shoe or slipper." In Maine it was called Valerian and Nerve-Root, "much esteemed as a nerve-sedative, collected and used by the nervous" (Perkins, 1929). The USD reports that it "appears to be a gentle nervous stimulant or antispasmodic, and has been used for the same purpose as valerian."

"Everywhere now in dry pitch pine woods stand the red lady's slipper over the red pine leaves on the forest floor, rejoicing in June, with their two broad curving green leaves,—some even in swamps. Uphold their rich, striped red, drooping sack" (Thoreau, 1856).

## Yellow Lady's-Slipper

*Cypripedium pubscens*. Venus slipper; downy. (Also found in Eurasia.)

American-Valerian, Bleeding-Heart, Ducks, Golden-Slipper, Indian-Shoe, Male-Nervine, Moccasin-Flower, Noah's-Ark, Monkey-Flower, Nerve-Root, Pine-Tulip, *Sabot de la Vierge* (P.Q.), Slipper-Root, Sysper-Root, Umbil-Root, Venus'-Cup, Venus'-Shoe, Water-Stealer, Whippoorwill-Shoe (N.Y.), Yellow, Yellow Downy Lady's-Slipper, Yellow Indian-Shoe, Yellows, Yellow-Umbil

Dr. Porcher reported that "it is employed by the Indians, and held in high estimation in domestic practice as a sedative and antispasmodic, acting like valerian in alleviating nervous systems; said to have proved useful in hysteria, and even in chorea." Thus it was called American-Valerian by the early settlers. It has been listed in the USP and NF. The Cherokees used the plant as a vermifuge. This

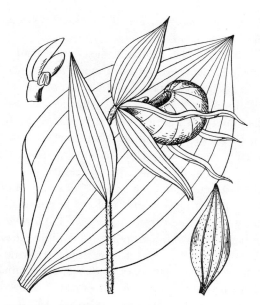

*Yellow Lady's-Slipper*

## Showy Orchid

*Galearis spectabilis.* Helmetlike (the hood over the column); showy.

Gay-Orchis, Heal-All, Kirtle-Pink, Mauve-Hood-Orchis, Preacher-in-the-Pulpit, Purple-Hooded Orchis, Purple-Orchis (N.Y.), Shinplasters, Spring Orchis, Two-Leaved Orchis

"Leafy bracts sheathe the ovaries, and the white sepals unite in an arch bending over the anther cells in such a way as to give the name 'Preacher in the Pulpit' to the orchid, from the fancied resemblance to two little men standing in a canopied pulpit" (Gibson, 1905). A kirtle is a skirt or tunic.

is "one of the few circumboreal species among orchids, being found throughout Europe and extending into Asia where it is occasionally found in the Himalaya mountains at 12,000 feet" (Correll, 1950). "In Western New York, all the Indians call the yellow Lady's Slipper, Whip-Poor-Will's shoes" (Perkins, 1929).

## Showy Lady's-Slipper

*Cypripedium reginae.* Venus slipper; of the queen.

Big Pink-and-White, Ducks, Female-Nervine, Gay Lady's-Slipper, Nerve-Root (N.B.), Pink Lady's-Slipper, Purple-Blush, Queen Lady's-Slipper, Queen's-Slipper, Royal Lady's-Slipper, Shepherd's-Purse (N.B.), Showy-Moccasin-Flower, Showy-Slipper, Silver-Slipper, Whippoorwill-Shoes (Conn.), White-Wing-Moccasin, White-Petaled Lady's-Slipper

This "moccasin flower," wrote Kalm (1750) in upper New York state, "which is found quite generally in the woods here, is said to be rather good for women in the throes of childbirth."

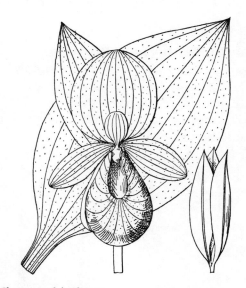

*Showy Lady's-Slipper*

## Rattlesnake-Plantains

*Goodyera.* Of Goodyer (John Goodyer, 1592–1664).

Lattice-Leaf, Rattlesnake-Violet (N.Y.)

John Goodyer, who was born and died in Hampshire, England, was an amateur naturalist and expert on elms. He botanized with Thomas Johnson (who was responsible for the revised edition of Gerard's *Herbal*), and together they planned a British flora. But

Johnson, who rose from apothecary to colonel in the Royalist army of the English Civil War, was killed in battle, and Goodyer retired to the country to translate the *De Materia Medica* of Dioscorides. His handwritten translation was discovered 250 years later and first published in 1934.

Marie-Victorin wrote, "In America, all the species are known by the common name of Rattlesnake-Plantain: these plants superficially resemble the Plantains; on the other hand, the leaf patterns, which resemble a snake skin, suggested the idea (doctrine of signatures) to the first American settlers to use the Goodyers as antidotes to snake venom."

## Downy Rattlesnake-Plantain

*Goodyera pubescens.* Of Goodyer; downy.
Adder's-Tongue (Maine), Adder-Tongue-Cactus (Maine), Adder's-Violet, Cancer-Weed, Canker-Root, Net-Leaf, Net-Leaf-Plantain, Networt, Ratsbane (N.C.), Rattlesnake-Leaf, Rattlesnake-Orchid, Rattlesnake-Root, Rattlesnake-Tongue (N.J.), Scrofula-Weed, Spotted-Plantain

Thoreau (1851) liked the name Rattlesnake-Plantain "very well, though it may not be easy to convince a quibbler and proser of its fitness. We want some name to express the mystic wildness of its rich leaves. Such work as men imitate in their embroidery, unaccountably agreeable to the eye, as if it answered its end only when it met the eye of man; a reticulated leaf, visible only on one side; little things which make one pause in the woods, take captive the eye." "Pursh says it has a wide reputation as an infallible cure for hydrophobia, and a New England divine tells us that the leaves of Rattlesnake Plantain were used by country folk to make a decoction to cure skin diseases" (Gibson, 1905).

## Fringed Orchids

*Platanthera.* Broad anther.
Frogspear, Frogspike, Gypsy-Spike, Monkey-Face, Naked-Gland Orchis, Rein Orchis

## Leafy White Orchid

*Platanthera dilatata.* Broad anther; dilated (lip).
Bog-Candle, Bog-Torch, Boreal Bog-Orchis, Fragrant Orchis, Marsh-Lily (Nfd.), Northern-Orchis, Scent-Bottle, Smelling-Bottle (Nfd.), Tall Bog-Orchis

This was a charm plant for the Thompson Indians of British Columbia: "Young men use it as a wash to make them lucky, good looking, and sweet smelling. Women use the wash to gain a mate and have success in love. Both sexes use it to obtain riches and property. When they dig up the plant they chant, 'Friend. I want wealth and much property'" (Teit). Northwest Indians and Eskimos gather and eat the corms, which when cooked evidently taste of potatoes.

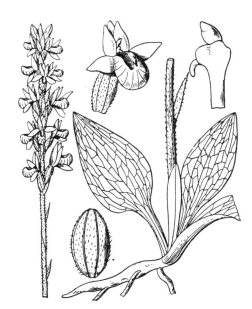

*Downy Rattlesnake-Plantain*

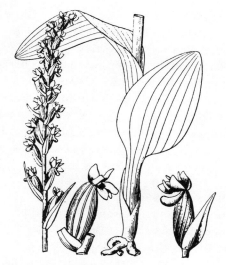

*Northern Green-Orchid*

## Northern Green-Orchid

*Platanthera hyperborea.* Broad anther; far northern. (Also found in Iceland and northeastern Asia.)

Green-Flowered Bog-Orchis, Leafy Northern-Green-Orchis, Marsh-Lily (Nfd.), Smelling-Bottles (Nfd.), Tall Leafy-Green-Orchis

"When occurring as a small few-flowered form in damp New England woods, this orchid is very inconspicuous and only the most persistent search will enable one to observe it. On the other hand, I have seen it in willow thickets on alluvial deposits along the Sikanni Chief river in northern British Columbia where it is so abundant that it is one of the dominant herbaceous plants" (Correll, 1950).

## Round-Leaved Orchid

*Plantanthera orbiculata.* Broad anther; rounded.

Bear's-Ears, Elephant's-Ears, Gall-of-the-Earth, Great Green-Orchis, Heal-All, Large-Orchis, Moon-Set, Round-Leaved Rein-Orchis, Shin-Plasters, Solomon's-Plaster (N.S.), Solomon's-Seal (Vt.)

In Vermont "the common names of the Round-Leaved orchises hereabout are 'Shin-plaster' and 'Heal-all,' since they are applied to bruised shins, and are used as plasters for weak lungs" (Niles, 1904). "In Barre, Vt., the leaves . . . are thought to be a valuable application for lameness or soreness. I have known of a farmer recently using them on a lame colt" (Bergen, 1892).

## Purple Fringed-Orchid

*Platanthera psycodes.* Broad anther; like a butterfly.

Butterfly-Orchis, Dead-Man's-Fingers, Dead-Man's-Thumbs, Fairy-Fringe, Flaming-Orchis, Lady's-Plume, Long-Purples, Meadow-Pink (Mass.), Plume-Royal, Soldier's-Plume (N.Y.), Tattered Fringed-Orchis, Wild-Hyacinth (Maine)

Manasseh Cutler called this plant Lady's-Plume and Female-Handed Orchis. In 1850 Susan Cooper wrote that in Cooperstown, New York, "the handsome, large purple-fringed orchis is also found here. The country people call it soldier's plume." In *Hamlet,* Ophelia made fantastic garlands

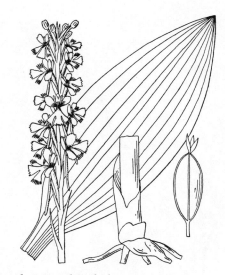

*Purple Fringed-Orchid*

*Of crowflowers, nettles, daisies, and*
*    long purples,*
*That liberal shepherds give a grosser*
*    name,*
*But our cold maids do dead men's fin-*
*    gers call them.*

In Britain Long-Purples and Dead-Man's-Fingers or Thumbs (for the fingerlike lobes on the tubers) are names of *Orchis macula*.

## Rose Pogonia, Snake-Mouth

*Pogonia ophioglossoides.* Beard; like *Ophioglossum* (the Adder's-Tongue fern).
Adder's-Mouth Pogonia, Adder's-Tongue-Arethusa (Mass.), Beard-Flower, Crested-Ettercap, Ettercap, Rose Crest-Lip, Sweet Crest-Orchis, Snake-Mouthed-Arethusa (Mass.)

"The adder's-tongue arethusa smells exactly like a snake. How singular that in nature, too, beauty and offensiveness should be thus combined! In flowers, as well as in men, we demand a beauty pure and fragrant, which perfumes the air. The flower which is showy but has no, or an offensive, odor expresses the character of too many mortals" (Thoreau, 1852). Actually, the fresh flower has a sweet scent, "odor of raspberries," according to Gibson (1905). The snaky smell is only apparent in withered flowers. Ettercap is a variant of attercap, a spider (from Old English *atter*, "poison," *coppa*, "spider"). It also meant a malignant person. Presumably it sounded like "adder" and so was applied to this and other adder-named Orchids.

## Ladies'-Tresses

*Spiranthes.* Spiral flower.
Bayonet-Lily (Nfd.), Ladies'-Dresses, Ladies'-Traces, Pearl-Twist, Spiral-Orchid (N.H.)

"The full and sappy roots of Ladie traces eaten, or boyled in milke and drunke, provoke venery, nourish and strengthen the bodye, and be good for such as are fallen into a consumption or Fever Hectique" (Gerard, 1633).

## Nodding Ladies'-Tresses

*Spiranthes cernua.* Spiral flower; nodding.
Autumn-Tresses, Common Ladies'-Tresses, Drooping Ladies'-Tresses, Fragrant Ladies'-Tresses (var.

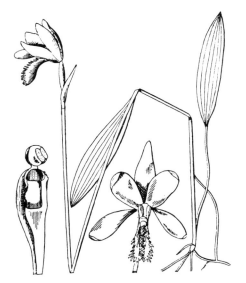

*Rose Pogonia*

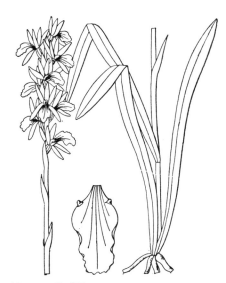

*Nodding Ladies'-Tresses*

*odorata*), Hen's-Toes (Maine), Nodding-Tresses, Screw-Auger (N.S.), Swamp Ladies'-Tresses (var. *odorata*), Sweet Ladies'-Tresses (var *odorata*), Water-Orchid (var. *odorata*), Wild Lily-of-the-Valley (Maine), Wild-Tuberose

## Slender Ladies'-Tresses

*Spiranthes lacera.* Spiral flower; slashed.
Corkscrew-Plant, Green-Lip Ladies'-Tresses, Green Pearl-Twist, Green Spiral-Orchis, Long-Tresses, Northern Slender-Ladies'-Tresses, Twisted-Stalk (W.Va.)

"The *gracilis* has its crystalline white flowers arranged in a dense spiral cone like the thread of a screw, standing out nearly at right-angles with the stem, curved downward a little" (Thoreau, 1853); *gracilis* was the previous epithet.

# BIBLIOGRAPHY

American Council of Learned Societies. *Dictionary of American Biography.* New York: Scribner's, 1928–1936.

Arber, Agnes. *Herbals: Their Origin and Evolution. A Chapter in the History of Botany, 1470–1670.* 2d ed. Cambridge: Cambridge University Press, 1953.

Armstrong, Margaret. *Field Book of Western Wild Flowers.* New York: Putnam's, 1915.

Aubrey, John. *Three Prose Works: Miscellanies; Remaines of Gentilism and Judaisme; Observations.* Edited by John Buchanan-Brown. Carbondale, Ill.: Southern Illinois University Press, 1972.

Banckes, Rycharde. *Here begynneth a new mater, the whiche sheweth and treateth of ye vertues and proprytes of herbes the whiche is called an Herball.* London, 1525.

Banister, John. *See* Ewan.

Bartlett, John Russell. *Dictionary of Americanisms.* Boston, 1859.

Barton, Benjamin H., and Thomas Castle. *The British Flora Medica: A History of the Medicinal Plants of Great Britain.* Rev. ed. London: Chatto & Windus, 1877.

Barton, Benjamin Smith. *Collections for an Essay towards a Materia Medica of the United-States.* Parts 1 and 2. 1798, 1804.

Reprint. Bulletin of the Lloyd Library, No. 1. Cincinnati, 1900.

Bartram, John. "A brief account of those plants that are most troublesome in our pastures and fields, in Pennsylvania; most of which were brought from Europe." 1758. In *Memorials of John Bartram and Humphry Marshall.* By William Darlington. 1849. Reprint. New York: Hafner, 1967.

———. Preface, Notes and Appendix ("Containing a Description of a Number of Plants Peculiar to America, their Uses, Virtues &c."). In *Medicina Britannica; or a Treatise . . .* By Thomas Short. 3d ed. Philadelphia, 1751.

Bartram, William. *Travels through North & South Carolina, Georgia, East & West Florida.* 1791. Reprinted as *Travels of William Bartram.* Edited by Mark Van Doren. 1928. Reprint. New York: Dover, 1955.

Beaumont, W.M. "Onondoga plant-names." *Daily Journal,* Syracuse, N.Y., April 13, 1891.

Bergen, Fanny D. "Popular American plant names." *Journal of American Folk-Lore* 5 (1892): 89–106; 6 (1893): 135–42; 7 (1894): 89–104; 9 (1896): 179–93; 10 (1897): 49–54, 143–48; 11 (1898): 221–30, 273–83.

———. "Some bits of plant lore." *Journal of American Folk-Lore* 5 (1892): 19–22.

Betts, Edwin M., ed. *Thomas Jefferson's Garden Book, 1766–1824.* Philadelphia: American Philosophical Society, 1944.

Beverley, Robert. *The History and Present State of Virginia.* 1705. Edited by Louis B. Wright. Chapel Hill, N.C.: University of North Carolina Press, 1947.

Bianchini, Francesco, and Francesco Corbetta. *The Complete Book of Health Plants.* 1975. Reprint. New York: Crescent Books, 1985.

Bigelow, Jacob. *American Medical Botany, Being a Collection of the Native Medicinal Plants of the United States.* 3 vols. Boston, 1817–1820.

————. *Florula Bostoniensis. A Collection of Plants of Boston and its Environs, with their Generic and Specific Characters, Synonyms, Descriptions, Places of Growth and Time of Flowering, and Occasional Remarks.* Boston, 1814.

Biggar, H.P., ed. *The Voyages of Jacques Cartier.* Public Archives of Canada, 11. Ottawa: 1924. Cited in *Medicinal and Other Uses of North American Plants: A Historical Survey with Special Reference to the Eastern Indian Tribes.* By Charlotte Erichsen-Brown. 1979. Reprint. New York: Dover, 1989.

Bocek, Barbara R. "Ethnobotany of Costanoan Indians, California, based on collections by John P. Harrington." *Economic Botany* 38 (1984): 240–55.

Bolyard, J. L. *Medicinal Plants and Home Remedies of Appalachia.* Springfield, Ill.: Thomas, 1981.

Bradstreet, Anne. *The Works of Anne Bradstreet.* Edited by Jeannine Hensley. Cambridge: Harvard University Press, 1967.

Braunschweig, Hieronymus. *Liber de arte distillandi. de Simplicibus.* 1500. Translated as *The vertuose Boke of Distyllacyon of the waters of all maner of Herbes* . . . By Laurens Andrewe. London, 1527

Britten, James, and Robert Holland. *A Dictionary of English Plant-Names.* London: Trübner, 1886.

Britton, Nathaniel Lord, and Addison Brown. *An Illustrated Flora of the United States and Canada.* 3 vols. New York: Scribner's, 1896. [The 2d edition of 1913 has been reprinted by Dover Publications, New York, 1970.]

Bryant, Charles. *Flora Diaetetica: Or History of Esculent Plants both Domestic and Foreign.* London, 1783.

Bullein, William. *Bulwarke of Defence against all Sicknesse, Sornesse and Woundes that doe dayly assaulte mankinde.* London, 1562.

Burros, Marian. "The Culinary Signs of Spring across the Land." *The New York Times,* April 30, 1986.

Burroughs, John. *Riverby.* Boston: Houghton Mifflin, 1894.

————. *Under the Maples.* Edited by Clara Barrus. Boston: Houghton, Mifflin, 1921.

Byrd, William. "A progress to the mines, 1732." In *The Writings of Colonel William Byrd of Westover in Virginia, Esqr.* Edited by J. S. Bassett. New York, 1901.

————. "Letters of William Byrd II and Sir Hans Sloane relative to plants and minerals in Virginia." *William and Mary Quarterly,* 2d Ser, 1 (1921): 186–200.

————. *William Byrd's Histories of the Dividing Line betwixt Virginia and North Carolina.* 1728. Reprint. New York: Dover, 1967.

Carmer, Carl. *Stars Fell on Alabama.* New York: Farrar & Rhinehart, 1934.

Cartier, Jacques. *See* Biggar.

Carver, Jonathan. *Three Years Travel through the Interior Parts of North America in the years 1766, 1767 and 1768.* London, 1778.

Castiglioni, Luigi. *Luigi Castiglioni's Viaggio. Travels in the United States of North America, 1785–87.* Edited and translated by Antonio Pace. Syracuse: Syracuse University Press, 1983.

Catesby, Mark. *Natural History of Carolina, Florida and the Bahama Islands.* 2 vols. London: 1730–1747.

Chamberlin, Ralph V. "The ethno-botany of the Gosiute Indians of Utah." *Memoirs of the American Anthropological Association* 2 (1911): 329–405.

Chapman, Jefferson, Robert B. Stewart, and Richard A. Yarnell. "Archaeological evidence for preColumbian introduction of *Portulaca oleracea* and *Molluga verticillata* into Eastern North America." *Economic Botany* 28 (1974): 411–12.

Chaucer, Geoffrey. *The Canterbury Tales.* Translated into Modern English by Nevill Coghill. London: Penguin, 1951.

Chesnut, V. K. "Plants used by the Indians of Mendocino County, California." *Contributions from the U.S. National Herbarium* 7 (1902): 295–422.

Clapp, Asahel. *A Synopsis; or, Systematic Catalogue of the Medicinal Plants of the United States.* Presented to the American Medical Association, May 1852. Philadelphia, 1852.

Clark, Lewis J. *Wild Flowers of the Pacific Northwest, from Alaska to Northern California.* Edited by John G. Trelawny. Sidney, B.C.: Gray's Publishing; 1976.

Clayton, John. *Flora Virginica.* Edited by L. T. Gronovius. Leyden, 1762.

Clayton, Rev. John. "Letter from Virginia to Dr. Grew in answer to several quaerys sent to him by that learned gentleman, 1687." British Museum, Add. MSS 4437: 85–97. Cited in *Medicinal and Other Uses of North American Plants: A Historical Survey with Special Reference to the Eastern Indian Tribes.* By Charlotte Erichsen-Brown. 1979. Reprint. New York: Dover, 1989.

Clute, Willard N. *A Dictionary of American Plant Names.* Joliet, Ill.: 1923.

Colden, Jane. *Botanic Manuscript of Jane Colden, 1724–1766.* Edited by H. W. Rickett and Elizabeth C. Hall. New York: Garden Club of Orange & Duchess Counties, 1963.

Cole, William. *Adam in Eden: or, Natures Paradise. The History of Plants, Fruits, Herbs and Flowers.* London, 1657.

———. *The Art of Simpling. An Introduction to the Knowledge and Gathering of Plants.* London, 1656.

Coombes, Allen J. *A Dictionary of Plant Names.* Portland, Ore.: Timber Press, 1987.

Cooper, James Fenimore. *Satanstoe; or, The Littlepage Manuscripts.* New York, 1845.

Cooper, Susan Fenimore. *Rural Hours.* 1850. Reprint. Syracuse, N.Y.: Syracuse University Press, 1968.

Copley, Alfred Lewin, and Helen Boswell. "Aconite the love poison." *Bulletin of the History of Medicine* 15 (1944): 420–26.

Core, Earl L. "Ethnobotany of the Southern Appalachian aborigines." *Economic Botany* 21 (1967): 198–214.

Cornut, Jacques Philippe. *Canadensium plantarum, aliarumque nondum editarum historia . . .* Paris, 1635.

Correll, Donovan Stewart. *Native Orchids of North America North of Mexico.* 1950. Reprint. Stanford, Calif.: Stanford University Press, 1978.

Coues, Elliott, ed. *The History of the Lewis and Clark Expedition.* 3 vols. 1893. Reprint. New York: Dover, 1965.

Coville, Frederick V. "Notes on the plants used by the Klamath Indians of Oregon." *Contributions from the U.S. National Herbarium* 5 (1897): 87–108.

———. "The Panamint Indians of California." *American Anthropologist* 5 (1892): 351–61.

Craighead, John J., Frank C. Craighead, Jr., and Ray J. Davis. *A Field Guide to Rocky Mountain Wildflowers.* Boston: Houghton Mifflin, 1963.

Crellin, John K., and Jane Philpott. *Herbal Medicine Past and Present.* 2 vols. Durham, N.C.: Duke University Press, 1990.

Cronquist, Arthur. *An Integrated System of*

*Classification of Flowering Plants.* New York: Columbia University Press, 1981.

———. *The Evolution and Classification of Flowering Plants.* 2d ed. Bronx, N.Y.: New York Botanical Garden, 1988.

Culpeper, Nicholas. *The English Physician Or an Astrologo-physical Discourse of the Vulgar Herbs of this Nation Being a Compleat Method of Physick . . .* London, 1652.

Cutler, Manasseh. "An account of some of the vegetable productions naturally growing in this part of America, botanically arranged." American Academy of Arts and Sciences, *Memoirs* 1 (1785): 396–493. [*Bulletin of the Lloyd Library,* No. 7, 1903.]

Dana, Mrs. William Dana Starr. *How to Know the Wild Flowers: A Guide to the Names, Haunts, and Habits of Our Common Wild Flowers.* 1900. Rev. ed. Edited by Clarence J. Hylander. New York: Dover, 1963.

Darlington, William. *Agricultural Botany: An Enumeration and Description of Useful Plants and Weeds.* Philadelphia: 1847.

———. *Memorials of John Bartram and Humphry Marshall.* 1849. Reprint. New York: Hafner, 1967.

Darwin, Erasmus. *The Botanic Garden. Part I. The Economy of Vegetation. Part II. The Loves of the Plants. A Poem with Philosophical Notes.* 1789. Reprint. New York: Garland, 1978.

Davies, John. *Douglas of the Forests: The North American Journals of David Douglas.* Seattle: University of Washington Press, 1980.

Densmore, Frances. *How Indians Use Wild Plants for Food, Medicine and Crafts.* 1928. Reprint. New York: Dover, 1974.

De Smet, Pierre-Jean. *Life, Letters and Travels of Father Pierre-Jean De Smet, S.J., 1801–1873.* Edited by H. M. Chittenden and A. T. Richardson. New York: Harper, 1905.

Dioscorides. *The Greek Herbal of Dioscorides. Illustrated by a Byzantine A.D. 512. Englished by John Goodyer A.D. 1655.* Edited by Robert T. Gunther. 1934. Reprint. New York: Hafner, 1968.

Dodoens, Rembert, or Rembertus Dodonaeus. *Cruydeboeck.* 1554. Translated into English as *A Niewe Herball or Historie of Plantes,* by Henry Lyte. London, 1578.

Don, George. *A General System of Gardening and Botany.* London, 1831–1837.

Douglas, David. *See* Davies.

Duffy, David Cameron. "Land of milk and honey." *Natural History* 7 (July 1990): 4–8.

Duke, James A. *Handbook of Medicinal Herbs.* Boca Raton: CRC Press, 1985.

———. *Handbook of Northeastern Indian Medicinal Plants.* Lincoln, Mass.: Quaterman, 1986.

Earle, Alice Morse. *Home Life in Colonial Days.* New York: Macmillan, 1913.

Eaton, Amos. *Manual of Botany for North America.* Albany, N.Y., 1818.

Erichsen-Brown, Charlotte. *Medicinal and Other Uses of North American Plants: A Historical Survey with Special Reference to the Eastern Indian Tribes.* 1979. Reprint. New York: Dover, 1989.

Everard, Barbara, and Brian D. Morley. *Wild Flowers of the World.* New York: Putnam's, 1970.

Evelyn, John. *Acetaria. A Discourse of Sallets.* London, 1699.

Ewan, Joseph, and Nesta Ewan. *John Banister and his Natural History of Virginia, 1678–1692.* Urbana, Ill.: University of Illinois Press, 1970.

Fantz, Paul R. "Ethnobotany of Clitoria (Leguminosae)." *Economic Botany* 45 (1991): 511–21.

Fitzherbert, John. *The Boke of Husbandrie.* London, 1523.

Fernald, Merritt Lyndon. *Gray's Manual of Botany.* 8th ed. New York: American Book Company, 1950.

———, and Alfred Charles Kinsey. *Edible Wild*

*Plants of Eastern North America.* 1943. Reprint. New York: Harper, 1958.

Foster, Steven. *Echinacea: Nature's Immune Enhancer.* Rochester, Vt.: Healing Arts Press, 1991.

Foster, Steven, and James A. Duke. *A Field Guide to Medicinal Plants.* Boston: Houghton Mifflin, 1990.

Frazer, James George. *Balder the Beautiful: The Fire-Festivals of Europe and the Doctrine of the External Soul.* 1913. Reprint. New York: Macmillan, 1935.

Frémont, John Charles. *The Expeditions of John Charles Frémont,* edited by Donald Jackson and Mary Lee Spence. Urbana, Ill.: University of Illinois Press, 1970.

Frick, George Frederick, and Raymond Phineas. *Mark Catesby: The Colonial Audubon.* Urbana, Ill.: University of Illinois Press, 1961.

Gannett, Lewis. *New York Herald Tribune,* 1944. Cited in *The Gardener's World.* By Joseph Wood Krutch. New York: Putnam's, 1959.

Gardner, Helen, ed. *The Metaphysical Poets.* Baltimore: Penguin Books, 1972.

Gerard, John. *The Herball or General Historie of Plantes.* London: 1597.

———. *The Herball or Generall Historie of Plantes . . . Very Much Enlarged and Amended by Thomas Johnson.* 1633. Reprint. New York: Dover, 1975.

Geyer, Carl A. "Notes on the vegetation and general character of the Missouri and Oregon Territories, made during a botanical journey from the State of Missouri, across the South-Pass of the Rocky Mountains, to the Pacific, during the years 1843 and 1844. *Journal of Botany* (London) 5 (1846): 285–310.

Gibson, William Hamilton. *Our Native Orchids: A Series of Drawings from Nature of All the Species Found in the Northeastern United States.* New York: Doubleday, 1905.

Gilmore, Melvin R. *Uses of Plants by the Indians of the Missouri River Region.* 1914. Reprint. Lincoln, Nebr.: University of Nebraska Press, 1977.

Gleason, Henry A. *The New Britton & Brown's Illustrated Flora of the Northeastern United States and Adjacent Canada.* New York: New York Botanical Garden, 1952.

Gleason, Henry A., and Arthur Cronquist. *Manual of the Vascular Plants of Northeastern United States and Adjacent Canada.* 2d ed. Bronx, N.Y.: New York Botanical Garden, 1991.

Gledhill, D. *The Names of Plants.* New York: Cambridge University Press, 1985.

Graustein, Jeannette E. "Nuttall's travels into the Old Northwest: an unpublished 1810 diary." *Chronica Botanica* 14, no. 1/2 (1951): 1–88.

Gray, Asa. *Scientific Papers of Asa Gray.* Selected by Charles Sprague Sargent. 1899. Reprint. New York: Kraus Reprint, 1969.

Greene, Robert. *A Quip for an Upstart Courtier.* London, 1592.

Grete Herball. *The grete herball which geveth parfyt knowlege and understanding of all maner of herbes & there gracyous vertues . . .* London, 1526.

Grieve, Maud. *A Modern Herbal. The Medicinal, Culinary, Cosmetic and Economic Properties, Cultivation and Folk-Lore of Herbs, Grasses, Fungi, Shrubs & Trees.* Edited by Hilda Winifred Leyel. 1931. Reprint. New York: Dover, 1971.

Grigson, Geoffrey. *The Englishman's Flora.* 1955. Reprint. London: Hart-Davis, MacGibbon, 1975.

Grinnel, George Bird. "Some Cheyenne plant medicines." *American Anthropologist* 7 (1905): 37–43.

Gronovius. *See* Clayton, John.

Gunn, John D. *New Domestic Physician or Home Book of Health . . .* Cincinnati: 1857.

Gunther, Erna. *Ethnobotany of Western Washington: The Knowledge and Use of Indigenous Plants by Native Americans.* Rev. ed.

Seattle: University of Washington Press, 1973.

Hamel, Paul B., and Mary U. Chiltoskey. *Cherokee Plants*. Sylva, N.C.: Herald Publishing, 1975.

Harington, Sir John. *The Englishman's Doctor. Or the Schoole of Salerne*. 1607. Cited in *The Englishman's Flora*. By Geoffrey Grigson. 1955. Reprint. London: Hart-Davis, MacGibbon, 1975.

Harriot, Thomas. *A briefe and true report of the new found land of Virginia*. 1590. Reprint. New York: Dover, 1972.

Harris, Joel Chandler. *Nights with Uncle Remus*. 1883. Reprint. Boston, 1911.

Hart, Jeffrey A. "The ethnobotany of the Northern Cheyenne Indians of Montana." *Journal of Ethnopharmacology* 4 (1980): 1–55.

Hayward, Sylvanus. "Popular names of American plants." *Journal of American Folk-Lore* 4 (1891): 147–50.

Heiser, Charles B., Jr. *The Fascinating World of the Nightshades*. 1969. Reprint. New York: Dover, 1987.

Henkel, Alice. *Weeds Used in Medicine*. U.S. Department of Agriculture. Farmer's Bulletin No. 188. Washington, D.C.: U.S. Government Printing Office, 1904.

———. *Wild Medicinal Plants of the United States*. U.S. Department of Agriculture. Bureau of Plant Industry, Bulletin No. 89. Washington, D.C.: U.S. Government Printing Office, 1906.

Heywood, V. H., ed. *Flowering Plants of the World*. Englewood Cliffs, N.J.: Prentice Hall, 1985.

Hill, John. *The Family Herbal* . . . London, 1755.

Hoffman, W. J. "The Midē'wiwin or 'Grand Medicine Society' of the Ojibwa. In *Seventh Annual Report of the Bureau of Ethnology*. Washington, D.C.: U.S. Government Printing Office, 1891.

Holloway, Patricia, and Ginny Alexander. "Ethnobotany of the Fort Yukon Region, Alaska." *Economic Botany* 44 (1990): 214–25.

Hu, Shiu Ying. "The genus Panax (Ginseng) in Chinese medicine." *Economic Botany* 30 (1976): 11–28.

Hughes, Thomas P. *Medicine in Virginia, 1607–1699*. Jamestown 350th Anniversary Historical Booklet 21. Williamsburg, Va., 1957.

Hunter, John D. *Manners and Customs of Several Indian Tribes Located West of the Mississippi*. Philadelphia, 1823.

Hurston, Zora Neale. *Mules and Men*. Philadelphia: Lippincott, 1935.

Hylander, Clarence J. *The World of Plant Life*. New York: Macmillan, 1939.

Isham, James. *Observations on Hudson's Bay and Notes and Observations on a Book Entitled "A Voyage to Hudson Bay in the Dobbs Galley 1746–7."* Edited by E. E. Rich and A. M. Johnson. London: Hudson's Bay Record Society, 1949. Cited in *Medicinal and Other Uses of North American Plants: A Historical Survey with Special Reference to the Eastern Indian Tribes*. By Charlotte Erichsen-Brown. 1979. Reprint. New York: Dover, 1989.

Jacobs, Marion Lee, and Henry M. Burlage. *Index of Plants of North Carolina with Reputed Medicinal Uses*. 1958.

James, Thomas. "The Strange and Dangerous Voyage of Captain Thomas James by Himself." 1633. In *Ordeal by Ice*. Edited by Farley Mowat. Toronto: McLelland & Stewart, 1960.

Jefferson, Thomas. *See* Betts.

Johnson, Thomas. *See* Gerard.

Johnston, Alex. "Blackfoot Indian utilization of the flora of the northwestern Great Plains." *Economic Botany* 24 (1970): 301–24.

Jordan, Philip D. "The secret six: an inquiry into the basic materia medica of the Thomsonian system of botanic medicine." *Ohio*

*State Archaeologial and Historical Quarterly* 52 (1943): 347–55.

Josselyn, John. *An Account of Two Voyages to New-England Made during the Years 1638, 1663.* 1674. Reprint. Boston: Veazie, 1865.

———. *New-England's Rarities Discovered in Birds, Beasts, Fishes, Serpents, and Plants of that Country.* Edited by Edward Tuckerman. 1672. Reprint. Boston: Veazie, 1865.

Kalm, Peter. *The America of 1750: Peter Kalm's Travels in North America. The English Version of 1770, Revised from the Original Swedish by Adolph B. Benson.* 2 vols. 1937. Reprint. New York: Dover, 1966.

Kartesz, John T. *A Synonymized Checklist of the Vascular Flora of the United States, Canada, and Greenland.* 2d ed. Portland, Ore.: Timber Press. In press.

———. *Common Names for North American Plants.* Portland, Ore: Timber Press. In press.

Kartesz, John T., and John W. Thieret. "Common names for vascular plants: guidelines for use and application." *Sida* 14 (1991): 421–34.

Kelly, Howard A. *Some American Medical Botanists.* Troy, N.Y.: Southworth Co., 1914.

Kennedy, Diana. *The Cuisines of Mexico.* New York: Harper & Row, 1972.

Kindscher, Kelly. "Ethnobotany of Purple Coneflower (*Echinacea angustifolia,* Asteraceae) and other Echinacea species." *Economic Botany* 43 (1989): 498–507.

King, John, and R. S. Newton. *The Eclectic Dispensatory of the United States of America.* Cincinnati, 1852.

Kingsbury, John M. *Poisonous Plants of the United States and Canada.* Englewood Cliffs, N.J.: Prentice-Hall, 1964.

Krutch, Joseph Wood. *Herbal.* Boston: Godine, 1976.

———. *The Gardener's World.* New York: Putnam's, 1959.

Latrobe, Benjamin Henry. *The Virginia Journals of Benjamin Henry Latrobe, 1795–1798.* Edited by E. C. Carter, II. New Haven: Yale University Press, 1977.

Lawson, John. *A New Voyage to Carolina.* London, 1709.

Leighton, Ann. *American Gardens of the Nineteenth Century: "For Comfort and Affluence."* Amherst: University of Massachusetts Press, 1987.

———. *American Gardens in the Eighteenth Century: "For Use or for Delight."* Amherst: University of Massachusetts Press, 1986.

———. *Early American Gardens: "For Meate or Medicine."* Boston: Houghton Mifflin, 1970.

Leopold, Aldo. *A Sand County Almanac and Sketches Here and There.* New York: Oxford University Press, 1949.

Lewis, Meriwether, and William Clark. *See* Coues.

Lewis, Walter H., and Memory P. F. Elvin-Lewis. *Medical Botany: Plants Affecting Man's Health.* New York: Wiley, 1977.

Liddell, Henry George, and Robert Scott. *A Greek–English Lexicon.* 9th ed. Oxford: Oxford University Press, 1940.

Lloyd, I. U. *History of the Vegetable Drugs of the Pharmacopeia of the United States.* Bulletin of the Lloyd Library, No. 18. Cincinnati, 1911.

———. *Origin and History of All the Pharmacopeial Vegetable Drugs, Chemicals and Preparations.* Cincinnati; Lloyd Library, 1929.

Lloyd, I.U., and C. G. Lloyd. *Drugs and Medicines of North America.* 2 vols. 1884–1887. Reprint. Bulletin of the Lloyd Library, No. 29. Cincinnati, 1930.

Lust, John. *The Herb Book.* New York: Bantam Books, 1974.

Lyte, Henry. *See* Dodoens.

Mabberly, D. J. *The Plant Book: A Portable Dictionary of Higher Plants.* Cambridge: Cambridge University Press, 1990.

McAtee, W. L. "Some folk and scientific names for plants." *Publication of the American Dialect Society* No. 15 (April 1951): 3–25.

———. "Some local names of plants." *Torreya* 13 (1913): 225–36; 16 (1916): 235–42; 20 (1920): 17–27; 26 (1926): 3–10; 33 (1933): 81–6; 37 (1937): 93–103; 41 (1941): 43–55; 42 (1942): 153–68.

M'Mahon, Bernard. *The American Gardener's Calendar, Adapted to the Climates and Seasons of the United States.* 8th ed. Philadelphia, 1830.

Marie de l'Incarnation. *Word from New France. The Selected Letters of Marie de l'Incarnation, Founder and First Mother Superior of the Ursuline Monastery and School in Quebec City.* Edited by Joyce Marshall. Toronto: Oxford University Press, 1967.

Marie-Victorin, Frère. *Flore laurentienne.* Montreal: Les Frères des Écoles Chrétiennes, 1935.

Mather, Cotton. *The Angel of Bethesda.* 1724. Edited by Gordon W. Jones. Barre, Mass.: American Antiquarian Society and Barre Publishers, 1972.

Mathew, Brian. "Iris tenax." *The Kew Magazine* 8 (1991): 8–12.

———. *The Genus Lewisia.* Kew, England: The Royal Botanic Gardens, in association with Christopher Helm & Timber Press, 1989.

Maximilian, Prince of Wied. *Travels in the Interior of North America.* Translated by H. E. Lloyd. London, 1843.

Medsger, Oliver Perry. *Edible Wild Plants.* 1939. Reprint. New York: Collier Books, 1966.

Miller, Philip. *The Gardener's Dictionary.* London, 1741

Millspaugh, Charles F. *American Medicinal Plants: An Illustrated and Descriptive Guide to Plants Indigenous to and Naturalized in the United States Which Are Used in Medicine.* 1892. Reprint. New York: Dover, 1974.

Minsheu, John. *Hegemon eis tas glossas. id est, Ductor in Linguas. The Guide into Tongues.* London, 1617.

Mitgang, Herbert. Obituary of E. B. White. *The New York Times,* October 2, 1985.

Moerman, Daniel E. *Medicinal Plants of Native America.* Ann Arbor: University of Michigan, Museum of Anthropology, 1986.

Moldenke, Harold N. *American Wild Flowers.* New York: Van Nostrand, 1949.

Mooney, James. "Folklore of the Carolina mountains." *Journal of American Folk-Lore* 2 (1889): 95–104.

———. "The sacred formulas of the Cherokees." In *Seventh Annual Report of the Bureau of American Ethnology.* Washington, D.C., U.S. Government Printing Office, 1891.

Moore, Michael. *Medicinal Plants of the Desert and Canyon West.* Albuquerque: Museum of New Mexico Press, 1989

More, Thomas. Thomas More's first and second letters to William Sherard from New England. Dated at Boston, 27 October 1722 and 12 December 1723. Sherard Letters, IV, Nos. 560 and 561. In *Mark Catesby: The Colonial Audubon.* By George Frederick Frick and Raymond Phineas Stearns. Urbana, Ill.: University of Illinois Press, 1961.

Morton, Julia F. "Cattails (Typha spp.)——Weed problem or potential crop?" *Economic Botany* 29 (1975): 7–29.

———. "Principal wild food plants of the United States, excluding Alaska and Hawaii." *Economic Botany* 17 (1963): 319–30.

Munz, Philip A., and David D. Keck. *A California Flora.* Berkeley: University of California Press, 1959.

Niehaus, Theodore F., and Charles L. Ripper. *A Field Guide to Pacific States Wildflowers.* Boston: Houghton Mifflin, 1976.

Niehaus, Theodore F., Charles L. Ripper, and Virginia Savage. *A Field Guide to Southwestern and Texas Wildflowers*. Boston: Houghton Mifflin, 1984.

Niering, William A., and Nancy C. Olmstead. *The Audubon Society Field Guide to North American Wildflowers. Eastern Region*. New York: Knopf, 1979.

Niles, Grace Greylock. *Bog-Trotting for Orchids*. New York: Putnam's, 1904.

Nuttall, Thomas. *A Journal of Travel into the Arkansas Territory*. Philadelphia, 1821.

Osol, Arthur, and George E. Farrar, Jr. *The Dispensatory of the United States of America*. 25th ed. Philadelphia: Lippincott, 1955.

Palmer, Edward. *See* Vasey and Rose.

Parkinson, John. *A Garden of Pleasant Flowers (Paradisi in Sole: Paradisus Terrestris)*. 1629. Reprint. New York: Dover, 1976.

———. *Theatrum Botanicum: The Theater of Plants or a Herball of a Large Extent*. London, 1640.

Pechey, John. *The Compleat Herbal of Physical Plants*. London, 1694.

Perkins, Anne E. "Colloquial names of Maine plants." *Torreya* 29 (1929): 149–51.

Peterson, Lee Allen. *A Field Guide to Edible Wild Plants of Eastern and Central North America*. Boston: Houghton Mifflin, 1977.

Peterson, Roger Tory, and Margaret McKenny. *A Field Guide to Wildflowers of Northeastern and North-Central North America*. Boston: Houghton Mifflin, 1968.

Petiver, James. *Botanicum Anglicum, or the English Herbal*. London, 1715.

Pickard, Madge E., and R. Carlyle Buley. *The Midwest Pioneer: His Ills, Cures, & Doctors*. 1945. Reprint. New York: Henry Schuman, 1946.

Pliny. Gaius Plinius Secundus. *Natural History. With an English Translation in Ten Volumes*. Cambridge: Harvard University Press, 1951.

Plowden, C. C. *A Manual of Plant Names*. 2d ed. London: Allen & Unwin, 1970.

Plowman, Timothy. "Folk uses of New World aroids." *Economic Botany* 23 (1969): 97–122.

Porcher, Francis Peyre. *Resources of the Southern Fields and Forests, Medical, Economical, and Agricultural . . . Prepared and Published by Order of the Surgeon-General, Richmond, Va*. 1863. Reprint. New York: Arno Press, 1970.

Purchas, Samuel. *Hakluytus Posthumus or Purchas His Pilgrims: Containing a History of the World in Sea Voyages . . .* 1625. Reprint. New York: Macmillan, 1906.

Pursh, Frederick. *Flora Americana Septentrionalis; or, A Systematic Arrangement and Description of the Plants of North America*. London, 1814.

Rabelais, François. *The Five Books of Gargantua and Pantagruel*. Translated by J. Le Clerq. New York: Modern Library, 1936.

Rafinesque, Constantine Samuel. *Medical Flora; or, Manual of the Medical Botany of the United States of North America*. Philadelphia, 1828–1830.

*Range Plant Handbook*. *See* United States Department of Agriculture.

Ray, John. *Synopsis stirpium Britannicarum . . .* London, 1696.

Reid, Bessie M. "Vernacular names of Texas plants." *Publication of the American Dialect Society* No. 15 (April 1951): 26–50.

Richardson, John. "Account of the Cree Indians" and "Botanical Appendix." In *Narrative of a Journey to the Shores of the Polar Sea in the Years 1819, 20, 21, and 22*. By John Franklin. London, 1823

Rickett, Harold William. "English names of plants." *Bulletin of the Torrey Botanical Club* 92 (1965): 137–39.

———. *Wildflowers of the United States*. 6 vols. New York: McGraw-Hill, 1966.

Ridley, Henry N. *The Dispersal of Plants throughout the World.* Ashford, England: Reeve, 1930.

Riley, James Whitcomb. *Rhymes of Childhood.* Indianapolis, 1894.

Robbins, Wilfred William, John Peabody Harrington, and Barbara Freire-Marreco, B. *Ethnobotany of the Tewa Indians.* Smithsonian Institution, Bureau of American Ethnology, Bulletin 55. Washington, D.C.: U.S. Government Printing Office, 1916.

Rohde, Eleanour Sinclair. *The Old English Herbals.* 1922. Reprint. New York: Dover, 1971.

Rothstein, William G. *American Physicians in the Nineteenth Century: From Sects to Science.* Baltimore: John Hopkins University Press, 1972.

Ruskin, John. *Proserpina. Studies of Wayside Flowers.* London, 1879.

Sagard, Father Théodat Gabriel. *Le gran voyage du pays des Hurons . . .* Paris, 1632. Translation published by the Champlain Society, 1939. Cited in *Medicinal and Other Uses of North American Plants: A Historical Survey with Special Reference to the Eastern Indian Tribes.* By Charlotte Erichsen-Brown. 1979. Reprint. New York: Dover, 1989.

Saunders, Charles Francis. *Edible and Useful Wild Plants of the United States and Canada.* 1934. Reprint. New York: Dover, 1976.

Schöpf, Johann David. *Travels in the Confederation* [1783–1784]. 1788. Translated by A. J. Morrison. Philadelphia: Campbell, 1911.

Smith, A. W. *A Gardener's Dictionary of Plant Names.* Rev. ed. New York: St. Martin's, 1972.

Smith, Huron H. *Ethnobotany of the Forest Potawatomi Indians.* Bulletin of the Public Museum of the City of Milwaukee. Vol. 7, no. 1 (1933): 1–230.

———. *Ethnobotany of the Menomini Indians.* Bulletin of the Public Museum of the City of Milwaukee. Vol. 4, no. 1 (1923): 1–174.

———. *Ethnobotany of the Meskwaki Indians.* Bulletin of the Public Museum of the City of Milwaukee. Vol. 4, no. 2 (1928): 175–326.

———. *Ethnobotany of the Ojibwe Indians.* Bulletin of the Public Museum of the City of Milwaukee. Vol. 4, no. 3 (1932): 327–525.

Smith, John. *A Map of Virginia. With a Description of the Countrey, the Commodities, People, Government and Religion. Written by Captaine Smith.* Oxford, 1612.

Speck, Francis G. "A list of plant curatives obtained from the Houma Indians of Louisiana." *Primitive Man* 14 (1941): 49–75.

———. "Medicine practices of the Northeastern Algonquians." In *Proceedings of the 19th International Congress of Americanists.* Washington, D.C., 1917.

Spellenberg, Richard. *The Audubon Society Field Guide to North American Wildflowers. Western Region.* New York: Knopf, 1979.

Spencer, Neal R. "Velvetleaf, *Abutilon theophrasti* (Malvaceae); history and economic impact in the United States." *Economic Botany* 38 (1984): 407–416.

Stansbury, Howard. *An Expedition to the Great Salt Lake of Utah.* London, 1852.

Stearn, William T. *Botanical Latin: History, Grammar, Syntax, Terminology and Vocabulary.* 3d ed. North Pomfret, Vt.: David & Charles, 1983.

Stearns, Samuel. *The American Herbal, or Materia Medica.* Walpole, N.H.: 1801.

Stevenson, Matilda Coxe. "Ethnobotany of the Zuñi Indians." In *Thirtieth Annual Report of the Bureau of American Ethnology.* Washington, D.C.: U.S. Government Printing Office, 1915.

Still, James. *Early Recollections and Life of*

*Dr. James Still*. 1877. Reprint. New Brunswick, N.J.: Rutgers University Press, 1973.

Strachey, William. *For the colony in Virginea Brittanica . . .* London, 1612.

Sturtevant, E. Lewis. "Kitchen garden esculents of American origin." *American Naturalist* 19 (1885): 444–57.

———. *Sturtevant's Edible Plants of the World.* Edited by U. P. Hedrick. 1919. Reprint. New York: Dover, 1972.

Sturtevant, Louis. "History of garden vegetables." *American Naturalist* 22 (1888): 420–33.

Swem, Earl G. *Brothers of the Spade. Correspondence of Peter Collinson of London and of John Custis of Wiliamsburg, Virginia, 1734–1746.* 1949. Reprint. Barre, Mass.: Barre Gazette, 1957.

Tabor, Edward. "Plant poisons in Shakespeare." *Economic Botany* 24 (1970): 81–9.

Teit, James A. "Ethnobotany of the Thompson Indians of British Columbia." Edited by Elsie Viault Steedman. In *Forty-Fifth Annual Report of the Bureau of American Ethnology.* Washington, D.C.: U.S. Government Printing Office, 1930.

Thiselton-Dyer, T. F. *The Folk-Lore of Plants.* New York: Appleton, 1889.

Thomson, Samuel. *Life and Medical Discoveries.* Boston, 1822.

Thoreau, Henry David. *Cape Cod.* 1864. Reprint. Boston: Houghton Mifflin; 1893.

———. *The Journals of Henry D. Thoreau.* Edited by Bradford Torrey and Francis H. Allen. 14 vols. 1906. Reprint. 2 vols. New York: Dover, 1962.

———. *The Maine Woods.* 1864. Reprint. Boston: Houghton Mifflin, 1892.

Threlkeld, Caleb. *Synopsis stirpium Hibernicarum.* 1727. Cited in *The Englishman's Flora.* By Geoffrey Grigson. 1955. Reprint. London: Hart-Davis, MacGibbon, 1975.

Todd, John E. *John Todd: The Story of His Life . . .* New York, 1876.

Torrey, Bradford. *A Florida Sketchbook.* Boston, 1894.

Touchstone, Samuel J. *Herbal and Folk Medicine of Louisiana and Adjacent States.* Princeton, La.: Folk-Life Books, 1983.

Traill, Catherine Parr. *The Canadian Settler's Guide.* 1855. Reprint. Toronto: McClelland & Stewart, 1969.

Train, Percy, James R. Henrichs, and W. Andrew Archer. *Medicinal Uses of Plants by Indian Tribes of Nevada.* 1941. Reprint. Lawrence, Mass.: Quarterman, 1978.

Trollope, Frances. *Domestic Manners of the Americans.* London, 1832.

Tuckerman, Edward, ed. *New England's Rarities . . .* By John Josselyn. Boston, 1865.

Turner, William. *The first and seconde partes of the Herbal of William Turner Doctor in Phisick lately oversene corrected and enlarged with the Thirde parte.* Cologne, 1568.

———. *The names of herbes in Greke, Latin, Englishe, Duche, and Frenche wyth the commune names that Herbaries and Apotecaries use.* London, 1548.

United Society, New Gloucester, Maine. *Herbs, Roots, Barks, Powdered Articles, &c.* Catalog. 1864. Reprint. Sabbathday Lake, Maine: United Society of Shakers, 1972.

United States Department of Agriculture, Forest Service. *Range Plant Handbook.* 1937. Reprint. New York: Dover, 1988.

United States Dispensatory. *See* Osol and Farrar.

Van Wijk, H. L. G. *A Dictionary of Plant Names.* 2 vols. 1909–1916. Reprint. Amsterdam: Asher, 1971.

Vasey, George, and J. N. Rose. "List of plants collected by Dr. Edward Palmer in 1889, in the region of Lower California, with notes and descriptions of new species." *Contri-*

*butions from the U.S. National Herbarium* 1 (1890): 9–28.

Venning, Frank D., and Manabu C. Saito. *Wildflowers of North America. A Guide to Field Identification.* New York: Golden Press, 1984.

Vestal, Paul A. *Ethnobotany of the Ramah Navaho.* Reports of the Ramah Project No. 4. Cambridge, Mass.: Peabody Museum of American Archaeology and Ethnology, Harvard University, 1952.

Virgil. *The Aeneid of Virgil: A New Verse Translation.* By C. Day Lewis. New York: Doubleday Anchor, 1953.

Vogel, Virgil J. *American Indian Medicine.* Norman, Okla.: University of Oklahoma Press, 1970.

Walton, Izaac. *The Compleat Angler, or the Contemplative Man's Recreation.* London, 1676.

Ward-Harris, J. *More Than Meets the Eye: the Life and Lore of Western Wildflowers.* Toronto: Oxford University Press, 1983.

Wernert, Susan J., ed. *North American Wildlife.* Pleasantville, N.Y.: Reader's Digest, 1982.

Whitcher, Frances Miriam Berry. *The Widow Bedott Papers.* New York, 1856.

Whittle, Tyler, and Christopher Cook. *Curtis's Flower Garden Displayed: 120 Plates from the Years 1787–1807 with New Descriptions.* New York: Oxford University Press, 1981.

Williams, Roger. *A Key into the Language of America: or, An help to the Language of the Natives in that part of America called New-England.* London, 1643.

Williamson, William D. *History of the State of Maine.* Hollowell, Maine, 1832.

Withering, William. *A Botanical Arrangement of All the Vegetables Naturally Growing in Great Britain.* Birmingham, England, 1776.

———. *An Account of the Foxglove, and Some of Its Medical Uses.* London, 1785.

Wolley, Charles. *A Two Year's Journal in New York and Part of Its Territories in America. Reprinted from the original edition of 1701, with an Introduction and Notes by Edward Gaylord Bourne.* Cleveland: Burrows Brothers, 1902.

Wood, William. *New England's Prospect.* London, 1634.

Wyman, Leland C., and Stuart K. Harris. *Navajo Indian Medical Ethnobotany.* Albuquerque, N.M.: University of New Mexico Press, 1941.

Young, Andrew. *A Prospect of Flowers: A Book about Wild Flowers.* 1945. Reprint. New York: Penguin, 1986.

Zohary, Michael. *Plants of the Bible.* New York: Cambridge University Press, 1982.

# INDEX OF NAMES OF PERSONS
## Cited or Quoted and Selected Publications

An asterisk indicates where biographical information about the person cited may be found;
† indicates a footnote. A few names from mythology are also included in this index.

# INDEX OF FAMILIES, GENERA AND COMMON PLANT NAMES

A few names of genera that appeared in many field guides to wildflowers have since been eliminated and thus do not appear in the text of this book, where new names have been introduced. Old and new names are cross-referenced in the index: "see" cross-references send the reader from a previously used name to the name used in this book; "see also" cross-references indicate that a genus has been spilt into one or more genera. Vernacular names are not indexed, but can be found in the text under the common and botanical plant names.

## DATE DUE